Cases and Materials on Constitutional and Administrative Law

Authors

Christopher Costigan

Neil Hurden

Alex Lawson

Consultant Editor(s)

Neil Hurden

Editor-in-Chief

Christopher Costigan LL.B. (Hons), Barrister

Senior Lecturer

First edition July 2010

Second edition August 2012

Published ISBN: 9781 4453 9951 5

Previous ISBN: 9781 4453 0710 7

British Library Cataloguing-in-Publication Data
A catalogue record for this book is available
from the British Library

Published by
BPP Learning Media Ltd
BPP House, Aldine Place
London W12 8AA
www.bpp.com/learningmedia

Printed in the United Kingdom by Polestar Wheatons

Polestar Wheatons
Hennock Road
Marsh Barton
Exeter
EX2 8RP

Your learning materials, published by BPP Learning Media Ltd, are printed on paper sourced from sustainable, managed forests.

Contents

A note about copyright

Dear Customer

What does the little © mean and why does it matter?

Your market-leading BPP books, course materials and e-learning materials do not write and update themselves. People write them: on their own behalf or as employees of an organisation that invests in this activity. Copyright law protects their livelihoods. It does so by creating rights over the use of the content.

Breach of copyright is a form of theft – as well as being a criminal offence in some jurisdictions, it is potentially a serious breach of professional ethics.

With current technology, things might seem a bit hazy but, basically, without the express permission of BPP Learning Media:

Photocopying our materials is a breach of copyright

Scanning, ripcasting or conversion of our digital materials into different file formats, uploading them to Facebook or e-mailing them to your friends is a breach of copyright

You can, of course, sell your books, in the form in which you have bought them – once you have finished with them. (Is this fair to your fellow students? We update for a reason.) But the e-products are sold on a single user licence basis: we do not supply 'unlock' codes to people who have bought them second-hand.

And what about outside the UK? BPP Learning Media strives to make our materials available at prices students can afford by local printing arrangements, pricing policies and partnerships which are clearly listed on our website. A tiny minority ignore this and indulge in criminal activity by illegally photocopying our material or supporting organisations that do. If they act illegally and unethically in one area, can you really trust them?

Index of Cases

A

B

C

D

E

G

H

I

J

M

P

R

S

T

Part A

Constitutional Law

1

Sources of the Constitution

Topic List

Alex Lawson and Christopher Costigan

Introduction

The uncodified nature of the United Kingdom's constitution means that its sources are far more dispersed than those constitutions which can be found in a single, codified document. However, while students of constitutional law in the United States, for instance, may be able to read their constitution and its amendments and have an almost entire picture of how that system functions, that understanding would not be complete. No system can work effectively through a document alone. Certain statutes will be of constitutional significance, as will the way in which a constitution is interpreted by the courts, when dealing with key cases. How a constitution operates in practice will be crucial to a proper and full understanding of the rules.

The UK's constitution – uniquely – places more emphasis on decisions of the courts, how the constitution operates in practice, and the key constitutional principle of parliamentary sovereignty. The cases which are of relevance to UK constitutional law are pervasive throughout this book and the growing dominance of the rule of law, as protected by the courts, will be a vital recurring theme. Parliamentary sovereignty will be dealt with in Chapter 4.

The UK constitution has a number of legal sources, such as key constitutional statutes and common law decisions. However, this chapter will focus on how a non-legal source of constitutional rules, the convention, governs the operation of the constitution in practice, by looking at two key cases.

1 Conventions

Professor A.V. Dicey, in his work 'Introduction to the Study of the Law of Constitutions', 1885, described the non-legal rules of a constitution as:

> ...conventions, understandings, habits or practices, which, though they may regulate the conduct of officials, are not in reality laws at all since they are not enforced by the courts.

Dicey thought that conventions were descriptive rules of behaviour, whereas Sir Ivor Jennings thought they were binding, although not enforced in fact by the courts. Conventions are at the heart of the two cases considered in this chapter.

***Attorney-General v Jonathan Cape Ltd. and Others; Attorney-General v Times Newspapers Ltd.* [1976] QB 752**

Panel: Lord Widgery CJ

Facts: The facts of the case are clearly set out in the judgment of Lord Widgery CJ.

> LORD WIDGERY CJ
>
> These are two actions for injunctions to restrain the publication, either in whole or in part, of the political diaries of the late Richard Crossman. Mr. Crossman was a Cabinet Minister in the Labour government of 1964 to 1970, and during this period he kept a

detailed diary, and kept this diary to the knowledge of his colleagues in the Cabinet. When the government fell in 1970 and he was no longer employed as a Cabinet Minister, Mr. Crossman began to collate his diaries with a view to their publication. He obtained the assistance for research purposes of Dr. Janet Morgan, and he was soon in touch with the Secretary of the Cabinet in order to refresh his memory by reference to the relevant Cabinet papers of the times. For many years former Cabinet Ministers have been allowed the privilege of looking at Cabinet papers prepared while they were in the Cabinet in order to refresh their memory for this purpose, and this was undoubtedly being done by Mr. Crossman up to shortly before his death, which occurred on April 5, 1974.

Mr. Crossman had appointed three literary executors, and these executors were naturally concerned to proceed with preparing the diaries for publication, and correspondence between the literary executors or their representatives and the Secretary of the Cabinet now ensued...

On June 22 there is a long letter from Sir John Hunt to Mr. Graham Greene containing Sir John's comments on the first volume of the Diaries, and therefore obviously very important:

"When you called here on June 21 I explained why I felt unable to agree to the publication of the first volume of Mr. Richard Crossman's Diaries which you had sent me for official scrutiny. You felt it would be helpful if I were briefly to restate the reasons in this letter.

Alert

"The conventions which in the public interest govern the publication of works by former Ministers have evolved over many years and been accepted by successive administrations. They flow from the two complementary principles of the collective responsibility of the government as a whole and the personal responsibility of individual Ministers.

"As regards the first of these, the Cabinet meets in secret and the records of its proceedings are secret until of historical interest only when they become available to public scrutiny under the Public Records Act 1967. Only in this way can completely frank discussion take place between Ministers in the Cabinet and in Cabinet committees without the risk of extraneous pressure and controversy. It has also always been held vital for good government that other confidential communications between Ministers, or between Ministers and their senior civil servants, should be protected from untoward disclosure. This is not a matter which depends on the Official Secrets Act ... It is based upon the inherent needs of government, and the mutual trust which needs to exist between Ministers and between Ministers and their senior advisers. It is an essential feature of the doctrine of collective responsibility which is at the centre of our system of government. To put it another way, Ministers will not feel free frankly to discuss and to surrender their personal and departmental preferences to the achievement of a common view, nor can they be expected to abide by a common decision, if they know that the stand they have taken and the points they have surrendered will sooner rather than later become public knowledge. Since Cabinet government depends on the mutual confidence of collective responsibility, its basis can be eroded by the premature disclosure of what has passed within the confidential relationship."

There, I pause to observe, is a statement of the attitude of Sir John Hunt which is really repeated and supported by the Attorney-General in his argument before this court in the present proceedings. It is a convenient statement of the case for the Attorney-General, the plaintiff.

I can pass on now a little more quickly. On July 2, 1974, we find Mr. Montgomerie, a partner in the solicitors' firm of Goodman, Derrick & Co., writing to Sir Henry Ware, the Treasury Solicitor, and he says:

"I am writing formally to confirm the undertaking which Lord Goodman" - the senior partner of the solicitors' firm in question - "gave to you on behalf of the executors and literary executors of the late Richard Crossman that the book will not be published and no review or other copies will be distributed without giving you first 14 days' notice to enable you to take such action, if any, as you are advised. This undertaking is given on the understanding that discussions will be undertaken as soon as possible to see whether the objections of the Cabinet Office can be obviated."

At this stage solicitors had come into the matter and an attempt to compromise the issue had already begun.

The matter is continued in correspondence by a letter from Sir John Hunt to Lord Goodman on August 7, 1974. Sir John Hunt has been looking at amendments proposed by Mr. Montgomerie to the first 145 pages of the Diaries, and Sir John Hunt is now commenting on Mr. Montgomerie's editorship of that matter. He says:

"I considered the amendments against the parameters which we discussed when you called here on July 10. These were:

Cabinet discussions.

There was no objection to references to meetings of the Cabinet or Cabinet committees as such. Nor would we object to reference in appropriate cases to the fact that the Cabinet had considered proposals put forward by Mr. Crossman. We could not however agree to publication of the 'blow by blow' accounts of Cabinet or Cabinet committee discussions, the revelation of differences between members of the Cabinet and the detailed discussions of other Ministers' policies."

Sir John then goes on to make similar objections to references in the Diaries which disclose advice given by civil servants, and discussion on the suitability of senior civil servants for appointment. Later in the letter he says:

"These parameters" - that word, I may say, has been much abused in the course of this case - "were the minimum which I considered necessary to meet the central point which I had put earlier in letters to the literary executors, namely that the Cabinet meets in secret and the records of its proceedings are secret until of historical interest only when they become available to public scrutiny."

Sir John then apologises for having written a long letter, but he has clearly, as can be seen, brought out again the real objections which have been put forward on behalf of the Attorney-General to the publication of these Diaries.

...

I can go on now to the point at which, I think it can fairly be said, issue was joined. On December 24, 1974, Sir John Hunt is writing to Lord Goodman and he says:

"I have now been able to study the extracts submitted ... It is clear, as you will I am sure agree, that the extracts do not conform with these parameters and accordingly you will understand that I am not able to give clearance of them."

That, in a sense, is his final word on the discussion. It is answered on January 20, 1975, by a letter written by Lord Goodman on behalf of the would-be publishers, to Sir John Hunt, in which he sets out the defendants' case in these terms:

"The literary executors, and also, I believe, the Sunday Times, feel very strongly that the parameters laid down in your correspondence go beyond those established by Sir Burke Trend in his evidence before the Franks Committee. ...

They have therefore granted a licence to the Sunday Times to publish extracts."

In fact, on January 26, 1975, without any specific consent from Sir John Hunt, or anybody else on the government side, the first extract from the Diaries was published in the "Sunday Times." Thereafter for a time an uneasy truce persisted between Sir John Hunt and the representatives of the "Sunday Times." The editor of the newspaper submitted extracts from the Diaries proposed for publication for Sir John's comment; Sir John commented upon these extracts and, in some instances, his comments were adopted; in others they were not. The "Sunday Times" and its editor were, I think, quite clearly asserting their right to be their own judges of what matter was eventually included for publication, but as a matter of fact many matters which Sir John Hunt suggested should be excised from the extracts were in fact so excised.

Eventually, however, proceedings began on June 18 and 24, 1975, in the form of the two actions now before me. The first action is concerned with preventing the literary executors from proceeding with publication of the Diaries, and the second with preventing the "Sunday Times" from proceeding further with the publication of extracts.

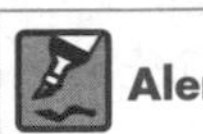

It has always been assumed by lawyers and, I suspect, by politicians, and the Civil Service, that Cabinet proceedings and Cabinet papers are secret, and cannot be publicly disclosed until they have passed into history. It is quite clear that no court will compel the production of Cabinet papers in the course of discovery in an action, and the Attorney-General contends that not only will the court refuse to compel the production of such matters, but it will go further and positively forbid the disclosure of such papers and proceedings if publication will be contrary to the public interest.

The basis of this contention is the confidential character of these papers and proceedings, derived from the convention of joint Cabinet responsibility whereby any policy decision reached by the Cabinet has to be supported thereafter by all members of the Cabinet whether they approve of it or not, unless they feel compelled to resign.

It is contended that Cabinet decisions and papers are confidential for a period to the extent at least that they must not be referred to outside the Cabinet in such a way as to disclose the attitude of individual Ministers in the argument which preceded the decision. Thus, there may be no objection to a Minister disclosing (or leaking, as it was called) the fact that a Cabinet meeting has taken place, or, indeed, the decision taken, so long as the individual views of Ministers are not identified.

There is no doubt that Mr. Crossman's manuscripts contain frequent references to individual opinions of Cabinet Ministers, and this is not surprising because it was his avowed object to obtain a relaxation of the convention regarding memoirs of ex-Ministers to which Sir John Hunt referred. There have, as far as I know, been no previous attempts in any court to define the extent to which Cabinet proceedings should be treated as secret or confidential, and it is not surprising that different views on this subject are contained in the evidence before me. The Attorney-General does not attempt a final definition but his contention is that such proceedings are confidential and their publication is capable of control by the courts at least as far as they include (a) disclosure of Cabinet documents or proceedings in such a way as to reveal the individual views or attitudes of Ministers; (b) disclosure of confidential advice from civil servants, whether contained in Cabinet papers or not; (c) disclosure of confidential discussions affecting the appointment or transfer of such senior civil servants.

The Attorney-General contends that all Cabinet papers and discussions are prima facie confidential, and that the court should restrain any disclosure thereof if the public interest in concealment outweighs the public interest in a right to free publication. The Attorney General further contends that, if it is shown that the public interest is involved, he has the right and duty to bring the matter before the court. In this contention he is well supported by Lord Salmon in Reg. v. Lewes Justices, Ex parte Secretary of State for the Home Department [1973] A.C. 388, 412...

I do not understand Lord Salmon to be saying, or the Attorney-General to be contending, that it is only necessary for him to evoke the public interest to obtain an order of the court. On the contrary, it must be for the court in every case to be satisfied that the public interest is involved, and that, after balancing all the factors which tell for or against publication, to decide whether suppression is necessary.

The defendants' main contention is that whatever the limits of the convention of joint Cabinet responsibility may be, there is no obligation enforceable at law to prevent the publication of Cabinet papers and proceedings, except in extreme cases where national security is involved. In other words, the defendants submit that the confidential character of Cabinet papers and discussions is based on a true convention as defined in the evidence of Professor Henry Wade, namely, an obligation founded in conscience only. Accordingly, the defendants contend that publication of these Diaries is not capable of control by any order of this court.

If the Attorney-General were restricted in his argument to the general proposition that Cabinet papers and discussion are all under the seal of secrecy at all times, he would be in difficulty. It is true that he has called evidence from eminent former holders of office to the effect that the public interest requires a continuing secrecy, and he cites a powerful passage from the late Viscount Hailsham to this effect. The extract comes from a copy of the Official Report (House of Lords) for December 21, 1932, in the course of a debate on Cabinet secrecy. Lord Hailsham said...

"It is absolutely essential in the public interest that discussions which take place between Cabinet Ministers shall take place in the full certainty of all of them that they are speaking their minds with absolute freedom to colleagues on whom they can explicitly rely, upon matters on which it is their sworn duty to express their opinions with complete frankness and to give all information, without any haunting fear that what happens may hereafter by publication create difficulties for themselves or, what is far more grave, may create complications for the King and country that they are trying to serve. For those reasons I hope that the inflexible rule which has hitherto prevailed will be maintained in its integrity, and that if there has been any relaxation or misunderstanding, of which I say nothing, the debate in this House will have done something to clarify the position and restate the old rule in all its rigour and all its inflexibility."

The defendants, however, in the present action, have also called distinguished former Cabinet Ministers who do not support this view of Lord Hailsham, and it seems to me that the degree of protection afforded to Cabinet papers and discussion cannot be determined by a single rule of thumb. Some secrets require a high standard of protection for a short time. Others require protection until a new political generation has taken over. In the present action against the literary executors, the Attorney-General asks for a perpetual injunction to restrain further publication of the Diaries in whole or in part. I am far from convinced that he has made out a case that the public interest requires such a Draconian remedy when due regard is had to other public interests, such as the freedom of speech: see Lord Denning M.R. in In re X (A Minor) (Wardship: Jurisdiction) [1975] Fam. 47.

...It seems to me, therefore, that the Attorney-General must first show that whatever obligation of secrecy or discretion attaches to former Cabinet Ministers, that obligation is binding in law and not merely in morals.

...

In recent years, successive Secretaries of the Cabinet, when giving advice on the publication of a Minister's memoirs, were much concerned about (a) disclosure of individual views of Members of the Cabinet in defiance of the principle of joint responsibility; (b) disclosure of advice given by civil servants still in office; (c) disclosure of discussions relating to the promotion or transfer of senior civil servants.

Mr. Crossman, as appears from the introduction to volume one of his Diaries, disapproved of the submission of manuscripts to the Secretary of the Cabinet. He made no attempt to admit the three categories of information just referred to, and expressed the intention to obtain publication whilst memories were green.

Mr. Crossman made no secret of the fact that he kept a diary which he intended to use for the writing of his memoirs. It was contended on behalf of the literary executors that any bond of confidence or secrecy normally attending upon Cabinet material had been lifted in Mr. Crossman's case by consent of his colleagues. Even if, as a matter of law, a Minister can release himself from a bond of secrecy in this way, I do not find that Mr. Crossman effectively did so. It is not enough to show that his colleagues accepted the keeping of the diary. It was vital to show that they accepted Mr. Crossman's intention to use the diary whether it passed the scrutiny of the Secretary of the Cabinet or not. ...

The main framework of the defence is to be found in eight submissions from Mr. Comyn. The first two have already been referred to, the allegation being that there is no power in law for the court to interfere with publication of these diaries or extracts, and that the Attorney-General's proper remedy lies in obtaining a change of the statute law.

I have already indicated some of the difficulties which face the Attorney-General when he relied simply on the public interest as a ground for his actions. ...

However, the Attorney-General has a powerful reinforcement for his argument in the developing equitable doctrine that a man shall not profit from the wrongful publication of information received by him in confidence. This doctrine, said to have its origin in *Prince Albert v. Strange* (1849) 1 H. & T. 1, has been frequently recognised as a ground for restraining the unfair use of commercial secrets transmitted in confidence. Sometimes in these cases there is a contract which may be said to have been breached by the breach of confidence, but it is clear that the doctrine applies independently of contract: see *Saltman Engineering Co. Ltd. v. Campbell Engineering Co. Ltd.* (1948) 65 R.P.C. 203. Again in *Coco v. A. N. Clark (Engineers) Ltd.* [1969] R.P.C. 41 Megarry J., reviewing the authorities, set out the requirements necessary for an action based on breach of confidence to succeed. He said, at p. 47:

"In my judgment three elements are normally required if, apart from contract, a case of breach of confidence is to succeed. First, the information itself, in the words of Lord Greene M.R.... must 'have the necessary quality of confidence about it.' Secondly, that information must have been imparted in circumstances importing an obligation of confidence. Thirdly, there must be an unauthorised use of that information to the detriment of the party communicating it."

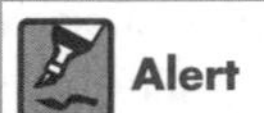

It is not until the decision in *Duchess of Argyll v. Duke of Argyll* [1967] Ch. 302, that the same principle was applied to domestic secrets such as those passing between husband and wife during the marriage. It was there held by Ungoed-Thomas J. that the plaintiff wife could obtain an order to restrain the defendant husband from communicating such secrets, and the principle is well expressed in the headnote in these terms, at p. 304:

"A contract or obligation of confidence need not be expressed but could be implied, and a breach of contract or trust or faith could arise independently of any right of property or contract... and that the court, in the exercise of its equitable jurisdiction, would restrain a breach of confidence independently of any right at law.

This extension of the doctrine of confidence beyond commercial secrets has never been directly challenged, and was noted without criticism by Lord Denning M.R. in Fraser v.

Evans [1969] 1 Q.B. 349, 361. I am sure that I ought to regard myself, sitting here, as bound by the decision of Ungoed-Thomas J.

Even so, these defendants argue that an extension of the principle of the Argyll case to the present dispute involves another large and unjustified leap forward, because in the present case the Attorney-General is seeking to apply the principle to public secrets made confidential in the interests of good government. I cannot see why the courts should be powerless to restrain the publication of public secrets, while enjoying the Argyll powers in regard to domestic secrets. Indeed, as already pointed out, the court must have power to deal with publication which threatens national security, and the difference between such a case and the present case is one of degree rather than kind. I conclude, therefore, that when a Cabinet Minister receives information in confidence the improper publication of such information can be restrained by the court, and his obligation is not merely to observe a gentleman's agreement to refrain from publication.

Alert

It is convenient next to deal with Mr. Comyn's third submission, namely, that the evidence does not prove the existence of a convention as to collective responsibility, or adequately define a sphere of secrecy. I find overwhelming evidence that the doctrine of joint responsibility is generally understood and practised and equally strong evidence that it is on occasion ignored. The general effect of the evidence is that the doctrine is an established feature of the English form of government, and it follows that some matters leading up to a Cabinet decision may be regarded as confidential. Furthermore, I am persuaded that the nature of the confidence is that spoken for by the Attorney-General, namely, that since the confidence is imposed to enable the efficient conduct of the Queen's business, the confidence is owed to the Queen and cannot be released by the members of Cabinet themselves. I have been told that a resigning Minister who wishes to make a personal statement in the House, and to disclose matters which are confidential under the doctrine obtains the consent of the Queen for this purpose. Such consent is obtained through the Prime Minister. ...I cannot accept the suggestion that a Minister owes no duty of confidence in respect of his own views expressed in Cabinet. It would only need one or two Ministers to describe their own views to enable experienced observers to identify the views of the others.

The other defence submissions are either variants of those dealt with, or submissions with regard to relief.

The Cabinet is at the very centre of national affairs, and must be in possession at all times of information which is secret or confidential. Secrets relating to national security may require to be preserved indefinitely. Secrets relating to new taxation proposals may be of the highest importance until Budget day, but public knowledge thereafter. To leak a Cabinet decision a day or so before it is officially announced is an accepted exercise in public relations, but to identify the Ministers who voted one way or another is objectionable because it undermines the doctrine of joint responsibility.

It is evident that there cannot be a single rule governing the publication of such a variety of matters. In these actions we are concerned with the publication of diaries at a time when 11 years have expired since the first recorded events. The Attorney-

General must show (a) that such publication would be a breach of confidence; (b) that the public interest requires that the publication be restrained, and (c) that there are no other facts of the public interest contradictory of and more compelling than that relied upon. Moreover, the court, when asked to restrain such a publication, must closely examine the extent to which relief is necessary to ensure that restrictions are not imposed beyond the strict requirement of public need.

Alert

Applying those principles to the present case, what do we find? In my judgment, the Attorney-General has made out his claim that the expression of individual opinions by Cabinet Ministers in the course of Cabinet discussion are matters of confidence, the publication of which can be restrained by the court when this is clearly necessary in the public interest.

The maintenance of the doctrine of joint responsibility within the Cabinet is in the public interest, and the application of that doctrine might be prejudiced by premature disclosure of the views of individual Ministers.

There must, however, be a limit in time after which the confidential character of the information, and the duty of the court to restrain publication, will lapse. ...

It may, of course, be intensely difficult in a particular case, to say at what point the material loses its confidential character, on the ground that publication will no longer undermine the doctrine of joint Cabinet responsibility. ...The court should intervene only in the clearest of cases where the continuing confidentiality of the material can be demonstrated. In less clear cases - and this, in my view, is certainly one - reliance must be placed on the good sense and good taste of the Minister or ex-Minister concerned.

In the present case there is nothing in Mr. Crossman's work to suggest that he did not support the doctrine of joint Cabinet responsibility. The question for the court is whether it is shown that publication now might damage the doctrine notwithstanding that much of the action is up to 10 years old and three general elections have been held meanwhile. So far as the Attorney-General relies in his argument on the disclosure of individual ministerial opinions, he has not satisfied me that publication would in any way inhibit free and open discussion in Cabinet hereafter.

In his judgment Lord Widgery CJ confirmed the traditional orthodoxy that a court of law could not enforce a convention directly. He was, though, prepared to acknowledge that the convention of collective ministerial responsibility existed. And, interestingly, while he could not enforce the convention in its own right, he did feel able to use its existence to assist in the development of the common law duty of confidence (which had already been extended beyond purely commercial dealings) to include the relationship between cabinet colleagues where a matter fell under the doctrine of collective ministerial responsibility. This does seem to suggest that a convention could be given quasi-legal effect where the claimant can find an existing cause of action that can be enlarged or developed to incorporate the conventional rule.

***Reference re Questions Concerning Amendment of Constitution of Canada* [1981] 6 WWR 1**

Panel: Laskin CJC, Martland, Ritchie, Dickson, Beetz, Estey, McIntyre, Chouinard and Lamer JJ

Facts: Canada was created as a federal state by the British North America Act 1867. However, reflecting its status as a former British colony, any amendment to the constitution had to be approved in Westminster. The Act stated that Westminster would only make such changes on request from 'Canada', but did not define what 'Canada' meant. A convention emerged to the effect that the Canadian federal government would make such requests, but would not send a Bill altering the balance of federal/provincial governmental power without the support of the provinces. A Bill to 'patriate' the constitution was proposed which would have allowed the federal government to amend the constitution without provincial support. This would have meant the federal government could, if it chose to, unilaterally abolish or reduce provincial powers. The Canadian Supreme court was asked several questions, of which questions two and three are relevant here.

References were made to the Manitoba Court of Appeal, the Newfoundland Court of Appeal, and the Quebec Court of Appeal by the respective governments of those three provinces. The questions posed in the Manitoba reference were:

...

2. Is it a constitutional convention that the House of Commons and Senate of Canada will not request Her Majesty the Queen to lay before the Parliament of the United Kingdom of Great Britain and Northern Ireland a measure to amend the Constitution of Canada affecting federal-provincial relationships or the powers, rights or privileges granted or secured by the Constitution of Canada to the provinces, their legislatures or governments without first obtaining the agreement of the provinces?

3. Is the agreement of the provinces of Canada constitutionally required for amendment to the Constitution of Canada where such amendment affects federal-provincial relationships or alters the powers, rights or privileges granted or secured by the Constitution of Canada to the provinces, their legislatures or governments?

CHIEF JUSTICE OF CANADA LASKIN AND JUSTICES DICKSON, BEETZ, ESTEY, MCINTYRE, CHOUINARD AND LAMER

...

VII

39. Coming now to Q. 3 in the Manitoba and Newfoundland references and Q. B (on its legal side) in the Quebec reference: by reason of the use of the words "constitutionally required" in Q. 3, the question imports both legal and conventional issues and, as the latter are dealt with in separate reasons, what follows is concerned only with the legal side of Q. 3 in the Manitoba and Newfoundland references and Q. B (on its legal side) in the Quebec reference, which meets the submissions of all counsel on this issue.

40. There are two broad aspects to the matter under discussion, which divide into a number of separate issues: (1) the authority of the two federal Houses to proceed by resolution where provincial powers and federal-provincial relationships are thereby affected; and (2) the role or authority of the Parliament of the United Kingdom to act on the resolution. The first point concerns the need of legal power to initiate the process in Canada; the second concerns legal power, or want of it, in the Parliament of the United Kingdom to act on the resolution when it does not carry the consent of the provinces.

...

43. The proposition was advanced on behalf of the Attorney General of Manitoba that a convention may crystallize into law and that the requirement of provincial consent to the kind of resolution that we have here, although in origin political, has become a rule of law. (No firm position was taken on whether the consent must be that of the governments or that of the legislatures.)

44. In our view, this is not so. No instance of an explicit recognition of a convention as having matured into a rule of law was produced. The very nature of a convention, as political in inception and as depending on a consistent course of political recognition by those for whose benefit and to whose detriment (if any) the convention developed over a considerable period of time, is inconsistent with its legal enforcement.

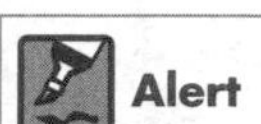

45. The attempted assimilation of the growth of a convention to the growth of the common law is misconceived. The latter is the product of judicial effort, based on justiciable issues which have attained legal formulation and are subject to modification and even reversal by the courts which gave them birth when acting within their role in the state in obedience to statutes or constitutional directives. No such parental role is played by the courts with respect to conventions.

46. It was urged before us that a host of cases have given legal force to conventions. This is an overdrawn proposition. One case in which direct recognition and enforcement of convention was sought is *Madzimbamuto v. Lardner-Burke*, [1969] 1 A.C. 645. There, the Privy Council rejected the assertion that a convention formally recognized by the United Kingdom as established, namely, that it would not legislate for Southern Rhodesia on matters within the competence of the latter's legislature without its government's consent, could not be overridden by British legislation made applicable to Southern Rhodesia after the unilateral declaration of independence by the latter's government. Speaking for the Privy Council, Lord Reid pointed out that, although the convention was a very important one, "it had no legal effect in limiting the legal power of Parliament" (at p. 723). And, again (at the same page):

...It may be that it would have been thought, before 1965, that it would be unconstitutional to disregard this convention. But it may also be that the unilateral Declaration of Independence released the United Kingdom from any obligation to observe the convention. Their Lordships in declaring the law are not concerned with these matters. They are only concerned with the legal powers of Parliament.

47. Counsel for Manitoba sought to distinguish this case on the ground that the Statute of Westminster did not embrace Southern Rhodesia, a point to which the Privy Council adverted. The Statute of Westminster will be considered later in these reasons, but if it had been in force in Southern Rhodesia it would be only under its terms, and not through any conventional rule per se, that the Parliament of the United Kingdom would have desisted from legislating for Southern Rhodesia.

48. Quite a number of cases were cited on which counsel for Manitoba relied to support his contention of conventions crystallizing into law. The chief support put forward for the "crystallization into law" proposition was the opinion of Duff C.J.C. in *Reference re Weekly Rest in Industrial Undertakings Act, etc.*, [1936] S.C.R. 461, [1936] 3 D.L.R. 673, affirmed in part (sub nom. *A.G. Can v. A.G. Ont.*) [1937] A.C. 326, [1937] 1 W.W.R. 299, [1937] 1 D.L.R. 673, better known as "the Labour Conventions case" when appealed to the Privy Council, which took a different view on the constitutional merits than did the equally divided Supreme Court of Canada. The issue, so far as it touched the matter under discussion here, concerned the alleged want of power of the Governor-General in Council, the federal executive, to enter into a treaty or accept an international obligation toward and with a foreign state, especially where the substance of the treaty or obligation related to matters which legislatively within Canada were within exclusive provincial competence.

49. The following portion of the reasons of Duff C.J.C. contains the passage relied on ... (at pp. 476-77):

...As a rule, the crystallization of constitutional usage into a rule of constitutional law to which the Courts will give effect is a slow process extending over a long period of time; but the Great War accelerated the pace of development in the region with which we are concerned, and it would seem that the usages to which I have referred, the practice, that is to say, under which Great Britain and the Dominions enter into agreements with foreign countries in the form of agreements between governments and of a still more informal character, must be recognized by the Courts as having the force of law.

...

50. What the learned Chief Justice was dealing with was an evolution which is characteristic of customary international law: the attainment by the Canadian federal executive of full and independent power to enter into international agreements. ...International law perforce has had to develop, if it was to exist at all, through commonly recognized political practices of states, there being no governing constitution, no legislating authority, no executive enforcement authority and no generally accepted judicial organ through which international law could be developed. The situation is entirely different in domestic law, in the position of a state having its own governing legislative, executive and judicial organs and, in most cases, an overarching written constitution.

51. Duff C.J.C. indicated his view of convention as allegedly maturing into law in a domestic setting in *Reference re Power of Disallowance and Power of Reservation,*

[1938] S.C.R. 71, [1938] 2 D.L.R. 8. There, it was urged that a certain portion of s.90 of the B.N.A. Act, 1867 (incorporating, in respect of the provinces, ss. 56 and 57, with some modification) had by reason of convention become spent and was suspended by the alleged convention. As to this, the Chief Justice said (at p. 78):

...We are concerned with questions of law...

[W]e are not concerned with constitutional usage or constitutional practice.

52. There is nothing in the other judgments delivered in the *Labour Conventions* case, supra, either in the Supreme Court or in the Privy Council, that takes the matter there beyond its international law setting or lends credence to the crystallization proposition urged by counsel for the Attorney General of Manitoba and, it should be said, supported by other provinces and by observations in the reasons of the Newfoundland Court of Appeal. Other cases cited for the proposition turn out, on examination, to be instances where the courts proceeded on firm statutory or other legal principles. ...

53. A close look at some other cases and issues raised on so called crystallization reveals no support for the contention. ...

[The Justices considered some cases in detail and continued:]

60. As to all the cases cited, it must be said that there is no independent force to be found in selective quotations from a portion of the reasons unless regard is had to issues raised and the context in which the quotations are found.

61. We were invited to consider academic writings on the matter under discussion. There is no consensus among the author-scholars, but the better and prevailing view is that expressed in an article by Munro, "Laws and Conventions Distinguished" (1975), 91 L.Q. Rev. 218, where he says (at p. 228):

The validity of conventions cannot be the subject of proceedings in a court of law. Reparation for breach of such rules will not be effected by any legal sanction. There are no cases which contradict these propositions. In fact, the idea of a court enforcing a mere convention is so strange that the question hardly arises.

Another passage from this article deserves mention, as follows (at p. 224):

If in fact laws and conventions are different in kind, as is my argument, then an accurate and meaningful picture of the constitution may only be obtained if this distinction is made. If the distinction is blurred, analysis of the constitution is less complete; this is not only dangerous for the lawyer, but less than helpful to the political scientist.

There is no difference in approach whether the issue arises in a unitary state or in a federal state: see Hogg, Constitutional Law of Canada (1977), at pp. 7-11.

62. A contrary view relied on by the provincial appellants is that expressed by Professor W.R. Lederman in two published articles, one entitled "Process of Constitutional Amendment for Canada" (1967), 12 McGill L.J. 371, and the second entitled "Constitutional Amendment and Canadian Unity," [1978] L. Soc. of Upper Can. Lectures 17. As a respected scholar, Professor Lederman's views deserve more

than cursory consideration. He himself recognizes that there are contrary views, including those of an equally distinguished scholar, Professor F.R. Scott: see Scott, Essays on the Constitution (1977), pp. 144, 169, 204-205, 245, 370-71 and 402. There is also the contrary view of Professor Hogg, already cited.

63. Professor Lederman relies in part on a line of cases that has already been considered, especially the reasons of Duff C.J.C. in the *Labour Conventions* case, supra. The leap from convention to law is explained almost as if there was a common law of constitutional law, but originating in political practice. That is simply not so. What is desirable as a political limitation does not translate into a legal limitation, without expression in imperative constitutional text or statute. The position advocated is all the more unacceptable when substantial provincial compliance or consent is by him said to be sufficient. Although Professor Lederman would not give a veto to Prince Edward Island, he would to Ontario or Quebec or British Columbia or Alberta. This is an impossible position for a court to manage. ...

XIV

JUSTICES MARTLAND, RITCHIE, DICKSON, BEETZ, CHOUINARD AND LAMER

233. The second question in the Manitoba reference [[1981] 2 W.W.R. 193, 117 D.L.R. (3d) 1 at 10, 7 Man. R. (2d) 269] and the Newfoundland reference [29 N. & P.E.I.R. 503, 118 D.L.R. (3d) 1 at 7, 82 A.P.R. 503] is the same:

2. Is it a constitutional convention that the House of Commons and Senate of Canada will not request Her Majesty the Queen to lay before the Parliament of the United Kingdom of Great Britain and Northern Ireland a measure to amend the Constitution of Canada affecting federal-provincial relationships or the powers, rights or privileges granted or secured by the Constitution of Canada to the provinces, their legislatures or governments without first obtaining the agreement of the provinces?

[the Justices also set out the translation of the question from Quebec and continued:]

...

237. As will be seen later, counsel for several provinces strenuously argued that the convention exists and requires the agreement of all the provinces. However, we did not understand any of them to have taken the position that the second question in the Manitoba and Newfoundland references should be dealt with and answered as if the last part of the question read "without obtaining the agreement of all the provinces".

238. Be that as it may, the question should not, in our view, be so read.

239. It would have been easy to insert the word "all" into the question had it been intended to narrow its meaning. But we do not think it was so intended. The issue raised by the question is essentially whether there is a constitutional convention that the House of Commons and Senate of Canada will not proceed alone. The thrust of the question is accordingly on whether or not there is a conventional requirement for provincial agreement, not on whether the agreement should be unanimous, assuming that it is required. ...

240. If the questions are thought to be ambiguous, this court should not, in a constitutional reference, be in a worse position than that of a witness in a trial... . Should it find that a question might be misleading, or should it simply wish to avoid the risk of misunderstanding, the court is free either to interpret the question ... or it may qualify both the question and the answer... .

The Nature of Constitutional Conventions

241. A substantial part of the rules of the Canadian constitution are written. They are contained, not in a single document called a "constitution", but in a great variety of statutes... .

242. Another part of the constitution of Canada consists of the rules of the common law. ...

245. Those parts of the constitution of Canada which are composed of statutory rules and common law rules are generically referred to as "the law of the constitution". In cases of doubt or dispute, it is the function of the courts to declare what the law is and, since the law is sometimes breached, it is generally the function of the courts to ascertain whether it has in fact been breached in specific instances and, if so, to apply such sanctions as are contemplated by the law, whether they be punitive sanctions or civil sanctions, such as a declaration of nullity. Thus, when a federal or a provincial statute is found by the courts to be in excess of the legislative competence of the legislature which has enacted it, it is declared null and void and the courts refuse to give effect to it. In this sense, it can be said that the law of the constitution is administered or enforced by the courts.

246. But many Canadians would perhaps be surprised to learn that important parts of the constitution of Canada, with which they are the most familiar because they are directly involved when they exercise their right to vote at federal and provincial elections, are nowhere to be found in the law of the constitution. For instance, it is a fundamental requirement of the constitution that, if the opposition obtains the majority at the polls, the government must tender its resignation forthwith. But, fundamental as it is, this requirement of the constitution does not form part of the law of the constitution.

247. It is also a constitutional requirement that the person who is appointed Prime Minister or Premier by the Crown and who is the effective head of the government should have the support of the elected branch of the legislature; in practice, this means in most cases the leader of the political party which has won a majority of seats at a general election. Other ministers are appointed by the Crown on the advice of the Prime Minister or Premier when he forms or reshuffles his cabinet. Ministers must continuously have the confidence of the elected branch of the legislature, individually and collectively. Should they lose it, they must either resign or ask the Crown for a dissolution of the legislature and the holding of a general election. Most of the powers of the Crown under the prerogative are exercised only upon the advice of the Prime Minister or the cabinet, which means that they are effectively exercised by the latter, together with the innumerable statutory powers delegated to the Crown in council.

248. Yet none of these essential rules of the constitution can be said to be a law of the constitution. It was apparently Dicey who, in the first edition of his Law of the Constitution, in 1885, called them "the conventions of the constitution", an expression which quickly became current (W.S. Holdsworth, "The Conventions of the Eighteenth Century Constitution" (1932), 17 Iowa L. Rev. 161). What Dicey described under these terms are the principles and rules of responsible government, several of which are stated above and which regulate the relations between the Crown, the Prime Minister, the cabinet and the two Houses of Parliament. These rules developed in Great Britain by way of custom and precedent during the 19th century, and were exported to such British colonies as were granted self-government.

249. Dicey first gave the impression that constitutional conventions are a peculiarly British and modern phenomenon. But he recognized in later editions that different conventions are found in other constitutions. As Sir William Holdsworth wrote at p. 162:

In fact conventions must grow up at all times and in all places where the powers of government are vested in different persons or bodies - where in other words there is a mixed constitution. 'The constituent parts of a State,' said Burke, [French Revolution, 28] 'are obliged to hold their public faith with each other, and with all those who derive any serious interest under their engagements, as much as the whole state is bound to keep its faith with separate communities.' Necessarily conventional rules spring up to regulate the working of the various parts of the constitution, their relations to one another, and to the subject.

Alert

250. Within the British Empire, powers of government were vested in different bodies, which provided a fertile ground for the growth of new constitutional conventions unknown to Dicey, whereby self-governing colonies acquired equal and independent status within the commonwealth. ...

251. A federal constitution provides for the distribution of powers between various legislatures and governments, and may also constitute a fertile ground for the growth of constitutional conventions between those legislatures and governments. ...It was to this possibility that Duff C.J.C. alluded when he referred to "constitutional usage or constitutional practice" in Reference *re Power of Disallowance and Power of Reservation*, [1938] S.C.R. 71 at 78, [1938] 2 D.L.R. 8. ...

252. The main purpose of constitutional conventions is to ensure that the legal framework of the constitution will be operated in accordance with the prevailing constitutional values or principles of the period. For example, the constitutional value which is the pivot of the conventions stated above and relating to responsible government is the democratic principle that the powers of the state must be exercised in accordance with the wishes of the electorate, and the constitutional value or principle which anchors the conventions regulating the relationship between the members of the Commonwealth is the independence of the former British colonies.

Alert

253. Being based on custom and precedent, constitutional conventions are usually unwritten rules. Some of them, however, may be reduced to writing and expressed in

the proceedings and documents of Imperial conferences, or in the preamble of statutes such as the Statute of Westminster, 1931, or in the proceedings and documents of federal-provincial conferences. They are often referred to and recognized in statements made by members of governments.

254. The conventional rules of the constitution present one striking peculiarity. In contradistinction to the laws of the constitution, they are not enforced by the courts. One reason for this situation is that, unlike common law rules, conventions are not judge-made rules. They are not based on judicial precedents but on precedents established by the institutions of government themselves. Nor are they in the nature of statutory commands which it is the function and duty of the courts to obey and enforce. Furthermore, to enforce them would mean to administer some formal sanction when they are breached. But the legal system, from which they are distinct, does not contemplate formal sanctions for their breach.

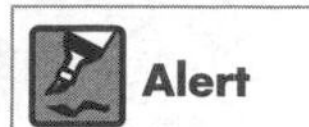

255. Perhaps the main reason why conventional rules cannot be enforced by the courts is that they are generally in conflict with the legal rules which they postulate, and the courts are bound to enforce the legal rules. The conflict is not of a type which would entail the commission of any illegality. It results from the fact that legal rules create wide powers, discretions and rights which conventions prescribe should be exercised only in a certain limited manner, if at all.

[The Justices use some examples to illustrate the point and continued:]

259. This conflict between convention and law, which prevents the courts from enforcing conventions, also prevents conventions from crystallizing into laws, unless it be by statutory adoption.

260. It is because the sanctions of convention rest with institutions of government other than courts, such as the Governor-General or the Lieutenant-Governor, or the Houses of Parliament, or with public opinion and, ultimately, with the electorate that it is generally said that they are "political".

261. We respectfully adopt the definition of a "convention" given by the learned Chief Justice of Manitoba, Freedman C.J.M., in the Manitoba reference at pp. 13–14:

> What is a constitutional convention? ...[T]here is general agreement that a convention occupies a position somewhere in between a usage or custom on the one hand and a constitutional law on the other. There is general agreement that if one sought to fix that position with greater precision he would place convention nearer to law than to usage or custom. There is also general agreement that 'a convention is a rule which is regarded as obligatory by the officials to whom it applies': Hogg, Constitutional Law of Canada (1977), p. 9. There is, if not general agreement, at least weighty authority, that the sanction for breach of a convention will be political rather than legal.

262. It should be borne in mind, however, that, while they are not laws, some conventions may be more important than some laws. Their importance depends on that of the value or principle which they are meant to safeguard. Also, they form an integral part of the constitution and of the constitutional system. ...

263. That is why it is perfectly appropriate to say that to violate a convention is to do something which is unconstitutional, although it entails no direct legal consequence. But the words "constitutional" and "unconstitutional" may also be used in a strict legal sense, for instance, with respect to a statute which is found ultra vires, or unconstitutional. The foregoing may perhaps be summarized in an equation: constitutional conventions plus constitutional law equal the total constitution of the country.

Alert

II – Whether the Questions should be Answered

[The Justices outlined Counsel's arguments and concluded:]

267. Question 2 is not confined to an issue of pure legality, but it has to do with a fundamental issue of constitutionality and legitimacy. Given the broad statutory basis upon which the governments of Manitoba, Newfoundland and Quebec are empowered to put questions to their three respective Courts of Appeal, they are, in our view, entitled to an answer to a question of this type.

...

270. In so recognizing conventional rules, the courts have described them, sometimes commented upon them and given them such precision as is derived from the written form of a judgment. They did not shrink from doing so on account of the political aspects of conventions, nor because of their supposed vagueness, uncertainty or flexibility.

271. In our view, we should not, in a constitutional reference, decline to accomplish a type of exercise that courts have been doing of their own motion for years.

III – Whether the Convention Exists

(1) The class of constitutional amendments contemplated by the question

276. Constitutional amendments fall into three categories: (1) amendments which may be made by a provincial legislature acting alone ...; (2) amendments which may be made by the Parliament of Canada acting alone ...; and (3) all other amendments.

277. The first two categories are irrelevant for the purposes of these references. While the wording of the second and third questions of the Manitoba and Newfoundland references may be broad enough to embrace all amendments in the third category, it is not necessary for us to consider those amendments which affect federal-provincial relationship only indirectly.

...

280. Therefore, in essence, although not in terms, the issue raised by the second question in the Manitoba and Newfoundland references is whether there is a constitutional convention for agreement of the provinces to amendments which change legislative powers and provide for a method of effecting such change. The same issue is raised by Q. B of the Quebec reference, above quoted in part.

(2) Requirements for establishing a convention

281. The requirements for establishing a convention bear some resemblance with those which apply to customary law. Precedents and usage are necessary but do not suffice. They must be normative. We adopt the following passage of Sir W. Ivor Jennings in The Law and the Constitution, 5th ed. (1959), p. 136:

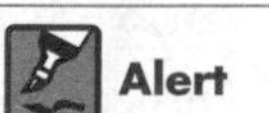

> We have to ask ourselves three questions: first, what are the precedents; secondly, did the actors in the precedents believe that they were bound by a rule; and thirdly, is there a reason for the rule? A single precedent with a good reason may be enough to establish the rule. A whole string of precedents without such a reason will be of no avail, unless it is perfectly certain that the persons concerned regarded them as bound by it.

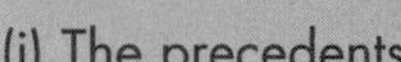

(i) The precedents

282. An account of the statutes enacted by the Parliament of Westminster to modify the constitution of Canada is found in a white paper published in 1965 under the authority of the Honourable Guy Favreau, then Minister of Justice for Canada, under the title of "The Amendment of the Constitution of Canada" ("the White Paper"). This account is quoted in the Senate Reference, supra, but we find it necessary to reproduce it here for convenience:

[The Justices set out 22 examples and continued:]

...

284. For reasons already stated, these precedents must be considered selectively. They must also be considered in positive as well as in negative terms.

285. Of these 22 amendments or groups of amendments, five directly affected federal-provincial relationships, in the sense of changing provincial legislative powers; they are the amendment of 1930, the Statute of Westminster, 1931, and the amendments of 1940, 1951 and 1964.

....

288. The 1940 amendment is of special interest, in that it transferred an exclusive legislative power from the provincial legislatures to the Parliament of Canada.

289. In 1938, the Speech from the Throne (House of Commons Debates (1938), p. 2) stated:

> The co-operation of the provinces has been sought with a view to an amendment of the British North America Act, which would empower the parliament of Canada to enact forthwith a national scheme of unemployment insurance. My ministers hope the proposal may meet with early approval, in order that unemployment insurance legislation may be enacted during the present session of parliament.

290. In November 1937, the government of Canada had communicated with the provinces and asked for their views in principle. A draft amendment was later circulated. By March 1938, five of the nine provinces had approved the draft amendment. Ontario had agreed in principle, but Alberta, New Brunswick and Quebec had declined to join in. The proposed amendment was not proceeded with

until June 1940, when Prime Minister King announced to the House of Commons that all nine provinces had assented to the proposed amendment: Gerin-Lajoie at p. 106.

291. The 1951 and 1964 amendments changed the legislative powers: areas of exclusive provincial competence became areas of concurrent legislative competence. They were agreed upon by all the provinces.

292. These five amendments are the only ones which can be viewed as positive precedents whereby federal-provincial relationships were directly affected in the sense of changing legislative powers.

293. Every one of these five amendments was agreed upon by each province whose legislative authority was affected.

294. In negative terms, no amendment changing provincial legislative powers has been made since Confederation when agreement of a province whose legislative powers would have been changed was withheld.

295. There are no exceptions.

296. Furthermore, in even more telling negative terms, in 1951 an amendment was proposed to give the provinces a limited power of indirect taxation. Ontario and Quebec did not agree, and the amendment was not proceeded with: House of Commons Debates (1951), pp. 2682, 2726-43.

297. The Constitutional Conference of 1960 devised a formula for the amendment of the constitution of Canada. Under this formula, the distribution of legislative powers could have been modified. The great majority of the participants found the formula acceptable, but some differences remained, and the proposed amendment was not proceeded with: White Paper, p. 29.

298. In 1964, a conference of first ministers unanimously agreed on an amending formula that would have permitted the modification of legislative powers. Quebec subsequently withdrew its agreement, and the proposed amendment was not proceeded with: Professor Lederman, Senate-House of Commons Special Joint Committees on Constitution of Canada (23rd August 1978), vol. 5, p. 14.

299. Finally, in 1971, proposed amendments which included an amending formula were agreed upon by the federal government and eight of the ten provincial governments. Quebec disagreed, and Saskatchewan, which had a new government, did not take a position, because it was believed that the disagreement of Quebec rendered the question academic. The proposed amendments were not proceeded with: Gerald A. Beaudoin, Le Partage des Pouvoirs (1980), p. 349.

300. The accumulation of these precedents, positive and negative, concurrent and without exception, does not of itself suffice in establishing the existence of the convention, but it unmistakedly (sic) points in its direction. Indeed, if the precedents stood alone, it might be argued that unanimity is required.

...

317. Finally, it was noted in the course of argument that, in the case of four of the five amendments mentioned above, where provincial consent effectively had been obtained, the statutes enacted by the Parliament of Westminster did not refer to this consent. This does not alter the fact that consent was obtained.

(ii) The actors treating the rule as binding

318. In the White Paper, one finds this passage at pp. 10-11:

PROCEDURES FOLLOWED IN THE PAST IN SECURING AMENDMENTS TO THE BRITISH NORTH AMERICA ACT

...

319. There follows a list of 14 constitutional amendments thought to "have contributed to the development of accepted constitutional rules and principles". The White Paper then goes on to state these principles, at p. 15:

The first general principle that emerges in the foregoing resume is that although an enactment by the United Kingdom is necessary to amend the British North America Act, such action is taken only upon formal request from Canada. No Act of the United Kingdom Parliament affecting Canada is therefore passed unless it is requested and consented to by Canada.

Conversely, every amendment requested by Canada in the past has been enacted.

The second general principle is that the sanction of Parliament is required for a request to the British Parliament for an amendment to the British North America Act. This principle was established early in the history of Canada's constitutional amendments, and has not been violated since 1895.

The procedure invariably is to seek amendments by a joint Address of the Canadian House of Commons and Senate to the Crown.

The third general principle is that no amendment to Canada's Constitution will be made by the British Parliament merely upon the request of a Canadian province. A number of attempts to secure such amendments have been made, but none has been successful. The first such attempt was made as early as 1868, by a province which was at that time dissatisfied with the terms of Confederation. This was followed by other attempts in 1869, 1874 and 1887.

The British Government refused in all cases to act on provincial government representations on the grounds that it should not intervene in the affairs of Canada except at the request of the federal government representing all of Canada.

The fourth general principle is that the Canadian Parliament will not request an amendment directly affecting federal-provincial relationships without prior consultation and agreement with the provinces. This principle did not emerge as early as others but since 1907, and particularly since 1930, has gained increasing recognition and acceptance. The nature and the degree of provincial participation in the amending process, however, have not lent themselves to easy definition.

320. The text which precedes the four general principles makes it clear that it deals with conventions. It refers to the laws and conventions by which a country is governed, and to constitutional rules which are not binding in any strict sense (that is, in a legal sense) but which have come to be recognized and accepted in practice as part of the amendment process in Canada. The first three general principles are statements of well-known constitutional conventions governing the relationships between Canada and the United Kingdom with respect to constitutional amendments.

321. In our view, the fourth general principle equally and unmistakedly (sic) states and recognizes as a rule of the Canadian constitution the convention referred to in the second question of the Manitoba and Newfoundland references, as well as in Q.B of the Quebec reference, namely, that there is a requirement for provincial agreement to amendments which change provincial legislative powers.

322. This statement is not a casual utterance. It is contained in a carefully drafted document which had been circulated to all the provinces prior to its publication and been found satisfactory by all of them... . It was published as a white paper, that is, as an official statement of government policy, under the authority of the federal Minister of Justice as member of a government responsible to Parliament, neither House of which, so far as we know, has taken issue with it. This statement is a recognition by all the actors in the precedents that the requirement of provincial agreement is a constitutional rule.

...

337. [W]hile the precedents point at unanimity, it does not appear that all the actors in the precedents have accepted the unanimity rule as a binding one.

338. In 1965, the White Paper had stated that: "The nature and the degree of provincial participation in the amending process ... have not lent themselves to easy definition."

339. Nothing has occurred since then which would permit us to conclude in a more precise manner.

340. Nor can it be said that this lack of precision is such as to prevent the principle from acquiring the constitutional status of a conventional rule. If a consensus had emerged on the measure of provincial agreement, an amending formula would quickly have been enacted and we would no longer be in the realm of conventions. To demand as much precision as if this were the case and as if the rule were a legal one is tantamount to denying that this area of the Canadian constitution is capable of being governed by conventional rules.

341. Furthermore, the government of Canada and the governments of the provinces have attempted to reach a consensus on a constitutional amending formula in the course of ten federal-provincial conferences, held in 1927, 1931, 1935, 1950, 1960, 1964, 1971, 1978, 1979 and 1980: Beaudoin, p. 346. A major issue at these conferences was the quantification of provincial consent. No consensus was reached on this issue. But the discussion of this very issue for more than 50 years postulates a

clear recognition by all the governments concerned of the principle that a substantial degree of provincial consent is required.

342. It would not be appropriate for the court to devise in the abstract a specific formula which would indicate in positive terms what measure of provincial agreement is required for the convention to be complied with. Conventions by their nature develop in the political field and it will be for the political actors, not this court, to determine the degree of provincial consent required.

343. It is sufficient for the court to decide that at least a substantial measure of provincial consent is required, and to decide further whether the situation before the court meets with this requirement. The situation is one where Ontario and New Brunswick agree with the proposed amendments, whereas the eight other provinces oppose it. By no conceivable standard could this situation be thought to pass muster. It clearly does not disclose a sufficient measure of provincial agreement. Nothing more should be said about this.

(iii) A reason for the rule

344. The reason for the rule is the federal principle. Canada is a federal union. The preamble of the B.N.A. Act states that "the provinces of Canada, Nova Scotia, and New Brunswick have expressed their Desire to be federally united".

345. The federal character of the Canadian constitution was recognized in innumerable judicial pronouncements. We will quote only one, that of Lord Watson in *Liquidators of Maritime Bank*, supra, at pp. 441-42:

> The object of the Act was neither to weld the provinces into one, nor to subordinate provincial governments to a central authority, but to create a federal government in which they should all be represented, entrusted with the exclusive administration of affairs in which they had a common interest, each province retaining its independence and autonomy.

346. The federal principle cannot be reconciled with a state of affairs where the modification of provincial legislative powers could be obtained by the unilateral action of the federal authorities. It would, indeed, offend the federal principle that "a radical change to [the] constitution [be] taken at the request of a bare majority of the members of the Canadian House of Commons and Senate": Report of Dominion-Provincial Conference (1931), p. 3.

347. This is an essential requirement of the federal principle which was clearly recognized by the Dominion-Provincial Conference of 1931. This conference had been convened to consider the proposed Statute of Westminster, as well as a draft of s. 7, which dealt exclusively with the Canadian position.

348. At the opening of the Conference, Prime Minister Bennett said (pp. 3-4):

> It should be noted that nothing in the Statute confers on the Parliament of Canada the power to alter the constitution.

The position remained that nothing in the future could be done to amend the British North America Act except as the result of appropriate action taken in Canada and in London. In the past such appropriate action had been an address by both Houses of the Canadian Parliament to the Parliament of Westminster. It was recognized, however, that this might result in a radical change to our constitution taken at the request of a bare majority of the members of the Canadian House of Commons and Senate. The original draft of the Statute appeared, in the opinion of some provincial authorities, to sanction such a procedure, but in the draft before the conference this was clearly not the case.

349. This did not satisfy Premier Taschereau of Quebec, who, the next day, said (p. 12):

Do we wish the British North America Act to be amended at the request of the Dominion only, without the consent of the Provinces? Do we wish it to be amended by the Parliament of Canada? Quebec could not accept either of these suggestions. She was not prepared to agree that the British North America Act might be amended without the consent of the Provinces.

...

357. Then followed the positive precedents of 1940, 1951 and 1964, as well as the abortive ones of 1951, 1960 and 1964, all discussed above. By 1965, the rule had become recognized as a binding constitutional one, formulated in the fourth general principle of the White Paper already quoted, reading, in part, as follows:

The fourth general principle is that the Canadian Parliament will not request an amendment directly affecting federal-provincial relationships without prior consultation and agreement with the provinces.

358. The purpose of this conventional rule is to protect the federal character of the Canadian constitution and prevent the anomaly that the House of Commons and Senate could obtain by simple resolutions what they could not validly accomplish by statute.

359. It was contended by counsel for Canada, Ontario and New Brunswick that the proposed amendments would not offend the federal principle and that, if they became law, Canada would remain a federation. The federal principle would even be reinforced, it was said, since the provinces would as a matter of law be given an important role in the amending formula.

360. It is true that Canada would remain a federation if the proposed amendments became law. But it would be a different federation, made different at the instance of a majority in the Houses of the federal Parliament acting alone. It is this process itself which offends the federal principle.

361. It was suggested by counsel for Saskatchewan that the proposed amendments were perhaps severable; that the proposed Charter of Rights offended the federal principle, in that it would unilaterally alter legislative powers, whereas the proposed amending formula did not offend the federal principle.

362. To this suggestion we cannot accede. Counsel for Canada (as well as counsel for other parties and all intervenors) took the firm position that the proposed amendment formed an unseverable package. Furthermore, and, to repeat, whatever the result, the process offends the federal principle. It was to guard against this process that the constitutional convention came about.

IV – Conclusion

363. We have reached the conclusion that the agreement of the provinces of Canada, no views being expressed as to its quantification, is constitutionally required for the passing of the "Proposed Resolution for a joint Address to Her Majesty respecting the Constitution of Canada" and that the passing of this resolution without such agreement would be unconstitutional in the conventional sense.

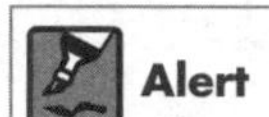

This case is a very interesting one on several levels. First, it confirms the view, expressed by academics and Lord Widgery CJ, that conventions are not laws and are therefore not enforceable *per se* by the courts. In paragraph 44 of a judgment of almost 400 paragraphs the provinces effectively lost their legal case and yet the Supreme Court continued to deliver a full judgment. It had been suggested by Counsel for the federal government that it would be inappropriate for the court to deliver judgment on the second question once it had been established that the constitution could not 'crystallise' into law. However, the court clearly disagreed with that submission and spent a considerable time in discussing question 2, finally concluding that not only did the convention exist but that the federal government's actions, if they continued, would be 'unconstitutional'.

The Supreme Court clearly felt that it had a role to play as an arbiter of the constitution, even in the field of political action. The Supreme Court must have known that its conclusion, after full and reasoned argument, that the federal government's actions were unconstitutional would have an effect, even though that effect would not be in law. And indeed, as a result of this case, the federal government did feel obliged to re-negotiate with the provinces.

On a more general level, while courts may be excluded from passing binding judgment on the political aspects of the constitution, they clearly still feel they have a role to play. This will be seen throughout this book, and is especially notable in the judiciary's statements both on and off the bench concerning limitations on the sovereignty of Parliament.

Further Reading

Dicey A V, Introduction to the Study of the Law of the Constitution, 1885, Part III

Colin Munro, Studies in Constitutional Law, Chapter 3

Jack Beatson, Reforming an Unwritten Constitution, [2010] *LQR* 48

2

Separation of Powers

Topic List

1 The separation of powers
2 Implications of the separation of powers
3 The separation of powers in the United Kingdom
4 The separation of powers and constitutional reform

Alex Lawson and Christopher Costigan

Introduction

Some of the key principles relating to the separation of powers are very usefully set out in the following article by Eric Barendt. Though written 15 years ago, it will be noted that many of the issues he mentions are still highly relevant today.

1 The Separation of Powers

The separation of powers has been a central concept in modern constitutionalism. The clearest expression of this perspective may be found in Article 16 of the French Declaration of the Rights of Man of 1789: "Any society in which the safeguarding of rights is not assured, and the separation of powers is not observed, has no constitution." The principle was also discussed extensively in *The Federalist Papers,* the best analysis of the fundamental principles of a liberal constitution ever written in the English language. It is reflected in Articles I, II and III of the United States Constitution: Article I vests the legislative power in Congress, Article II the executive power in the President, and Article III the judicial power in a supreme court and other lower courts established by Congress. ...

Yet commentators on United Kingdom constitutional law have paid relatively little attention to the principle. Dicey set in this, as in other matters, a very bad example. Virtually the only mention made of it in the *Introduction to the Study of the* Law *of the Constitution* occurs in his treatment of *droit administratif* in France, when he explains the doctrine's influence on the administration's independence from judicial review by the ordinary courts. In contrast Sir Ivor Jennings did discuss the separation of powers at some length. He devoted much of the opening chapter of *The* Law *and the* Constitution, as well as an entire appendix, to the doctrine, only to dismiss its coherence and significance for the protection of civil liberties. ... Other treatments tend to be either brief or dismissive...

On one view this apparent lack of concern for the separation of powers is hard to explain. After all, Montesquieu based his famous exposition of the doctrine on his understanding of the British constitution. Admittedly, that is now regarded as flawed. Even the eighteenth-century constitution did not observe a separation of powers, as the idea was formulated at the end of that century in the United States and in France. There was, for example, no bar then (or now) on government ministers, the executive, from sitting in either the House of Commons or the House of Lords, the two branches of the legislature. Indeed they are required to do so by convention. But there was a balance of powers in the constitution, which for Madison, the principal author of *The Federalist Papers,* served the same purpose as the stricter pure separation principle. Indeed, it is far from clear that he would have regarded his version of the separation of powers theory, the *partial* separation of powers with its emphasis on reciprocal checks and balances between the three branches of government, as significantly different from the fundamental principles of the contemporary British constitution.

1.1 The values served by the separation of powers

...The classic formulation is that there are three distinct functions of government – the legislative, executive, and the judicial – which should be discharged by three separate agencies – the legislature, the executive (or government), and the judiciary (or courts) – and that no individual should be a member of more than one of them. ...

Montesquieu was in no doubt about the importance of the principle. It was to be valued as a guarantee against tyranny.

When the legislative and executive powers are united in the same person, or in the same body of magistrates, there can be no liberty; because apprehensions may arise, lest the same monarch or senate should enact tyrannical laws to execute them in a tyrannical manner.

He added, in his most distinctive contribution to separation of powers theory, that it was equally important for the judicial power to be wholly independent of the other two branches of government. Otherwise the legislature, or executive, could pass laws, knowing that it could enforce them selectively against a chosen individual or section of society. ...

1.2 The partial separation theory

...[T]he separation of powers should not be explained in terms of a strict distribution of *functions* between the three branches of government, but in terms of a network of rules and principles which ensure that power is not concentrated in the hands of one branch. (In practice the danger now is that the executive has too much power, though it is worth remembering that at other times there was more anxiety about self-aggrandizement of the legislature.) That does not mean that the allocation of functions is wholly irrelevant. I will explain in the next section of this article how in civil liberties cases courts may properly insist that general rules be made by the legislature and that the executive does not act without legislative authorization to deprive individuals of their rights. But the importance of a correct definition and allocation of functions should not be exaggerated. Madison for instance was not troubled by these questions, though nobody has argued so cogently for the separation of powers principle.

Outside the context of court rulings in civil liberties cases, the principle is most frequently applied in the architecture of the constitution itself. Powers are allocated to different institutions. The legislature is normally divided into two branches, a procedure recommended by Madison on the ground that otherwise it would be too powerful. Each branch is empowered to check the others by exercising a *partial agency* or *control* over their acts. That is why, for example, in the United States Constitution the Senate must give its advice and consent to the appointment of ministers, ambassadors and judges, and the President may veto Bills passed by the House of Representatives and the Senate, subject to an override by a two-thirds majority vote in each House. It is not very helpful to ask whether in the former instance the Senate is exercising an executive power and whether in the latter the President acts as a third branch of the legislature. What is important is that there is a system of checks and balances between institutions which otherwise might exercise excessive power. As Madison put it in *Federalist Paper 51*, the structure of government should be so arranged "that its several constituent parts may, by their mutual relations, be the means of keeping each other in their proper places."

2 Implications of the separation of powers

Link

See Rule of Law for further discussion on the use of the Human Rights Act to protect fundamental rights by the courts.

It is worth exploring some of the implications of commitment to the separation of powers found in other legal systems before turning to the significance of the principle in the modern United Kingdom constitution. For it has been argued that the principle is too ambivalent to be useful. It is also said that it has been compromised by, for example, the need to tolerate extensive executive law-making under the welfare state. Yet there are a number of cases in the United States, and more recently France and Germany, where separation of powers arguments have been decisive in litigation. In particular (though not exclusively) they have been used to bolster claims that a citizen's fundamental rights have been violated.

This coupling of the two arguments is no accident. For the litigant may be uncertain whether his right will prevail against the substantial public interest which, according to the government, justifies its infringement. Alternatively the contours of the right may be uncertain or controversial. It may be relatively easier to deploy an argument that the decision has been taken unconstitutionally by the executive when it was only appropriate for the legislature to act. Moreover, under this argument judicial review is less susceptible to the charge that it is fundamentally undemocratic. Indeed, when a court requires the legislature to impose clearer standards on the executive or the police, it would be reinforcing democratic values. Individuals and pressure groups enjoy readier access to legislators than they do to ministers, civil servants or police officers, and so may in theory exercise some influence on the drafting of legislation. Equally, the courts should be particularly willing to strike down retrospective criminal legislation, insofar as it interferes with the general liberty of the defendants and also with their rights to a fair trial. In these circumstances, the civil rights argument reinforces the case that the legislature is violating the structural limits on its powers.

Courts are, therefore, right to look with particular suspicion on acts of the executive which affect individuals and which are entirely unauthorised by statute. This is exemplified by a number of United States cases, among them the famous Supreme Court decisions in the *Steel Seizure* and *Pentagon Papers* cases. In the former the Court held President Truman had violated the separation of powers when he issued an order directing seizure of all steel mills. Put simply there was neither constitutional nor Congressional authority for the order, which at least two members of the majority, Black J. and Douglas J. regarded as an attempt on the part of the President to exercise legislative power. Moreover, it trespassed on the mill owners' constitutional property right guaranteed by the Fifth Amendment. The right at issue in the *Pentagon Papers* case was the First Amendment freedom of speech and of the press. The federal government had applied for an injunction to restrain publication of classified Defence

Department documents in the *New York Times* and the *Washington Post*. The most important reason for denial of the remedy was the hostility in the United States to any prior restraint on speech, but several members of the Court stressed the absence of any Congressional statute, which authorised the government to take proceedings in these circumstances or which prohibited publication of such documents. In contrast, the English courts have been quite willing to apply the law on breach of confidence at the request of the executive without prior Parliamentary enactment, as shown by the Crossman Diaries and *Spycatcher* cases.

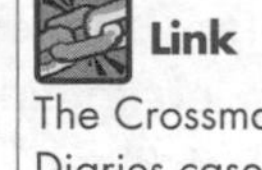
Link
The Crossman Diaries case is A-G v Jonathan Cape Ltd [1976] QB 752 in Chapter 1.

In other First Amendment cases the Supreme Court has invalidated legislation conferring wide licensing powers on city officials or police officers. In *Lovell v. Griffin* it struck down an ordinance giving a City Manager unfettered discretion to ban the public distribution of circulars and pamphlets. Other decisions have applied the same principle in the context of the allocation of permits to use loudspeakers, and to hold public meetings. In all these cases the official was free to formulate for himself the grounds on which he determined the applications. In effect the city ordinance gave him a legislative as well as an executive power. This is clearly undesirable. Without detailed standards to constrain official discretion, it is unlikely that due regard will be paid to the constitutional rights at issue. Moreover, such wide power can be applied selectively, say, to political groups favoured by the official or chief of police, without any opportunity for democratic control.

There are similar decisions of the Conseil constitutionnel in France. Under the Constitution of the Fifth Republic, there is a complex division of legislative authority between Parliament and the government. Broadly, the former has power under Article 34 to enact *lois* over certain specified topics, while under Article 37 other matters "fall within the field of rule-making". In other words, it would appear that government enjoys a wide residuary power to issue *règlements.* However, the jurisprudence of the Conseil has interpreted these provisions in favour of Parliament, recognising *inter alia* that it alone may enact rules which affect the general principles of French law (*principes généraux du droit*), and rules which impose penal sanctions involving a deprivation of personal liberty. In addition, as already mentioned, it has insisted that statutes grant the judiciary the authority to determine issues of personal liberty and not delegate such authority without clear standards to the police.

The separation of powers principle may also be relevant to constitutional disputes or litigation, even where there is no immediate or direct impact on the rights and liberties of individuals. This may be illustrated by reference to two different sets of circumstances. The first concerns the organization and powers of broadcasting authorities. In a number of cases the German Constitutional Court has said that it is for the state legislature to lay down the fundamental rules about membership of the regulatory bodies, its powers, and the standards by which public and private broadcasters are to operate. These matters are too important to be left to administrative regulation or to the discretion of the authority itself. This is really a constitutional point: the legislature, and not the executive, nor even an independent agency, should take responsibility for framing these rules which touch on the exercise of fundamental liberties.

The second set of circumstances involves political parties and the rights of members of the legislature. Continental European constitutions recognise the distinctive role of political parties and other groups, a matter on which both United Kingdom and United States constitutions are silent. One of the earliest decisions of the Conseil constitutionnel held a rule of the National Assembly unconstitutional with regard to Article 4 of the Constitution. That guarantees the right to form parties, though "[T]hey must respect the principles of national sovereignty and democracy". Article 19-3 of a draft Assembly regulation would have given it the power to decide whether a party respected these principles and hence should be recognised for parliamentary purposes.

The Conseil clearly thought it undesirable to leave this sensitive matter to the judgement of the majority party or coalition in the Assembly, in effect to the will of the government. In Germany the Basic Law reserves this assessment for the Constitutional Court. Only it may decide that a political party is unconstitutional because it "seeks to impair or abolish the free democratic basic order or to endanger the existence" of the country. In principle, it must be right to allocate this decision to the judicial branch, since both legislature and executive have an interest in its outcome, which may run counter to democratic values.

Somewhat similar issues may be raised in the context of disputes about whether a member should be expelled from the legislature for financial or other misconduct. In the United Kingdom this has been left for the Houses of Parliament themselves to regulate, and it is inconceivable that the ordinary courts would interfere with a decision to expel or suspend a member. In contrast the United States Supreme Court has held that it may review the exclusion of an elected member by the House of Representatives; his claim was not barred by the "political questions" doctrine and was justiciable. Article 1, section 5 of the Constitution provides that a member may be expelled for disorderly behaviour, but that provision was not invoked by the House. Warren C.J. rightly concluded that for the House to claim further powers to exclude an elected member would be dangerous to a representative democracy. The Court has also upheld an appeal against conviction for contempt of Congress, imposing significant limits on its power to conduct investigations. These procedures carried the risk that Congress would cease to act as a legislature and would assume an executive or judicial role. Under the Basic Law the Bundestag is free to determine election disputes, but is subject in this respect to the control of the Constitutional Court.

The separation of powers principle is therefore not simply a formal guide to the organization of state power. It can be given teeth by constitutional courts to reinforce the protection conferred by the constitution on individual rights, and to prevent one branch of government from accumulating excessive powers. Whatever its theoretical defects may be, case law in other systems shows that it is not as vacuous as its English critics have alleged.

3 The separation of powers in the United Kingdom

One of Walter Bagehot's best known remarks is that "[t]he efficient secret of the English *[sic]* Constitution may be described as the close union, the nearly complete fusion, of the executive and legislative powers." He contrasted this with the Presidential system in the United States, where the President and Congress are totally separate from each other. The former is not chosen by or responsible to the latter. In the United Kingdom, on the other hand, the executive is formed from the majority party in the legislature. Ministers sit in Parliament, so there is no separation of membership of the legislative and executive organs as there is in the United States and in France. The Prime Minister is able to control the House of Commons through his power to recommend to the Crown a dissolution of Parliament. For Bagehot this was entirely satisfactory, though it is hard to see why he reached this conclusion when he admitted that parliamentary government is in essence "sectarian government".

When Bagehot wrote, there was perhaps still a system of "checks and balances" in the U.K. constitution. Admittedly it was a shadow of the eighteenth-century balance of powers, when the Commons, Lords, and the King (with his Court) still constituted distinct social interests, participating almost equally in the formation of legislative policy. But the House of Lords balanced the Commons to some extent until its legislative powers were reduced by the Parliament Acts 1911-49. During the nineteenth-century Members of Parliament were conscious of their independent representative role as advocated by Burke, and were more willing to act independently of political party loyalties and constraints than they are now. Bagehot argued that excesses of sectarian zeal could be checked by the Prime Minister's power to dissolve Parliament. He seems to have ignored the possibility that the government and Parliament might be party to the same excesses. Overall his attempts to find the constitution's "supposed checks and balances" (to use his term) were very unconvincing.

The truth is that there is no effective separation of powers between legislature and executive in the United Kingdom in the sense of a system of "checks and balances". The advent of mass political parties has destroyed the semblance of such a system which existed a century ago. Except on the rare occasions when there is a significant party split, the government effectively controls the legislature. For Members of Parliament are, it can be said, selected by party members or activists, and are certainly in practice answerable to them for their conduct and voting record. The chief concern of party loyalists is to support the government, or to bring it down when it is controlled by the other party. Hence the executive is able to control members of the legislature through the device of party. This phenomenon is of course not confined to the United Kingdom. Even in the United States, Jackson J. observed that the party system had significantly increased the effective power of the President by enabling him to apply pressure on the legislators who are supposed to check him.

In fact the constitutional settlement achieved by the Glorious Revolution nearly introduced an institutional separation of legislative and executive powers. During the

1690s there was considerable apprehension that a Hanoverian King would attempt to control Parliament. The Act of Settlement 1701, therefore, provided that, after the date of his succession, no minister or Crown appointee could sit in the Commons. But the provision was never brought into operation; instead, it was replaced by more moderate rules against placemen which precluded civil servants, and army and navy officers, from membership of the House. At the beginning of the nineteenth century William Cobbett thought it desirable to re-introduce the stronger prohibition. Even now some deference to institutional separation is shown by the limit on the number of ministers who may sit in the Commons.

There is, however, an effective separation of the judicial power from the other branches. Judges may not sit in the House of Commons and they are protected from summary removal under the Act of Settlement 1701. By convention lay peers may not take part in the deliberations of the House of Lords as an appeal court. On the other hand, the position of the Lord Chancellor and the freedom, increasingly exploited, of the Law Lords to participate in the legislative debates of the Upper House, contravene the principle, albeit moderately and perhaps acceptably.

Decipher
Note that, since Barendt wrote this article, the Constitutional Reform Act 2005 has changed the role of Lord Chancellor and created a new Court.

While there is in practice a fusion of legislative and executive *powers*, there is in principle a distinction between the two *functions*. In other words, government may control the legislature (and certainly there is overlapping membership), but it must still legislate through Acts of Parliament. Since the *Case of Proclamations* the Crown has had no power to change the law without resort to parliamentary enactment. Nor can it levy taxation, suspend a statute or dispense anyone from complying with its provisions. All three of these prerogative legislative powers were swept away by the Bill of Rights 1689. Recently the House of Lords had a marvellous opportunity to restate these principles in the *Criminal Injuries Compensation Board* case. Clearly the Home Secretary was trying to legislate, when he used his prerogative power to introduce the tariff compensation scheme. The House of Lords should have simply held it was unconstitutional for the executive to legislate. The point is important. Individuals and pressure groups almost certainly find it easier to persuade MPs to move amendments to a Bill than to induce the government to change course. Judicial intervention on this straightforward constitutional principle would have struck a blow for the values of democracy.

Link
This case is extracted below.

The Home Secretary's powers to determine the effective length of discretionary life sentences of imprisonment also raise delicate separation of functions questions. The European Court of Human Rights has twice ruled that a court must decide whether a prisoner may be detained again, subsequent to his release following expiry of the minimum tariff period of his sentence. These rulings were determined by the text of Article 5(4) of the Human Rights Convention, which provides that anyone suffering deprivation of liberty has a right to have its legality determined speedily by a court. The separation of powers principle is also at issue here. The executive is ill-fitted to decide issues of personal liberty. It is much more susceptible than a court to media and other pressure which is likely to give individual liberty less weight than public order and safety considerations.

The courts are generally anxious to safeguard the judicial function against attempts by the executive to take it over. This is clearly evidenced by the number of administrative law cases, where they have interpreted statutes not to oust their jurisdiction to determine questions of legal entitlement or liability. In effect they disregard provisions which appear on their face to preclude judicial review of administrative decisions. One common justification for these rulings is that there is a presumption Parliament does not intend the courts' jurisdiction to be excluded, so the judges are giving effect to the will of the legislature. But this is very artificial. The separation of powers principle provides a much more cogent explanation, and in effect justifies what is in practice a restraint on the principle of parliamentary legal supremacy.

It remains, of course, unclear whether United Kingdom courts would be prepared to follow the Privy Council rulings which have invalidated retrospective penal legislations as contrary to the separation principle. Adherence to the familiar doctrine of parliamentary sovereignty might lead to the application of even the most monstrous retrospective legislation. It can safely be assumed that the courts would strive as hard as they could to avoid that course, and it would be relevant in this context that the European Human Rights Convention precludes such legislation in most circumstances.

Lords Diplock and Scarman have observed that the constitution is based on the separation of powers. But they made this point to reinforce the argument for judicial restraint in interpreting statutes; the role of the courts is not to make law, but to interpret the words used by the legislature. Interestingly, the only Law Lord to make explicit reference to the separation of powers in the *Criminal Injuries Compensation Board* case was Lord Mustill, who dissented from the majority conclusion that the Home Secretary had abused his powers. For him the principle indicated that the courts should be hesitant to expand their rapidly developing power of judicial review. In a sense all these statements support the traditional French or pure theory of the separation of powers, which has emphasised the discrete and exclusive functions of the three branches rather than the "checks and balances" approach.

The same attitude is surely implicit in those cases where the courts refuse to intervene because they fear that, if they did so, they would be trespassing on the province of the House of Commons. For example, Lord Browne-Wilkinson has recently said that Article 9 of the Bill of Rights, providing that freedom of speech in Parliament may not be questioned, manifests a wider constitutional principle that courts and Parliament recognise their discrete roles. Judges should not allow any challenge to what is said or done within Parliament in pursuance of its legislative functions. The effect of this pronouncement was that the defendant could not rely on speeches made by the plaintiff in the New Zealand House of Representatives to substantiate a defence of justification to the latter's libel action. That might lead to an injustice to the defendant (though the Privy Council conceded that in extreme cases proceedings should be stayed if in the absence of this evidence the issue could not be tried fairly). On the alternative "checks and balances" understanding of the separation principle, a court should have no hesitation in interfering here. Judicial control of parliamentary privilege is vital to prevent the legislature, or one branch of it, abusing its powers.

4 The separation of powers and constitutional reform

Separation of powers issues are as much ignored in discussion of constitutional reform as they have generally been in constitutional analysis. That is not surprising. There is no obvious constituency to whom they appeal. In comparison, there is national pressure in Scotland and Wales for devolution, while civil liberties groups campaign for incorporation of the European Convention on Human Rights. Moreover, the legal relationship of the legislature and the executive, much the most important and complex aspect of the principle, was for the most part settled three hundred years ago in the wake of the Glorious Revolution. Finally, it should not be forgotten that the agenda for constitutional reform is mostly drawn up by the two major political parties. The only reason why it is conceivable that the United Kingdom may soon experience devolution and incorporation of the Convention is that the Labour Party is now sympathetic to both causes. But it is most unlikely that the Labour party, or any other, would favour constitutional reform which would impose more effective checks and balances on the executive. After all it was the rise of the modern mass political party which has largely led to the erosion of that balance of power which characterised the constitution in the eighteenth, and to some extent even in the nineteenth, centuries.

Decipher

note that all three of these reforms have now come about.

Nevertheless, there is one serious reform proposal, which is arguably inspired by the separation of powers principle: the institution of fixed term Parliaments, with consequent abolition of the Crown's prerogative to dissolve the House of Commons and call a general election. As Bagehot pointed out, the power in effect enables the executive, and in particular the Prime Minister, to discipline a legislature which might otherwise be too independent or unruly. During the nineteenth century it may have been desirable for the government to be able to check Parliament in this way. But it is now crucial to strengthen the latter. Removal of the dissolution power would make it easier for the House of Commons to resist what it considered to be unwarranted government measures, albeit by strengthening the position of dissident members of the majority party who would be immune from the threat of an immediate dissolution and possible loss of their seats. The legislature in short would be in a position to check the executive more effectively. A comparative point is that in Germany the Federal President has very limited discretion to dissolve the Bundestag. Under Article 68 of the Basic Law he may only do this if the Chancellor's confidence motion is not passed by a majority of its members; further, the Constitutional Court may review the exercise of both the Chancellor's and the President's discretion in this context.

Another more controversial proposal would be to reduce the number of ministers entitled to sit in the House of Commons. At the moment the limit is 95, about 15 per cent of the total number of MPs. Questions should be asked about whether it is really necessary to have so many ministers in the Commons, or whether it would matter much if more were drawn from the Lords or if some, at junior level, were not even members of either House. It might be worth paying the price of a loss of ministerial accountability to Parliament to reduce the size of the pay-roll vote. More balance of a different kind would be achieved by *increasing* the powers of the Second Chamber. This desirable step could not, of course, be taken unless its composition were first changed, and its members elected on an acceptable basis, perhaps as in a federal system to represent constituent national or regional communities. What would clearly be unacceptable on separation of powers grounds is for all members of the Upper House to be appointed, even temporarily, by the government, once hereditary peers lose their voting rights. This would be a monstrous expedient, for the head of the executive would be claiming a right to choose one branch of the legislature.

Decipher
Note that this is the system that has existed since the House of Lords Act 1999.

The courts could also take the separation of powers more seriously, though in the absence of a codified constitution it is hard for them to articulate or develop appropriate principles. In particular, they should scrutinize even more carefully administrative decisions which impinge on individual rights without clear legislative authority. The applications for injunctions in the *Crossman Diaries and Spycatcher* cases should have been rejected on separation of powers grounds alone – as they would have been in the United States. The courts should also reconsider their pusillanimous attitude to parliamentary privilege and contempt cases, where abstention from review may lead to real injustice to individuals.

Whatever the shape of future constitutional reform, MPs should be careful to ensure that legislation is precise and does not delegate power to the executive or to administrative agencies without any standards to guide its exercise. Such vigilance strengthens the democratic process, and further assists the courts to check that power is not abused. Finally, there should be a comprehensive review of the legal arrangements governing the Boundary Commissions, the National Audit Office, the Audit Commission and all other bodies which are concerned with accountability. Their independence must be guaranteed against undue interference from either the legislature or executive. One means of achieving this end would be to provide that Parliament and government check each other, both at the stage of appointing members and at the time for implementation of their proposals. All these developments and arrangements are implicit in the separation of powers, a principle too long ignored in United Kingdom constitutional law.

As will have been noted from Barendt's article, the key concern behind the principle of separation of powers is the need to avoid excessive concentrations of power. While this danger could in theory come from the legislature, far greater concern has generally been directed towards the problem of the executive becoming too powerful. In the UK there has been a significant domination of the legislature by the executive, given the partial fusion of the two bodies and a traditionally strong party political system. In response to this the courts have shown themselves willing to check the executive and ensure that it does not encroach on either the courts' or the legislature's role.

4.1 Control of the Executive

Relationship with the Courts

In the case of *Re M* [1994] 1 AC 377 it was argued by the government that the executive could not be subject to an order of the court and that, if any order was followed, it would be on a voluntary basis. If correct, this would have subverted the courts' ability to safeguard the rule of law. In the Court of Appeal, Nolan L J stated that:

> It goes without saying that judgments and orders of the courts are meaningless without the willingness and ability of the executive to enforce them - and to enforce them, where necessary, against individual members of the executive itself. To that extent I accept ... the submission of the executive to orders of the court is voluntary. Equally, it is fundamental to the rule of law. So far as mutual respect is concerned, I would for my part adopt [the] submission that the proper constitutional relationship of the executive with the courts is that the courts will respect all acts of the executive within its lawful province, and that the executive will respect all decisions of the court as to what its lawful province is.

The case eventually reached the House of Lords.

***In Re M* [1994] 1 AC 377**

Panel: Lord Keith of Kinkel, Lord Templeman, Lord Griffiths, Lord Browne-Wilkinson and Lord Woolf

Facts: 'M' was a Zairian national who came to the UK seeking political asylum. His claim was rejected and his application for judicial review of that decision was refused. Immediately before his scheduled removal, he applied to the High Court for leave to apply for judicial review on allegedly fresh grounds. Mr Justice Garland indicated that he wished the applicant's departure to be postponed pending consideration, and Garland J's understanding was that counsel for the Secretary of State had given an undertaking to that effect; counsel's understanding was that no undertaking had been given. Home Office officials did nothing to stay M's removal and, during the night of M's removal, the judge made an order requiring the Secretary of State to seek to return M to the jurisdiction of the High Court. The Secretary of State, relying on legal advice that the judge's order, being an injunction against an officer of the Crown, had been made without jurisdiction, cancelled arrangements for M's return. The Home Secretary was found in contempt of court for ignoring the injunction and appealed. The key separation of powers question was whether the Crown was bound by the jurisdiction of the courts. A secondary question was, if the answer to the main question was yes, whether officers of the Crown could be held personally liable for contempt of such jurisdiction.

Injunctions and the Crown

> LORD WOOLF
>
> ...[T]he issue [of whether the court can make coercive orders against the Crown] is of constitutional importance since it goes to the heart of the relationship between the executive and the courts. Is the relationship based ... on trust and co-operation or ultimately on coercion?
>
> Mr. Richards submits that the answer to this question is provided by the decision of *Reg. v. Secretary for State for Transport, Ex parte Factortame Ltd.* [1990] 2 A.C. 85

.... The question ... arose as to whether the applicants were entitled to interim relief pending the outcome of the reference [to the ECJ]. ... Lord Bridge initially ... concluded that no relief could be granted... .

Lord Bridge went on to give a second reason for his decision which is directly relevant to the present appeal. The second reason is that injunctive relief is not available against the Crown or an officer of the Crown, when acting as such, in judicial review proceedings.

...

Before examining the second reason that Lord Bridge gave for his conclusion I should point out that I was a party to the judgment of the majority in the *Smith Kline* case. In my judgment in that case I indicated that injunctive relief was available in judicial review proceedings not only against an officer of the Crown but also against the Crown. Although in reality the distinction between the Crown and an officer of the Crown is of no practical significance in judicial review proceedings, in the theory which clouds this subject the distinction is of the greatest importance. My judgment in the earlier case may have caused some confusion in *Factortame* by obscuring the important fact that, as was the position prior to the introduction of judicial review, while prerogative orders are made regularly against ministers in their official capacity, they are never made against the Crown.

Decipher

The reason prerogative orders cannot be made against the Crown is because the Queen would, in effect, be ordering herself to do something.

...

In support of their respective submissions as to the correct answer to this issue, Mr. Richards and Mr. Kentridge relied on principles which had been repeatedly reiterated down the centuries since medieval times. The principles on which Mr. Richards founded his argument are that the King can do no wrong and that the King cannot be sued in his own courts. Mr. Kentridge on the other hand relied on the equally historic principle which is intimately linked with the name of Professor Dicey that

"when we speak of the 'rule of law' as a characteristic of our country, [we mean] not only that with us no man is above the law, but (what is a different thing) that here every man, whatever be his rank or condition, is subject to the ordinary law of the realm and amenable to the jurisdiction of the ordinary tribunals. In England the idea of legal equality, or of the universal subjection of all classes to one law administered by the ordinary courts, has been pushed to its utmost limit. With us every official, from Prime Minister down to a constable or a collector of taxes, is under the same responsibility for every act done without legal justification as any other citizen. The reports abound with cases in which officials have been brought before the courts, and made, in their personal capacity, liable to punishment, or to the payment of damages, for acts done in their official character but in excess of their lawful authority. A colonial governor, a secretary of state, a military officer, and all subordinates, though carrying out the commands of their official superiors, are as responsible for any act which the law does not authorise as is any private and unofficial person:" *Dicey on the Law of the Constitution*, 10th ed. (1959), pp. 193-194.

...

Prior to the introduction of judicial review, the principal remedies which were available were certiorari, mandamus, prohibition and habeas corpus. As we are primarily concerned with the possible availability of injunction, I will focus on mandamus and prohibition since they are indistinguishable in their effect from final injunctions. ...

The prerogative remedies could not be obtained against the Crown directly as was explained by Lord Denman C.J. in *Reg. v. Powell* (1841) 1 Q.B. 352, 361:

"both because there would be an incongruity in the Queen commanding herself to do an act, and also because the disobedience to a writ of mandamus is to be enforced by attachment."

Originally this difficulty could not be avoided by bringing the proceedings against named ministers of the Crown... . But, where a duty was imposed by statute for the benefit of the public upon a particular minister, so that he was under a duty to perform that duty in his official capacity, then orders of prohibition and mandamus were granted regularly against the minister. The proceedings were brought against the minister in his official name and according to the title of the proceedings by the Crown. The title of the proceedings would be *Reg. v. Minister, Ex parte the applicant...*, so that unless the minister was treated as being distinct from the Crown the title of the proceedings would disclose the "incongruity" of the Crown suing the Crown. This did not mean that the minister was treated as acting other than in his official capacity and the order was made against him in his official name. In accordance with this practice there have been numerous cases where prerogative orders, including orders of prohibition and mandamus, have been made against ministers. ...

After the introduction of judicial review in 1977 it was ... not necessary to draw any distinction between an officer of the Crown "acting as such" and an officer acting in some other capacity in public law proceedings.

...

Why then did Lord Bridge come to the conclusion that an injunction could not be granted against a minister in proceedings for judicial review?

A primary cause for Lord Bridge's taking this view was that he concluded that it would be a dramatic departure from what was the position prior to the introduction of judicial review for an injunction to be available against the Crown or a minister of the Crown, so that the change was one which could be expected to be made only by express legislation. His conclusion was not, however, based on as comprehensive an argument of the history of both civil and prerogative proceedings as was available to your Lordships. In particular he did not have an account of the developments which had taken place in the granting of prerogative orders against ministers, which meant that in practical terms the only consequence of treating section 31 [of the Senior Courts Act 1981] as enabling injunctions to be granted against ministers acting in their official capacity would be to provide an alternative in name only to the orders of prohibition and mandamus which were already available and to allow interim relief other than a stay for the first time.

...

I do not regard it [Lord Bridge's speech] as justifying limiting the natural interpretation of section 31 so as to exclude the jurisdiction to grant injunctions, including interim injunctions, on applications for judicial review against ministers of the Crown. ...

I am, therefore, of the opinion that, the language of section 31 being unqualified in its terms, there is no warrant for restricting its application so that in respect of ministers and other officers of the Crown alone the remedy of an injunction, including an interim injunction, is not available. In my view the history of prerogative proceedings against officers of the Crown supports such a conclusion. So far as interim relief is concerned, which is the practical change which has been made, there is no justification for adopting a different approach to officers of the Crown from that adopted in relation to other respondents in the absence of clear language... . The fact that in any event a stay could be granted against the Crown under Ord. 53, r. 3(10) emphasises the limits of the change in the situation which is involved. It would be most regrettable if an approach which is inconsistent with that which exists in Community law should be allowed to persist if this is not strictly necessary. ...

The fact that, in my view, the court should be regarded as having jurisdiction to grant interim and final injunctions against officers of the Crown does not mean that that jurisdiction should be exercised except in the most limited circumstances. In the majority of situations so far as final relief is concerned, a declaration will continue to be the appropriate remedy on an application for judicial review involving officers of the Crown. As has been the position in the past, the Crown can be relied upon to co-operate fully with such declarations. To avoid having to grant interim injunctions against officers of the Crown, I can see advantages in the courts being able to grant interim declarations. ...

4.2 Jurisdiction to make a finding of contempt

The Court of Appeal were of the opinion that a finding of contempt could not be made against the Crown, a government department or a minister of the Crown in his official capacity. Although it is to be expected that it will be rare indeed that the circumstances will exist in which such a finding would be justified, I do not believe there is any impediment to a court making such a finding, when it is appropriate to do so, not against the Crown directly, but against a government department or a minister of the Crown in his official capacity.

...

However, the finding under appeal is one made against Mr. Baker personally in respect of an injunction addressed to him in his official capacity as the Secretary of State for the Home Department. It was appropriate to direct the injunction to the Secretary of State in his official capacity since, as previously indicated, remedies on an application for judicial review which involve the Crown are made against the appropriate officer in his official capacity. This does not mean that it cannot be appropriate to make a finding of contempt against a minister personally rather than

> against him in his official capacity provided that the contempt relates to his own default. Normally it will be more appropriate to make the order against the office which a minister holds where the order which has been breached has been made against that office since members of the department concerned will almost certainly be involved and investigation as to the part played by individuals is likely to be at least extremely difficult, if not impossible, unless privilege is waived (as commendably happened in this case). In addition the object of the exercise is not so much to punish an individual as to vindicate the rule of law by a finding of contempt. This can be achieved equally by a declaratory finding of the court as to the contempt against the minister as representing the department. By making the finding against the minister in his official capacity the court will be indicating that it is the department for which the minister is responsible which has been guilty of contempt. The minister himself may or may not have been personally guilty of contempt. The position so far as he is personally concerned would be the equivalent of that which needs to exist for the court to give relief against the minister in proceedings for judicial review. There would need to be default by the department for which the minister is responsible.
>
> ...I would dismiss this appeal and cross-appeal save for substituting the Secretary of State for Home Affairs as being the person against whom the finding of contempt was made. This was the alternative decision which was the subject of the cross-appeal, except that there the order was sought against the Home Office rather than the Home Secretary.

Link

Note the interplay between the separation of powers between judiciary and executive, and the importance of the rule of law.

In *Re M* it was made clear that the Crown as monarch is above the law and no prerogative order or injunction could be made against the Queen directly. However, the Crown as government (and the persons who from time to time represent the Crown), are bound by injunctions as coercive tools and not merely by trust and co-operation.

4.3 Relationship with Parliament

The core executive (the Secretaries of State and junior ministers) are all drawn from Parliament. This fusion led Lord Hailsham to describe the British system as an 'elective dictatorship': the executive, after election, is in effect able to control the timetable of Parliament and to force through its legislative programme. However, despite this *de facto* degree of fusion and control, the courts have taken a much stricter view of the relationship between the executive and Parliament in law. This can be clearly seen in the seminal case of *Re De Keyser's Royal Hotel Ltd* [1920] AC 508 where Lord Dunedin said: 'Inasmuch as the Crown is a party to every Act of Parliament it is logical enough to consider that when the Act deals with something which before the Act could be effected by the prerogative, and specially empowers the Crown to do the same thing, but subject to conditions, the Crown assents to that, and by that Act, to the prerogative being curtailed'. However, an even stronger statement of the principle can be found in the next case which dealt with legislation which, although it had been passed, had not yet been brought into force. This case was referred to in Barendt's article as the *Criminal Injuries Compensation Board* case.

***Regina v Secretary of State for the Home Department, Ex parte Fire Brigades Union and Others* [1995] 2 AC 513**

Panel: Lord Keith of Kinkel, Lord Browne-Wilkinson, Lord Mustill, Lord Lloyd of Berwick and Lord Nicholls of Birkenhead

Facts: The Criminal Injuries Compensation scheme, which awarded damages to victims of crime based on common law principles of assessment applicable in tort (and which was set up originally using prerogative powers), was put onto a statutory footing in the Criminal Justice Act 1988. However, the relevant provisions were only to come into force "on such day as the Secretary of State may . . . appoint". No date was ever appointed and the original prerogative scheme continued in existence. The Home Secretary later indicated that the statutory scheme would not be brought into force, but that a new, amended scheme would be brought in, using prerogative power, and which would make payments on an ex-gratia, tariff basis. A declaration was sought by the Fire Brigades Union (representing members likely to be the victims of criminal injuries), that the new scheme was an abuse of power while the statutory scheme remained on the 'statute book'; and that it was not open to the Home Secretary to fetter his discretion by stating that the statutory scheme would not now come into effect.

LORD BROWNE-WILKINSON

If, as I think, that is the clear purpose for which the power in section 171(1) was conferred on the Secretary of State, two things follow. First, the Secretary of State comes under a clear duty to keep under consideration from time to time the question whether or not to bring the sections (and therefore the statutory scheme) into force. In my judgment he cannot lawfully surrender or release the power contained in section 171(1) so as to purport to exclude its future exercise either by himself or by his successors. In the course of argument, the Lord Advocate accepted that this was the correct view of the legal position. It follows that the decision of the Secretary of State to give effect to the statement in paragraph 38 of the White Paper (Cm. 2434) that "the provisions in the Act of 1988 will not now be implemented" was unlawful. The Lord Advocate contended, correctly, that the attempt by the Secretary of State to abandon or release the power conferred on him by section 171(1), being unlawful, did not bind either the present Secretary of State or any successor in that office. It was a nullity. But, in my judgment, that does not alter the fact that the Secretary of State made the attempt to bind himself not to exercise the power conferred by section 171(1) and such attempt was an unlawful act.

There is a second consequence of the power in section 171(1) being conferred for the purpose of bringing the sections into force. As I have said, in my view the Secretary of State is entitled to decide not to bring the sections into force if events subsequently occur which render it undesirable to do so. But if the power is conferred on the Secretary of State with a view to bringing the sections into force, in my judgment the Secretary of State cannot himself procure events to take place and rely on the occurrence of those events as the ground for not bringing the statutory scheme into force. In claiming that the introduction of the new tariff scheme renders it undesirable now to bring the statutory scheme into force, the Secretary of State is, in effect, claiming that the purpose of the statutory power has been frustrated by his own act in choosing to introduce a scheme inconsistent with the statutory scheme approved by Parliament.

4.4 The lawfulness of the decision to introduce the tariff scheme

The tariff scheme, if validly introduced under the Royal Prerogative, is both inconsistent with the statutory scheme ... and intended to be permanent. In practice, the tariff scheme renders it now either impossible or at least more expensive to reintroduce the old scheme or the statutory enactment of it contained in the Act of 1988. The tariff scheme involves the winding-up of the old Criminal Injuries Compensation Board together with its team of those skilled in assessing compensation on the common law basis and the creation of a new body, the Criminal Injuries Compensation Authority, set up to assess compensation on the tariff basis at figures which, in some cases, will be very substantially less than under the old scheme. All this at a time when Parliament has expressed its will that there should be a scheme based on the tortious measure of damages, such will being expressed in a statute which Parliament has neither repealed nor (for reasons which have not been disclosed) been invited to repeal.

My Lords, it would be most surprising if, at the present day, prerogative powers could be validly exercised by the executive so as to frustrate the will of Parliament expressed in a statute and, to an extent, to pre-empt the decision of Parliament whether or not to continue with the statutory scheme even though the old scheme has been abandoned. It is not for the executive, as the Lord Advocate accepted, to state as it did in the White Paper (paragraph 38) that the provisions in the Act of 1988 "will accordingly be repealed when a suitable legislative opportunity occurs." It is for Parliament, not the executive, to repeal legislation. The constitutional history of this country is the history of the prerogative powers of the Crown being made subject to the overriding powers of the democratically elected legislature as the sovereign body. The prerogative powers of the Crown remain in existence to the extent that Parliament has not expressly or by implication extinguished them. But under the principle in *Attorney-General v. de Keyser's Royal Hotel Ltd.* [1920] A.C. 508, if Parliament has conferred on the executive statutory powers to do a particular act, that act can only thereafter be done under the statutory powers so conferred: any pre-existing prerogative power to do the same act is pro tanto excluded.

How then is it suggested that the executive has power in the present case to introduce under the prerogative power a scheme inconsistent with the statutory scheme? First, it is said that since sections 108 to 117 of the Act are not in force they confer no legal rights on the victims of crime and impose no duties on the Secretary of State. The *De Keyser* principle does not apply since it only operates to the extent that Parliament has conferred statutory powers which in fact replace pre-existing powers: unless and until the statutory provisions are brought into force, no statutory powers have been conferred and therefore the prerogative powers remain. Moreover, the abandonment of the old scheme and the introduction of the new tariff scheme does not involve any interference by the executive with private rights. The old scheme, being a scheme for ex gratia payments, conferred no legal rights on the victims of crime. The new tariff scheme, being also an ex gratia scheme, confers benefits not detriments on the victims of crime. How can it be unlawful to confer benefits on the citizen, provided that Parliament has voted the necessary funds for that purpose?

In my judgment, these arguments overlook the fact that this case is concerned with public, not private, law. If this were an action in which some victim of crime were suing for the benefits to which he was entitled under the old scheme, the arguments which I have recited would have been fatal to his claim: such a victim has no legal right to any benefits. But these are proceedings for judicial review of the decisions of the Secretary of State in the discharge of his public functions. The well known passage in the speech of Lord Diplock in the *G.C.H.Q.* case, *Council of Civil Service Unions v. Minister for the Civil Service* [1985] A.C. 374, 408-410, demonstrates two points relevant to the present case. First, an executive decision which affects the legitimate expectations of the applicant (even though it does not infringe his legal rights) is subject to judicial review. Second, judicial review is as applicable to decisions taken under prerogative powers as to decisions taken under statutory powers save to the extent that the legality of the exercise of certain prerogative powers (e.g. treaty-making) may not be justiciable.

...

In his powerful dissenting judgment in the Court of Appeal Hobhouse L.J., ante, pp. 523C et seq., decided that, since the statutory provisions had not been brought into force, they had no legal significance of any kind. He held, in my judgment correctly, that the *De Keyser* principle did not apply to the present case: since the statutory provisions were not in force they could not have excluded the pre-existing prerogative powers. Therefore the prerogative powers remained. He then turned to consider whether it could be said that the Secretary of State had abused those prerogative powers and again approached the matter on the basis that since the sections were not in force they had no significance in deciding whether or not the Secretary of State had acted lawfully. I cannot agree with this last step. In public law the fact that a scheme approved by Parliament was on the statute book and would come into force as law if and when the Secretary of State so determined is in my judgment directly relevant to the question whether the Secretary of State could in the lawful exercise of prerogative powers both decide to bring in the tariff scheme and refuse properly to exercise his discretion under section 171(1) to bring the statutory provisions into force.

4.5 Judicial Law Making

The ability of the courts to establish legal rules and principles through development of the common law is often seen as a breach of the theory separation of powers. The extent of this can be overstated, however. It must be borne in mind that, ultimately in the UK, Parliament is sovereign and, if it disagrees with a principle of law that has been developed by the courts, it has the power to exercise its law-making function and amend the general law, because statute is seen as a higher form of law than case law. In extreme cases Parliament can even legislate with retrospective effect so that the legal principle established in a case cannot be enforced in relation to events occurring after or before the Act was passed. An example of Parliament legislating with retrospective effect can be seen in the War Damages Act of 1965, which was passed to annul the House of Lords' decision in the case of *Burmah Oil Company (Burma Trading) Ltd. v Lord Advocate* [1965] AC 75.

Nevertheless, it has been argued that excessive judicial activism can represent a usurpation of the legislative function. The following provide some often quoted examples.

***Shaw v DPP* [1962] AC 220**

Panel: Lord Parker CJ, Streatfeild and Ashworth JJ

Facts: The appellant published a booklet detailing where prostitutes could be contacted and their services procured. He was convicted of 'conspiracy to corrupt public morals'. His main point of appeal was that there was no such offence at common law, nor was it to be found within the statutory rules relating to prostitution. The appellant's appeal was rejected in the Court of Criminal Appeal and the House of Lords. This extract picks up on the judgment of the Court of Criminal Appeal.

MR JUSTICE ASHWORTH

The first count, with which we now deal, raises in some ways a more difficult problem. The charge was one of conspiracy, and it is convenient to set out the relevant portion of the indictment: "Statement of Offence: Conspiracy to corrupt public morals. Particulars of Offence: On divers days between the 1st day of October 1959 and the 23rd day of July 1960 within the jurisdiction of the Central Criminal Court, conspired with certain persons who inserted advertisements in issues of a magazine entitled 'Ladies' Directory' numbered 7, 7 revised, 8, 9, 10 and a supplement thereto, and with certain other persons whose names are unknown, by means of the said magazine and the said advertisements to induce readers thereof to resort to the said advertisers for the purposes of fornication and of taking part in or witnessing other disgusting and immoral acts and exhibitions, with intent thereby to debauch and corrupt the morals as well of youth as of divers other liege subjects of Our Lady the Queen and to raise and create in their minds inordinate and lustful desires."

Conspiracy is an offence which takes many different forms but in the present appeal the matter was greatly simplified when Mr. Buzzard, on behalf of the prosecution, made it clear that the form of conspiracy, which he had alleged at the trial and to which he adhered, was a conspiracy to commit an unlawful act, and not a conspiracy to commit a lawful act by unlawful means. He reserved the right to contend, should it be necessary, that a conspiracy to corrupt the morals of a particular individual was an indictable offence by reason of the conspiracy, even if such corruption if done by one person would not be an offence. The unlawful act which he alleged was said to be a common law misdemeanour, namely, the corruption of public morals. His proposition was two-fold: at common law any act calculated or intended to corrupt the morals of the public or a portion thereof in general, as opposed to the morals of a particular individual or individuals, is indictable as a substantive offence. Secondly, an act calculated or intended to outrage public decency is also indictable as a substantive offence. Both parts of this proposition were naturally contested by Mr. Rees Davies and the main issue before us on this first count is whether the first of Mr. Buzzard's propositions is well-founded.

We were referred to a large number of cases, but before alluding to any of them in detail we may usefully refer to the speech of Lord Sumner in *Bowman v. Secular Society Ltd.*, in which is set out an illuminating survey of this branch of the law from the beginning of the seventeenth century. He said: "The time of Charles II was one of notorious laxity both in faith and morals, and for a time it seemed as if the old safeguards were in abeyance or had been swept away. Immorality and irreligion were cognisable in the Ecclesiastical Courts, but spiritual censures had lost their sting and those civil courts were extinct, which had specially dealt with such matters viewed as offences against civil order. The Court of King's Bench stepped in to fill the gap."

The first reported occasion on which the Court of King's Bench thus stepped in appears to be *Rex v. Sidney*. Amongst other acts alleged against Sir Charles Sidney were his exposure of his naked body upon a balcony in Covent Garden before a large gathering of people and making water on the persons below. In addition he was said to have thrown down bottles upon such persons' heads. This latter conduct was plainly within the jurisdiction of the Court of King's Bench but there was evidently an issue whether the other conduct was such as could be dealt with in that court. In the short report of the case there appears the statement that "this court is custos morum of all the King's subjects and that it is high time to punish such profane conduct." In 1780, in *Reg. v. Read*, the court expressed a different view when considering a charge of publishing an obscene libel, but the judgment in the defendant's favour was only a "judgment nisi," that is, a provisional judgment. Not long afterwards the case of *Rex v. Curl* came before the Court of King's Bench, in which the charge against the accused was that of publishing an obscene libel. Reliance was naturally placed on *Read*'s case by defending counsel, but the Attorney-General's argument to the contrary prevailed: "What I insist upon is, that this is an offence at common law, as it tends to corrupt the morals of the King's subjects, and is against the peace of the King. ... I do not insist that every immoral act is indictable, such as telling a lie, or the like; but if it is destructive of morality in general, if it does, or may, affect all the King's subjects, it then is an offence of a public nature."

Lord Raymond C.J., in giving judgment, said: "... if it reflects on religion, virtue, or morality, if it tends to disturb the civil order of society, I think it is a temporal offence." After the case had been adjourned the court "gave it as their unanimous opinion that this was a temporal offence. They said it was plain that the force used in *Sidney*'s case was but a small ingredient in the judgment of the court who fined him £2,000. And if the force was all they went upon, there was no occasion to talk of the court's being censor morum of the King's subjects. They said that if *Read*'s case was to be adjudged, they should rule it otherwise: and therefore in this case they gave judgment for the King."

In 1875, in *Reg. v. Saunders*, the main issue seems to have been whether a booth on Epsom Downs was a public place, but the decision is of importance as confirmation of the existence of a common law misdemeanour if conduct takes place which openly outrages decency and is injurious to public morality.

Similarly, in *Reg. v. Wellard*, Grove J. said "I am of opinion that this case comes within the ordinary and reasonable meaning of the principle which makes it a misdemeanour to outrage public decency and morality." Huddleston B. said: "the principle is well established which is laid down in Blackstone and in Hawkins' Pleas of the Crown, viz., that whatever openly outrages decency, and is injurious to public morals, is a common nuisance, and indictable as a misdemeanour at common law."

Lastly, in 1927, the case of *Rex v. Berg, Britt, Carré and Lummies* came before this court. This court has seen the original indictment in that case. It contains two counts, the second of which alleged a conspiracy to corrupt morals, and it is suggested that all the accused named in that count pleaded guilty to it. The issues raised in the appeal related only to the first count which charged all the accused with keeping a disorderly house, but in our view it is impossible to suppose, having regard to the eminence of the counsel engaged in the case, that if the charge in the second count alleged an offence unknown to the law, the indictment would have been drafted in that way, that the prisoners would have been allowed to plead guilty or that the point would not have been taken by the court itself, presided over by Avory J.

...

In our opinion, having regard to the long line of cases to which we have been referred, it is an established principle of common law that conduct calculated or intended to corrupt public morals (as opposed to the morals of a particular individual) is an indictable misdemeanour. As the reports show, the conduct to which that principle is applicable may vary considerably, but the principle itself does not, and in our view the facts of the present case fall plainly within it.

The contrary view put forward by Mr. Rees Davies may be summarised as follows: He accepted for the purposes of his argument the claim of the Court of King's Bench to be custos morum but he contended that acting in that role the court had, so to speak, from time to time declared particular conduct to be an offence, thereby creating an offence rather than applying existing law to particular facts. He went on to contend that Parliament in the last 100 years had concerned itself with legislation on issues of morality, decency and the like, that such legislation must be taken to be in effect a comprehensive code, and that there is no longer any occasion for the court to create new offences in its capacity as custos morum. We are unable to agree with this argument, which fails to give sufficient weight to the repeated statements of the established principle of common law to which we have already referred. The courts in the relevant cases were not creating new offences or making new law: they were applying existing law to new facts.

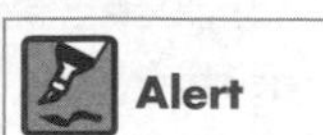

Gillick v West Norfolk and Wisbech Area Health Authority and Another [1984] QB 581

Panel: Woolf J

Facts: The NHS issued a guidance notice regarding the prescription of contraception to minors. It said that it would be unusual to provide contraceptive advice and treatment without parental consent, but that in exceptional cases it was for a doctor, exercising his clinical judgment, to decide whether contraceptive advice or treatment should be provided. The plaintiff wrote to her local area health authority seeking an assurance from them that no contraceptive advice or treatment would be given to any of her children without her consent. The area health authority refused to give the assurance and the plaintiff applied for a declaration that the advice in the notice was unlawful. Mr Justice Woolf refused to grant the declaration. The Court of Appeal reversed that decision, but on further appeal to the House of Lords the appeal was allowed. Below is an extract from the judgment of Woolf J.

MR JUSTICE WOOLF

There are two principal limbs to the argument of Mr. Wright on behalf of the plaintiff. ...The second limb is that the guidance authorises doctors to give advice and treatment to children under 16 without their parents' consent, which, if it is not a criminal offence under the foregoing provisions, is inconsistent with the rights of the parents of that child and the ability of the parents properly and effectively to discharge their duties as parents of supervising the physical and moral welfare of their children.

...

Is the giving of advice or the prescribing of contraceptives without parental consent unlawful?

Turning to the second limb of the argument, this only arises in what is described in the revised section G as "exceptional cases" which are left to the clinical judgment of a doctor. Unlike the first limb of the argument, this argument cannot apply when, in what is assumed in the guidance to be the usual situation. The advice about contraception will take place with parental consent, so there can be no interference with the "rights" of the parents.

For advice to be given and contraceptives prescribed without their consent, Mr. Wright submitted, would be inconsistent with the fundamental rights of the parents. However, he cited no authority to establish such "rights," and the interest of parents, I consider, are more accurately described as responsibilities or duties. The interference in the exceptional case with "parental rights" could only make the doctor's acts unlawful if his conduct also amounts to a trespass. This limb can only therefore apply where the doctor does some physical act to the child without there being a consent which would amount to a defence for the purpose of the law of trespass.

It is most surprising that there is no previous authority of the courts in this country as to whether a child under 16 can consent to medical treatment. ...

In the absence of binding authority, the position seems to me to be as follows: the fact that a child is under the age of 16 does not mean automatically that she cannot give consent to any treatment. Whether or not a child is capable of giving the necessary consent will depend upon the child's maturity and understanding and the nature of the consent which is required. The child must be capable of making a reasonable assessment of the advantages and disadvantages of the treatment proposed, so the consent if given can be properly and fairly described as a true consent. If the child is not capable of giving consent, then her parents can do so on the child's behalf. If what is involved is some treatment of a minor nature, and the child is of normal intelligence and approaching 16, it will be easier to show that the child is capable of giving the necessary consent; otherwise if the implications of the treatment are long-term. Taking an extreme case, I would have thought it is unlikely that a child under the age of 16 will ever be regarded by the courts as being capable of giving consent to sterilisation.

Mr. Wright submitted that the explanation for the absence of authority is that at least in Victorian times it would never have been suggested that anything but parental consent would suffice for a child under 16. I do not know whether he is justified in making this submission, though I recognise that he could be. However, even assuming that he is right, it does not mean that I am required to ignore the change in attitudes since the Victorian era. I would respectfully rely for support on the vivid language of Lord Denning M.R. in Hewer v. Bryant [1970] 1 Q.B. 357, where he said, at p. 369F: "The common law can, and should, keep pace with the times." (I would add "where there is no authority to the contrary.")

In contrast to the two preceding cases, the next reveals a rather more deferential and less activist approach by the court. Here it clearly felt that it would be constitutionally inappropriate for it as a non-elected and non-political institution to develop law on a matter of wide and significant public importance.

***Malone v Metropolitan Police Commissioner* [1979] Ch 344**

Panel: Sir Robert Megarry V-C

Facts: The Metropolitan Police had been authorised, through a warrant issued by the Home Office, to tap Malone's telephone, pursuant to a criminal investigation. Malone contended that this violated his right to enjoy private property, confidentiality and certain human rights. The court refused to find a right to privacy in English law and stated that in a matter as complex as telephone tapping it was for Parliament, and not the courts, to intervene.

SIR ROBERT MEGARRY V-C

Finally, there is the contention that as no power to tap telephones has been given by either statute or common law, the tapping is necessarily unlawful. The underlying assumption of this contention, of course, is that nothing is lawful that is not positively authorised by law. As I have indicated, England is not a country where everything is forbidden except what is expressly permitted.

...

Third, there is the right of privacy. Here the contention is that although at present no general right of privacy has been recognised by English law, there is a particular right of privacy, namely, the right to hold a telephone conversation in the privacy of one's home without molestation. This, it was said, ought to be recognised and declared to be part of English law, despite the absence of any English authority to this effect. As I have indicated, I am not unduly troubled by the absence of English authority: there has to be a first time for everything, and if the principles of English law, and not least analogies from the existing rules, together with the requirements of justice and common sense, pointed firmly to such a right existing, then I think the court should not be deterred from recognising the right.

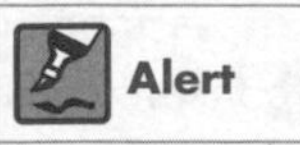

On the other hand, it is no function of the courts to legislate in a new field. The extension of the existing laws and principles is one thing, the creation of an altogether new right is another. At times judges must, and do, legislate; but as Holmes J. once said, they do so only interstitially, and with molecular rather than molar motions: see Southern Pacific Co. v. Jensen (1917) 244 U.S. 205 , 221, in a dissenting judgment. Anything beyond that must be left for legislation. No new right in the law, fully-fledged with all the appropriate safeguards, can spring from the head of a judge deciding a particular case: only Parliament can create such a right.

...

One of the factors that must be relevant in such a case is the degree of particularity in the right that is claimed. The wider and more indefinite the right claimed, the greater the undesirability of holding that such a right exists. Wide and indefinite rights, while conferring an advantage on those who have them, may well gravely impair the position of those who are subject to the rights. To create a right for one person, you have to impose a corresponding duty on another. In the present case, the alleged right to hold a telephone conversation in the privacy of one's own home without molestation is wide and indefinite in its scope, and in any case does not seem to be very apt for covering the plaintiff's grievance. He was not "molested" in holding his telephone conversations: he held them without "molestation," but without their retaining the privacy that he desired. If a man telephones from his own home, but an open window makes it possible for a near neighbour to overhear what is said, and the neighbour, remaining throughout on his own property, listens to the conversation, is he to be a tortfeasor? Is a person who overhears a telephone conversation by reason of a so-called "crossed line" to be liable in damages? What of an operator of a private switchboard who listens in? Why is the right that is claimed confined to a man's own home, so that it would not apply to private telephone conversations from offices, call boxes or the houses of others? If they were to be included, what of the greater opportunities for deliberate overhearing that they offer? In any case, why is the telephone to be subject to this special right of privacy when there is no general right?

That is not all. Suppose that there is what for brevity I may call a right to telephonic privacy, sounding in tort. What exceptions to it, if any, would there be? Would it be a breach of the right if anyone listened to a telephone conversation in which some act of criminal violence or dishonesty was being planned? Should a listener be restrained by injunction from disclosing to the authorities a conversation that would lead to the release of someone who has been kidnapped? There are many, many questions that can, and should, be asked.

Further Reading

The United States Constitution

3

The Rule of Law

Topic List

Alex Lawson and Christopher Costigan

Introduction

The rule of law is, together with the separation of powers, one of the fundamental principles underpinning the study of constitutions. In the UK system the trinity is completed by the principle of parliamentary sovereignty (or supremacy).

The rule of law can be distinguished from the separation of powers in that it is descriptive of one of the fundamental qualities of a constitutional system, namely that the law exists to control the rulers as much as the ruled. It is not concerned purely with technical distinctions, but rather with substance as well. For this reason the rule of law is indispensible in a constitution. A constitution with a structure which does not entirely accord with separation of powers principles could still produce an effective system of government. However, a constitution where the rule of law is not observed, is very likely to create a distorted and corrupt system of government.

The cases highlighted on the rule of law show a steady progression in judicial understanding of the concept and a willingness to engage with it more actively. Some commentators believe, however, that the post Human Rights Act era may have witnessed an increase in judicial activism in this area.

The classical rule of law case is *Entick v Carrington* [1765] 95 ER 807. It was one of the key cases used by Dicey in the formulation of his rule of law theory and use of the reasoning in the case can be seen in several more modern judgments, such as that of Lord Denning MR in *Inland Revenue Commissioners and Another Appellants v Rossminster Ltd. and Others Respondents* [1980] AC 952.

There are many cases which are relevant to study of the rule of law and, as you progress you will see that many of the cases in this Casebook are linked back to this concept. One particularly important case is *R (on the application of Jackson) v Attorney General* [2006] 1 AC 262 which is dealt with in detail in Chapter 4 of this Case book.

However, this chapter will concentrate on two key cases, as they are illustrative of the tension between the rule of law and other constitutional concepts, and of the courts' approach following the introduction of the Human Rights Act 1998.

1 The Rule of Law

Inland Revenue Commissioners and Another Appellants v Rossminster Ltd. and Others Respondents [1980] AC 952

Panel: House of Lords: Lord Wilberforce, Viscount Dilhorne, Lord Diplock, Lord Salmon and Lord Scarman; Court of Appeal: Lord Denning MR, Browne and Goff LJJ

Statute: Taxes Management Act 1970 s 20C

Facts: The Taxes Management Act 1970 allowed for the issue of a search warrant on suspicion of tax fraud having been being committed. Rossminster Ltd had its premises searched under such a warrant and challenged the warrant on the basis of the lack of specificity it seemed to require with regard to the nature of the suspected offence.

In the Court of Appeal, Lord Denning MR took a robust approach to statutory interpretation, reading in a set of requirements that were particularly heavily influenced by his own, substantive attachment to certain rule of law principles. In the House of Lords, however, their Lordships arguably placed more emphasis on the principles of separation of powers and parliamentary sovereignty and the Court of Appeal decision was overturned. The decision of Lord Denning MR in the Court of Appeal is extracted below, followed by Lord Wilberforce's in the House of Lords.

LORD DENNING MR

It was a military style operation. It was carried out by officers of the Inland Revenue in their war against tax frauds. Zero hour was fixed for 7 a.m. on Friday, July 13, 1979. Everything was highly secret. The other side must not be forewarned. There was a briefing session beforehand. Some 60 officers or more of the Inland Revenue attended. They were given detailed instructions. They were divided into teams, each with a leader. Each team had an objective allotted to it. It was to search a particular house or office, marked, I expect, on a map: and to seize any incriminating documents found therein. Each team leader was on the day to be handed a search warrant authorising him and his team to enter the house or office. It would be empowered to use force if need be. Each team was to be accompanied by a police officer. Sometimes more than one. The role of the police was presumably to be silent witnesses: or maybe to let it be known that this was all done with the authority of the law: and that the householder had better not resist - or else!

Everything went according to plan. On Thursday, July 12, Mr. Quinlan, the senior inspector of the Inland Revenue, went to the Central Criminal Court and put before a circuit judge - the Common Serjeant - the suspicions which the Revenue [sic] held. The circuit judge signed the warrants. The officers made photographs of the warrants, and distributed them to the team leaders. Then in the early morning of Friday, July 13 - the next day - each team started off at first light. Each reached its objective. Some in London. Others in the Home Counties. At 7 a.m. there was a knock on each door. One was the home in Kensington of Mr. Ronald Anthony Plummer, a chartered accountant. It was opened by his daughter aged 11. He came downstairs in his dressing-gown. The officers of the Inland Revenue were at the door accompanied by a detective inspector. The householder Mr. Plummer put up no resistance. He let them in. They went to his filing cabinet and removed a large number of files. They went to the safe and took building society passbooks, his children's cheque books and passports. They took his daughter's school report. They went to his bedroom, opened a suitcase, and removed a bundle of papers belonging to his mother. They searched the house. They took personal papers of his wife.

Another house was the home near Maidstone of Mr. Roy Clifford Tucker, a fellow of the Institute of Chartered Accountants. He was away on business in Guernsey. So his wife opened the door. The officers of the Inland Revenue produced the search warrant. She let them in. She did not know what to do. She telephoned her husband in Guernsey. She told him that they were going through the house taking all the documents they could find. They took envelopes addressed to students who were tenants. They went up to the attic and took papers stored there belonging to Mr. Tucker's brother. They took Mr. Tucker's passport.

The main attack was reserved for the offices at no. 1, Hanover Square of the Rossminster group of companies of which Mr. Plummer and Mr. Tucker were directors. They were let in by one of the employees. Many officers of the Inland Revenue went in accompanied by police officers. It was a big set of offices with many rooms full of files, papers and documents of all kinds. They took large quantities of them, pushed them into plastic bags, carried them down in the lift, and loaded them into a van. They carried them off to the offices of the Inland Revenue at Melbourne House in the Aldwych. Twelve van loads. They cleared out Mr. Tucker's office completely: and other rooms too. They spent the whole day on it from 7 a.m. until 6.30 at night. They did examine some of the documents carefully, but there were so many documents and so many files that they could not examine them all. They simply put a number on each file, included it in a list, and put it into the plastic bag. Against each file they noted the time they did it. It looks as if they averaged one file a minute. They did not stop at files. They took the shorthand notebooks of the typists - I do not suppose they could read them. They took some of the financial newspapers in a bundle. In one case the "top half" of a drawer was taken in the first instalment and the balance of the drawer was taken in the second.

Another set of offices was next door in St. George Street - I think along the same corridor. It was the office of A. J. R. Financial Services Ltd. The director Mr. Hallas was not there, of course, at seven o'clock. He arrived at 9.10 a.m. He found the officers of the Inland Revenue packing the company's files into bags for removal. He said that it amounted to several hundreds of documents. Police officers were in attendance there too.

At no point did any of the householders make any resistance. They did the only thing open to them. They went off to their solicitors. They saw counsel. They acted very quickly. By the evening they had gone to a judge of the Chancery Division, Walton J., and asked for and obtained an injunction to stop any trespassing on the premises. They telephoned the injunction through to Hanover Square at about a quarter to six at night. The officers therefore brought the search and seizure to an end. They had, however, by this time practically completed it. So the injunction made very little difference. If the lawyers had had more time to think about it, they would have realised that it was not a case where an injunction would lie against the officers of the [R]evenue. They were officers of the Crown: and under section 31 of the Crown Proceedings Act 1947 no injunction would lie against the Crown or its officers. So the lawyers did not proceed with their claim for an injunction. They took further advice. Counsel advised them that there might be a remedy under a new procedure recently available. It is to restrain abuse of power under R.S.C., Ord. 53. Counsel advised that they might now apply for a declaration - a declaration which, if made, the Crown would be expected to obey. If the circumstances justified it - and if a declaration was made that the seizure was bad - that might be an efficient and expeditious remedy. Before that rule was enacted, the only thing to do would have been to submit to the seizure: to wait until everything had happened: and then to bring an action for damages. But under the new rule, there might be an expeditious remedy available by way of judicial review.

So end the facts. As far as my knowledge of history goes, there has been no search like it - and no seizure like it - in England since that Saturday, April 30, 1763, when the Secretary of State issued a general warrant by which he authorised the King's messengers to arrest John Wilkes and seize all his books and papers. They took everything - all his manuscripts and all papers whatsoever. His pocket-book filled up the mouth of the sack. He applied to the courts. Pratt C.J. struck down the general warrant. You will find it all set out in *Rex v. Wilkes* (1763) 2 Wils. 151; *Huckle v. Money* (1763) 2 Wils. 205 and *Entick v. Carrington* (1765) 2 Wils. 275. Pratt C.J. said, at p. 207:

"To enter a man's house by virtue of a nameless warrant, in order to procure evidence, is worse than the Spanish inquisition; a law under which no Englishman would wish to live an hour; it was a most daring public attack made upon the liberty of the subject."

Now we have to see in this case whether this warrant was valid or not. It all depends of course upon the statute. By the common law no search or seizure at any man's house can be made except for stolen goods. I set it all out in *Chic Fashions (West Wales) Ltd. v. Jones* [1968] 2 Q.B. 299. Search and seizure is only authorised - and has been authorised - by many statutes in recent years. The one which concerns us was only passed in July 1976. It is Schedule 6 to the Finance Act 1976. It is by section 20C. As it is so important, I will read it:

"(1) If the appropriate judicial authority" - and he is defined as the circuit judge - "is satisfied on information on oath given by an officer of the board that - (a) there is reasonable ground for suspecting that an offence involving any form of fraud in connection with, or in relation to, tax has been committed and that evidence of it is to be found on premises specified in the information; and (b) in applying under this section, the officer acts with the approval of the board given in relation to the particular case, the authority may issue a warrant in writing authorising an officer of the board to enter the premises, if necessary by force, at any time within 14 days from the time of issue of the warrant, and search them. ... (3) On entering the premises with a warrant under this section, the officer may seize and remove any things whatsoever found there which he has reasonable cause to believe may be required as evidence for the purposes of proceedings in respect of such an offence as is mentioned in subsection (1) above. ..."

That is the statute. It is under that statute that Mr. Quinlan went to the appropriate judicial authority - in this case a circuit judge - the Common Serjeant of the City of London. I would much like to know the information which was given to the judge - the nature of the evidence which was put before him to found the suspicion - and the offence of which the accused were suspected. I would also like to know why these private homes were believed to hold incriminating material. But we have not been given any information as to what the Common Serjeant was told. The [R]evenue take the view that it would not be appropriate for us at this stage to know what were the grounds of their suspicion. If this court were told them, it would follow equally that Mr.

Bateson and his clients would be told them also. So we must remain in ignorance of the information which was laid before the Common Serjeant. But I must say - and I think it is right to say - that we should assume that there was laid before the Common Serjeant material which did justify the view that there was reasonable ground for suspecting that the applicants had been guilty of an offence involving some fraud on the Revenue; and also that incriminating documents would be found in these offices and homes.

Whilst I say that, I would like to emphasise that it is suspicion only. In our law every man is presumed to be innocent until he is proved to be guilty. Suspicion is not by itself enough to prove guilt. So I think we should proceed on the presumption that these were innocent - or presumably innocent - men: and so far there was only a suspicion.

This brings me to the validity of the warrant - and indeed to consider the statute.

The validity of the warrant

Beyond all doubt this search and seizure was unlawful unless it was authorised by Parliament. As to the statute, we are not allowed to read Hansard - but you can. You can find it if you turn up the debate of May 17, 1976, columns 981 to 1050; and July 15, 1976, columns 923 to 1006. The government of the day put forward the clause. It was opposed by many as being a dangerous encroachment on individual freedom. It was passed by a narrow majority.

Many will ask: why has Parliament done this? Why have they allowed this search and seizure by the Revenue officers? It did it here because the Board of Inland Revenue were very worried by the devices used by some wicked people, such as those - and we often see such cases in our courts - who keep two sets of books: one for themselves to use; the other to be shown to the [R]evenue. Those who make out two invoices. One for the customer. The other to be shown to the taxman. Those who enter into fictitious transactions and write them into their books as genuine. Those who show losses when they have in fact made gains. In the tax evasion pool, there are some big fish who do not stop at tax avoidance. They resort to frauds on a large scale. I can well see that if the legislation were confined - or could be confined - to people of that sort, it would be supported by all honest citizens. Those who defraud the [R]evenue in this way are parasites who suck out the life-blood of our society. The trouble is that the legislation is drawn so widely that in some hands it might be an instrument of oppression. It may be said that "honest people need not fear: that it will never be used against them: that tax inspectors can be trusted, only to use it in the case of the big, bad frauds." This is an attractive argument, but I would reject it. Once great power is granted, there is a danger of it being abused. Rather than risk such abuse, it is, as I see it, the duty of the courts so to construe the statute as to see that it encroaches as little as possible upon the liberties of the people of England.

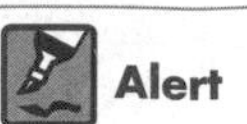

The warrant and the challenge to it

The warrant is challenged on the ground that it does not specify any particular offence. I must read it in full, because this was what was given to all the teams of inspectors who went round:

"*Search Warrant.* To: Raymond Quinlan and to the persons named in the first schedule annexed to this warrant. Officers of the Board of Inland Revenue. Information on oath having been laid this day by Raymond Quinlan in accordance with the provisions of section 20C of the Taxes Management Act 1970 stating that there is reasonable ground for suspecting that an offence involving fraud in connection with or in relation to tax has been committed and that evidence of it is to be found on the premises described in the second schedule annexed hereto. You are hereby authorised to enter those premises, together with all or any of the officers of the Board of Inland Revenue named in the first schedule hereto and together with such constables as you may require, if necessary by force, at any time within 14 days from the time of issue of this warrant, and search them; and on entering those premises with this warrant you may seize and remove any things whatsoever found there which you have reasonable cause to believe may be required as evidence for the purposes of proceedings in respect of such an offence. Dated July 12, 1979" - signed by the circuit judge.

Then in the first schedule there are a whole number of names - over 60 officers. And in the second schedule annexed to this particular warrant is the address 1, Hanover Square: and there would be similar warrants in respect of the other premises which were searched.

I come back to the challenge to the warrant. The challenge which is made here is that it does not specify any particular offence involving fraud. There may be 20 different kinds of fraud, as someone suggested, and this warrant does not specify which one of them is suspected. Each of the applicants, in complaining to the court, complain of this. There is a paragraph which each of them makes in his affidavit:

"Despite requests by my solicitor so to do, the Inland Revenue have refused to disclose the nature of the offence or offences they have in mind and neither I, nor I verily believe my fellow directors, have the slightest idea what offence or offences they do have in mind, or, even who is supposed to have committed it or them."

That is acknowledged by the [R]evenue: and they give their justification for it in an affidavit which was put forward - I think at the request of the Divisional Court. It is an affidavit by Mr. Dermit. He said:

"In the course of my duties I am responsible for initiating and conducting many inquiries some of which may lead to proceedings for offences of fraud in relation to tax. I verily believe that it would be greatly detrimental to and obstructive of inquiries of this nature to disclose at this stage the precise nature of the offences in respect of which proceedings may be taken and in which the documents seized may be required as evidence. Such disclosure, in my view, would be harmful because, inter alia, it might reveal to those suspected of having committed offences not only that those persons have been identified by the Inland Revenue but also the extent and nature of the information in the [R]evenue's possession concerning such offences."

So there it is. The justification is: "We do not wish to tell more to those we suspect because we do not want them to know too much about what we intend to do. Otherwise they will be on their guard."

Is this a just excuse? The words "an offence involving any form of fraud in connection with, or in relation to, tax" are very wide words. We were taken by Mr. Davenport through a number of offences which might be comprised in them. There is no specific section in the Act itself. But there are a number of other offences which involve fraud. There is "false accounting" under section 17 of the Theft Act 1968. There is "evasion of liability by deception" in section 2 of the Theft Act 1978. There is perjury, forgery, conspiracy, and false statements relating to income tax. You will find all those set out in Archbold, Criminal Pleading Evidence & Practice, 40th ed. (1979). They are all offences which involve fraud. But I myself would not be prepared to limit it to those half-dozen which Mr. Davenport put before us. It seems to me that these words "fraud ... in relation to ... tax" are so vague and so general that it must be exceedingly difficult for the officers of the Inland Revenue themselves to know what papers they can take or what they cannot take. Take an instance, for example, which Mr. Davenport put before us. They may say to themselves, "This man must have been guilty of some fraud on the tax. His income is only £1,000 a year - let us say - and he is spending at a rate of £5,000 a year. He must be fiddling the tax in some way. Let us see how he gets his money and what he spends it on." That, as we know in these courts, is the sort of evidence relied on by the [R]evenue when they are charging a person with a tax fraud.

If such is the ground of suspicion, if such is the sort of evidence which points to fraud, see how wide a scope it gives to the inspectors of the Inland Revenue. It enables them to pick up all a man's papers, saying to themselves: "This looks as though there may be something useful in it. Let's take it." The vice of a general warrant of this kind - which does not specify any particular offence - is two-fold. It gives no help to the officers when they have to exercise it. It means also that they can roam wide and large, seizing and taking pretty well all a man's documents and papers.

There is some assistance to be found in the cases. I refer to the law about arrest - when a man is arrested under a warrant for an offence. ...

Lord Simonds put it more graphically when he said, at p. 592:

"Arrested with or without a warrant the subject is entitled to know why he is deprived of his freedom, if only in order that he may, without a moment's delay, take such steps as will enable him to regain it."

So here. When the officers of the Inland Revenue come armed with a warrant to search a man's home or his office, it seems to me that he is entitled to say: "Of what offence do you suspect me? You are claiming to enter my house and to seize my papers." And when they look at the papers and seize them, he should be able to say: "Why are you seizing these papers? Of what offence do you suspect me? What have these to do with your case?" Unless he knows the particular offence charged, he cannot take steps to secure himself or his property. So it seems to me, as a matter of construction of the statute and therefore of the warrant - in pursuance of our traditional role to protect the liberty of the individual - it is our duty to say that the warrant must particularise the specific offence which is charged as being fraud on the [R]evenue.

If this be right, it follows necessarily that this warrant is bad. It should have specified the particular offence of which the man is suspected. On this ground I would hold that certiorari should go to quash the warrant.

If this be right, there is no need to go further. But I must go further in case it be wrong. The warrant was issued under judicial authority. The circuit judge - the Common Serjeant of the City of London - issued it. But the seizure - the subsequent conduct of the officers at Hanover Square and in the homes of these men - was not subject to any judicial supervision. And as far as I know without any police check at all. The police were there, but not doing anything except keeping the peace. The question is whether or not that seizure came within the provisions of the statute, which I will repeat: "... the officer may seize and remove any things whatsoever found there which he has reasonable cause to believe may be required as evidence. ..." Is he exempt from supervision in that regard? Or is he the sole arbiter of "which he has reasonable cause to believe"? surely not. In this regard I need only quote the words of Lord Radcliffe in *Nakkuda Ali v. Jayaratne* [1951] A.C. 66 on those very words "reasonable cause to believe." Lord Radcliffe said, at p. 77:

"After all, words such as these are commonly found when a legislature or law-making authority confers powers on a minister or official. However read, they must be intended to serve in some sense as a condition limiting the exercise of an otherwise arbitrary power. But if the question whether the condition has been satisfied is to be conclusively decided by the man who wields the power the value of the intended restraint is in effect nothing."

Alert

So it cannot be that these officers are the people conclusively to decide whether there is reasonable cause to believe. The courts must be able to exercise some supervision over them. If the courts cannot do so, no one else can. Just see what these officers did here. Mr. Bateson went through the evidence of what they did. Minute by minute. File after file. From their own lists. They could not possibly have had time to examine all these documents or to come to a proper decision as to whether they were reasonably required as evidence. Instead of examining them on the premises, they bundled them into plastic bags and took them off to Melbourne House. But, in fairness to the Inland Revenue, I will read what Mr. Quinlan said was done. The description given by Mr. Plummer's manager, he said:

"is not an accurate description of the way the search was carried out. For example, during the day I went through the two-volume securities register page by page with the manager of Rossminster sitting beside me and selected only certain objects in such register. I went through a very thick correspondence file of a Mr. Glatt and released it all. I also went through all the incoming telex messages and the manager's outgoing post, and released it all. I carried out a sample check of the ledger cards and made special arrangements with the manager to have them photocopied on the premises in order that the originals could remain. These are but examples of some of the detailed searching which I, and I verily believe, other officers carried out on the day in question. But in a very great many instances files and bundles of documents were removed when their title or subject matter made it clear that their contents were such that the officers had reasonable cause to believe that they might be required as evidence for the purpose of proceedings in respect of any such offences."

Mr. Quinlan tells us about the documents which he released. But he does not tell us what documents he retained and on what ground and for what purpose, or which particular fraud he had in mind. We are left to guess. I would ask, on what grounds did these officers decide whether or not there was reasonable cause for believing that they would be required in evidence? What about the shorthand notebooks, the diaries and all that kind of thing - would they be reasonably required? Mr. Davenport said that at this stage the [R]evenue would not wish to go further than they had. They would not tell us on what grounds they required these documents. At this stage, he said, it is not desirable. ...

This brings me to the end. This case has given us much concern. No one would wish that any of those who defraud the revenue should go free. They should be found out and brought to justice. But it is fundamental in our law that the means which are adopted to this end should be lawful means. A good end does not justify a bad means. The means must not be such as to offend against the personal freedom, the privacy and the elemental rights of property. Every man is presumed to be innocent until he is found guilty. If his house is to be searched and his property seized on suspicion of an offence, it must be done by due process of law. And due process involves that there must be a valid warrant specifying the offence of which he is suspected: and the seizure is limited to those things authorised by the warrant. In this case, as I see it, the warrant was invalid for want of particularity: and the search and seizure were not in accordance with anything which was authorised by the warrant. It was an illegal and excessive use of power.

Alert

I would therefore allow the appeal, quash the warrant, and make the declaration.

The opinion of Lord Wilberforce in the House of Lords follows.

LORD WILBERFORCE

My Lords, the organised searches by officers of the Inland Revenue on Friday, July 13, 1979, on the respondents' offices and private premises were carried out under powers claimed to be conferred by Act of Parliament - the Finance Act 1976, section 57, and Schedule 6, section 20C amending the Taxes Management Act 1970, section 20.

The integrity and privacy of a man's home, and of his place of business, an important human right has, since the second world war, been eroded by a number of statutes passed by Parliament in the belief, presumably, that this right of privacy ought in some cases to be over-ridden by the interest which the public has in preventing evasions of the law. Some of these powers of search are reflections of dirigisme and of heavy taxation, others of changes in mores. Examples of them are to be found in the Exchange Control Act 1947, the Finance Act 1972 (in relation to VAT) and in statutes about gaming or the use of drugs. A formidable number of officials now have powers to enter people's premises, and to take property away, and these powers are frequently exercised, sometimes on a large scale. Many people, as well as the respondents, think that this process has gone too far; that is an issue to be debated in Parliament and in the press.

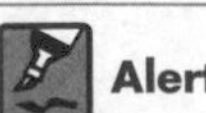

The courts have the duty to supervise, I would say critically, even jealously, the legality of any purported exercise of these powers. They are the guardians of the citizens' right to privacy. But they must do this in the context of the times, i.e. of increasing Parliamentary intervention, and of the modern power of judicial review. In my respectful opinion appeals to 18th century precedents of arbitrary action by Secretaries of State and references to general warrants do nothing to throw light on the issue. Furthermore, while the courts may look critically at legislation which impairs the rights of citizens and should resolve any doubt in interpretation in their favour, it is no part of their duty, or power, to restrict or impede the working of legislation, even of unpopular legislation; to do so would be to weaken rather than to advance the democratic process.

It is necessary to be clear at once that Parliament, in conferring these wide powers, has introduced substantial safeguards. Those relevant to this case are three:

(1) No action can be taken under section 20C without the approval of the Board of Inland Revenue - viz., two members, at least, acting personally. This board consists of senior and responsible officials expert in the subject matter, who must be expected to weigh carefully the issues of public interest involved.

(2) No warrant to enter can be issued except by a circuit judge, not, as is usually the case, by a magistrate. There has to be laid before him information on oath, and on this he must be satisfied that there is reasonable ground for suspecting the commission of a "tax fraud" and that evidence of it is to be found in the premises sought to be searched. If the judge does his duty (and we must assume that the learned Common Serjeant did in the present case) he must carefully consider for himself the grounds put forward by the Revenue officer and judicially satisfy himself, in relation to each of the premises concerned, that these amount to reasonable grounds for suspecting, etc. It would be quite wrong to suppose that he acts simply as a rubber stamp on the [R]evenue's application.

(3) The courts retain their full powers of supervision of judicial and executive action. There is nothing in section 20C which cuts these down: on the contrary, Parliament, by using such phrases as "is satisfied," "has reasonable cause to believe" must be taken to accept the restraints which courts in many cases have held to be inherent in them. The courts are concerned, in this case, only with two matters bearing upon legality.

First, were the warrants valid? Secondly, can the actual action taken under subsection (3) be challenged on the ground that the officers did not have, or could not have had, reasonable cause to believe that the documents they seized might be required as evidence for the purposes of proceedings in respect of a "tax fraud"? A third possible issue, namely, that there was not before the judge sufficient material on which to be satisfied as the section requires was not pursued, nor thought sustainable by the Court of Appeal. It is not an issue now.

The two first mentioned are the only issues in the case. Three judges have decided them in favour of each side. For myself I have no doubt that the view taken by the Divisional Court on each was correct and I am willing to adopt their judgment. I add a few observations of my own.

1. I can understand very well the perplexity, and indeed indignation, of those present on the premises, when they were searched. Beyond knowing, as appears in the warrant, that the search is in connection with a "tax fraud," they were not told what the precise nature of the fraud was, when it was committed, or by whom it was committed. In the case of a concern with numerous clients, for example, a bank, without this knowledge the occupier of the premises is totally unable to protect his customers' confidential information from investigation and seizure. I cannot believe that this does not call for a fresh look by Parliament. But, on the plain words of the enactment, the officers are entitled if they can persuade the board and the judge, to enter and search premises regardless of whom they belong to: a warrant which confers this power is strictly and exactly within the parliamentary authority, and the occupier has no answer to it. I accept that some information as regards the person(s) who are alleged to have committed an offence and possibly as to the approximate dates of the offences must almost certainly have been laid before the board and the judge. But the occupier has no right to be told of this at this stage, nor has he the right to be informed of the "reasonable grounds" of which the judge was satisfied. Both courts agree as to this: all this information is clearly protected by the public interest immunity which covers investigations into possible criminal offences. With reference to the police, Lord Reid stated this in these words:

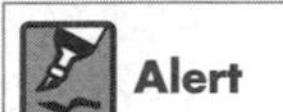

"The police are carrying on an unending war with criminals many of whom are today highly intelligent. So it is essential that there should be no disclosure of anything which might give any useful information to those who organise criminal activities. and (sic) it would generally be wrong to require disclosure in a civil case of anything which might be material in a pending prosecution: but after a verdict has been given or it has been decided to take no proceedings there is not the same need for secrecy." *(Conway v. Rimmer* [1968] A.C. 910, 953-954).

The Court of Appeal took the view that the warrants were invalid because they did not sufficiently particularise the alleged offence(s). The court did not make clear exactly what particulars should have been given - and indeed I think that this cannot be done. The warrant followed the wording of the statute "fraud in connection with or in relation to tax": a portmanteau description which covers a number of common law (cheating) and statutory offences (under the Theft Act 1968 et al.). To require specification at this investigatory stage would be impracticable given the complexity of "tax frauds" and the different persons who may be involved (companies, officers of companies, accountants, tax consultants, taxpayers, wives of taxpayers etc.). Moreover, particularisation, if required, would no doubt take the form of a listing of one offence and/or another or others and so would be of little help to those concerned. Finally, there would clearly be power, on principles well accepted in the common law, after entry had been made in connection with one particular offence, to seize material bearing upon other offences within the portmanteau. So, particularisation, even if practicable, would not help the occupier.

I am unable, therefore, to escape the conclusion, that adherence to the statutory formula is sufficient.

The warrants, being valid, confer an authority to enter and search: see section 20C (1). This being in terms stated in the Act, I do not appreciate the relevance of an inquiry into the form of search warrants at common law (which in any case admitted of some flexibility in operation) still less into that of warrants of arrest. There is no mystery about the word "warrant": it simply means a document issued by a person in authority under power conferred in that behalf authorising the doing of an act which would otherwise be illegal. The person affected, of course, has the right to be satisfied that the power to issue it exists: therefore the warrant should (and did) contain a reference to that power. It would be wise to add to it a statement of satisfaction on the part of the judicial authority as to the matters on which he must be satisfied but this is not a requirement and its absence does not go to validity. To complain of its absence in the present case when, as is admitted, no challenge can be made as to the satisfaction, in fact, of the judge, would be technical and indeed irrational. I can find no ground for holding these warrants invalid.

2. The second matter, on which the intervention of the court may be called for, arises under section 20C (3). This confers a statutory power independent of any authority in the warrant to seize and remove. Like all statutory powers conferred on executive officers it is subject to supervision by the courts exercising their classic and traditional powers of judicial review. It is undisputed that the words "has reasonable cause to believe" are open to examination in spite of their subjective form: see *Nakkuda Ali v. Jayaratne* [1951] A.C. 66 et al. The existence of this reasonable cause and of the belief founded upon it is ultimately a question of fact to be tried on evidence.

So far as regards these appeals this issue is complicated in three ways. First, it has been raised at an interlocutory stage, and at the very beginning of the investigation, upon affidavit evidence. Secondly, the [R]evenue have refused, so far, to disclose their reasonable grounds, claiming immunity from so doing, on the grounds stated above. Thirdly, the defendants being, in effect, the Crown or Crown servants, an interlocutory injunction cannot be granted (section 21 of the Crown Proceedings Act 1947).

The Court of Appeal sought to meet this situation by granting a declaration: and recognising, rightly in my opinion, that an interim declaration could not be granted, gave a final declaration in effect that the [R]evenue had exceeded their powers. I regret that I cannot agree that this was correct. It is to me apparent that there was a substantial conflict of evidence as to the manner in which the searches were carried out, the respondents broadly contending that the officers gave no real consideration to the question whether individual documents might be required as evidence: the [R]evenue asserting that they had detailed instructions what to look for and seize and that these were complied with. I shall not further analyse this issue which was fully and satisfactorily treated by the Divisional Court, for I am satisfied that even if, which I doubt, there might have been enough evidence to justify the granting of interlocutory relief, this fell very far short of supporting a final declaration. I believe that the Court of Appeal was itself really of this opinion. The final declaration granted must clearly be set aside.

...

Appeals allowed.

This case clearly demonstrates the interplay between the three constitutional concepts of the rule of law, the separation of powers and parliamentary sovereignty. Lord Denning MR's judgment is focused heavily on rule of law concerns, notably his attachment to what he saw as the vital role of the courts in upholding the rights of individuals against the state. However, the opinion of Lord Wilberforce arguably shows more respect for the other two principles, the separation of powers and parliamentary sovereignty, reflected in the final decision to adopt a more literal interpretation of the relevant statute.

The next case was heard after the coming into force of the Human Rights Act 1998 and shows the development of the rule of law, with a trend towards a more substantive rule of law focused approach.

***A (FC) and others (FC) v Secretary of State for the Home Department; X (FC) and another (FC) (Appellants) v. Secretary of State for the Home Department* [2004] UKHL 56, [2005] 2 AC 68**

Panel: Lord Bingham of Cornhill, Lord Nicholls of Birkenhead, Lord Hoffmann, Lord Hope of Craighead, Lord Scott of Foscote, Lord Rodger of Earlsferry, Lord Walker of Gestingthorpe, Baroness Hale of Richmond and Lord Carswell

Statutes: European Convention on Human Rights Arts 5, 14 and 15; Human Rights Act 1998; Anti-terrorism, Crime and Security Act 2001 s 23

Facts: Following the terrorist attacks on America on 11 September 2001 the UK derogated from its obligations under Article 5(1) of the European Convention on Human Rights, requiring it to declare (under Art 15) that a public emergency existed, 'threatening the life of the nation'. Parliament subsequently passed the Anti-terrorism, Crime and Security Act 2001 which, under s 23, enabled the detention of non-nationals who the Home Secretary suspected of being international terrorists but who, for practical reasons, could not be deported. The appellants were detained under the Act and appealed to the Special Immigration Appeals Commission which found that the Government had complied with Art 15. However, the Order was quashed and a declaration of incompatibility made in relation to s 23 on the basis that it was incompatible with Articles 5 and 14 of the Convention because it was discriminatory. The Court of Appeal allowed the Secretary of State's appeal and dismissed the cross-appeal. The appellants appealed to the House of Lords, which held (Lord Hoffmann dissenting) that there was a public emergency, but that the measures adopted were not strictly required by the exigencies of the situation.

LORD BINGHAM OF CORNHILL

...

The background

5. In July 2000 Parliament enacted the Terrorism Act 2000. This was a substantial measure, with 131 sections and 16 Schedules, intended to overhaul, modernise and strengthen the law relating to the growing problem of terrorism. ...

6. On 11 September 2001 terrorists launched concerted attacks in New York, Washington DC and Pennsylvania. The main facts surrounding those attacks are too well known to call for recapitulation here. It is enough to record that they were atrocities on an unprecedented scale, causing many deaths and destroying property of immense value. They were intended to disable the governmental and commercial power of the United States. The attacks were the product of detailed planning. They were committed by terrorists fired by ideological hatred of the United States and willing to sacrifice their own lives in order to injure the leading nation of the western world. The mounting of such attacks against such targets in such a country inevitably caused acute concerns about their own security in other western countries, particularly those which, like the United Kingdom, were particularly prominent in their support for the United States and its military response to Al-Qaeda, the organisation quickly identified as responsible for the attacks. Before and after 11 September Osama bin Laden, the moving spirit of Al-Qaeda, made threats specifically directed against the United Kingdom and its people.

7. Her Majesty's Government reacted to the events of 11 September in two ways directly relevant to these appeals. First, it introduced (and Parliament, subject to amendment, very swiftly enacted) what became Part 4 of the Anti-terrorism, Crime and Security Act 2001. Secondly, it made the Human Rights Act 1998 (Designated Derogation) Order 2001 (SI 2001/3644) ("the Derogation Order"). Before summarising the effect of these measures it is important to understand their underlying legal rationale.

[Lord Bingham went on to find that] there was no warrant for the long-term or indefinite detention of a non-UK national whom the Home Secretary wished to remove. [and continued:]

10. The European Convention gives member states a limited right to derogate from some articles of the Convention (including article 5, although not article 3). The governing provision is article 15...

It was in exercise of his power ... that the Home Secretary, on 11 November 2001, made the Derogation Order, which came into force two days later, although relating to what was at that stage a proposed derogation.

The Derogation Order

11. The derogation related to article 5(1), in reality article 5(1)(f), of the Convention. The proposed notification by the United Kingdom was set out in a Schedule to the Order. The first section of this, entitled "Public emergency in the United Kingdom",

referred to the attacks of 11 September and to United Nations Security Council resolutions recognising those attacks as a threat to international peace and security and requiring all states to take measures to prevent the commission of terrorist attacks, "including by denying safe haven to those who finance, plan, support or commit terrorist attacks". It was stated in the Schedule:

"There exists a terrorist threat to the United Kingdom from persons suspected of involvement in international terrorism. In particular, there are foreign nationals present in the United Kingdom who are suspected of being concerned in the commission, preparation or instigation of acts of international terrorism, of being members of organisations or groups which are so concerned or of having links with members of such organisations or groups, and who are a threat to the national security of the United Kingdom."

The next section summarised the effect of what was to become the 2001 Act. A brief account was then given of the power to detain under the Immigration Act 1971 and reference was made to the decision in *R v Governor of Durham Prison, Ex p Hardial Singh* [1984] 1 WLR 709. In a section entitled "Article 5(1)(f) of the Convention" the effect of the court's decision in *Chahal* was summarised. In the next section it was recognised that the extended power in the new legislation to detain a person against whom no action was being taken with a view to deportation might be inconsistent with article 5(1)(f). Hence the need for derogation. Formal notice of derogation was given to the Secretary General on 18 December 2001. Corresponding steps were taken to derogate from article 9 of the International Covenant on Civil and Political Rights 1966, which is similar in effect to article 5, although not (like article 5) incorporated into domestic law.

The 2001 Act

12. The 2001 Act is a long and comprehensive statute. Only Part 4 ("Immigration and Asylum") has featured in argument in these appeals, because only Part 4 contains the power to detain indefinitely on reasonable suspicion without charge or trial of which the appellants complain, and only Part 4 is the subject of the United Kingdom derogation. Section 21 provides for certification of a person by the Secretary of State...

14. Section 23(1) is the provision most directly challenged in these appeals. It provides:

"23. Detention

"(1) A suspected international terrorist may be detained under a provision specified in subsection (2) despite the fact that his removal or departure from the United Kingdom is prevented (whether temporarily or indefinitely) by—(a) a point of law which wholly or partly relates to an international agreement, or (b) a practical consideration."

...

Public emergency

16. The appellants repeated before the House a contention rejected by both SIAC and the Court of Appeal, that there neither was nor is a "public emergency threatening the life of the nation" within the meaning of article 15(1). Thus, they contended, the threshold test for reliance on article 15 has not been satisfied.

17. The European Court considered the meaning of this provision in *Lawless v Ireland (No 3)* (1961) 1 EHRR 15, a case concerned with very low-level IRA terrorist activity in Ireland and Northern Ireland between 1954 and 1957. The Irish Government derogated from article 5 in July 1957 in order to permit detention without charge or trial and the applicant was detained between July and December 1957. He could have obtained his release by undertaking to observe the law and refrain from activities contrary to the Offences against the State (Amendment) Act 1940, but instead challenged the lawfulness of the Irish derogation. He failed. In para 22 of its judgment the court held that it was for it to determine whether the conditions laid down in article 15 for the exercise of the exceptional right of derogation had been made out. In paras 28-29 it ruled:

"28. In the general context of article 15 of the Convention, the natural and customary meaning of the words 'other public emergency threatening the life of the nation' is sufficiently clear; they refer to an exceptional situation of crisis or emergency which affects the whole population and constitutes a threat to the organised life of the community of which the state is composed. Having thus established the natural and customary meaning of this conception, the court must determine whether the facts and circumstances which led the Irish Government to make their Proclamation of 5 July 1957 come within this conception. The court, after an examination, finds this to be the case; the existence at the time of a 'public emergency threatening the life of the nation' was reasonably deduced by the Irish Government from a combination of several factors, namely: in the first place, the existence in the territory of the Republic of Ireland of a secret army engaged in unconstitutional activities and using violence to attain its purposes; secondly, the fact that this army was also operating outside the territory of the state, thus seriously jeopardising the relations of the Republic of Ireland with its neighbour; thirdly, the steady and alarming increase in terrorist activities from the autumn of 1956 and throughout the first half of 1957.

"29. Despite the gravity of the situation, the Government had succeeded, by using means available under ordinary legislation, in keeping public institutions functioning more or less normally, but the homicidal ambush on the night of 3 to 4 July 1957 in the territory of Northern Ireland near the border had brought to light, just before 12 July—a date, which, for historical reasons, is particularly critical for the preservation of public peace and order—the imminent danger to the nation caused by the continuance of unlawful activities in Northern Ireland by the IRA and various associated groups, operating from the territory of the Republic of Ireland."

18. In *The Greek Case* (1969) 12 YB 1 the Government of Greece failed to persuade the commission that there had been a public emergency threatening the life of the

nation such as would justify derogation. In para 153 of its opinion the commission described the features of such an emergency:

"Such a public emergency may then be seen to have, in particular, the following characteristics: (1) It must be actual or imminent. (2) Its effects must involve the whole nation. (3) The continuance of the organised life of the community must be threatened. (4) The crisis or danger must be exceptional, in that the normal measures or restrictions, permitted by the Convention for the maintenance of public safety, health and order, are plainly inadequate."

In *Ireland v United Kingdom* (1978) 2 EHRR 25 the parties were agreed, as were the commission and the court, that the article 15 test was satisfied. This was unsurprising, since the IRA had for a number of years represented (para 212) "a particularly far-reaching and acute danger for the territorial integrity of the United Kingdom, the institutions of the six counties and the lives of the province's inhabitants". The article 15 test was accordingly not discussed, but the court made valuable observations about its role where the application of the article is challenged:

"(a) The role of the court

"207. The limits on the court's powers of review are particularly apparent where article 15 is concerned.

"It falls in the first place to each contracting state, with its responsibility for 'the life of [its] nation', to determine whether that life is threatened by a 'public emergency' and, if so, how far it is necessary to go in attempting to overcome the emergency. By reason of their direct and continuous contact with the pressing needs of the moment, the national authorities are in principle in a better position than the international judge to decide both on the presence of such an emergency and on the nature and scope of derogations necessary to avert it. In this matter, article 15(1) leaves those authorities a wide margin of appreciation.

Alert

"Nevertheless, the states do not enjoy an unlimited power in this respect. The court, which, with the commission, is responsible for ensuring the observance of the states' engagements (article 19), is empowered to rule on whether the states have gone beyond the 'extent strictly required by the exigencies' of the crisis. The domestic margin of appreciation is thus accompanied by a European supervision."

...

24. The appellants submitted that detailed information pointing to a real and imminent danger to public safety in the United Kingdom had not been shown. In making this submission they were able to rely on a series of reports by the Joint Committee on Human Rights. In its Second Report of the Session 2001-2002 (HL Paper 37, HC 372), made on 14 November 2001 when the 2001 Act was a Bill before Parliament, the Joint Committee stated, in para 30:

"Having considered the Home Secretary's evidence carefully, we recognise that there may be evidence of the existence of a public emergency threatening the life of the nation, although none was shown by him to this committee."

It repeated these doubts in para 4 of its Fifth Report of the Session 2001-2002 (HL Paper 51, HC 420) (3 December 2001). In para 20 of its Fifth Report of the Session 2002-2003 (HL Paper 59, HC 462, 24 February 2003), following the decisions of SIAC and the Court of Appeal, the Joint Committee noted that SIAC had had sight of closed as well as open material but suggested that each House might wish to seek further information from the Government on the public emergency issue. In its report of 23 February 2004 (Sixth Report of the Session 2003-2004, HL Paper 38, HC 381), the Joint Committee stated, in para 34:

"Insufficient evidence has been presented to Parliament to make it possible for us to accept that derogation under ECHR article 15 is strictly required by the exigencies of the situation to deal with a public emergency threatening the life of the nation."

It adhered to this opinion in paras 15-19 of its Eighteenth Report of the Session 2003-2004 (HL Paper 158, HC 713), drawing attention (para 82) to the fact that the UK was the only country out of 45 countries in the Council of Europe which had found it necessary to derogate from article 5. The appellants relied on these doubts when contrasting the British derogation with the conduct of other Council of Europe member states which had not derogated, including even Spain which had actually experienced catastrophic violence inflicted by Al-Qaeda.

25. The Attorney General, representing the Home Secretary, answered these points. He submitted that an emergency could properly be regarded as imminent if an atrocity was credibly threatened by a body such as Al-Qaeda which had demonstrated its capacity and will to carry out such a threat, where the atrocity might be committed without warning at any time. The Government, responsible as it was and is for the safety of the British people, need not wait for disaster to strike before taking necessary steps to prevent it striking. As to the requirement that the emergency be temporary, the Attorney General did not suggest that an emergency could ever become the normal state of affairs, but he did resist the imposition of any artificial temporal limit to an emergency of the present kind, and pointed out that the emergency which had been held to justify derogation in Northern Ireland in 1988 had been accepted as continuing for a considerable number of years: see *Marshall v United Kingdom* (Application No 41571/98), para 18 above. Little help, it was suggested, could be gained by looking at the practice of other states. It was for each national government, as the guardian of its own people's safety, to make its own judgment on the basis of the facts known to it. In so far as any difference of practice as between the United Kingdom and other Council of Europe members called for justification, it could be found in this country's prominent role as an enemy of Al-Qaeda and an ally of the United States. The Attorney General also made two more fundamental submissions. First, he submitted that there was no error of law in SIAC's approach to this issue and accordingly, since an appeal against its decision lay only on a point of law, there was no ground upon which any appellate court was entitled to disturb its conclusion. Secondly, he submitted that the judgment on this question was pre-eminently one within the discretionary area of judgment reserved to the Secretary of State and his colleagues, exercising their judgment with the benefit of official advice, and to Parliament.

26. The appellants have in my opinion raised an important and difficult question, as the continuing anxiety of the Joint Committee on Human Rights, the observations of the Commissioner for Human Rights and the warnings of the UN Human Rights Committee make clear. In the result, however, not without misgiving (fortified by reading the opinion of my noble and learned friend Lord Hoffmann), I would resolve this issue against the appellants, for three main reasons.

27. First, it is not shown that SIAC or the Court of Appeal misdirected themselves on this issue. SIAC considered a body of closed material, that is, secret material of a sensitive nature not shown to the parties. The Court of Appeal was not asked to read this material. The Attorney General expressly declined to ask the House to read it. From this I infer that while the closed material no doubt substantiates and strengthens the evidence in the public domain, it does not alter its essential character and effect. But this is in my view beside the point. It is not shown that SIAC misdirected itself in law on this issue, and the view which it accepted was one it could reach on the open evidence in the case.

28. My second reason is a legal one. The European Court decisions in *Ireland v United Kingdom* 2 EHRR 25; *Brannigan and McBride v United Kingdom* 17 EHRR 539; *Aksoy v Turkey* 23 EHRR 553 and *Marshall v United Kingdom* (Application No 41571/98) seem to me to be, with respect, clearly right. In each case the member state had actually experienced widespread loss of life caused by an armed body dedicated to destroying the territorial integrity of the state. To hold that the article 15 test was not satisfied in such circumstances, if a response beyond that provided by the ordinary course of law was required, would have been perverse. But these features were not, on the facts found, very clearly present in *Lawless v Ireland* (No 3) 1 EHRR 15. That was a relatively early decision of the European Court, but it has never to my knowledge been disavowed and the House is required by section 2(1) of the 1998 Act to take it into account. The decision may perhaps be explained as showing the breadth of the margin of appreciation accorded by the court to national authorities. It may even have been influenced by the generous opportunity for release given to Mr Lawless and those in his position. If, however, it was open to the Irish Government in *Lawless* to conclude that there was a public emergency threatening the life of the Irish nation, the British Government could scarcely be faulted for reaching that conclusion in the much more dangerous situation which arose after 11 September.

29. Thirdly, I would accept that great weight should be given to the judgment of the Home Secretary, his colleagues and Parliament on this question, because they were called on to exercise a pre-eminently political judgment. ...Reasonable and informed minds may differ, and a judgment is not shown to be wrong or unreasonable because that which is thought likely to happen does not happen. It would have been irresponsible not to err, if at all, on the side of safety. As will become apparent, I do not accept the full breadth of the Attorney General's argument on what is generally called the deference owed by the courts to the political authorities. It is perhaps preferable to approach this question as one of demarcation of functions or what Liberty in its written case called "relative institutional competence". The more purely political (in a broad or narrow sense) a question is, the more appropriate it will be for political

resolution and the less likely it is to be an appropriate matter for judicial decision. The smaller, therefore, will be the potential role of the court. It is the function of political and not judicial bodies to resolve political questions. Conversely, the greater the legal content of any issue, the greater the potential role of the court, because under our constitution and subject to the sovereign power of Parliament it is the function of the courts and not of political bodies to resolve legal questions. The present question seems to me to be very much at the political end of the spectrum: see *Secretary of State for the Home Department v Rehman* [2003] 1 AC 153, para 62, per Lord Hoffmann. The appellants recognised this by acknowledging that the Home Secretary's decision on the present question was less readily open to challenge than his decision (as they argued) on some other questions. This reflects the unintrusive approach of the European court to such a question. I conclude that the appellants have shown no ground strong enough to warrant displacing the Secretary of State's decision on this important threshold question.

...

LORD NICHOLLS OF BIRKENHEAD

74. My Lords, indefinite imprisonment without charge or trial is anathema in any country which observes the rule of law. It deprives the detained person of the protection a criminal trial is intended to afford. Wholly exceptional circumstances must exist before this extreme step can be justified.

Alert

...

81. In the present case I see no escape from the conclusion that Parliament must be regarded as having attached insufficient weight to the human rights of non-nationals. The subject matter of the legislation is the needs of national security. This subject matter dictates that, in the ordinary course, substantial latitude should be accorded to the legislature. But the human right in question, the right to individual liberty, is one of the most fundamental of human rights. Indefinite detention without trial wholly negates that right for an indefinite period. With one exception all the individuals currently detained have been imprisoned now for three years and there is no prospect of imminent release. It is true that those detained may at any time walk away from their place of detention if they leave this country. Their prison, it is said, has only three walls. But this freedom is more theoretical than real. This is demonstrated by the continuing presence in Belmarsh of most of those detained. They prefer to stay in prison rather than face the prospect of ill treatment in any country willing to admit them.

...

LORD HOFFMANN

86. ...This is one of the most important cases which the House has had to decide in recent years. It calls into question the very existence of an ancient liberty of which this country has until now been very proud: freedom from arbitrary arrest and detention. The power which the Home Secretary seeks to uphold is a power to detain people indefinitely without charge or trial. Nothing could be more antithetical to the instincts and traditions of the people of the United Kingdom.

87. At present, the power cannot be exercised against citizens of this country. First, it applies only to foreigners whom the Home Secretary would otherwise be able to deport. But the power to deport foreigners is extremely wide. Secondly, it requires that the Home Secretary should reasonably suspect the foreigners of a variety of activities or attitudes in connection with terrorism, including supporting a group influenced from abroad whom the Home Secretary suspects of being concerned in terrorism. If the finger of suspicion has pointed and the suspect is detained, his detention must be reviewed by the Special Immigration Appeals Commission. They can decide that there were no reasonable grounds for the Home Secretary's suspicion. But the suspect is not entitled to be told the grounds upon which he has been suspected. So he may not find it easy to explain that the suspicion is groundless. In any case, suspicion of being a supporter is one thing and proof of wrongdoing is another. Someone who has never committed any offence and has no intention of doing anything wrong may be reasonably suspected of being a supporter on the basis of some heated remarks overheard in a pub. The question in this case is whether the United Kingdom should be a country in which the police can come to such a person's house and take him away to be detained indefinitely without trial.

88. The technical issue in this appeal is whether such a power can be justified on the ground that there exists a "war or other public emergency threatening the life of the nation" within the meaning of article 15 of the European Convention on Human Rights. But I would not like anyone to think that we are concerned with some special doctrine of European law. Freedom from arbitrary arrest and detention is a quintessentially British liberty, enjoyed by the inhabitants of this country when most of the population of Europe could be thrown into prison at the whim of their rulers. It was incorporated into the European Convention in order to entrench the same liberty in countries which had recently been under Nazi occupation. The United Kingdom subscribed to the Convention because it set out the rights which British subjects enjoyed under the common law.

89. The exceptional power to derogate from those rights also reflected British constitutional history. There have been times of great national emergency in which habeas corpus has been suspended and powers to detain on suspicion conferred on the Government. It happened during the Napoleonic Wars and during both World Wars in the 20th century. These powers were conferred with great misgiving and, in the sober light of retrospect after the emergency had passed, were often found to have been cruelly and unnecessarily exercised. But the necessity of draconian powers in moments of national crisis is recognised in our constitutional history. Article 15 of the

Convention, when it speaks of "war or other public emergency threatening the life of the nation", accurately states the conditions in which such legislation has previously been thought necessary.

Alert

90. Until the Human Rights Act 1998, the question of whether the threat to the nation was sufficient to justify suspension of habeas corpus or the introduction of powers of detention could not have been the subject of judicial decision. There could be no basis for questioning an Act of Parliament by court proceedings. Under the 1998 Act, the courts still cannot say that an Act of Parliament is invalid. But they can declare that it is incompatible with the human rights of persons in this country. Parliament may then choose whether to maintain the law or not. The declaration of the court enables Parliament to choose with full knowledge that the law does not accord with our constitutional traditions.

Link

See also the separation of powers and parliamentary sovereignty.

91. What is meant by "threatening the life of the nation"? The "nation" is a social organism, living in its territory (in this case, the United Kingdom) under its own form of government and subject to a system of laws which expresses its own political and moral values. When one speaks of a threat to the "life" of the nation, the word life is being used in a metaphorical sense. The life of the nation is not coterminous with the lives of its people. The nation, its institutions and values, endure through generations. In many important respects, England is the same nation as it was at the time of the first Elizabeth or the Glorious Revolution. The Armada threatened to destroy the life of the nation, not by loss of life in battle, but by subjecting English institutions to the rule of Spain and the Inquisition. The same was true of the threat posed to the United Kingdom by Nazi Germany in the Second World War. This country, more than any other in the world, has an unbroken history of living for centuries under institutions and in accordance with values which show a recognisable continuity.

...

94. The Home Secretary has adduced evidence, both open and secret, to show the existence of a threat of serious terrorist outrages. The Attorney General did not invite us to examine the secret evidence, but despite the widespread scepticism which has attached to intelligence assessments since the fiasco over Iraqi weapons of mass destruction, I am willing to accept that credible evidence of such plots exist. The events of 11 September 2001 in New York and Washington and 11 March 2003 in Madrid make it entirely likely that the threat of similar atrocities in the United Kingdom is a real one.

95. But the question is whether such a threat is a threat to the life of the nation. The Attorney General's submissions and the judgment of the Special Immigration Appeals Commission treated a threat of serious physical damage and loss of life as necessarily involving a threat to the life of the nation. But in my opinion this shows a misunderstanding of what is meant by "threatening the life of the nation". Of course the Government has a duty to protect the lives and property of its citizens. But that is a duty which it owes all the time and which it must discharge without destroying our constitutional freedoms. There may be some nations too fragile or fissiparous to withstand a serious act of violence. But that is not the case in the United Kingdom.

When Milton urged the government of his day not to censor the press even in time of civil war, he said: "Lords and Commons of England, consider what nation it is whereof ye are, and whereof ye are the governours".

96. This is a nation which has been tested in adversity, which has survived physical destruction and catastrophic loss of life. I do not underestimate the ability of fanatical groups of terrorists to kill and destroy, but they do not threaten the life of the nation. Whether we would survive Hitler hung in the balance, but there is no doubt that we shall survive Al-Qaeda. The Spanish people have not said that what happened in Madrid, hideous crime as it was, threatened the life of their nation. Their legendary pride would not allow it. Terrorist violence, serious as it is, does not threaten our institutions of government or our existence as a civil community.

97. For these reasons I think that the Special Immigration Appeals Commission made an error of law and that the appeal ought to be allowed. Others of your Lordships who are also in favour of allowing the appeal would do so, not because there is no emergency threatening the life of the nation, but on the ground that a power of detention confined to foreigners is irrational and discriminatory. I would prefer not to express a view on this point. I said that the power of detention is at present confined to foreigners and I would not like to give the impression that all that was necessary was to extend the power to United Kingdom citizens as well. In my opinion, such a power in any form is not compatible with our constitution. The real threat to the life of the nation, in the sense of a people living in accordance with its traditional laws and political values, comes not from terrorism but from laws such as these. That is the true measure of what terrorism may achieve. It is for Parliament to decide whether to give the terrorists such a victory.

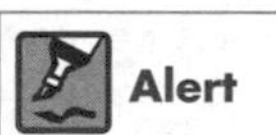
Alert

LORD HOPE OF CRAIGHEAD

...

107. The Attorney General ... submitted that a wide margin of discretion should be accorded at each stage in the analysis to the executive and to Parliament. He based this submission on the claim of these branches of government to democratic legitimacy, on the fact that the executive was best placed to consider the risks and on the special nature of the intelligence exercise. I accept at once that the executive and the legislature are to be accorded a wide margin of discretion in matters relating to national security, especially where the Convention rights of others such as the right to life may be put in jeopardy... . But the width of the margin depends on the context. Here the context is set by the nature of the right to liberty which the Convention guarantees to everyone, and by the responsibility that rests on the court to give effect to the guarantee to minimise the risk of arbitrariness and to ensure the rule of law: *Aksoy v Turkey* (1996) 23 EHRR 553, 588, para 76. Its absolute nature, save only in the circumstances that are expressly provided for by article 5(1), indicates that any interference with the right to liberty must be accorded the fullest and most anxious scrutiny.

Link

See the separation of powers.

108. Put another way, the margin of the discretionary judgment that the courts will accord to the executive and to Parliament where this right is in issue is narrower than will be appropriate in other contexts. We are not dealing here with matters of social or economic policy, where opinions may reasonably differ in a democratic society and where choices on behalf of the country as a whole are properly left to government and to the legislature. We are dealing with actions taken on behalf of society as a whole which affect the rights and freedoms of the individual. This is where the courts may legitimately intervene, to ensure that the actions taken are proportionate. It is an essential safeguard, if individual rights and freedoms are to be protected in a democratic society which respects the principle that minorities, however unpopular, have the same rights as the majority. The intensity of the scrutiny will nevertheless vary according to the point that has to be considered at each stage as one examines the question that was referred to the Special Immigration Appeals Commission ("SIAC") under section 30 of the 2001 Act. This is whether the Derogation Order and Part 4 of the 2001 Act are incompatible with the appellants' Convention rights.

...

115. The question whether there is a public emergency of the kind contemplated by article 15(1) requires the exercise of judgment. The primary meaning of the word is an occurrence that is sudden or unexpected. It has an extended meaning—a situation of pressing need. A patch of fog on the motorway or a storm which brings down power lines may create a situation of emergency without the life of the nation being under threat. It is a question of degree. The range of situations which may demonstrate such a threat will extend from the consequences of natural disasters of all kinds to the consequences of acts of terrorism. Few would doubt that it is for the executive, with all the resources at its disposal, to judge whether the consequences of such events amount to an emergency of that kind. But imminent emergencies arouse fear and, as has often been said, fear is democracy's worst enemy. So it would be dangerous to ignore the context in which the judgment is to be exercised. Its exercise needs to be watched very carefully if it is a preliminary to the invoking of emergency powers, especially if they involve actions which are incompatible with Convention rights.

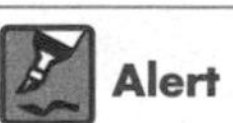
Alert

116. I am content therefore to accept that the questions whether there is an emergency and whether it threatens the life of the nation are pre-eminently for the executive and for Parliament. The judgment that has to be formed on these issues lies outside the expertise of the courts, including SIAC in the exercise of the jurisdiction that has been given to it by Part 4 of the 2001 Act. But in my opinion it is nevertheless open to the judiciary to examine the nature of the situation that has been identified by government as constituting the emergency, and to scrutinise the submission by the Attorney General that for the appellants to be deprived of their fundamental right to liberty does not exceed what is "strictly required" by the situation which it has identified. The use of the word "strictly" invites close scrutiny of the action that has been taken. Where the rights of the individual are in issue the nature of the emergency must first be identified, and then compared with the effects on the individual of depriving him of those rights. In my opinion it is the proper function of the judiciary to subject the Government's reasoning on these matters in this case to very close analysis. ...

Alert

LORD SCOTT OF FOSCOTE

154. The Secretary of State's case that this threshold criterion has been met is based upon the horrific example of the 11 September attack on the Twin Towers in New York, on the belief that those responsible may target allies of the United States for similar atrocities (a belief given credibility by the recent attack in Madrid) and on the assertion that available intelligence indicates the reality and imminence of a comparable terrorist attack on the United Kingdom. The Secretary of State is unfortunate in the timing of the judicial examination in these proceedings of the "public emergency" that he postulates. It is certainly true that the judiciary must in general defer to the executive's assessment of what constitutes a threat to national security or to "the life of the nation". But judicial memories are no shorter than those of the public and the public have not forgotten the faulty intelligence assessments on the basis of which United Kingdom forces were sent to take part, and are still taking part, in the hostilities in Iraq. For my part I do not doubt that there is a terrorist threat to this country and I do not doubt that great vigilance is necessary, not only on the part of the security forces but also on the part of individual members of the public, to guard against terrorist attacks. But I do have very great doubt whether the "public emergency" is one that justifies the description of "threatening the life of the nation". None the less, I would, for my part, be prepared to allow the Secretary of State the benefit of the doubt on this point and accept that the threshold criterion of article 15 is satisfied.

"To the extent strictly required by the exigencies of the situation"

155. Section 23 constitutes, in my opinion, a derogation from article 5(1) at the extreme end of the severity spectrum. An individual who is detained under section 23 will be a person accused of no crime but a person whom the Secretary of State has certified that he "reasonably ... suspects ... is a terrorist" (section 21(1)). The individual may then be detained in prison indefinitely. True it is that he can leave the United Kingdom if he elects to do so but the reality in many cases will be that the only country to which he is entitled to go will be a country where he is likely to undergo torture if he does go there. He can challenge before the SIAC the reasonableness of the Secretary of State's suspicion that he is a terrorist but has no right to know the grounds on which the Secretary of State has formed that suspicion. The grounds can be made known to a special advocate appointed to represent him but the special advocate may not inform him of the grounds and, therefore, cannot take instructions from him in refutation of the allegations made against him. Indefinite imprisonment in consequence of a denunciation on grounds that are not disclosed and made by a person whose identity cannot be disclosed is the stuff of nightmares, associated whether accurately or inaccurately with France before and during the Revolution, with Soviet Russia in the Stalinist era and now associated, as a result of section 23 of the 2001 Act, with the United Kingdom. I can understand, conceptually, that the circumstances constituting the "public emergency threatening the life of the nation" might be of such an order as to justify describing section 23 as a measure "strictly required by the exigencies of the situation". But I am unable to accept that the Secretary of State has established that section 23 is "strictly required" by the public emergency. He should, at the least, in my

opinion, have to show that monitoring arrangements or movement restrictions less severe than incarceration in prison would not suffice.

...

BARONESS HALE OF RICHMOND

226. The courts' power to rule on the validity of the derogation is another of the safeguards enacted by Parliament in this carefully constructed package. It would be meaningless if we could only rubber-stamp what the Home Secretary and Parliament have done. But any sensible court, like any sensible person, recognises the limits of its expertise. Assessing the strength of a general threat to the life of the nation is, or should be, within the expertise of the Government and its advisers. They may, as recent events have shown, not always get it right. But courts too do not always get things right. It would be very surprising if the courts were better able to make that sort of judgment than the Government. Protecting the life of the nation is one of the first tasks of a Government in a world of nation states. That does not mean that the courts could never intervene. Unwarranted declarations of emergency are a familiar tool of tyranny. If a government were to declare a public emergency where patently there was no such thing, it would be the duty of the court to say so. But we are here considering the immediate aftermath of the unforgettable events of 11 September 2001. The attacks launched on the United States on that date were clearly intended to threaten the life of that nation. SIAC were satisfied that the open and closed material before them justified the conclusion that there was also a public emergency threatening the life of this nation. I, for one, would not feel qualified or even inclined to disagree.

227. But what is then done to meet the emergency must be no more than "is strictly required by the exigencies of the situation". The Government wished to solve a problem which had three components: (1) it suspected certain people living here of being international terrorists—in the very broad definition given to that term by the Act; but (2) either it could not or it did not wish to prove this beyond reasonable doubt by evidence admissible in a court of law; and (3) it could not solve the problem by deporting them, either for practical or for legal reasons.

228. The Government knew about certain foreign nationals presenting this problem, because they were identified during the usual immigration appeals process. But there is absolutely no reason to think that the problem applies only to foreigners. Quite the reverse. There is every reason to think that there are British nationals living here who are international terrorists within the meaning of the Act; who cannot be shown to be such in a court of law; and who cannot be deported to another country because they have every right to be here. Yet the Government does not think that it is necessary to lock them up. Indeed, it has publicly stated that locking up nationals is a Draconian step which could not at present be justified. But it has provided us with no real explanation of why it is necessary to lock up one group of people sharing exactly the same characteristics as another group which it does not think necessary to lock up.

229. The Attorney General's arguments were mainly directed to the entirely different question of whether it is justifiable in international law to treat foreigners differently

from nationals. The unsurprising answer is that some differences in treatment are indeed allowed. Foreigners do not have to be given the same rights to participate in the politics and government of the country as have citizens (see article 16 of the Convention). Nor do they have to be given the same rights to come or to stay here; if they are here, they may be refused entry or deported (and detained for that purpose under article 5(1)(f)). But while they are here they have the same human rights as everyone else. This includes not being forcibly removed to a place where they are liable to suffer torture or other severe ill-treatment contrary to article 3 of the Convention. It also includes not being locked up except in the circumstances allowed under article 5.

230. The Attorney General did argue that it would have been discriminatory to lock up the nationals as well as the foreigners, because the foreigners are free to leave this country if they can and want to do so, but nationals have no other country which has an obligation to receive them. It is correct that we have no power to force our nationals to go, unless some other country wishes to extradite them. But if it is necessary to lock anyone up in a 'prison with three walls', the reality is that it will depend upon the personal circumstances of each individual whether he has in fact somewhere else to go. Some nationals may, for example, have dual nationality or friends in foreign countries which are happy to receive them. But the very fact that it is a prison with only three walls also casts doubt upon whether it is "strictly required by the exigencies of the situation". What sense does it make to consider a person such a threat to the life of the nation that he must be locked up without trial, but allow him to leave, as has happened, for France where he was released almost immediately?

231. The conclusion has to be that it is not necessary to lock up the nationals. Other ways must have been found to contain the threat which they present. And if it is not necessary to lock up the nationals it cannot be necessary to lock up the foreigners. It is not strictly required by the exigencies of the situation.

232. It is also inconsistent with our other obligations under international law from which there has been no derogation, principally article 14 of the European Convention. ...

233. This has five components, some of which overlap: (i) people belonging to a particular group or status (ii) must not be singled out for less favourable treatment (iii) from that given to other people who are in the same situation (iv) in relation to the enjoyment of their Convention rights (v) unless there is an objective justification for the difference in treatment.

234. Article 14 would make it unlawful to single out foreign nationals for less favourable treatment in respect of their article 5 rights whether or not the derogation from those rights was "strictly required by the exigencies of the situation". It is wrong to single them out for detention without trial if detention without trial is not strictly required to meet the exigencies of the situation. It is also wrong to single them out for detention without trial if detention without trial is strictly required, if there are other people who are in the same situation and there is no objective justification for the difference in treatment. Like cases must be treated alike.

235. Are foreigners and nationals alike for this purpose? The Attorney General argued that they are not. The foreigners have no right to be here and we would expel them if we could. We only have to allow them to stay to protect them from an even worse invasion of their human rights. Hence, he argued, the true comparison is not with suspected international terrorists who are British nationals but with foreign suspected international terrorists who can be deported. This cannot be right. The foreigners who can be deported are not like the foreigners who cannot. These foreigners are only being detained because they cannot be deported. They are just like a British national who cannot be deported. The relevant circumstances making the two cases alike for this purpose are the same three which constitute the problem: a suspected international terrorist, who for a variety of reasons cannot be successfully prosecuted, and who for a variety of reasons cannot be deported or expelled.

236. Even then, the difference in treatment might have an objective justification. But to do so it must serve a legitimate aim and be proportionate to that aim. Once again, the fact that it is sometimes permissible to treat foreigners differently does not mean that every difference in treatment serves a legitimate aim. If the situation really is so serious, and the threat so severe, that people may be detained indefinitely without trial, what possible legitimate aim could be served by only having power to lock up some of the people who present that threat? This is even more so, of course, if the necessity to lock people up in this way has not been shown.

237. Democracy values each person equally. In most respects, this means that the will of the majority must prevail. But valuing each person equally also means that the will of the majority cannot prevail if it is inconsistent with the equal rights of minorities. As Thomas Jefferson said in his inaugural address:

"Though the will of the majority is in all cases to prevail, that will to be rightful must be reasonable ... The minority possess their equal rights, which equal law must protect, and to violate would be oppression."

238. No one has the right to be an international terrorist. But substitute "black", "disabled", "female", "gay", or any other similar adjective for "foreign" before "suspected international terrorist" and ask whether it would be justifiable to take power to lock up that group but not the "white", "able-bodied", "male" or "straight" suspected international terrorists. The answer is clear.

239. I would therefore allow the appeals, quash the derogation order, and declare section 23 of the 2001 Act incompatible with the right to liberty in article 5(1) of the European Convention.

This case reveals that the key motivation underlying the strong support for the idea of the rule of law is the need properly to constrain and control executive action. Very notably too, the nature of the rule of law principles upheld by the modern judiciary can be seen as substantive; in other words the mechanisms of constraint are not just procedural, but impute certain moral, substantive values, notably the importance of fundamental human rights. As you progress through this Case Book, especially when you reach the Human Rights section, you will see a strong trend towards a more determined judicial culture that seeks to restrain executive power on a substantive basis.

Further Reading

The Rule of Law, Sixth Annual Sir David Williams Lecture given by the Rt Hon Lord Bingham of Cornhill KG, 16 November 2006

Jowell J and Oliver D, *The Changing Constitution*, (5th Edition), OUP, Chapter 1 – The Rule of Law Today

Tom Bingham, The Rule of Law, (1st Edition)

4

Parliamentary Sovereignty

Topic List

Alex Lawson and Neil Hurden

Introduction

The single greatest conceptual difference between the UK's model of constitutionalism and that of most other democracies is the operation of the doctrine of Parliamentary sovereignty. Most other constitutional systems, for instance the USA, possess a constitutional document which forms the fundamental law and ultimate sovereign element of the state. Such constitutional frameworks are often protected or 'entrenched' by a special amendment procedure. In the UK, there is no formal, special protection given to the combination of laws and other rules that comprise the constitution; in this sense, all law has traditionally been seen as 'regular' law. Importantly too, the courts in the UK (including the new Supreme Court) have not had the power to strike down primary legislation that constitutional courts in other countries have. This has meant that ultimate sovereignty in the UK has rested in the institution of Parliament itself, because this body has the legal ability to pass legislation on any matter it sees fit. The courts have played an important role in interpreting such legislation but, as seen in the chapter on separation of powers, this function is essentially a secondary one; interpretation should not in principle move into the realm of amendment, just as development of the common law should not veer towards judicial "law-making".

1 Parliamentary Sovereignty

For Dicey, Parliamentary sovereignty meant that Parliament had 'the right to make or unmake any law whatsoever; ... and further that no person or body is recognised by the law of England as having the right to override or set aside the legislation of Parliament'. Sovereignty in this sense means that Parliament is not legally subordinate to any other body, and a key aspect of his doctrine was that no Parliament could bind its successor or be bound by its predecessor: every Parliament enjoyed an unfettered legislative power, which neither the courts nor King could interfere with.

The inability of the courts to challenge the validity of an Act of Parliament was illustrated well in the following case.

British Railways Board Appellants v Pickin **[1974] AC 765**

Panel: Lord Reid, Lord Morris of Borth-y-Gest, Lord Wilberforce, Lord Simon of Glaisdale and Lord Cross of Chelsea

Facts: Pickin owned some land next to a railway line and his property rights were affected by the passing of the British Railways Act 1968, which was a private Act of Parliament. He alleged that the Board of British Railways has misled Parliament at the time when sponsoring the Bill and that the statute was therefore invalid. The Board initially managed to have the claim struck out as an abuse of process but the Court of Appeal reversed the decision.

LORD MORRIS OF BORTH-y-GEST

In my view, it is beyond question that the substance of the plea advanced by the two paragraphs is that the court is entitled to and should disregard what Parliament has enacted in section 18. The question of fundamental importance which arises is whether the court should entertain the proposition that an Act of Parliament can so be assailed in the courts that matters should proceed as though the Act or some part of it had never been passed. I consider that such doctrine would be dangerous and impermissible. It is the function of the courts to administer the laws which Parliament has enacted. In the processes of Parliament there will be much consideration whether a Bill should or should not in one form or another become an enactment. When an enactment is passed there is finality unless and until it is amended or repealed by Parliament. In the courts there may be argument as to the correct interpretation of the enactment: there must be none as to whether it should be on the Statute Book at all.

...

The conclusion which I have reached results, in my view, not only from a settled and sustained line of authority which I see no reason to question and which I think should be endorsed but also from the view that any other conclusion would be constitutionally undesirable and impracticable. It must surely be for Parliament to lay down the procedures which are to be followed before a Bill can become an Act. It must be for Parliament to decide whether its decreed procedures have in fact been followed. It must be for Parliament to lay down and to construe its Standing Orders and further to decide whether they have been obeyed: it must be for Parliament to decide whether in any particular case to dispense with ampleness with such orders. It must be for Parliament to decide whether it is satisfied that an Act should be passed in the form and with the wording set out in the Act. It must be for Parliament to decide what documentary material or testimony it requires and the extent to which Parliamentary privilege should attach. It would be impracticable and undesirable for the High Court of Justice to embark upon an inquiry concerning the effect or the effectiveness of the internal procedures in the High Court of Parliament or an inquiry whether in any particular case those procedures were effectively followed.

The very clear message conveyed by Lord Morris illustrates how, for policy reasons, the courts have traditionally not thought it constitutionally appropriate to interfere with the function and product of Parliament. In accordance with the so-called "enrolled bill rule" the courts were intent on observing perceived separation of powers boundaries and respecting the notion of parliamentary privilege by refusing to look behind the manner in which a statute may have been passed.

Modern developments

The primacy of the doctrine of Parliamentary sovereignty as the most basic element of the UK constitutional set-up has been subjected to pressure and criticism in recent years and developments in this area represent the most interesting source of change in the modern constitution.

Probably the most significant of the modern developments has been the entry of the UK into the EEC, now the European Union. This has involved a certain amount of 'pooling' of sovereignty across the Union's Member States and, in legal terms, a recognition that, for as long as the UK remains a member of the EU, its domestic law is obliged to comply with the higher authority of EU law, representing a radical departure from the traditional Diceyan position.

After a number of years of gradual accommodation to the new legal order of the EU, the UK courts finally confirmed the supremacy of EU law in rather unusual circumstances. The following case brought about a landmark change, as this was the first occasion on which a piece of UK legislation was so clearly inconsistent with EU law that the courts could not employ even a highly purposive form of statutory interpretation to try to engineer consistency.

R v Secretary of State for Transport, Ex parte Factortame Ltd. and Others (No. 2) [1991] 1 AC 603

Panel: Lord Bridge of Harwich, Lord Brandon of Oakbrook, Lord Oliver of Aylmerton, Lord Goff of Chieveley and Lord Jauncey of Tullichettle

Facts: the applicant companies, which were incorporated under UK law, owned 95 fishing vessels. The companies were mainly owned and managed by Spanish nationals but their vessels were registered as British under an Act of 1894. The law in this area was significantly reformed, however, with the passing of Part II of the Merchant Shipping Act 1988 and related regulations. The statutory changes meant that vessels, previously registered as British, had to be re-registered under the Act of 1988, and the applicants' vessels failed to qualify under the new regime because they were largely managed and controlled from Spain. The companies therefore sought to challenge the legality of the relevant new statutory provisions on the ground that they contravened the provisions of the EEC Treaty and other aspects of EU law, as incorporated into domestic UK law by the European Communities Act 1972. The Divisional Court requested a preliminary ruling from the European Court of Justice and it ordered that, pending the ECJ ruling, the applicants should be allowed interim, financial relief by 'disapplying' the domestic provisions. The Court of Appeal subsequently set aside the interim relief order and the companies appealed to the House of Lords, which (in case No. 1) upheld the Court of Appeal's decision but referred the matter to the ECJ for a ruling on whether Community law effectively obliged the UK courts to provide interim relief notwithstanding the established position regarding the status of a UK Act of Parliament. The ECJ held that in a case concerning EU law, if a national court considered that the only obstacle which precluded it from granting an application of interim relief was a rule of national law, that rule should be set aside.

LORD BRIDGE OF HARWICH

My Lords, when this appeal first came before the House last year (*Reg. v. Secretary of State for Transport, Ex parte Factortame Ltd.* [1990] 2 A.C. 85) your Lordships held that, as a matter of English law, the courts had no jurisdiction to grant interim relief in terms which would involve either overturning an English statute in advance of any decision by the European Court of Justice that the statute infringed Community law or granting an injunction against the Crown. It then became necessary to seek a preliminary ruling from the European Court of Justice as to whether Community law itself invested us with such jurisdiction. In the speech I delivered on that occasion, with which your Lordships agreed, I explained the reasons which led us to those conclusions. It will be remembered that, on that occasion, the House never directed its attention to the question how, if there were jurisdiction to grant the relief sought, discretion ought to be exercised in deciding whether or not relief should be granted.

Decipher

The decision in *Factortame (No 1)* can be seen as upholding Parliamentary sovereignty.

In June of this year we received the judgment of the European Court of Justice (Case C 213/89), ante, pp. 640 et seq., replying to the questions we had posed and affirming that we had jurisdiction, in the circumstances postulated, to grant interim relief for the protection of directly enforceable rights under Community law and that no limitation on our jurisdiction imposed by any rule of national law could stand as the sole obstacle to preclude the grant of such relief. In the light of this judgment we were able to conclude the hearing of the appeal in July and unanimously decided that relief should be granted in terms of the orders which the House then made, indicating that we would give our reasons for the decision later.

My noble and learned friend, Lord Goff of Chieveley, whose speech I have had the advantage of reading in draft, has given a very full account of all the relevant circumstances arising since our decision last year in the light of which our final disposal of the appeal fell to be made. I gratefully adopt this account. I also agree with his exposition of the principles applicable in relation to the grant of interim injunctive relief where the dispute involves a conflict between private and public interests and where damages are not a remedy available to either party, leading, in the circumstances of this case, to the conclusion that it was appropriate to grant relief in terms of the orders made by the House. But I add some observations of my own in view of the importance of the subject matter.

Some public comments on the decision of the European Court of Justice, affirming the jurisdiction of the courts of member states to override national legislation if necessary to enable interim relief to be granted in protection of rights under Community law, have suggested that this was a novel and dangerous invasion by a Community institution of the sovereignty of the United Kingdom Parliament. But such comments are based on a misconception. If the supremacy within the European Community of Community law over the national law of member states was not always inherent in the E.E.C. Treaty (Cmnd. 5179-II) it was certainly well established in the jurisprudence of the European Court of Justice long before the United Kingdom joined the Community. Thus, whatever limitation of its sovereignty Parliament accepted when it enacted the European Communities Act 1972 was entirely voluntary. Under the terms of the Act of 1972 it has always been clear that it was the duty of a United Kingdom court, when delivering final judgment, to override any rule of national law found to be in conflict with any directly enforceable rule of Community law. Similarly, when decisions of the European Court of Justice have exposed areas of United Kingdom statute law which failed to implement Council directives, Parliament has always loyally accepted the obligation to

Decipher

This is a novel idea. Under Dicey's theory sovereignty cannot be limited, even voluntarily.

make appropriate and prompt amendments. Thus there is nothing in any way novel in according supremacy to rules of Community law in those areas to which they apply and to insist that, in the protection of rights under Community law, national courts must not be inhibited by rules of national law from granting interim relief in appropriate cases is no more than a logical recognition of that supremacy.

Although affirming our jurisdiction, the judgment of the European Court of Justice does not fetter our discretion to determine whether an appropriate case for the grant of interim relief has been made out. While agreeing with Lord Goff's exposition of the general principles by which the discretion should be guided, I would wish to emphasise the salient features of the present case which, at the end of the argument, left me in no doubt that interim relief should be granted. A decision to grant or withold interim relief in the protection of disputed rights at a time when the merits of the dispute cannot be finally resolved must always involve an element of risk. If, in the end, the claimant succeeds in a case where interim relief has been refused, he will have suffered an injustice. If, in the end, he fails in a case where interim relief has been granted, injustice will have been done to the other party. The objective which underlies the principles by which the discretion is to be guided must always be to ensure that the court shall choose the course which, in all the circumstances, appears to offer the best prospect that eventual injustice will be avoided or minimised. Questions as to the adequacy of an alternative remedy in damages to the party claiming injunctive relief and of a cross-undertaking in damages to the party against whom the relief is sought play a primary role in assisting the court to determine which course offers the best prospect that injustice may be avoided or minimised. But where, as here, no alternative remedy will be available to either party if the final decision does not accord with the interim decision, choosing the course which will minimise the risk presents exceptional difficulty.

If the applicants were to succeed after a refusal of interim relief, the irreparable damage they would have suffered would be very great. That is now beyond dispute. On the other hand, if they failed after a grant of interim relief, there would have been a substantial detriment to the public interest resulting from the diversion of a very significant part of the British quota of controlled stocks of fish from those who ought in law to enjoy it to others having no right to it. In either case, if the final decision did not accord with the interim decision, there would have been an undoubted injustice. But the injustices are so different in kind that I find it very difficult to weigh the one against the other.

If the matter rested there, I should be inclined to say, for the reasons indicated by Lord Goff of Chieveley, that the public interest should prevail and interim relief be refused. But the matter does not rest there. Unlike the ordinary case in which the court must decide whether or not to grant interlocutory relief at a time when disputed issues of fact remain unresolved, here the relevant facts are all ascertained and the only unresolved issues are issues of law, albeit of Community law. Now, although the final decision of such issues is the exclusive prerogative of the European Court of Justice, that does not mean that an English court may not reach an informed opinion as to how such issues are likely to be resolved. In this case we are now in a position to derive much assistance in that task from the decisions of the European Court of Justice in *Reg. v. Ministry of Agriculture, Fisheries and Food, Ex parte Agegate Ltd.* (Case C 3/87) [1990] 2 Q.B. 151 and *Reg. v. Ministry of Agriculture, Fisheries and Food, Ex parte Jaderow Ltd.* (Case C 216/87) [1990] 2 Q.B. 193 and the interim decision of the President in the proceedings brought by the European Commission against the United Kingdom (*Commission of the European Communities v. United Kingdom* (Case 246/89 R) [1989] E.C.R. 3125) to which Lord Goff of Chieveley has referred. In the circumstances I believe that the most logical course in seeking a decision least likely to occasion injustice is to make the best prediction we can of the final outcome and to give to that prediction decisive weight in resolving the interlocutory issue.

It is now, I think, common ground that the quota system operated under the common fisheries policy, in order to be effective and to ensure that the quota of a member state enures to the benefit of its local fishing industry, entitles the member state to derogate from rights otherwise exerciseable under Community law to the extent necessary to ensure that only fishing vessels having a genuine economic link with that industry may fish against its quota. The narrow ground on which the Secretary of State resists the applicants' claim is that the requirements of section 14 of the Merchant Shipping Act 1988 that at least 75 per cent. of the beneficial ownership of a British fishing vessel must be vested in persons resident and domiciled in the United Kingdom is necessary to ensure that the vessel has a genuine economic link with the British fishing industry. Before the decision of the European Court of Justice in *Agegate* that would have seemed to me a contention of some cogency. But in *Agegate* it was held that a licensing condition requiring 75 per cent. of the crew of a vessel fishing against the quota of a member state to be resident within the member state could not be justified on the ground that it was "irrelevant to the aim of the quota system:" p. 261. I confess that I find some difficulty in understanding the reasoning in the judgment which leads to this conclusion. But if a residence requirement relating to crew members cannot be justified as necessary to the maintenance of a genuine economic link with the local industry, it is difficult to see how residence or domicile requirements relating to beneficial owners could possibly fare any better.

The broader contention on behalf of the Secretary of State that member states have an unfettered right to determine what ships may fly their flag raises more difficult issues. It would not be appropriate in the context of the present interlocutory decision to enter upon a detailed examination of the wide-ranging arguments bearing upon those issues. I believe the best indication that we have of the prospect of success of that contention is found in the interlocutory judgment of President Due in the case brought by the Commission against the United Kingdom. He concluded that the contention was of insufficient weight to preclude him from granting an interim order suspending the application of the nationality requirements of section 14 of the Act of 1988 to nationals of other member states. His reasoning persuaded me that we should reach the same conclusion in relation to the residence and domicile requirements.

It is interesting to see from Lord Bridge's speech that he rationalises the decision to grant interim relief to the applicants by looking at what he calls the "misconception" of constitutional traditionalists about an "invasion" of UK sovereignty. Following reassurance from the ECJ Lord Bridge is conscious of the need to emphasise the logic of the EEC Treaty and subsequent case law in the ECJ pointed very firmly to the view that the UK had voluntarily limited some of its sovereignty in passing the ECA 1972.

Thoburn v Sunderland City Council **[2003] QB 151, [2002] EWHC 195 (Admin)**

Panel: Laws LJ and Crane J

Facts: Thoburn was a campaigner, known along with others as the "Metric Martyrs", who sought to preserve the use of the imperial system of measuring the weight of goods sold in markets. These individual traders were prosecuted by various local authority trading standards departments for failing to sell goods in metric units. Their argument was a complex one but in essence they rejected the councils' position that the Units of Measurement Regulations 1994 (made under exercise of powers conferred by the European Communities Act 1972) prohibited the sale of goods in imperial units, which had been allowed under the Weights and Measures Act 1985. The traders argued that that the various local authorities had acted unlawfully, because the 1985 Act had impliedly repealed the 1972 Act. They were convicted and appealed by way of case stated.

LORD JUSTICE LAWS

62. ...In the present state of its maturity the common law has come to recognise that there exist rights which should properly be classified as constitutional or fundamental: see for example such cases as *R v Secretary of State for the Home Department, Ex p Simms* [2000] 2 AC 115, 131 per Lord Hoffmann, *R v Secretary of State for the Home Department, Ex p Pierson* [1998] AC 539, *R v Secretary of State for the Home Department, Ex p Leech* [1994] QB 198, *Derbyshire County Council v Times Newspapers Ltd* [1993] AC 534 and *R v Lord Chancellor, Ex p Witham* [1998] QB 575. And from this a further insight follows. We should recognise a hierarchy of Acts of Parliament: as it were "ordinary" statutes and "constitutional" statutes. The two categories must be distinguished on a principled basis. In my opinion a constitutional statute is one which (a) conditions the legal relationship between citizen and state in some general, overarching manner, or (b) enlarges or diminishes the scope of what we would now regard as fundamental constitutional rights. (a) and (b) are of necessity closely related: it is difficult to think of an instance of (a) that is not also an instance of (b). The special status of constitutional statutes follows the special status of constitutional rights. Examples are Magna Carta 1297 (25 Edw 1), the Bill of Rights 1689 (1 Will & Mary sess 2 c 2), the Union with Scotland Act 1706 (6 Anne c 11), the Reform Acts which distributed and enlarged the franchise (Representation of the People Acts 1832 (2 & 3 Will 4 c 45), 1867 (30 & 31 Vict c 102) and 1884 (48 & 49 Vict c 3)), the Human Rights Act 1998, the Scotland Act 1998 and the Government of Wales Act 1998. The 1972 Act clearly belongs in this family. It incorporated the whole corpus of substantive Community rights and obligations, and gave overriding domestic effect to the judicial and administrative machinery of Community law. It may be there has never

been a statute having such profound effects on so many dimensions of our daily lives. The 1972 Act is, by force of the common law, a constitutional statute.

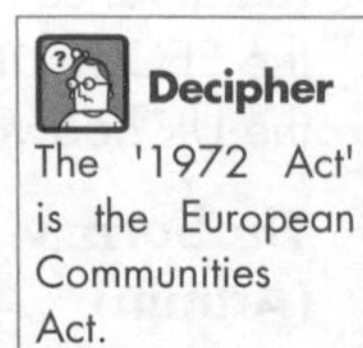
Decipher
The '1972 Act' is the European Communities Act.

63 Ordinary statutes may be impliedly repealed. Constitutional statutes may not. For the repeal of a constitutional Act or the abrogation of a fundamental right to be effected by statute, the court would apply this test: is it shown that the legislature's *actual*— not imputed, constructive or presumed—intention was to effect the repeal or abrogation? I think the test could only be met by express words in the later statute, or by words so specific that the inference of an actual determination to effect the result contended for was irresistible. The ordinary rule of implied repeal does not satisfy this test. Accordingly, it has no application to constitutional statutes. I should add that in my judgment general words could not be supplemented, so as to effect a repeal or significant amendment to a constitutional statute, by reference to what was said in Parliament by the minister promoting the Bill pursuant to Pepper v Hart [1993] AC 593. A constitutional statute can only be repealed, or amended in a way which significantly affects its provisions touching fundamental rights or otherwise the relation between citizen and state, by unambiguous words on the face of the later statute.

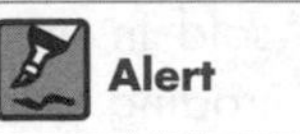
Alert

64 This development of the common law regarding constitutional rights, and as I would say constitutional statutes, is highly beneficial. It gives us most of the benefits of a written constitution, in which fundamental rights are accorded special respect. But it preserves the sovereignty of the legislature and the flexibility of our uncodified constitution. It accepts the relation between legislative supremacy and fundamental rights is not fixed or brittle: rather the courts (in interpreting statutes and, now, applying the Human Rights Act 1998) will pay more or less deference to the legislature, or other public decision-maker, according to the subject in hand. Nothing is plainer than that this benign development involves, as I have said, the recognition of the 1972 Act as a constitutional statute.

Alert

In terms of the actual case, Laws LJ's reading of the relevant legislation meant that he upheld the validity of the regulations under which the traders had been prosecuted. The case is far more interesting and significant, though, for what he says more generally about the differing status of various Acts of Parliament. The idea that some statutes effectively have a higher and more fundamental status, based on their subject matter, than regular statutes clearly does not comply with Diceyan orthodoxy relating to the idea of implied repeal. Nor, however, does it mean that these constitutional statutes are permanently entrenched, as he also makes plain, because all statutes can be expressly repealed on the basis of a majority vote in Parliament.

A similar line of argument was pursued by Lord Hoffmann in the case of *R v Secretary of State for the Home Department, Ex p Simms* [2000] 2 AC 115 in the specific context of human rights protection. As with the impact of the ECA 1972 s 2, it is notable that under the Human Rights Act the courts' use of s3 interpretive powers effectively mean that Convention rights can only be overridden by the express intention of Parliament, with all the political consequences that that may entail:

Parliamentary sovereignty means that Parliament can, if it chooses, legislate contrary to fundamental principles of human rights. The Human Rights Act 1998 will not detract from this power. The constraints upon its exercise by Parliament are ultimately political, not legal. But the principle of legality means that Parliament must squarely confront what it is doing and accept the political cost. Fundamental rights cannot be overridden by general or ambiguous words. This is because there is too great a risk that the full implications of their unqualified meaning may have passed unnoticed in the democratic process. In the absence of express language or necessary implication to the contrary, the courts therefore presume that even the most general words were intended to be subject to the basic rights of the individual. In this way the courts of the United Kingdom, though acknowledging the sovereignty of Parliament, apply principles of constitutionality little different from those which exist in countries where the power of the legislature is expressly limited by a constitutional document.

The Human Rights Act 1998 will make three changes to this scheme of things. First, the principles of fundamental human rights which exist at common law will be supplemented by a specific text, namely the European Convention on Human Rights and Fundamental Freedoms. But much of the Convention reflects the common law: see *Derbyshire County Council v. Times Newspapers Ltd.* [1993] A.C. 534, 551. That is why the United Kingdom government felt able in 1950 to accede to the Convention without domestic legislative change. So the adoption of the text as part of domestic law is unlikely to involve radical change in our notions of fundamental human rights. Secondly, the principle of legality will be expressly enacted as a rule of construction in section 3 and will gain further support from the obligation of the minister in charge of a Bill to make a statement of compatibility under section 19. Thirdly, in those unusual cases in which the legislative infringement of fundamental human rights is so clearly expressed as not to yield to the principle of legality, the courts will be able to draw this to the attention of Parliament by making a declaration of incompatibility. It will then be for the sovereign Parliament to decide whether or not to remove the incompatibility.

Although the views of judges such as Laws LJ and Lord Hoffmann in the preceding two cases had implications for the orthodox doctrine of Parliamentary sovereignty, they did not directly challenge it or undermine it. In the unlikely context of a case relating to the validity of the Hunting Act 2004, however, some of the law lords did, however, venture into potentially more radical territory, questioning the centrality of Parliamentary sovereignty as the primary doctrine in the UK constitution.

***R (on the application of Jackson) v Attorney General* [2006] 1 AC 262, [2005] UKHL 56**

Panel: Lord Bingham of Cornhill, Lord Nicholls of Birkenhead, Lord Steyn, Lord Hope of Craighead, Lord Rodger of Earlsferry, Lord Walker of Gestingthorpe, Baroness Hale of Richmond, Lord Carswell and Lord Brown of Eaton-under-Heywood

Statutes: Parliament Act 1911 and Parliament Act 1949

Facts: The case was brought by pro-hunting lobbyists to challenge the legislative ban on hunting with hounds in the Hunting Act 2004. The basis of the challenge was not the content of the Hunting Act but how it was passed into law, because it was enacted through the use of the procedure set up under the Parliament Act 1949. The claimants argued that the Parliament Act 1949 was not in itself validly enacted and hence any Acts passed under it (*inter alia*, the Hunting Act 2004) were similarly enacted invalidly.

This argument was based on their interpretation of the earlier Parliament Act 1911. This Act limited the powers of the House of Lords to block legislation passed by the House of Commons, following a political impasse in the preceding two years. According to this Act, a bill rejected by the Lords in three successive sessions could become law, provided that two years lapsed between the Second Reading and the Final Approval given by the Commons. The 1911 Act was itself amended in 1949 in order to reduce the delaying power of the House of Lords further, effectively allowing only a one year delay. Significantly, the Parliament Act 1949 became law using the Parliament Act 1911 procedure. This was the basis of the challenge to the 1949 (and hence 2004) Act: that the 1911 Act was never designed to be used to amend or extend itself.

Most of the comments of wider constitutional interest are *obiter*.

LORD BINGHAM OF CORNHILL

My Lords,

1 The appellants all, in differing ways, have an interest in fox-hunting. They wish that activity to continue. They challenge the legal validity of the Hunting Act 2004 which, on its face, makes it an offence to hunt a wild mammal with a dog save in limited circumstances. The appellants acknowledge that the legislative procedure adopted to enact the Hunting Act was in accordance with the procedure laid down in the Parliament Act 1949. But they contend that the 1949 Act was itself invalid: it did not, as they correctly say, receive the consent of the House of Lords; and the Parliament Act 1911 did not, they submit, permit an Act such as the 1949 Act to be enacted without the consent of the House of Lords. Thus, although the Hunting Act gives rise to the present issue between the appellants and the Attorney General, the real question turns on the validity of the 1949 Act and that in turn depends on the true effect of the 1911 Act. The merits and demerits of the Hunting Act, on which opinion is sharply divided, have no bearing on the legal issue which the House, sitting judicially, must resolve.

2 In these proceedings the appellants sought a declaration that

"1. The Parliament Act 1949 is not an Act of Parliament and is consequently of no legal effect.

2. Accordingly, the Hunting Act 2004 is not an Act of Parliament and is of no legal effect."

...

The 1949 Act

4 The 1949 Act was very short. It was described in its long title as "An Act to amend the Parliament Act, 1911." Its words of enactment were as for the Hunting Act, save that the only statutory reference was to the 1911 Act. Its substantial effect was to reduce the number of successive sessions referred to in section 2(1) of the 1911 Act

from three to two, and to reduce the lapse of time referred to in the proviso to section 2(1) of the 1911 Act from two years to one.

...

The appellants' submissions

7 Sir Sydney helpfully encapsulated the appellants' submissions in a series of key propositions, which he elaborated in written and oral argument. The propositions are these:

(1) Legislation made under the 1911 Act is delegated or subordinate, not primary.

(2) The legislative power conferred by section 2(1) of the 1911 Act is not unlimited in scope and must be read according to established principles of statutory interpretation.

(3) Among these is the principle that powers conferred on a body by an enabling Act may not be enlarged or modified by that body unless there are express words authorising such enlargement or modification.

(4) Accordingly, section 2(1) of the 1911 Act does not authorise the Commons to remove, attenuate or modify in any respect any of the conditions on which its law-making power is granted.

(5) Even if, contrary to the appellants' case, the Court of Appeal was right to regard section 2(1) of the 1911 Act as wide enough to authorise "modest" amendments of the Commons' law-making powers, the amendments in the 1949 Act were not "modest", but substantial and significant.

Decipher

Sir Sydney Kentridge QC was leading counsel for the appellants in this case.

The intervening sections retread the historical circumstances surrounding the passage of the 1911 Act.

...

The status of legislation passed under the 1911 Act

22 Sir Sydney submits that whereas legislation duly enacted by the Crown in Parliament commands general obedience and recognition as such, and is the ultimate political fact upon which the whole system of legislation hangs, legislation made under the 1911 Act is required to state on its face that it is made by the authority of the 1911 Act. Such legislation is not primary because it depends for its validity on a prior enactment, and legislation is not primary where that is so. Legislation under the 1911 Act is not similar to other delegated or subordinate legislation, such as statutory instruments and bylaws made under the authority of statute, but it is delegated or subordinate or derivative in the sense that its validity is open to investigation in the courts, which would not be permissible in the case of primary legislation.

...

23 The Divisional Court rejected this argument for reasons very clearly and succinctly given by Maurice Kay LJ (paras 23–25 of his judgment) and Collins J (paras 39–45). The Court of Appeal, in part at least, accepted it (paras 30–48).

24 Despite the skill with which the argument is advanced and the respect properly due to the authorities relied on, I am of opinion that the Divisional Court was right to reject it, for two main reasons. First, sections 1(1) and 2(1) of the 1911 Act provide that legislation made in accordance with those provisions respectively shall "become an Act of Parliament on the Royal Assent being signified". The meaning of the expression "Act of Parliament" is not doubtful, ambiguous or obscure. It is as clear and well understood as any expression in the lexicon of the law. It is used, and used only, to denote primary legislation. If there were room for doubt, which to my mind there is not, it would be resolved by comparing the language of the second resolution, quoted in para 15 above, with the language of section 2(1) as enacted. The resolution provided that a measure meeting the specified conditions "shall become Law without the consent of the House of Lords on the Royal Assent being declared". Section 2(1), as just noted, provides that a measure shall become an Act of Parliament. The change can only have been made to preclude just such an argument as the appellants are advancing. The 1911 Act did, of course, effect an important constitutional change, but the change lay not in authorising a new form of sub-primary parliamentary legislation but in creating a new way of enacting primary legislation.

25 I cannot, secondly, accept that the 1911 Act can be understood as a delegation of legislative power or authority by the House of Lords, or by Parliament, to the House of Commons. The implausibility of this interpretation can perhaps be most readily seen in relation to money bills. As noted in para 13, the Lords' rejection of the Finance Bill was a departure from convention and precedent because supply had come to be recognised as the all but exclusive preserve of the Commons. Section 1 of the 1911 Act involved no delegation of legislative power and authority to the Commons but a statutory recognition of where such power and authority in relation to supply had long been understood to lie. It would be hard to read the very similar language in section 2 as involving a delegation either, since the overall object of the Act was not to enlarge the powers of the Commons but to restrict those of the Lords. This is, in my opinion, clear from the historical context and from the Act itself. The first resolution (see para 15 above) was that "it is expedient that the House of Lords be disabled by Law from ..." The second resolution (para 15 above) was that "it is expedient that the powers of the House of Lords, as respects Bills other than Money Bills, be restricted by Law ..." The effect of section 1 of the 1911 Act is to restrict the power of the Lords to amend or reject money bills. The effect of section 2(1) is, despite the different conditions, the same, and is aptly summarised in the sidenote: "Restriction of the powers of the House of Lords as to Bills other than Money Bills". The certification of a money bill by the Speaker under section 1 and of a bill other than a money bill under section 2 is mandatory, and the presentation of a bill to the monarch for the royal assent to be signified under sections 1(1) and 2(1) is automatic, "unless the House of Commons direct to the contrary". If it be permissible to resort to the preamble of the 1911 Act, one finds reference to the expediency of making "such provision as in this Act appears for restricting the existing powers of the House of Lords". The overall object of the 1911 Act was not to delegate power: it was to restrict, subject to compliance with the specified statutory conditions, the power of the Lords to defeat measures supported by a majority of the Commons, and thereby obviate the need for the monarch to create (or

for any threat to be made that the monarch would create) peers to carry the government's programme in the Lords. This was a procedure necessarily unwelcome to a constitutional monarch, rightly anxious to avoid any appearance of participation in politics, and one which constitutionally-minded politicians were accordingly reluctant to invoke.

26 It is true, as the appellants point out, that section 4 of the 1911 Act requires the words of enactment of a Bill presented to the monarch under section 1 or section 2 of the Act, to record that the measure is enacted "in accordance with the Parliament Act 1911, and by authority of the same", and reference is now added to the 1949 Act also. But the inclusion of these words does not in my opinion mean that measures so enacted should be regarded as delegated or subordinate. The standard words of enactment make reference to the Lords Spiritual and Temporal and Commons and provide for the measure to be enacted "by the authority of the same". This language is plainly inappropriate where the Lords have not consented, and it is unsurprising that reference is instead made to the measure which makes it lawful to enact a measure in the absence of such consent. I do not think this reference can support the weight of argument the appellants seek to build on it.

27 Like the Court of Appeal (see paras 11–13 of its judgment), I feel some sense of strangeness at the exercise which the courts have (with the acquiescence of the Attorney General) been invited to undertake in these proceedings. The authority of *Pickin v British Railways Board* [1974] AC 765 is unquestioned, and it was there very clearly decided that "the courts in this country have no power to declare enacted law to be invalid" (per Lord Simon of Glaisdale at p 798). I am, however, persuaded that the present proceedings are legitimate, for two reasons. First, in *Pickin*, unlike the present case, it was sought to investigate the internal workings and procedures of Parliament to demonstrate that it had been misled and so had proceeded on a false basis. This was held to be illegitimate: see Lord Reid at p 787, Lord Morris of Borth-y-Gest at p 790, Lord Wilberforce at p 796, Lord Simon of Glaisdale at p 800 and Lord Cross of Chelsea at p 802. Lord Reid quoted with approval a passage of Lord Campbell's opinion in *Edinburgh and Dalkeith Railway Co v Wauchope* (1842) 8 Cl & F 710, 725, where he said:

"All that a Court of Justice can do is to look to the Parliamentary roll: if from that it should appear that a bill has passed both Houses and received the Royal assent, no Court of Justice can inquire into the mode in which it was introduced into Parliament, nor into what was done previous to its introduction, or what passed in Parliament during its various stages through both Houses".

Here, the court looks to the parliamentary roll and sees bills (the 1949 Act, and then the 2004 Act) which have not passed both Houses. The issue concerns no question of parliamentary procedure such as would, and could only, be the subject of parliamentary inquiry, but a question whether, in Lord Simon's language, these Acts are "enacted law". My second reason is more practical. The appellants have raised a question of law which cannot, as such, be resolved by Parliament. But it would not be satisfactory, or consistent with the rule of law, if it could not be resolved at all. So it

Decipher
Note the emphasis being placed on the rule of law, despite criticism that review is contrary to Parliamentary sovereignty.

seems to me necessary that the courts should resolve it, and that to do so involves no breach of constitutional propriety.

The scope of section 2(1)

28 Sir Sydney submits that, in accordance with long-established principles of statutory interpretation, the courts will often imply qualifications into the literal meaning of wide and general words in order to prevent them having some unreasonable consequence which Parliament could not have intended. He cites such compelling authority as *Stradling v Morgan* (1560) 1 Plow 199; *R (Edison First Power Limited) v Central Valuation Officer* [2003] UKHL 20, [2003] 4 All ER 209, para 25; *R v Secretary of State for the Home Department, Ex p Pierson* [1998] AC 539, 573–575, 588; *R v Secretary of State for the Home Department, Ex p Simms* [2000] 2 AC 115, 131; and *R (Morgan Grenfell & Co Ltd) v Special Commissioner of Income Tax* [2003] 1 AC 563, paras 8, 44–45. He relies on these authorities as establishing (as it is put in the appellants' printed case)

"that general words such as section 2(1) should not be read as authorising the doing of acts which adversely affect the basic principles on which the law of the United Kingdom is based in the absence of clear words authorising such acts. There is no more fundamental principle of law in the UK than the identity of the sovereign body. Section 2(1) should not be read as modifying the identity of the sovereign body unless its language admits of no other interpretation".

The Divisional Court did not accept that the 1911 Act, properly construed, precluded use of the procedure laid down in that Act to amend the conditions specified in section 2 : see Maurice Kay LJ in paras 17–19 of his judgment, and Collins J in paras 41–44 of his. The Court of Appeal took a different view (paras 40–41); it concluded that section 2(1) conferred powers which could be used for some purposes but not others (paras 42–45).

29 The Attorney General does not, I think, take issue with the general principles relied on by the appellants, which are indeed familiar and well-established. But he invites the House to focus on the language of the 1911 Act, and in this he is right, since a careful study of the statutory language, read in its statutory and historical context and with the benefit of permissible aids to interpretation, is the essential first step in any exercise of statutory interpretation. Here, section 2(1) makes provision, subject to three exceptions, for any public bill which satisfies the specified conditions to become an Act of Parliament without the consent of the Lords. The first exception relates to money bills, which are the subject of section 1 and to which different conditions apply. The second relates to bills containing any provision to extend the maximum duration of Parliament beyond five years. I consider this exception in detail below. The third relates to bills for confirming a provisional order, which do not fall within the expression "public bill" by virtue of section 5. Subject to these exceptions, section 2(1) applies to "any" public bill. I cannot think of any broader expression the draftsman could have used. Nor can I see any reason to infer that "any" is used in a sense other than its colloquial, and also its dictionary, sense of "no matter which, or what". The expression is repeatedly used in this sense in the 1911 Act, and it would be surprising if it were used in any other

sense: see section 1(2) ("any of the following subjects", "any such charges", "any loan", "those subjects or any of them", "any taxation, money, or loan"); section 2(4) ("any amendments", "any further amendments", "any such suggested amendments"); section 3 ("Any certificate", "any court of law"); section 4(2) ("Any alteration"); section 5 ("any Bill"). "Any" is an expression used to indicate that the user does not intend to discriminate, or does not intend to discriminate save to such extent as is indicated.

30 Sir Sydney is of course correct in submitting that the literal meaning of even a very familiar expression may have to be rejected if it leads to an interpretation or consequence which Parliament could not have intended. But in this case it is clear from the historical background that Parliament did intend the word "any", subject to the noted exceptions, to mean exactly what it said. Sir Henry Campbell-Bannerman's resolution of June 1907, adopted by the Commons before rejection of the 1909 Finance Bill, referred quite generally to "Bills passed by this House" (para 12 above). The second of the resolutions adopted on 14 April 1910 (para 15 above) referred to "Bills other than Money Bills". Attempts to amend the resolution so as to enlarge the classes of bill to which the new procedure would not apply were all rejected (para 15 above). During the constitutional Conference which followed the death of the King there was provisional agreement to exclude "the Act which is to embody this agreement" from application of the new procedure, but such a provision was never included in the Bill (para 17 above). During the passage of the Bill through Parliament, there were again repeated attempts to enlarge the classes of bill to which the new procedure would not apply, but save for the amendment related to bills extending the maximum duration of Parliament they were uniformly rejected (para 20 above). The suggestion that Parliament intended the conditions laid down in section 2(1) to be incapable of amendment by use of the Act is in my opinion contradicted both by the language of the section and by the historical record. This was certainly the understanding of Dicey, who was no friend of the 1911 Act. In the first edition of his Introduction after 1911 (the 8th edition, 1915), he wrote at p xxiii:

"The simple truth is that the Parliament Act has given to the House of Commons, or, in plain language, to the majority thereof, the power of passing any Bill whatever, provided always that the conditions of the Parliament Act, section 2, are complied with."

31 The Court of Appeal concluded (in paras 98–100 of its judgment) that there was power under the 1911 Act to make a "relatively modest and straightforward amendment" of the Act, including the amendment made by the 1949 Act, but not to making "changes of a fundamentally different nature to the relationship between the House of Lords and the Commons from those which the 1911 Act had made". This was not, as I understand, a solution which any party advocated in the Court of Appeal, and none supported it in the House. I do not think, with respect, that it can be supported in principle. The known object of the Parliament Bill, strongly resisted by the Conservative party and the source of the bitterness and intransigence which characterised the struggle over the Bill, was to secure the grant of Home Rule to Ireland. This was, by any standards, a fundamental constitutional change. So was the disestablishment of the Anglican Church in Wales, also well known to be an objective of the government.

Attempts to ensure that the 1911 Act could not be used to achieve these objects were repeatedly made and repeatedly defeated (paras 15 and 20 above). Whatever its practical merits, the Court of Appeal solution finds no support in the language of the Act, in principle or in the historical record. Had the government been willing to exclude changes of major constitutional significance from the operation of the new legislative scheme, it may very well be that the constitutional Conference of 1910 would not have broken down and the 1911 Act would never have been enacted.

32 It is unnecessary for resolution of the present case to decide whether the 1911 (and now the 1949) Act could be relied on to extend the maximum duration of Parliament beyond five years. It does not seem likely that such a proposal would command popular and parliamentary support (save in a national emergency such as led to extensions, by consent of both Houses, during both world wars), knowledge of parliamentary tyranny during the Long Parliament would weigh against such a proposal and article 3 of the First Protocol to the European Convention on Human Rights now requires elections at reasonable intervals. The Attorney General, however, submits that the 1911, and now the 1949, Act could in principle be used to amend or delete the reference to the maximum duration of Parliament in the parenthesis to section 2(1), and that a further measure could then be introduced to extend the maximum duration. Sir Sydney contends that this is a procedure which section 2(1) very clearly does not permit, stressing that the timetable in section 2(1) was very closely linked to the maximum duration of Parliament which the Act laid down. It is common ground that section 2(1) in its unamended form cannot without more be relied on to extend the maximum duration of Parliament, because a public bill to do so is outside the express terms of section 2(1). But there is nothing in the 1911 Act to provide that it cannot be amended, and even if there were such a provision it could not bind a successor Parliament. Once it is accepted, as I have accepted, that an Act passed pursuant to the procedures in section 2(1), as amended in 1949, is in every sense an Act of Parliament having effect and entitled to recognition as such, I see no basis in the language of section 2(1) or in principle for holding that the parenthesis in that subsection, or for that matter section 7, are unamendable save with the consent of the Lords. It cannot have been contemplated that if, however improbably, the Houses found themselves in irreconcilable deadlock on this point, the government should have to resort to the creation of peers. However academic the point may be, I think the Attorney General is right.

Enlargement of powers

33 Sir Sydney relies on what Hood Phillips and Jackson describe as the general principle of logic and law that delegates (the Queen and Commons) cannot enlarge the authority delegated to them: Constitutional and Administrative Law, 8th edn (2001), p 80. He also prays in aid the observations of Lord Donaldson of Lymington speaking extra-judicially in support of his Parliament Acts (Amendment) Bill (HL Hansard, 19 January 2001, cols 1308–1309):

"As your Lordships well know, it is a fundamental tenet of constitutional law that, prima facie, where the sovereign Parliament — that is to say, the Monarch acting on the advice and with the consent of both Houses of Parliament — delegates power to legislate, whether to one House unilaterally, to the King or Queen in Council, to a Minister or to whomsoever, the delegate cannot use that power to enlarge or vary the powers delegated to him. The only exception is where the primary legislation, in this case the 1911 Act, expressly authorises the delegate to do so. In other words there has to be a Henry VIII clause."

To support his argument Sir Sydney cites a number of cases relating to colonial and Dominion legislatures, the most significant of these cases perhaps being *R v Burah* (1878) 3 App Cas 889, 904–905; *Taylor v Attorney General of Queensland* (1917) 23 CLR 457; *McCawley v The King* [1920] AC 691, 703–704, 710–711; *Minister of the Interior v Harris* 1952 (4) SA 769, 790; *Clayton v Heffron* (1960) 105 CLR 214 and *Bribery Commissioner v Ranasinghe* [1965] AC 172, 196–198. In written submissions in reply this argument was elaborated and the authorities further analysed.

34 The Divisional Court was not persuaded by this line of argument. Maurice Kay LJ, with whom Collins J agreed, said in para 27 of his judgment:

"Moreover, the whole line of authority relied upon by the claimants, dealing as it does with the relationship between the Westminster Parliament and the devolved legislatures of former colonies with (in Lord Birkenhead's phrase — McCawley, p 703) "controlled constitutions", is not strictly analogous to the context of the Parliament Acts. In my judgment there is no established principle applicable to this case which denies a power of amendment of the earlier statute in the absence of the express conferral of one specifically dealing with amendment. What is important is the language of the earlier statute. I do not doubt that it is sufficient to permit amendment in the manner that was achieved by the 1949 Act."

35 The Court of Appeal (para 62) regarded this approach as being an over-simplification, but reached the same conclusion. It accepted (para 66) the Attorney General's submission that, although in many instances the relevant legislation discussed in the cases contained an express power to make amendments to the constitution, the authorities did not establish a principle that such constitutions may not be appropriately amended without such an express power. It found (para 68) no constitutional principle or principle of statutory construction which prevents a legislature from altering its own constitution by enacting alterations to the very instrument from which its powers derive by virtue of powers in that same instrument if the powers, properly understood, extend that far. The Court of Appeal adopted (para 69) the opinion of Lord Pearce on behalf of the Privy Council in *Bribery Commissioner v Ranasinghe*, above, at p 198, where he held that a constitution can be altered or amended by the legislature

"if the regulating instrument so provides and if the terms of those provisions are complied with: and the alteration or amendment may include the change or abolition of those very provisions."

The question was one of construction (para 69), and the Court of Appeal did not detect anything in the language of section 2(1) which would prevent the amendment made by the 1949 Act.

36 I cannot accept the appellants' submissions on this issue, for three main reasons. First, for reasons given in para 25 above, the 1911 Act did not involve a delegation of power and the Commons, when invoking the 1911 Act, cannot be regarded as in any sense a subordinate body. Secondly, the historical context of the 1911 Act was unique. The situation was factually and constitutionally so remote from the grant of legislative authority to a colonial or Dominion legislature as to render analogies drawn from the latter situation of little if any value when considering the former. Thirdly, the Court of Appeal distilled from the authorities what is in my judgment the correct principle. The question is one of construction. There was nothing in the 1911 Act to preclude use of the procedure laid down by the Act to amend the Act. As explained in paras 29–32 above, the language of the Act was wide enough, as the Divisional Court and the Court of Appeal held, to permit the amendment made by the 1949 Act, and also (in my opinion) to make much more far-reaching changes. For the past half century it has been generally, even if not universally, believed that the 1949 Act had been validly enacted, as evidenced by the use made of it by governments of different political persuasions. In my opinion that belief was well-founded.

The scope of the power to amend the conditions to which section 2(1) is subject

37 This submission is in essence a conclusion drawn from the propositions which precede it: see the summary in para 7 above. It necessarily follows from the reasons I have given for rejecting those propositions that I cannot accept that section 2(1) of the 1911 Act "does not authorise the Commons to remove, attenuate or modify in any respect any of the conditions on which its law-making power is granted". As should be clear, I reject the premises on which that conclusion is founded. If the appellants were right, it would, I think, follow that the 1911 Act could not be invoked, for instance, to shorten (or even, perhaps, lengthen) the period allowed in section 1(1) for passing money bills, or to provide that a bill for confirming a provisional order should rank as a public bill: a government bent on achieving such an object with a clear and recent mandate to do so would have either to accept the veto of the Lords or resort to the creation of peers. That would seem an extravagant, and unhistorical, intention to attribute to Parliament.

The significance of the 1949 Act

38 I agree with the appellants that the change made by the 1949 Act was not, as the Court of Appeal described it (para 98), "relatively modest", but was substantial and significant. But I also agree with them and also the Attorney General that the breadth of the power to amend the 1911 Act in reliance on section 2(1) cannot depend on whether the amendment in question is or is not relatively modest. I have given my reasons for sharing that conclusion in paras 29–32 above. Such a test would be vague in the extreme, and impose on the Speaker a judgment which Parliament cannot have contemplated imposing.

Conclusion

39 I would dismiss this appeal for the reasons I have given. The 1949 Act and the 2004 Act are Acts of Parliament of full legal effect.

Following Lord Bingham's clear rejection of the various arguments put forward by the appellants, the other Law Lords also came to similar conclusions on the facts. Very importantly, however, they used the opportunity presented by this case to pronounce more generally on the subject of Parliamentary sovereignty. The theoretical dominance of this doctrine in UK constitutional thinking had become more contentious in recent years and the radical *obiter* thoughts of various members of the higher judiciary, extracted below, clearly indicate real concerns about the perceived imbalance in the UK constitution's framework.

LORD STEYN

I. The dominance of the Government

71 My Lords, the power of a government with a large majority in the House of Commons is redoubtable. That has been the pattern for almost 25 years. In 1979, 1983 and 1987 Conservative Governments were elected respectively with majorities of 43, 144 and 100. In 1997, 2001 and 2005 New Labour was elected with majorities of respectively 177, 165 and 67. As Lord Hailsham of St Marylebone explained in *The Dilemma of Democracy* (1978), p 126, the dominance of a government elected with a large majority over Parliament has progressively become greater. This process has continued and strengthened inexorably since Lord Hailsham warned of its dangers in 1978.

...

XVI. The consequences of the decision

100 The Administrative Court did not comment on the drastic implications of its decision. Rightly, the Court of Appeal was intensely aware of the consequences of its decision. That is the context in which the Court of Appeal held that abolishing the House of Lords would be a constitutional change so fundamental that it could only be enacted by Parliament as ordinarily constituted and not by the attenuated process: paras 98-100. [The powers in the Parliament Acts]

101 The potential consequences of a decision in favour of the Attorney General are far-reaching. The Attorney General said at the hearing that the Government might wish to use the 1949 Act to bring about constitutional changes such as altering the composition of the House of Lords. The logic of this proposition is that the procedure of the 1949 Act could be used by the Government to abolish the House of Lords. Strict legalism suggests that the Attorney General may be right. But I am deeply troubled about assenting to the validity of such an exorbitant assertion of government power in our bi-cameral system. It may be that such an issue would test the relative merits of strict legalism and constitutional legal principle in the courts at the most fundamental level.

102 But the implications are much wider. If the Attorney General is right the 1949 Act could also be used to introduce oppressive and wholly undemocratic legislation. For example, it could theoretically be used to abolish judicial review of flagrant abuse of power by a government or even the role of the ordinary courts in standing between the executive and citizens. This is where we may have to come back to the point about the supremacy of Parliament. We do not in the United Kingdom have an uncontrolled constitution as the Attorney General implausibly asserts. In the European context the second *Factortame* decision [1991] 1 AC 603 made that clear. The settlement contained in the Scotland Act 1998 also point to a divided sovereignty. Moreover, the European Convention on Human Rights as incorporated into our law by the Human Rights Act 1998, created a new legal order. One must not assimilate the European Convention on Human Rights with multilateral treaties of the traditional type. Instead it is a legal order in which the United Kingdom assumes obligations to protect fundamental rights, not in relation to other states, but towards all individuals within its jurisdiction. The classic account given by Dicey of the doctrine of the supremacy of Parliament, pure and absolute as it was, can now be seen to be out of place in the modern United Kingdom. Nevertheless, the supremacy of Parliament is still the general principle of our constitution. It is a construct of the common law. The judges created this principle. If that is so, it is not unthinkable that circumstances could arise where the courts may have to qualify a principle established on a different hypothesis of constitutionalism. In exceptional circumstances involving an attempt to abolish judicial review or the ordinary role of the courts, the Appellate Committee of the House of Lords or a new Supreme Court may have to consider whether this is constitutional fundamental which even a sovereign Parliament acting at the behest of a complaisant House of Commons cannot abolish. It is not necessary to explore the ramifications of this question in this opinion. No such issues arise on the present appeal.

Alert

LORD HOPE OF CRAIGHEAD

104 My Lords, I start where my learned friend, Lord Steyn, has just ended. Our constitution is dominated by the sovereignty of Parliament. But parliamentary sovereignty is no longer, if it ever was, absolute. It is not uncontrolled in the sense referred to by Lord Birkenhead LC in McCawley v The King [1920] AC 691, 720. It is no longer right to say that its freedom to legislate admits of no qualification whatever. Step by step, gradually but surely, the English principle of the absolute legislative sovereignty of Parliament which Dicey derived from Coke and Blackstone is being qualified.

...

107 Nor should we overlook the fact that one of the guiding principles that were identified by Dicey at p 35 was the universal rule or supremacy throughout the constitution of ordinary law. Owen Dixon, "The Law and Constitution" (1935) 51 LQR 590, 596 was making the same point when he said that it is of the essence of supremacy of the law that the courts shall disregard as unauthorised and void the acts of any organ of government, whether legislative or administrative, which exceed the limits of the power that organ derives from the law. In its modern form, now reinforced

by the European Convention on Human Rights and the enactment by Parliament of the Human Rights Act 1998, this principle protects the individual from arbitrary government. The rule of law enforced by the courts is the ultimate controlling factor on which our constitution is based. The fact that your Lordships have been willing to hear this appeal and to give judgment upon it is another indication that the courts have a part to play in defining the limits of Parliament's legislative sovereignty.

BARONESS HALE OF RICHMOND

159 ... The concept of parliamentary sovereignty which has been fundamental to the constitution of England and Wales since the 17th century (I appreciate that Scotland may have taken a different view) means that Parliament can do anything. The courts will, of course, decline to hold that Parliament has interfered with fundamental rights unless it has made its intentions crystal clear. The courts will treat with particular suspicion (and might even reject) any attempt to subvert the rule of law by removing governmental action affecting the rights of the individual from all judicial scrutiny. Parliament has also, for the time being at least, limited its own powers by the European Communities Act 1972 and, in a different way, by the Human Rights Act 1998 . It is possible that other qualifications may emerge in due course. In general, however, the constraints upon what Parliament can do are political and diplomatic rather than constitutional.

...

163 ... If the sovereign Parliament can redefine itself downwards, to remove or modify the requirement for the consent of the Upper House, it may very well be that it can also redefine itself upwards, to require a particular parliamentary majority or a popular referendum for particular types of measure. In each case, the courts would be respecting the will of the sovereign Parliament as constituted when that will had been expressed. But that is for another day.

This case provides the most thorough critique and assessment of the place of Parliamentary sovereignty in the modern age. It is clear that a significant degree of tension exists between this traditional doctrine and the concept of the rule of law and that several leading members of the modern judiciary, as Lord Hope shows here, believe that there should be a finer equilibrium between these two key constitutional principles. It is very important to cross-refer between this area and the chapter on the rule of law, therefore.

The article below gives some further valuable academic insight into this very important area of constitutional debate.

1.1 Considering *Jackson*

Hunting sovereignty: Jackson v Her Majesty's Attorney-General, Alison L. Young, [2006] PL 187

...

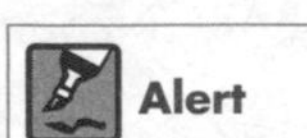
Alert

H.L.A. Hart drew a distinction between continuing and self-embracing parliamentary sovereignty. Continuing parliamentary sovereignty regards each separate Parliament as a sovereign law-making body. Self-embracing parliamentary sovereignty views "Parliament" as a whole over time as sovereign. The historically first "Parliament" has unlimited law-making powers which it can use to bind its successors. Although that successor does not enjoy unlimited law-making authority, multiple Parliaments taken together over time are sovereign. This challenges the traditional rejection of the "new" view as being limited to non-sovereign legislative bodies, such as the Dominion legislators. For Hart, it is possible for Parliament to be sovereign and have restrictions placed upon its law-making powers by a previous Parliament. Further difficulties arise when assessing whether the "old" view is a correct description of English law, particularly following the European Communities Act 1972, the Human Rights Act 1998 and the statutes regulating devolution. For advocates of self-embracing parliamentary legislative supremacy, *Factortame* and *Thoburn* illustrate not only that Parliament can, but that it did bind its successors when it enacted s.2(4) of the European Communities Act 1972. In *Factortame,* directly effective provisions of EC law, incorporated into English law through s.2(1) and (4) of the European Communities Act 1972, conflicted with the provisions of the Merchant Shipping Act 1988. The doctrine of implied repeal, which preserves continuing parliamentary legislative supremacy, would require the later statute to repeal the provisions of the earlier contradictory statute. However, the House of Lords granted an interim injunction to suspend the application of the 1988 Act; suggesting that the provisions of the European Communities Act 1972 could not be repealed by implication. Alternatively, *Factortame* can be explained through principles of construction: the Merchant Shipping Act 1988 did not repeal the provisions of the European Communities Act 1972, as its provisions could be "read and given effect subject to" directly effective provisions of European Community law.

In *Thoburn* Laws L.J. distinguishes between constitutional and other statutes, stating that constitutional statutes cannot be repealed by implication, suggesting in turn a shift towards self-embracing parliamentary legislative supremacy where constitutional statutes are "entrenched" in that they can only be expressly repealed. Alternatively, Laws L.J. could be interpreted as supporting a constructivist interpretation: principles of interpretation will be used to ensure that later statutes are interpreted in a manner compatible with earlier constitutional statutes, thus ensuring that constitutional statutes cannot be repealed by implication. Such principles of interpretation would not be able to preserve provisions of a constitutional statute that were expressly modified or repealed.

It was to be hoped, therefore, that the panel of nine Law Lords in *Jackson* would bring clarity to such a confused picture, using the opportunity to establish whether English law supported a continuing or a self-embracing theory of parliamentary legislative supremacy. Despite a greater judicial willingness to discuss parliamentary legislative supremacy, any hopes of clarification were dashed, given the plethora of conceptions referred to by their Lordships: ranging from Lord Bingham who stated that "[t]he bedrock of the British Constitution ... is the supremacy of the Crown in Parliament", where the Crown could in 1911 and can now "make or unmake any law" that it wishes, to Lord Steyn who, whilst admitting that the supremacy of Parliament remained the "*general* principle of our constitution", nevertheless stated that "[t]he classic account given by Dicey of the doctrine of the supremacy of Parliament, pure and absolute as it was, can now be seen to be out of place in the modern United Kingdom", analysing the conflict between the 1911 and 1949 Act using self-embracing theories of parliamentary legislative supremacy. However, *Jackson* goes beyond providing more grist to the mill of the sovereignty debate. It provides one essential clarification that has the potential to move the sovereignty debate to more fruitful territory. It recognises that whether the United Kingdom does or should support continuing or self-embracing parliamentary legislative supremacy is a different argument from whether statutory provisions could or should be entrenched. Rather, our account of parliamentary legislative supremacy depends upon an assessment of the nature of law-making authority. To understand this, we need to examine the legal background to the case, in particular the way in which the case challenged continuing parliamentary legislative supremacy and how their Lordships resolved this challenge.

...

Challenges to continuing parliamentary legislative supremacy

Jurisdiction

It was unanimously held that the court had jurisdiction to ascertain whether the Hunting Act 2004 was an Act of Parliament, with four of their Lordships providing detailed justification for their conclusions. It might appear that this challenges Dicey's theory of continuing parliamentary legislative supremacy, which requires that "no person or body is recognised by the law of England as having a right to override or set aside the legislation of Parliament". Here, the House of Lords had jurisdiction to assess the validity of the Hunting Act 2004. The House of Lords could have determined that the Hunting Act 2004 was invalid; implying that the court could set aside legislation. However, this is not the case. The House of Lords had jurisdiction to determine whether the Hunting Act 2004 is an Act of Parliament. If the House of Lords were to have concluded that the Hunting Act 2004 was not an Act of Parliament, this would not amount to overriding or setting aside the legislation of Parliament. Rather, the courts would be concluding that a purported Act of Parliament was not an Act of Parliament.

The jurisdiction of the court to determine whether a purported statute really is an Act of Parliament has been long-recognised by the common law. It does not contradict continuing parliamentary legislative supremacy. Dicey grants parliamentary sovereignty to the "Queen in Parliament" –the Commons, Lords and the Monarch–arguing that "Parliament thus defined has ... the right to make or unmake any law whatsoever". By determining whether a purported Act of Parliament has been validly enacted by the Queen in Parliament, the courts are reinforcing parliamentary legislative supremacy, ensuring that Parliament alone may enact statutes.

It is clear, therefore, that courts do and should have the power to ascertain the validity of a purported Act of Parliament. Problems arise, however, when ascertaining the criteria that the courts may use to determine this validity. It is an established principle of the common law that courts ascertain whether a statute is valid by examining the parliamentary roll. In *Jackson,* however, the House of Lords examined the provisions of the Parliament Act 1911 to determine the validity of the Parliament Act 1949. Does this challenge Dicey's theory of parliamentary legislative supremacy? The four Law Lords who examined this issue provided two reasons why the House of Lords had jurisdiction to act in this manner. First, *Pickin v British Railway Board* was regarded as authority for the provision that the courts could not question the way in which legislation is passed. This is prevented by Art.9 of the Bill of Rights 1689, which provides a statutory basis for the parliamentary privilege of freedom of expression, preventing the courts from questioning proceedings in Parliament. In *Pickin* the court was asked to investigate allegations of fraud in the passing of legislation, requiring the court to question proceedings in Parliament. No such questioning of proceedings in Parliament was required in *Jackson.* There is also an established power of the court to look beyond the parliamentary roll when this contains an error on the face of the record, for example when it is stated that consent has been given when it has not. In *Jackson,* the court would be determining whether there was a legal error, by interpreting the provisions of the Parliament Act 1911.

This provides the second reason why the court has jurisdiction to determine the validity of the Parliament Act 1949. Questions of statutory interpretation are within the inherent jurisdiction of the court. However, the use of the Parliament Act 1911 to ascertain the validity of the Parliament Act 1949 itself indirectly challenges continuing parliamentary legislative supremacy. No challenge arises from the ratio of the decision. As there was no contradiction between the two provisions, the later Act was merely interpreted in line with the earlier statutory provisions – raising no problem for continuing parliamentary legislative supremacy. Difficulties arise, however, as there is the suggestion that, were the Parliament Act 1949 to have contradicted the provisions of the Parliament Act 1911, then the Parliament Act 1949 would have been invalid. This does raise problems for continuing parliamentary legislative supremacy and it is to this issue that we now turn.

Parliament Act 1911, s.2(1)

It will be recalled that s.2(1) prevents the use of the Parliament Act 1911 procedure to extend the life of Parliament beyond five years. Seven of their Lordships held that, were a statute to be passed extending the life of Parliament beyond five years without the consent of the House of Lords, the courts would refuse to recognise this statute as a valid Act of Parliament. In addition, five of their Lordships stated that it would not be possible to use the Parliament Act procedure to amend s.2(1), so as to remove the provision preventing the use of the Parliament Act procedure to extend the life of Parliament. Section 2(1) would itself imply this further restriction, ensuring that what could not be done by one step could also not be done by two steps. These conclusions appear to challenge Dicey's account of parliamentary legislative supremacy; holding first that s.2(1) cannot be repealed by implication and second that it is not subject to express repeal. This can best be explained by means of examples.

Example One

The Commons and Monarch use the Parliament Acts 1911-49 to enact the Parliament Act 2006, s.1 of which extends the life of Parliament to 10 years. Section 2(1) of the Parliament Act 1911 expressly prevents the use of the Parliament Act 1911 in this manner. There is a conflict between s.1 of the 2006 Act and s.2(1) of the Parliament Act 1911. As the 2006 Parliament cannot be bound by the provisions of the 1911 Parliament, the provisions of the 2006 Act are held to repeal the provisions of the 1911 Act by implication. To apply the 1911 Act ensures that legislation passed without the consent of the House of Lords cannot impliedly repeal s.2(1) of the Parliament Act 1911.

Example Two

Parliament passes the Parliament Act 1911 (Amendment) Act 2006, the sole provision of which expressly overturns the restriction in s.2(1) of the Parliament Act 1911 preventing the use of the Parliament Act procedure to enact legislation to extend the life of Parliament beyond five years. Parliament then enacts the Parliament Act 2006 as in example one. Continuing parliamentary legislative supremacy would again dictate that the provisions of the later Act repeal the provisions of the earlier Act. To apply the provisions of the 1911 Act is to refuse to allow s.2(1) to be expressly repealed by legislation passed through the Parliament Act 1911.

In essence s.2(1) of the Parliament Act 1911 is entrenched. It binds future Parliaments. Parliaments wishing to overturn its provisions can only do so by adopting a specific manner and form – legislation that has the consent of the House of Lords as opposed to legislation passed without its consent. It is for this reason that H.W.R. Wade concluded that legislation passed under the provisions of the Parliament Acts 1911-1949 was delegated legislation. This method of preserving continuing parliamentary legislative supremacy is not open to their Lordships, all of whom concluded that legislation passed under the Parliament Act procedure was primary legislation. Does this mean, therefore, that a majority of their Lordships advocate self-embracing parliamentary legislative supremacy?

It is easy to conclude that Lord Steyn and Baroness Hale would support this conclusion. By passing the 1911 Act, Parliament partially redefined its composition, enabling the Commons and the Monarch to pass Acts of Parliament without the consent of the House of Lords. This definition binds the courts. Parliament, when composed of the House of Commons and the Monarch, cannot pass legislation extending the life of Parliament. Consequently, the Parliament Act 2006 would not be recognised as valid law; being beyond the scope of s.2(1) it cannot be enacted by Parliament as defined in the 1911 Act.

However, Lords Hope, Nicholls and Carswell provide an alternative explanation that does not challenge continuing parliamentary legislative supremacy. The 1911 Act modified the way in which valid legislation can be enacted. In doing so it claims to modify the rule of recognition, the rule used to define valid legal enactments. The rule of recognition is both a legal rule and a political fact. As a legal rule, courts are bound to apply the rule of recognition. However, as a political fact, it cannot be modified and changed by Parliament alone. When recognising a change in the rule of recognition, courts are acknowledging a change in political fact. The Parliament Act 1949, for example, is accepted as valid not merely because it satisfies the legal requirements of s.2(1), but also because its validity is recognised as a political fact, implying that the change in the rule of recognition instigated by the Parliament Act 1911 is also recognised as a political fact. Parliament is bound by the provisions of the Parliament Act 1911. But it is so bound not merely because the Parliament Act 1911 is a valid Act of Parliament, but also because the change in the rule of recognition, derived from the constitutional crisis resolved by this Act, has been recognised as a political fact. Consequently the Parliament of 1911 was not able to bind future Parliaments in and of itself. If future Parliaments are bound, they are bound by the rule of recognition, which was changed due to the new provisions being accepted internally by at least a core of officials administering the legal system. Continuing parliamentary legislative supremacy is preserved. As Wade recognised, the definition of a valid law-making authority and the procedures required to make valid law are logically prior rules. Dicey affords parliamentary legislative supremacy to a particular definition of Parliament passing legislation according to a particular procedure. This particular definition and procedure cannot be made by Parliament alone if continuing parliamentary legislative supremacy is to be preserved.

It is possible to achieve the same practical effect as entrenchment whilst preserving continuing parliamentary legislative supremacy. Modifications of the definition of Parliament or the way in which legislation is passed occur through a change in the rule of recognition. A change in the rule of recognition cannot be enacted by Parliament alone; it needs to be internally accepted by officials of the UK constitution, which includes the courts. The desirability of entrenchment should not determine whether the United Kingdom adopts a self-embracing theory of parliamentary legislative supremacy. Nor should it depend upon whether one accepts the claims of common law constitutionalism that empower the courts to challenge legislation which overturns fundamental principles of the constitution. Our description of the nature of parliamentary legislative supremacy depends upon our assessment of the fundamental constitutional rule that determines the identity of the sovereign law-making body and the procedures used to enact valid legislation and, more precisely, the way in which this can be modified. Continuing parliamentary legislative supremacy requires that modification cannot be achieved by Parliament acting alone. If, for example, we identify this fundamental provision as part of the rule of recognition, its modification requires internal acceptance by at least some of the officials of the legal system. Self-embracing parliamentary legislative supremacy regards the fundamental rule as one that can be modified by Parliament alone. Jennings, for example, regarded this rule as part of the common law. As statutory provisions could override the common law, Parliament could modify the common law provisions governing the identity of the sovereign and its functions.

Conclusion

Parliamentary sovereignty is a complex concept. Parliament can be politically sovereign whilst enjoying a limited legislative power through acceptance of self-embracing theories of parliamentary legislative supremacy. The effect of entrenchment can be achieved whilst maintaining continuing parliamentary legislative supremacy. The distinction between continuing and self-embracing parliamentary legislative supremacy depends upon the way in which one modifies the fundamental rules defining the law-making authority and the process it adopts for enacting valid legislation. The European Communities Act 1972, the devolution statutes and the Human Rights Act of 1998 and, following *Jackson,* the Parliament Acts 1911-49 may well question whether it is possible for Parliament effectively to bind its successors. However, this need not question our acceptance of continuing parliamentary legislative supremacy. Dicey's belief in the sovereignty of the electorate led to his support for continuing parliamentary legislative supremacy. Continuing parliamentary legislative supremacy also recognises the important role of both the courts and Parliament in determining whether political facts have shifted our definition of the sovereign or the law-making process. A discussion of whether the English constitution should change to self-embracing parliamentary legislative supremacy requires further analysis of the nature of these fundamental rules as opposed to an attempt to ascertain whether Parliament can bind its successors.

Further Reading

Gordon, Michael 'The conceptual foundations of parliamentary sovereignty: reconsidering Jennings and Wade' [2009] *PL* 519

Munro, Colin *Studies in Constitutional Law*, Oxford University Press (2nd Edition), Chapter 5

Lord Steyn, 'Civil liberties in modern Britain', [2009] *PL* 228

Tomkins, Adam *Public Law*, Clarendon Law Series, Chapter 4

5

Prerogative Power

Topic List

Alex Lawson and Neil Hurden

Introduction

Dicey described the royal prerogative as 'the residue of discretionary or arbitrary authority, which at any time is legally left in the hands of the Crown... Every act which the executive government can lawfully do without the authority of an Act of Parliament is done in virtue of this prerogative.' The description of the prerogative as an 'arbitrary' power is in clear contravention of the rule of law, and the courts' attempt to reconcile the rule of law with the nature of prerogative power will be seen as a key feature in this chapter.

As is also clear from Dicey's words, prerogative powers are 'residual' of the absolute authority enjoyed by monarchs under the ancient doctrine of the Divine Right of kings. Following the constitutional settlement in 1688-89 with the Glorious Revolution and the Bill of Rights, the absolutist monarchy of the Stuart and earlier dynasties was replaced by a form of government in which Parliament gained supremacy. This led in turn to a very slow evolutionary change over subsequent centuries towards a full, modern constitutional democracy in the twentieth century. As part of the process of change many of the powers exercised by governments came to be based not on traditional powers held by the Crown but on statutory authority, as granted by Parliament.

However, some powers retained by the Crown and today exercised by the executive on behalf of the Crown, are still derived from the prerogative and not from statute. This is partly a matter of historical accident – these powers were simply not transferred anywhere, so they must still be within the possession of the Crown where they originated. It is also very arguable that such powers are useful for the executive, because they enable governments to act effectively and efficiently without the need for prior political approval. This presents issues in relation to the perceived legitimacy of this type of governmental power and there is a strong body of opinion which would argue that all prerogative powers should be codified, particularly as these powers include some of the most far-reaching aspects of governmental authority, including maintenance of national defence and regulation of foreign affairs.

The ability of the courts to review prerogative power has been the most important theme in the developing case law in this area. Until the mid 1980s the extent to which it was thought that the courts could intervene was very limited; it was a question largely of adjudicating on whether a prerogative power existed and whether it had been supplanted by a more modern, statutory authority regulating the same area or issue.

1 The Royal Prerogative

1.1 Statute and Prerogative

***Attorney-General v De Keyser's Royal Hotel, Limited* [1920] AC 508**

Panel: Lord Dunedin, Lord Atkinson, Lord Moulton, Lord Sumner and Lord Parmoor

Facts: during the First World War the War Office took over De Keyser's Royal Hotel. The parties could not agree on rent payments. The Defence of the Realm Regulations would have entitled the owners to full compensation, but the War Office argued the seizure had actually been made pursuant to a prerogative power enabling requisitioning of property in wartime without the need for the Crown to pay compensation. The question was thus whether the statutory regulations, which were more advantageous to the hotel owners, took precedence over the prerogative power and effectively put it into abeyance.

LORD ATKINSON

...The late Master of the Rolls in the following pregnant passage of his judgment put a rather unanswerable question. He said:

"Those powers which the executive exercises without Parliamentary authority are comprised under the comprehensive term of the prerogative. Where, however, Parliament has intervened and has provided by statute for powers, previously within the prerogative, being exercised in a particular manner and subject to the limitations and provisions contained in the statute, they can only be so exercised. Otherwise, what use would there be in imposing limitations, if the Crown could at its pleasure disregard them and fall back on prerogative?"

Alert

It was not contended, it could not, I think, be successfully contended, that the Act of 1842 and the Defence of the Realm Consolidation Act of 1914 (hereinafter referred to as the Act of 1914) do not bind the Crown, seeing that they deal with what is the special trust and duty of the King to provide for - namely, the defence and security of the realm - and prescribe the mode in which, and the methods by which, land or its use is to be acquired by the Crown's officers, the Ordnance Department, the Admiralty, the Army Council, the members of His Majesty's forces, and other persons acting on his behalf, for these very purposes. Whether one applies the test suggested in Bacon's Abridgement, 7th ed., vol. vii., 462, quoted, apparently, with approval by Jessel M.R. in *Ex parte Postmaster-General* or that laid down by Lord Lindley in *Wheaton v. Maple*, that the Crown is never bound by a statutory enactment unless the intention of the Legislature to bind the Crown is clear and unmistakable, I think these statutes and Regulations satisfy both those tests. Before dealing with them I desire to express my complete concurrence in the conclusion at which the late Master of the Rolls arrived as to the result of the searches made by the Crown touching the nature and particulars of the commissions issued in early times, in order to determine what sums were paid ex gratia where lands were taken by the Crown or its officers for the defence of the realm, and the occupation of them connected therewith by the military. The conclusion, as I understand it, is this: that it does not appear that the Crown has ever taken for these purposes the land of the subject without paying for it, and that there is no trace of the Crown having, even in the times of the Stuarts, exercised or asserted the power or right to do so by virtue of the Royal Prerogative. I also concur with the conclusion at which that distinguished and learned judge arrived as to the purpose, object, and effect of the body of legislation passed from the year 1708 to the year 1798, enabling land, or the use of it, to be compulsorily acquired by the Crown on the terms of the owner being paid for it.

I further concur with him in his analysis of the provisions of the Acts passed in 1803, 1804, 1819, dealing with the public service. I agree that in all this legislation there is not a trace of a suggestion that the Crown was left free to ignore these statutory provisions, and by its unfettered prerogative do the very things the statutes empowered the Crown to do, but free from the conditions and restrictions imposed by the statutes.

It is quite obvious that it would be useless and meaningless for the Legislature to impose restrictions and limitations upon, and to attach conditions to, the exercise by the Crown of the powers conferred by a statute, if the Crown were free at its pleasure to disregard these provisions, and by virtue of its prerogative do the very thing the statutes empowered it to do. One cannot in the construction of a statute attribute to the Legislature (in the absence of compelling words) an intention so absurd. It was suggested that when a statute is passed empowering the Crown to do a certain thing which it might theretofore have done by virtue of its prerogative, the prerogative is merged in the statute. I confess I do not think the word "merged" is happily chosen. I should prefer to say that when such a statute, expressing the will and intention of the King and of the three estates of the realm, is passed, it abridges the Royal Prerogative while it is in force to this extent: that the Crown can only do the particular thing under and in accordance with the statutory provisions, and that its prerogative power to do that thing is in abeyance. Whichever mode of expression be used, the result intended to be indicated is, I think, the same - namely, that after the statute has been passed, and while it is in force, the thing it empowers the Crown to do can thenceforth only be done by and under the statute, and subject to all the limitations, restrictions and conditions by it imposed, however unrestricted the Royal Prerogative may theretofore have been.

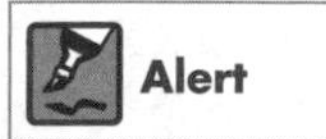

The reasoning in this case can be seen to uphold the doctrine of Parliamentary sovereignty and also the separation of powers. The reasoning in this case was followed in the later case of *Regina v Secretary of State for the Home Department, Ex parte Fire Brigades Union and Others* [1995] 2 AC 513 which was extracted in Chapter 2.

1.2 Judicial Control of the Prerogative

In the seminal rule of law case *Entick v Carrington* [1765] 95 ER 807, the courts made it clear that it was their role to establish the existence and scope of the Royal prerogative. Where in that case they found that the prerogative power purported to be exercised did not exist, Carrington was subject to the ordinary law of the land. However, once the existence of a prerogative power had been established and its scope identified there was no role for the courts to examine the legality of the exercise of the power. The tension between the rule of law and the Royal prerogative is evident as without review of the exercise Dicey's description of the powers as 'arbitrary' becomes manifest.

The case that changed the landscape in terms of the courts' control over exercise of prerogative power by the government was *Council of Civil Service Unions and Others v Minister for the Civil Service ("GCHQ")* [1985] AC 374 (known as *GCHQ*). Until this case the courts, as illustrated above, were able to pronounce upon the existence and the scope of prerogative powers but judicial review of how prerogative power was exercised in practice had not been conceded. Consequently, even though it had been established for a considerable time that the executive could be held to account under the courts' judicial review powers for the legality and fairness and reasonableness of public law decisions and actions taken under statutory authority, the same was not the case for use of prerogative powers.

1.3 The *GCHQ* Case

Council of Civil Service Unions and Others v Minister for the Civil Service ("GCHQ") [1985] AC 374

Panel: Lord Fraser of Tullybelton, Lord Scarman, Lord Diplock, Lord Roskill and Lord Brightman

Facts: Civil service staff employed at Government Communications Headquarters (GCHQ), a listening centre in Cheltenham, had for nearly 40 years been allowed to belong to national trade unions. During this time there was an established pattern of consultation between management and trade unions if any important changes in working conditions and terms were proposed. On 22 December 1983, the Prime Minister, Margaret Thatcher (also the Civil Service Minister), used a form of prerogative power to order that membership of trade unions would no longer be permitted for GCHQ staff because of the nature of their work. This measure was taken immediately without any prior consultation. The applicants, a trade union and a number of individuals, sought judicial review of the decision on the ground that the lack of prior consultation represented an unfair frustration of their legitimate expectation to be consulted, established by consistent previous practice. The Minister put forward two main arguments in her defence: first, and most fundamental, was that she had taken this step using prerogative powers and therefore the court was powerless to review the manner in which these had been exercised; and (in the alternative) that these powers had been exercised in relation to a matter involving national security and were therefore not amenable to judicial review.

LORD DIPLOCK

My Lords, the English law relating to judicial control of administrative action has been developed upon a case to case basis which has virtually transformed it over the last three decades. The principles of public law that are applicable to the instant case are in my view well established by authorities that are sufficiently cited in the speech that will be delivered by my noble and learned friend, Lord Roskill. ...

Judicial review ... provides the means by which judicial control of administrative action is exercised. The subject matter of every judicial review is a decision made by some person (or body of persons) whom I will call the "decision-maker" or else a refusal by him to make a decision.

To qualify as a subject for judicial review the decision must have consequences which affect some person (or body of persons) other than the decision-maker, although it may affect him too. It must affect such other person either:

(a) by altering rights or obligations of that person which are enforceable by or against him in private law; or

(b) by depriving him of some benefit or advantage ...

For a decision to be susceptible to judicial review the decision-maker must be empowered by public law (and not merely, as in arbitration, by agreement between private parties) to make decisions that, if validly made, will lead to administrative action or abstention from action by an authority endowed by law with executive powers, which have one or other of the consequences mentioned in the preceding paragraph. The ultimate source of the decision-making power is nearly always nowadays a statute or subordinate legislation made under the statute; but in the absence of any statute regulating the subject matter of the decision the source of the decision-making power may still be the common law itself, i.e., that part of the common law that is given by lawyers the label of "the prerogative." Where this is the source of decision-making power, the power is confined to executive officers of central as distinct from local government and in constitutional practice is generally exercised by those holding ministerial rank.

It was the prerogative that was relied on as the source of the power of the Minister for the Civil Service in reaching her decision of 22 December 1983 that membership of national trade unions should in future be barred to all members of the home civil service employed at GCHQ.

My Lords, I intend no discourtesy to counsel when I say that, intellectual interest apart, in answering the question of law raised in this appeal, I have derived little practical assistance from learned and esoteric analyses of the precise legal nature, boundaries and historical origin of "the prerogative," or of what powers exercisable by executive officers acting on behalf of central government that are not shared by private citizens qualify for inclusion under this particular label. It does not, for instance, seem to me to matter whether today the right of the executive government that happens to be in power to dismiss without notice any member of the home civil service upon which perforce it must rely for the administration of its policies, and the correlative disability of the executive government that is in power to agree with a civil servant that his service should be on terms that did not make him subject to instant dismissal, should be ascribed to "the prerogative" or merely to a consequence of the survival, for entirely different reasons, of a rule of constitutional law whose origin is to be found in the theory that those by whom the administration of the realm is carried on do so as personal servants of the monarch who can dismiss them at will, because the King can do no wrong.

Nevertheless, whatever label may be attached to them there have unquestionably survived into the present day a residue of miscellaneous fields of law in which the executive government retains decision-making powers that are not dependent upon any statutory authority but nevertheless have consequences on the private rights or legitimate expectations of other persons which would render the decision subject to judicial review if the power of the decision-maker to make them were statutory in origin. From matters so relatively minor as the grant of pardons to condemned criminals, of honours to the good and great, of corporate personality to deserving bodies of persons, and of bounty from moneys made available to the executive government by Parliament, they extend to matters so vital to the survival and welfare of the nation as the conduct of relations with foreign states and - what lies at the heart of the present case - the defence of the realm against potential enemies. Adopting the phraseology used in the European Convention on Human Rights 1953 (Convention for the Protection of Human Rights and Fundamental Freedoms (1953) (Cmd. 8969)) to which the United Kingdom is a party it has now become usual in statutes to refer to the latter as "national security".

My Lords, I see no reason why simply because a decision-making power is derived from a common law and not a statutory source, it should for that reason only be immune from judicial review. Judicial review has I think developed to a stage today when without reiterating any analysis of the steps by which the development has come about, one can conveniently classify under three heads the grounds upon which administrative action is subject to control by judicial review. The first ground I would call "illegality," the second "irrationality" and the third "procedural impropriety". That is not to say that further development on a case by case basis may not in course of time add further grounds. I have in mind particularly the possible adoption in the future of the principle of "proportionality" which is recognised in the administrative law of several of our fellow members of the European Economic Community; but to dispose of the instant case the three already well-established heads that I have mentioned will suffice.

...

My Lords, that a decision of which the ultimate source of power to make it is not a statute but the common law (whether or not the common law is for this purpose given the label of "the prerogative") may be the subject of judicial review on the ground of illegality is, I think, established by the cases cited by my noble and learned friend, Lord Roskill, and this extends to cases where the field of law to which the decision relates is national security, as the decision of this House itself in *Burmah Oil Co. Ltd. v. Lord Advocate*, 1964 S.C. (H.L.) 117 shows. While I see no a priori reason to rule out "irrationality" as a ground for judicial review of a ministerial decision taken in the exercise of "prerogative" powers, I find it difficult to envisage in any of the various fields in which the prerogative remains the only source of the relevant decision-making power a decision of a kind that would be open to attack through the judicial process upon this ground. Such decisions will generally involve the application of government policy. The reasons for the decision-maker taking one course rather than another do not normally involve questions to which, if disputed, the judicial process is adapted to provide the right answer, by which I mean that the kind of evidence that is admissible under judicial procedures and the way in which it has to be adduced tend to exclude from the attention of the court competing policy considerations which, if the executive discretion is to be wisely exercised, need to be weighed against one another - a balancing exercise which judges by their upbringing and experience are ill-qualified to perform. So I leave this as an open question to be dealt with on a case to case basis if, indeed, the case should ever arise.

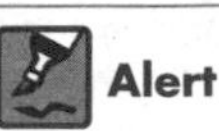

As respects "procedural propriety" I see no reason why it should not be a ground for judicial review of a decision made under powers of which the ultimate source is the prerogative. Such indeed was one of the grounds that formed the subject matter of judicial review in *Reg. v. Criminal Injuries Compensation Board, Ex parte Lain* [1967] 2 Q.B. 864. Indeed, where the decision is one which does not alter rights or obligations enforceable in private law but only deprives a person of legitimate expectations, "procedural impropriety" will normally provide the only ground on which the decision is open to judicial review. But in any event what procedure will satisfy the public law requirement of procedural propriety depends upon the subject matter of the decision, the executive functions of the decision-maker (if the decision is not that of an administrative tribunal) and the particular circumstances in which the decision came to be made.

My Lords, in the instant case the immediate subject matter of the decision was a change in one of the terms of employment of civil servants employed at GCHQ. That the executive functions of the Minister for the Civil Service, in her capacity as such, included making a decision to change any of those terms, except in so far as they related to remuneration, expenses and allowances, is not disputed. It does not seem to me to be of any practical significance whether or not as a matter of strict legal analysis this power is based upon the rule of constitutional law to which I have already alluded that the employment of any civil servant may be terminated at any time without notice and that upon such termination the same civil servant may be re-engaged on different terms. The rule of terminability of employment in the civil service without notice, of which the existence is beyond doubt, must in any event have the consequence that the continued enjoyment by a civil servant in the future of a right under a particular term of his employment cannot be the subject of any right enforceable by him in private law; at most it can only be a legitimate expectation.

Prima facie, therefore, civil servants employed at GCHQ who were members of national trade unions had, at best, in December 1983, a legitimate expectation that they would continue to enjoy the benefits of such membership and of representation by those trade unions in any consultations and negotiations with representatives of the management of that government department as to changes in any term of their employment. So, but again prima facie only, they were entitled, as a matter of public law under the head of "procedural propriety," before administrative action was taken on a decision to withdraw that benefit, to have communicated to the national trade unions by which they had theretofore been represented the reason for such withdrawal, and for such unions to be given an opportunity to comment on it.

The reason why the Minister for the Civil Service decided on 22 December 1983 to withdraw this benefit was in the interests of national security. National security is the responsibility of the executive government; what action is needed to protect its interests is, as the cases cited by my learned friend, Lord Roskill, establish and common sense itself dictates, a matter upon which those upon whom the responsibility rests, and not the courts of justice, must have the last word. It is par excellence a non-justiciable question. The judicial process is totally inept to deal with the sort of problems which it involves.

The executive government likewise decided, and this would appear to be a collective decision of cabinet ministers involved, that the interests of national security required that no notice should be given of the decision before administrative action had been taken to give effect to it. The reason for this was the risk that advance notice to the national unions of the executive government's intention would attract the very disruptive action prejudicial to the national security the recurrence of which the decision barring membership of national trade unions to civil servants employed at GCHQ was designed to prevent.

There was ample evidence to which reference is made by others of your Lordships that this was indeed a real risk; so the crucial point of law in this case is whether procedural propriety must give way to national security when there is conflict between (1) on the one hand, the prima facie rule of "procedural propriety" in public law, applicable to a case of legitimate expectations that a benefit ought not to be withdrawn until the reason for its proposed withdrawal has been communicated to the person who has theretofore enjoyed that benefit and that person has been given an opportunity to comment on the reason, and (2) on the other hand, action that is needed to be taken in the interests of national security, for which the executive government bears the responsibility and alone has access to sources of information that qualify it to judge what the necessary action is. To that there can, in my opinion, be only one sensible answer. That answer is "Yes."

I agree with your Lordships that this appeal must be dismissed.

LORD ROSKILL

My Lords, the right of the executive to do a lawful act affecting the rights of the citizen, whether adversely or beneficially, is founded upon the giving to the executive of a power enabling it to do that act. The giving of such a power usually carries with it legal sanctions to enable that power if necessary to be enforced by the courts. In most cases that power is derived from statute though in some cases, as indeed in the present case, it may still be derived from the prerogative. In yet other cases, as the decisions show, the two powers may coexist or the statutory power may by necessary implication have replaced the former prerogative power. If the executive in pursuance of the statutory power does an act affecting the rights of the citizen, it is beyond question that in principle the manner of the exercise of that power may today be challenged on one or more of the three grounds which I have mentioned earlier in this speech. If the executive instead of acting under a statutory power acts under a prerogative power and in particular a prerogative power delegated to the respondent under article 4 of the Order in Council of 1982, so as to affect the rights of the citizen, I am unable to see, subject to what I shall say later, that there is any logical reason why the fact that the source of the power is the prerogative and not statute should today deprive the citizen of that right of challenge to the manner of its exercise which he would possess were the source of the power statutory. In either case the act in question is the act of the executive. To talk of that act as the act of the sovereign savours of the archaism of past centuries. In reaching this conclusion I find myself in agreement with my noble and

learned friends Lord Scarman and Lord Diplock whose speeches I have had the advantage of reading in draft since completing the preparation of this speech.

But I do not think that that right of challenge can be unqualified. It must, I think, depend upon the subject matter of the prerogative power which is exercised. Many examples were given during the argument of prerogative powers which as at present advised I do not think could properly be made the subject of judicial review. Prerogative powers such as those relating to the making of treaties, the defence of the realm, the prerogative of mercy, the grant of honours, the dissolution of Parliament and the appointment of ministers as well as others are not, I think susceptible to judicial review because their nature and subject matter are such as not to be amenable to the judicial process. The courts are not the place wherein to determine whether a treaty should be concluded or the armed forces disposed in a particular manner or Parliament dissolved on one date rather than another.

In my view the exercise of the prerogative which enabled the oral instructions of 22 December 1983 to be given does not by reason of its subject matter fall within what for want of a better phrase I would call the "excluded categories" some of which I have just mentioned. It follows that in principle I can see no reason why those instructions should not be the subject of judicial review.

...

I have little doubt that were management to seek to alter without prior consultation the terms and conditions of civil servants in a field which had no connection whatever with national security or perhaps, though the matter does not arise in this appeal, with urgent fiscal emergency, such action would in principle be amenable to judicial review.

But that is not the present issue. It is asserted on behalf of the respondent that the reason for the instructions being given without prior consultation was that it was feared that so to consult would have given rise to grave risk of industrial action through the reaction of the appellants and others and thus have brought about the very situation which the oral instructions were themselves designed to avoid, namely the risk of industrial action by the staff at GCHQ caused or at least facilitated by a membership of trade unions, and damaging to national security. GCHQ was, it was said, and is, highly vulnerable to industrial action and prior consultation would have revealed to those who had previously organised disruption that high degree of vulnerability.

My Lords, the conflict between private rights and the rights of the state is not novel either in our political history or in our courts. Historically, at least since 1688, the courts have sought to present a barrier to inordinate claims by the executive. But they have also been obliged to recognise that in some fields that barrier must be lowered and that on occasions, albeit with reluctance, the courts must accept that the claims of executive power must take precedence over those of the individual. One such field is that of national security. The courts have long shown themselves sensitive to the assertion by the executive that considerations of national security must preclude judicial investigation of a particular individual grievance. But even in that field the courts will not act on a mere assertion that questions of national security were involved. Evidence is required that the decision under challenge was in fact founded on those grounds.

That that principle exists is I think beyond doubt. In a famous passage in *The Zamora* [1916] 2 A.C. 77, 107 Lord Parker of Waddington, delivering the opinion of the Judicial Committee said:

"Those who are responsible for the national security must be the sole judges of what the national security requires. It would be obviously undesirable that such matters should be made the subject of evidence in a court of law or otherwise discussed in public."

Although the trade union's case eventually fell at the last hurdle, as its legitimate expectation was allowed to be frustrated for reasons of apparent, over-riding national security concerns, the principle had clearly been firmly established that, in determining whether government powers could be judicially reviewed, the source of those powers was no longer a relevant factor. Instead Lord Roskill sought to analyse the issue from a different perspective, differentiating between the nature of the various areas of prerogative power. Some areas would in his view be inherently unamenable to judicial review, because of the political nature of the power being exercised. This brought up many of the key factors at play in the delicate separation of powers balance that has applied in the UK, demonstrating the courts' awareness of both the respective institutional competences of judiciary and executive and of the democratic mandate held by elected politicians.

Subsequent case law in this area has involved a gradual erosion of what Lord Roskill called the "excluded categories" and the scope of judicial review of the exercise of prerogative powers has widened further in recent decades. In the following two cases the House of Lords was prepared to consider and address challenges made to government decisions taken under prerogative powers relating to defence of the realm and foreign affairs.

1.4 Erosion of Lord Roskill's List

Regina v Ministry of Defence ex parte Smith [1996] QB 517

Panel: Sir Thomas Bingham MR, Henry and Thorpe LJJ

Facts: Smith and others were homosexuals, who were discharged from their jobs in the armed forces on the basis of their sexuality, in accordance with contemporary Ministry of Defence policy. They challenged the decision on the grounds of unreasonableness. In theory, as the case directly involved exercise of prerogative powers in one of the areas on Lord Roskill's "list" (defence of the realm/disposition of armed forces), this could have been regarded as a non-justiciable matter but instead the court reviewed the issues with a relatively intense degree of scrutiny.

SIR THOMAS BINGHAM MR

The policy which currently governs homosexuals (male and female) in the British armed forces is clear:

"The Ministry of Defence's policy is that homosexuality is incompatible with service in the Armed Forces. Service personnel who are known to be homosexual or who engage in homosexual activity are administratively discharged from the Armed Forces."

As this statement makes plain, proof of homosexual activity is not needed. A reliable admission of homosexual orientation is enough. Where homosexual orientation or activity is clear, the service authorities give themselves no choice but to discharge the member involved without regard to the member's service record or character or the consequences of discharge to the member personally.

These four applicants, three men and one woman, were administratively discharged from the armed forces because they were homosexual. None of them had committed any offence against the general criminal law, nor any offence against the special law governing his or her service. None of them had committed any homosexual act on service premises nor (save in one instance, said to be unwitting) any act involving another member of the service. All of them had shown the qualities required of loyal and efficient service personnel. All of them had looked forward to long service careers, now denied them. Their lives and livelihoods have been grossly disrupted by their involuntary discharge.

The applicants challenge the lawfulness of their discharge and thus, indirectly, of the policy which required them to be discharged. They say that the policy is irrational, and in breach of the European Convention for the Protection of Human Rights and Fundamental Freedoms, and contrary to Council Directive (76/207/E.E.C.) (the Equal Treatment Directive). They accept without reservation that any member of the armed services who acts inappropriately towards any other member, or who is guilty of any harassment, or who commits any offence or breach of service discipline, may be discharged administratively, if not on disciplinary grounds. So too if a member's sexual orientation undermines that member's efficiency as a member of the service or is shown to cause demonstrable damage to the service. They claim no right or liberty to commit homosexual acts or to make homosexual advances on the mess-deck or in the barrack-room or in any other service setting. They accept that membership of a disciplined fighting force involves a curtailment of freedoms enjoyed by others in civilian employments, and recognise that the exigencies of service life may properly justify restrictions on homosexual activity and manifestations of homosexual orientation. Their challenge is, and is only, to the blanket, non-discretionary, unspecific nature of the existing policy.

The applicants' challenge was rejected by the Queen's Bench Divisional Court (Simon Brown L.J. and Curtis J.) on 7 June 1995: see, ante, pp. 523A et seq. But the court urged the Ministry of Defence to re-examine its policy in the light of changing attitudes and circumstances, and of all available evidence, and we are told that such a review is now in progress. Meanwhile, the applicants contend that the Divisional Court were wrong to reject their challenge.

Background

There can be no doubt that public attitudes to homosexuals and homosexuality have in the past varied widely from country to country, and within the same country at different times, and among different social groups in the same country. Almost any generalisation can be faulted. But there has in this country been a discernible trend, over the last half century or so, towards greater understanding and greater tolerance of homosexuals by heterosexuals, and towards greater openness and honesty by homosexuals. In part this trend has prompted, in part it may have been a result of, legislative change.

Section 1(1) of the Sexual Offences Act 1967 decriminalised homosexual acts between consenting adults in private. It only applied to males, since homosexual acts between women were not criminal anyway. This legislative change, now nearly 30 years ago, followed and gave effect to the Report of the Committee on Homosexual Offences and Prostitution, 1957 (Cmnd. 247, chaired by Sir John Wolfenden). At that time very few European countries took cognisance of homosexual behaviour between consenting parties in private: see paragraph 59 and Appendix III of the Report. It does not appear that that committee addressed the issues with specific reference to the armed forces. But it is important to note that section 1(1) of the Act did not, by virtue of section 1(5), prevent a homosexual act being an offence (other than a civil offence) under the statutes governing the three services. Any person subject to those statutes remained liable to punishment for homosexual acts. So, by section 2 of the Act of 1967, did the crew of British merchant ships. Plainly, the view was then taken that to permit homosexual acts by or between members of the armed services, or in the special conditions pertaining aboard ship, would be subversive of discipline, efficiency and good order.

The routine quinquennial review of the statutes governing the armed forces has the effect that issues such as the treatment of homosexuals are reconsidered periodically. In 1986 a Select Committee of the House of Commons, despite argument that service law should be brought into line with civilian law, concluded that the law should remain as it then stood. But opinion did not stand still. In 1991 another House of Commons Select Committee returned to the subject. Submissions were then made that service law should be brought into line with civilian law and that homosexual orientation *alone* should not be a bar to membership of the armed forces. The select committee accepted the first of these submissions, seeing "no reason why service personnel should be liable to prosecution under service law for homosexual activity which would be legal in civilian law." But they rejected the second submission, concluding that there was "considerable force to the M.O.D.'s argument that the presence of people known to be homosexual can cause tension in a group of people required to live and work sometimes under great stress and physically at very close quarters, and thus damage its cohesion and fighting effectiveness." The select committee were not persuaded in 1991 that the time had yet come to permit the armed forces to accept homosexuals or homosexual activity.

In 1992 the responsible minister announced that in future individuals who engaged in homosexual activity that was legal in civilian law would not be prosecuted under service law. For want of parliamentary time, legislative effect was not given to this change until 1994, when section 146(1) of the Criminal Justice and Public Order Act 1994 was enacted. But section 146(4) provided that this change should not prevent a homosexual act (with or without other acts or circumstances) from constituting a ground for discharging a member of the armed forces.

In upholding the existing policy that homosexual activity or orientation should be an absolute bar to membership of the armed forces the 1991 [S]elect [C]ommittee undoubtedly reflected the overwhelming consensus of service and official opinion in this country. It does not appear that the select committee required or received any evidence of actual harm done by sexual orientation alone or by private homosexual activity outside the context of service life. Nor does the select committee appear to have considered whether the objectives of the existing policy could be met by a rule less absolute in its effect than that which was then applied.

In other areas of national life opinion has shifted. In July 1991 the Prime Minister announced that neither homosexual orientation nor private homosexual activity should henceforth preclude appointment even to sensitive posts in the home civil service and the diplomatic service. The Lord Chancellor has made similar announcements in relation to judicial office. In July 1994 the Royal Fleet Auxiliary introduced an equal opportunities policy stating that it did not discriminate on grounds of homosexuality. A majority of police forces now follow the same policy.

Outside the United Kingdom also, opinion has not stood still. Very few N.A.T.O. countries bar homosexuals from their armed forces. This practice does not appear to have precluded the closest co-operation between such forces and our own. In the course of 1992-93 Australia, New Zealand and Canada relaxed their ban on homosexuals in their armed services but, importantly, introduced codes of conduct which defined the forms of homosexual conduct which were judged to be unacceptable. In the United States, on the other hand, as an authoritative report in 1993 made plain, military opinion remained overwhelmingly against allowing homosexuals to serve. The lawfulness of the legislative compromise adopted in that country is in doubt: see *Able v. United States* (1995) 44 F.3 d 128. In arguing that case the U.S. Government "recognised that a policy mandating discharge of homosexuals merely because they have a homosexual orientation or status could not withstand judicial scrutiny."

I regard the progressive development and refinement of public and professional opinion at home and abroad, here very briefly described, as an important feature of this case. A belief which represented unquestioned orthodoxy in year X may have become questionable by year Y and unsustainable by year Z. Public and professional opinion are a continuum. The four applicants were discharged towards the end of 1994. The lawfulness of their discharge falls to be judged as of that date.

(a) The test

Mr. David Pannick, who represented three of the applicants, and whose arguments were adopted by the fourth, submitted that the court should adopt the following approach to the issue of irrationality:

"The court may not interfere with the exercise of an administrative discretion on substantive grounds save where the court is satisfied that the decision is unreasonable in the sense that it is beyond the range of responses open to a reasonable decision-maker. But in judging whether the decision-maker has exceeded this margin of appreciation the human rights context is important. The more substantial the interference with human rights, the more the court will require by way of justification before it is satisfied that the decision is reasonable in the sense outlined above."

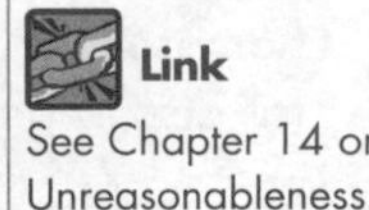

Link

See Chapter 14 on Unreasonableness.

This submission is in my judgment an accurate distillation of the principles laid down by the House of Lords in *Reg. v. Secretary of State for the Home Department, Ex parte Bugdaycay* [1987] A.C. 514 and *Reg. v. Secretary of State for the Home Department, Ex parte Brind* [1991] 1 A.C. 696. In the first of these cases Lord Bridge of Harwich said, at p. 531:

"I approach the question raised by the challenge to the Secretary of State's decision on the basis of the law stated earlier in this opinion, viz. that the resolution of any issue of fact and the exercise of any discretion in relation to an application for asylum as a refugee lie exclusively within the jurisdiction of the Secretary of State subject only to the court's power of review. The limitations on the scope of that power are well known and need not be restated here. Within those limitations the court must, I think, be entitled to subject an administrative decision to the more rigorous examination, to ensure that it is in no way flawed, according to the gravity of the issue which the decision determines. The most fundamental of all human rights is the individual's right to life and when an administrative decision under challenge is said to be one which may put the applicant's life at risk, the basis of the decision must surely call for the most anxious scrutiny."

Lord Templeman, at p. 537H, spoke to similar effect. In the second case, having concluded that it was not open to an English court to apply the European Convention on Human Rights, Lord Bridge said [1991] 1 A.C. 696, 748-749:

"But I do not accept that this conclusion means that the courts are powerless to prevent the exercise by the executive of administrative discretions, even when conferred, as in the instant case, in terms which are on their face unlimited, in a way which infringes fundamental human rights. Most of the rights spelled out in terms in the Convention, including the right to freedom of expression, are less than absolute and must in some cases yield to the claims of competing public interests. Thus, article 10(2) of the Convention spells out and categorises the competing public interests by reference to which the right to freedom of expression may have to be curtailed. In exercising the power of judicial review we have neither the advantages nor the disadvantages of any comparable code to which we may refer or by which we are bound. But again, this surely does not mean that in deciding whether the Secretary of State, in the exercise of his discretion, could reasonably impose the restriction he has imposed on the broadcasting organisations, we are not perfectly entitled to start from the premise that any restriction of the right to freedom of expression requires to be justified and that nothing less than an important competing public interest will be sufficient to justify it. The primary judgment as to whether the particular competing public interest justifies the particular restriction imposed falls to be made by the Secretary of State to whom Parliament has entrusted the discretion. But we are entitled to exercise a secondary judgment by asking whether a reasonable Secretary of State, on the material before him, could reasonably make that primary judgment."

Again, Lord Templeman spoke to similar effect, at p. 751:

"It seems to me that the courts cannot escape from asking themselves whether a reasonable Secretary of State, on the material before him, could reasonably conclude that the interference with freedom of expression which he determined to impose was justifiable."

It is important to note that, in considering whether English law satisfies the requirement in article 13 of the European Convention that there should be a national remedy to enforce the substance of the Convention rights and freedoms, the European Court of Human Rights has held that it does, attaching very considerable weight to the power of the English courts to review administrative decisions by way of judicial review: see *Vilvarajah v. United Kingdom* (1991) 14 E.H.R.R. 248, 291, 292.

It was argued for the ministry in reliance on *Reg. v. Secretary of State for the Environment, Ex parte Nottinghamshire County Council* [1986] A.C. 240 and *Reg. v. Secretary of State for the Environment, Ex parte Hammersmith and Fulham London Borough Council* [1991] 1 A.C. 521 that a test more exacting than *Wednesbury (Associated Provincial Picture Houses Ltd. v. Wednesbury Corporation* [1948] 1 K.B. 223) was appropriate in this case. The Divisional Court rejected this argument and so do I. The greater the policy content of a decision, and the more remote the subject matter of a decision from ordinary judicial experience, the more hesitant the court must necessarily be in holding a decision to be irrational. That is good law and, like most good law, common sense. Where decisions of a policy-laden, esoteric or security-based nature are in issue even greater caution than normal must be shown in applying the test, but the test itself is sufficiently flexible to cover all situations.

The present cases do not affect the lives or liberty of those involved. But they do concern innate qualities of a very personal kind and the decisions of which the applicants complain have had a profound effect on their careers and prospects. The applicants' rights as human beings are very much in issue. It is now accepted that this issue is justiciable. This does not of course mean that the court is thrust into the position of the primary decision-maker. It is not the constitutional role of the court to regulate the conditions of service in the armed forces of the Crown, nor has it the expertise to do so. But it has the constitutional role and duty of ensuring that the rights of citizens are not abused by the unlawful exercise of executive power. While the court must properly defer to the expertise of responsible decision-makers, it must not shrink from its fundamental duty to "do right to all manner of people. . . ."

(b) The facts

The reasons underlying the present policy were given in an affidavit sworn by Air Chief Marshal Sir John Willis K.C.B., C.B.E., the Vice-Chief of the Defence Staff, an officer of great seniority and experience. The relevant paragraphs of his affidavit have been recited in full by Simon Brown L.J. in his judgment in the Divisional Court, ante, pp. 316F-318A, and it is unnecessary to duplicate that recital. Sir John advanced three reasons. The first related to morale and unit effectiveness, the second to the role of the services as guardian of recruits under the age of 18 and the third to the requirement of communal living in many service situations. Sir John described the ministry's policy as based not on a moral judgment but on a practical assessment of the implications of homosexual orientation on military life. By "a practical assessment" Sir John may have meant an assessment of past experience in practice, or he may have meant an assessment of what would be likely to happen in practice if the present policy were varied. His affidavit makes no reference to any specific past experience, despite the fact that over the years very many homosexuals must have served in the armed forces. He does, however, make clear the apprehension of senior service authorities as to what could happen if the existing policy were revoked or varied, and the grounds upon which he relies were the subject of consideration by the House of Commons [S]elect [C]ommittees to which reference has already been made.

The first factor relied on by Sir John, morale and unit effectiveness, was the subject of searing criticism by Mr. Pannick. He submitted that the effect of a homosexual member of any military unit would depend on the character, ability and personality of the member involved. He pointed out that many homosexuals had successfully served in the services over the years. He drew attention to the experience of other disciplined forces such as the police. He submitted that inappropriate behaviour by homosexual members of the armed forces could be effectively regulated. He submitted that the ministry should not be deterred from doing what fairness and good sense demanded by apprehensions of irrational and prejudiced behaviour on the part of others.

Mr. Pannick also criticised the second factor relied on by Sir John. He pointed out that any service member behaving inappropriately towards an under-age member of the service could be disciplined and punished in the same way as in society at large. He rejected the suggestion that homosexuals were less able to control their sexual impulses than heterosexuals. Again he suggested that the policy of the ministry was pandering to ignorant prejudice.

Mr. Pannick accepted, of course, that members of the services could in many situations find themselves living together in conditions of very close proximity, although he pointed out that one of the applicants (by reason of his seniority) and another of the applicants (by reason of her particular occupation) were in no foreseeable situation likely to share accommodation with anyone. The lack of privacy in service life was, he suggested, a reason for imposing strict rules and discipline, but not a reason for banning the membership of any homosexual. He drew attention to the experience of other disciplined services. He pointed out that each of the applicants had worked in the armed forces for a number of years without any concern being expressed or complaints made about inappropriate behaviour. Each of them had earned very favourable reports. The same, it was said, was true of many other homosexual members of the services.

Above all, Mr. Pannick criticised the blanket nature of the existing rule. He placed great emphasis on the practice of other nations whose rules were framed so as to counter the particular mischiefs to which homosexual orientation or activity might give rise. He pointed out that other personal problems such as addiction to alcohol, or compulsive gambling, or marital infidelity were dealt with by the service authorities on a case by case basis and not on the basis of a rule which permitted no account to be taken of the peculiar features of the case under consideration.

The arguments advanced by Mr. Pannick are in my opinion of very considerable cogency. They call to be considered in depth, with particular reference to specific evidence of past experience in this country, to the developing experience of other countries and to the potential effectiveness or otherwise of a detailed prescriptive code along the lines adopted elsewhere in place of the present blanket ban. Such a reassessment of the existing policy is already, as I have noted, in train, and I note that the next Select Committee quinquennial review of the policy is to receive a departmental paper of evidence covering all the matters canvassed on this appeal. What the outcome of that review will be, I do not know.

The existing policy cannot in my judgment be stigmatised as irrational at the time when these applicants were discharged. It was supported by both Houses of Parliament and by those to whom the ministry properly looked for professional advice. There was, to my knowledge, no evidence before the ministry which plainly invalidated that advice. Changes made by other countries were in some cases very recent. The Australian, New Zealand and Canadian codes had been adopted too recently to yield much valuable experience. The ministry did not have the opportunity to consider the full range of arguments developed before us. Major policy changes should be the product of mature reflection, not instant reaction. The threshold of irrationality is a high one. It was not crossed in this case.

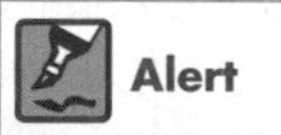
Alert

...

Appeal dismissed.

Although *Smith* was seemingly in a banned area under Lord Roskill's list the court was willing to intervene. In the original application, Simon Brown LJ had justified review on the following basis:

I have no hesitation in holding this challenge justiciable. To my mind only the rarest cases will today be ruled strictly beyond the court's purview - only cases involving national security properly so called and where in addition the courts really do lack the expertise or material to form a judgment on the point at issue. This case does not fall into that category. True, it touches on the defence of the realm but it does not involve determining "whether . . . the armed forces [should be] disposed of in a particular manner" (which Lord Roskill in *Council of Civil Service Unions v. Minister for the Civil Service* [1985] A.C. 374 thought plainly unreviewable - as indeed had been held in *China Navigation Co. Ltd. v. Attorney-General* [1932] 2 K.B. 197). No operational considerations are involved in this policy. Now, indeed, that the "security implications" have disappeared, there appears little about it which the courts are not perfectly well qualified to judge for themselves.

Similar reasoning can be seen in the Court of Appeal where Sir Thomas Bingham MR's reasoning for feeling able to review was the fact that this case touched not on high policy, so much as individual rights. A similar pattern can be seen in the following case which engaged the prerogative relating to diplomatic relations with other countries and foreign affairs in the wider sense.

***The Queen on the Application of Abbasi & Another v Secretary of State for Foreign and Commonwealth Affairs & Secretary of State for the Home Department* [2003] UKHRR 76, [2002] EWCA Civ 1598**

Panel: Lord Phillips of Worth Matravers MR, Waller and Carnwath LJJ

Facts: The applicants had been detained by the US authorities as part of the 'global war on terror'. Their families argued that the UK government was under a legal obligation pursuant to a legitimate expectation to try to intercede on their behalf (using the prerogative power of foreign affairs). This area of power was also one of the "excluded categories" in Lord Roskill's "list". While the case did throw up wider issues such as the basic legality of Abbasi's detention under international law, these are peripheral. The case does address them in places, but not in an especially comprehensive or convincing manner.

LORD PHILLIPS OF WORTH MATRAVERS MR

This is the judgment of the Court to which all members have contributed.

Introduction

1. Feroz Ali Abbasi, the first claimant, is a British national. He was captured by United States forces in Afghanistan. In January 2002 he was transported to Guantanamo Bay in Cuba, a naval base on territory held by the United States on long lease pursuant to a treaty with Cuba. By the time of the hearing before us he had been held captive for eight months without access to a court or any other form of tribunal or even to a lawyer. These proceedings, brought on his behalf by his mother, the second claimant, are founded on the contention that one of his fundamental human rights, the right not to be arbitrarily detained, is being infringed. They seek, by judicial review, to compel the Foreign Office to make representations on his behalf to the United States Government or to take other appropriate action or at least to give an explanation as to why this has not been done.

2. On 15 March 2002 Richards J. refused the application for permission to seek judicial review. However, on 1 July 2002 this court granted that permission, retained the matter for itself, and directed that the substantive hearing commence on 10 September 2002. It did so because the unusual facts of this case raise important issues. To what extent, if at all, can the English court examine whether a foreign state is in breach of treaty obligations or public international law where fundamental human rights are engaged? To what extent, if at all, is a decision of the executive in the field of foreign relations justiciable in the English court? More particularly, are there any circumstances in which the court can properly seek to influence the conduct of the executive in a situation where this may impact on foreign relations? Finally, in the light of the answers to these questions, is any form of relief open to Mr Abbasi and his mother against the Secretary of State for Foreign and Commonwealth Affairs?

Alert

Mr Abbasi's predicament

4. Evidence of action taken by the United Kingdom Government in relation to Mr Abbasi and the other British detainees in Guantanamo Bay has been provided in a witness statement by Mr Fry, a Deputy Under-Secretary of State for Foreign and Commonwealth Affairs. He speaks of close contact between the United Kingdom Government and the United States Government about the situation of the detainees and their treatment and of the consistent endeavour of the government to secure their welfare and ensure their proper treatment. To that end, we are told, the circumstances of the British detainees have been the subject of regular representations by the British Embassy in Washington to the United States Government. They have also been the subject of direct discussions between the Foreign Secretary and the United States Secretary of State as well as 'numerous communications at official level'.

5. The government was able to obtain permission from the United States Government to visit detainees at Guantanamo Bay on three occasions, between 19 and 20 January, between 26 February and 1 March and between 27 and 31 May. These visits were conducted by officials of the Foreign and Commonwealth Office and members of the security services. The former were able to assure themselves that the British prisoners, including Mr Abbasi, were being well treated and appeared in good physical health. By the time of the third visit, facilities had been purpose built to house detainees. Each was held in an individual cell with air ventilation, a washbasin and a toilet. It is not suggested by the claimants that Mr Abbasi is not being treated humanely.

6. The members of the security services took advantage of these visits to question Mr Abbasi with a view to obtaining information about possible threats to the safety of the United Kingdom. Initially this was the subject of independent complaint by the claimants, but before us the argument has focussed on the allegation that the Foreign and Commonwealth Office is not reacting appropriately to the fact that Mr Abbasi is being arbitrarily detained in violation of his fundamental human rights.

7. The position of the Foreign and Commonwealth Office is summarised by Mr Fry in the following terms:

"In cases that come to us with a request for assistance, Foreign and Commonwealth Ministers and Her Majesty's diplomatic and consular officers have to make an informed and considered judgement about the most appropriate way in which the interests of the British national may be protected, including the nature, manner and timing of any diplomatic representations to the country concerned. Assessments of when and how to press another State require very fine judgements to be made, based on experience and detailed information gathered in the course of diplomatic business.

In cases where a person is detained in connection with international terrorism, these judgements become particularly complex. As regards the issue of the detainees now at Guantanamo Bay, as well as satisfying the clear need to safeguard the welfare of British nationals, the conduct of United Kingdom international relations has had to take account of a range of factors, including the duty of the Government to gather information relevant to United Kingdom national security and which might be important in averting a possible attack against the United Kingdom or British nationals or our allies; and the objectives of handling the detainees securely and of bringing any terrorist suspects to justice."

8. In or about February 2002 the claimants initiated habeas corpus proceedings in the District Court of Columbia. As we shall explain, rulings in proceedings brought by other detainees in a similar position demonstrate that Mr Abbasi's proceedings have, at present, no prospect of success.

...

Is the conduct of the Secretary of State justiciable?

68 Mr Blake submitted that we should find that the Foreign Secretary owed Mr Abbasi a duty to respond positively to his, and his mother's, request for diplomatic assistance. He founded this submission on (i) the assertion that international law is moving towards the recognition of such a duty and that customary international law forms part of our common law; (ii) the alleged recognition of such a duty under the constitutions of Germany and, possibly, other states; (iii) the assertion that such a duty arises under the Human Rights Convention together with the Human Rights Act.

The court undertook a full analysis of the arguments put forward to the effect that Abbasi had a right to diplomatic assistance under domestic law that, through either the incorporation of international law or under the Human Rights Act, but did not find in his favour.

80 If Mr Blake is unable to demonstrate that, either through the incorporation of international law or under the Human Rights Act, Mr Abbasi enjoys a right to diplomatic assistance under our domestic law, do the authorities relied upon by Mr Greenwood close the door to any possibility of establishing such a right by way, as Mr Blake would contend, of a beneficial development of our public law? The authorities relied upon by Mr Greenwood, of which we have cited relevant passages at paragraphs 37 and 38 above, are powerful indeed. There are, however, three considerations which have led us to reject the proposition that there is no scope for judicial review of a refusal to render diplomatic assistance to a British subject who is suffering violation of a fundamental human right as the result of the conduct of the authorities of a foreign state.

81 The first consideration is the development of the law of judicial review in relation (i) to the doctrine of legitimate expectation and (ii) to the invasion of areas previously immune from review, such as the exercise of the prerogative.

82 As to the first, under the modern law of judicial review, the doctrine of "legitimate expectation" provides a well-established and flexible means for giving legal effect to a settled policy or practice for the exercise of an administrative discretion. The expectation may arise from an express promise or "from the existence of a regular practice which the claimant can reasonably expect to continue", per Lord Fraser, Council of Civil Service Unions v Minister for Civil Service [1985] AC 374, 401; and

see de Smith, Judicial Review 5 th Ed p.419ff. The expectation is not that the policy or practice will necessarily remain unchanged, or, if unchanged, that it will not be overridden by other policy considerations. However, so long as it remains unchanged, the subject is entitled to have it properly taken into account in considering his individual case; see de Smith pp.574–5, citing Re Findlay [1985] AC 318, 388, per Lord Scarman.

83 For the second development, it is necessary to refer to the landmark decision in Council of Civil Service Unions -v- Minister for the Civil Service [1985] AC 374 (the 'GCHQ' case), which established that the mere fact that a power derived from the Royal Prerogative did not necessarily exclude it from the scope of judicial review. The House of Lords did, however, accept that there were certain areas which remain outside the area of justiciability. Thus, at p.398, Lord Fraser referred to:

"many of the most important prerogative powers concerned with control of the armed forces and with foreign policy and with other matters which are unsuitable for discussion or review in the Law Courts".

84 Lord Scarman said, at p.407, that the controlling factor in considering whether a particular exercise of prerogative power was subject to review was "not its source but its subject matter." Lord Diplock, at p.411, expanded on the categories of prerogative decision which remained unsuitable for judicial review:

"Such decisions will generally involve the application of Government policy. The reasons for the decision-maker taking one course rather than another do not normally involve questions to which, if disputed, the judicial process is adapted to provide the right answer, by which I mean that the kind of evidence that is admissible under judicial procedures and the way in which it has to be adduced tend to exclude from the attention of the court competing policy considerations which, if the Executive discretion is to be wisely exercised, need to weighed against one another – a balancing exercise which judges by their upbringing and experience are ill-qualified to perform."

85 Those extracts indicate that the issue of justiciability depends, not on general principle, but on subject matter and suitability in the particular case. That is illustrated by the subsequent case of R -v- Foreign Secretary ex p. Everett [1989] 1QB 811. This court held, following the GCHQ case, that a decision taken under the prerogative whether or not to issue a passport was subject to judicial review, although relief was refused on the facts of that particular case. Lord Justice Taylor, at p.820, summarised the effect of the GCHQ case as making clear that the powers of the court "cannot be ousted merely by invoking the word 'prerogative'":

"The majority of their Lordships indicated that whether judicial review of the exercise of a prerogative power is open depends upon the subject matter and in particular whether it is justiciable. At the top of the scale of executive functions under the Prerogative are matters of high policy, of which examples were given by their Lordships; making treaties, making war, dissolving parliament, mobilising the armed forces. Clearly those matters and no doubt a number of others are not justiciable but the grant or refusal of a passport is in a quite different category. It is a matter of administrative decision affecting the right of individuals and their freedom of travel. It raises issues which are just as justiciable as, for example, the issues arising in immigration cases."

86 The interaction of these two developments in the law of judicial review can be seen in R -v- Home Secretary ex p. Ahmed and Patel [1998] INLR 570. The applicants were illegal immigrants who had married persons with indefinite leave to remain in the UK and had children in the UK. In support of their applications for leave to remain on the basis of their marriages, they relied on legitimate expectations created by the UK's ratification of two international conventions relating to the rights of the child and of the family. Lord Woolf MR accepted that in principle a legitimate expectation could be created by the State's act in entering into a treaty. He relied, at p.584, on the approach of the High Court of Australia in Minister for Immigration -v- Teoh [1995] 183 CLR 273:

"... Ratification of a convention is a positive statement by the Executive Government of this country to the world and the Australian people that the Executive Government and its agencies will act in accordance with convention that positive statement is an adequate foundation for a legitimate expectation, *absent statutory or executive indications to the contrary*, that administrators will act in conformity with the Convention ..." (p.291, per Mason CJ and Deane J — Lord Woolf's emphasis).

At p.592 Hobhouse LJ also accepted the approach of the Australian case, but emphasised that where the Secretary of State had adopted a specific policy, as he had in the instant case, it was not possible to derive any expectation from the treaty going beyond the scope of the policy.

87 The second consideration is that, to a degree, the Foreign and Commonwealth Office have promulgated a policy which, so it seems to us, is capable of giving rise to a legitimate expectation.

88 The practice of the United Kingdom Government in respect of diplomatic protection was explained in 1999, in comments presented to the United Nations General Assembly, as part of the discussion of a report of the International Law Commission (reproduced in British Yearbook of International Law 1999 at p.526). Under the heading "Diplomatic protection: United Kingdom Practice", the paper notes that this is a matter "falling within the prerogative of the Crown" and that "there is no general legislation or case law governing this area in domestic law". It distinguishes between "formal claims" and "informal representations".

89 In relation to formal claims, "a considered statement of the Government's policy" is contained in "rules" issued by the Foreign Office, based on "general principles of customary international law". It is said, citing Mutasa v Attorney General [1980] 1 QB 114 (see below), that the rules are "a statement of general policy and have no direct effect in domestic law". We have been shown the current version of the rules (reproduced in (1988) 37 ICLQ p.1006). It is not suggested that any are directly relevant to this case, but we note rule VIII, which provides:

"If, in exhausting any municipal remedies, the claimant has met with prejudice or obstruction, which are a denial of justice, HMG may intervene on his behalf in order to secure justice."

90 In relation to informal representations, the 1999 British Year Book of International Law records two further Ministerial statements of policy. The first refers to a "review of our policy" on making such representations about convictions and sentencing of British prisoners abroad:

"At present we consider making representations if, when all legal remedies have been exhausted, the British national and their lawyer have evidence of a miscarriage or denial of justice. We are extending this to cases where fundamental violations of the British national's human rights had demonstrably altered the course of justice. In such cases, we would consider supporting their request for an appeal to any official human rights body in the country concerned, and subsequently giving advice on how to take their cases to relevant international human rights mechanisms."

91 This review was further explained in a Parliamentary Answer on 16th December 1999 by Baroness Scotland. Having referred to the revised policy, she said:

"We are very conscious of the other government's obligations to ensure the respect of the rights of British citizens within their jurisdiction. This includes the right to a fair trial. In cases where a British citizen may have suffered a miscarriage of justice we believe that the most appropriate course of action is for the defendant's lawyers to take action through the local courts. If concerns remain, their lawyers can take the case to the United Nations Human Rights Committee, where the State in question has accepted the right of individual petition under the ICCPR. *The UK Government would also consider making direct representations to third governments on behalf of British citizens where we believe that they were in breach of their international obligations.*" (emphasis added)

92 Taken together, these statements indicate a clear acceptance by the government of a role in relation to protecting the rights of British citizens abroad, where there is evidence of miscarriage or denial of justice. In the present case none of the avenues suggested in the last quotation is available. The words emphasised contain no more than a commitment "to consider" making representations, which will be triggered by the "belief" that there is a breach of the international obligations. This seems to imply that such consideration will at least start from a formulated view as to whether there is such a breach, and as to the gravity of the resulting denial of rights.

...

96 In *Al Adsani v United Kingdom* the Government contended, as recorded at paragraph 50, that:

"There were other, traditional means of redress for wrongs of this kind available to the applicant, namely diplomatic representations or an inter-State claim."

97 In *Rasul* the United States District Court expressed the "serious concern" that the court's decision would leave the prisoners without any rights, and recorded the government's recognition that:

"these aliens fall within the protections of certain provisions of international law and that diplomatic channels remain an ongoing and viable means to address the claims raised by these aliens." (p.2)

98 These statements reflect the fact that, to use the words of *Everett*, it must be a 'normal expectation of every citizen' that, if subjected abroad to a violation of a fundamental right, the British Government will not simply wash their hands of the matter and abandon him to his fate.

99 What then is the nature of the expectation that a British subject in the position of Mr Abbasi can legitimately hold in relation to the response of the government to a request for assistance? The policy statements that we have cited underline the very limited nature of the expectation. They indicate that where certain criteria are satisfied, the government will "consider" making representations. Whether to make any representations in a particular case, and if so in what form, is left entirely to the discretion of the Secretary of State. That gives free play to the "balance" to which Lord Diplock referred in GCHQ. The Secretary of State must be free to give full weight to foreign policy considerations, which are not justiciable. However, that does not mean the whole process is immune from judicial scrutiny. The citizen's legitimate expectation is that his request will be "considered", and that in that consideration all relevant factors will be thrown into the balance.

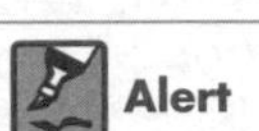
Alert

100 One vital factor, as the policy recognises, is the nature and extent of the injustice, which he claims to have suffered. Even where there has been a gross miscarriage of justice, there may perhaps be overriding reasons of foreign policy which may lead the Secretary of State to decline to intervene. However, unless and until he has formed some judgment as to the gravity of the miscarriage, it is impossible for that balance to be properly conducted.

101 Although Mr Blake did not rest his case on "legitimate expectation", the position as it emerges from the authorities to which we have referred seems very close to what he was ultimately contending should be the content of the "duty" which he asserts. As he said in his reply:—

"The claimants are not seeking relief against the US Government and nor are they seeking to dictate to the Executive how it should conduct foreign policy and by what means; they are merely stating their case why the Government should intervene with another foreign sovereign state".

Orally he made clear what he wanted was the case considered by the Foreign and Commonwealth Office.

...

104 The extreme case where judicial review would lie in relation to diplomatic protection would be if the Foreign and Commonwealth Office were, contrary to its

stated practice, to refuse even to consider whether to make diplomatic representations on behalf of a subject whose fundamental rights were being violated. In such, unlikely, circumstances we consider that it would be appropriate for the court to make a mandatory order to the Foreign Secretary to give due consideration to the applicant's case.

105 Beyond this we do not believe it is possible to make general propositions. In some cases it might be reasonable to expect the Secretary of State to state the result of considering a request for assistance, in others it might not. In some cases he might be expected to give reasons for his decision, in others he might not. In some cases such reasons might be open to attack, in others they would not.

106 We would summarise our views as to what the authorities establish as follows:

i) It is not an answer to a claim for judicial review to say that the source of the power of the Foreign Office is the prerogative. It is the subject matter that is determinative.

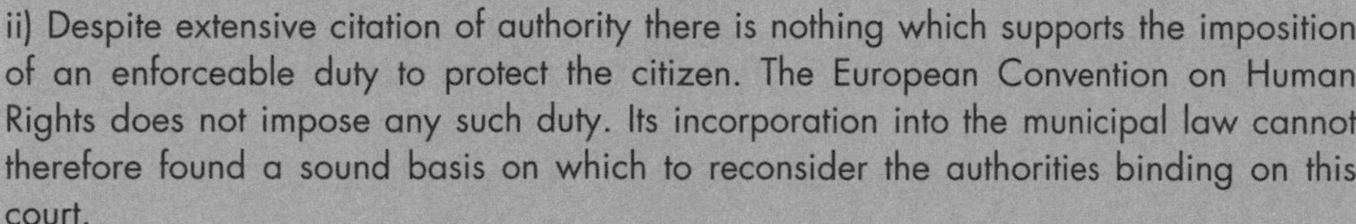

ii) Despite extensive citation of authority there is nothing which supports the imposition of an enforceable duty to protect the citizen. The European Convention on Human Rights does not impose any such duty. Its incorporation into the municipal law cannot therefore found a sound basis on which to reconsider the authorities binding on this court.

iii) However the Foreign Office has discretion whether to exercise the right, which it undoubtedly has, to protect British citizens. It has indicated in the ways explained what a British citizen may expect of it. The expectations are limited and the discretion is a very wide one but there is no reason why its decision or inaction should not be reviewable if it can be shown that the same were irrational or contrary to legitimate expectation; but the court cannot enter the forbidden areas, including decisions affecting foreign policy.

iv) It is highly likely that any decision of the Foreign and Commonwealth Office, as to whether to make representations on a diplomatic level, will be intimately connected with decisions relating to this country's foreign policy, but an obligation to consider the position of a particular British citizen and consider the extent to which some action might be taken on his behalf, would seem unlikely itself to impinge on any forbidden area.

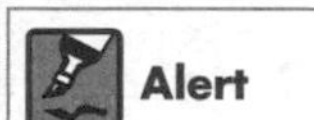

v) The extent to which it may be possible to require more than that the Foreign Secretary give due consideration to a request for assistance will depend on the facts of the particular case.

Are the applicants entitled to relief in the present case?

107 We have made clear our deep concern that, in apparent contravention of fundamental principles of law, Mr Abbasi may be subject to indefinite detention in territory over which the United States has exclusive control with no opportunity to challenge the legitimacy of his detention before any court or tribunal. However, there are a number of reasons why we consider that the applicants' claim to relief must be rejected:

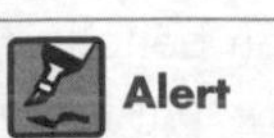

i) It is quite clear from Mr Fry's evidence that the Foreign and Commonwealth Office have considered Mr Abbasi's request for assistance. He has also disclosed that the British detainees are the subject of discussions between this country and the United States both at Secretary of State and lower official levels. We do not consider that Mr Abbasi could reasonably expect more than this. In particular, if the Foreign and Commonwealth Office were to make any statement as to its view of the legality of the detention of the British prisoners, or any statement as to the nature of discussions held with United States officials, this might well undermine those discussions.

ii) On no view would it be appropriate to order the Secretary of State to make any specific representations to the United States, even in the face of what appears to be a clear breach of a fundamental human right, as it is obvious that this would have an impact on the conduct of foreign policy, and an impact on such policy at a particularly delicate time.

iii) The position of detainees at Guantanamo Bay is to be considered further by the appellate courts in the United States. It may be that the anxiety that we have expressed will be drawn to their attention. We wish to make it clear that we are only expressing an anxiety that we believe was felt by the court in *Rasul*. As is clear from our judgment, we believe that the United States courts have the same respect for human rights as our own.

iv) The Inter-American Commission on Human Rights has taken up the case of the detainees. It is as yet unclear what the result of the Commission's intervention will be. It is not clear that any activity on the part of the Foreign and Commonwealth Office would assist in taking the matter further while it is in the hands of that international body.

108 For all these reasons the application before us must be dismissed.

...

1. Appeal dismissed.

Similarly to the approach taken in *Smith*, the court in *Abbasi* was prepared to accept the case as justiciable in the pure sense of the word – the case was addressed and fully adjudicated upon. The court again reiterated the essential point of principle from *GCHQ* and alluded to the Roskill "list" issue. However, it took the more modern view on this point preferring to see the issue as one of the appropriate intensity of review rather than a matter of justiciability in the basic sense. On the facts of the case all that was effectively required of the Foreign Office was that it had considered making representations on Abbasi's behalf in the context of the unusual circumstances that prevailed. This it had done and so the challenge was ultimately ineffective. However, had the family's requests for Foreign Office not even been considered, it was conceivable that the court would have held it to had acted contrary to the legitimate expectation.

Further Reading

Cohn, Margit 'Judicial review of non-statutory executive powers after Bancoult: a unified anxious model', [2010] *PL* 260

Cohn, Margit 'Medieval chains, invisible inks: on non-statutory powers of the executive', (2005) 25(1) *OJLS* 97

Kilroy, Charlotte 'R. (Abbasi) v Secretary of State for Foreign and Commonwealth Affairs: reviewing the prerogative', [2003] 2 *EHRLR* 222

6

Accountability of Government: Responsible Government

Topic List

Alex Lawson

Introduction

Responsible government is largely governed by the internal rules and practices of Parliament and government. In the United Kingdom the concept stems form the fact that the core executive is drawn from Parliament: what Walter Baghot describes as the 'efficient secret' of the Constitution. This means all ministers are accountable to Parliament for the exercise of power, and is another manifestation of Parliament's sovereignty.

Because responsible government deals with politicians regulating, scrutinising and controlling the actions of other politicians it is largely based on convention and so there is little scope for the judiciary to get involved or for a heavy emphasis on case law. Perhaps the most important case in this area is *Attorney-General v Jonathan Cape Ltd. and Others; Attorney-General v Times Newspapers Ltd.* [1976] QB 752, which was extracted in Chapter 1. You should refresh your memory of that case.

1 Accountability

At the heart of the doctrine of responsible government is the idea of accountability. In this area accountability is for political activity where the courts may be unable to perform the role of holding the executive to account. However, in this area, due to the evolutionary nature and developmental potential of conventions, ministers have been able to weaken the value of Parliament's accountability role by redefining the conventions in such a way that they are only responsible (in the sense of having to resign) for policy failure; and for operational failures which may be the fault of civil servants they are only required to account. However, since the minister themselves is able to decide if the failure is one of operation or policy this leads to inevitable problems and lacuna in accountability.

The Treasury and Civil Service Committee tried to remedy the problem in their 1993 – 1994 report, *The Role of the Civil Service* where they said:

'We do not believe that Ministerial power to intervene in the actions and decisions of Agencies justifies the retention of Ministerial accountability for the actions and decisions of Agencies for which the Chief Executives are responsible... The delegation of responsibility should be accompanied by a commensurate delegation of accountability. Agency Chief Executives should be directly and personally accountable to Select Committees in relation to their annual performance agreements.'

This would have closed the accountability gap, but was roundly rejected by the government who maintained that it was the minister who was required to account for operational matters, but that they could only be held accountable for policy.

The article that follows looks at some of the issues of accountability under ministerial responsibility, picking up on this operational/policy divide.

The reconstruction of constitutional accountability, Diana Woodhouse, [2002] PL 73

During the last decade, constitutional accountability, as delivered through the convention of ministerial responsibility, became confused with, and by, managerial accountability. This focuses on the performance of those who deliver government programmes and as an adjunct to ministerial responsibility could contribute to an extended and improved model of accountability. However, the potential of managerial accountability has not always been realised and, on occasions, it has been used as a substitute for, rather than an aid to, constitutional accountability. Part of the problem lies in a construction of ministerial responsibility which focuses on "causal" responsibility, that is on the direct involvement of ministers in any errors or misjudgments. This has resulted in ministers seeking to distance themselves from the cause of any departmental failings through the employment of the "operations/policy" and "accountability/responsibility" distinctions. At times it has also resulted in the transfer of blame from ministers to officials and a confusion of managerial and constitutional accountability.

The issue is therefore how to reconstruct constitutional accountability so as to avoid such confusion. One way forward could be to reformulate the convention of ministerial responsibility so that, using H. L. A. Hart's terminology, it centres on "role", rather than "causal", responsibility. This would move the emphasis of the convention away from direct personal culpability towards the minister's role, that is, towards the requirements of the ministerial job. By so doing, it would provide a more workable distinction between the accountability of ministers and officials and reduce the opportunity for ministers to hide behind the uncertainties of their job descriptions. Role responsibility not only stresses the supervisory nature of a minister's responsibilities but reinforces his or her duty, as minister, to account to Parliament, both in terms of explanation and, where appropriate, amendatory action.

Constitutional accountability

The convention of ministerial responsibility requires ministers to be accountable to Parliament for their own actions and those of their departments, and most interpretations of the convention focus on causal responsibility. Where the behaviour or personal conduct of a minister is concerned, such a focus is appropriate, as ministers can be assumed to have control over their own actions and therefore to be personally to blame for any ensuing political repercussions. Problems relating to the meaning and location of accountability therefore do not arise. Causal responsibility means that ministers are accountable in the sense both of "giving an account" and "being held to account". In the terminology introduced by Sir Robin (now Lord) Butler, when Cabinet Secretary, ministers are "accountable" and "responsible", that is personally to blame, and if the consequences of their actions are such as to cast doubt on their ability to fulfil their ministerial duties or undermine their standing in government, resignation may be required. However, matters are seldom so clear cut when there are errors within a department and the need to find ministerial involvement, and thus locate causal responsibility in the minister, has contributed to the sparsity of resignations in this category. Indeed, in the second half of the twentieth century only the resignations of Dugdale (1954), Carrington (1982) and Brittan (1986) can, with any degree of

certainty, be attributed to departmental fault. How much ministerial involvement is necessary depends on the circumstances. Notions of vicarious or "consequential" responsibility, that is, the acceptance of responsibility for the consequences of the actions of officials, regardless of their distance from the minister, are unsupported by precedent, although where the consequences are very serious, as when the Falkland Islands were invaded, any involvement of the minister, in that instance Lord Carrington, may be sufficient for resignation to be required.

The emphasis on causal responsibility has resulted in a general acceptance that resignation may be required for serious departmental errors in which ministers were involved, or of which they knew or should have known, and the corollary position that ministers "cannot be expected to shoulder the blame for decisions of which they knew nothing or could be expected to know nothing". However, this has raised questions about what a minister "could be expected to know" and has resulted in attempts by ministers to minimise expectations and distance themselves from culpability. Hence the employment of the distinction between "policy" and "operations", which implies that ministers cannot be expected to know anything about operational matters, and that between "responsibility" and "accountability", which implies that they therefore cannot be blamed for any operational error or for a series of such errors.

Nowhere was the use of these distinctions more evident than when the Home Secretary, Michael Howard, dismissed the Director General of the Prison Service Agency in 1995 after a series of incidents concerning prison security. Howard insisted that these were the result of operational failures for which the Director General, through the agency framework agreement, was responsible and that while he, as minister, was accountable to Parliament, in terms of "giving an account", responsibility, in the sense of culpability, lay with the Director General. Such a division assumes that in instances of serious departmental fault the requirements of ministerial responsibility are fulfilled by the minister accounting for what had happened. However, this is not necessarily the case, for, as was evident from Howard's handling of the Prison Service incident, accounting may have more to do with self-preservation and blame avoidance than with giving full information and explanations. Howard, it seems, failed to lay a full report of what had happened before Parliament. The division also allows ministers to escape blame for operational errors which may amount to negligence or mismanagement on the minister's part, on the basis that no individual mistake is his or her own. In this instance, as far as the Prison Service was concerned, the Home Secretary became responsible for virtually nothing, the "cause" was tied to the responsibilities of the Director General, and managerial accountability was substituted for constitutional accountability.

This is not to say that the Director General should have remained in office, although the Agency's progress against its targets, on which managerial accountability centres, would seem to indicate that his performance was more than adequate, at least according to the criteria against which he was assessed. Nor is it suggested that the Home Secretary should have resigned, there being no precedent for Home Secretaries resigning over prison escapes. The point is that managerial accountability, which centres on the direct accountability of officials to the minister for their responsibilities, should ensure better constitutional accountability, that is the accountability of ministers to Parliament and the public, not substitute for it.

Causal responsibility would therefore seem to be an inappropriate basis on which to found ministerial responsibility, particularly given that, as Honoré suggests, what "is picked out as the cause in a given context depends on how far back the inquiry is taken and this depends on its purpose". The possible cause of death of someone killed in a road accident therefore ranges through "internal bleeding, the driver's mistake, the ice on the road with which the driver failed to cope, [and] the shortage of funds that led to the local authority not removing the ice in time". In a similar way, the cause of serious departmental error may be an operational mistake by an official, a system's failure, a misguided policy and a lack of resources. However, while in the case of the road accident a number of inquiries, each with a different purpose, will be instigated to determine the cause, with rare exceptions the purpose of inquiries set up to investigate the cause of departmental errors will be primarily to uncover what happened on the ground. Indeed, the terms of reference of the inquiry may prevent it from looking at matters of policy or from going beyond the immediate cause which, almost inevitably, will be "operational", thus enabling ministers to blame officials. The problem is that both directly, as in the case of departmental inquiries, and indirectly, as with select committee investigations, ministers control the inquiry process and can therefore ensure that they are distanced from the cause and hence escape the constitutional consequences of being held culpable themselves.

The reformulation of ministerial responsibility

The answer may therefore be a concentration on role, rather than causal, responsibility. Role responsibility arises from the minister's "distinctive place or office", that is from his or her job, and therefore distinguishes more clearly between the positions of officials and ministers. It implies that ministers are constitutionally responsible for their departments, not because of their involvement in the detail of departmental affairs, but because their position as politicians lays upon them certain duties, both personal and organisational, and the responsibility for ensuring that these are fulfilled. Their responsibilities are therefore not confined to matters of policy, which in any case usually fall under the cover of collective responsibility, but encompass the supervision of their departments.

Ideas which can be equated with role responsibility are not new. They were, for instance, given voice in 1972 by the Home Secretary, Reginald Maudling, when he said that ministers are "responsible not only for their personal decisions but also for seeing that there is a system in their Departments by which they are informed of important matters which arise. They are also responsible for minimising the danger of errors and mistakes so far as is possible, and clearly, they are responsible for the general efficiency of their Department". This view was echoed some 10 years later by Sir Ian Bancroft, a former head of the Home Civil Service, who argued that the minister was "responsible and accountable to Parliament for the effectiveness of his department's policies and the efficient and economic use of the resources allocated to it". He continued, "[i]t is part of that responsibility to ensure that his department has the systems, procedures, organisation and staffing necessary to promote efficient management".

The 1994 government publication, *Taking Forward Continuity and Change,* also set out some of the responsibilities that fall to ministers. These included "the policies of the department", "the framework through which these policies are delivered", "the resources allocated", "such implementation decisions any agency framework document may require to be referred or agreed with the Minister", and "responding to major failures or expressions of Parliamentary or public concern". The document therefore reflected some of the responsibilities listed previously. Moreover, it took account of new ones which arose because of executive agencies. However, as an outline of the ministerial job description it failed in a number of respects. There was, for instance, no reference to the responsibility of ministers for their informal interventions in agencies nor for any decision not to intervene when a matter was brought to their attention. Yet ministers can neither escape responsibility for the way in which they exercise such judgment nor claim that non-intervention removes responsibility. Nor was there any mention of mismanagement by the minister which results in a succession of errors, or in the department "prevent[ing] a Minister knowing about things that he should have known about". Indeed, the document failed to encompass the general supervisory responsibility implied by both Maudling and Bancroft.

Despite its omissions, *Taking Forward Continuity and Change* represented further support for some notion of role responsibility, albeit narrowly defined, and this support was again evident in the statement made by Jack Straw when he became Home Secretary in 1997. Straw told Parliament that, in contrast to his predecessor, Michael Howard, he would be taking "proper ministerial responsibility for the Prison Service". Straw was seeking to make a political point. He was also making a constitutional point, for while stressing that he was not culpable "if a cell door has been left open by accident"– in other words he was not to blame for an action far removed from him hierarchically and geographically – he said he was "responsible for checking whether the right procedures [were] in place and that effective management decisions [had] been made through the Director General of the Prison Service to ensure that sort of thing doesn't happen again".

The statements of Maudling, Bancroft and Straw suggest that the ministerial role encompasses a supervisory responsibility which centres on ensuring that standards are maintained, both in terms of what is delivered and how this is accomplished. Ministers are therefore responsible for seeing that mechanisms are in place to provide them with the necessary and correct information so that they can respond to problems, if appropriate by taking direct control, and account to Parliament and the public. They are also responsible for ensuring that their departments have adequate human and financial resources to implement government policies, that those appointed as heads of executive agencies are suitably qualified, and that there are systems and procedures in place which minimise the danger of errors being made. Such responsibilities can be described as "positive" responsibilities and they constitute a large part of a minister's job description. They are supplemented by "negative" responsibilities, so that the failure of ministers to intervene, when they should have done so, is not an appropriate excuse; neither is not knowing that something has happened when they should have known. Thus, as the Public Administrative Committee noted, "politicians should not offer ignorance as a defence".

The focus on role, rather than causal, responsibility means that the need to find direct ministerial involvement in departmental fault is diminished. The artificial division between operations and policy therefore becomes largely irrelevant and the distinction between responsibility and accountability even less appropriate than previously. Instead there are two main issues. The first is whether the minister has been negligent or incompetent in the overall supervision of his or her department. The second, linked to the first, is whether he or she fulfils the requirements of explanation and amendatory action when things go wrong, for ministers are accountable to Parliament not only for their own actions but also for those of their department and this means giving information and explanations and, on occasions, making amends for departmental errors. The failure of a minister on either count may result in him or her being seen as culpable.

Ministerial negligence and incompetence

Ministers may be judged to be negligent or incompetent in fulfilling their role responsibility when they have failed adequately to supervise their departments, with the result that there has been "recurring or systematic poor performance". In such circumstances they are "responsible and accountable, even if the day-to-day administrative authority has been delegated". Role responsibility therefore reduces the situations in which ministers can abdicate responsibility by classifying all failures as "operational" and thus nothing to do with them. This was the response of ministers in 1994 when the newly established Child Support Agency failed by a long way to meet its performance targets or to accord with the standards of administration required of a public body. The chief executive resigned. However, the Committee on the Parliamentary Commissioner for Administration reported that maladministration within the Agency "could not be divorced from the responsibility of Ministers for the framework" which gave a greater priority to saving money than to the quality of the service, while the Social Security Committee noted that the agency's ability to operate effectively had been directly affected by the failure of ministers to ensure that the agency was properly established and adequately staffed and financed. Thus ministers had failed to fulfil the responsibility required by their role, namely to ensure that the agency was in a position to implement a new and complex government policy.

The judgment of negligence or incompetence may also be made when an inquiry into a specific incident finds systemic failures within the department. Such findings may promote "a reified conception of responsibility borne by an impersonal entity", but if the "manifest integrity of government systems" is to be sustained, it is essential for those in charge to bear responsibility, even when there is no direct causal link. There have been findings of systemic failures in a number of recent cases. Sir Richard Scott's 1996 investigation into the export of arms to Iraq reported such failings, as did Sir Thomas Legg's inquiry in 1998 into allegations that the Foreign Office had secretly sanctioned the supply of military equipment to Sierra Leone. Legg concluded that there had been no policy to breach the arms embargo and no conspiracy by officials to undermine government policy. He did, however, find that mistakes had been made and while some of these were attributed to individual officials, "systemic and cultural factors" were mainly responsible. No blame attached to the Foreign Secretary, Robin Cook, whose party had been in office for less than a year. However, Cook accepted that it was his responsibility to ensure that these failings were addressed and did not reoccur (see below for further discussion).

The Commission of Inquiry into the Cave Creek tragedy in New Zealand in 1995 also found "substantial systemic failure". Fourteen people had died after a viewing platform had collapsed in New Zealand's South Island. The Commission concluded that while the "proximate or dominant" cause of the collapse was that the platform had not been built in accordance with sound building practice, the "most significant secondary cause" was the Department of Conservation's failure to maintain an adequate project management system. The question was whether responsibility for such failure lay with the chief executive or the minister. The relationship between the two was a contractual one and a model of ministerial responsibility, based on causal responsibility, distanced the minister from responsibility, attributing blame away from him. As noted by Gregory:

In this view, under the terms of the contractual relationship between a minister and his/her chief executive, based on a reassertion of the old "policy/administration" dichotomy, the minister could not be held responsible for the failure of the DOC's chief executive and his staff to ensure that systems were in place to guarantee that the platform was correctly and safely built.

However, the inquiry had also found that the Department was underfunded. Thus, if the responsibility of the minister was seen as encompassing the supervision of the Department, the minister was not only "accountable to Parliament and the public for the actions of his departmental staff, he also had to accept responsibility for the tragedy, if only on the grounds that inadequate funding of the DOC had reinforced a culture of trying to do more with less". The result seems to have been a compromise. The Minister of Conservation resigned his conservation portfolio, "to express my sorrow for what happened", but assumed different departmental responsibilities and thus retained his position in Cabinet, while the chief executive remained in office for a further two years with a brief to take the appropriate corrective action to prevent a reoccurrence of such a disaster.

"Systemic failure" was also the finding of the Parliamentary Ombudsman, when he upheld claims of maladministration against the Department of Social Security in 2000. The Department had failed to inform those who might be affected that from April 2000 widows and widowers would only inherit half of their spouses' State Earnings Related Pension (SERPS). The Ombudsman's conclusion was supported by the Public Administration Committee which saw the omission as "a political and administrative failure that will cost the public purse many billions of pounds". It sought to determine who should take responsibility, recognising that systems cannot, of course, do so. In the event it was unable to locate responsibility in any one person, the errors having spanned too many years, but, nevertheless, explored the broader question of responsibility for systems failure.

In evidence before the Committee the permanent secretary of the Department of Social Security, Rachel Lomax, believed that responsibility for inadequate systems rested with Accounting Officers, that is with the official heads of departments, a view contested by Alistair Darling, the Secretary of State, who, speaking of the SERPS failure, said: "What I am clear about is that Ministers ... are responsible for what went on in their department at that time not the permanent secretary ... if you let the ministers off then you are never going to hold anyone to account really". Darling's response recognised the difference between the constitutional positions of ministers and permanent secretaries, whereby political responsibility resides with the individual minister, even after he or she has left office, but "administrative responsibility is indivisible and inherited by each incumbent of office from the last". Moreover, his view that it was ultimately the minister's responsibility to ensure that appropriate systems were in place in his department was supported by Peter Lilley, a previous Secretary of State for the department, who told the committee, "I accept full responsibility for everything which did or did not happen during the period I was Secretary of State". He also considered that, even though when in office his stated policy had been that he should be told bad news, "whether I was aware or not, in my view, does not affect my ultimate responsibility for it".

The implication of the statements by Darling and Lilley was that they saw themselves having a supervisory responsibility, which arose from their role or position as minister and which meant they were responsible for ensuring that systems were in place to prevent errors occurring and to provide them with the appropriate information. The Public Administration Committee concurred, concluding that ministers "are responsible for ensuring staff keep them fully informed and that their Departments have administrative systems that are in good working order".

As well as being subject to the charge of negligence or incompetence when systemic failures become evident, ministers may also find the charge levelled against them when they have failed to intervene in a department or agency within their responsibility. This was the position of the Scottish Minister, Sam Galbraith, after the credibility of the Scottish examination system was brought into question during the summer of 2000. A number of candidates, who had sat the Scottish Higher examinations, received inaccurate examination results. The body responsible was the Scottish Qualifying Authority, a non-departmental public body which not only operates at arm's length from the government but receives only 21 per cent of its funding from it, and in its inquiry into the incident the Enterprise and Lifelong Learning Committee found that "the failure ... occurred at an operational level within the organisation, below the level of governance". Moreover, it found "no evidence that Ministers, or their officials neglected their monitoring role". Indeed, the Committee stated: "[g]iven that the real problems were not being communicated by SQA staff to the Board, it is difficult to argue that Ministers should have been aware of, or responded to, these specific problems". Responsibility was, in fact, taken by the chief executive, who resigned from his position, and subsequently by the Chairman of the Board, who likewise relinquished office.

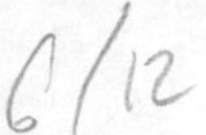

However, while there was no suggestion that there was a direct causal link between Galbraith and the errors made by the SQA, the Committee questioned "whether the appointment of the former chief executive, a Ministerial one, was appropriate, given his level of experience in managing a large organisation". It was also critical of Galbraith for lacking "a clearer overview of the strains present on the organisation". Thus the Minister was unable to escape blame completely. His role in relation to the agency required that he accepted responsibility for appointing a chief executive who, it seems, was not up to the job and for not recognising that changes in the examination requirements would inevitably create difficulties for the agency.

More serious, however, was the issue debated in the Scottish Parliament, which centred on whether Galbraith had failed to fulfil his responsibility as a minister by not taking action to minimise the consequences of the SQA's errors. He therefore had to answer for his role in the handling of the crisis which, some argued, was "not only complacent, but negligent – if not reckless". In the first motion of no confidence brought in the Scottish Parliament, Galbraith was criticised for not having exercised his power "to give SQA directions of a general or specific character with regard to the discharge of its functions" as soon as he knew there were difficulties in delivering accurate and timely results.

His detractors argued that he had the choice to "do something and delay the results, or do nothing and let them go out". In the event, rather than dismissing the chief executive and taking charge of the situation himself, he "chose to do nothing", and thus the results were released. Galbraith was also attacked for his decision to remain in office to "sort things out" which, his critics maintained, he had failed to do. Galbraith was in fact moved to another ministerial post after two months. For opponents this was an admission of fault. However, his government colleagues denied any culpability, arguing that the move had been necessary because "in an unfair world that has damaged the lives of many young people, their parents and their teachers, it would have seemed wrong to many of us if the minister with responsibility had stayed in post".

This suggested that Galbraith's relinquishing of responsibility for the SQA was a symbolic gesture, which showed acceptance of the notion that ministers have to take the bad along with the good. Like the Cave Creek tragedy, it seemed to be a compromise position, in which the government was saying – we do not accept the minister was culpable but, because of the impact of the errors, we will move him to another position. It was thus not any direct link between the minister and the cause which required him to take responsibility, but his failure to fulfil his supervisory role to the satisfaction of the public.

Explanatory and amendatory responsibility

The second issue on which role responsibility focuses is whether the minister responds adequately, in terms of explanation and amendatory action, when a serious error is made, for ministers, like all those whose responsibility arises because of their position or role, have "a moral obligation to do something to put [the error] right, for example to acknowledge it and to apologise, even though they are not morally to blame". As far as ministers are concerned this is also a political requirement. The emphasis in the political arena is on giving information and satisfying Parliament and the public that mistakes have been rectified and mechanisms established to prevent a reoccurrence of similar errors. This requires openness from ministers and accords with Sir Richard Scott's belief that the "key to ministerial accountability must surely be the *obligation to give information*". It also accords with the 1997 Parliamentary Resolution, embodied within the Ministerial Code, which states: "It is of paramount importance that ministers give accurate and truthful information to this House and its Committees ..." and are "as open as possible with this House and its Committees, refusing to provide information only when disclosure would not be in the public interest ...". Recognition of this obligation to provide information and explanation and to take appropriate amendatory action was apparent in Robin Cook's handling of the Sandline affair in 1998 and Jack Straw's response to the passport crisis in 1999.

When allegations were made that Foreign Office officials had sanctioned the supply of military equipment to Sierra Leone, the Foreign Secretary, Robin Cook, moved quickly to deny any ministerial involvement or knowledge and to state that any breach of the embargo would be a "serious matter" and contrary to British policy. He told the House that he was "trying to be frank and open about what has happened" and that he would return with more information when he had investigated further. Within a week, he was expressing confidence in his officials, stating that "in all the papers on this affair, I have found no evidence that officials in the Africa department were involved in any kind of conspiracy with Sandline [the company concerned] or gave any prior approval to a breach of the arms embargo". He, nevertheless, set up an inquiry, chaired by Sir Thomas Legg, to determine what had happened and subsequently published Legg's report. Moreover, he informed Parliament that he would be implementing a programme of 60 measures to improve the management of the Foreign Office and address Sir Thomas' concerns about the systemic and culture failures. He invited Parliament, through the Foreign Affairs Committee, to make sure that "the Foreign Office and I are harried, pursued and kept up to scratch in putting in place the program of reform".

This involvement of Parliament suggested a completion of the accountability cycle, whereby the giving of information and explanation is followed by amendatory action, the outcome of which is monitored by Parliament. On this occasion, it was marred by the Foreign Secretary's earlier lack of co-operation with the investigation by the Foreign Affairs Committee which, he maintained, merely duplicated that being undertaken by Legg. On this basis he initially refused any access to telegrams concerning events in Sierra Leone, or even to provide a summary of their contents, verified by nominated members of the committee. Access was granted subsequently but only on the proviso that confidentiality was respected until after Legg had reported. He also refused to allow departmental officials, other than the permanent secretary, to appear before the committee and even after the publication of the Legg Report he did not let the committee question all the officials concerned. However, while his actions impeded the Foreign Affairs Committee's inquiry, Cook seems to have been motivated by a belief that his officials should be protected from public blame rather than by a desire to be

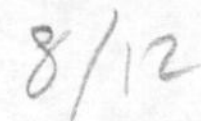

obstructive. Moreover, his speed in taking amendatory action and his involvement of the Foreign Affairs Committee as a monitor suggested an acceptance that his role as minister required him to exercise explanatory and amendatory accountability.

The second incident where an acceptance of this aspect of role responsibility was evident, was in the Home Secretary's handling of the Passport Agency crisis in the summer of 1999. Difficulties with a new computer system coincided with the requirement that children should be issued with their own passports, an unexpected upsurge in seasonal demand and a "run on the bank" as passport applications took longer to process. The resulting backlog of over 50,000 applications produced a loss in public confidence in the Agency and further pressure on it as applications were made in person rather than by post.

The Home Secretary not only explained what had happened but apologised personally to those queuing at the Petty France Passport Office. He also took amendatory action, intervening in some cases to ensure that passports were issued in time, compensation was paid to those whose travel plans had been disrupted and extra staff were employed to clear the backlog. Moreover, while his explanations and actions implied that the crisis was the result of agency mismanagement, he did not publicly blame and punish the chief executive, as Michael Howard had done in the case of the Prison Service Agency. His emphasis was rather on putting things right, although this did, in fact, include a change of chief executive. Before the Home Affairs select committee, the permanent secretary, David Ormand, gave a full explanation, stating that the fault lay with "inadequate planning", which meant that "the agency was operating on a very fine margin in terms of whether it would get through this summer". As it happened, despite "active management of this matter by ministers and the chief executive throughout", " 'the run on the bank' factor was more than it could cope with". Ormand apologised on behalf of the Home Office but noted: "The chain of command in the Passport Office is very clear. It is an executive agency, and the Home Secretary is accountable to Parliament for its activities. The [C]hief [E]xecutive is accountable to the Home Secretary for his performance." As performance was at fault, the chief executive designate was asked to take up his position early and, as a sign of its failure, the government removed the agency's Chartermark.

Although a question can be raised as to whether the "inadequate planning", held responsible for triggering the problem, was entirely the fault of the Agency, the Passport Office incident suggests a coming together of constitutional and managerial accountability, with the minister holding the chief executive to account for the responsibilities delegated under the agency framework agreement, while accepting role responsibility himself. Moreover, the removal of the Chartermark, which was a recognition of the Agency's accountability to consumers, indicated that a minister's supervisory responsibility not only includes ensuring the accountability of officials to select committees. It also includes ensuring their accountability to users. Role responsibility therefore acts to reinforce the changed government culture and managerial accountability.

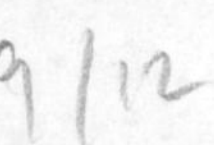

The effect of reformulation

The above cases suggest some recognition that ministerial responsibility is not only concerned with the personal actions or behaviour of ministers, in the sense of their direct involvement in errors, but with the responsibilities which attach to them because of their role or job. These responsibilities include the supervision of their departments and agencies, so that appropriate systems and procedures are in place, adequate resources are available for the effective implementation of policies, and chief executives have the necessary experience. They also include assuming direct control when things go wrong and fulfilling the requirements of explanatory and amendatory accountability. Such a formulation of ministerial responsibility which moves away from causal towards role responsibility is significant for accountability. It could be argued that the seeming concentration on role responsibility in the incidents considered only arose because there was no direct causal link between departmental errors and the minister. However, this link is seldom evident, although much political energy is spent trying to find it. In any case, the examples provide some useful indications of the requirements of role responsibility.

They also provide some indication of the effects of a reformulation of ministerial responsibility on officials, for it is not only the responsibility of ministers which become more transparent: so too do those of civil servants. Moreover, the emphasis on openness, "giving an account" and taking amendatory action makes it inevitable that they will be exposed to criticism and blame when things go wrong. This is not to suggest that such exposure has not happened in the past. Maxwell Fyfe's statement after *Crichel Down* suggested that ministers were not required to support officials who acted contrary to their policy and reports have, exceptionally, named and blamed officials for acting in such a way or for other failings. Moreover, the use of the policy/operations division, and its formalisation with the establishment of Next Steps agencies, has resulted in ministers themselves attributing blame to identified, or identifiable, officials, as was evident in the context of the Prison Service Agency, considered above. The problem lies in the thinness of the line between a minister reasonably blaming officials and unreasonably attributing blame in order to distance him or herself from culpability. The disciplining of an official in private, as part of the internal process of accountability, is one thing and is supported by the performance culture of managerial accountability and by the need for the minister to take amendatory action. The removal of an official in the full glare of publicity is another and confuses managerial and constitutional accountability.

Hence the need to move away from causal responsibility, with its emphasis on determining whether there has been direct ministerial involvement. This will not prevent the locating of blame in officials, which would seem unavoidable, and may, on occasions, be desirable, as part of being forthcoming about what has happened. However, it should minimise the extent to which ministers seek unreasonably to locate culpability, particularly if officials are given the opportunity to defend themselves before select committees against unfair accusations. The time has surely come when officials, who have delegated responsibilities, should be allowed to speak on their own behalf for these responsibilities. The Osmotherly Rules, which were designed to give effect to the principle that ministerial responsibility protects officials from public accountability, are now outdated, particularly as they apply to chief executives of Next Steps agencies, and, in reality, are frequently ignored where non-contentious agencies are concerned. The continued insistence of governments that they retain their current form would therefore seem to have little to do with protecting chief executives and more to do with protecting ministers from possible embarrassment.

The move towards greater government openness, including the Freedom of Information Act, will increase the exposure of officials, but could also expose instances where ministers have failed to give the required information and explanation to Parliament, or where they have been negligent or incompetent in the supervision of their departments. This could include failing to give officials adequate resources to fulfil their delegated responsibilities, failing to intervene when things start to go wrong, and failing to ensure that they are kept informed of potential, as well as actual, problems. Thus role responsibility does not narrow constitutional accountability by absolving ministers when things go wrong but suggests a more appropriate model of accountability which accords with the changes in the structure and culture of government and is supported by it. Moreover, the direct accountability of chief executives to the minister for their delegated responsibilities should work to strengthen the ability of the minister to assume a supervisory role. This strengthening of ministerial control over officials was part of the rationale for the establishment of agencies, and the subsequent extension of agency principles to heads of departments, in New Zealand and Australia. Such an aim has not been articulated in Britain. However, the effect of managerial accountability should be the same, namely, to provide ministers with the mechanisms for better oversight and control.

The need for such mechanisms was stressed by the Secretary of State for Social Security, Alistair Darling, when he told the Public Administration Committee's inquiry into the failings of the SERPS reforms that he had reorganised the department to "address the lack of end to end accountability". This included giving responsibility for the pensions directorate to a single official, "to ensure not only that the policy is right but also that the operational side of things functions effectively". As the Public Administration Committee commented, "the return of operational matters to the department might be thought to be at odds with the original purpose of the agency system". It would also seem to undermine the notion that policy and operations can be neatly separated. It was, however, deemed necessary by Darling if he was to exercise a supervisory responsibility for this activity.

Similarly, after the SQA crisis over examinations results, the Enterprise and Lifelong Learning Committee recommended "a strengthening of the relationship between the Minister and the SQA, and a move towards a much more rigorous performance management framework". It suggested that "this should involve reports on a monthly basis from the SQA, containing the 'hard core' management information". Moreover, it noted, "that similar proposals were made at UK level following the difficulties faced by the Passport Agency". The assumption by the minister of a supervisory responsibility thus requires the appropriate structures of managerial accountability to be in place.

Role responsibility locates the minister firmly at the head of his department. It also emphasises the fact that, under our system, ministers, not officials, take constitutional responsibility which should not be confused with, or by, managerial responsibility. There therefore needs to be an acceptance by ministers that they cannot abdicate responsibility for the oversight of their department. Thus when there have been serious departmental errors, they may be required to resign not because they personally caused them but because they are judged to have failed to fulfil the supervisory responsibility required of their role. Of course, whether a minister resigns will always depend on political considerations and the support, or otherwise, of the prime minister and party. Instances of resignation will therefore continue to be rare and the emphasis on role responsibility is not intended, necessarily, to increase them. Indeed, there is an argument for ministers remaining in office to correct errors and ensure they cannot be repeated. However, role responsibility could make constitutional accountability more open and more honest and prevent ministers from hiding behind the policy/operations division or arguing that they are "accountable" but not "responsible", for the emphasis will not be on finding a direct link between the minister and the cause, in the sense of determining whether he personally made the decision or took the action, but rather on whether he fulfilled his responsibilities as minister.

Conclusion

The reformulation of ministerial responsibility is not by itself sufficient to forward the cause of constitutional accountability, for while the focus on role responsibility may improve accountability at the macro, or political, level, there needs to be a corresponding improvement at the micro level. This requires adjustments to the way in which managerial accountability operates so that the division of responsibilities between ministers and officials is clear and the scope of delegation accurate. It is also essential that the information provided to select committees, which are ill-suited to the task of on-going audit and have little interest in it, is relevant and digestible, thus enabling meaningful scrutiny of routine departmental activities and specific matters of public concern.

For some, developments in managerial accountability, which may include further structural changes in government, need to precede any reform of constitutional accountability and there is logic in this view. However, there is a danger that a concentration on managerial accountability could result in mechanisms for accountability seeking to mirror the accounting regimes of private companies and focusing primarily on performance and the interests of efficiency. Such regimes are insufficient for the public sector, partly because the "preoccupation with technical competence and efficiency arguably tends to venerate the need of accountability as organisational control rather than promote the likelihood of responsibility as individual integrity". They may therefore undermine constitutional accountability. Moreover, while the interests of efficiency may be served by "bottom-line accountability", that is accountability for performance or results, those of constitutional accountability may not. They require scrutiny of policy and process, as well as results. They also require that those charged with holding government to account should set the agenda, rather than having it set for them, and that ministers, as part of the elected government, should be part of the accountability process, not detached from it. Managerial accountability, while important in its own right, should therefore be considered in the context of constitutional accountability, as an aid to improving it and making it easier for Parliament and its select committees and the public to hold government to account. This requires some rethinking of constitutional accountability. An emphasis on role, rather than causal, responsibility would seem to be a useful starting point for the process.

The debate about what exactly ministerial responsibility is, is by no means over and even though many years have passed since this article was written whether accountability is only for policy, or also for operational failures is by no means clear. However, what has been seen in recent years is an increase in Parliament's role in relation to high policy areas. In situations such as declarations of war, the ratification of Treaties and most recently the dissolution of Parliament ministers have not come to Parliament to inform, but to seek permission. This trend is seeing the diminution of prerogative powers as being in the exclusive hands of the executive, unfettered either by the courts or the legislature.

Further Reading

Blackburn, Robert 'The prerogative power of dissolution of Parliament: law, practice, and reform' [2009] *PL* 766

Feldman, David 'Parliamentary scrutiny of legislation and human rights', [2002] *PL* 323

Oliver, Dawn 'Improving the scrutiny of bills: the case for standards and checklists', [2006] *PL* 219

Woodhouse, Diana 'Ministerial responsibility: something old, something new', [1997] *PL* 262

Part B

Human Rights

7

The Human Rights Act – s6

Topic List

Christopher Costigan

Introduction

The Human Rights Act 1998 was one of a number of important constitutional reforms introduced by the New Labour government in its first term of office. It enables people within the United Kingdom to bring an action in the domestic courts against public authorities for breaches of rights contained in the European Convention on Human Rights. In addition, it places an obligation on the courts to try to interpret legislation in a Convention-compatible way, or gives them discretion to declare a piece of legislation incompatible with a Convention right.

1 The Human Rights Act: Definition of Public Authority

In the preface to the White Paper the then Prime Minister, Tony Blair, set out his reasons for enacting the Human Rights Act.

'Rights Brought Home: The Human Rights Bill': Command Paper No Cm 3782, Preface

It [The Human Rights Bill] will give people in the United Kingdom opportunities to enforce their rights under the European Convention in British courts rather than having to incur the cost and delay of taking a case to the European Human Rights Commission and Court in Strasbourg. It will enhance the awareness of human rights in our society. And it stands alongside our decision to put the promotion of human rights at the forefront of our foreign policy.

It was estimated that bringing an action before the European Court of Human Rights could take up to five years and cost a litigant up to £30,000.

The three central provisions in the Human Rights Act are sections 3, 4 and 6.

Section 6 and the definition of 'public authority'

Section 6 is the cornerstone of the Human Rights Act.

Following the wide-scale abuse of human rights in the Second World War the European Convention was written to place an obligation on sovereign states to protect the rights of people within their jurisdictions. If a state failed to protect the rights of people within its jurisdiction there were mechanisms either for individuals or for another signatory state to bring an action in international law to punish the offending country.

The Human Rights Act was designed with the same purpose in mind: it places an obligation on UK public authorities to protect Convention rights within the UK and creates a cause of action if a public authority fails to do so. The key to the effective protection of human rights is therefore bound up in how widely or narrowly the definition of 'public authority' in section 6 is interpreted.

While no definition of public authority was given in the Human Rights Act, it was emphasised in the White Paper that the term should be interpreted widely.

'Rights Brought Home: The Human Rights Bill': Command Paper No Cm 3782, Para 2.2

> The definition of what constitutes a public authority is in wide terms. Examples of persons or organisations whose acts or omissions it is intended should be able to be challenged include central government (including executive agencies); local government; the police; immigration officers; prisons; courts and tribunals themselves; and, to the extent that they are exercising public functions, companies responsible for areas of activity which were previously within the public sector, such as the privatised utilities.

This was echoed by the sponsors of the Bill in Parliament, but the matter was then left to the courts.

The Court of Appeal, led by the then Lord Chief Justice, Lord Woolf, got the opportunity to begin to define the term 'public authority' in two key early cases. In *Poplar Housing and Regeneration Community Association Ltd v Donoghue* [2001] EWCA Civ 595, [2002] QB 48 it was determined that a housing association, to which the local authority had transferred all its housing stock and retained a high level of control, was a public authority for the purpose of the Human Rights Act s 6(3)(b), with Lord Woolf CJ concluding:

> ... As is the position on applications for judicial review, there is no clear demarcation line which can be drawn between public and private bodies and functions. In a borderline case, such as this, the decision is very much one of fact and degree. Taking into account all the circumstances, we have come to the conclusion that while activities of housing associations need not involve the performance of public functions, in this case, in providing accommodation for the defendant and then seeking possession, the role of Poplar is so closely assimilated to that of Tower Hamlets that it was performing public and not private functions. Poplar therefore is a functional public authority, at least to that extent. We emphasise that this does not mean that all Poplar's functions are public.

R (on the application of Heather and others) v Leonard Cheshire Foundation and another [2002] EWCA Civ 366, [2002] 2 All ER 936 concerned the status of a charitable organisation which provided accommodation to the elderly. Some of its residents were privately funded, and others were housed pursuant to contracts with the local authority which was under an obligation to provide such housing. In deciding that the charity was not a public authority, Lord Woolf CJ said:

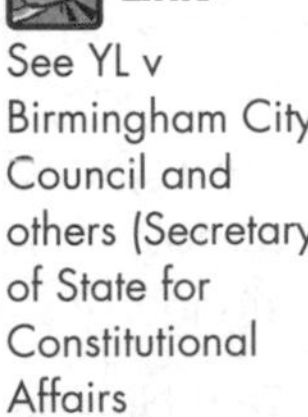

Link

See YL v Birmingham City Council and others (Secretary of State for Constitutional Affairs interviewing) [2007] UKHL27 [2008] 1 AC 95

> [35] ... In our judgment the role that LCF was performing manifestly did not involve the performance of public functions. The fact that LCF is a large and flourishing organisation does not change the nature of its activities from private to public. (i) It is not in issue that it is possible for LCF to perform some public functions and some private functions. In this case it is contended that this was what has been happening in regard to those residents who are privately funded and those residents who are publicly funded. But in this case except for the resources needed to fund the residents of the different occupants of Le Court, there is no material distinction between the nature of

the services LCF has provided for residents funded by a local authority and those provided to residents funded privately. While the degree of public funding of the activities of an otherwise private body is certainly relevant as to the nature of the functions performed, by itself it is not determinative of whether the functions are public or private... (ii) There is no other evidence of there being a public flavour to the functions of LCF or LCF itself. LCF is not standing in the shoes of the local authorities... LCF is not exercising statutory powers in performing functions for the appellants. (iii) In truth, all that Mr Gordon can rely upon is the fact that if LCF is not performing a public function the appellants would not be able to rely upon art 8 as against LCF. However, this is a circular argument. If LCF was performing a public function, that would mean that the appellants could rely in relation to that function on art 8, but, if the situation is otherwise, art 8 cannot change the appropriate classification of the function. On the approach adopted in *Poplar Housing and Regeneration Community Association Ltd v Donoghue* [2001] 4 All ER 604, [2002] QB 48, it can be said that LCF is clearly not performing any public function.

These two cases both dealt with situations where a local authority had 'contracted out' its obligations. However, in both cases the court (headed by Lord Woolf CJ) came to a different conclusion. In *Poplar* the court decided that the housing authority was a hybrid public authority because of the level of 'enmeshment' between the local authority and the housing authority: there was a close relationship between the two bodies. However, in *Leonard Cheshire Foundation* that degree of proximity was not present: the Foundation acted independently of the local authority and provided the same service to both its privately and publicly funded clients. Lord Woolf CJ could see no reason why a private company providing a service through contracting-out arrangement with a public authority should thereby take on obligations under the Human Rights Act. These judgments were criticised as creating a gap in human rights protection, where the rights of the most vulnerable in society would not be protected because of the service arrangements of local authorities.

House of Lords and House of Commons Joint Select Committee on Human Rights: The Meaning of Public Authority under the Human Rights Act (Seventh Report of Sessions 2003-4) HL Paper 39

Public authorities under the Human Rights Act: the parliamentary debates

18. Ministerial statements during debates on the Human Rights Bill indicated that the purpose of the "public function" test under section 6(3)(b) was to make the Act comprehensive rather than restrictive in its application, in accordance with the principle that delegation did not absolve the State of responsibility. The then Lord Chancellor, Lord Irvine of Lairg, noted that the drafting of the relevant provisions was designed to "provide as much protection as possible for the rights of the individual against the misuse of power by the State". There was a deliberate and considered decision to reject a more prescriptive approach and list those bodies subject to responsibilities under the Act...

19. Statements by the then Home Secretary and the then Lord Chancellor in the parliamentary debates in both Houses made it clear that privatised or contracted-out public services were intended to be brought within the scope of the Act by the "public function" provision. It was also made clear that the Government intended the provisions of the Act to be adaptable to the changing structures of public realm, and to changes in the distribution of power and responsibility for factors affecting individual rights—

The Government have a direct responsibility for core bodies, such as central Government and the police, but they also have a responsibility for other public authorities, in so far as the actions of such authorities impinge on private individuals. The Bill had to have a definition ... that went at least as wide and took account of the fact that, over the past 20 years, an increasingly large number of private bodies, such as companies and charities, have come to exercise public functions that were previously exercised by public authorities.

...

For example, charities that operate ... in the area of homelessness, no doubt do exercise public functions. The NSPCC, for example, exercises statutory functions which are of a public nature, although it is a charity.

20. It was left to the courts to interpret the legislation to determine exactly where the lines between public and private functions should be drawn. It is quite clear that Parliament envisaged that the scope of section 6(3)(b) should be based primarily on the nature of the function being performed by a private body, rather than the intrinsic nature of the body itself. In a key statement the Home Secretary explained—

As we are dealing with public functions and with an evolving situation, we believe that the test must relate to the substance and nature of the act, not to the form and legal personality.

A gap in human rights protection?

41. The tests being applied by the courts to determine whether a function is a "public function" within the meaning of section 6(3)(b) of the Human Rights Act are, in human rights terms, highly problematic. Their application results in many instances where an organisation "stands in the shoes of the State" and yet does not have responsibilities under the Human Rights Act. It means that the protection of human rights is dependent not on the type of power being exercised, nor on its capacity to interfere with human rights, but on the relatively arbitrary (in human rights terms) criterion of the body's administrative links with institutions of the State. The European Convention on Human Rights provides no basis for such a limitation, which calls into question the capacity of the Human Rights Act to bring rights home to the full extent envisaged by those who designed, debated and agreed the Act.

...

43. We asked the Secretary of State for Constitutional Affairs whether he considered the current legal position to be unsatisfactory. He expressed some concern at the way the law was developing but noted—

It is early days. I can fully understand why some people believe that the words "public authority" have been drawn too narrowly, compared with what was said at the time. All I can say at this stage is that I shall keep this concern under close review, and will pay particular attention to the need to intervene in future cases on the meaning of section 6(3)(b)...

44. **This is not just a theoretical legal problem. The development of the case law has significant and immediate practical implications.**

The House of Lords had its first opportunity to consider the issue of the definition of 'public authority' in 2003.

***Aston Cantlow and Wilmcote with Billesley Parochial Church Council v Wallbank and Another* [2003] UKHL 37, [2004] 1 AC 546**

Statute: The Human Rights Act 1998 s 6

Panel: Lord Nicholls of Birkenhead, Lord Hope of Craighead, Lord Hobhouse of Woodborough, Lord Scott of Foscote and Lord Rodger of Earlsferry

Facts: The defendants, as lay rectors of the parish of Aston Cantlow, were responsible for maintenance of the church chancel. In 1994 the claimant served the defendant with a notice for repair. The defendants disputed liability and the claimant brought an action. The Court of Appeal decided the cost of repair could not be recovered because this would represent a breach of part of the Convention, and the claimant was deemed to be a public authority within the meaning of the Human Rights Act s 6 and therefore could not act incompatibly with Convention rights. The claimant appealed.

LORD NICHOLLS OF BIRKENHEAD

6. The expression "public authority" is not defined in the Act, nor is it a recognised term of art in English law, that is, an expression with a specific recognised meaning. The word "public" is a term of uncertain import, used with many different shades of meaning: public policy, public rights of way, public property, public authority (in the Public Authorities Protection Act 1893 (56 & 57 Vict c 61)), public nuisance, public house, public school, public company. So in the present case the statutory context is all important. As to that, the broad purpose sought to be achieved by section 6(1) is not in doubt. The purpose is that those bodies for whose acts the state is answerable before the European Court of Human Rights shall in future be subject to a domestic law obligation not to act incompatibly with Convention rights. If they act in breach of this legal obligation victims may henceforth obtain redress from the courts of this country. In future victims should not need to travel to Strasbourg.

7 Conformably with this purpose, the phrase "a public authority" in section 6(1) is essentially a reference to a body whose nature is governmental in a broad sense of that expression. It is in respect of organisations of this nature that the government is answerable under the European Convention on Human Rights. Hence, under the Human Rights Act 1998 a body of this nature is required to act compatibly with Convention rights in everything it does. The most obvious examples are government

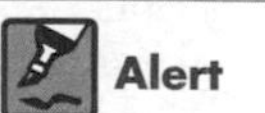
Alert

departments, local authorities, the police and the armed forces. Behind the instinctive classification of these organisations as bodies whose nature is governmental lie factors such as the possession of special powers, democratic accountability, public funding in whole or in part, an obligation to act only in the public interest, and a statutory constitution: see the valuable article by Professor Dawn Oliver, "The Frontiers of the State: Public Authorities and Public Functions under the Human Rights Act": [2000] PL 476.

8. A further, general point should be noted. One consequence of being a "core" public authority, namely, an authority falling within section 6 without reference to section 6(3), is that the body in question does not itself enjoy Convention rights. It is difficult to see how a core public authority could ever claim to be a victim of an infringement of a Convention rights... This feature, that a core public authority is incapable of having Convention rights of its own, is a matter to be borne in mind when considering whether or not a particular body is a core public authority. In itself this feature throws some light on how the expression "public authority" should be understood and applied. It must always be relevant to consider whether Parliament can have been intended that the body in question should have no Convention rights.

9. In a modern developed state governmental functions extend far beyond maintenance of law and order and defence of the realm. Further, the manner in which wide ranging governmental functions are discharged varies considerably. In the interests of efficiency and economy, and for other reasons, functions of a governmental nature are frequently discharged by non-governmental bodies. Sometimes this will be a consequence of privatisation, sometimes not. One obvious example is the running of prisons by commercial organisations. Another is the discharge of regulatory functions by organisations in the private sector, for instance, the Law Society. Section 6(3)(b) gathers this type of case into the embrace of section 6 by including within the phrase "public authority" any person whose functions include "functions of a public nature". This extension of the expression "public authority" does not apply to a person if the nature of the act in question is "private".

10. Again, the statute does not amplify what the expression "public" and its counterpart "private" mean in this context. But, here also, given the statutory context already mentioned and the repetition of the description "public", essentially the contrast being drawn is between functions of a governmental nature and functions, or acts, which are not of that nature. I stress, however, that this is no more than a useful guide. The phrase used in the Act is public function, not governmental function.

11. Unlike a core public authority, a "hybrid" public authority, exercising both public functions and non-public functions, is not absolutely disabled from having Convention rights. A hybrid public authority is not a public authority in respect of an act of a private nature. Here again, as with section 6(1), this feature throws some light on the approach to be adopted when interpreting section 6(3)(b). Giving a generously wide scope to the expression "public function" in section 6(3)(b) will further the statutory aim of promoting the observance of human rights values without depriving the bodies in question of the ability themselves to rely on Convention rights when necessary.

12. What, then, is the touchstone to be used in deciding whether a function is public for this purpose? Clearly there is no single test of universal application. There cannot be, given the diverse nature of governmental functions and the variety of means by which these functions are discharged today. Factors to be taken into account include the extent to which in carrying out the relevant function the body is publicly funded, or is exercising statutory powers, or is taking the place of central government or local authorities, or is providing a public service.

Appeal allowed.

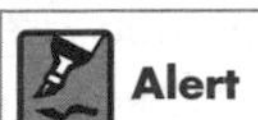

Following this case, it is possible to say that there are three types of public authority for the purposes of the HRA. First, there are courts and tribunals which are specified in section 6(3)(a) of the Act. Second, there are 'core' public authorities, which are, according to Lord Nicholls, instinctively governmental in nature and are created by use of the term 'public authority' in s 6(1). These authorities must act compatibly in relation to everything they do, and do not themselves have Convention rights. In order to determine whether a body is a core public authority, it is necessary to look at the nature of the body itself, and Lord Nicholls gives helpful guidance on the sorts of characteristics that body might have. The third type of public authority are functional or 'hybrid' public authorities. The courts will determine these by applying a combination of sections 6(3)(b) and 6(5) and by identifying the function being performed by the body and secondly assessing its nature: whether it can be seen as public or private. Again, Lord Nicholls gives helpful guidance as to the sorts of characteristics this function may have.

After *Aston Cantlow* a question still remained over the position of private organisations providing services to the public through contracting-out arrangements. Their Lordships had not directly dealt with the issue, but the breadth of Lord Nicholls' characteristics of what would make a function 'public' is arguably broad enough to have impliedly overruled *Leonard Cheshire*. The House of Lords got the opportunity to decide this question in 2007 in a case which was factually very similar to the *Leonard Cheshire* case. In this case, the Lord Chancellor, Jack Straw (who was the sponsor of the Human Rights Bill during its passage through the House of Commons), appeared as an intervener arguing that the service provider *should* be defined as a functional or hybrid public authority.

YL v Birmingham City Council and others (Secretary of State for Constitutional Affairs intervening) **[2007] UKHL 27, [2008] 1 AC 95**

See also *Leonard Cheshire*

Statutes: The European Convention on Human Rights art. 8; National Assistance Act 1948 ss 21 and 26; The Human Rights Act 1998 s 6

Panel: Lord Bingham of Cornhill, Lord Scott of Foscote, Baroness Hale of Richmond, Lord Mance and Lord Neuberger of Abbotsbury

Facts: The defendant council was under a duty to house the claimant. The council discharged that duty by using public funds (save for a small top-up fee) to place the claimant with the second defendant, a private provider of health and social care services. The care home sought to terminate the contract and the claimant brought an action arguing that in the provision of care the second defendant was performing a public function and it was therefore required to protect her Convention rights. The judge and Court of Appeal held that the second defendant was not exercising a public function. YL appealed.

LORD BINGHAM OF CORNHILL

20. When the 1998 Act was passed, it was very well known that a number of functions formerly carried out by public authorities were now carried out by private bodies. Section 6(3)(b) of the 1998 Act was clearly drafted with this well-known fact in mind. The performance by private body A by arrangement with public body B, and perhaps at the expense of B, of what would undoubtedly be a public function if carried out by B is, in my opinion, precisely the case which section 6(3)(b) was intended to embrace. It is, in my opinion, this case.

LORD SCOTT OF FOSCOTE

25. ... Southern Cross is a company carrying on a socially useful business for profit. It is neither a charity nor a philanthropist. It enters into private law contracts with the residents in its care homes and with the local authorities with whom it does business. It receives no public funding, enjoys no special statutory powers, and is at liberty to accept or reject residents as it chooses (subject, of course, to anti-discrimination legislation which affects everyone who offers a service to the public) and to charge whatever fees in its commercial judgment it thinks suitable. It is operating in a commercial market with commercial competitors.

...

27. A number of the features which have been relied on by YL and the intervenors seems to me to carry little weight. It is said, correctly, that most of the residents in the Southern Cross care homes, including YL, are placed there by local authorities pursuant to their statutory duty under section 21 of the 1948 Act and that their fees are, either wholly or partly, paid by the local authorities or, where special nursing is required, by health authorities. But the fees charged by Southern Cross and paid by local or health authorities are charged and paid for a service. There is no element whatever of subsidy from public funds. It is a misuse of language and misleading to describe Southern Cross as publicly funded. If an outside private contractor is engaged on ordinary commercial terms to provide the cleaning services, or the catering and cooking services, or any other essential services at a local authority owned care home, it seems to me absurd to suggest that the private contractor, in earning its commercial fee for its business services, is publicly funded or is carrying on a function of a public nature. It is simply carrying on its private business with a customer who happens to be a public authority. The owner of a private care home taking local authority funded residents is in no different position. It is simply providing a service or services for which it charges a commercial fee.

BARONESS HALE OF RICHMOND

Functions of a public nature

65. ...While there cannot be a single litmus test of what is a function of a public nature, the underlying rationale must be that it is a task for which the public, in the shape of the state, have assumed responsibility, at public expense if need be, and in the public interest.

66. One important factor is whether the state has assumed responsibility for seeing that this task is performed. In this case, there can be no doubt that the state has undertaken the responsibility of securing that the assessed community care needs of the people to whom section 21(1)(a) of the National Assistance Act 1948 applies are met. In the modern "mixed economy of care", those needs may be met in a number of ways. But it is artificial and legalistic to draw a distinction between meeting those needs and the task of assessing and arranging them, when the state has assumed responsibility for seeing that both are done.

67. Another important factor is the public interest in having that task undertaken. In a state which cares about the welfare of the most vulnerable members of the community, there is a strong public interest in having people who are unable to look after themselves, whether because of old age, infirmity, mental or physical disability or youth, looked after properly. They must be provided with the specialist care, including the health care, that they need even if they are unable to arrange or pay for it themselves. No-one can doubt that providing health care can be a public function, even though it can also be provided purely privately. This home was providing health care by arrangement with the National Health Service as well as social care by arrangement with the local social services authority. It cannot be doubted that the provision of health care was a public function.

68. Another important factor is public funding. Not everything for which the state pays is a public function. The supply of goods and ancillary services such as laundry to a care home may well not be a public function. But providing a service to individual members of the public at public expense is different. These are people for whom the public have assumed responsibility. There may be other residents in the home for whom the public have not assumed responsibility. They may not have a remedy against the home under the Human Rights Act, although there may well be circumstances in which they would. But they will undoubtedly benefit from the human rights values which must already infuse the home's practices as a result of clause 55.1 of the service provision contract.

...

71. Finally, then, there is the close connection between this service and the core values underlying the Convention rights and the undoubted risk that rights will be violated unless adequate steps are taken to protect them.

Conclusion

73. Taken together, these factors lead inexorably to the conclusion that the company, in providing accommodation, health and social care for the appellant, was performing a function of a public nature. This was a function performed for the appellant pursuant to statutory arrangements, at public expense and in the public interest. I have no doubt that Parliament intended that it be covered by section 6(3)(b).

LORD MANCE

106. ...Of some interest is however a power conferred on the Secretary of State by section 5 of the Freedom of Information Act to designate as a public authority for the purposes of the Act any person not listed who either "(a) appears ... to exercise functions of a public nature, or (b) is providing under a contract made with a public authority any service whose provision is a function of that authority". The careful distinction between (a) and (b) highlights the point that a person with whom a public authority contracts for a service which it is the function of that authority to provide is not axiomatically exercising a function of a public nature. Under the Freedom of Information Act, there might be reason to extend the benefit of the Act to such a person. But section 6(3)(b) of the 1998 Act only extends the concept of a public authority to a person within (a).

LORD NEUBERGER OF ABBOTSBURY

The argument based on "contracting-out"

152. ...I consider that, in answer to the policy argument for allowing this appeal on the basis of contracting-out, there is a policy argument for dismissing it on the same basis. It is thought to be desirable, in some circumstances, to encourage core public authorities to contract-out services, and it may well be inimical to that policy if section 6(1) automatically applied to the contractor as it would to the authority. Indeed, unattractive though it may be to some people, one of the purposes of contracting-out at least certain services previously performed by local authorities may be to avoid some of the legal constraints and disadvantages which apply to local authorities but not to private operators. I am in no position to decide on the relative strength of the two competing policy arguments: that is a matter for the legislature. However, the fact that there are competing arguments makes it hard to justify the courts resolving the instant issue by reference to policy.

153. ...[I]t does not seem to me that, as a matter of ordinary language, an activity is " a function of a public nature" merely because it is contracted-out, as opposed to its being provided directly, by a core public authority. If an activity were thereby automatically rendered such a function, it would mean that activities such as providing meals or cleaning and repairing buildings could be caught. Referring again to the Ministry of Defence contracting for the manufacture of military materiel, it seems to me that the private manufacturer's activities would not be within section 6(3)(b) even though the Ministry could have manufactured the materiel in its own factory.

...

Conclusion

170 Accordingly, for the reasons given by Lord Mance, as well for those given by Lord Scott, and for the additional reasons I have set out, I am of the view that the provision of care and accommodation by Southern Cross to Mrs YL, even though it was arranged, and is being paid for, by Birmingham pursuant to sections 21 to 26 of the 1948 Act, does not constitute a "function of a public nature" within section 6(3)(b) . Accordingly, I would dismiss this appeal.

171. Finally, it is right to add this. It may well be thought to be desirable that residents in privately owned care homes should be given Convention rights against the proprietors. That is a subject on which there are no doubt opposing views, and I am in no position to express an opinion. However, if the legislature considers such a course appropriate, then it would be right to spell it out in terms, and, in the process, to make it clear whether the rights should be enjoyed by all residents of such care homes, or only certain classes (eg those whose care and accommodation is wholly or partly funded by a local authority).

Appeal dismissed.

This decision clears up the position regarding 'contracting out': the mere fact of contracting out, without more, does not make the provision of a service a public function. However, the decision was a close one, with their Lordships split three to two.

In his final paragraph, Lord Neuberger suggests that the competing policy decisions make this a matter for Parliament, and that it should express in terms whether the Human Rights Act would apply to private and publicly funded residents. Parliament in fact responded to this in the Health and Social Care Act 2008 s 145, which specifically states that social care contracted-out through the National Assistance Act is a function of a public nature for the purposes of the Human Rights Act s 6(3)(b). However, in relation to the provision of other contracted-out services, the law as stated in *YL* is still good law: without more, the function is private.

The cases of *Leonard Cheshire*, *YL* and *Aston Cantlow* focused on the Human Rights Act section 6(3)(b): whether the function was public. Because in these cases it was found that the nature of the function was not public, consideration was not given as to s 6(5), which focuses not on the function but the actual act being performed. This distinction was not drawn in *Poplar*, but was discussed in *R (on the application of Weaver) v London & Quadrant Housing Trust* [2009] EWCA Civ 587, [2010] 1 WLR 363.

R (on the application of Weaver) v London & Quadrant Housing Trust [2009] EWCA Civ 587, [2010] 1 WLR 363

Panel: Rix and Collins LJ (now Lord Collins of Mapesbury) and Elias LJ

Statute: The Human Rights Act 1998 ss 6(1), (3)(b) and (5)

Facts: Weaver was an assured tenant of London & Quadrant Housing Trust. Quadrant served her with an order for possession for non-payment of rent. Weaver challenged this in the Divisional Court on the basis of a legitimate expectation and her Article 8 Convention rights. The Convention argument relied on the establishment of the legitimate expectation. The Divisional Court found that there was no legitimate expectation and so the claim failed. However, they granted a declaration that Quadrant was a hybrid public authority in relation to the management and allocation of its housing stock. Quadrant appealed against this decision.

LORD JUSTICE ELIAS

27. The effect of these provisions [section 6(1), (3)(b) and (5)] is that some bodies, conventionally referred to as "core authorities", are public authorities for all purposes. They must at all times act in accordance with Convention rights; subsection (5) is inapplicable to such bodies. By contrast, subsection (3)(b) identifies and brings within the scope of the Act what is termed a "hybrid authority" i.e. one which exercises both public and private functions. Where its acts are in issue, the relevant question is whether the nature of the act is private. If it is then subsection (5) provides that it will not be deemed to be a public authority with respect to that particular act.

28. Accordingly, once it is determined that the body concerned is a hybrid authority - in other words that it exercises functions at least some of which are of a public nature - the only relevant question is whether the act in issue is a private act. Even if the particular act under consideration is connected in some way with the exercise of a public function, it may nonetheless be a private one. Not all acts concerned with carrying out a public function will be public acts. Conversely, it is also logically possible for an act not to be a private act notwithstanding that the function with which it is most closely connected is a private function, although it is difficult to envisage such a case. Such situations are likely to be extremely rare.

29. The concept of "functions" is not altogether straightforward, nor is the distinction between functions and acts...

The authorities

34. It is not necessary to analyse in detail the individual speeches of their Lordships in these two cases [*YL* and *Aston Cantlow*], not least because the principles which they establish are relatively clear and were not in dispute before us. The real issue lies not in identifying the principles, but rather in determining the result of their application to the particular circumstances of this case.

...

36. Their Lordships ... identified certain factors which will generally have little, if any, weight when determining the public status. First, the fact that the function is one which is carried out by a public body does not mean that it is a public function when carried out by a potentially hybrid body. The point was powerfully and cogently made by Lord Scott in *YL*, paras 30-31. He highlighted the anomalies and absurdities that would result if this were the case. Second, it will often be of no real relevance that the functions are subject to detailed statutory regulation. Again, as Lord Neuberger pointed out in *YL* (para. 134):

"the mere fact that the public interest required a service to be closely regulated and supervised pursuant to statutory rules, cannot mean the provision of a service, as opposed to its regulation and supervision, is a function of a public nature. Otherwise, for example, companies providing financial services, running restaurants, or manufacturing hazardous materials, would ipso facto be susceptible to be within the ambit of section 6(1)."

...

Discussion and conclusions

66. The essential question is whether the act of terminating the tenancy is a private act. When considering how to characterise the nature of the act, it is in my view important to focus on the context in which the act occurs; the act cannot be considered in isolation simply asking whether it involves the exercise of a private law power or not. As Lord Mance observed in *YL*, both the source and nature of the activities need to be considered when deciding whether a function is public or not, and in my view the same [is] required when determining whether an act is a private act or not within the meaning of section 6(5). Indeed, the difficulty of distinguishing between acts and functions reinforces that conclusion.

67. In this case there are a number of features which in my judgment bring the act of terminating a social tenancy within the purview of the Human Rights Act.

68. A useful starting point is to analyse the Trust's function of allocating and managing housing with respect to the four criteria identified by Lord Nicholls in paragraph 12 in the *Aston Cantlow* case, reproduced above. First, there is a significant reliance on public finance; there is a substantial public subsidy which enables the Trust to achieve its objectives. This does not involve, as in *YL*, the payment of money by reference to specific services provided but significant capital payments designed to enable the Trust to meet its publicly desirable objectives.

69. Second, although not directly taking the place of local government, the Trust in its allocation of social housing operates in very close harmony with it, assisting it to achieve the authority's statutory duties and objectives. In this context the allocation agreements play a particularly important role and in practice severely circumscribe the freedom of the Trust to allocate properties. This is not simply the exercise of choice by the RSL but is the result of a statutory duty to co-operate. That link is reinforced by the extent to which there has been a voluntary transfer of housing stock from local authorities to RSLs.

70. Third, the provision of subsidised housing, as opposed to the provision of housing itself, is, in my opinion a function which can properly be described as governmental. Almost by definition it is the antithesis of a private commercial activity. The provision of subsidy to meet the needs of the poorer section of the community is typically, although not necessarily, a function which government provides. The Trust, as one of the larger RSLs, makes a valuable contribution to achieving the government's objectives of providing subsidised housing. For similar reasons it seems to me that it can properly be

described as providing a public service of a nature described in the Lord Nicholls' fourth factor.

71. Furthermore, these factors, which point in favour of treating its housing functions as public functions, are reinforced by the following considerations. First, the Trust is acting in the public interest and has charitable objectives. I agree with the Divisional Court that this at least places it outside the traditional area of private commercial activity. Second, the regulation to which it is subjected is not designed simply to render its activities more transparent, or to ensure proper standards of performance in the public interest. Rather the regulations over such matters as rent and eviction are designed, at least in part, to ensure that the objectives of government policy with respect to this vulnerable group in society are achieved and that low cost housing is effectively provided to those in need of it. Moreover, it is intrusive regulation on various aspects of allocation and management, and even restricts the power to dispose of land and property.

72. None of these factors taken in isolation would suffice to make the functions of the provision of housing public functions, but I am satisfied that when considered cumulatively, they establish sufficient public flavour to bring the provision of social housing by this particular RSL within that concept. That is particularly so given that their Lordships have emphasised the need to give a broad and generous construction to the concept of a hybrid authority.

Is termination of a tenancy a private act?

73. That still leaves the central question whether the act of termination itself can nonetheless be treated as a private act. Can it be said that since it involves the exercise of a contractual power, it is therefore to be characterised solely as a private act? It is true that in both *Aston Cantlow* and *YL* it is possible to find observations which appear to support an affirmative answer to that question...

75. In my judgment, that would be a misreading of those decisions. The observations about private acts in *Aston Cantlow* and *YL* were in a context where it had already been determined that the function being exercised was not a public function. I do not consider that their Lordships would have reached the same conclusion if they had found that the nature of the functions in issue in those cases were public functions.

76. In my judgment, the act of termination is so bound up with the provision of social housing that once the latter is seen, in the context of this particular body, as the exercise of a public function, then acts which are necessarily involved in the regulation of the function must also be public acts. The grant of a tenancy and its subsequent termination are part and parcel of determining who should be allowed to take advantage of this public benefit. This is not an act which is purely incidental or supplementary to the principal function, such as contracting out the cleaning of the windows of the Trust's properties. That could readily be seen as a private function of a kind carried on by both public and private bodies. No doubt the termination of such a contract would be a private act (unless the body were a core public authority).

77. In my opinion, if an act were necessarily a private act because it involved the exercise of rights conferred by private law, that would significantly undermine the protection which Parliament intended to afford to potential victims of hybrid authorities. Public bodies necessarily fulfil their functions by entering into contractual arrangements. It would severely limit the significance of identifying certain bodies as hybrid authorities if the fact that the act under consideration was a contractual act meant that it was a private act falling within section 6(5).

...

80. A point which then arises is whether the protection afforded by the Human Rights Act will extend to all tenants of the Trust who are in social housing or only those in properties which were acquired as a result of state grants. I agree with the Divisional Court that it should be all those in social housing. The effect of the grant is not merely to assist the Trust (and other RSLs similarly placed) in being able to provide low cost housing to the tenants in the properties acquired by the grant; it necessarily has a wider impact, and bears upon its ability to provide social housing generally. Furthermore, it would be highly unsatisfactory if the protection of human rights' law depended upon the fortuitous fact whether a tenant happened to be allocated to housing acquired with a grant or not.

81. It does not follow, however, that all tenants of the Trust will receive the same protection. Mr Drabble conceded, I think probably correctly, that human rights' principles will not apply to those tenants of the Trust (a relatively small proportion, it seems) who are not housed in social housing at all. If the tenants are paying market rents in the normal way, then no question of subsidy arises. It is not obvious why the tenant should be in any different position to tenants in the private sector where human rights principles are inapplicable.

82. The effect of drawing this distinction does not lead to the unattractive consequence which would have resulted had the care home been held to have been a hybrid authority in *YL*, namely that two persons, each subject to the same level of care in the same care home, could be subject to different degrees of legal protection. Indeed, the distinction between those in social housing and those paying market rates merely mirrors the current distinction between those housed in local authority accommodation, who do have human rights protection with respect to evictions, and those housed in the private sector who do not.

LORD COLLINS OF MAPESBURY

96. ...[M]any acts which are in pursuance of performance of functions of a public nature will be private acts. Even if the provision of social housing were a public function, it could not be suggested that the termination of a contract with a builder to repair one of the houses in the housing stock was other than a private act.

100. Elias LJ is of the view that the source of the power will be a relevant factor in determining whether the act in question is in the nature of a private act or not. I would go somewhat further. It is not easy to envisage circumstances where an act could be of

a public nature where it is not done in pursuance, or purportedly in pursuance, of public functions.

101. I also agree with Elias LJ that the following features in particular are highly relevant to the question whether the functions of the Trust are public functions (although none of them on its own is in any sense conclusive): the substantial public subsidy which enables the Trust to achieve its objectives; the way in which the allocation agreements circumscribe the freedom of the Trust to allocate properties; and the nature of the regulation to which the Trust is subject. In addition, the vast majority of RSL tenants enjoy statutory protection as regards the circumstances in which a social housing tenancy may be terminated. Secure, assured and assured shorthold tenancies (the vast bulk of RSL tenancies) can only be determined by a process of service of statutorily prescribed notices, court proceedings and a court order which ends the tenancy... Although I do not attach significance to the concession that the Trust is a hybrid authority because it can obtain anti-social behaviour orders, I do attach some significance to that power in conjunction with the other powers relied on by the Equality and Human Rights Commission and referred to above.

102. Consequently it does not follow that the termination of a tenancy is necessarily a private act simply because it originates from the exercise of contractual rights. In any event, I do not read *Aston Cantlow* and *YL* as doing more than treating the private law source of the right and obligation as a factor in determining whether the act is a private act or a public act. In my judgment the act of termination is inextricably linked to the provision of social housing as part of the Trust's public function. Consequently I have come to the conclusion that the Divisional Court's decision on this point was right.

The combination of the decisions in *Aston Cantlow*, *YL* and *Weaver* seem to suggest that a four-stage approach applies to the question of whether or not there is a public authority. First, is the defendant a court or tribunal? If it is, then it is a public authority by virtue of s 6(3)(a). Second, is the defendant a core public authority? This will be assessed by looking at the nature of the body itself. If it is a core public authority, it must act in a Convention compatible way in relation to all its actions and cannot rely on s 6(5). Third, is the defendant a hybrid public authority? This must be assessed by looking at the functions the defendant performs. If any of them are public, then it is a hybrid public authority. Finally, if the defendant is a hybrid public authority is the specific act undertaken nevertheless private in nature? If it is, the defendant will be able to rely on s 6(5) and will not be subject to the Human Rights Act in relation to this action. If the action is public in nature, the authority must respect the claimant's human rights in relation to that action.

Further Reading

Blackstone's Guide to the Human Rights Act 1998, (5th Edition pp 60 – 67)

Hoffmann and Rowe QC, *Human Rights in the UK*, (3rd Edition pp 77 – 83)

Oliver, Dawn 'The Frontiers of the State: Public Authorities and Public Functions under the Human Rights Act', [2000] *PL* 46

8

The Human Rights Act 1998 – ss 3 and 4

Topic List

Christopher Costigan

Introduction

In addition to putting an obligation on public authorities to respect human rights, the motivation for introducing the Act was also to make observation of human rights pervasive throughout UK law. This was to be achieved through the mechanism of section 3 which places an obligation on the courts to interpret legislation in a Convention-compatible way. However, they are only entitled to do so 'as far as it is possible'. If it is not deemed possible, the courts may instead make a declaration of incompatibility under section 4. The scope of what is 'possible' has proved to be controversial and this issue has come to the House of Lords on several occasions.

1 The Human Rights Act 1998: Interpretation and Declarations of Incompatibility

Regina v A (No 2) **[2001] UKHL 25, [2002] 1 AC 45**

Panel: Lord Slynn of Hadley, Lord Steyn, Lord Hope of Craighead, Lord Clyde and Lord Hutton

Statutes: The European Convention on Human Rights Article 6; Human Rights Act 1998 s 6; Youth and Criminal Evidence Act 1999 s 41

Facts: The defendant was charged with rape. He sought permission to introduce evidence of his previous sexual history with the complainant, but was prevented from doing so by the application of the Youth Justice and Criminal Evidence Act 1999 s 41. The judge acknowledged that this would entail a breach of the defendant's right to a fair trial under Article 6 of the Convention. The Court of Appeal reversed that decision and the Director of Public Prosecutions appealed.

LORD STEYN

VII. The interpretation of section 41

Alert

...[T]he interpretative obligation under section 3 of the 1998 Act is a strong one. It applies even if there is no ambiguity in the language in the sense of the language being capable of two different meanings. It is an emphatic adjuration by the legislature... The White Paper made clear that the obligation goes far beyond the rule which enabled the courts to take the Convention into account in resolving any ambiguity in a legislative provision: see Rights Brought Home: The Human Rights Bill (1997) (Cm 3782), para 2.7. The draftsman of the Act had before him the slightly weaker model in section 6 of the New Zealand Bill of Rights Act 1990 but preferred stronger language. Parliament specifically rejected the legislative model of requiring a reasonable interpretation. Section 3 places a duty on the court to strive to find a possible interpretation compatible with Convention rights. Under ordinary methods of interpretation a court may depart from the language of the statute to avoid absurd consequences: section 3 goes much further. Undoubtedly, a court must always look for a contextual and purposive interpretation: section 3 is more radical in its effect. It is a general principle of the interpretation of legal instruments that the text is the primary source of interpretation: other sources are subordinate to it: compare, for example, articles 31 to 33 of the Vienna Convention on the Law of Treaties (1980) (Cmnd 7964). Section 3 qualifies this general principle because it requires a court to find an interpretation compatible with Convention rights if it is possible to do so. In the progress of the Bill through Parliament the Lord Chancellor observed that "in 99% of the cases that will arise, there will be no need for judicial declarations of incompatibility" and the Home Secretary said "We expect that, in almost all cases, the courts will be able to interpret the legislation compatibility with the Convention": Hansard (HL Debates), 5 February 1998, col 840 (3rd Reading) and Hansard (HC Debates), 16 February 1998, col 778 (2nd Reading). For reasons which I explained in a recent paper, this is at least relevant as an aid to the interpretation of section 3 against the executive: "Pepper v Hart; A Re-examination" (2001) 21 Oxford Journal of Legal Studies 59; see also Professor J H Baker, "Statutory Interpretation and Parliamentary Intervention" (1993) 52 CLJ 353. In accordance with the will of Parliament as reflected in section 3 it will sometimes be necessary to adopt an interpretation which linguistically may appear strained. The techniques to be used will not only involve the reading down of express language in a statute but also the implication of provisions. A declaration of incompatibility is a measure of last resort. It must be avoided unless it is plainly impossible to do so. If a clear limitation on Convention rights is stated in terms, such an impossibility will arise: *R v Secretary of State for the Home Department, Ex p* Simms [2000] 2 AC 115, 132a-b, per Lord Hoffmann. There is, however, no limitation of such a nature in the present case.

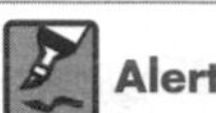

In my view section 3 requires the court to subordinate the niceties of the language of section 41(3)(c), and in particular the touchstone of coincidence, to broader considerations of relevance judged by logical and common sense criteria of time and circumstances. After all, it is realistic to proceed on the basis that the legislature would not, if alerted to the problem, have wished to deny the right to an accused to put forward a full and complete defence by advancing truly probative material. It is therefore possible under section 3 to read section 41, and in particular section 41(3)(c), as subject to the implied provision that evidence or questioning which is required to ensure a fair trial under article 6 of the Convention should not be treated as inadmissible. The result of such a reading would be that sometimes logically relevant sexual experiences between a complainant and an accused may be admitted under section 41(3)(c). On the other hand, there will be cases where previous sexual experience between a complainant and an accused will be irrelevant, eg an isolated episode distant in time and circumstances. Where the line is to be drawn must be left to the judgment of trial judges. On this basis a declaration of incompatibility can be avoided. If this approach is adopted, section 41 will have achieved a major part of its objective but its excessive reach will have been attenuated in accordance with the will of Parliament as reflected in section 3 of the 1998 Act. That is the approach which I would adopt.

LORD HOPE OF CRAIGHEAD

I should like to add … that I would find it very difficult to accept that it was permissible under section 3 of the Human Rights Act 1998 to read in to section 41(3)(c) a provision to the effect that evidence or questioning which was required to ensure a fair trial under article 6 of the Convention should not be treated as inadmissible. The rule of construction which section 3 lays down is quite unlike any previous rule of statutory interpretation. There is no need to identify an ambiguity or absurdity. Compatibility with Convention rights is the sole guiding principle. That is the paramount object which the rule seeks to achieve. But the rule is only a rule of interpretation. It does not entitle the judges to act as legislators. As Lord Woolf CJ said in *Poplar Housing and Regeneration Community Association Ltd v Donoghue* [2001] QB 48, section 3 does not entitle the court to legislate; its task is still one of interpretation. The compatibility is to be achieved only so far as this is possible. Plainly this will not be possible if the legislation contains provisions which expressly contradict the meaning which the enactment would have to be given to make it compatible. It seems to me that the same result must follow if they do so by necessary implication, as this too is a means of identifying the plain intention of Parliament: see Lord Hoffmann's observations in *R v Secretary of State for the Home Department, Ex p Simms* [2000] 2 AC 115, 131f-g.

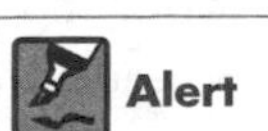

In the present case it seems to me that the entire structure of section 41 contradicts the idea that it is possible to read into it a new provision which would entitle the court to give leave whenever it was of the opinion that this was required to ensure a fair trial. The whole point of the section, as was made clear during the debates in Parliament, was to address the mischief which was thought to have arisen due to the width of the discretion which had previously been given to the trial judge. A deliberate decision was taken not to follow the examples which were to be found elsewhere, such as in section 275 of the Criminal Procedure (Scotland) Act 1995, of provisions which give an overriding discretion to the trial judge to allow the evidence or questioning where it would be contrary to the interests of justice to exclude it. Section 41(2) forbids the exercise of such a discretion unless the court is satisfied as to the matters which that subsection identifies. It seems to me that it would not be possible, without contradicting the plain intention of Parliament, to read in a provision which would enable the court to exercise a wider discretion than that permitted by section 41(2).

I would not have the same difficulty with a solution which read down the provisions of subsections (3) or (5), as the case may be, in order to render them compatible with the Convention right. But if that were to be done it would be necessary to identify precisely (a) the words used by the legislature which would otherwise be incompatible with the Convention right and (b) how these words were to be construed, according to the rule which section 3 lays down, to make them compatible. That, it seems to me, is what the rule of construction requires. The court's task is to read and give effect to the legislation which it is asked to construe. The allegations about the complainant's previous sexual behaviour with the respondent are so exiguous that I do not think that it would be possible for your Lordships in this case with any degree of confidence to embark upon that exercise. I would leave that exercise to be undertaken by the trial judge in the light of such further information about the nature and circumstances of his relationship with the complainant that the respondent can make available if and when he renews his application. If he finds it necessary to apply the interpretative obligation under section 3 of the Human Rights Act 1998 to the words used in section 41(3)(c) of the 1999 Act, he should do so by construing those words, so far as it is possible to do so, by applying the test indicated in paragraph 46 of the speech of my noble and learned friend Lord Steyn.

Although all of their Lordships dismissed the appeal, there is an obvious disparity in the approach of Lords Steyn and Hope. Both agree that section 3 is a robust provision, but the suggested breadth of its use by Lord Steyn is wider than that advocated by Lord Hope, who takes a constitutionally more traditional line.

In Re S (Minors) (Care Order: Implementation of Care Plan); In Re W (Minors) (Care Order: Adequacy of Care Plan) [2002] UKHL 10, [2002] 2 AC 291

Statutes: The European Convention on Human Rights Articles 6 and 8; Children Act 1989 s 38; the Human Rights Act ss 3 and 4

Panel: Lord Nicholls of Birkenhead, Lord Mackay of Clashfern, Lord Browne-Wilkinson, Lord Mustill and Lord Hutton

Facts: The cases concerned the implementation of care orders. The Court of Appeal heard both appeals together and regarded elements in the way care orders were made and implemented as incompatible with the rights of parents and children under Articles 6(1) and 8 of the Convention. Utilising section 3 of the Human Rights Act, the Court reinterpreted the Children Act 1989 to introduce a 'starring' system, whereby essential milestones of a care plan were identified and 'starred'. If a starred milestone was not achieved within a reasonable time after the date set at trial, the local authority was obliged to inform the child's guardian of the position. Either the guardian or the local authority would then have the right to apply to the court for further directions. The court also laid down guidelines to give judges a wider discretion to make an interim care order and to defer making a final care order.

The local authority in the second case and the Secretary of State for Health appealed against the introduction of the new procedures by the Court of Appeal.

LORD NICHOLLS OF BIRKENHEAD

Starred milestones

25. ...The [Children] Act delineated the boundary of responsibility with complete clarity. Where a care order is made the responsibility for the child's care is with the authority rather than the court. The court retains no supervisory role, monitoring the authority's discharge of its responsibilities. That was the intention of Parliament.

29. ...The system does not always work well. Shortages of money, of suitable trained staff and of suitable foster carers and prospective adopters for difficult children are among the reasons. There have been delays in placing children in accordance with

their care plans, unsatisfactory breakdown rates and delays in finding substitute placements.

31. ...One suggestion was that a court review could be triggered by failure to implement "starred" key factors in the care plan within specified time-scales. The guardian ad litem would be the appropriate person to intervene.

32. This was the source of the innovation which found expression in the judgments of the Court of Appeal in the present appeals...

33. The jurisprudential route by which the Court of Appeal found itself able to bring about this development was primarily by recourse to section 3 of the Human Rights Act 1998...

Section 3 of the Human Rights Act 1998

35. It is entirely understandable that the Court of Appeal should seek some means to alleviate these problems... The question is whether the courts have power to introduce into the working of the Children Act a range of rights and liabilities not sanctioned by Parliament.

36. On this I have to say at once, respectfully but emphatically, that I part company with the Court of Appeal. I am unable to agree that the court's introduction of a "starring system" can be justified as a legitimate exercise in interpretation of the Children Act 1989 in accordance with section 3 of the Human Rights Act 1998. Even if the Children Act is inconsistent with articles 6 or 8 of the Convention, which is a question I will consider later, section 3 does not in this case have the effect suggested by the Court of Appeal.

37. Section 3(1) provides: "So far as it is possible to do so, primary legislation ... must be read and given effect in a way which is compatible with the Convention rights." This is a powerful tool whose use is obligatory. It is not an optional canon of construction. Nor is its use dependent on the existence of ambiguity. Further, the section applies retrospectively. So far as it is possible to do so, primary legislation "must be read and given effect" to in a way which is compatible with Convention rights. This is forthright, uncompromising language.

38. But the reach of this tool is not unlimited. Section 3 is concerned with interpretation. This is apparent from the opening words of section 3(1): "so far as it is possible to do so". The side heading of the section is "Interpretation of legislation". Section 4 (power to make a declaration of incompatibility) and, indeed, section 3(2)(b) presuppose that not all provisions in primary legislation can be rendered Convention compliant by the application of section 3(1). The existence of this limit on the scope of section 3(1) has already been the subject of judicial confirmation, more than once: see, for instance, Lord Woolf CJ in *Poplar Housing and Regeneration Community Association Ltd v Donoghue* [2002] QB 48, 72-73, para 75 and Lord Hope of Craighead in *R v Lambert* [2001] 3 WLR 206, 233-235, paras 79-81.

39. In applying section 3 courts must be ever mindful of this outer limit. The Human Rights Act reserves the amendment of primary legislation to Parliament. By this means

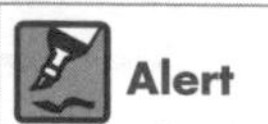
Alert

the Act seeks to preserve parliamentary sovereignty. The Act maintains the constitutional boundary. Interpretation of statutes is a matter for the courts; the enactment of statutes, and the amendment of statutes, are matters for Parliament.

40. Up to this point there is no difficulty. The area of real difficulty lies in identifying the limits of interpretation in a particular case. This is not a novel problem. If anything, the problem is more acute today than in past times. Nowadays courts are more "liberal" in the interpretation of all manner of documents. The greater the latitude with which courts construe documents, the less readily defined is the boundary. What one person regards as sensible, if robust, interpretation, another regards as impermissibly creative. For present purposes it is sufficient to say that a meaning which departs substantially from a fundamental feature of an Act of Parliament is likely to have crossed the boundary between interpretation and amendment. This is especially so where the departure has important practical repercussions which the court is not equipped to evaluate. In such a case the overall contextual setting may leave no scope for rendering the statutory provision Convention compliant by legitimate use of the process of interpretation. The boundary line may be crossed even though a limitation on Convention rights is not stated in express terms. Lord Steyn's observations in *R v A (No 2)* [2002] 1 AC 45, 68d-e, para 44 are not to be read as meaning that a clear limitation on Convention rights in terms is the only circumstance in which an interpretation incompatible with Convention rights may arise.

Alert

41. I should add a further general observation in the light of what happened in the present case. Section 3 directs courts on how legislation shall, as far as possible, be interpreted. When a court, called upon to construe legislation, ascribes a meaning and effect to the legislation pursuant to its obligation under section 3, it is important the court should identify clearly the particular statutory provision or provisions whose interpretation leads to that result. Apart from all else, this should assist in ensuring the court does not inadvertently stray outside its interpretation jurisdiction. ...

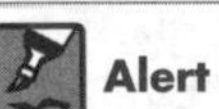
Alert

43. In his judgment Thorpe LJ noted that the starring system "seems to breach the fundamental boundary between the functions and responsibilities of the court and the local authority": see [2001] 2 FLR 582 , 596, para 31. I agree. I consider this judicial innovation passes well beyond the boundary of interpretation. I can see no provision in the Children Act which lends itself to the interpretation that Parliament was thereby conferring this supervisory function on the court. No such provision was identified by the Court of Appeal. On the contrary, the starring system is inconsistent in an important respect with the scheme of the Children Act. It would constitute amendment of the Children Act, not its interpretation. It would have far-reaching practical ramifications for local authorities and their care of children. The starring system would not come free from additional administrative work and expense. It would be likely to have a material effect on authorities' allocation of scarce financial and other resources. This in turn would affect authorities' discharge of their responsibilities to other children. Moreover, the need to produce a formal report whenever a care plan is significantly departed from, and then await the outcome of any subsequent court proceedings, would affect the whole manner in which authorities discharge, and are able to discharge, their parental responsibilities.

44. These are matters for decision by Parliament, not the courts. It is impossible for a court to attempt to evaluate these ramifications or assess what would be the views of Parliament if changes are needed. I echo the wise words of Cooke P in the New Zealand case of *R v Stack* [1986] 1 NZLR 257, 261-262:

"It would amount to amending the Act by judicial legislation. In a sensitive and controversial field which the New Zealand Parliament may be said to have taken to itself, we do not consider that this court would be justified in such a course. If the Act is to be amended it should be done by Parliament after full consideration of the arguments of policy."

In my view, in the present case the Court of Appeal exceeded the bounds of its judicial jurisdiction under section 3 in introducing this new scheme.

Appeal of mother dismissed. Appeals of local authority and Secretary of State allowed.

In his judgment Lord Nicholls also acknowledged that the Human Rights Act s 3 is a robust provision, but stated that there are limitations to its use which the Court of Appeal had crossed. Central to his argument that the use of s 3 was inappropriate was the concern that the scheme introduced by the Court of Appeal went against a fundamental feature of the original Act. Second, the starred system would have had practical implications for the way that local authorities work, notably an impact on local authority finance, which in his view was a matter for Parliament rather than the courts.

One further criticism of the approach adopted by the Court of Appeal was that they were unable to identify a section in the Children Act that they were interpreting. Lord Nicholls is clearly stating that, in order not to cross the boundary between interpretation and legislation, the court must be able to point to a specific section of an Act and say it is "reading" a provision in a particular way. If a court cannot do so, then use of the Human Rights Act s 3 would in his view be inappropriate.

Last, Lord Nicholls considered that it would not have been appropriate to declare a particular section of the Children Act incompatible with the Convention because of the way in which the statute was written.

R (Anderson) v Secretary of State for the Home Department; R (Taylor) v Secretary of State for the Home Department [2002] UKHL 46, [2003] 1 AC 837

Statutes: The European Convention on Human Rights Article 6; Murder (Abolition of the Death Penalty) Act 1965 s 1(1); The Human Rights Act 1998 ss 3 and 4; Crime (Sentences) Act 1997 s 29

Facts: The claimant had been convicted of two murders for which he received mandatory life sentences. In accordance with his stated practice the Secretary of State received advice from the trial judge, the Lord Chief Justice and departmental officials before deciding the appropriate tariff. In fixing the claimant's tariff, he set a longer period than that recommended by the judiciary. The claimant challenged his decision on the grounds, *inter alia*, that in fixing the tariff the Secretary of State, as a member of the executive, had acted incompatibly with the claimant's right to a fair trial under Article 6(1) of the Convention. The Divisional Court dismissed his application and his appeal was also dismissed by the Court of Appeal. The claimant further appealed.

LORD BINGHAM OF CORNHILL

20. Mr Fitzgerald's argument for the appellant involved the following steps. (1) Under article 6(1) of the Convention a criminal defendant has a right to a fair trial by an independent and impartial tribunal. (2) The imposition of sentence is part of the trial. (3) Therefore sentence should be imposed by an independent and impartial tribunal. (4) The fixing of the tariff of a convicted murderer is legally indistinguishable from the imposition of sentence. (5) Therefore the tariff should be fixed by an independent and impartial tribunal. (6) The Home Secretary is not an independent and impartial tribunal. (7) Therefore the Home Secretary should not fix the tariff of a convicted murderer...

28. ...I accept each of Mr Fitzgerald's steps (1) to (7) save that, in the light of *Benjamin and Wilson v United Kingdom*, it must now be held that the Home Secretary should play no part in fixing the tariff of a convicted murderer, even if he does no more than confirm what the judges have recommended. To that extent the appeal succeeds.

30. The question of relief therefore arises. Section 29 of the Crime (Sentences) Act 1997 ... appears to stand in the way of the appellant. It is unrepealed primary legislation. Mr Fitzgerald contended that it was possible to read and give effect to section 29 in a manner compatible with the Convention, and that the House should do so in exercise of the interpretative power conferred by section 3(1) of the Human Rights Act 1998. Mr Pannick contended that, even if the House were to accept Mr Fitzgerald's argument summarised in paragraph 20 above, the only relief which the appellant could obtain would be a declaration of incompatibility under section 4 of the 1998 Act. On this point I am satisfied that Mr Pannick is right... Parliament did not attempt to prescribe the procedures to be followed in fixing the tariff of a convicted murderer. But some things emerge clearly from this not very perspicuous section. The power to release a convicted murderer is conferred on the Home Secretary. He may not exercise that power unless recommended to do so by the Parole Board. But the Parole Board may not make such a recommendation unless the Home Secretary has referred the case to it. And the section imposes no duty on the Home Secretary either to refer a case to the board or to release a prisoner if the board recommends release. Since, therefore, the section leaves it to the Home Secretary to decide whether or when to refer a case to the board, and he is free to ignore its recommendation if it is favourable to the prisoner, the decision on how long the convicted murderer should remain in prison for punitive purposes is his alone. It cannot be doubted that Parliament intended this result when enacting section 29 and its predecessor sections. An entirely different regime was established, in the case of discretionary life sentence prisoners, in section 28... To read section 29 as precluding participation by the Home Secretary, if it were possible to do so, would not be judicial interpretation but judicial vandalism: it would give the section an effect quite different from that which Parliament intended and would go well beyond any interpretative process sanctioned by section 3 of the 1998

Act (*In re S (Minors) (Care Order: Implementation of Care Plan)* [2002] 2 AC 291, 313-314 , para 41).

LORD STEYN

VI. The issues on the appeal

48. It is manifest, and conceded by the Home Secretary, that if the fixing of tariff is appropriately to be classified as a judicial function under article 6(1), it follows that the existing system is in breach of article 6(1) since the Home Secretary, as a member of the executive, is undoubtedly not independent within the meaning of article 6(1). There are therefore two principal issues, namely: ... (2) ... what the appropriate remedy under the Human Rights Act 1998 is.

VIII. The remedy

59. Counsel for the appellant invited the House to use the interpretative obligation under section 3 to read into section 29 alleged Convention rights, viz to provide that the tariff set by the Home Secretary may not exceed the judicial recommendation. It is impossible to follow this course. It would not be interpretation but interpolation inconsistent with the plain legislative intent to entrust the decision to the Home Secretary, who was intended to be free to follow or reject judicial advice. Section 3(1) is not available where the suggested interpretation is contrary to express statutory words or is by implication necessarily contradicted by the statute: *In re S (Minors) (Care Order: Implementation of Care Plan)* [2002] 2 AC 291, 313-314, para 41, per Lord Nicholls of Birkenhead. It is therefore impossible to imply the suggested words into the statute or to secure the same result by a process of construction.

60. It follows that there must be a declaration of incompatibility.

This case clearly echoes the approach in *Re S* that the courts cannot, under section 3 of the Human Rights Act, depart from a fundamental feature of the statute. It is also interesting to note Lord Steyn's words in paragraph 60 that the court 'must' make a declaration of incompatibility. Under section 4 such a declaration is in fact discretionary. That a declaration will be made where the statute cannot be read compatibly can clearly be seen in the next case, however.

Bellinger v Bellinger (Lord Chancellor intervening) [2003] UKHL 21, [2003] 2 AC 467

Statutes: The European Convention on Human Rights Articles 8 and 14; Matrimonial Causes Act 1973 s 11(c); Human Rights Act 1998 ss 3 and 4

Panel: Lord Nicholls of Birkenhead, Lord Hope of Craighead, Lord Hobhouse of Woodborough, Lord Scott of Foscote and Lord Rodger of Earlsferry

Facts: The petitioner was a transsexual female who had been correctly classified and registered at birth as male but had undergone gender reassignment surgery and treatment. In 1981 she went through a ceremony of marriage with a man who supported her petition for a declaration that the marriage was valid at its inception and was subsisting. The judge refused to grant the declaration on the ground that 'male' and 'female' in section 11(c) of the Matrimonial Causes Act 1973 were to be determined by reference to biological criteria and that the petitioner was a male and not a woman for the purposes of marriage. The Court of Appeal dismissed the petitioner's appeal, and she further appealed.

LORD NICHOLLS OF BIRKENHEAD

42. ...Plainly, there must be some objective, publicly available criteria by which gender reassignment is to be assessed. If possible the criteria should be capable of being applied readily so as to produce a reasonably clear answer. Parties proposing to enter into a marriage relationship need to know whether their marriage will be valid. Other people need to know whether a marriage was valid. Marriage has legal consequences in many directions: for instance, housing and residential security of tenure, social security benefits, citizenship and immigration, taxation, pensions, inheritance, life insurance policies, criminal law (bigamy). There must be an adequate degree of certainty. Otherwise, as the majority of the Court of Appeal observed, the applicability of the law to an individual suffering from gender identity disorder would be in a state of complete confusion: see [2002] 2 Fam 150, 177, para 104.

43. Your Lordships' House is not in a position to decide where the demarcation line could sensibly or reasonably be drawn. Where this line should be drawn is far from self-evident. The antipodean decisions of *Attorney General v Otahuhu Family Court* [1995] 1 NZLR 603 and *In re Kevin (Validity of Marriage of Transsexual)* [2001] Fam CA 1074 and Appeal No EA 97/2001 have not identified any clear, persuasive principle in this regard. Nor has the dissenting judgment of Thorpe LJ in the present case. Nor has the decision of the European Court of Human Rights in *Goodwin v United Kingdom* 35 EHRR 447. Nor is there uniformity among the 13 member states of the European Union which afford legal recognition to a transsexual person's acquired gender. The preconditions for recognition vary considerably.

44. Further, the House is not in a position to give guidance on what other preconditions should be satisfied before legal recognition is given to a transsexual person's acquired gender. Some member states of the European Union insist on the applicant being single or on existing marriages being dissolved. Some insist on the applicant being sterile. Questions arise about the practical mechanisms and procedures for obtaining recognition of acquired gender, and about the problem of people who "revert" to their original gender after a period in their new gender role.

45. Secondly, the recognition of gender reassignment for the purposes of marriage is part of a wider problem which should be considered as a whole and not dealt with in a piecemeal fashion. There should be a clear, coherent policy. The decision regarding recognition of gender reassignment for the purpose of marriage cannot sensibly be made in isolation from a decision on the like problem in other areas where a distinction is drawn between people on the basis of gender. These areas include education, child care, occupational qualifications, criminal law (gender-specific offences), prison regulations, sport, the needs of decency, and birth certificates. Birth certificates, indeed, are one of the matters of most concern to transsexual people, because birth

certificates are frequently required as proof of identity or age or place of birth. When, and in what circumstances, should these certificates be capable of being reissued in a revised form which does not disclose that the person has undergone gender reassignment?

46. Thirdly, even in the context of marriage, the present question raises wider issues. Marriage is an institution, or relationship, deeply embedded in the religious and social culture of this country. It is deeply embedded as a relationship between two persons of the opposite sex. There was a time when the reproductive functions of male and female were regarded as the primary raison d'être of marriage. The Church of England Book of Common Prayer of 1662 declared that the first cause for which matrimony was ordained was the "procreation of children". For centuries this was proclaimed at innumerable marriage services. For a long time now the emphasis has been different. Variously expressed, there is much more emphasis now on the "mutual society, help and comfort that the one ought to have of the other".

47. Against this background there are those who urge that the special relationship of marriage should not now be confined to persons of the opposite sex. It should be possible for persons of the same sex to marry. This, it is said, is the appropriate way to resolve problems such as those confronting Mrs Bellinger.

48. It hardly needs saying that this approach would involve a fundamental change in the traditional concept of marriage. Here again, this raises a question which ought to be considered as part of an overall review of the most appropriate way to deal with the difficulties confronting transsexual people.

49. For these reasons I would not make a declaration that the marriage celebrated between Mr and Mrs Bellinger in 1981 was valid. A change in the law as sought by Mrs Bellinger must be a matter for deliberation and decision by Parliament when the forthcoming [Gender Recognition] Bill is introduced.

Declaration of incompatibility

50. Mrs Bellinger advanced a further, alternative claim for a declaration that in so far as section 11(c) of the Matrimonial Causes Act 1973 makes no provision for the recognition of gender reassignment it is incompatible with articles 8 and 12 of the Convention...

51. Mr Sales advanced several arguments on why such a declaration should not be made. There is, he submitted, no present incompatibility between the statute and the Convention. The European Court of Human Rights, in its decision in *Goodwin*, envisaged that the government should have a reasonable period in which to amend domestic law on a principled and coherent basis. The court said it "will be for the United Kingdom Government in due course to implement such measures as it considers appropriate to fulfil its obligations": see 35 EHRR 447, 483, para 120 (emphasis added).

52. I cannot accept this submission.

53. ...What was held to be incompatible in July 2002 has not now, for the purposes of section 4, become compatible. The government's announcement of forthcoming legislation has not had that effect, nor could it. That would make no sense.

54. Then Mr Sales submitted that a declaration of incompatibility would serve no useful purpose. A declaration of incompatibility triggers the ministerial powers to amend the offending legislation under the "fast track" procedures set out in section 10 and Schedule 2 of the Human Rights Act 1998. But the minister's powers have already been triggered in the present case under section 10(1)(b), by reason of the decisions of the European Court of Human Rights in the *Goodwin* case and the associated case of *I v United Kingdom* (Application No 25680/94) (unreported) 11 July 2002. Further, the Government has already announced its intention to bring forward primary legislation on this subject. For this reason also, counsel submitted, making a declaration of incompatibility would serve no useful purpose.

55. I am not persuaded by these submissions. If a provision of primary legislation is shown to be incompatible with a Convention right the court, in the exercise of its discretion, may make a declaration of incompatibility under section 4 of the Human Rights Act 1998. In exercising this discretion the court will have regard to all the circumstances. In the present case the government has not sought to question the decision of the European Court of Human Rights in *Goodwin* 35 EHRR 447. Indeed, it is committed to giving effect to that decision. Nevertheless, when proceedings are already before the House, it is desirable that in a case of such sensitivity this House, as the court of final appeal in this country, should formally record that the present state of statute law is incompatible with the Convention. I would therefore make a declaration of incompatibility as sought. I would otherwise dismiss this appeal.

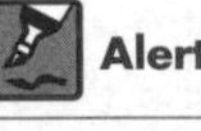
Alert

This case revolved around the interpretation of the words 'male' and 'female' in the Matrimonial Causes Act. For the marriage to have been valid, the word 'female' would have had to have been interpreted to include Mrs Bellinger. However, Lord Nicholls was clearly of the opinion that this was not possible and he characterised the request as one for a 'change in the law', which (as seen in *Re S*), he clearly believed to have been beyond the scope of s 3 interpretation. Lord Nicholls felt that this would have amounted to a change in the law for three reasons. First, it was not clear when somebody would change from one gender to another, nor importantly was that a question which the courts were competent to answer. Second, a s 3 interpretation would have had wider implications in other areas of law and he believed that reform of the law in this area should be dealt with holistically by Parliament. And finally, such an interpretation would have come into conflict with more traditional views on the institution of marriage. Again, he felt that reform therefore had to take into account ethical, religious and other complex considerations, which were more properly the preserve of Parliament and not the courts. These reasons add further valuable insight, therefore, into what is possible under the s 3 power of interpretation.

These conclusions led Lord Nicholls to consider whether to make a declaration of incompatibility. Mr Sales, Counsel for the Government, argued that a declaration should not be made because this would serve little purpose: the Government had already indicated that reform was in the process of being introduced in this area in the form of the Gender Recognition Bill. Although a persuasive argument, this was rejected by the court which went on to make a declaration, partly for symbolic reasons. This might suggest that, even though the making of a declaration is discretionary, the courts are likely to exercise that discretion whenever a s 3 interpretation cannot be made and (unlike in *Re S*) the offending provision can be identified.

These early cases relating to ss 3 and 4 attracted a good deal of academic debate around the extent of the interpretative obligation placed on the courts. Two articles written in 2004 argued against each other on whether the courts' approach was consistent or appropriate.

Statutory interpretation and human rights after *Anderson*, Danny Nicol, [2004] PL 274

The section 3/section 4 interplay and the nature of the HRA

Section 3 enjoins courts and tribunals "so far as it is possible to do so", to read and give effect to legislation in a way which is compatible with Convention rights. At the same time, s.3 acknowledges that not everything can be construed in a Convention-compliant fashion, and stipulates that the courts must continue to enforce incompatible primary legislation. The delineation of s.3's outer limits has sharply divided judges and academic commentators because the relationship between ss.3 and 4 is pivotal to the view one takes of the HRA as a whole. Those who wish the HRA to ensure that the Convention rights as interpreted by the European Court of Human Rights become the supreme law of the land, tend to favour an approach to s.3 which confers upon the courts extensive power to accord legislation the most Convention-friendly meaning possible, even if this conflicts with clear statutory language or purposes. Sometimes this may involve extremely creative feats of statutory interpretation, but this is considered preferable to running the risk inherent in making a declaration of incompatibility under s.4, namely that government and Parliament may disagree with it and decline to act upon it, thereby obstructing the transmission of rights norms from the Strasbourg jurisprudence into domestic law. Conversely, those who would prefer the HRA to be a unique participatory instrument which involves legislature and executive, not just judiciary, in the delineation of rights, tend to argue for a less expansive reading of s.3, obliging courts to eschew overly fanciful interpretations and instead make greater use of s.4 declarations, thereby opening up decision-making on rights to the state's elected officials. It is this fundamental normative difference as to the nature of the HRA as a whole, rather than disagreements over s.3's precise wording and structure, which truly lies at the heart of controversy over the section's scope. The forensic textual examination undertaken by some academic lawyers should not obscure the fact that when the judges set the boundaries of s.3 they are really making a decision about constitutional fundamentals.

Indeed, the judges' dilemma regarding the interplay between ss.3 and 4 is not unlike the choice which confronted them over the European Communities Act 1972 (ECA). The question of whether the ECA was subject to the full rigours of traditional parliamentary sovereignty–including the rule that Parliament cannot bind its successors–

or whether it would allow EC law to prevail over subsequent statute, was not resolved by analysis of s.2(4)'s delphic wording. Rather, their Lordships in *Factortame (No.2)* embraced the supremacy of EC law in order to bring constitutional doctrine in line with the political reality of Britain's long-term EC membership, the increasing acceptance of EC law as part of our law, and the acceptance by the majority of the population of Britain's EC membership as a political norm. The decision therefore represented a form of "constitutional catch-up", in which the judiciary brought constitutional law into line with the broad sweep of constitutional politics. The House's interpretation of the ECA was driven by these great issues, not by the finer details of the statute's text.

R v A (No.2)

The evolution of their Lordships' approach to s.3 can be seen by comparing three cases: *R v A (No.2), Re S (Minors) (Care Order: Implementation of Care Plan)* and *Anderson* itself. The first case involved the interpretation of s.41 of the Youth Justice and Criminal Evidence Act 1999 which related to the protection of complainants in proceedings for sexual offences ... But the court's discretion was highly circumscribed. Plainly, the intention of Parliament was severely to restrict the circumstances in which complainants could be interrogated about their sexual histories.

This clarity of parliamentary purpose in no way inhibited the House of Lords... In Lord Steyn's words, s.3 required the court to subordinate the niceties of the language of s.41 to broader considerations of relevance.

...This suggested that Parliament would need to enact words to the effect that it realised its legislation might infringe Convention rights but had nonetheless elected so to legislate. In the absence of such words, s.3 would seemingly always allow the courts to *transform* statutory provisions in a way which accorded with their interpretation of the Convention rights.

Their Lordships' use of s.3 in *A* proved controversial. Lord Hope clearly felt uncomfortable with Lord Steyn's approach, arguing that the entire structure of s.41 contradicted the idea that one could "read into" it a power of the court to give leave whenever it considered that this was necessary to ensure a fair trial.

Re S

S can be seen as a reaction to the judicial overkill of *A*... Hale L.J. contended that there was nothing in the Children Act to prohibit this new system: there was simply nothing to allow it; so the court could read it into the statute.

The House of Lords, however, held that the Court of Appeal had gone too far. Section 3 could not be used to accord a meaning to a provision which departed substantially from a fundamental feature of the Act of Parliament...

Anderson

In *Anderson* a seven-member Appellate Committee resoundingly confirmed *S* and made it clear that the new approach to s.3 rests on foundations of high constitutional principle.

...So how come Parliament's "unambiguous wish" was flouted in *A* but respected in *Anderson*? Why the change of heart? One explanation has been that *A* very much concerned the province of the courts. The problem with this argument is that *Anderson* also involved the province of the courts–their role in sentencing. Perhaps a more convincing explanation is that the case law has evolved on the basis of judicial politics. In *A* one panel of Law Lords adopted an approach designed to ensure the triumph of their interpretation of the ECHR over all other forms of law. In *S* and *Anderson* two differently-constituted panels drew back from this position, recognising that if judges take too many liberties with interpretation, this serves to undermine parliamentary sovereignty by transferring the right to "make or unmake any law" from the elected and accountable Parliament to themselves. This was not what the mass of legislators intended in 1998 – the broad design of the HRA makes that perfectly plain – nor is it any more tolerable to them today. Indeed, too much judicial legislating might well prompt government and Parliament to rebalance the HRA in favour of politicians.

Whilst *Anderson* is replete with references to parliamentary sovereignty, their Lordships could additionally justify a restrictive reading of s.3 by reference to the rule of law, in the sense that the law must be adequately accessible and formulated with sufficient precision so that the citizen can regulate his or her conduct accordingly. With a s.4 declaration, the individual knows where he or she stands: for good or ill, the courts will enforce the clear words of Parliament, whilst at the same time encouraging legislators to reform the law. With an outlandish s.3 interpretation, the statute book becomes a minefield, with provisions such as s.41 of the Youth Justice and Criminal Evidence Act 1999 turning out to mean the opposite of what one would think they mean. Thus a rape victim might have started co-operating in a prosecution in the belief that her previous sex life will not be placed under the microscope, only to discover, once *A* was decided, that the plain statutory words which seemed to protect her could no longer be relied upon. Legal certainty – one of the pervasive requirements of the ECHR – goes by the board.

Will *Anderson* stick?

Before *Anderson,* lower courts sometimes relied upon a skewed selection of judicial dicta to justify extravagant interpretations under the s.3 obligation. This will no longer be defensible. *Anderson* was, after all, decided by a seven-Law Lord panel. Their Lordships were unanimous. The case did not create new principles from out of the blue, but affirmed as authoritative those enunciated in *S,* another unanimous decision, so the House can be seen to be building up consistency of approach. Lord Steyn, who had seemingly assumed the leadership role in the far-fetched interpretation in *A,* abandoned his earlier approach, rejecting the notion that " interpretations" could conflict with clear statutory words and upholding parliamentary sovereignty as the country's supreme constitutional doctrine. In the interests of legal certainty it is imperative that from now on courts and tribunals loyally adhere to the *S/Anderson* limitations on the interpretative obligation.

The authority of *S* and *Anderson* has been further strengthened by the House's post-*Anderson* case law. In *R v Att-Gen Ex p Rusbridger* Lord Steyn again cited Lord

Nicholls' position in *S* as authoritative. In *Bellinger v Bellinger* the House ... held that it was not possible to give the expressions "male" or "female" the extended meaning capable of accommodating Mrs Bellinger's case. Indeed, such an interpretation would constitute a legislative exercise of amendment, with the court making a legislative choice as to what precise amendment was appropriate. The case raised wider issues about the very nature of marriage and these were best addressed by Parliament. Moreover the interpretative approach would be irresponsible, since piecemeal law reform in the context of transsexuals would be profoundly unsatisfactory. What was needed was a clear, coherent policy, deliberated upon by Parliament, and dealing with the recognition of gender reassignment in diverse aspects of human life. Accordingly the House made a declaration of incompatibility. The case confirms judicial reluctance to use s.3 when interpretation would involve the exercise of legislative discretion.

The effect of *Bellinger* is further to isolate *A*, where their Lordships' use of s.3 did indeed usurp Parliament's exercise of legislative choice. Had the House instead made a declaration of incompatibility, then even supposing Parliament had agreed with the judiciary that the law needed to be changed, it could have substituted a spectrum of measures for the impugned "rape-shield" provision, ranging from those which gave a high degree of discretion for trial judges to those which still involved fairly tight restrictions on admissibility. Instead their Lordships took advantage of the interpretative obligation to make the choice themselves, and opted to give trial judges very wide discretion.

Conclusion

The emphatic rejection of over-zealous interpretation in *Anderson, S* and *Bellinger* confirms that the House of Lords has made up its mind in favour of restricting its use of s.3 and correspondingly availing itself more readily of s.4 declarations. In *Anderson* the House rooted this approach in parliamentary sovereignty, reflecting the necessity in a democratic society that those who are politically accountable should have the last word on what the law should be. Thus the declaration of incompatibility is not to be avoided at all costs, but rather used to involve executive and legislature in the task of defining and furthering human rights.

In fashioning this approach the House has provided valuable guidance to help chart the elusive frontier between permissible interpretation and impermissible legislative amendment. Section 3 may not be used to contradict the clear words of a statute (Anderson), nor to undermine fundamental features implicit in a statute (S), nor to deprive Parliament of its legislative discretion (Bellinger), nor to effect piecemeal reform in a legal regime requiring coherence (S, Bellinger), nor to engage in law reform where change in one field would have important "spillover" effects elsewhere (S, Bellinger). These principles cast doubt on the constitutional legitimacy of their Lordships' use of s.3 rather than s.4 in *A*. The majority of the Appellate Committee now appears to have concluded that the HRA is different from earlier human rights instruments, in that it takes the inherent contestability of rights to its logical conclusion by giving the judiciary the task of raising the questions and giving government and Parliament the

task of deciding the solutions. These solutions will themselves be amenable to judicial scrutiny under the HRA, thereby fostering a dialogue on rights between our governing institutions. In a society which increasingly recognises that fundamental rights are matters on which reasonable people disagree, this constitutes a more attractive vision of the HRA than the assertion of a judicial monopoly of wisdom underlying *A*.

A response to Nicol's article appeared shortly afterwards in the same journal.

Statutory interpretation and human rights after *Anderson*: a more contextual approach, Alieen Kavanagh [2004] PL 537

A key question under the Human Rights Act 1998 (HRA) is the extent of the interpretative power given to the judiciary by s.3(1). In a recent issue of this journal, Danny Nicol has argued that in three recent decisions (*Anderson, Re S* and *Bellinger*), the House of Lords has "settled" this complex issue in favour of "restricting its use of s.3 and correspondingly availing itself more readily of s.4 declarations". Moreover, Nicol claims that these cases are a reaction to, and departure from, the interpretative approach adopted by the House of Lords in *R. v A* - a decision which he characterises as "far-fetched", "outlandish" and amounting to "judicial overkill". The aim here is to question the cogency of these views and to suggest an alternative explanation for the difference of approach in *A* to the later cases. The argument will be that it is the context and individual circumstances of the cases which explains the difference of judicial approach, rather than any fundamental change of mind about the possibilities of s.3(1).

Contrasting *R. v A* and *Re S*

We can begin by examining the decisions in *A* and *Re S*. *R. v A* concerned s.41 of the Youth Justice and Criminal Evidence Act 1999... The House of Lords held that this provision was so restrictive that it "amounted to legislative overkill"... In order to remedy this, their Lordships relied on s.3(1) HRA to read s.41 subject to an "implied provision" that evidence which was necessary to ensure a fair trial should not be treated as inadmissible by the trial judge.

In *Re S*, the House of Lords examined the interpretative approach taken by the Court of Appeal in that case under s.3(1) HRA... The Court of Appeal's decision was reversed unanimously by the House of Lords. They held that the introduction of these innovations into the statutory scheme was an inappropriate use of s.3(1). A fundamental and pervasive feature of the Children Act was that the courts were not empowered to intervene in the way local authorities discharged their parental responsibilities in care orders...

His Lordship [Lord Nicholls] also stressed that:

[W]hen a court, called upon to construe legislation, ascribes a meaning and effect to the legislation pursuant to its obligation under s.3, it is important that the court should identify clearly the particular statutory provision or provisions whose interpretation leads to that result.

This was not done in this case. As Hale L.J. pointed out in the Court of Appeal, the appellants "found it difficult to identify particular provisions of the 1989 Act which might be declared incompatible: the problem is more with what the Act does not say than with what it does". In introducing a new scheme to fill in what the Act did not say, the Court of Appeal "exceeded the bounds of its judicial jurisdiction under s.3". The question that now arises is whether the decision in *Re S* constitutes a retreat from the reasoning adopted in *R. v A*. In other words, if *R. v A* were decided after *Re S*, would it be decided differently? In arguing that *Re S* does not constitute such a retreat, it is necessary to outline the considerable factual differences between both cases. First, in *R. v A*, it *was* possible to identify a particular statutory provision which could be construed in a Convention-compatible way under s.3(1). This was not possible in *Re S* due to the terms of the Children Act 1989. Therefore, to the extent that the decision in *Re S* was based on this point, it does not challenge or impugn the interpretive methodology adopted in *A*. Secondly, although the decision in *R. v A* increased judicial discretion about the admissibility of certain types of evidence in rape cases, this did not require the setting up of whole new procedures or mechanisms to implement the decision. It could take place within the framework provided by s.41 of the Youth Justice and Criminal Evidence Act and the judicial decision-making power prescribed by it. In *Re* S, the proposed innovation purported to set up a novel monitoring procedure for the courts which was no part of the existing Children Act, involving them in the delivery of services to which they were ill-suited. Moreover, this innovation would have had far-reaching practical ramifications for local authorities and their care of children, including the authority's allocation of scarce financial and other resources. In contrast, the decision about whether to admit certain evidence in the interests of a fair trial as guaranteed by Art.6 ECHR (the subject-matter of *R. v A*) is one which lies within the traditional decision-making expertise of the courts. In sum, the type of legal reform which seemed necessary to the Court of Appeal in *Re S* to achieve Convention-compatibility was much more radical in scope and effect than that which was necessary to achieve the same aim in *R. v A*.

The contrast between these two cases highlights the fact that judicial decisions about whether an interpretation under s.3(1) HRA is "possible" will depend in part on contextual factors, such as (crucially) the terms of the legislation under scrutiny, as well as the impact and consequences of the proposed interpretation. When viewed in light of these factors, the decision in *Re S* does not seem to be based on a rejection of the reasoning or interpretative methodology adopted in *R. v A*. Rather, it is due to the significant differences in legislative context between the two cases. Indeed, if *Re S* was meant to be an "emphatic rejection of the overzealous interpretation" adopted in *A*, one might have expected their Lordships to discuss and then explain such a rejection in emphatic terms. However, this does not take place. In fact, *A* is only mentioned once in *Re S*, where Lord Nicholls noted in passing that Lord Steyn's observations in *A* "are not to be read as meaning that a clear limitation on Convention rights in terms is the only circumstance in which an interpretation incompatible with Convention rights may arise". In my view, this comment refers to the fact that there will sometimes be contextual factors which limit the power of the judiciary to engage in legal reform via s.3(1) HRA. In particular, whilst it may be possible to rectify a particular statutory provision in order to render it Convention-compatible, that possibility will be restricted due to the partial and piecemeal way in which the judicial law-making power generally operates. In some cases, the necessary reform to achieve Convention-compatibility will be so radical that it may be impossible or inappropriate for the courts to attempt to carry it out.

Re S makes clear that s.3(1) should not be used as a way of radically reforming a whole statute or writing a quasi-legislative code granting new powers and setting out new procedures to replace that statute. However, that does not necessarily mean that the decision rules out the type of "reading in" which was adopted in *R. v A.* As Lord Irvine pointed out, "*Re S* does not preclude s.3 from producing unexpected, yet acceptable results; results that clarify and improve the law, and achieve compliance with the Convention. With s.3, Parliament has invited the courts to use the Convention creatively in order to find the right answer." When viewed contextually in light of the circumstances in *Re S,* Lord Nicholl's reference to the judicial reluctance to depart from fundamental features of statutes must refer to those features that are so embedded in the fabric of the statute, they cannot be removed or changed by way of the necessarily piecemeal tool of judicial rectification. Of course, whether this is appropriate or not will depend on the "overall contextual setting" of the statute in question, and will be especially sensitive to whether the legal change has far-reaching practical ramifications which the court is not equipped to assess. Lord Nicholl's comments in *Re S* clarify that radical legislative reform of the type proposed in that case is best undertaken by Parliament, rather than the courts. However, it does not rule out creative judicial decision-making under s.3(1) to engage in law reform which is not of this type.

Bellinger, Anderson and the piecemeal nature of judicial law-making under section 3(1) HRA

We have seen from *Re S* that the senior judiciary are reluctant to engage in *radical* statutory reform under the auspices of s.3(1). This goes to a general point about the differences between the judicial power to make law and the legislative law-making power, namely, that the former tends to be more limited in scope and effect. Legislators can decide to reform a whole area of the law in a root-and-branch fashion. Such radical and broad-ranging reform is generally not open to judges. Judges must operate within existing legal structures and can only make law on a case-by-case basis in response to the accidents of litigation. It is therefore difficult for them to provide a blueprint of reform for an entire area of the law. In other words, judges generally possess the power to engage in partial and piecemeal reform, whereas Parliament has the power to engage in more radical and wide-ranging reform.

This general point is illustrated by the decision in *Bellinger v Bellinger,* where the House of Lords declined to interpret "male" and "female" in s.11(c) of the Matrimonial Causes Act 1973 to include a transsexual female under s.3 HRA...

Therefore, although the interpretation proposed by Mrs Bellinger under s.3(1) may have been linguistically and legally possible, the resulting change in the law would have far-reaching practical ramifications, raising issues whose solution calls for extensive inquiry and the widest public consultation and discussion which was more appropriate for Parliament than the courts. Again, the decision is not based on a rejection of the very idea of "reading in" or of engaging in law reform through s.3(1). It is based on a rejection of a particular type of law reform, namely, that which is so radical in effect, and so interlinked to reform in other areas of the law, that to attempt it by way of the necessarily piecemeal tool of the judicial rectification would be inappropriate.

However, this was not the only relevant contextual factor at play in *Bellinger*. When deciding the case, the House of Lords knew that the European Court of Human Rights (ECtHR) had handed down a recent decision holding the United Kingdom to be in breach of Arts 8 and 12 for denying legal recognition of cases of gender reassignment. This decision prompted three significant developments, described by Lord Nicholls as having "an important bearing on the outcome of this appeal". First, the Interdepartmental Working Group on Transsexual People had been reconvened to re-examine the implications of granting full legal status to transsexual people in their acquired gender in light of the *Goodwin* judgment. Secondly, in December 2002 (*i.e.* a month before the *Bellinger* decision was handed down) the government announced its intention to bring forward primary legislation that would allow transsexual people to marry in their acquired gender. Thirdly, the Lord Chancellor accepted that since the ECtHR decision, those parts of English law that failed to give legal recognition to the acquired gender transsexual persons were in principle incompatible with Arts 8 and 12 ECHR. Domestic law, including s.11 of the 1973 Act, would have to change.

...

Danny Nicol claims that *Anderson* demonstrates that the House of Lords has now "made up its mind in favour of restricting its use of s.3 and correspondingly availing itself more readily of s.4 declarations". However, before rushing to such conclusions, we need to examine *Anderson* contextually in light of all the factors influencing the decision to grant a declaration of incompatibility in that case. Of central importance in *Anderson* was the fact that the ECtHR had handed down two recent decisions indicating that the power exercised by the Home Secretary under s.29 violated the Convention right contained in Art.6. Moreover, there was *Hansard* evidence that, in response to *Stafford,* the Home Secretary acknowledged that some of the administrative arrangements for the review and release of mandatory life sentence prisoners needed to be changed in order to give effect to that decision. Finally, the *Stafford* ruling provided that even if the Secretary of State's discretion under s.29 was removed, and he was obliged to follow the judicial recommendation on tariffs, this would still be in violation of Art.6, because it would be objectionable from a "separation of powers" point of view.

These factors combined to assure the House of Lords that the government was going to change provisions like s.29, indeed was legally obliged to do so, following the ruling in *Stafford*. Therefore, there was no need to adopt a strained construction under s.3(1) HRA in this case. The more appropriate course of action was to grant a declaration of incompatibility. Moreover, even if they attempted some judicial rectification under s.3(1) to remove the Home Secretary's discretion, the judgment in *Stafford* indicated that this would be insufficient to remove the violation of Art.6 ECHR. For these reasons, a declaration of incompatibility under s.4 was a preferable and more effective judicial option than a strained interpretation under s.3. The existence of these factors casts doubt on the claim that this case is clear authority for the proposition that the House of Lords will *generally* restrict its use of s.3, and tends to prefer declarations of incompatibility under s.4 as a general matter. *Anderson* merely shows that in cases where the ECtHR has already pronounced on an issue and there is evidence that the government intends to change the law in light of this, the courts may well prefer to issue a declaration of incompatibility, rather than engaging in difficult and perhaps strained modes of interpretation under s.3.

As Nicol rightly points out, one of the reasons why judges may be reluctant to issue a declaration of incompatibility is the fear or risk that Parliament will not reform the law to comply with Convention rights. It would be naive to think that considerations about whether Parliament is already prepared to change the law would not influence the judicial decision about whether to adopt an interpretation under s.3, or a declaration of incompatibility under s.4 HRA. Both *Anderson* and *Bellinger* are cases where the declaration of incompatibility was the easiest and most obvious solution. They are not cases where the judges decided to restrict their use of s.3 and rely on s.4, on the basis of a general view that the latter is preferable. It was simply that it was obviously preferable in the context of these particular cases.

It is perhaps worth noting that in his judgment in *A,* Lord Steyn asserted that "in order to carry out the will of Parliament as expressed in s.3, it will sometimes be necessary to adopt an interpretation which linguistically may appear strained". He did not say that it will *always* be necessary or possible - simply that it would sometimes be so. *Re S, Bellinger* and *Anderson* are all examples of cases where it was either impossible, unnecessary or inappropriate to adopt a strained interpretation under s.3(1). Simply because a s.3(1) interpretation is impossible or undesirable in one case, does not mean that it will be impossible or undesirable in all cases. It all depends on the reasons given for that impossibility in the context and circumstances of the individual case.

One final point to be addressed concerns the relationship between *Anderson* and *Re S.* This is an important issue, because it is central to Nicol's claim that *Re S, Bellinger* and *Anderson* are evidence of an interpretative trend which differs from that adopted in *A.* According to Nicol, *Anderson* "resoundingly confirmed *S*", thus making it clear that a new interpretative approach was being favoured by the House of Lords. Whilst it is true that the three judges who gave full judgment in *Anderson* cited *Re S* in support of their conclusions, it is worth examining the exact citations they chose and the exact use they made of them in their reasoning. All three judges in *Anderson* cited *Re S* in support of the general proposition that there is an important distinction between interpretation and legislation in adjudication under the HRA. Lord Steyn and Lord Bingham cited [41] of Lord Nicholls' judgment in *Re* S, which simply contained the observation that it was important for judges fulfilling their obligation under s.3(1) to identify clearly a particular statutory provision. Lord Hutton cited [39] of the same judgment which itself contains some general statements about the appropriate constitutional boundary between interpretation of statutes and the enactment of statutes.

Two points should be noted about these citations. First, the distinction between interpretation and legislation is often used by the judiciary in a rhetorical way and its mere statement (without more explanation or elaboration) does not determine or resolve difficult questions about the nature of the interpretative process under s.3 or indeed its possible limits. Secondly, the paragraph cited by Lords Steyn and Bingham contains an entirely uncontroversial point, which in no way contradicts the method of interpretation adopted in *R. v A.* If *Anderson* is a resounding confirmation of these points, then much more argument is needed to show that this entails a new departure in interpretive method under s.3. Moreover, the three judges who gave a full judgment in the *Anderson* case, left the issue of the interpretative obligation under s.3 to the very end of their judgments, dedicating only a few lines each to the issue of what would be "possible" in this particular case. It is perhaps unwise to attribute to such terse remarks the far-reaching significance which Nicol does on the complex issue of the appropriate interpretative method prescribed by s.3(1).

Conclusion

Whether it is "possible" to adopt an interpretation under s.3 HRA will depend on the terms of those provisions, their interrelationship, as well as their relationship to the wider area of law of which they are a part. As I have attempted to show, it may also depend on other factors, such as whether Parliament is willing to reform the law, whether that reform is imminent, whether there is a ECtHR case on the issue, whether the disadvantages of a particular strained interpretation outweigh its advantages in terms of justice for the individual litigants, etc. The case analysis presented here shows that mere linguistic possibility is not the only factor in deciding whether to adopt an interpretation under s.3(1). In making that decision, the courts will also take account of the possible consequences of such an interpretation whether it is desirable or appropriate all things considered. We now have examples of cases where a proposed interpretation of certain statutory provisions is possible, but was not adopted by the court for other (legitimate) reasons. The case law must be viewed in the context of these reasons, not in isolation from them.

Further consideration was given to the issue of what was possible under the Human Rights Act s 3 in the case of *Ghaidan v Godin-Mendoza* [2004] UKHL 30, [2004] 2 AC 557.

Ghaidan v Godin-Mendoza [2004] UKHL 30, [2004] 2 AC 557

Statutes: The European Convention on Human Rights Articles 8 and 14; Rent Act 1977 s 76(1); Housing Act 1988 s 39(2); The Human Rights Act 1998 s 3

Panel: Lord Nicholls of Birkenhead, Lord Steyn, Lord Millett, Lord Rodger of Earlsferry and Baroness Hale of Richmond

Facts: The defendant had lived in a stable and permanent homosexual relationship with the protected tenant of a flat; the claimant was the freehold owner. In possession proceedings brought by the claimant on the tenant's death the judge granted a declaration that the defendant could not succeed to the tenancy of the flat, as the surviving spouse of the original tenant, but became entitled to an assured tenancy of the flat by succession as a member of the original tenant's family. On the defendant's appeal the Court of Appeal held that the interpretation of 'spouse' placed a surviving homosexual partner in a less secure position than the survivor of a heterosexual partner and as such infringed the defendant's rights under articles 8 and 14 of the Convention. The court, utilising the Human Rights Act s 3, held that it was possible to give effect to the law in a way that was compatible with Convention rights by reading it as extending to persons living with the original tenant as if they were his or her wife or husband, with the result that the defendant's longstanding homosexual relationship with the original tenant allowed him to succeed to the tenancy. The claimant appealed.

LORD NICHOLLS OF BIRKENHEAD

5. On an ordinary reading of this language paragraph 2(2) draws a distinction between the position of a heterosexual couple living together in a house as husband and wife and a homosexual couple living together in a house. The survivor of a heterosexual couple may become a statutory tenant by succession, the survivor of a homosexual couple cannot. That was decided in *Fitzpatrick*'s case.

6. Mr Godin-Mendoza's claim is that this difference in treatment infringes article 14 of the European Convention on Human Rights read in conjunction with article 8...

7. That is the first step in Mr Godin-Mendoza's claim. That step would not, of itself, improve Mr Godin-Mendoza's status in his flat. The second step in his claim is to pray in aid the court's duty under section 3 of the Human Rights Act 1998 to read and give effect to legislation in a way which is compliant with the Convention rights. Here, it is said, section 3 requires the court to read paragraph 2 so that it embraces couples living together in a close and stable homosexual relationship as much as couples living together in a close and stable heterosexual relationship. So read, paragraph 2 covers Mr Godin-Mendoza's position. Hence he is entitled to a declaration that on the death of Mr Wallwyn-James he succeeded to a statutory tenancy.

...

Section 3 of the Human Rights Act 1998

25. I turn next to the question whether section 3 of the Human Rights Act 1998 requires the court to depart from the interpretation of paragraph 2 enunciated in *Fitzpatrick*'s case [2001] 1 AC 27.

26. Section 3 is a key section in the Human Rights Act 1998. It is one of the primary means by which Convention rights are brought into the law of this country. Parliament has decreed that all legislation, existing and future, shall be interpreted in a particular way. All legislation must be read and given effect to in a way which is compatible with the Convention rights "so far as it is possible to do so". This is the intention of Parliament, expressed in section 3, and the courts must give effect to this intention.

27. Unfortunately, in making this provision for the interpretation of legislation, section 3 itself is not free from ambiguity. Section 3 is open to more than one interpretation. The difficulty lies in the word "possible". Section 3(1), read in conjunction with section 3(2) and section 4, makes one matter clear: Parliament expressly envisaged that not all

legislation would be capable of being made Convention-compliant by application of section 3. Sometimes it would be possible, sometimes not. What is not clear is the test to be applied in separating the sheep from the goats. What is the standard, or the criterion, by which "possibility" is to be judged? A comprehensive answer to this question is proving elusive. The courts, including your Lordships' House, are still cautiously feeling their way forward as experience in the application of section 3 gradually accumulates.

28. One tenable interpretation of the word "possible" would be that section 3 is confined to requiring courts to resolve ambiguities. Where the words under consideration fairly admit of more than one meaning the Convention-compliant meaning is to prevail. Words should be given the meaning which best accords with the Convention rights.

29. This interpretation of section 3 would give the section a comparatively narrow scope. This is not the view which has prevailed. It is now generally accepted that the application of section 3 does not depend upon the presence of ambiguity in the legislation being interpreted. Even if, construed according to the ordinary principles of interpretation, the meaning of the legislation admits of no doubt, section 3 may none the less require the legislation to be given a different meaning. The decision of your Lordships' House in *R v A (No 2)* [2002] 1 AC 45 is an instance of this...

30. From this it follows that the interpretative obligation decreed by section 3 is of an unusual and far-reaching character. Section 3 may require a court to depart from the unambiguous meaning the legislation would otherwise bear. In the ordinary course the interpretation of legislation involves seeking the intention reasonably to be attributed to Parliament in using the language in question. Section 3 may require the court to depart from this legislative intention, that is, depart from the intention of the Parliament which enacted the legislation. The question of difficulty is how far, and in what circumstances, section 3 requires a court to depart from the intention of the enacting Parliament. The answer to this question depends upon the intention reasonably to be attributed to Parliament in enacting section 3.

31. On this the first point to be considered is how far, when enacting section 3, Parliament intended that the actual language of a statute, as distinct from the concept expressed in that language, should be determinative. Since section 3 relates to the "interpretation" of legislation, it is natural to focus attention initially on the language used in the legislative provision being considered. But once it is accepted that section 3 may require legislation to bear a meaning which departs from the unambiguous meaning the legislation would otherwise bear, it becomes impossible to suppose Parliament intended that the operation of section 3 should depend critically upon the particular form of words adopted by the parliamentary draftsman in the statutory provision under consideration. That would make the application of section 3 something of a semantic lottery. If the draftsman chose to express the concept being enacted in one form of words, section 3 would be available to achieve Convention-compliance. If he chose a different form of words, section 3 would be impotent.

32. From this the conclusion which seems inescapable is that the mere fact the language under consideration is inconsistent with a Convention-compliant meaning does not of itself make a Convention-compliant interpretation under section 3 impossible. Section 3 enables language to be interpreted restrictively or expansively. But section 3 goes further than this. It is also apt to require a court to read in words which change the meaning of the enacted legislation, so as to make it Convention-compliant. In other words, the intention of Parliament in enacting section 3 was that, to an extent bounded only by what is "possible", a court can modify the meaning, and hence the effect, of primary and secondary legislation.

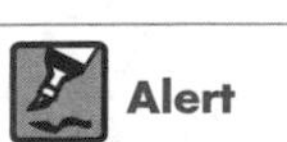
Alert

33. Parliament, however, cannot have intended that in the discharge of this extended interpretative function the courts should adopt a meaning inconsistent with a fundamental feature of legislation. That would be to cross the constitutional boundary section 3 seeks to demarcate and preserve. Parliament has retained the right to enact legislation in terms which are not Convention-compliant. The meaning imported by application of section 3 must be compatible with the underlying thrust of the legislation being construed. Words implied must, in the phrase of my noble and learned friend, Lord Rodger of Earlsferry, "go with the grain of the legislation". Nor can Parliament have intended that section 3 should require courts to make decisions for which they are not equipped. There may be several ways of making a provision Convention-compliant, and the choice may involve issues calling for legislative deliberation.

34. Both these features were present in *In re S (Minors) (Care Order: Implementation of Care Plan)* [2002] 2 AC 29. There the proposed "starring system" was inconsistent in an important respect with the scheme of the Children Act 1989, and the proposed system had far-reaching practical ramifications for local authorities. Again, in *R (Anderson) v Secretary of State for the Home Department* [2003] 1 AC 837 section 29 of the Crime (Sentences) Act 1997 could not be read in a Convention-compliant way without giving the section a meaning inconsistent with an important feature expressed clearly in the legislation. In *Bellinger v Bellinger (Lord Chancellor intervening)* [2003] 2 AC 467 recognition of Mrs Bellinger as female for the purposes of section 11(c) of the Matrimonial Causes Act 1973 would have had exceedingly wide ramifications, raising issues ill-suited for determination by the courts or court procedures.

35. In some cases difficult problems may arise. No difficulty arises in the present case. Paragraph 2 of Schedule 1 to the Rent Act 1977 is unambiguous. But the social policy underlying the 1988 extension of security of tenure under paragraph 2 to the survivor of couples living together as husband and wife is equally applicable to the survivor of homosexual couples living together in a close and stable relationship. In this circumstance I see no reason to doubt that application of section 3 to paragraph 2 has the effect that paragraph 2 should be read and given effect to as though the survivor of such a homosexual couple were the surviving spouse of the original tenant. Reading paragraph 2 in this way would have the result that cohabiting heterosexual couples and cohabiting homosexual couples would be treated alike for the purposes of succession as a statutory tenant. This would eliminate the discriminatory effect of paragraph 2 and would do so consistently with the social policy underlying paragraph

2. The precise form of words read in for this purpose is of no significance. It is their substantive effect which matters.

LORD STEYN

49. ...[T]here has sometimes been a tendency to approach the interpretative task under section 3(1) in too literal and technical a way. In practice there has been too much emphasis on linguistic features. If the core remedial purpose of section 3(1) is not to be undermined a broader approach is required. That is, of course, not to gainsay the obvious proposition that inherent in the use of the word "possible" in section 3(1) is the idea that there is a Rubicon which courts may not cross. If it is not possible, within the meaning of section 3, to read or give effect to legislation in a way which is compatible with Convention rights, the only alternative is to exercise, where appropriate, the power to make a declaration of incompatibility. Usually, such cases should not be too difficult to identify...

50. Having had the opportunity to reconsider the matter in some depth, I am not disposed to try to formulate precise rules about where section 3 may not be used. Like the proverbial elephant such a case ought generally to be easily identifiable. What is necessary, however, is to emphasise that interpretation under section 3(1) is the prime remedial remedy and that resort to section 4 must always be an exceptional course. In practical effect there is a strong rebuttable presumption in favour of an interpretation consistent with Convention rights. Perhaps the opinions delivered in the House today will serve to ensure a balanced approach along such lines.

LORD MILLETT

57. ...I have given long and anxious consideration to the question whether, in the interests of unanimity, I should suppress my dissent, but I have come to the conclusion that I should not. The question is of great constitutional importance, for it goes to the relationship between the legislature and the judiciary, and hence ultimately to the supremacy of Parliament. Sections 3 and 4 of the Human Rights Act were carefully crafted to preserve the existing constitutional doctrine, and any application of the ambit of section 3 beyond its proper scope subverts it. This is not to say that the doctrine of Parliamentary supremacy is sacrosanct, but only that any change in a fundamental constitutional principle should be the consequence of deliberate legislative action and not judicial activism, however well meaning.

59. Several points may be made at the outset. First, the requirement in section 3 is obligatory...

60. Secondly, the obligation arises (or at least has significance) only where the legislation in its natural and ordinary meaning, that is to say as construed in accordance with normal principles, is incompatible with the Convention...

62. Thirdly, there are limits to the extent to which section 3 may be applied to render existing legislation compatible with the Convention. The presence of section 4 alone shows this to be the case, for it presupposes the existence of cases where the offending

legislation cannot be rendered compatible with the Convention by the application of section 3.

63. There are two limitations to its application which are expressed in section 3 itself. In the first place, the exercise which the court is called on to perform is still one of interpretation, not legislation: (legislation must be "read and given effect to")...

66. In the second place, section 3 requires the court to read legislation in a way which is compatible with the Convention only "so far as it is possible to do so". It must, therefore, be possible, by a process of interpretation alone, to read the offending statute in a way which is compatible with the Convention.

67. This does not mean that it is necessary to identify an ambiguity or absurdity in the statute ... It means only that the court must take the language of the statute as it finds it and give it a meaning which, however unnatural or unreasonable, is intellectually defensible. It can read in and read down; it can supply missing words, so long as they are consistent with the fundamental features of the legislative scheme; it can do considerable violence to the language and stretch it almost (but not quite) to breaking point. The court must "strive to find a possible interpretation compatible with Convention rights" (emphasis added): *R v A* [2002] 1 AC 45, 67, para 44, per Lord Steyn. But it is not entitled to give it an impossible one, however much it would wish to do so.

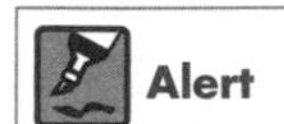

68. In my view section 3 does not entitle the court to supply words which are inconsistent with a fundamental feature of the legislative scheme; nor to repeal, delete, or contradict the language of the offending statute...

69. I doubt that the principles which I have endeavoured to state would be disputed; disagreement is likely to lie in their application in a particular case...

The cases on the appropriate use of ss 3 and 4 appear to show a significant level of consistency at least in terms of theory. Their Lordships agree that s 3 is a strong and robust provision and that the court can depart from the apparent intention of Parliament. However, while definition of what is 'possible' in principle has proved consistent, there has been some disagreement in the application of the principle. This can be seen in the case of *Ghaidan*. Lord Millett was correct that the principles he set out were undisputed. Yet, even though the House agreed on what the principles were, he still felt unable to agree with the majority on their application. This may cause problems in practice. While the lottery may not be a semantic one in terms of what 'possible' means, to use Lord Nicholls' phrase in *Ghaidan*, the application of the principles could be seen as a lottery dependent on which judge is hearing the case.

Further Reading

Blackstone's Guide to the Human Rights Act 1998, (5th Edition) pp 60 – 67

Hoffmann and Rowe QC, *Human Rights in the UK*, (3rd Edition) pp 68 – 77

Lord Irvine of Lairg, *Human Rights, Constitutional Law and Development of the English Legal System*, Part 1 Chapter 5

9

"Absolute rights" – Articles 2 and 3

Topic List

Alex Lawson and Neil Hurden

Introduction

The European Convention on Human Rights Articles 2 and 3 are generally known as the 'absolute rights'. These are, respectively, the right to life and the prohibition against torture and inhuman or degrading treatment. However, the term can only be loosely applied as the State can be justified in taking someone's life. There are a number of scenarios in which this may not be merely unavoidable, but arguably legally and morally necessary. It is important to consider the wording of Article 2(2) in particular, which lays down three broad justifications for state-sanctioned killing, using force that is 'no more than absolutely necessary'.

The problem with Article 3 is slightly different. There are no scenarios in which torture or its slightly less serious variants of causing inhuman or degrading treatment are legally allowed. Rather, the two-fold problem is in first defining at what level treatment falls into Article 3 at all. There are plenty of activities and forms of treatment one might find unpleasant, but do they cross into Article 3? The second problem is that Article 3 involves two broad concepts and so identifying the dividing lines is also important.

This chapter will look at two leading cases, the first involving the use of force by agents of the State leading to deaths, therefore engaging Article 2. And the second a case brought by the Republic of Ireland against the United Kingdom alleging violations of Article 3.

1 Article 2

***McCann, Farrell and Savage v UK* (1996) 21 EHRR 97**

Panel: The President, Judge Ryssdal; Judges Bernhardt, Thór Vilhjálmsson, Gölcüklü, Russo, Spielman, Valticos, Palm, Pekkanen, Morenilla, Freeland, Baka, Lopes Rocha, Mifsud Bonnici, Makarczyk, Repik, Jambrek, Kuris and Lohmus

Statute: European Convention on Human Rights Article 2

Facts: The applicants were relatives of three alleged Provisional IRA terrorists who had been killed by British military personnel (members of the SAS) in Gibraltar. The UK Government's position was that the killings, which had been carried out with little in the way of warning or concerted attempt to capture the individuals alive, was a proportionate response to the intelligence assessment which indicated that the individuals were about to explode a bomb, threatening serious loss of life. The case was critical in establishing that, when the state takes the life of individuals, an adequate investigation must be carried out. This is a very important, secondary obligation inherent within Article 2. If the investigation discloses serious errors in training, command and control, then that also will disclose a violation of the more substantive element of Article 2, namely the lawfulness of the killing in the first place. The case is notable for establishing many of the key principles in this area – note the lack of reference to other cases in the text.

JUDGMENT

Alleged violation of Article 2 of the Convention

The obligation to protect life in Article 2(1)

Compatibility of national law and practice with Article 2 standards

151. The applicants submitted under this head that Article 2(1) of the Convention imposed a positive duty on States to "protect" life. In particular, the national law must strictly control and limit the circumstances in which a person may be deprived of his life by agents of the State. The State must also give appropriate training, instructions and briefing to its soldiers and other agents who may use force and exercise strict control over any operations which may involve the use of lethal force.

In their view, the relevant domestic law was vague and general and did not encompass the Article 2 standard of absolute necessity. This in itself constituted a violation of Article 2(1). There was also a violation of this provision in that the law did not require that the agents of the State be trained in accordance with the strict standards of Article 2(1).

152. For the Commission, with whom the Government agreed, Article 2 was not to be interpreted as requiring an identical formulation in domestic law. Its requirements were satisfied if the substance of the Convention right was protected by domestic law.

153. The Court recalls that the Convention does not oblige contracting parties to incorporate its provisions into national law. Furthermore, it is not the role of the Convention institutions to examine in abstracto the compatibility of national legislative or constitutional provisions with the requirements of the Convention.

154. Bearing the above in mind, it is noted that Article 2 of the Gibraltar Constitution is similar to Article 2 of the Convention with the exception that the standard of justification for the use of force which results in the deprivation of life is that of "reasonably justifiable" as opposed to "absolutely necessary" in Article 2(2). While the Convention standard appears on its face to be stricter than the relevant national standard, it has been submitted by the Government that, having regard to the manner in which the standard is interpreted and applied by the national courts, there is no significant difference in substance between the two concepts.

155. In the Court's view, whatever the validity of this submission, the difference between the two standards is not sufficiently great that a violation of Article 2(1) could be found on this ground alone.

156. As regards the applicants' arguments concerning the training and instruction of the agents of the State and the need for operational control, the Court considers that these are matters which, in the context of the present case, raise issues under Article 2(2) concerning the proportionality of the State's response to the perceived threat of a terrorist attack. It suffices to note in this respect that the Rules of Engagement issued to the soldiers and the police in the present case provide a series of rules governing the use of force which carefully reflect the national standard as well as the substance of the Convention standard.

Adequacy of the Inquest proceedings as an investigative mechanism

157. The applicants also submitted under this head, with reference to the relevant standards contained in the UN Force and Firearms Principles, that the State must provide an effective ex post facto procedure for establishing the facts surrounding a killing by agents of the State through an independent judicial process to which relatives must have full access.

Together with the amici curiae, Amnesty International and British-Irish Rights Watch and Others, they submitted that this procedural requirement had not been satisfied by the Inquest procedure because of a combination of shortcomings. In particular, they complained that no independent police investigation took place of any aspect of the operation leading to the shootings; that normal scene-of-crime procedures were not followed; that not all eye witnesses were traced or interviewed by the police; that the Coroner sat with a jury which was drawn from a "garrison" town with close ties to the military; that the Coroner refused to allow the jury to be screened to exclude members who were Crown servants; that the public interest certificates issued by the relevant government authorities effectively curtailed on examination of the overall operation.

They further contended that they did not enjoy equality of representation with the Crown in the course of the Inquest proceedings and were thus severely handicapped in their efforts to find the truth since, *inter alia*, they had had no legal aid and were only represented by two lawyers; witness statements had been made available in advance to the Crown and to the lawyers representing the police and the soldiers but, with the exception of ballistic and pathology reports, not to their lawyers; they did not have the necessary resources to pay for copies of the daily transcript of the proceedings which amounted to £500–£700.

158. The Government submitted that the Inquest was an effective, independent and public review mechanism which more than satisfied any procedural requirement which might be read into Article 2(1) of the Convention. In particular, they maintained that it would not be appropriate for the Court to seek to identify a single set of standards by which all investigations into the circumstances of death should be assessed. Moreover, it was important to distinguish between such an investigation and civil proceedings brought to seek a remedy for an alleged violation of the right to life. Finally, they invited the Court to reject the contention by the intervenors British-Irish Rights Watch and Others that a violation of Article 2(1) will have occurred whenever the Court finds serious differences between the UN Principles on Extra-Legal Executions and the investigation conducted into any particular death.

159. For the Commission, the Inquest subjected the actions of the State to extensive, independent and highly public scrutiny and thereby provided sufficient procedural safeguards for the purposes of Article 2 of the Convention.

160. The Court considers that it is unnecessary to decide in the present case whether a right of access to court to bring civil proceedings in connection with deprivation of life can be inferred from Article 2(1) since this is an issue which would be more

appropriately considered under Articles 6 and 13 of the Convention—provisions that have not been invoked by the applicants.

161. It confines itself to noting, like the Commission, that a general legal prohibition of arbitrary killing by the agents of the State would be ineffective, in practice, if there existed no procedure for reviewing the lawfulness of the use of lethal force by State authorities. The obligation to protect the right to life under this provision, read in conjunction with the State's general duty under Article 1 of the Convention to "secure to everyone within their jurisdiction the rights and freedoms defined in [the] Convention", requires by implication that there should be some form of effective official investigation when individuals have been killed as a result of the use of force by, inter alios, agents of the State.

Alert

162. However, it is not necessary in the present case for the Court to decide what form such an investigation should take and under what conditions it should be conducted, since public Inquest proceedings, at which the applicants were legally represented and which involved the hearing of 79 witnesses, did in fact take place. Moreover, the proceedings lasted 19 days and, as is evident from the Inquest's voluminous transcript, involved a detailed review of the events surrounding the killings. Furthermore, it appears from the transcript, including the Coroner's summing up to the jury, that the lawyers acting on behalf of the applicants were able to examine and cross-examine key witnesses, including the military and police personnel involved in the planning and conduct of the anti-terrorist operation, and to make the submissions they wished to make in the course of the proceedings.

163. In light of the above, the Court does not consider that the alleged various shortcomings in the Inquest proceedings, to which reference has been made by both the applicants and the intervenors, substantially hampered the carrying out of a thorough, impartial and careful examination of the circumstances surrounding the killings.

164. It follows that there has been no breach of Article 2(1) of the Convention on this ground.

Application of Article 2 to the facts of the case

General approach to the evaluation of the evidence

165. While accepting that the Convention institutions are not in any formal sense bound by the decisions of the Inquest jury, the Government submitted that the verdicts were of central importance to any subsequent examination of the deaths of the deceased. Accordingly, the Court should give substantial weight to the verdicts of the jury in the absence of any indication that those verdicts were perverse or ones which no reasonable tribunal of fact could have reached. In this connection, the jury was uniquely well placed to assess the circumstances surrounding the shootings. The members of the jury heard and saw each of the 79 witnesses giving evidence, including extensive cross-examination. With that benefit they were able to assess the credibility and probative value of the witnesses' testimony. The Government pointed out

that the jury also heard the submissions of the various parties, including those of the lawyers representing the deceased.

166. The applicants, on the other hand, maintained that inquests are by their very nature ill-equipped to be full and detailed enquiries into controversial killings such as in the present case. Moreover, the Inquest did not examine the killings from the standpoint of concepts such as "proportionality" or "absolute necessity" but applied the lesser tests of "reasonable force" or "reasonable necessity". Furthermore, the jury focused on the actions of the soldiers as they opened fire as if it were considering their criminal culpability and not on matters such as the allegedly negligent and reckless planning of the operation.

167. The Commission examined the case on the basis of the observations of the parties and the documents submitted by time, in particular the transcript of the Inquest. It did not consider itself bound by the findings of the jury.

168. The Court recalls that under the scheme of the Convention the establishment and verification of the facts is primarily a matter for the Commission. Accordingly, it is only in exceptional circumstances that the Court will use its powers in this area. The Court is not, however, bound by the Commission's findings of fact and remains free to make its own appreciation in the light of all the material before it.

169. In the present case neither the Government nor the applicants have, in the proceedings before the Court, sought to contest the facts as they have been found by the Commission although they differ fundamentally as to the conclusions to be drawn from them under Article 2 of the Convention.

Having regard to the submissions of those appearing before the Court and to the Inquest proceedings, the Court takes the Commission's establishment of the facts and findings on the points summarised in paragraphs 13 to 132 above to be an accurate and reliable account of the facts underlying the present case.

170. As regards the appreciation of these facts from the standpoint of Article 2, the Court observes that the jury had the benefit of listening to the witnesses at first hand, observing their demeanour and assessing the probative value of their testimony.

Nevertheless, it must be borne in mind that the jury's finding was limited to a decision of lawful killing and, as is normally the case, did not provide reasons for the conclusion that it reached. In addition, the focus of concern of the Inquest proceedings and the standard applied by the jury was whether the killings by the soldiers were reasonably justified in the circumstances as opposed to whether they were "absolutely necessary" under Article 2(2) in the sense developed above.

171. Against this background, the Court must make its own assessment whether the facts as established by the Commission disclose a violation of Article 2 of the Convention.

172. The applicants further submitted that in examining the actions of the State in a case in which the use of deliberate lethal force was expressly contemplated in writing, the Court should place on the Government the onus of proving, beyond reasonable

doubt, that the planning and execution of the operation was in accordance with Article 2 of the Convention. In addition, it should not grant the State authorities the benefit of the doubt as if its criminal liability were at stake.

173. The Court, in determining whether there has been a breach of Article 2 in the present case, is not assessing the criminal responsibility of those directly or indirectly concerned. In accordance with its usual practice therefore it will assess the issues in the light of all the material placed before it by the applicants and by the Government or, if necessary, material obtained of its own motion.

Applicant's allegation that the killings were premeditated

174. The applicants alleged that there had been a premeditated plan to kill the deceased. While conceding that there was no evidence of a direct order from the highest authorities in the Ministry of Defence, they claimed that there was strong circumstantial evidence in support of their allegation. They suggested that a plot to kill could be achieved by other means such as hints and innuendoes, coupled with the choice of a military unit like the SAS which, as indicated by the evidence given by their members at the Inquest, was trained to neutralise a target by shooting to kill. Supplying false information of the sort that was actually given to the soldiers in this case would render a fatal shooting likely. The use of the SAS was, in itself, evidence that the killing was intended.

175. They further contended that the Gibraltar police would not have been aware of such an unlawful enterprise. They pointed out that the SAS officer E gave his men secret briefings to which the Gibraltar police were not privy. Moreover, when the soldiers attended the police station after the shootings, they were accompanied by an army lawyer who made it clear that the soldiers were there only for the purpose of handing in their weapons. In addition, the soldiers were immediately flown out of Gibraltar without ever having been interviewed by the police.

176. The applicants referred to the following factors, amongst others, in support of their contention:

— The best and safest method of preventing an explosion and capturing the suspects would have been to stop them and their bomb from entering Gibraltar. The authorities had their photographs and knew their names and aliases as well as the passports they were carrying;

— If the suspects had been under close observation by the Spanish authorities from Malaga to Gibraltar, as claimed by the journalist, Mr Debelius, the hiring of the white Renault car would have been seen and it would have been known that it did not contain a bomb;

— The above claim is supported by the failure of the authorities to isolate the bomb and clear the area around it in order to protect the public. In Gibraltar there were a large number of soldiers present with experience in the speedy clearance of suspect bomb sites. The only explanation for this lapse in security procedures was that the security services knew that there was no bomb in the car;

– Soldier G, who was sent to inspect the car and who reported that there was a suspect car bomb, admitted during the Inquest that he was not an expert in radio signal transmission. This was significant since the sole basis for his assessment was that the radio aerial looked older than the car. A real expert would have thought of removing the aerial to nullify the radio detonator, which could have been done without destabilising the explosive, as testified by Dr Scott. He would have also known that if the suspects had intended to explode a bomb by means of a radio signal they would not have used a rusty aerial—which would reduce the capacity to receive a clear signal—but a clean one. It also emerged from his evidence that he was not an explosive expert either. There was thus the possibility that the true role of Soldier G was to report that he suspected a car bomb in order to induce the Gibraltar police to sign the document authorising the SAS to employ lethal force.

177. In the Government's submission it was implicit in the jury's verdicts of lawful killing that they found as facts that there was no plot to kill the three terrorists and that the operation in Gibraltar had not been conceived or mounted with this aim in view. The aim of the operation was to effect the lawful arrest of the three terrorists and it was for this purpose that the assistance of the military was sought and given. Furthermore, the jury must have also rejected the applicants' contention that Soldiers A, B, C and D had deliberately set out to kill the terrorists, whether acting on express orders or as a result of being given "a nod and a wink".

178. The Commission concluded that there was no evidence to support the applicants' claim of a premeditated plot to kill the suspects.

179. The Court observes that it would need to have convincing evidence before it could conclude that there was a premeditated plan, in the sense developed by the applicants.

180. In the light of its own examination of the material before it, the Court does not find it established that there was an execution plot at the highest level of command in the Ministry of Defence or in the Government, or that Soldiers A, B, C and D had been so encouraged or instructed by the superior officers who had briefed them prior to the operation, or indeed that they had decided on their own initiative to kill the suspects irrespective of the existence of any justification for the use of lethal force and in disobedience to the arrest instructions they had received. Nor is there evidence that there was an implicit encouragement by the authorities or hints and innuendoes to execute the three suspects.

181. The factors relied on by the applicants amount to a series of conjectures that the authorities must have known that there was no bomb in the car. However, having regard to the intelligence information that they had received, to the known profiles of the three terrorists, all of whom had a background in explosives, and the fact that Mr Savage was seen to "fiddle" with something before leaving the car, the belief that the car contained a bomb cannot be described as either implausible or wholly lacking in foundation.

182. In particular, the decision to admit them to Gibraltar, however open to criticism given the risks that it entailed, was in accordance with the arrest policy formulated by the Advisory Group that no effort should be made to apprehend them until all three were present in Gibraltar and there was sufficient evidence of a bombing mission to secure their convictions.

183. Nor can the Court accept the applicants' contention that the use of the SAS, in itself, amounted to evidence that the killing of the suspects was intended. In this respect it notes that the SAS is a special unit which has received specialist training in combating terrorism. It was only natural, therefore, that in light of the advance warning that the authorities received of an impending terrorist attack they would resort to the skill and experience of the SAS in order to deal with the threat in the safest and most informed manner possible.

184. The Court therefore rejects as unsubstantiated the applicants' allegations that the killing of the three suspects were premeditated or the product of a tacit agreement amongst those involved in the operation.

Conduct and planning of the operation

Arguments of those appearing before the Court

The applicants

185. The applicants submitted that it would be wrong for the Court, as the Commission had done, to limit its assessment to the question of the possible justification of the soldiers who actually killed the suspects. It must examine the liability of the Government for all aspects of the operation. Indeed, the soldiers may well have been acquitted at a criminal trial if they could have shown that they honestly believed the ungrounded and false information they were given.

186. The soldiers had been told by Officer E (the attack commander) that the three suspects had planted a car bomb in Gibraltar, whereas Soldier G—the bomb disposal expert—had reported that it was merely a suspect bomb; that it was a remote-control bomb; that each of the suspects could detonate it from anywhere in Gibraltar by the mere flicking of a switch and that they would not hesitate to do so the moment they were challenged. In reality, these "certainties" and "facts" were no more than suspicions or at best dubious assessments. However they were conveyed as facts to soldiers who not only had been trained to shoot at the merest hint of a threat but also, as emerged from the evidence given during the Inquest, to continue to shoot until they had killed their target.

In sum, they submitted that the killings came about as a result of incompetence and negligence in the planning and conduct of the anti-terrorist operation to arrest the suspects as well as a failure to maintain a proper balance between the need to meet the threat posed and the right to life of the suspects.

The Government

187. The Government submitted that the actions of the soldiers were absolutely necessary in defence of persons from unlawful violence within the meaning of Article

2(2) (a) of the Convention. Each of them had to make a split second decision which could have affected a large number of lives. They believed that the movements which they saw the suspects make at the moment they were intercepted gave the impression that the terrorists were about to detonate a bomb. This evidence was confirmed by other witnesses who saw the movements in question. If it is accepted that the soldiers honestly and reasonably believed that the terrorists upon whom they opened fire might have been about to detonate a bomb by pressing a button, then they had no alternative but to open fire.

188. They also pointed out that much of the information available to the authorities and many of the judgments made by them proved to be accurate. The three deceased were an IRA active service unit which was planning an operation in Gibraltar; they did have in their control a large quantity of explosives which were subsequently found in Spain; and the nature of the operation was a car bomb. The risk to the lives of those in Gibraltar was, therefore, both real and extremely serious.

189. The Government further submitted that in examining the planning of the anti-terrorist operation it should be borne in mind that intelligence assessments are necessarily based on incomplete information since only fragments of the true picture will be known. Moreover, experience showed that the IRA were exceptionally ruthless and skilled in counter-surveillance techniques and that they did their best to conceal their intentions from the authorities. In addition, experience in Northern Ireland showed that the IRA is constantly and rapidly developing new technology. They thus had to take into account the possibility that the terrorists might be equipped with more sophisticated or more easily concealable radio-controlled devices than the IRA had previously been known to use. Finally, the consequences of underestimating the threat posed by the active service unit could have been catastrophic. If they had succeeded in detonating a bomb of the type and size found in Spain, everyone in the car park would have been killed or badly maimed and grievous injuries would have been caused to those in adjacent buildings, which included a school and an old people's home.

190. The intelligence assessments made in the course of the operation were reasonable ones to make in the light of the inevitably limited amount of information available to the authorities and the potentially devastating consequences of underestimating the terrorists' abilities and resources. In this regard the Government made the following observations:

— It was believed that a remote-controlled device would be used because it would give the terrorists a better chance of escape and would increase their ability to maximise the proportion of military rather than civilian casualties. Moreover, the IRA had used such a device in Brussels only six weeks before;

— It was assumed that any remote control such as that produced to the Court would be small enough to be readily concealed about the person. The soldiers themselves successfully concealed radios of a similar size about their persons;

— As testified by Captain Edwards at the Inquest, tests carried out demonstrated that a bomb in the car park could have been detonated from the spot where the terrorists were shot;

— Past experience strongly suggested that the terrorists' detonation device might have been operated by pressing a single button;

— As explained by witness O at the Inquest, the use of a blocking car would have been unnecessary because the terrorists would not be expected to have any difficulty in finding a free space on 8 March. It was also dangerous because it would have required two trips into Gibraltar, thereby significantly increasing the risk of detection;

— There was no reason to doubt the *bona fides* of Soldier G's assessment that the car was a suspect car bomb. In the first place his evidence was that he was quite familiar with car bombs. Moreover, the car had been parked by a known bomb-maker who had been seen to "fiddle" with something between the seats and the car aerial appeared to be out of place. IRA car bombs had been known from experience to have specially fitted aerials and G could not say for certain from an external examination that the car did not contain a bomb. Furthermore, all three suspects appeared to be leaving Gibraltar. Finally the operation of cordoning-off the area around the car began only 20 minutes after the above assessment had been made because of the shortage of available manpower and the fact that the evacuation plans were not intended for implementation until 7 or 8 March;

— It would have been reckless for the authorities to assume that the terrorists might not have detonated their bomb if challenged. The IRA were deeply committed terrorists who were, in their view, at war with the United Kingdom and who had in the past shown a reckless disregard for their own safety. There was still a real risk that if they had been faced with a choice between an explosion causing civilian casualties and no explosion at all, the terrorists would have preferred the former.

The Commission

191. The Commission considered that, given the soldiers' perception of the risk to the lives of the people of Gibraltar, the shooting of the three suspects could be regarded as absolutely necessary for the legitimate aim of the defence of others from unlawful violence. It also concluded that, having regard to the possibility that the suspects had brought in a car bomb which, if detonated, would have occasioned the loss of many lives and the possibility that the suspects could have been able to detonate it when confronted by the soldiers, the planning and execution of the operation by the authorities did not disclose any deliberate design or lack of proper care which might have rendered the use of lethal force disproportionate to the aim of saving lives.

The Court's assessment

Preliminary considerations

192. In carrying out its examination under Article 2 of the Convention, the Court must bear in mind that the information that the United Kingdom authorities received that there would be a terrorist attack in Gibraltar presented them with a fundamental dilemma. On the one hand, they were required to have regard to their duty to protect the lives of the people in Gibraltar including their own military personnel and, on the other, to have minimum resort to the use of lethal force against those suspected of

posing this threat in the light of the obligations flowing from both domestic and international law.

193. Several other factors must also be taken into consideration.

In the first place, the authorities were confronted by an active service unit of the IRA composed of persons who had been convicted of bombing offences and a known explosives expert. The IRA, judged by its actions in the past, had demonstrated a disregard for human life, including that of its own members.

Secondly, the authorities had had prior warning of the impending terrorist action and thus had ample opportunity to plan their reaction and, in co-ordination with the local Gibraltar authorities, to take measures to foil the attack and arrest the suspects. Inevitably, however, the security authorities could have been in possession of the full facts and were obliged to formulate their policies on the basis of incomplete hypotheses.

194. Against this background, in determining whether the force used was compatible with Article 2, the Court must carefully scrutinise, as noted above, not only whether the force used by the soldiers was strictly proportionate to the aim of protecting persons against unlawful violence but also whether the anti-terrorist operation was planned and controlled by the authorities so as to minimise, to the greatest extent possible, recourse to lethal force. The Court will consider each of these points in turn.

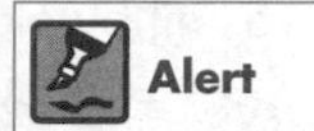

Actions of the soldiers

195. It is recalled that the soldiers who carried out the shooting (A, B, C and D) were informed by their superiors, in essence, that there was a car bomb in place which could be detonated by any of the three suspects by means of a radio control device which might have been concealed on their persons; that the device could be activated by pressing a button; that they would be likely to detonate the bomb if challenged, thereby causing heavy loss of life and serious injuries, and were also likely to be armed and to resist arrest.

196. As regards the shooting of Mr McCann and Ms Farrell, the Court recalls the Commission's finding that they were shot at close range after making what appeared to Soldiers A and B to be threatening movements with their hands as if they were going to detonate the bomb. The evidence indicated that they were shot as they fell to the ground but not as they lay on the ground. Four witnesses recalled hearing a warning shout. Officer P corroborated the soldiers' evidence as to the hand movements. Officer Q and Police Constable Parody also confirmed that Ms Farrell had made a sudden, suspicious move towards her handbag.

197. As regards the shooting of Mr Savage, the evidence revealed that there was only a matter of seconds between the shooting at the Shell garage (McCann and Farrell) and the shooting at Landport tunnel (Savage). The Commission found that it was unlikely that Soldiers C and D witnessed the first shooting before pursuing Mr Savage who had turned around after being alerted by either the police siren or the shooting.

Soldier C opened fire because Mr Savage moved his right arm to the area of his jacket pocket, thereby giving rise to the fear that he was about to detonate the bomb. In addition, Soldier C had seen something bulky in his pocket which he believed to be a detonating transmitter. Soldier D also opened fire believing that the suspect was trying to detonate the supposed bomb. The soldiers' version of events was corroborated in some respects by Witnesses H and J who saw Mr Savage spin round to face the soldiers in apparent response to the police siren or the first shooting.

The Commission found that Mr Savage was shot at close range until he hit the ground and probably in the instant as or after he had hit the ground. This conclusion was supported by the pathologists' evidence at the Inquest.

198. It was subsequently discovered that the suspects were unarmed, that they did not have a detonator device on their persons and that there was no bomb in the car.[74]

199. All four soldiers admitted that they shot to kill. They considered that it was necessary to continue to fire at the suspects until they were rendered physically incapable of detonating a device. According to the pathologists' evidence Ms Farrell was hit by eight bullets, Mr McCann by five and Mr Savage by 16.

200. The Court accepts that the soldiers honestly believed, in the light of the information that they had been given, as set out above, that it was necessary to shoot the suspects in order to prevent them from detonating a bomb and causing serious loss of life. The actions which they took, in obedience to superior orders, were thus perceived by them as absolutely necessary in order to safeguard innocent lives.

It considers that the use of force by agents of the State in pursuit of one of the aims delineated in Article 2(2) of the Convention may be justified under this provision where it is based on an honest belief which is perceived, for good reasons, to be valid at the time but which subsequently turns out to be mistaken. To hold otherwise would be to impose an unrealistic burden on the State and its law enforcement personnel in the execution of their duty, perhaps to the detriment of their lives and those of others.

Alert

It follows that, having regard to the dilemma confronting the authorities in the circumstances of the case, the actions of the soldiers do not, in themselves, give rise to a violation of this provision.

201. The question arises, however, whether the anti-terrorist operation as a whole was controlled and organised in a manner which respected the requirements of Article 2 and whether the information and instructions given to the soldiers which, in effect, rendered inevitable the use of lethal force, took adequately into consideration the right to life of the three suspects.

Alert

Control and organisation of the operation

202. The Court first observes that, as appears from the Operational Order of the Commissioner, it had been the intention of the authorities to arrest the suspects at an appropriate stage. Indeed evidence was given at the Inquest that arrest procedures had been practised by the soldiers before 6 March and that efforts had been made to find a suitable place in Gibraltar to detain the suspects after their arrest.

203. It may be questioned why the three suspects were not arrested at the border immediately on their arrival in Gibraltar and why, as emerged from the evidence given by Inspector Ullger, the decision was taken not to prevent them from entering Gibraltar if they were believed to be on a bombing mission. Having had advance warning of the terrorists' intentions it would certainly have been possible for the authorities to have mounted an arrest operation. Although surprised at the early arrival of the three suspects, they had a surveillance team at the border and an arrest group nearby. In addition, the security services and the Spanish authorities had photographs of the three suspects, knew their names as well as their aliases and would have known what passports to look for.

204. On this issue, the Government submitted that at that moment there might not have been sufficient evidence to warrant the detention and trial of the suspects. Moreover, to release them, having alerted them to the authorities' state of awareness but leaving them or others free to try again, would obviously increase the risks. Nor could the authorities be sure that those three were the only terrorists they had to deal with or of the manner in which it was proposed to carry out the bombing.

205. The Court confines itself to observing in this respect that the danger to the population of Gibraltar—which is at the heart of the Government's submissions in the case—in not preventing their entry must be considered to outweigh the possible consequences of having insufficient evidence to warrant their detention and trial. In its view, either the authorities knew that there was no bomb in the car—which the Court has already discounted—or there was a serious miscalculation by those responsible for controlling the operation. As a result, the scene was set in which the fatal shooting, given the intelligence assessments which had been made, was a foreseeable possibility if not a likelihood.

The decision not to stop the three terrorists from entering Gibraltar is thus a relevant factor to take into account under this head.

206. The Court notes that at the briefing on 5 March attended by Soldiers A, B, C and D it was considered likely that the attack would be by way of a large car bomb. A number of key assessments were made. In particular, it was thought that the terrorists would not use a blocking car; that the bomb would be detonated by a radio-control device; that the detonation could be effected by the pressing of a button; that it was likely that the suspects would detonate the bomb if challenged; that they would be armed and would be likely to use their arms if confronted.

207. In the event, all of these crucial assumptions, apart from the terrorists' intentions to carry out an attack, turned out to be erroneous. Nevertheless, as has been demonstrated by the Government, on the basis of their experience in dealing with the IRA, they were all possible hypotheses in a situation where the true facts were unknown and where the authorities operated on the basis of limited intelligence information.

208. In fact, insufficient allowances appear to have been made for other assumptions.

For example, since the bombing was not expected until 8 March when the changing of the guard ceremony was to take place, there was equally the possibility that the three terrorists were on a reconnaissance mission. While this was a factor which was briefly considered, it does not appear to have been regarded as a serious possibility.

In addition, at the briefings or after the suspects had been spotted, it might have been thought unlikely that they would have been prepared to explode the bomb, thereby killing many civilians, as Mr McCann and Ms Farrell strolled towards the border area since this would have increased the risk of detection and capture. It might also have been thought improbable that at that point they would set up the transmitter in anticipation to enable them to detonate the supposed bomb immediately if confronted.

Moreover, even if allowances are made for the technological skills of the IRA, the description of the detonation device as a "button job" without the qualifications subsequently described by the experts at the Inquest, of which the competent authorities must have been aware, over-simplifies the true nature of these devices.

209. It is further disquieting in this context that the assessment made by Soldier G, after a cursory external examination of the car, that there was a "suspect car bomb" was conveyed to the soldiers, according to their own testimony, as a definite identification that there was such a bomb. It is recalled that while Soldier G had experience in car bombs, it transpired that he was not an expert in radio communications or explosives; and that his assessment that there was a suspect car bomb, based on his observation that the car aerial was out of place, was more in the nature of a report that a bomb could not be ruled out.

210. In the absence of sufficient allowances being made for alternative possibilities, and the definite reporting of the existence of a car bomb which, according to the assessments that had been made, could be detonated at the press of a button, a series of working hypotheses were conveyed to Soldiers A, B, C and D as certainties, thereby making the use of lethal force almost unavoidable.

211. However, the failure to make provision for a margin of error must also be considered in combination with the training of the soldiers to continue shooting once they opened fire until the suspect was dead. As noted by the Coroner in his summing up to the jury at the Inquest, all four soldiers shot to kill the suspects. Soldier E testified that it had been discussed with the soldiers that there was an increased chance that they would have to shoot to kill since there would be less time where there was a "button" device. Against this background, the authorities were bound by their obligation to respect the right to life of the suspects to exercise the greatest of care in evaluating the information at their disposal before transmitting it to soldiers whose use of firearms automatically involved shooting to kill.

212. Although detailed investigation at the Inquest into the training received by the soldiers was prevented by the public interest certificates which had been used, it is not clear whether they had been trained or instructed to assess whether the use of firearms to wound their targets may have been warranted by the specific circumstances that confronted them at the moment of arrest.

Their reflex action in this vital respect lacks the degree of caution in the use of firearms to be expected from law enforcement personnel in a democratic society, even when dealing with dangerous terrorist suspects, and stands in marked contrast to the standard of care reflected in the instructions in the use of firearms by the police which had been drawn to their attention and which emphasised the legal responsibilities of the individual officer in the light of conditions prevailing at the moment of engagement.

This failure by the authorities also suggests a lack of appropriate care in the control and organisation of the arrest operation.

213. In sum, having regard to the decision not to prevent the suspects from travelling into Gibraltar, to the failure of the authorities to make sufficient allowances for the possibility that their intelligence assessments might, in some respects at least, be erroneous and to the automatic recourse to lethal force when the soldiers opened fire, the Court is not persuaded that the killing of the three terrorists constituted the use of force which was no more than absolutely necessary in defence of persons from unlawful violence within the meaning of Article 2(2)(a) of the Convention.

214. Accordingly, it finds that there has been a breach of Article 2 of the Convention.

2 Article 3

The following case is primarily of relevance in terms of Article 3. It provides a useful indication of how the European Court of Human Rights in Strasbourg has differentiated between cases of torture and those involving lesser variants and breaches of the Article, namely the imposition of inhuman and degrading treatment or punishment. It is significant, though, that this case was decided in the late 1970s and it is highly arguable that a more censorious attitude would be taken today in similar circumstances.

The Republic of Ireland v The United Kingdom (1979-80) 2 EHRR 25

Panel: The President, Judge Balladore Pallieri; Judges Wiarda, Zekia, Cremona, O'Donoghue, Pedersen, Vilhjàlmsson, Ryssdal, Ganshof van der Meersch, Fitzmaurice, Bindscheidler-Robert, Evrigenis, Teitgen, Lagergren, Liesch, Gölcüklü and Matscher

Decipher

it is possible for one signatory state to make allegations about another, as in this case.

Statute: European Convention on Human Rights Article 3

Facts: the British government had introduced detention without trial in Northern Ireland. This directly infringed the key principle in Article 5, for which a derogation had been lodged (under Article 15). The more important aspect of the case for present purposes was that, while subject to detention, individuals were subjected to the so-called 'five techniques', which included wall-standing, hooding and deprivation of sleep and food. The case was about whether these interrogation practices engaged Article 3, and if so, whether they amounted to torture or the less serious variant of inhuman and degrading treatment. (Note that it is not possible for a state to derogate from either Article 3 or 2.)

JUDGMENT

148. Paragraph (*d*) of the application of 10 March 1976 states that the object of bringing the case before the Court (rule 31 (1) (*d*) of the Rules of Court) is 'to ensure the observance in Northern Ireland of the engagements undertaken by the respondent

Government as a High Contracting Party to the Convention and in particular of the engagements specifically set out by the applicant Government in the pleadings filed and the submissions made on their behalf and described in the evidence adduced before the Commission in the hearings before them'. 'To this end', the Court is invited 'to consider the report of the Commission and to confirm the opinion of the Commission that breaches of the Convention have occurred and also to consider the claims of the applicant Government with regard to other alleged breaches and to make a finding of breach of the Convention where the Court is satisfied that a breach has occurred'.

In their written and oral pleadings before the Court, the Irish Government allege breaches of Articles 1, 3, 5 (taken together with Article 15), 6 (taken together with Article 15) and 14 (taken together with Articles 5 and 6).

They also maintain – though they do not ask the Court to make a specific finding—that the British Government failed on several occasions in their duty to furnish the necessary facilities for the effective conduct of the investigation. The Commission does not go as far as that; however, at various places in its report, the Commission points out, in substance, that the respondent Government did not always afford it the assistance desirable. The Court regrets this attitude on the part of that Government; it must stress the fundamental importance of the principle, enshrined in Article 28 (*a*) *in fine,* that the Contracting States have a duty to co-operate with the Convention institutions.

149. The Court notes first of all that it is not called upon to take cognisance of every single aspect of the tragic situation prevailing in Northern Ireland. For example, it is not required to rule on the terrorist activities in the six counties of individuals or of groups, activities that are in clear disregard of human rights. The Court has only to give a decision on the claims made before it by the Irish Republic against the United Kingdom. However, in so doing, the Court cannot lose sight of the events that form the background to this case.

ON ARTICLE 3

150. Article 3 provides that 'no one shall be subjected to torture or to inhuman or degrading treatment or punishment'.

PRELIMINARY QUESTIONS

151. In their memorial of 26 October 1976 and at the hearings in February 1977, the United Kingdom Government raised two preliminary questions on the alleged violations of Article 3. The first concerns the violations which they no longer contest, the second certain of the violations whose existence they dispute.

Preliminary question on the non-contested violations of Article 3

152. The United Kingdom Government contest neither the breaches of Article 3 as found by the Commission (see para. 147 above), nor – a point moreover that is beyond doubt – the Court's jurisdiction to examine such breaches. However, relying *inter alia* on the case law of the International Court of Justice, they argue that the European Court has power to decline to exercise its jurisdiction where the objective of an application has been accomplished or where adjudication on the merits would be

devoid of purpose. Such, they claim, is the situation here. They maintain that the findings in question not only are not contested but also have been widely publicised and that they do not give rise to problems of interpretation or application of the Convention sufficiently important to require a decision by the Court. Furthermore, for them the subject-matter of those findings now belongs to past history in view of the abandonment of the five techniques (1972), the solemn and unqualified undertaking not to reintroduce these techniques (8 February 1977) and the other measures taken by the United Kingdom to remedy, impose punishment for, and prevent the recurrence of, the various violations found by the Commission.

This argument is disputed by the applicant Government. Neither is it accepted in a general way by the delegates of the Commission; they stated, however, that they would express no conclusion as to whether or not the above-mentioned undertaking had deprived the claim concerning the five techniques of its object.

153. The Court takes formal note of the undertaking given before it, at the hearing on 8 February 1977, by the United Kingdom Attorney-General on behalf of the respondent Government. The terms of this undertaking were as follows: The Government of the United Kingdom have considered the question of the use of the 'five techniques' with very great care and with particular regard to Article 3 of the Convention. They now give this unqualified undertaking, that the 'five techniques' will not in any circumstances be reintroduced as an aid to interrogation. The Court also notes that the United Kingdom has taken various measures designed to prevent the recurrence of the events complained of and to afford reparation for their consequences. For example, it has issued to the police and the army instructions and directives on the arrest, interrogation and treatment of persons in custody, reinforced the procedures for investigating complaints, appointed commissions of enquiry and paid or offered compensation in many cases (see paras. 99–100, 107, 110–111, 116–118, 121–122, 124, 128–130, 132, 135–139 and 142–143 above).

154. Nevertheless, the Court considers that the responsibilities assigned to it within the framework of the system under the Convention extend to pronouncing on the non-contested allegations of violation of Article 3. The Court's judgments in fact serve not only to decide those cases brought before the Court but, more generally, to elucidate, safeguard and develop the rules instituted by the Convention, thereby contributing to the observance by the States of the engagements undertaken by them as Contracting Parties (Art. 19).

158. Following the Order of 11 February 1977 (see para. 8 above), the Irish Government indicated, at the hearings in April 1977, that they were asking the Court to hold that there had been in Northern Ireland, from 1971 to 1974, a practice or practices in breach of Article 3 and to specify, if need be, where they had occurred. They also declared that they were no longer seeking specific findings in relation to the cases of T3 and T5. [Cases T3 and T5 were cases in which the five techniques had been used.]

159. A practice incompatible with the Convention consists of an accumulation of identical or analogous breaches which are sufficiently numerous and inter-connected to

amount not merely to isolated incidents or exceptions but to a pattern or system; a practice does not of itself constitute a violation separate from such breaches.

It is inconceivable that the higher authorities of a State should be, or at least should be entitled to be, unaware of the existence of such a practice. Furthermore, under the Convention those authorities are strictly liable for the conduct of their subordinates; they are under a duty to impose their will on subordinates and cannot shelter behind their inability to ensure that it is respected.

The concept of practice is of particular importance for the operation of the rule of exhaustion of domestic remedies. This rule, as embodied in Article 26 of the Convention, applies to State applications (Art. 24), in the same way as it does to 'individual' applications (Art. 25), when the applicant State does no more than denounce a violation or violations allegedly suffered by 'individuals' whose place, as it were, is taken by the State. On the other hand and in principle, the rule does not apply where the applicant State complains of a practice as such, with the aim of preventing its continuation or recurrence, but does not ask the Commission or the Court to give a decision on each of the cases put forward as proof or illustrations of that practice. The Court agrees with the opinion which the Commission, following its earlier case law, expressed on the subject in its decision of 1 October 1972 on the admissibility of the Irish Government's original application. Moreover, the Court notes that that decision is not contested by the respondent Government.

QUESTIONS OF PROOF

160. In order to satisfy itself as to the existence or not in Northern Ireland of practices contrary to Article 3, the Court will not rely on the concept that the burden of proof is borne by one or other of the two Governments concerned. In the cases referred to it, the Court examines all the material before it, whether originating from the Commission, the Parties or other sources, and, if necessary, obtains material proprio motu.

161. The Commission based its own conclusions mainly on the evidence of the 100 witnesses heard in, and on the medical reports relating to, the 16 'illustrative' cases it had asked the applicant Government to select. The Commission also relied, but to a lesser extent, on the documents and written comments submitted in connection with the '41 cases' and it referred to the numerous 'remaining cases' (see para. 93 above). As in *The Greek Case*, the standard of proof the Commission adopted when evaluating the material it obtained was proof 'beyond reasonable doubt'.

The Irish Government see this as an excessively rigid standard for the purposes of the present proceedings. They maintain that the system of enforcement would prove ineffectual if, where there was a prima facie case of violation of Article 3, the risk of a finding of such a violation was not borne by a State which fails in its obligation to assist the Commission in establishing the truth (Art. 28 (*a*) *in fine* of the Convention). In their submission, this is how the attitude taken by the United Kingdom should be described.

The respondent Government dispute this contention and ask the Court to follow the same course as the Commission.

The Court agrees with the Commission's approach regarding the evidence on which to base the decision whether there has been violation of Article 3. To assess this evidence, the Court adopts the standard of proof 'beyond reasonable doubt' but adds that such proof may follow from the coexistence of sufficiently strong, clear and concordant inferences or of similar unrebutted presumptions of fact. In this context, the conduct of the Parties when evidence is being obtained has to be taken into account.

QUESTIONS CONCERNING THE MERITS

162. As was emphasised by the Commission, ill-treatment must attain a minimum level of severity if it is to fall within the scope of Article 3. The assessment of this minimum is, in the nature of things, relative; it depends on all the circumstances of the case, such as the duration of the treatment, its physical or mental effects and, in some cases, the sex, age and state of health of the victim, etc.

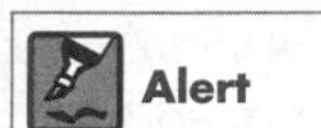

163. The Convention prohibits in absolute terms torture and inhuman or degrading treatment or punishment, irrespective of the victim's conduct. Unlike most of the substantive clauses of the Convention and of Protocols 1 and 4, Article 3 makes no provision for exceptions and, under Article 15 (2), there can be no derogation therefrom even in the event of a public emergency threatening the life of the nation.

164. In the instant case, the only relevant concepts are 'torture' and 'inhuman or degrading treatment', to the exclusion of 'inhuman or degrading punishment'.

The unidentified interrogation centre or centres

The 'five techniques'

165. The facts concerning the five techniques are summarised at paragraphs 96–104 and 106–107 above. In the Commission's estimation, those facts constituted a practice not only of inhuman and degrading treatment but also of torture. The applicant Government ask for confirmation of this opinion which is not contested before the Court by the respondent Government.

166. The police used the five techniques on 14 persons in 1971, that is, on 12, including T6 and T13, in August before the Compton Committee was set up, and on two in October whilst that Committee was carrying out its enquiry. Although never authorised in writing in any official document, the five techniques were taught orally by the English Intelligence Centre to members of the RUC at a seminar held in April 1971. There was accordingly a practice.

167. The five techniques were applied in combination, with premeditation and for hours at a stretch; they caused, if not actual bodily injury, at least intense physical and mental suffering to the persons subjected thereto and also led to acute psychiatric disturbances during interrogation. They accordingly fell into the category of inhuman treatment within the meaning of Article 3. The techniques were also degrading since they were such as to arouse in their victims feelings of fear, anguish and inferiority capable of humiliating and debasing them and possibly breaking their physical or moral resistance.

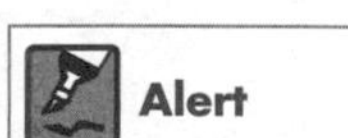

On these two points, the Court is of the same view as the Commission.

In order to determine whether the five techniques should also be qualified as torture, the Court must have regard to the distinction, embodied in Article 3, between this notion and that of inhuman or degrading treatment.

In the Court's view, this distinction derives principally from a difference in the intensity of the suffering inflicted.

The Court considers in fact that, whilst there exists on the one hand violence which is to be condemned both on moral grounds and also in most cases under the domestic law of the Contracting States but which does not fall within Article 3 of the Convention, it appears on the other hand that it was the intention that the Convention, with its distinction between 'torture' and 'inhuman or degrading treatment' , should by the first of these terms attach a special stigma to deliberate inhuman treatment causing very serious and cruel suffering.

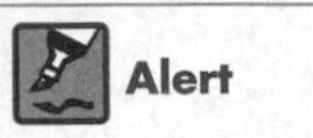

Moreover, this seems to be the thinking lying behind Article 1 *in fine* of Resolution 3452 (XXX) adopted by the General Assembly of the United Nations on 9 December, 1975, which declares: 'Torture constitutes an *aggravated* and deliberate form of cruel, inhuman or degrading treatment or punishment.'

Although the five techniques, as applied in combination, undoubtedly amounted to inhuman and degrading treatment, although their object was the extraction of confessions, the naming of others and/or information and although they were used systematically, they did not occasion suffering of the particular intensity and cruelty implied by the word torture as so understood.

168. The Court concludes that recourse to the five techniques amounted to a practice of inhuman and degrading treatment, which practice was in breach of Article 3.

It is notable in this case that the distinction made by the Strasbourg Court between torture and a lesser breach of Article 3 was that the former, in order to meet the high threshold and 'special stigma' implicit in the term, had to involve an 'aggravated and deliberate' form of treatment causing 'serious and cruel suffering'. There appears also to have been some differentiation between infliction of actual bodily injury and of psychological pressure and humiliation, though it is arguable that a more modern assessment of these types of interrogation technique would take a stricter approach with regard to the psychological impact on detainees.

Further Reading

Susan Nash, 'Human rights and wrongs', (2010) 160 *NLJ* 683

10

Freedom of the Person and "Due Process" rights – Articles 5 and 6

Topic List

Alex Lawson and Neil Hurden

Introduction

The preceding chapter dealt with fundamental principles relating to two of the most basic human rights, enshrined in Articles 2 and 3 of the Convention. The Articles highlighted in this chapter could be argued to be as important because they enable individuals to enjoy liberty and a fair legal process, which open up access to enforcement of all other rights.

Both these Articles are longer and structured in a more complex way than many others in the Convention and have application to different parts of the criminal and civil legal process. This chapter will focus on two key cases relating to the Article 5 rights of those arrested and detained by the state before moving on to a further two cases concerned with the fairness of the legal process more generally, as protected by Article 6.

1 Article 5

The first case deals with the most important of the six limitations to the right to liberty, justifiable under Article 5(1), the requirement of reasonable suspicion before an individual can be deprived of their liberty.

***Fox, Campbell and Hartley v UK* (1990) 13 EHRR 157**

Panel: The President, Judge Ryssdal; Judges Cremona, Pinheiro Farinha, Sir Vincent Evans, Bernhardt, Martens and Palm

Statute: European Convention on Human Rights Article 5

Facts: Under terrorist legislation operating in Northern Ireland it was only necessary for the police to demonstrate 'suspicion' rather than the more normal 'reasonable suspicion', before an arrest could be brought about. The question was whether this involved a violation of Article 5. A second issue was whether or not persons so detained needed to be told directly why they had been arrested, or whether it was sufficient under Article 5(2) that they be able to ascertain this based upon the types of questions being asked.

JUDGMENT

General approach

28. The applicants' complaints are directed against their arrest and detention under criminal legislation enacted to deal with acts of terrorism connected with the affairs of Northern Ireland.

Over the last 20 years, the campaign of terrorism waged in Northern Ireland has taken a heavy toll, especially in terms of human life and suffering. The Court has already recognised the need, inherent in the Convention system, for a proper balance between the defence of the institutions of democracy in the common interest and the protection of individual rights. Accordingly, when examining these complaints the Court will, as it did in the *Brogan and Others* judgment, take into account the special nature of terrorist crime and the exigencies of dealing with it, as far as is compatible with the applicable provisions of the Convention in the light of their particular wording and its overall object and purpose.

Alleged breach of Article 5(1)

29. The applicants alleged a breach of Article 5(1) of the Convention, which, in so far as relevant, provides:

'Everyone has the right to liberty and security of person. No one shall be deprived of his liberty save in the following cases and in accordance with a procedure prescribed by law:

... (c) the lawful arrest or detention of a person effected for the purpose of bringing him before the competent legal authority on reasonable suspicion of having committed an offence ...;

...'

They did not dispute that their arrest was 'lawful' under Northern Ireland law for the purposes of this provision and, in particular, 'in accordance with a procedure prescribed by law.'

30. They did, however, argue that they had not been arrested and detained on 'reasonable' suspicion of having committed an offence. Section 11(1) of the 1978 Act provided that 'any constable may arrest without warrant any person whom he suspects of being a terrorist.' In their submission, this section was itself in direct conflict with Article 5(1)(c) in that it did not contain any requirement of reasonableness. They further agreed with the Commission's opinion that their arrests had not been shown on the facts to have been based on reasonable suspicion.

In addition, they maintained that the purpose of their arrest was not to bring them before the 'competent legal authority' but rather to gather information without necessarily intending to charge them with a criminal offence. Both the respondent Government and the Commission rejected this contention.

31. For an arrest to be lawful under section 11(1) of the 1978 Act, as construed by the House of Lords in the case of *McKee v. Chief Constable for Northern Ireland,* the suspicion needed only to be honestly held. In his report to Parliament in 1984, the Right Honourable Sir George Baker highlighted the fact that the test for section 11 was a 'subjective one.' On the other hand, where the requirement was 'reasonable suspicion' he considered that the test was 'objective' and that it was 'for the court to judge the reasonableness of the suspicion.'

Article 5(1) (c) speaks of a 'reasonable suspicion' rather than a genuine and *bona fide* suspicion. The Court's task, however, is not to review the impugned legislation in abstracto but to examine its application in these particular cases.

32. The 'reasonableness' of the suspicion on which an arrest must be based forms an essential part of the safeguard against arbitrary arrest and detention which is laid down in Article 5(1) (c). The Court agrees with the Commission and the Government that having a 'reasonable suspicion' presupposes the existence of facts or information which would satisfy an objective observer that the person concerned may have committed the offence. What may be regarded as 'reasonable' will however depend upon all the circumstances.

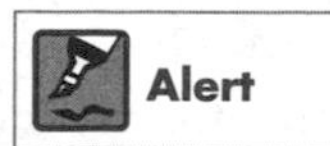

In this respect, terrorist crime falls into a special category. Because of the attendant risk of loss of life and human suffering, the police are obliged to act with utmost urgency in following up all information, including information from secret sources. Further, the police may frequently have to arrest a suspected terrorist on the basis of information which is reliable but which cannot, without putting in jeopardy the source of the information, be revealed to the suspect or produced in court to support a charge.

As the Government pointed out, in view of the difficulties inherent in the investigation and prosecution of terrorist-type offences in Northern Ireland, the 'reasonableness' of the suspicion justifying such arrests cannot always be judged according to the same standards as are applied in dealing with conventional crime. Nevertheless, the exigencies of dealing with terrorist crime cannot justify stretching the notion of 'reasonableness' to the point where the essence of the safeguard secured by Article 5(1)(c) is impaired.

33. The majority of the Commission, with whom the applicants agreed, were of the opinion that 'the Government [had] not provided any information which would allow the Commission to conclude that the suspicions against the applicants at the time of their arrest were "reasonable" within the meaning of Article 5(1)(c) of the Convention or that their arrest was based on anything more than the "honestly held suspicion" which was required under Northern Ireland law.'

The Government argued that it was unable to disclose the acutely sensitive material on which the suspicion against the three applicants was based because of the risk of disclosing the source of the material and thereby placing in danger the lives and safety of others. In support of its contention that there was nevertheless reasonable suspicion, it pointed to the facts that the first two applicants had previous convictions for serious acts of terrorism connected with the Provisional IRA and that all three applicants were questioned during their detention about specific terrorist acts of which they were suspected. In the Government's submission these facts were sufficient to confirm that the arresting officer had a *bona fide* or genuine suspicion and it maintained that there was no difference in substance between a *bona fide* or genuine suspicion and a reasonable suspicion. The Government observed moreover that the applicants themselves did not contest that they were arrested and detained in connection with acts of terrorism.

The Government also stated that, although it could not disclose the information or identify the source of the information which led to the arrest of the applicants, there did exist in the case of the first and second applicants strong grounds for suggesting that at the time of their arrest the applicants were engaged in intelligence gathering and courier work for the Provisional IRA and that in the case of the third applicant there was available to the police material connecting him with the kidnapping attempt about which he was questioned.

34. Certainly Article 5(1)(c) of the Convention should not be applied in such a manner as to put disproportionate difficulties in the way of the police authorities of the Contracting States in taking effective measures to counter organised terrorism. It follows that the Contracting States cannot be asked to establish the reasonableness of the suspicion grounding the arrest of a suspected terrorist by disclosing the confidential sources of supporting information or even facts which would be susceptible of indicating such sources or their identity.

Nevertheless the Court must be enabled to ascertain whether the essence of the safeguard afforded by Article 5(1)(c) has been secured. Consequently the respondent Government has to furnish at least some facts or information capable of satisfying the Court that the arrested person was reasonably suspected of having committed the alleged offence. This is all the more necessary where, as in the present case, the domestic law does not require reasonable suspicion, but sets a lower threshold by merely requiring honest suspicion.

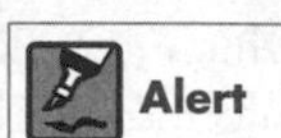
Alert

35. The Court accepts that the arrest and detention of each of the present applicants was based on a *bona fide* suspicion that he or she was a terrorist, and that each of them, including Mr. Hartley, was questioned during his or her detention about specific terrorist acts of which he or she was suspected.

The fact that Mr. Fox and Ms. Campbell both have previous convictions for acts of terrorism connected with the IRA, although it could reinforce a suspicion linking them to the commission of terrorist-type offences, cannot form the sole basis of a suspicion justifying their arrest in 1986, some seven years later.

The fact that all the applicants, during their detention, were questioned about specific terrorist acts does no more than confirm that the arresting officers had a genuine suspicion that they had been involved in those acts, but it cannot satisfy an objective observer that the applicants may have committed these acts.

The aforementioned elements on their own are insufficient to support the conclusion that there was 'reasonable suspicion'. The Government has not provided any further material on which the suspicion against the applicants was based. Its explanations therefore do not meet the minimum standard set by Article 5(1)(c) for judging the reasonableness of a suspicion for the arrest of an individual.

36. The Court accordingly holds that there has been a breach of Article 5(1). This being so, it is not considered necessary to go into the question of the purpose of the applicants' arrests.

Alleged breach of Article 5(2)

37. The applicants alleged a violation of Article 5(2) , which reads:

'Everyone who is arrested shall be informed promptly, in a language which he understands, of the reasons for his arrest and of any charge against him.'

The Commission upheld this claim which was rejected by the Government.

38. In the applicants' submission Article 5(1)(c) refers to the grounds justifying the arrest and these are what should be communicated to detainees. They argued that suspected terrorism in itself is not necessarily an offence justifying an arrest under section 11. Accordingly, in breach of Article 5(2) they were not given at the time of their arrest adequate and understandable information of the substantive grounds for their arrest. In particular, they maintained that the national authorities' duty to 'inform' the person is not complied with where, as in their cases, the person is left to deduce from the subsequent police interrogation the reasons for his or her arrest.

39. The Government submitted that the purpose of Article 5(2) is to enable an arrested person to judge the unlawfulness of the arrest and take steps to challenge it if he sees fit. It argued that the information given need not be detailed and that it was enough that the arrested person should be informed promptly of the legal basis of his detention and of the 'essential facts relevant under (domestic law) for the determination of the lawfulness of his detention.' Applying these principles to the facts of the present case it contended that the requirements of Article 5(2) were clearly met.

40. Paragraph (2) of Article 5 contains the elementary safeguard that any person arrested should know why he is being deprived of his liberty. This provision is an integral part of the scheme of protection afforded by Article 5: by virtue of paragraph (2) any person arrested must be told, in simple, non-technical language that he can understand, the essential legal and factual grounds for his arrest, so as to be able, if he sees fit, to apply to a court to challenge its lawfulness in accordance with paragraph (4). Whilst this information must be conveyed 'promptly' (in French: 'dans le plus court délai'), it need not be related in its entirety by the arresting officer at the very moment of the arrest. Whether the content and promptness of the information conveyed were sufficient is to be assessed in each case according to its special features.

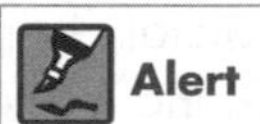
Alert

41. On being taken into custody, Mr. Fox, Ms. Campbell and Mr. Hartley were simply told by the arresting officer that they were being arrested under section 11(1) of the 1978 Act on suspicion of being terrorists. This bare indication of the legal basis for the arrest, taken on its own, is insufficient for the purposes of Article 5(2), as the Government conceded.

However, following their arrest all of the applicants were interrogated by the police about their suspected involvement in specific criminal acts and their suspected membership of proscribed organisations. There is no ground to suppose that these interrogations were not such as to enable the applicants to understand why they had been arrested. The reasons why they were suspected of being terrorists were thereby brought to their attention during their interrogation.

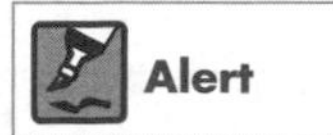
Alert

42. Mr. Fox and Ms. Campbell were arrested at 3.40 p.m. on 5 February 1986 at Woodbourne RUC station and then separately questioned the same day between 8.15 p.m. and 10.00 p.m. at Castlereagh Police Office. Mr. Hartley, for his part, was arrested at his home at 7.55 a.m. on 18 August 1986 and taken to Antrim Police Station where he was questioned between 11.05 a.m. and 12.15 p.m. In the context

of the present case these intervals of a few hours cannot be regarded as falling outside the constraints of time imposed by the notion of promptness in Article 5(2) .

43. In conclusion there was therefore no breach of Article 5(2) in relation to any of the applicants.

The key point to take from this case is that the Article 5(1) right to liberty can only be denied in the context of an arrest in accordance with Article 5(1)(c) if the arrest has been carried out in accordance with a procedure prescribed by law and the state is able to show some *objectively* verifiable evidence on which to justify its suspicion that an individual has committed an offence or is about to do so.

Additionally *Fox* provides an important authority qualifying the protection afforded by Article 5(2). As elsewhere in the Convention, the wording of Articles will be construed in a non-absolute, proportionate way. Even if suspects are not specifically informed of the technical offence they are suspected of, there is unlikely to be a breach of Article 5(2) if the nature and essence of the suspected offence becomes apparent during questioning.

***Brogan & Others v UK* (1989) 11 EHRR 117**

Panel: The President, Judge Ryssdal; Judges Cremona, Thór Vilhjálmsson, Bindschedler-Robert, Gölcüklü, Matscher, Pinheiro Farinha, Pettiti, Mever, Carrilo Salcedo, Valticos, Martens and Palm

Statute: European Convention on Human Rights Article 5

Facts: following his arrest, the applicant was detained for over four days without judicial oversight, as allowed under the exceptional legislation applying to Northern Ireland in that period. The applicant contended that this violated the essence of Article 5(3), namely that detained individuals should be brought before a judicial authority as promptly as possible, or else released.

JUDGMENT

Relevant domestic law and practice

Introduction

...

Power to arrest without warrant under the 1984 and other Acts

30. The relevant provisions of section 12 of the 1984 Act, substantially the same as those of the 1974 and 1976 Acts, are as follows:

'... [A] constable may arrest without warrant a person who he has reasonable grounds for suspecting to be:

...

(b) a person who is or has been concerned in the commission, preparation or instigation of acts of terrorism to which this Part of this Act applies;

...

The acts of terrorism to which this Part of this Act applies are:

(a) acts of terrorism connected with the affairs of Northern Ireland;

...

(4) A person arrested under this section shall not be detained in right of the arrest for more than 48 hours after his arrest; but the Secretary of State may, in any particular case, extend the period of 48 hours by a period or periods specified by him.

(5) Any such further period or periods shall not exceed five days in all.

The following provisions (requirement to bring accused person before the court after his arrest) shall not apply to a person detained in right of the arrest

...

(d) Article 131 of the Magistrates' Courts (Northern Ireland) Order 1981;

...

(8) The provisions of this section are without prejudice to any power of arrest exercisable apart from this section.'

31. According to the definition given in section 14(1) of the 1984 Act, terrorism 'means of the use of violence for political ends, and includes any use of violence for the purpose of putting the public or any section of the public in fear' was held to be 'in wide terms' by the House of Lords, which rejected an interpretation of the word 'terrorist' that would have been 'in narrower terms than popular usage of the word "terrorist" might connote to a police officer or a layman' .

32. Article 131 of the Magistrates' Courts (Northern Ireland) Order 1981, declared inapplicable by section 12(6)(d) of the 1984 Act, provides that where a person arrested without warrant is not within 24 hours released from custody, he must be brought before a Magistrates' Court as soon as practicable thereafter but not later than 48 hours after his arrest.

33. The Northern Ireland (Emergency Provisions) Act 1978 also conferred special powers of arrest without warrant. Section 11 provided that a constable could arrest without warrant any person who he suspected of being a terrorist. Such a person could be detained for up to 72 hours without being brought before a court.

The 1978 Act has been amended by the Northern Ireland (Emergency Provisions) Act 1987, which came into force on 15 June 1987. The powers of arrest under the 1978 Act have been replaced by a power to enter and search premises for the purpose of arresting a suspected terrorist under section 12 of the 1984 Act.

Exercise of the power to make an arrest under section 12(1)(b) of the 1984 Act

34. In order to make a lawful arrest under section 12(1)(b) of the 1984 Act, the arresting officer must have a reasonable suspicion that the person being arrested is or has been concerned in the commission, preparation or instigation of acts of terrorism.

In addition, an arrest without warrant is subject to the applicable common law rules laid down by the House of Lords in the case of *Christie v. Leachinsky* [1947] A.C. 573 at 578 and 600. The person being arrested must in ordinary circumstances be informed of the true ground of his arrest at the time he is taken into custody or, if special circumstances exist which excuse this, as soon thereafter as it is reasonably practicable to inform him. This does not require technical or precise language to be used provided the person being arrested knows in substance why.

In the case of *ex parte Lynch [1980]* N.I.R. 126 at 131, in which the arrested person sought a writ of habeas corpus, the High Court of Northern Ireland discussed section 12(1)(b). The arresting officer had told the applicant that he was arresting him under section 12 of the 1976 Act as he suspected him of being involved in terrorist activities. The High Court held that the officer had communicated the true ground of arrest and had done what was reasonable in the circumstances to convey to the applicant the nature of his suspicion, namely that the applicant was involved in terrorist activities. Accordingly, the High Court found that the lawfulness of the arrest could not be impugned in this respect.

35. The arresting officer's suspicion must be reasonable in the circumstances and to decide this the court must be told something about the sources and grounds of the suspicion.

Link
See *Fox* above.

Purpose of arrest and detention under section 12 of the 1984 Act

36. Under ordinary law, there is no power to arrest and detain a person merely to make enquiries about him. The questioning of a suspect on the ground of reasonable suspicion that he has committed an arrestable offence is a legitimate cause for arrest and detention without warrant where the purpose of such questioning is to dispel or confirm such a reasonable suspicion, provided he is brought before a court as soon as practicable.

On the other hand, Lord Lowry C.J. held in the case of *Ex parte Lynch* that under the 1984 Act no specific crime need be suspected to ground a proper arrest under section 12(1)(b). He added:

'... [I]t is further to be noted that an arrest under section 12(1) leads ... to a permitted period of detention without preferring a charge. No charge may follow at all; thus an arrest is not necessarily ... the first step in a criminal proceeding against a suspected person on a charge which was intended to be judicially investigated.'

Extension of period of detention

37. In Northern Ireland, applications for extended detention beyond the initial 48 hour period are processed at senior police level in Belfast and then forwarded to the Secretary of State for Northern Ireland for approval by him or, if he is not available, a junior minister.

There are no criteria in the 1984 Act (or its predecessors) governing decisions to extend the initial period of detention, though strict criteria that have been developed in practice are listed in the reports and reviews appended to the government's memorial.

According to statistics quoted by the Standing Advisory Commission on Human Rights in its written submissions, just over 2 per cent. of police requests for extended detention in Northern Ireland between the entry into force of the 1984 Act in March 1984 and June 1987 were refused by the Secretary of State.

...

General approach

48. The government has adverted extensively to the existence of particularly difficult circumstances in Northern Ireland, notably the threat posed by organised terrorism.

The Court, having taken notice of the growth of terrorism in modern society, has already recognised the need, inherent in the Convention system, for a proper balance between the defence of the institutions of democracy in the common interest and the protection of individual rights.

The government informed the Secretary General of the Council of Europe on 22 August 1984 that it was withdrawing a notice of derogation under Article 15 which had relied on an emergency situation in Northern Ireland. The government indicated accordingly that in their opinion 'the provisions of the Convention are being fully executed'. In any event, as they pointed out, the derogation did not apply to the area of law in issue in the present case.

Consequently, there is no call in the present proceedings to consider whether any derogation from the United Kingdom's obligations under the Convention might be permissible under Article 15 by reason of a terrorist campaign in Northern Ireland. Examination of the case must proceed on the basis that the Articles of the Convention in respect of which complaints have been made are fully applicable. This does not, however, preclude proper account being taken of the background circumstances of the case. In the context of Article 5, it is for the Court to determine the significance to be attached to those circumstances and to ascertain whether, in the instant case, the balance struck complied with the applicable provisions of that Article in the light of their particular wording and its overall object and purpose.

...

Alleged breach of Article 5(3)

55. Under the 1984 Act, a person arrested under section 12 on reasonable suspicion of involvement in acts of terrorism may be detained by police for an initial period of 48 hours, and, on the authorisation of the Secretary of State for Northern Ireland, for a further period or periods of up to five days.

The applicants claimed, as a consequence of their arrest and detention under this legislation, to have been the victims of a violation of Article 5(3) which provides;

'Everyone arrested or detained in accordance with the provisions of paragraph (1)(c) of this Article shall be brought promptly before a judge or other officer authorised by law to exercise judicial power and shall be entitled to trial within a reasonable time or to release pending trial. Release may be conditioned by guarantees to appear for trial.'

The applicants noted that a person arrested under the ordinary law of Northern Ireland must be brought before a Magistrates' Court within 48 hours; and that under the ordinary law in England and Wales (Police and Criminal Evidence Act 1984) the maximum period of detention permitted without charge is four days, judicial approval being required at the 36 hour stage. In their submission, there was no plausible reason why a seven-day detention period was necessary, marking as it did such a radical departure from ordinary law and even from the three-day period permitted under the special powers of detention embodied in the Northern Ireland (Emergency Provisions) Act 1978. Nor was there any justification for not entrusting such decisions to the judiciary of Northern Ireland.

56. The government has argued that in view of the nature and extent of the terrorist threat and the resulting problems in obtaining evidence sufficient to bring charges, the maximum statutory period of detention of seven days was an indispensable part of the effort to combat that threat, as successive parliamentary debates and reviews of the legislation had confirmed. In particular, they drew attention to the difficulty faced by the security forces in obtaining evidence which is both admissible and usable in consequence of training in anti-interrogation techniques adopted by those involved in terrorism. Time was also needed to undertake necessary scientific examinations, to correlate information from other detainees and to liaise with other security forces. The government claimed that the need for a power of extension of the period of detention was borne out by statistics. For instance, in 1987 extensions were granted in Northern Ireland in respect of 365 persons. Some 83 were detained in excess of five days and of this number 39 were charged with serious terrorist offences during the extended period.

As regards the suggestion that extensions of detention beyond the initial 48-hour period should be controlled or even authorised by a judge, the government pointed out the difficulty, in view of the acute sensitivity of some of the information on which the suspicion was based, of producing it in court. Not only would the court have to sit *in camera* but neither the detained person nor his legal advisers could be present or told any of the details. This would require a fundamental and undesirable change in the law and procedure of the United Kingdom under which an individual who is deprived of his liberty is entitled to be represented by his legal advisers at any proceedings before a court relating to his detention. If entrusted with the power to grant extensions of detention, the judges would be seen to be exercising an executive rather than a judicial function. It would add nothing to the safeguards against abuse which the present arrangements are designed to achieve and could lead to unanswerable criticism of the judiciary. In all the circumstances, the Secretary of State was better placed to take such decisions and to ensure a consistent approach. Moreover, the merits of each request to extend detention were personally scrutinised by the Secretary of State or, if he was unavailable, by another Minister.

57. The Commission, in its report, cited its established case law to the effect that a period of four days in cases concerning ordinary criminal offences and of five days in

exceptional cases could be considered compatible with the requirement of promptness in Article 5(3). In the Commission's opinion, given the context in which the applicants were arrested and the special problems associated with the investigation of terrorist offences, a somewhat longer period of detention than in normal cases was justified. The Commission concluded that the periods of four days and six hours (Mr. McFadden) and four days and eleven hours (Mr. Tracey) did satisfy the requirement of promptness, whereas the periods of five days and eleven hours (Mr. Brogan) and six days and sixteen and a half hours (Mr. Coyle) did not.

58. The fact that a detained person is not charged or brought before a court does not in itself amount to a violation of the first part of Article 5(3). No violation of Article 5(3) can arise if the arrested person is released 'promptly' before any judicial control of his detention would have been feasible. If the arrested person is not released promptly, he is entitled to a prompt appearance before a judge or judicial officer.

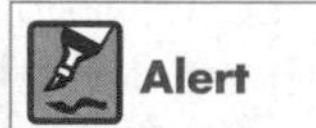

The assessment of 'promptness' has to be made in the light of the object and purpose of Article 5. The Court has regard to the importance of this Article in the Convention system: it enshrines a fundamental human right, namely the protection of the individual against arbitrary interferences by the State with his right to liberty. Judicial control of interferences by the executive with the individual's right to liberty is an essential feature of the guarantee embodied in Article 5(3), which is intended to minimise the risk of arbitrariness. Judicial control is implied by the rule of law, 'one of the fundamental principles of a democratic society ..., which is expressly referred to in the Preamble to the Convention' and 'from which the whole Convention draws its inspiration'.

59. The obligation expressed in English by the word 'promptly' and in French by the word 'aussitôt' is clearly distinguishable from the less strict requirement in the second part of paragraph 3 ('reasonable time' / 'délai raisonnable') and even from that in paragraph 4 of Article 5 ('speedily' / 'à bref délai'). The term 'promptly' also occurs in the English text of paragraph 2, where the French text uses the words 'dans le plus court délai'. As indicated in the *Ireland v. United Kingdom* judgment, 'promptly' in paragraph 3 may be understood as having a broader significance than 'aussitôt', which literally means immediately. Thus confronted with versions of a law-making treaty which are equally authentic but not exactly the same, the Court must interpret them in a way that reconciles them as far as possible and is most appropriate in order to realise the aim and achieve the object of the treaty.

The use in the French text of the word 'aussitôt', with its constraining connotation of immediacy, confirms that the degree of flexibility attaching to the notion of 'promptness' is limited, even if the attendant circumstances can never be ignored for the purposes of the assessment under paragraph 3. Whereas promptness is to be assessed in each case according to its special features, the significance to be attached to those features can never be taken to the point of impairing the very essence of the right guaranteed by Article 5(3), that is the point of effectively negativing the State's obligation to ensure a prompt release or a prompt appearance before a judicial authority.

60. The instant case is exclusively concerned with the arrest and detention, by virtue of powers granted under special legislation, of persons suspected of involvement in terrorism in Northern Ireland. The requirements under the ordinary law in Northern Ireland as to bringing an accused before a court were expressly made inapplicable to such arrest and detention by section 12(6) of the 1984 Act. There is no call to determine in the present judgment whether in an ordinary criminal case any given period, such as four days, in police or administrative custody would as a general rule be capable of being compatible with the first part of Article 5(3).

None of the applicants was in fact brought before a judge or judicial officer during his time in custody. The issue to be decided is therefore whether, having regard to the special features relied on by the government, each applicant's release can be considered as 'prompt' for the purposes of Article 5(3).

61. The investigation of terrorist offences undoubtedly presents the authorities with special problems, partial reference to which has already been made under Article 5(1). The Court takes full judicial notice of the factors adverted to by the government in this connection. It is also true that in Northern Ireland the referral of police requests for extended detention to the Secretary of State and the individual scrutiny of each police request by a Minister do provide a form of executive control. In addition, the need for the continuation of the special powers has been constantly monitored by Parliament and their operation regularly reviewed by independent personalities. The Court accepts that, subject to the existence of adequate safeguards, the context of terrorism in Northern Ireland has the effect of prolonging the period during which the authorities may, without violating Article 5(3), keep a person suspected of serious terrorist offences in custody before bringing him before a judge or other judicial officer.

The difficulties, alluded to by the government, of judicial control over decisions to arrest and detain suspected terrorists may affect the manner of implementation of Article 5(3), for example in calling for appropriate procedural precautions in view of the nature of the suspected offences. However, they cannot justify, under Article 5(3), dispensing altogether with 'prompt' judicial control.

62. As indicated above, the scope for flexibility in interpreting and applying the notion of 'promptness' is very limited. In the Court's view, even the shortest of the four periods of detention namely the four days and six hours spent in police custody by Mr. McFadden, falls outside the strict constraints as to time permitted by the first part of Article 5(3). To attach such importance to the special features of this case as to justify so lengthy a period of detention without appearance before a judge or other judicial officer would be an unacceptably wide interpretation of the plain meaning of the word 'promptly'. An interpretation to this effect would import into Article 5(3) a serious weakening of a procedural guarantee to the detriment of the individual and would entail consequences impairing the very essence of the individual and would entail consequences impairing the very essence of the right protected by this provision. The Court thus has to conclude that none of the applicants was either brought 'promptly' before a judicial authority or released 'promptly' following his arrest. The undoubted fact that the arrest and detention of the applicants were inspired by the legitimate aim

of protecting the community as a whole from terrorism is not on its own sufficient to ensure compliance with the specific requirements of Article 5(3).

There has thus been a breach of Article 5(3) in respect of all four applicants.

The essence of the protection afforded by Article 5(3) can be seen in the highlighted passages above, which reveal the attachment of the Strasbourg Court to key rule of law principles. Underlying more semantic arguments about the meaning of the word "promptly" in the Article is the more basic principle that, when an individual has been deprived of their liberty by the state, it is vitally important that their detention is properly sanctioned and supervised by a judicial authority.

2 Article 6

Article 6 is an unusually structured right. It is not limited in the same way as Article 5, nor is it qualified in the way that Articles 9 to 11 are. However, the various rights contained within it are not absolute either. Instead they are tempered and moderated by the application of the principle of proportionality.

It is important to pay close attention to the wording of this Article. Importantly it only becomes engaged when a person's civil rights and obligations or a criminal charge against them are being "determined". Article 6(1) contains the general point of principle relating to the importance of a fair and impartial legal process and this is supplemented by Article 6(2) relating to the presumption of innocence and Article 6(3) containing a range of 'minimum rights' following a criminal charge.

Murray (John) v UK (1996) 22 EHRR 29

Panel: The President, Judge Ryssdal; Judges Bernhardt, Matscher, Pettiti, Walsh, Valticos, Martens, Palm, Foighel, Pekkanen, Loizou, Bigi, Freeland, Lopes Rocha, Wildhaber, Makarczyk, Gotchev, Jungwiert and Lõhmus

Statute: European Convention on Human Rights Article 6

Facts: Murray was arrested, detained and later convicted of a terrorism-related offence in Northern Ireland. For the first 48 hours of his detention he had been denied access to legal advice and, on conviction, he was told that adverse inferences had been drawn from his refusal to answer police questions after his arrest. Murray complained to the Strasbourg Court that the combination of lack of legal advice and the drawing of the inferences by the criminal court had deprived him of a fair trial and legal process.

JUDGMENT

Alleged violation of Article 6 of the Convention

40. The applicant alleged that there had been a violation of the right to silence and the right not to incriminate oneself contrary to Article 6(1) and (2) of the Convention. He further complained that he was denied access to his solicitor in violation of Article 6(1) in conjunction with paragraph 3(c) of the Convention. The relevant provisions provide as follows:

1. In the determination of … any criminal charge against him, everyone is entitled to a fair and public hearing within a reasonable time by an independent and impartial tribunal established by law …

2. Everyone charged with a criminal offence shall be presumed innocent until proved guilty according to law.

Everyone charged with a criminal offence has the following minimum rights:

…

(c) to defend himself in person or through legal assistance of his own choosing or, if he has not sufficient means to pay for legal assistance, to be given it free when the interests of justice so require;

The Court will examine each of these allegations in turn.

Article 6(1) and (2): right to silence

41. In the submission of the applicant, the drawing of incriminating inferences against him under the Criminal Justice (Northern Ireland) Order 1988 ("the Order") violated Article 6(1) and (2) of the Convention. It amounted to an infringement of the right to silence, the right not to incriminate oneself and the principle that the prosecution bear the burden of proving the case without assistance from the accused.

He contended that a first, and most obvious element of the right to silence is the right to remain silent in the face of police questioning and not to have to testify against oneself at trial. In his submission, these have always been essential and fundamental elements of the British criminal justice system. Moreover the Commission in *Saunders v. United Kingdom* and the Court in *Funke v. France* have accepted that they are an inherent part of the right to a fair hearing under Article 6. In his view these are absolute rights which an accused is entitled to enjoy without restriction.

A second, equally essential element of the right to silence was that the exercise of the right by an accused would not be used as evidence against him in his trial. However, the trial judge drew very strong inferences, under Articles 4 and 6 of the Order, from his decision to remain silent under police questioning and during the trial. Indeed, it was clear from the trial judge's remarks and from the judgment of the Court of Appeal in his case that the inferences were an integral part of his decision to find him guilty.

Accordingly, he was severely and doubly penalised for choosing to remain silent: once for his silence under police interrogation and once for his failure to testify during the trial. To use against him silence under police questioning and his refusal to testify during trial amounted to subverting the presumption of innocence and the onus of proof resulting from that presumption: it is for the prosecution to prove the accused's guilt without any assistance from the latter being required.

42. Amnesty International submitted that permitting adverse inferences to be drawn from the silence of the accused was an effective means of compulsion which shifted the burden of proof from the prosecution to the accused and was inconsistent with the right not to be compelled to testify against oneself or to confess guilt because the accused is

left with no reasonable choice between silence—which will be taken as testimony against oneself—and testifying. It pointed out that Article 14(3)(g) of the United Nations International Covenant on Civil and Political Rights explicitly provides that an accused shall "not be compelled to testify against himself or to confess guilt". Reference was also made to Rule 42(A) of the Rules of Procedure and Evidence of the International Criminal Tribunal for the Former Yugoslavia which expressly provides that a suspect has the right to remain silent and to the Draft Statute for an International Criminal Court, submitted to the United Nations General Assembly by the International Law Commission, which in Draft Article 26(6)(a)(i) qualifies the right to silence with the words "without such silence being a consideration in the determination of guilt or innocence".

Liberty and others made similar submissions. Justice stressed that such encroachments on the right to silence increased the risk of miscarriages of justice.

The Northern Ireland Standing Advisory Commission on Human Rights, for its part, considered that the right to silence was not an absolute right, but rather a safeguard which might, in certain circumstances, be removed provided other appropriate safeguards for accused persons were introduced to compensate for the potential risk of unjust convictions.

43. The Government contended that what is at issue is not whether the Order as such is compatible with the right to silence but rather whether, on the facts of the case, the drawing of inferences under Articles 4 and 6 of the Order rendered the criminal proceedings against the applicant unfair contrary to Article 6 of the Convention.

They maintained, however, that the first question should be answered in the negative. They emphasised that the Order did not detract from the right to remain silent in the face of police questioning and explicitly confirmed the right not to have to testify at trial. They further noted that the Order in no way changed either the burden or the standard of proof: it remained for the prosecution to prove an accused's guilt beyond reasonable doubt. What the Order did was to confer a discretionary power to draw inferences from the silence of an accused in carefully defined circumstances. They maintained that this did not, of itself, violate the right to silence.

In this respect, they emphasised the safeguards governing the drawing of inferences under the Order which had been highlighted in national judicial decisions. In particular, it had been consistently stressed by the courts that the Order merely allows the trier of fact to draw such inferences as common sense dictates. The question in each case is whether the evidence adduced by the prosecution is sufficiently strong to call for an answer.

With regard to the international standards to which reference had been made by Amnesty International, it was contended that they did not demonstrate any internationally-accepted prohibition on the drawing of common sense inferences from the silence of an accused whether at trial or pre-trial. In particular, the Draft Statute for an International Criminal Court is far from final and cannot be said to have been adopted by the international community.

As to the question whether, on the facts of the case, the drawing of inferences under Articles 4 and 6 of the Order rendered the criminal proceedings against the applicant unfair, the Government comprehensively analysed the trial court's assessment of the evidence against the applicant. On the basis of this analysis they submitted that on the evidence adduced against the applicant by the Crown, the Court of Appeal was right to conclude that a formidable case has been made out against him which deeply implicated him in the false imprisonment of Mr L and that this case "called for an answer". The drawing of inferences therefore had been quite natural and in accordance with common sense.

44. The Court must, confining its attention to the facts of the case, consider whether the drawing of inferences against the applicant under Articles 4 and 6 of the Order rendered the criminal proceedings against him—and especially his conviction—unfair within the meaning of Article 6 of the Convention. It is recalled in this context that no inference was drawn under Article 3 of the Order. It is not the Court's role to examine whether, in general, the drawing of inferences under the scheme contained in the Order is compatible with the notion of a fair hearing under Article 6.

45. Although not specifically mentioned in Article 6 of the Convention, there can be no doubt that the right to remain silent under police questioning and the privilege against self-incrimination are generally recognised international standards which lie at the heart of the notion of a fair procedure under Article 6. By providing the accused with protection against improper compulsion by the authorities these immunities contribute to avoiding miscarriages of justice and to securing the aim of Article 6.

46. The Court does not consider that it is called upon to give an abstract analysis of the scope of these immunities and, in particular, of what constitutes in this context "improper compulsion". What is at stake in the present case is whether these immunities are absolute in the sense that the exercise by an accused of the right to silence cannot under any circumstances be used against him at trial or, alternatively, whether informing him in advance that, under certain conditions, his silence may be used, is always to be regarded as "improper compulsion" .

47. On the one hand, it is self-evident that is incompatible with the immunities under consideration to base a conviction solely or mainly on the accused's silence or on a refusal to answer questions or to give evidence himself. On the other hand, the Court deems it equally obvious that these immunities cannot and should not prevent that the accused's silence, in situations which clearly call for an explanation from him, be taken into account in assessing the persuasiveness of the evidence adduced by the prosecution.

Alert

Wherever the line between these two extremes is to be drawn, it follows from this understanding of "the right to silence" that the question whether the right is absolute must be answered in the negative.

It cannot be said therefore that an accused's decision to remain silent throughout criminal proceedings should necessarily have no implications when the trial court seeks to evaluate the evidence against him. In particular, as the Government has pointed out, established international standards in this area, while providing for the right to silence and the privilege against self-incrimination, are silent on this point.

Whether the drawing of adverse inferences from an accused's silence infringes Article 6 is a matter to be determined in the light of all the circumstances of the case, having particular regard to the situations where inferences may be drawn, the weight attached to them by the national courts in their assessment of the evidence and the degree of compulsion inherent in the situation.

48. As regards the degree of compulsion involved in the present case, it is recalled that the applicant was in fact able to remain silent. Notwithstanding the repeated warnings as to the possibility that inferences might be drawn from his silence, he did not make any statements to the police and did not give evidence during his trial. Moreover under Article 4(5) of the Order he remained a non-compellable witness (see para. 27 above). Thus his insistence in maintaining silence throughout the proceedings did not amount to a criminal offence or contempt of court. Furthermore, as has been stressed in national court decisions, silence, in itself, cannot be regarded as an indication of guilt.

49. The facts of the present case accordingly fall to be distinguished from those in *Funke v. France* where criminal proceedings were brought against the applicant by the customs authorities in an attempt to compel him to provide evidence of offences he had allegedly committed. Such a degree of compulsion in that case was found by the Court to be incompatible with Article 6 since, in effect, it destroyed the very essence of the privilege against self-incrimination.

50. Admittedly a system which warns the accused—who is possibly without legal assistance (as in the applicant's case)—that adverse inferences may be drawn from a refusal to provide an explanation to the police for his presence at the scene of a crime or to testify during his trial, when taken in conjunction with the weight of the case against him, involves a certain level of indirect compulsion. However, since the applicant could not be compelled to speak or to testify, as indicated above, this factor on its own cannot be decisive. The Court must rather concentrate its attention on the role played by the inferences in the proceedings against the applicant and especially in his conviction.

51. In this context, it is recalled that these were proceedings without a jury, the trier of fact being an experienced judge. Furthermore, the drawing of inferences under the Order is subject to an important series of safeguards designed to respect the rights of the defence and to limit the extent to which reliance can be placed on inferences.

In the first place, before inferences can be drawn under Article 4 and 6 of the Order appropriate warnings must have been given to the accused as to the legal effects of maintaining silence. Moreover, as indicated by the judgment of the House of Lords in *R. v. Kevin Sean Murray* the prosecutor must first establish a prima facie case against the accused, *i.e.* a case consisting of direct evidence which, if believed and combined with legitimate inferences based upon it, could lead a properly directed jury to be satisfied beyond reasonable doubt that each of the essential elements of the offence is proved.

The question in each particular case is whether the evidence adduced by the prosecution is sufficiently strong to require an answer. The national court cannot conclude that the accused is guilty merely because he chooses to remain silent. It is only if the evidence against the accused "calls" for an explanation which the accused ought to be in a position to give that a failure to give an explanation "may as a matter of common sense allow the drawing of an inference that there is no explanation and that the accused is guilty". Conversely if the case presented by the prosecution had so little evidential value that it called for no answer, a failure to provide one could not justify an inference of guilt. In sum, it is only common sense inferences which the judge considers proper, in the light of the evidence against the accused, that can be drawn under the Order.

In addition, the trial judge has a discretion whether, on the facts of the particular case, an inference should be drawn. As indicated by the Court of Appeal in the present case, if a judge accepted that an accused did not understand the warning given or if he had doubts about it, "we are confident that he would not activate Article 6 against him". Furthermore in Northern Ireland, where trial judges sit without a jury, the judge must explain the reasons for the decision to draw inferences and the weight attached to them. The exercise of discretion in this regard is subject to review by the appellate courts.

52. In the present case, the evidence presented against the applicant by the prosecution was considered by the Court of Appeal to constitute a "formidable" case against him. It is recalled that when the police entered the house some appreciable time after they knocked on the door, they found the applicant coming down the flight of stairs in the house where Mr L had been held captive by the IRA. Evidence had been given by Mr L—evidence which in the opinion of the trial judge had been corroborated—that he had been forced to make a taped confession and that after the arrival of the police at the house and the removal of his blindfold he saw the applicant at the top of the stairs. He had been told by him to go downstairs and watch television. The applicant was pulling a tape out of a cassette. The tangled tape and cassette recorder were later found on the premises. Evidence by the applicant's co-accused that he had recently arrived at the house was discounted as not being credible.

53. The trial judge drew strong inferences against the applicant under Article 6 of the Order by reason of his failure to give an account of his presence in the house when arrested and interrogated by the police. He also drew strong inferences under Article 4 of the Order by reason of the applicant's refusal to give evidence in his own defence when asked by the court to do so.

54. In the Court's view, having regard to the weight of the evidence against the applicant, as outlined above, the drawing of inferences from his refusal, at arrest, during police questioning and at trial, to provide an explanation for his presence in the house was a matter of common sense and cannot be regarded as unfair or unreasonable in the circumstances. As pointed out by the Delegate of the Commission, the courts in a considerable number of countries where evidence is freely assessed may have regard to all relevant circumstances, including the manner in which the accused

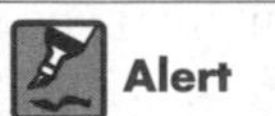
Alert

has behaved or has conducted his defence, when evaluating the evidence in the case. It considers that, what distinguishes the drawing of inferences under the Order is that, in addition to the existence of the specific safeguards mentioned above, it constitutes, as described by the Commission, "a formalised system which aims at allowing common sense implications to play an open role in the assessment of evidence".

Nor can it be said, against this background, that the drawing of reasonable inferences from the applicant's behaviour had the effect of shifting the burden of proof from the prosecution to the defence so as to infringe the principle of the presumption of innocence.

55. The applicant submitted that it was unfair to draw inferences under Article 6 of the Order from his silence at a time when he had not had the benefit of legal advice. In his view the question of access to a solicitor was inextricably entwined with that of the drawing of adverse inferences from pre-trial silence under police questioning. In this context he emphasised that under the Order once an accused has remained silent a trap is set from which he cannot escape: if an accused chooses to give evidence or to call witnesses, he is, by reason of his prior silence, exposed to the risk of an Article 3 inference sufficient to bring about a conviction; on the other hand, if he maintains his silence inferences may be drawn against him under other provisions of the Order.

56. The Court recalls that it must confine its attention to the facts of the present case. The reality of this case is that the applicant maintained silence right from the first questioning by the police to the end of his trial. It is not for the Court therefore to speculate on the question whether inferences would have been drawn under the Order had the applicant, at any moment after his first interrogation, chosen to speak to the police or to give evidence at his trial or call witnesses. Nor should it speculate on the question whether it was the possibility of such inferences being drawn that explains why the applicant was advised by his solicitor to remain silent.

Immediately after arrest the applicant was warned in accordance with the provisions of the Order but chose to remain silent. The Court, like the Commission, observed that there is no indication that the applicant failed to understand the significance of the warning given to him by the police prior to seeing his solicitor. Under these circumstances the fact that during the first 48 hours of his detention the applicant had been refused access to a lawyer does not detract from the above conclusion that the drawing of inferences was not unfair or unreasonable.

Nevertheless, the issue of denial of access to a solicitor, has implications for the rights of the defence which call for a separate examination.

57. Against the above background, and taking into account the role played by inferences under the Order during the trial and their impact on the rights of the defence, the Court does not consider that the criminal proceedings were unfair or that there had been an infringement of the presumption of innocence.

58. Accordingly, there has been no violation of Article 6(1) and (2) of the Convention.

Access to a lawyer

59. The applicant submitted that he was denied access to a lawyer at a critical stage of the criminal proceedings against him. He pointed out that in Northern Ireland the initial phase of detention is of crucial importance in the context of the criminal proceedings as a whole because of the possibility of inferences being drawn under Articles 3, 4 and 6 of the Order.

He was in fact denied access to any legal advice for 48 hours. During that time Article 3 and Article 6 cautions had been administered without his having had the benefit of prior legal advice. He was interviewed on 12 occasions without a solicitor being present to represent his interests. When he was finally granted access to his solicitor he was advised to remain silent partly because he had maintained silence already during the interview and partly because the solicitor would not be permitted to remain during questioning. The silence which had already occurred prior to seeing his solicitor would have triggered the operation on both Articles 3 and 6 at any subsequent trial, even had he chosen to give an account to the police. Having regard to the very strong inferences which the trial judge drew under Articles 4 and 6 of the Order, the decision to deny him access to a solicitor unfairly prejudiced the rights of the defence and rendered the proceedings against him unfair contrary to Article 6(1) and (3)(c) of the Convention.

60. In the submission of the Government, actual as opposed to notional or theoretical prejudice must be shown by an applicant in order to conclude that there had a breach of Article 6(1). The following matters were highlighted in this respect.

In the first place, the applicant did not seek to challenge by way of judicial review the exercise of the statutory power to delay access to a lawyer for up to 48 hours. The power is designed, *inter alia,* to limit the risk of interference with the vital information-gathering process and the risk that a person involved in an act of terrorism or still at large may be alerted. The denial of access was therefore a bona fide exercise of necessary and carefully designed statutory powers on reasonable grounds.

Secondly, as accepted by the Commission, the inferences drawn under Articles 4 and 6 of the Order were not the only evidence against the applicant. Furthermore the delay of access to a lawyer was for a limited period of 48 hours. Thereafter he had access to lawyers of his own choosing. He was represented both at his trial and on appeal by experienced solicitors and counsel and was in receipt of legal aid.

The Government did not accept that the applicant was irretrievably prejudiced in his defence because of the denial of access. They submitted that if, having consulted his solicitor, he had accounted for this presence at the scene of the crime and put forward an innocent explanation, it would have been extremely unlikely that Article 3 or Article 6 inferences would have been drawn. Moreover there was nothing to suggest, in his attitude or actions, that he would have acted differently had he seen a solicitor from the beginning. He had consistently refused to answer any questions put to him, both before and after he had consulted with his solicitor. In order to make out a case of actual prejudice it must be alleged by the applicant that if he had been able to consult his solicitor earlier he would have acted differently.

In sum, a limited delay of access to a lawyer did not cause any actual prejudice to the applicant's defence.

61. Amnesty International and Liberty and others, stressed that access to a lawyer when in police custody is an integral part of well-established international standards concerning protection against the dangers of *incommunicado* detention. It was also a vital element in enabling access to the procedural guarantees of the courts in respect of illegal detention. They both stressed, *inter alia,* that in the context of Northern Ireland where adverse inferences could be drawn from the applicant's failure to answer questions by the police it was particularly important to be assisted by a solicitor at an early stage.

The Northern Ireland Standing Advisory Commission on Human Rights considered that it was very much in the public interest that those detained for questioning should have immediate access to legal advice.

62. The Court observes that it has not been disputed by the Government that Article 6 applies even at the stage of the preliminary investigation into an offence by the police. In this respect it recalls its finding in *the Imbrioscia v. Switzerland judgment of 24 November 1993* that Article 6 — especially paragraph 3—may be relevant before a case is sent for trial if and so far as the fairness of the trial is likely to be seriously prejudiced by an initial failure to comply with its provisions. As it pointed out in that judgment, the manner in which Article 6(3)(c) is to be applied during the preliminary investigation depends on the special features of the proceedings involved and on the circumstances of the case.

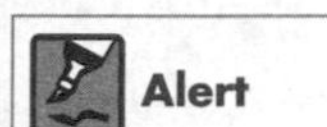

63. National laws may attach consequences to the attitude of an accused at the initial stages of police interrogation which are decisive for the prospects of the defence in any subsequent criminal proceedings. In such circumstances Article 6 will normally require that the accused be allowed to benefit from the assistance of a lawyer already at the initial stages of police interrogation. However, this right, which is not explicitly set out in the Convention, may be subject to restrictions for good cause. The question, in each case, is whether the restriction, in the light of the entirety of the proceedings, has deprived the accused of a fair hearing.

64. In the present case, the applicant's right of access to a lawyer during the first 48 hours of police detention was restricted under section 15 of the Northern Ireland (Emergency Provisions) Act 1987 on the basis that the police had reasonable grounds to believe that the exercise of the right of access would, *inter alia,* interfere with the gathering of information about the commission of acts of terrorism or make it more difficult to prevent such an act.

65. It is observed that the applicant did not seek to challenge the exercise of this power by instituting proceedings for judicial review although, before the Court, he now contests its lawfulness. The Court, however, has no reason to doubt that it amounted to a lawful exercise of the power to restrict access. Nevertheless, although it is an important element to be taken into account, even a lawfully exercised power of

restriction is capable of depriving an accused, in certain circumstances, of a fair procedure.

66. The Court is of the opinion that the scheme contained in the Order is such that it is of paramount importance for the rights of the defence that an accused has access to a lawyer at the initial stages of police interrogation. It observes in this context that, under the Order, at the beginning of police interrogation, an accused is confronted with a fundamental dilemma relating to his defence. If he chooses to remain silent, adverse inferences may be drawn against him in accordance with the provisions of the Order. On the other hand, if the accused opts to break his silence during the course of interrogation, he runs the risk of prejudicing his defence without necessarily removing the possibility of inferences being drawn against him.

Under such conditions the concept of fairness enshrined in Article 6 requires that the accused has the benefit of the assistance of a lawyer already at the initial stages of police interrogation. To deny access to a lawyer for the first 48 hours of police questioning, in a situation where the rights of the defence may well be irretrievably prejudiced, is—whatever the justification for such denial—incompatible with the rights of the accused under Article 6.

Alert

67. The Government has argued, that in order to complain under Article 6 of denial of access to a lawyer it must be clear that had the applicant been able to consult with his solicitor earlier, he would have acted differently from the way he did. It is contended that the applicant has not shown this to be the case.

68. It is true, as pointed out by the Government, that when the applicant was able to consult with his solicitor he was advised to continue to remain silent and that during the trial the applicant chose not to give evidence or call witnesses on his behalf. However, it is not for the Court to speculate on what the applicant's reaction, or his lawyer's advice, would have been had access not been denied during this initial period. As matters stand, the applicant was undoubtedly directly affected by the denial of access and the ensuing interference with the rights of the defence. The Court's conclusion as to the drawing of inferences does not alter that.

69. In his written submissions to the Court, the applicant appeared to make the further complaint under this head that his solicitor was unable to be present during police interviews. However, whether or not this issue formed part of the complaints admitted by the Commission, in any event its examination of the case was limited to that of the question of his access to a lawyer. Moreover, the case as argued before the Court was, in the main, confined to this issue. In these circumstances, and having regard to the Court's finding that he ought to have had access to a lawyer, it is not necessary to examine this point.

70. There has therefore been a breach of Article 6(1) in conjunction with paragraph 3(c) of the Convention as regards the applicant's denial of access to a lawyer during the first 48 hours of his police detention.

The findings in this case reveal some important features about the nature of Article 6 protection and the application of the proportionality test in this area. Even though the applicant strongly argued that the drawing of adverse inferences was in itself contrary to the spirit of Article 6(2) in particular, the court did not look at his claim in this absolutist way. Instead the judges assessed whether there was a justification, permitted by the law, for partial restriction of the 'right' to silence and against self-incrimination and decided that in the particular circumstances there was, especially as the applicant had been cautioned at the start of the process about the possibility of adverse inferences being drawn. However, the applicant was successful in his claim relating to the restriction of access to legal advice in the very important first stage of the criminal process following arrest. The court clearly thought that this applicant and criminal defendants generally are particularly vulnerable to possible abuse of process at this early stage and found that there had been a breach of Article 6(1) taken together with Article 6(3)(c) in these circumstances, irrespective of how a lawyer may have advised in the first place.

Saunders v UK (1997) 23 EHRR 313

Panel: The President, Judge Bernhardt; Judges Thór Vilhjálmsson, Gölcüklü, Pettiti, Walsh, Spielman, De Meyer, Valticos, Martens, Palm, Pekkanen, Loizou, Morenilla, Freeland, Wildhaber, Mifsud Bonnici, Makarczyk, Gotchev, Repik and Lōhmus

Statute: European Convention on Human Rights Article 6

Facts: Ernest Saunder, the former Chief Executive of Guinness plc, was investigated by Inspectors from the then Department of Trade and Industry (DTI) in relation to allegations of misconduct relating to Guinness's proposed takeover of another company. The evidence obtained in this investigation was subsequently used as part of the prosecution case against Saunders when he was subsequently tried and convicted of offences relating to false accounting, conspiracy and theft. He later took his case to Strasbourg alleging that he had been obliged to incriminate himself, and that use at his trial of statements he had had to make to the DTI inspectors under their compulsory powers deprived him of a fair hearing in accordance with Article 6(1).

JUDGMENT

67. The Court first observes that the applicant's complaint is confined to the use of the statements obtained by the DTI Inspectors during the criminal proceedings against him. While an administrative investigation is capable of involving the determination of a "criminal charge" in the light of the Court's case law concerning the autonomous meaning of this concept, it has not been suggested in the pleadings before the Court that Article 6(1) was applicable to the proceedings conducted by the Inspectors or that these proceedings themselves involved the determination of a criminal charge within the meaning of that provision. In this respect the Court recalls its judgment in *Fayed v. United Kingdom* where it held that the functions performed by the Inspectors under *section 432(2) of the Companies Act 1985* were essentially investigative in nature and that they did not adjudicate either in form or in substance. Their purpose was to ascertain and record facts which might subsequently be used as the basis for action by other competent authorities—prosecuting, regulatory, disciplinary or even legislative. As stated in that case, a requirement that such a preparatory investigation should be

subject to the guarantees of a judicial procedure as set forth in Article 6(1) would in practice unduly hamper the effective regulation in the public interest of complex financial and commercial activities.

Accordingly the Court's sole concern in the present case is with the use made of the relevant statements at the applicant's criminal trial.

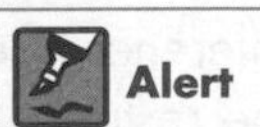

68. The Court recalls that, although not specifically mentioned in Article 6 of the Convention, the right to silence and the right not to incriminate oneself, are generally recognised international standards which lie at the heart of the notion of a fair procedure under Article 6. Their rationale lies, inter alia, in the protection of the accused against improper compulsion by the authorities thereby contributing to the avoidance of miscarriages of justice and to the fulfilment of the aims of Article 6. The right not to incriminate oneself, in particular, presupposes that the prosecution in a criminal case seek to prove their case against the accused without resort to evidence obtained through methods of coercion or oppression in defiance of the will of the accused. In this sense the right is closely linked to the presumption of innocence contained in Article 6(2) of the Convention.

69. The right not to incriminate oneself is primarily concerned, however, with respecting the will of an accused person to remain silent. As commonly understood in the legal systems of the Contracting Parties to the Convention and elsewhere, it does not extend to the use in criminal proceedings of material which may be obtained from the accused through the use of compulsory powers but which has an existence independent of the will of the suspect such as, *inter alia,* documents acquired pursuant to a warrant, breath, blood and urine samples and bodily tissue for the purpose of DNA testing.

In the present case the Court is only called upon to decide whether the use made by the prosecution of the statements obtained from the applicant by the Inspectors amounted to an unjustifiable infringement of the right. This question must be examined by the Court in the light of all the circumstances of the case. In particular, it must be determined whether the applicant has been subject to compulsion to give evidence and whether the use made of the resulting testimony at his trial offended the basic principles of a fair procedure inherent in Article 6(1) of which the right not to incriminate oneself is a constituent element.

70. It has not been disputed by the Government that the applicant was subject to legal compulsion to give evidence to the Inspectors. He was obliged under *sections 434 and 436 of the Companies Act 1985* to answer the questions put to him by the Inspectors in the course of nine lengthy interviews of which seven were admissible as evidence at his trial. A refusal by the applicant to answer the questions put to him could have led to a finding of contempt of court and the imposition of a fine or committal to prison for up to two years and it was no defence to such refusal that the questions were of an incriminating nature.

However, the Government have emphasised, before the Court, that nothing said by the applicant in the course of the interviews was self-incriminating and that he had merely given exculpatory answers or answers which, if true, would serve to confirm his defence. In their submission only statements which are self-incriminating could fall within the privilege against self-incrimination.

71. The Court does not accept the Government's premise on this point since some of the applicant's answers were in fact of an incriminating nature in the sense that they contained admissions to knowledge of information which tended to incriminate him. In any event, bearing in mind the concept of fairness in Article 6, the right not to incriminate oneself cannot reasonably be confined to statements of admission of wrongdoing or to remarks which are directly incriminating. Testimony obtained under compulsion which appears on its face to be of a non-incriminating nature—such as exculpatory remarks or mere information on questions of fact—may later be deployed in criminal proceedings in support of the prosecution case, for example to contradict or cast doubt upon other statements of the accused or evidence given by him during the trial or to otherwise undermine his credibility. Where the credibility of an accused must be assessed by a jury the use of such testimony may be especially harmful. It follows that what is of the essence in this context is the use to which evidence obtained under compulsion is made in the course of the criminal trial.

Alert

72. In this regard, the Court observes that part of the transcript of answers given by the applicant was read to the jury by counsel for the prosecution over a three-day period despite objections by the applicant. The fact that such extensive use was made of the interviews strongly suggests that the prosecution must have believed that the reading of the transcripts assisted their case in establishing the applicant's dishonesty. This interpretation of the intended impact of the material is supported by the remarks made by the trial judge in the course of the voir dire concerning the eighth and ninth interviews to the effect that each of the applicant's statements was capable of being a "confession" for the purposes of section 82(1) of the Police and Criminal Evidence Act 1984. Similarly, the Court of Appeal considered that the interviews formed "a significant part" of the prosecution's case against the applicant. Moreover, there were clearly instances where the statements were used by the prosecution to incriminating effect in order to establish the applicant's knowledge of payments to persons involved in the share support operation and to call into question his honesty. They were also used by counsel for the applicant's co-accused to cast doubt on the applicant's version of events.

In sum, the evidence available to the Court supports the claim that the transcripts of the applicant's answers, whether directly self-incriminating or not, were used in the course of the proceedings in a manner which sought to incriminate the applicant.

73. Both the applicant and the Commission maintained that the admissions contained in the interviews must have exerted additional pressure on the applicant to give testimony during the trial rather than to exercise his right to remain silent. However, it was the Government's view that the applicant chose to give evidence because of the damaging effect of the testimony of the chief witness for the prosecution, Mr Roux.

Although it cannot be excluded that one of the reasons which affected this decision was the extensive use made by the prosecution of the interviews, the Court finds it unnecessary to speculate on the reasons why the applicant chose to give evidence at his trial.

74. Nor does the Court find it necessary, having regard to the above assessment as to the use of the interviews during the trial, to decide whether the right not to incriminate oneself is absolute or whether infringements of it may be justified in particular circumstances.

It does not accept the Government's argument that the complexity of corporate fraud and the vital public interest in the investigation of such fraud and the punishment of those responsible could justify such a marked departure as that which occurred in the present case from one of the basic principles of a fair procedure. Like the Commission, it considers that the general requirements of fairness contained in Article 6, including the right not to incriminate oneself, apply to criminal proceedings in respect of all types of criminal offences without distinction, from the most simple to the most complex. The public interest cannot be invoked to justify the use of answers compulsorily obtained in a non-judicial investigation to incriminate the accused during the trial proceedings. It is noteworthy in this respect that under the relevant legislation statements obtained under compulsory powers by the Serious Fraud Office cannot, as a general rule, be adduced in evidence at the subsequent trial of the person concerned. Moreover the fact that statements were made by the applicant prior to his being charged does not prevent their later use in criminal proceedings from constituting an infringement of the right.

75. It follows from the above analysis and from the fact that section 434(5) of the Companies Act 1985 authorises, as noted by both the trial judge and the Court of Appeal, the subsequent use in criminal proceedings of statements obtained by the Inspectors that the various procedural safeguards to which reference has been made by the respondent Government cannot provide a defence in the present case since they did not operate to prevent the use of the statements in the subsequent criminal proceedings.

76. Accordingly, there has been an infringement in the present case of the right not to incriminate oneself.

The key point to take from *Saunders* is that it was the use of the statements, which he had earlier been obliged to make to the DTI inspectors, as evidence in the criminal trial which prompted the Strasbourg court to declare a breach of Article 6(1). The statements had been adduced in a way that suggested that Saunders had been dishonest, and that was sufficient to have tainted the legal process, whether or not the statements had actually contained an admission of guilt. Significantly, the court did recognise that use of such evidence could be justified in some circumstances and so a proportionality test was applied. However, in this particular case, the UK Government's argument that such a practice was justified in the fight against corporate fraud was not ultimately persuasive.

Further Reading

Forsyth, Christopher 'Control orders, conditions precedent and compliance with Article 6(1)', (2008) 67(1) *CLJ* 1

Landau, Jonny 'The right against self-incrimination and the right to silence under Article 6', (2007) 12(4) *JR* 261

Juss, Satvinder Singh 'Constitutionalising rights without a constitution: the British experience under article 6 of the Human Rights Act 1998', (2006) 27(1) *Stat LR* 29

11

Right to Privacy – Article 8

Topic List

1 Article 8

2 Privacy of the person – state interference

Alex Lawson and Neil Hurden

Introduction

It is important to note from the outset that Article 8 was designed to cover more than just a narrow right to privacy as a protection against press intrusion. It is concerned generally with the right to respect for one's private and family life and to one's home and correspondence. The Article is therefore one of the most wide-ranging of the various 'qualified' rights. It has been construed liberally by the Strasbourg court to take into account issues as varied as gender identity, sexual orientation, genetic identity (DNA profiling and records), and stop and search powers. Broadly speaking, the courts are likely to consider this Article to be engaged when the "physical and moral integrity" of the individual is in issue.

This chapter is primarily concerned, though, with the contentious issue of privacy in relation to alleged press intrusion. This is where the modern case law is at its most interesting and innovative. These cases also address another of the unusual aspects of Article 8, as applied under the Human Rights Act – it can be used as often to protect individuals from other (legal) individuals as it can to protect individuals from the state. This is because UK courts are deemed to be "public authorities" under the HRA s 6(3)(a) and so they have a duty to act in a way which is compatible with Convention rights. This creates the so-called 'horizontal effect' which now requires the domestic court to balance the competing rights represented by Articles 8 and 10, when there are disputes between two private legal entities.

1 The Right to Privacy – Article 8

The first case to consider, though, is a decision by the Strasbourg court which raises some of the most important, basic principles about privacy under the Convention. These are highlighted in the extracts from the case below.

***Von Hannover v Germany* (2005) 40 EHRR 1**

Panel: The President, Judge Cabral Barreto; Judges Ress, Caflisch, Türmen, Zupanĉiĉ, Hedigan and Traja

Statute: European Convention on Human Rights Article 8

Facts: The applicant, Princess Caroline of Monaco, had sought injunctions before the German domestic courts that would prevent the publication of photographs of her and her family in the German media. She argued that publication violated her Article 8 rights. The German courts had consistently adopted the view that, as a public figure of note, the applicant would essentially have to tolerate this level of press interest and intrusion, whereas she argued that such a situation should only apply when she was carrying out her official duties. Having been unsuccessful in the German courts, the applicant sought to argue at Strasbourg that the German state itself was at fault for not providing a mechanism by which people like her might protect themselves. Her case therefore was based on the important Convention principle of the 'positive obligation' which falls on signatory states.

Background to the case

9 Since the early 1990s the applicant has been trying—often through the courts—in a number of European countries to prevent the publication of photos about her private life in the tabloid press.

10 The photos that were the subject of the proceedings described below were published by the publishing company Burda in the German magazines *Bunte* and *Freizeit Revue* and by the publishing company Heinrich Bauer in the German magazine *Neue Post*.

The first series of photos

The five photos of the applicant published in Freizeit Revue magazine (edition No.30 of July 22, 1993)

11 These photos show her with the actor Vincent Lindon at the far end of a restaurant courtyard in Saint-Rémy-de-Provence. The first page of the magazine refers to "the tenderest photos of her romance with Vincent" and the photos themselves bear the caption "these photos are evidence of the tenderest romance of our time".

The two photos of the applicant published in *Bunte* magazine (edition No.32 of August 5, 1993)

12 The first photo shows her on horseback with the caption "Caroline and the blues. Her life is a novel with innumerable misfortunes, says the author Roig".

The second photo shows her with her children Peter and Andrea.

The photos are part of an article entitled "I don't think I could be a man's ideal wife".

The seven photos of the applicant published in *Bunte* magazine (edition No.34 of August 19, 1993)

13 The first photo shows her canoeing with her daughter Charlotte, the second shows her son Andrea with a bunch of flowers in his arms.

The third photo shows her doing her shopping with a bag slung over her shoulder, the fourth with Vincent Lindon in a restaurant and the fifth alone on a bicycle.

The sixth photo shows her with Vincent Lindon and her son Pierre.

The seventh photo shows her doing her shopping at the market, accompanied by her bodyguard.

The article is entitled "Pure happiness".

The second series of photos

The 10 photos of the applicant published in *Bunte* magazine (edition No.10 of February 27, 1997)

14 These photos show the applicant on a skiing holiday in Zürs/Arlberg. The accompanying article is entitled "Caroline ... a woman returns to life".

The 11 photos of the applicant published in *Bunte* magazine (edition No.12 of March 13, 1997)

15 Seven photos show her with Prince Ernst August von Hannover visiting a horse show in Saint-Rémy-de-Provence. The accompanying article is entitled "The kiss. Or: they are not hiding anymore".

Four other photos show her leaving her house in Paris with the caption "Out and about with Princess Caroline in Paris".

The seven photos of the applicant published in *Bunte* magazine (edition No.16 of April 10, 1997)

16 These photos show the applicant on the front page with Prince Ernst August von Hannover and on the inside pages of the magazine playing tennis with him or both putting their bicycles down.

The third series of photos

17 The sequence of photos published in *Neue Post* magazine (edition No.35/97) shows the applicant at the Monte Carlo Beach Club, dressed in a swimsuit and wrapped up in a bathing towel, tripping over an obstacle and falling down. The photos, which are quite blurred, are accompanied by an article entitled "Prince Ernst August played fisticuffs and Princess Caroline fell flat on her face".

There is some analysis of the German domestic law relating to privacy. It is important to note that there was law in this area, but that the Court regarded it as inadequately distinguishing when public figures were acting in a non-public environment.

JUDGMENT

Alleged violation of Article 8 of the Convention

43 The applicant submitted that the German court decisions had infringed her right to respect for her private and family life guaranteed by Art.8 of the Convention, which is worded as follows:

"1. Everyone has the right to respect for his private and family life, his home and his correspondence.

2. There shall be no interference by a public authority with the exercise of this right except such as is in accordance with the law and is necessary in a democratic society in the interests of national security, public safety or the economic well-being of the country, for the prevention of disorder or crime, for the protection of health or morals, or for the protection of the rights and freedoms of others".

Submissions of the parties and interveners

The applicant

44 The applicant stated that she had spent more than 10 years in unsuccessful litigation in the German courts trying to establish her right to the protection of her

private life. She alleged that as soon as she left her house she was constantly hounded by paparazzi who followed her every daily movement, be it crossing the road, fetching her children from school, doing her shopping, out walking, practising sport or going on holiday. In her submission, the protection afforded to the private life of a public figure like herself was minimal under German law because the concept of a "secluded place" as defined by the Federal Court of Justice and the Federal Constitutional Court was much too narrow in that respect. Furthermore, in order to benefit from that protection the onus was on her to establish every time that she had been in a secluded place. She was thus deprived of any privacy and could not move about freely without being a target for the paparazzi. She affirmed that in France her prior agreement was necessary for the publication of any photos not showing her at an official event. Such photos were regularly taken in France and then sold and published in Germany. The protection of private life from which she benefited in France was therefore systematically circumvented by virtue of the decisions of the German courts. On the subject of the freedom of the press the applicant stated that she was aware of the essential role played by the press in a democratic society in terms of informing and forming public opinion, but in her case it was just the entertainment press seeking to satisfy its readers' voyeuristic tendencies and make huge profits from generally anodyne photos showing her going about her daily business. Lastly, the applicant stressed that it was materially impossible to establish in respect of every photo whether or not she had been in a secluded place. As the judicial proceedings were generally held several months after publication of the photos, she was obliged to keep a permanent record of her every movement in order to protect herself from paparazzi who might photograph her. With regard to many of the photos that were the subject of this application it was impossible to determine the exact time and place at which they had been taken.

The Government

45 The Government submitted that German law, while taking account of the fundamental role of the freedom of the press in a democratic society, contained sufficient safeguards to prevent any abuse and ensure the effective protection of the private life of even public figures. In its submission, the German courts had in the instant case struck a fair balance between the applicant's rights to respect for her private life guaranteed by Art.8 and the freedom of the press guaranteed by Art.10, having regard to the margin of appreciation available to the State in this area. The courts had found in the first instance that the photos had not been taken in a secluded place and had, in the second instance, examined the limits on the protection of private life, particularly in the light of the freedom of the press and even where the publication of photos by the entertainment press were concerned. The protection of the private life of a figure of contemporary society "*par excellence*" did not require the publication of photos without his or her authorisation to be limited to showing the person in question engaged in their official duties. The public had a legitimate interest in knowing how the person behaved generally in public. The Government submitted that this definition of the freedom of the press by the Federal Constitutional Court was compatible with Art.10 and the European Court's relevant case law. Furthermore, the concept of a

secluded place was only one factor, albeit an important one, of which the domestic courts took account when balancing the protection of private life against the freedom of the press. Accordingly, while private life was less well protected where a public figure was photographed in a public place other factors could also be taken into consideration, such as the nature of the photos, for example, which should not shock the public. Lastly, the Government reiterated that the decision of the Federal Court of Justice—which had held that the publication of photos of the applicant with the actor Vincent Lindon in a restaurant courtyard in Saint-Rémy-de-Provence were unlawful—showed that the applicant's private life was protected even outside her home.

The interveners

46 The Association of Editors of German Magazines submitted that German law, which was half way between French law and United Kingdom law, struck a fair balance between the right to protection of private life and the freedom of the press. In its submission, it also complied with the principles set out in Resolution No.1165 of the Council of Europe on the right to privacy and the European Court's case law, which had always stressed the fundamental role of the press in a democratic society. The public's legitimate interest in being informed was not limited to politicians, but extended to public figures who had become known for other reasons. The press's role of "watchdog" could not be narrowly interpreted here. In that connection account should also be taken of the fact that the boundary between political commentary and entertainment was becoming increasingly blurred. Given that there was no uniform European standard concerning the protection of private life, the State had a wide margin of appreciation in this area.

47 Burda joined the observations of the Association of Editors of German Magazines and stated that German law required the courts to balance the competing interests of informing the public and protecting the right to control of the use of one's image very strictly and on a case by case basis. Even figures of contemporary society "*par excellence*" enjoyed a not inconsiderable degree of protection and recent case law had even tended towards reinforcing that protection. Since the death of her mother in 1982 the applicant had officially been First Lady of the reigning family in Monaco and was as such an example for the public. Moreover, the Grimaldi family had always sought to attract media attention and was therefore itself responsible for the public interest in it. The applicant could not therefore, especially if account were taken of her official functions, be regarded as a victim of the press. The publication of the photos in question had not infringed her right to control the use of her image because they had been taken while she was in public and had not been damaging to her reputation.

The Court's assessment

As regards the subject of the application

48 The Court notes at the outset that the photos of the applicant with her children are no longer the subject of this application, as it stated in its admissibility decision of July 8, 2003.

The same applies to the photos published in *Freizeit Revue* magazine showing the applicant with Vincent Lindon at the far end of a restaurant courtyard in Saint-Rémy-de-Provence. In its judgment of December 19, 1995 the Federal Court of Justice prohibited any further publication of the photos on the ground that they infringed the applicant's right to respect for her private life.

49 Accordingly, the Court considers it important to specify that the present application concerns the following photos, which were published as part of a series of articles about the applicant:

(i) the photo published in *Bunte* magazine showing the applicant on horseback;

(ii) the photos published in *Bunte* magazine showing the applicant shopping on her own; with Mr Vincent Lindon in a restaurant; alone on a bicycle; and with her bodyguard at a market;

(iii) the photos published in *Bunte* magazine showing the applicant on a skiing holiday in Austria;

(iv) the photos published in *Bunte* magazine showing the applicant with Prince Ernst August von Hannover or alone leaving her Parisian residence;

(v) the photos published in *Bunte* magazine showing the applicant playing tennis with Prince Ernst August von Hannover or both of them putting their bicycles down;

(vi) the photos published in *Neue Post* magazine showing the applicant tripping over an obstacle at the Monte Carlo Beach Club.

As regards the applicability of Article 8

50 The Court reiterates that the concept of private life extends to aspects relating to personal identity, such as a person's name, or a person's picture.

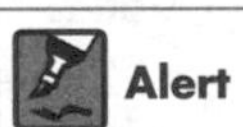

Furthermore, private life, in the Court's view, includes a person's physical and psychological integrity; the guarantee afforded by Art.8 of the Convention is primarily intended to ensure the development, without outside interference, of the personality of each individual in his relations with other human beings. There is therefore a zone of interaction of a person with others, even in a public context, which may fall within the scope of 'private life'.

51 The Court has also indicated that, in certain circumstances, a person has a "legitimate expectation" of protection and respect for his or her private life. Accordingly, it has held in a case concerning the interception of telephone calls on business premises that the applicant "would have had a reasonable expectation of privacy for such calls".

52 As regards photos, with a view to defining the scope of the protection afforded by Art.8 against arbitrary interference by public authorities, the Commission had regard to whether the photographs related to private or public matters and whether the material thus obtained was envisaged for a limited use or was likely to be made available to the general public.

53 In the present case there is no doubt that the publication by various German magazines of photos of the applicant in her daily life either on her own or with other people falls within the scope of her private life.

Compliance with Article 8

The domestic courts' position

54 The Court notes that, in its landmark judgment of December 15, 1999, the Federal Constitutional Court interpreted ss.22 and 23 of the Copyright (Arts Domain) Act by balancing the requirements of the freedom of the press against those of the protection of private life, that is, the public interest in being informed against the legitimate interests of the applicant. In doing so the Federal Constitutional Court took account of two criteria under German law, one functional and the other spatial. It considered that the applicant, as a figure of contemporary society "*par excellence*", enjoyed the protection of her private life even outside her home but only if she was in a secluded place out of the public eye "to which the person concerned retires with the objectively recognisable aim of being alone and where, confident of being alone, behaves in a manner in which he or she would not behave in public". In the light of those criteria the Federal Constitutional Court held that the Federal Court of Justice's judgment of December 19, 1995 regarding publication of the photos in question was compatible with the Basic Law. The court attached decisive weight to the freedom of the press, even the entertainment press, and to the public interest in knowing how the applicant behaved outside her representative functions.

55 Referring to its landmark judgment, the Federal Constitutional Court did not entertain the applicant's appeals in the subsequent proceedings brought by her.

The general principles governing the protection of private life and the freedom of expression

56 In the present case the applicant did not complain of an action by the State, but rather of the lack of adequate state protection of her private life and her image.

57 The Court reiterates that although the object of Art.8 is essentially that of protecting the individual against arbitrary interference by the public authorities, it does not merely compel the State to abstain from such interference: in addition to this primarily negative undertaking, there may be positive obligations inherent in an effective respect for private or family life. These obligations may involve the adoption of measures designed to secure respect for private life even in the sphere of the relations of individuals between themselves. That also applies to the protection of a person's picture against abuse by others.

The boundary between the State's positive and negative obligations under this provision does not lend itself to precise definition. The applicable principles are, nonetheless, similar. In both contexts regard must be had to the fair balance that has to be struck between the competing interests of the individual and of the community as a whole; and in both contexts the State enjoys a certain margin of appreciation.

58 That protection of private life has to be balanced against the freedom of expression guaranteed by Art.10 of the Convention. In that context the Court reiterates that the freedom of expression constitutes one of the essential foundations of a democratic society. Subject to para.2 of Art.10, it is applicable not only to "information" or "ideas" that are favourably received or regarded as inoffensive or as a matter of indifference, but also to those that offend, shock or disturb. Such are the demands of that pluralism, tolerance and broad-mindedness without which there is no "democratic society".

In that connection the press plays an essential role in a democratic society. Although it must not overstep certain bounds, in particular in respect of the reputation and rights of others, its duty is nevertheless to impart—in a manner consistent with its obligations and responsibilities—information and ideas on all matters of public interest. Journalistic freedom also covers possible recourse to a degree of exaggeration, or even provocation.

59 Although freedom of expression also extends to the publication of photos, this is an area in which the protection of the rights and reputation of others takes on particular importance. The present case does not concern the dissemination of "ideas", but of images containing very personal or even intimate "information" about an individual. Furthermore, photos appearing in the tabloid press are often taken in a climate of continual harassment that induces in the persons concerned a very strong sense of intrusion into their private life or even of persecution.

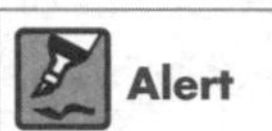

60 In the cases in which the Court has had to balance the protection of private life against the freedom of expression it has always stressed the contribution made by photos or articles in the press to a debate of general interest. The Court thus found, in one case, that the use of certain terms in relation to an individual's private life was not "justified by considerations of public concern" and that those terms did not "[bear] on a matter of general importance" and went on to hold that there had not been a violation of Art.10. In another case, however, the Court attached particular importance to the fact that the subject in question was a news item of "major public concern" and that the published photographs "did not disclose any details of [the] private life" of the person in question and held that there had been a violation of Art.10. Similarly, in a recent case concerning the publication by President Mitterand's former private doctor of a book containing revelations about the President's state of health, the Court held that "the more time passed the more the public interest in President Mitterand's two seven-year presidential terms prevailed over the requirements of the protection of his rights with regard to medical confidentiality" and held that there had been a breach of Art.10.

Application of these general principles by the Court

61 The Court points out at the outset that in the present case the photos of the applicant in the various German magazines show her in scenes from her daily life, thus engaged in activities of a purely private nature such as practising sport, out walking, leaving a restaurant or on holiday. The photos, in which the applicant appears sometimes alone

and sometimes in company, illustrate a series of articles with such anodyne titles as "Pure happiness", "Caroline ... a woman returning to life", "Out and about with Princess Caroline in Paris" and "The kiss. Or: they are not hiding anymore ...".

62 The Court also notes that the applicant, as a member of the Prince of Monaco's family, represents the ruling family at certain cultural or charitable events. However, she does not exercise any function within or on behalf of the State of Monaco or one of its institutions.

63 The Court considers that a fundamental distinction needs to be made between reporting facts—even controversial ones—capable of contributing to a debate in a democratic society relating to politicians in the exercise of their functions, for example, and reporting details of the private life of an individual who, moreover, as in this case, does not exercise official functions. While in the former case the press exercises its vital role of "watchdog" in a democracy by contributing to "impart[ing] information and ideas on matters of public interest" it does not do so in the latter case.

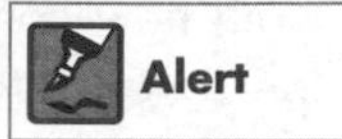

64 Similarly, although the public has a right to be informed, which is an essential right in a democratic society that, in certain special circumstances, can even extend to aspects of the private life of public figures, particularly where politicians are concerned, this is not the case here. The situation here does not come within the sphere of any political or public debate because the published photos and accompanying commentaries relate exclusively to details of the applicant's private life.

65 As in other similar cases it has examined, the Court considers that the publication of the photos and articles in question, of which the sole purpose was to satisfy the curiosity of a particular readership regarding the details of the applicant's private life, cannot be deemed to contribute to any debate of general interest to society despite the applicant being known to the public.

66 In these conditions freedom of expression calls for a narrower interpretation.

67 In that connection the Court also takes account of the resolution of the Parliamentary Assembly of the Council of Europe on the right to privacy, which stresses the "one-sided interpretation of the right to freedom of expression" by certain media which attempt to justify an infringement of the rights protected by Art.8 of the Convention by claiming that "their readers are entitled to know everything about public figures".

68 The Court finds another point to be of importance: even though, strictly speaking, the present application concerns only the publication of the photos and articles by various German magazines, the context in which these photos were taken—without the applicant's knowledge or consent—and the harassment endured by many public figures in their daily lives cannot be fully disregarded.

In the present case this point is illustrated in particularly striking fashion by the photos taken of the applicant at the Monte Carlo Beach Club tripping over an obstacle and falling down. It appears that these photos were taken secretly at a distance of several hundred metres, probably from a neighbouring house, whereas journalists and photographers' access to the club was strictly regulated.

69 The Court reiterates the fundamental importance of protecting private life from the point of view of the development of every human being's personality. That protection—as stated above—extends beyond the private family circle and also includes a social dimension. The Court considers that anyone, even if they are known to the general public, must be able to enjoy a "legitimate expectation" of protection of and respect for their private life.

70 Furthermore, increased vigilance in protecting private life is necessary to contend with new communication technologies which make it possible to store and reproduce personal data. This also applies to the systematic taking of specific photos and their dissemination to a broad section of the public.

Conclusion

76 As the Court has stated above, it considers that the decisive factor in balancing the protection of private life against freedom of expression should lie in the contribution that the published photos and articles make to a debate of general interest. It is clear in the instant case that they made no such contribution since the applicant exercises no official function and the photos and articles related exclusively to details of her private life.

77 Furthermore, the Court considers that the public does not have a legitimate interest in knowing where the applicant is and how she behaves generally in her private life even if she appears in places that cannot always be described as secluded and despite the fact that she is well known to the public.

Even if such a public interest exists, as does a commercial interest of the magazines in publishing these photos and these articles, in the instant case those interests must, in the Court's view, yield to the applicant's right to the effective protection of her private life.

80 There has therefore been a breach of Art.8 of the Convention.

Campbell v MGN Ltd [2004] 2 AC 457

Panel: Lord Nicholls of Birkenhead, Lord Hoffmann, Lord Hope of Craighead, Baroness Hale of Richmond and Lord Carswell

Statute: European Convention on Human Rights Article 8

Facts: The claimant in this case was the model Naomi Campbell, who had been depicted in a tabloid newspaper after coming out of a drug rehabilitation clinic. Her claim involved the application of the "horizontal effect" of the Human Rights Act, as the court was obliged to balance her claim that her rights to privacy had been infringed with the newspaper's defence that its Article 10 rights to free expression would be wrongly restricted if publication of the story and pictures of the incident were restrained. Part of the interest in the case stemmed from the fact that the applicant had publicly denied drug taking and criticised the practice within the fashion industry and so MGN used what could be called an "hypocrisy" defence.

LORD HOPE OF CRAIGHEAD

81 [F]or someone in Miss Campbell's position, there are few areas of the life of an individual that are more in need of protection on the grounds of privacy than the combating of addiction to drugs or to alcohol. It is hard to break the habit which has led to the addiction. It is all too easy to give up the struggle if efforts to do so are exposed to public scrutiny. The struggle, after all, is an intensely personal one. It involves a high degree of commitment and of self-criticism. The sense of shame that comes with it is one of the most powerful of all the tools that are used to break the habit. But shame increases the individual's vulnerability as the barriers that the habit has engendered are broken down. The smallest hint that the process is being watched by the public may be enough to persuade the individual to delay or curtail the treatment. At the least it is likely to cause distress, even to those who in other circumstances like to court publicity and regard publicity as a benefit.

...

Lord Hope was able to conclude that the fact of Campbell's treatment was of a private nature. The interesting area of analysis was whether or not there were reasons that would warrant its publication anyway – the balancing of Articles 8 and 10.

The competing rights of free speech and privacy

103 Morland J did not give any detailed reasons in para 70 of his judgment for his conclusion that, striking the balance between articles 8 and 10 and having full regard to section 12(4) of the Human Rights Act 1998, Miss Campbell was entitled to the remedy of damages. But he did recognise in para 98 that neither article 10 nor article 8 had pre-eminence, the one over the other. Court of Appeal's approach to the respondents' entitlement to publish what they described as the peripheral details was based on their view that the provision of these details as background to support the story that Miss Campbell was a drug addict was a legitimate part of the journalistic package which was designed to demonstrate that she had been deceiving the public when she said that she did not take drugs: [2003] QB 633, 662, para 62. In para 64 they said that its publication was justified in order to give a factual account that had the detail necessary to carry credibility. But they do not appear to have attempted to balance the competing Convention rights against each other. No doubt this was because they had already concluded that these details were peripheral and that their publication was not, in its context, sufficiently significant to amount to a breach of duty of confidence: para 58.

104 In my opinion the Court of Appeal's approach is open to the criticism that, because they wrongly held that these details were not entitled to protection under the law of confidence, they failed to carry out the required balancing exercise.

105 The context for this exercise is provided by articles 8 and 10 of the Convention. The rights guaranteed by these articles are qualified rights. Article 8(1) protects the right to respect for private life, but recognition is given in article 8(2) to the protection of the rights and freedoms of others. Article 10(1) protects the right to freedom of expression, but article 10(2) recognises the need to protect the rights and freedoms of

others. The effect of these provisions is that the right to privacy which lies at the heart of an action for breach of confidence has to be balanced against the right of the media to impart information to the public. And the right of the media to impart information to the public has to be balanced in its turn against the respect that must be given to private life.

106 There is nothing new about this, as the need for this kind of balancing exercise was already part of English law: *Attorney General v Guardian Newspapers Ltd (No 2) [1990] 1 AC 109, per Lord Goff of Chieveley*. But account must now be taken of the guidance which has been given by the European court on the application of these articles. As Sedley LJ pointed out in *Douglas v Hello! Ltd [2001] QB 967*, 1004, para 135:

"The European Court of Human Rights has always recognised the high importance of free media of communication in a democracy, but its jurisprudence does not—and could not consistently with the Convention itself—give article 10(1) the presumptive priority which is given, for example, to the First Amendment in the jurisprudence of the United States' courts. Everything will ultimately depend on the proper balance between privacy and publicity in the situation facing the court."

107 I accept, of course, that the importance which the Court of Appeal attached to the journalistic package finds support in the authorities. In *Jersild v Denmark (1994) 19 EHRR 1*, para 31 the European court, repeating what was said in *Observer and Guardian v United Kingdom (1991) 14 EHRR 153*, para 59, declared that freedom of expression constitutes one of the essential foundations of a democratic society and that the safeguards to be afforded to the press are of particular importance. It then added these comments in para 31:

"Whilst the press must not overstep the bounds set, inter alia, in the interest of 'the protection of the reputation and rights of others', it is nevertheless incumbent on it to impart information and ideas of public interest. Not only does the press have the task of imparting such information and ideas: the public also has a right to receive them. Were it otherwise, the press would be unable to play its vital role of 'public watchdog'."

...

Striking the balance

112 There is no doubt that the presentation of the material that it was legitimate to convey to the public in this case without breaching the duty of confidence was a matter for the journalists. The choice of language used to convey information and ideas, and decisions as to whether or not to accompany the printed word by the use of photographs, are pre-eminently editorial matters with which the court will not interfere. The respondents are also entitled to claim that they should be accorded a reasonable margin of appreciation in taking decisions as to what details needed to be included in the article to give it credibility. This is an essential part of the journalistic exercise.

113 But decisions about the publication of material that is private to the individual raise issues that are not simply about presentation and editing. Any interference with the public interest in disclosure has to be balanced against the interference with the right of the individual to respect for their private life. The decisions that are then taken are open to review by the court. The tests which the court must apply are the familiar ones. They are whether publication of the material pursues a legitimate aim and whether the benefits that will be achieved by its publication are proportionate to the harm that may be done by the interference with the right to privacy. The jurisprudence of the European Court of Human Rights explains how these principles are to be understood and applied in the context of the facts of each case. Any restriction of the right to freedom of expression must be subjected to very close scrutiny. But so too must any restriction of the right to respect for private life. Neither article 8 nor article 10 has any pre-eminence over the other in the conduct of this exercise. As Resolution 1165 of the Parliamentary Assembly of the Council of Europe (1998), para 11, pointed out, they are neither absolute not in any hierarchical order, since they are of equal value in a democratic society.

The article 10 right

114 In the present case it is convenient to begin by looking at the matter from the standpoint of the respondents' assertion of the article 10 right and the court's duty as a public authority under section 6(1) of the Human Rights Act 1998, which section 12(4) reinforces, not to act in a way which is incompatible with that Convention right.

Decipher

Decipher: The HRA s 12(4) states that courts must have particular regard to Article 10 rights.

115 The first question is whether the objective of the restriction on the article 10 right—the protection of Miss Campbell's right under article 8 to respect for her private life—is sufficiently important to justify limiting the fundamental right to freedom of expression which the press assert on behalf of the public. It follows from my conclusion that the details of Miss Campbell's treatment were private that I would answer this question in the affirmative. The second question is whether the means chosen to limit the article 10 right are rational, fair and not arbitrary and impair the right as minimally as is reasonably possible. It is not enough to assert that it would be reasonable to exclude these details from the article. A close examination of the factual justification for the restriction on the freedom of expression is needed if the fundamental right enshrined in article 10 is to remain practical and effective. The restrictions which the court imposes

Alert

on the article 10 right must be rational, fair and not arbitrary, and they must impair the right no more than is necessary.

116 In my opinion the factors that need to be weighed are, on the one hand, the duty that was recognised in **Jersild v Denmark 19 EHRR 1**, para 31 to impart information and ideas of public interest which the public has a right to receive, and the need that was recognised in **Fressoz and Roire v France 31 EHRR 28**, para 54 for the court to leave it to journalists to decide what material needs to be reproduced to ensure credibility; and, on the other hand, the degree of privacy to which Miss Campbell was entitled under the law of confidence as to the details of her therapy. Account should therefore be taken of the respondents' wish to put forward a story that was credible and to present Miss Campbell in a way that commended her for her efforts to overcome her addiction.

117 But it should also be recognised that the right of the public to receive information about the details of her treatment was of a much lower order than the undoubted right to know that she was misleading the public when she said that she did not take drugs. In *Dudgeon v United Kingdom (1981) 4 EHRR 149*, para 52 the European court said that the more intimate the aspects of private life which are being interfered with, the more serious must be the reasons for doing so before the interference can be legitimate. Clayton & Tomlinson, The Law of Human Rights (2000), para 15.162, point out that the court has distinguished three kinds of expression: political expression, artistic expression and commercial expression, and that it consistently attaches great importance to political expression and applies rather less rigorous principles to expression which is artistic and commercial. According to the court's well-established case law, freedom of expression constitutes one of the essential foundations of a democratic society and one of the basic conditions for its progress and the self-fulfilment of each individual: *Tammer v Estonia* (2001) 37 EHRR 857, para 59. But there were no political or democratic values at stake here, nor has any pressing social need been identified: contrast *Goodwin v United Kingdom (1996) 22 EHRR 123*, para 40.

Alert

118 As for the other side of the balance, Keene LJ said in *Douglas v Hello! Ltd [2001] QB 967*, 1012, para 168, that any consideration of article 8 rights must reflect the fact that there are different degrees of privacy. In the present context the potential for disclosure of the information to cause harm is an important factor to be taken into account in the assessment of the extent of the restriction that was needed to protect Miss Campbell's right to privacy.

The article 8 right

119 Looking at the matter from Miss Campbell's point of view and the protection of her article 8 Convention right, publication of details of the treatment which she was undertaking to cure her addiction—that she was attending Narcotics Anonymous, for how long, how frequently and at what times of day she had been attending this therapy, the nature of it and extent of her commitment to the process and the publication of the covertly taken photographs (the third, fourth and fifth of the five elements contained in the article)—had the potential to cause harm to her, for the

reasons which I have already given. So I would attach a good deal of weight to this factor.

120 As for the other side of the balance, a person's right to privacy may be limited by the public's interest in knowing about certain traits of her personality and certain aspects of her private life, as L'Heureux-Dubé and Bastarache JJ in the Supreme Court of Canada recognised in *Aubry v Éditions Vice-Versa Inc* [1998] 1 SCR 591, paras 57-58. But it is not enough to deprive Miss Campbell of her right to privacy that she is a celebrity and that her private life is newsworthy. A margin of appreciation must, of course, be given to the journalist. Weight must be given to this. But to treat these details merely as background was to undervalue the importance that was to be attached to the need, if Miss Campbell was to be protected, to keep these details private. And it is hard to see that there was any compelling need for the public to know the name of the organisation that she was attending for the therapy, or for the other details of it to be set out. The presentation of the article indicates that this was not fully appreciated when the decision was taken to publish these details. The decision to publish the photographs suggests that greater weight was being given to the wish to publish a story that would attract interest rather than to the wish to maintain its credibility.

121 Had it not been for the publication of the photographs, and looking to the text only, I would have been inclined to regard the balance between these rights as about even. Such is the effect of the margin of appreciation that must, in a doubtful case, be given to the journalist. In that situation the proper conclusion to draw would have been that it had not been shown that the restriction on the article 10 right for which Miss Campbell argues was justified on grounds of proportionality. But the text cannot be separated from the photographs. The words "Therapy: Naomi outside meeting" underneath the photograph on the front page and the words "Hugs: Naomi, dressed in jeans and baseball hat, arrives for a lunchtime group meeting this week" underneath the photograph on p 13 were designed to link what might otherwise have been anonymous and uninformative pictures with the main text. The reader would undoubtedly make that link, and so too would the reasonable person of ordinary sensibilities. The reasonable person of ordinary sensibilities would also regard publication of the covertly taken photographs, and the fact that they were linked with the text in this way, as adding greatly overall to the intrusion which the article as a whole made into her private life.

122 The photographs were taken of Miss Campbell while she was in a public place, as she was in the street outside the premises where she had been receiving therapy. The taking of photographs in a public street must, as Randerson J said *in Hosking v Runting* [2003] 3 NZLR 385, 415, para 138, be taken to be one of the ordinary incidents of living in a free community. The real issue is whether publicising the content of the photographs would be offensive: Gault and Blanchard JJ in the Court of Appeal [2004] NZCA 34, para 165. A person who just happens to be in the street when the photograph was taken and appears in it only incidentally cannot as a general rule object to the publication of the photograph, for the reasons given by L'Heureux-Dubé and Bastarache JJ in *Aubry v Éditions Vice-Versa Inc* [1998] 1 SCR 591, para 59. But the situation is different if the public nature of the place where a photograph is taken

was simply used as background for one or more persons who constitute the true subject of the photograph. The question then arises, balancing the rights at issue, where the public's right to information can justify dissemination of a photograph taken without authorisation: *Aubry*, para 61. The European court has recognised that a person who walks down a public street will inevitably be visible to any member of the public who is also present and, in the same way, to a security guard viewing the scene through closed circuit television: *PG and JH v United Kingdom Reports of Judgments and Decisions* 2001-ix, p 195, para 57. But, as the court pointed out in the same paragraph, private life considerations may arise once any systematic or permanent record comes into existence of such material from the public domain. In *Peck v United Kingdom* (2003) 36 EHRR 719, para 62 the court held that the release and publication of CCTV footage which showed the applicant in the process of attempting to commit suicide resulted in the moment being viewed to an extent that far exceeded any exposure to a passer-by or to security observation that he could have foreseen when he was in that street.

123 The same process of reasoning that led to the findings in *Peck* that the article 8 right had been violated and by the majority in *Aubry* that there had been an infringement of the claimant's right to respect for her private life can be applied here. Miss Campbell could not have complained if the photographs had been taken to show the scene in the street by a passer-by and later published simply as street scenes. But these were not just pictures of a street scene where she happened to be when the photographs were taken. They were taken deliberately, in secret and with a view to their publication in conjunction with the article. The zoom lens was directed at the doorway of the place where the meeting had been taking place. The faces of others in the doorway were pixelated so as not to reveal their identity. Hers was not, the photographs were published and her privacy was invaded. The argument that the publication of the photograph added credibility to the story has little weight. The photograph was not self-explanatory. Neither the place nor the person were instantly recognisable. The reader only had the editor's word as to the truth of these details.

124 Any person in Miss Campbell's position, assuming her to be of ordinary sensibilities but assuming also that she had been photographed surreptitiously outside the place where she been receiving therapy for drug addiction, would have known what they were and would have been distressed on seeing the photographs. She would have seen their publication, in conjunction with the article which revealed what she had been doing when she was photographed and other details about her engagement in the therapy, as a gross interference with her right to respect for her private life. In my opinion this additional element in the publication is more than enough to outweigh the right to freedom of expression which the defendants are asserting in this case.

Conclusion

125 Despite the weight that must be given to the right to freedom of expression that the press needs if it is to play its role effectively, I would hold that there was here an infringement of Miss Campbell's right to privacy that cannot be justified. In my opinion

publication of the third, fourth and fifth elements in the article (see para 88) was an invasion of that right for which she is entitled to damages. I would allow the appeal and restore the orders that were made by the trial judge.

The three elements referred to by Lord Hope above were the facts that she was being treated at a Narcotics Anonymous facility; the details of that treatment; and also, importantly, the photographs of her leaving the establishment. The other elements which he did not find to be an invasion of her privacy were the broader points of news, namely that she was addicted and that she was receiving treatment. It is significant here that the court can distinguish differing degrees of intrusion when trying to weigh up the competing interests between the individual and the media. The latter should have the right to report matters of public interest and concern but this should not infringe too much on specific areas of private life which may be gratuitous, in that they do not "add" anything to the story, or may be of a more sensitive, private nature, such as an individual's state of health, and so should only be reported when the justification for doing so is especially strong.

The following case provides another instructive example of how the courts have developed privacy law under the Human Rights Act and shows a more complete approach and methodology in this area, as the case law has settled into a more established pattern.

McKennitt v Ash [2006] EMLR 10

Panel: Eady J

Statute: European Convention on Human Rights Article 8

Facts: This case concerned the publication of an unauthorised biography about Loreena McKennitt, a Canadian folk singer, written by Niema Ash a (former) friend. McKennitt sought an injunction restraining further publication. The case is interesting for several reasons. One was the innovative argument put forward by Ash that the book was really about her and not McKennitt. While this argument could be disposed of relatively easily in this case, as no one knew who Ash was, it raises troubling possibilities for cases where both parties are famous (such as in celebrity divorce cases). Of principal interest, however, is the approach or methodology Eady J took to deciding whether or not Article 8 was engaged and whether other interests (such as the public interest) might defeat it. This was almost totally endorsed by three judges in the Court of Appeal, hence the reason why this technically inferior decision is extracted.

MR JUSTICE EADY

The modern approach to public interest

54 When addressing the tension between media rights under Art.10 and those of an individual under Art.8, the approach has been to balance the protection of private life against freedom of expression by reference to whether the intrusion makes any contribution to a debate of "general interest". The test was applied in one case of whether or not intrusive references to an individual's private life were "justified by

considerations of public concern" or bore on a matter of general importance: see, e.g. *Tammer v Estonia* (2003) 37 E.H.R.R. 43.

55 In the Princess Caroline case, the court drew a fundamental distinction between reporting facts capable of contributing to a debate in a democratic society, relating to politicians and the exercise of their functions, and reporting details of the private life of an individual who exercises no official functions. It is far less likely in the latter case that the press could ever be characterised as exercising its "vital role of watchdog". The court continued:

"The situation here does not come within the sphere of any political or public debate because the published photos and accompanying commentaries relate exclusively to details of the applicant's private life.

As in other similar cases it has examined, the Court considers that the publication of the photos and articles in question, of which the sole purpose was to satisfy the curiosity of a particular readership regarding the details of the applicant's private life, cannot be deemed to contribute to any debate of general interest to society despite the applicant being known to the public ...".

It was recognised (at [67]) that the readers of popular newspapers are not entitled to know "everything" about public figures.

57 It is important for courts in the United Kingdom to take these considerations into account. It is clear that there is a significant shift taking place as between, on the one hand, freedom of expression for the media and the corresponding interest of the public to receive information, and, on the other hand, the legitimate expectation of citizens to have their private lives protected. As was made clear at [77], even where there is a genuine public interest, alongside a commercial interest in the media in publishing articles or photographs, sometimes such interests would have to yield to the individual citizen's right to the effective protection of private life. As Lord Woolf C.J. observed in *A v B Plc* [2002] EWCA Civ 337; [2003] Q.B. 195 at 208, "... a public figure is entitled to a private life". Moreover, just as the European Court was not prepared to acknowledge a bright line boundary between private (or secluded) locations and public places, so too there was recognition that the protection of private life "... extends beyond the private family circle and also includes a social dimension".

58 It was shortly before the decision in *Von Hannover v Germany* that the House of Lords handed down its decision in *Campbell v MGN Ltd* (cited above). Nevertheless, it would appear that there is consistency between the approach of the court in Strasbourg and that now being adopted in the courts of the United Kingdom. It is interesting to note that the concept of a "reasonable expectation of privacy" is reflected also in the speeches of their Lordships. As Lord Nicholls observed at [20]–[21]:

"... but article 10(2), like article 8(2), recognises there are occasions when protection of the rights of others may make it necessary for the freedom of expression to give way. When both these articles are engaged a difficult question of proportionality may arise. This question is distinct from the initial question of whether the published information engaged article 8 at all by being within the sphere of the complainant's private or family life.

[21] Accordingly, in deciding what was the ambit of an individual's 'private life' in particular circumstances courts need to be on guard against using as a touchstone a test which brings into account considerations which should more properly be considered at the later stage of proportionality. Essentially the touchstone of private life is whether in respect of the disclosed acts the person in question had a reasonable expectation of privacy".

This would strongly suggest that the mere fact that information concerning an individual is "anodyne" or "trivial" will not necessarily mean that Art.8 is not engaged. For the purpose of determining that initial question, it seems that the subject-matter must be carefully assessed. If it is such as to give rise to a "reasonable expectation of privacy", then questions such as triviality or banality may well need to be considered at the later stage of bringing to bear an "intense focus" upon the comparative importance of the specific rights being claimed in the individual case. They will be relevant to proportionality.

59 Whether, in any given circumstances, an individual citizen can have a reasonable expectation that his privacy will be protected may depend simply upon the nature of the information itself or, on the other hand, it may depend upon a combination of factors. Sometimes such an expectation will arise from the circumstances in which the information has been voluntarily imparted to another person or persons. In particular, the expectation may be justified by a duty of confidence arising expressly or by implication at the time.

60 Having referred to the judgment of Lord Woolf C.J. in *A v B Plc* (cited above), Lord Hope observed in *Campbell v MGN Ltd* at [85], that "... a duty of confidence will arise whenever the party subject to the duty is in a situation where he knows or ought to know that the other person can reasonably expect his privacy to be protected. The difficulty will be as to the relevant facts, bearing in mind that, if there is an intrusion in a situation where a person can reasonably expect his privacy to be respected, that intrusion will be capable of giving rise to liability unless the intrusion can be justified".

61 Reference was made to the "three limiting principles" identified by Lord Goff in *Attorney General v Guardian Newspapers Ltd (No.2)* [1990] 1 A.C. 109 at 282:

"The first limiting principle (which is rather an expression of the scope of the duty) is highly relevant to this appeal. It is that the principle of confidentiality only applies to information to the extent that it is confidential. In particular, once it has entered what is usually called the public domain (which means no more than that the information in question is so generally accessible that, in all the circumstances, it cannot be regarded as confidential) then, as a general rule, the principle of confidentiality can have no application to it. ...

The second limiting principle is that the duty of confidence applies neither to useless information, nor to trivia. There is no need for me to develop this point.

The third limiting principle is of far greater importance. It is that, although the basis of the law's protection of confidence is that there is a public interest that confidences should be preserved and protected by the law, nevertheless that public interest may be outweighed by some other countervailing public interest which favours disclosure. This limitation may apply, as the learned judge pointed out, to all types of confidential information. It is this limiting principle which may require a court to carry out a balancing operation, weighing the public interest in maintaining confidence against a countervailing public interest favouring disclosure".

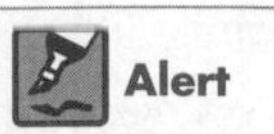

62 Lord Hope noted that the "language" has changed following the coming into operation of the Human Rights Act 1998; that is to say, the terminology used nowadays might differ, at least superficially, from that used by Lord Goff in 1988. Nevertheless, in Lord Hope's view the balancing exercise to be conducted today would be essentially the same, although it has to be more carefully focussed and more penetrating. Since the enactment of the 1998 statute, new breadth and strength is given to an action for breach of confidence by reference to Arts 8 and 10. That balancing exercise only begins, of course, once it has been decided that Art.8 is, in any particular respect, engaged.

How to decide whether Article 8 is engaged

63 It thus becomes clear that, with respect to any given piece of information, the first task confronting a court is to identify whether there would be a reasonable expectation of privacy such as to engage Art. 8 at all. If not, the balancing exercise becomes unnecessary and any claim based solely upon breach of confidence and/or privacy would fail. Another way of putting it, in the conventional language of claims for breach of confidence, would be to say that the relevant information does not have about it the necessary "quality of confidence": see, e.g. Coco v AN Clark (Engineers) Ltd [1969] R.P.C. 41; *Douglas v Hello! Ltd* [2003] 3 All E.R. 182 (sic); *SmithKline Beecham Plc v Generics (UK) Ltd BASF* [2003] EWCA Civ 1109; [2003] 4 All E.R. 1302 at [31].

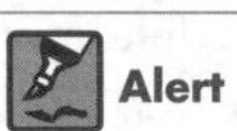

64 On the other hand, where information may be classified as inherently subject to a reasonable expectation of privacy, or it has been passed to another person in circumstances which would have given rise to such an expectation, that protection may be lost if the information has truly gone into the public domain. Courts would be less ready, however, in the case of personal private information (as opposed to commercial secrets) to assume that protection has gone forever by virtue of its having come to the attention of certain readers or categories of readers. In other words, so far as personal privacy is concerned, there may still be some rights vested in the individual citizen capable of protection: see e.g. *B v H Bauer Publishing Ltd* [2002] E.M.L.R. 8.

65 Again, information which would be subject to a prima facie obligation of confidence, and correspondingly entitled to legal protection, may turn out *not* to be so protected once the court has applied the "intense focus" to the circumstances. It may be concluded, for example, that protection in those particular circumstances would not be proportionate to the degree of interference which would be entailed for the defendant's Art.10 rights. Alternatively, as Lord Goff had in mind, there may be a countervailing public interest which would require the individual's right to be subordinated.

66 These are all considerations which arise on the facts of the present case. I shall need to consider the various arguments as they arise.

67 I need naturally to consider each of the passages in the book singled out for complaint separately, not only to decide whether in each case the threshold test for privacy is passed (that is to say, whether or not there would be a reasonable expectation of privacy), but also to consider, if that initial test has been satisfied, whether any other "limiting factor" comes into play such as public domain or public interest. In the light of Lord Nicholls' observations which I have cited above, it would seem to be at that second stage that I shall need to consider whether some item of information which is prima facie private should escape protection for reasons of being banal, anodyne or trivial.

The importance of this case is in Eady J's attempt to establish a firm methodology for approaching such disputes. Before they can be heard, there has to be a private law cause of action on which the Convention arguments can be "hung". The claimant then needs to show that they have a "reasonable expectation of privacy" relating to information or images that are not totally "anodyne" or already in the public domain. If they can show this, the court then has a duty to weigh up the respective rights of the parties to see whether there is sufficient justification to allow the exercise of freedom of expression to infringe on matters which engage the right to privacy. In this case he was clearly not persuaded that there were and so allowed publication of the book to be restrained.

2 Privacy of the person – state interference

The last case in this chapter deals with a completely different area in which Article 8 rights are relevant, this time in the context of direct interference by agents of the state with the privacy of individuals. It is an interesting case because it also reveals a different approach between the UK domestic courts, hearing Convention arguments under the Human Rights Act, and the Strasbourg court.

***Gillan and Quinton v United Kingdom* (2010) 50 EHRR 45**

Panel: The President, Judge Garlicki; Judges Bratza, Bonello, Mijović, Hirvelä, Bianku and Vučinić

Statute: European Convention on Human Rights Article 8

Facts: The two applicants were stopped and searched by the police en route to a demonstration under powers contained in the Terrorism Act 2000 s 44. Gillan was detained for around 20 minutes and Quinton, a journalist, was searched and ordered to stop filming. (In her case there was a factual dispute about how long she was stopped for.) The relevant statutory powers allowed a senior police officer to authorise the stopping of individuals within a specific area and physical searches of their person and belongings "for articles of a kind which could be used in connection with terrorism". The applicants complained that these actions had violated their rights under

Article 8 (and also their rights under Articles 5, 10 and 11). They were unsuccessful in the domestic courts and so took their case to Strasbourg.

JUDGMENT

Alleged violation of article 8 of the Convention

Whether there was an interference with the applicants' article 8 rights

58 The Court will first consider whether the stop-and-search measures amounted to an interference with the applicants' right to respect for their private life.

The parties' submissions

59 The applicants pointed out that the Court of Appeal had described s.44 as, "an extremely wide power to intrude on the privacy of members of the public" and the Metropolitan Police Commissioner had conceded in the domestic court that the exercise of the powers amounted to an interference with the individual's art.8 rights. They submitted that Lord Bingham had been wrong to conclude that art.8 was not engaged because, "an ordinary superficial search of the person and an opening of bags, of the kind to which passengers uncomplainingly submit at airports, for example, can scarcely be said to reach" the requisite level of seriousness. They reasoned that a person at an airport submitted to be searched because it was known that airport officials had coercive powers and because the freedom to travel by air was conditional upon agreeing to be searched. Such a person could, therefore, choose not to travel by air or leave behind any personal items which he would not wish to have examined in public. Section 44 was, however, qualitatively different. Citizens engaged in lawful business in any public place could, without any prior notice or any reasonable suspicion of wrongdoing whatsoever, be required to submit all their personal effects to a detailed coercive examination. They could not turn away and leave, as they could if they were, for example, hesitant to enter a public building with a search at the entrance. They would have no idea in advance that they were present in an area where active s.44 powers were in force. The Court's case law, for example *Peck v United Kingdom* (2003) 36 E.H.R.R. 41 at [57]–[63], made it clear that an individual did not automatically forfeit his privacy rights merely by taking his personal items into a public place such as a street. Moreover, the common thread running through art.8 was personal autonomy. That concept was substantially undermined by the police power to require submission to a coercive search in a public place, particularly since the lack of prior notice entailed that everyone had to assume that, wherever they went in public, they might be required to submit to a search.

60 The Government submitted that the searches of the applicants did not amount to an interference with their right to respect for their private lives. Not every act that might impinge upon a person's autonomy or physical integrity would entail such an interference. Whether or not the right to private life was engaged by a particular measure impinging on a person's autonomy or physical integrity would depend both upon the seriousness of that measure and upon the degree to which the person concerned had in the circumstances acted in a sphere where public life or the interests of other people were necessarily engaged. While the Government accepted that in

certain circumstances a particularly intrusive search might amount to an interference with art.8, it submitted that a normal, respectful search under s.45 of the 2000 Act would not and that there was no interference in the applicants' cases. The applicants were not searched at home, or even in a police station, but on the spot. In accordance with the Code, since neither applicant was asked to remove any articles of clothing, only an examination of outer garments and bags was conducted, of the type to which passengers regularly submit at airports. The applicants were not asked for personal details beyond their names, addresses and places of birth. In both cases, the intrusion was of relatively brief duration. Moreover, the applicants had brought themselves into contact with the public sphere through their voluntary engagement with a public demonstration. The fact that in other circumstances a more intrusive search might be conducted did not enable the present applicants to complain of any interference with their rights under art.8 : the Court did not examine the possible operation of legislation in abstracto.

The Court's assessment

61 As the Court has had previous occasion to remark, the concept of "private life" is a broad term not susceptible to exhaustive definition. It covers the physical and psychological integrity of a person. The notion of personal autonomy is an important principle underlying the interpretation of its guarantees. The article also protects a right to identity and personal development, and the right to establish relationships with other human beings and the outside world. It may include activities of a professional or business nature. There is, therefore, a zone of interaction of a person with others, even in a public context, which may fall within the scope of "private life". There are a number of elements relevant to a consideration of whether a person's private life is concerned in measures effected outside a person's home or private premises. In this connection, a person's reasonable expectations as to privacy may be a significant, though not necessarily conclusive, factor. In *Foka* at [85], where the applicant was subjected to a forced search of her bag by border guards, the Court held that "any search effected by the authorities on a person interferes with his or her private life."

62 Turning to the facts of the present case, the Court notes that ss.44–47 of the 2000 Act permit a uniformed police officer to stop any person within the geographical area covered by the authorisation and physically search the person and anything carried by him or her. The police officer may request the individual to remove headgear, footwear, outer clothing and gloves. Paragraph 3.5 of the related Code of Practice further clarifies that the police officer may place his or her hand inside the searched person's pockets, feel around and inside his or her collars, socks and shoes and search the person's hair. The search takes place in public and failure to submit to it amounts to an offence punishable by imprisonment or a fine or both. In the domestic courts, although the House of Lords doubted whether art.8 was applicable, since the intrusion did not reach a sufficient level of seriousness, the Metropolitan Police Commissioner conceded that the exercise of the power under s.44 amounted to an interference with the individual's art.8 rights and the Court of Appeal described it as, "an extremely wide power to intrude on the privacy of the members of the public".

63 The Government argues that in certain circumstances a particularly intrusive search may amount to an interference with an individual's art.8 rights, as may a search which involves perusing an address book or diary or correspondence, but that a superficial search which does not involve the discovery of such items does not do so. The Court is unable to accept this view. Irrespective of whether in any particular case correspondence or diaries or other private documents are discovered and read or other intimate items are revealed in the search, the Court considers that the use of the coercive powers conferred by the legislation to require an individual to submit to a detailed search of his person, his clothing and his personal belongings amounts to a clear interference with the right to respect for private life. Although the search is undertaken in a public place, this does not mean that art.8 is inapplicable. Indeed, in the Court's view, the public nature of the search may, in certain cases, compound the seriousness of the interference because of an element of humiliation and embarrassment. Items such as bags, wallets, notebooks and diaries may, moreover, contain personal information which the owner may feel uncomfortable about having exposed to the view of his companions or the wider public.

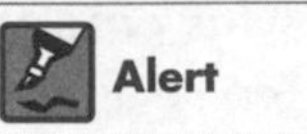

64 The Court is also unpersuaded by the analogy drawn with the search to which passengers uncomplainingly submit at airports or at the entrance of a public building. It does not need to decide whether the search of the person and of his bags in such circumstances amounts to an interference with an individual's art.8 rights, albeit one which is clearly justified on security grounds, since for the reasons given by the applicants the situations cannot be compared. An air traveller may be seen as consenting to such a search by choosing to travel. He knows that he and his bags are liable to be searched before boarding the aeroplane and has a freedom of choice, since he can leave personal items behind and walk away without being subjected to a search. The search powers under s.44 are qualitatively different. The individual can be stopped anywhere and at any time, without notice and without any choice as to whether or not to submit to a search.

65 Each of the applicants was stopped by a police officer and obliged to submit to a search under s.44 of the 2000 Act. For the reasons above, the Court considers that these searches constituted interferences with their right to respect for private life under art.8. Such an interference is justified by the terms of para.2 of art.8 only if it is, "in accordance with the law", pursues one or more of the legitimate aims referred to in para.2 and is, "necessary in a democratic society" in order to achieve the aim or aims.

Whether the interference was "in accordance with the law"

...

The Court's assessment

76 The Court recalls its well-established case law that the words, "in accordance with the law" require the impugned measure both to have some basis in domestic law and to be compatible with the rule of law, which is expressly mentioned in the preamble to the Convention and inherent in the object and purpose of art.8. The law must thus be

adequately accessible and foreseeable, that is, formulated with sufficient precision to enable the individual if—need be with appropriate advice—to regulate his conduct.

77 For domestic law to meet these requirements it must afford a measure of legal protection against arbitrary interferences by public authorities with the rights safeguarded by the Convention. In matters affecting fundamental rights it would be contrary to the rule of law, one of the basic principles of a democratic society enshrined in the Convention, for a legal discretion granted to the executive to be expressed in terms of an unfettered power. Consequently, the law must indicate with sufficient clarity the scope of any such discretion conferred on the competent authorities and the manner of its exercise. The level of precision required of domestic legislation—which cannot in any case provide for every eventuality—depends to a considerable degree on the content of the instrument in question, the field it is designed to cover and the number and status of those to whom it is addressed.

78 It is not disputed that the power in question in the present case has a basis in domestic law, namely ss.44–47 of the 2000 Act. In addition, the Code of Practice, which is a public document, sets out details of the manner in which the constable must carry out the search.

79 The applicants, however, complain that these provisions confer an unduly wide discretion on the police, both in terms of the authorisation of the power to stop and search and its application in practice. The House of Lords considered that this discretion was subject to effective control, and Lord Bingham identified 11 constraints on abuse of power. However, in the Court's view, the safeguards provided by domestic law have not been demonstrated to constitute a real curb on the wide powers afforded to the executive so as to offer the individual adequate protection against arbitrary interference.

80 The Court notes at the outset that the senior police officer referred to in s.44(4) of the Act is empowered to authorise any constable in uniform to stop and search a pedestrian in any area specified by him within his jurisdiction if he, "considers it expedient for the prevention of acts of terrorism". However, "expedient" means no more than "advantageous" or "helpful". There is no requirement at the authorisation stage that the stop-and-search power be considered "necessary" and therefore no requirement of any assessment of the proportionality of the measure. The authorisation is subject to confirmation by the Secretary of State within 48 hours. The Secretary of State may not alter the geographical coverage of an authorisation and although he or she can refuse confirmation or substitute an earlier time of expiry, it appears that in practice this has never been done. Although the exercise of the powers of authorisation and confirmation is subject to judicial review, the width of the statutory powers is such that applicants face formidable obstacles in showing that any authorisation and confirmation are ultra vires or an abuse of power.

81 The authorisation must be limited in time to 28 days, but it is renewable. It cannot extend beyond the boundary of the police force area and may be limited geographically within that boundary. However, many police force areas in the United Kingdom cover extensive regions with a concentrated populations. The Metropolitan

Police Force Area, where the applicants were stopped and searched, extends to all of Greater London. The failure of the temporal and geographical restrictions provided by Parliament to act as any real check on the issuing of authorisations by the executive are demonstrated by the fact that an authorisation for the Metropolitan Police District has been continuously renewed in a "rolling programme" since the powers were first granted.

82 An additional safeguard is provided by the independent reviewer. However, his powers are confined to reporting on the general operation of the statutory provisions and he has no right to cancel or alter authorisations, despite the fact that in every report from May 2006 onwards he has expressed the clear view that, "section 44 could be used less and I expect it to be used less".

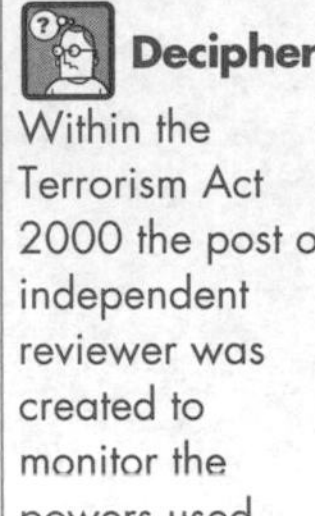

Within the Terrorism Act 2000 the post of independent reviewer was created to monitor the powers used under the Act.

83 Of still further concern is the breadth of the discretion conferred on the individual police officer. The officer is obliged, in carrying out the search, to comply with the terms of the Code. However, the Code governs essentially the mode in which the stop and search is carried out, rather than providing any restriction on the officer's decision to stop and search. That decision is, as the House of Lords made clear, one based exclusively on the "hunch" or "professional intuition" of the officer concerned. Not only is it unnecessary for him to demonstrate the existence of any reasonable suspicion; he is not required even subjectively to suspect anything about the person stopped and searched. The sole proviso is that the search must be for the purpose of looking for articles which could be used in connection with terrorism, a very wide category which could cover many articles commonly carried by people in the streets. Provided the person concerned is stopped for the purpose of searching for such articles, the police officer does not even have to have grounds for suspecting the presence of such articles. As noted by Lord Brown in the House of Lords, the stop-and-search power provided for by s 44, "radically ... departs from our traditional understanding of the limits of police power".

84 In this connection the Court is struck by the statistical and other evidence showing the extent to which resort is had by police officers to the powers of stop and search under s.44 of the Act. The Ministry of Justice recorded a total of 33,177 searches in 2004/5, 44,545 in 2005/6, 37,000 in 2006/7 and 117,278 in 2007/8. In his report into the operation of the Act in 2007, Lord Carlile noted that while arrests for other crimes had followed searches under s.44, none of the many thousands of searches had ever related to a terrorism offence; in his 2008 report Lord Carlile noted that examples of poor and unnecessary use of s.44 abounded, there being evidence of cases where the person stopped was so obviously far from any known terrorism profile that, realistically, there was not the slightest possibility of him/her being a terrorist, and no other feature to justify the stop.

Lord Carlile is the independent reviewer

85 In the Court's view, there is a clear risk of arbitrariness in the grant of such a broad discretion to the police officer. While the present cases do not concern black applicants or those of Asian origin, the risks of the discriminatory use of the powers against such persons is a very real consideration, as the judgments of Lord Hope, Lord Scott and Lord Brown recognised. The available statistics show that black and Asian persons are disproportionately affected by the powers, although the independent reviewer has also

noted, in his most recent report, that there has also been a practice of stopping and searching white people purely to produce greater racial balance in the statistics. There is, furthermore, a risk that such a widely framed power could be misused against demonstrators and protestors in breach of art.10 and/or 11 of the Convention.

86 The Government argues that safeguards against abuse are provided by the right of an individual to challenge a stop and search by way of judicial review or an action in damages. But the limitations of both actions are clearly demonstrated by the present case. In particular, in the absence of any obligation on the part of the officer to show a reasonable suspicion, it is likely to be difficult if not impossible to prove that the power was improperly exercised.

87 In conclusion, the Court considers that the powers of authorisation and confirmation as well as those of stop and search under ss.44 and 45 of the 2000 Act are neither sufficiently circumscribed nor subject to adequate legal safeguards against abuse. They are not, therefore, "in accordance with the law" and it follows that there has been a violation of art.8 of the Convention.

The most significant legal point to be taken from this case is the court's very strong view on the nature and use of the s 44 powers enjoyed by the police. Basing its criticism on fundamental rule of law principles, the court clearly considered that the very wide scope of the powers given to the police gave considerable potential and opportunity for abuse, a view reinforced by its statistical analysis of the extent of the use of the powers in recent years. The conclusion therefore was that the provision (and actions taken under it) were incompatible with Article 8 because they failed to match the standard required to pass the "prescribed by law" test, which forms a vital part of rights protection in the Convention.

Further Reading

Ashworth, A. J. 'Gillan and Quinton v United Kingdom: human rights - article 5 - stop and search as deprivation of liberty', [2010] *Crim. LR* 415

Beattie, Kate 'S and Marper v UK: privacy, DNA and crime prevention', [2009] *EHRLR* 229

Hunt, Murray 'The "horizontal effect" of the Human Rights Act, [1998]' *PL* 423

Morgan, Jonathan 'Privacy, confidence and horizontal effect: "Hello" trouble', (2003) 62(2) *CLJ* 444

12

Right of Freedom of Expression – Article 10

Topic List

Alex Lawson and Neil Hurden

Introduction

It is important that people are able to express themselves – it is part of what it means to be a human and is one explanation of why we possess rights in the first place. Yet it is also important that expression is protected as a mechanism for ensuring that we have the kind of democratic and well-informed society that the Convention and the Human Rights Act are designed to uphold and to enhance. For this reason press freedom is seen as particularly important under Article 10.

Yet Article 10 is by no means an absolute one; the difficulty with freedom of expression as a concept is that it can impact on the interests and feelings of others. As the Convention itself says, in Article 10(2), the freedom carries with it "duties and responsibilities". As with Article 8, Article 10 can be seen as a "qualified" right: it can be interfered with, but only if there is a legal basis for doing so, if the restriction is designed to achieve a "legitimate aim" and (in accordance with the proportionality principle) the restriction is no greater than is required to achieve this aim. The key phrase used in the Article is that the restriction has to be "necessary in a democratic society".

1 Article 10 Freedom of Expression

The cases on Article 10 address these issues by illustrating how states might justify interfering with freedom of expression. The following cases comprise some Strasbourg decisions and one important case decided by the UK courts. Reference should also be made back to the previous chapter on Article 8, as the right of privacy of others is of course one of the most clear-cut reasons for why it may be justifiable to limit and restrict freedom of expression.

Handyside v The United Kingdom (1979-80) 1 EHRR 737

Panel: Judges Mosler, Zekia, Wiarda, Pedersen, Thor Vilhjàlmsson, Petren, Ryssdal, Bozer, Ganshof van der Meersch, Fitzmaurice, Bindschedler-Robert, Evrigenis and Delvaux

Statute: European Convention on Human Rights Article 10

Facts: the applicant was the publisher of 'The Little Red Schoolbook' a publication aimed at children which, *inter alia*, discussed sex education. He was convicted under the Obscene Publications Acts 1959 and 1964. The books were seized and destroyed. He subsequently took his case to Strasbourg claiming that his right to free expression had been violated.

JUDGMENT

The Alleged Violation of Article 10 of the Convention

42. The applicant claims to be the victim of a violation of Article 10 of the Convention which provides:

1. Everyone has the right to freedom of expression. This right shall include freedom to hold opinions and to receive and impart information and ideas without interference by

public authority and regardless of frontiers. This Article shall not prevent States from requiring the licensing of broadcasting, television or cinema enterprises.

2. The exercise of these freedoms, since it carries with it duties and responsibilities, may be subject to such formalities, conditions, restrictions or penalties as are prescribed by law and are necessary in a democratic society, in the interests of national security, territorial integrity or public safety, for the prevention of disorder or crime, for the protection of health or morals, for the protection of the reputation or rights of others, for preventing the disclosure of information received in confidence, or for maintaining the authority and impartiality of the judiciary.

43. The various measures challenged—the applicant's criminal conviction, the seizure and subsequent forfeiture and destruction of the matrix and of hundreds of copies of the Schoolbook —were without any doubt, and the Government did not deny it, 'interferences by public authority' in the exercise of his freedom of expression which is guaranteed by paragraph 1 of the text cited above. Such interferences entail a 'violation' of Article 10 if they do not fall within one of the exceptions provided for in paragraph 2, which is accordingly of decisive importance in this case.

44. If the 'restrictions' and 'penalties' complained of by Mr. Handyside are not to infringe Article 10, they must, according to paragraph 2, in the first place have been 'prescribed by law'. The Court finds that this was the case. In the United Kingdom legal system, the basis in law for the measures in question was the 1959/1964 Acts. Besides, this was not contested by the applicant who further admitted that the competent authorities had correctly applied those Acts.

45. Having thus ascertained that the interferences complained of satisfied the first of the conditions in Article 10 (2), the Court then investigated whether they also complied with the others. According to the Government and the majority of the Commission, the interferences were 'necessary in a democratic society' , 'for the protection of ... morals'

46. Sharing the view of the Government and the unanimous opinion of the Commission, the Court first finds that the 1959/1964 Acts have an aim that is legitimate under Article 10 (2), namely, the protection of morals in a democratic society. Only this latter purpose is relevant in this case since the object of the said Acts—to wage war on 'obscene' publications, defined by their tendency to 'deprave and corrupt' —is linked far more closely to the protection of morals than to any of the further purposes permitted by Article 10 (2).

47. The Court must also investigate whether the protection of morals in a democratic society necessitated the various measures taken against the applicant and the Schoolbook under the 1959/1964 Acts. Mr. Handyside does not restrict himself to criticising these Acts as such: he also makes—from the viewpoint of the Convention and not of English law—several complaints concerning their application in his case.

The Commission's report and the subsequent hearings before the Court in June 1976 brought to light clear-cut differences of opinion on a crucial problem, namely, how to determine whether the actual 'restrictions' and 'penalties' complained of by the applicant were 'necessary in a democratic society', 'for the protection of morals'.

According to the Government and the majority of the Commission, the Court has only to ensure that the English courts acted reasonably, in good faith and within the limits of the margin of appreciation left to the Contracting States by Article 10 (2). On the other hand, the minority of the Commission sees the Court's task as being not to review the Inner London Quarter Sessions' judgment but to examine the Schoolbook directly in the light of the Convention and of nothing but the Convention.

48. The Court points out that the machinery of protection established by the Convention is subsidiary to the national systems safeguarding human rights. The Convention leaves to each Contracting State, in the first place, the task of securing the rights and freedoms it enshrines. The institutions created by it make their own contribution to this task but they become involved only through contentious proceedings and once all domestic remedies have been exhausted (Art. 26).

These observations apply, notably, to Article 10 (2). In particular, it is not possible to find in the domestic law of the various Contracting States a uniform European conception of morals. The view taken by their respective laws of the requirements of morals varies from time to time and from place to place, especially in our era which is characterised by a rapid and far-reaching evolution of opinions on the subject. By reason of their direct and continuous contact with the vital forces of their countries, State authorities are in principle in a better position than the international judge to give an opinion on the exact content of these requirements as well as on the 'necessity' of a 'restriction' or 'penalty' intended to meet them. The Court notes at this juncture that, whilst the adjective 'necessary', within the meaning of Article 10 (2), is not synonymous with 'indispensable', neither has it the flexibility of such expressions as 'admissible', 'ordinary', 'useful', 'reasonable' or 'desirable'. Nevertheless, it is for the national authorities to make the initial assessment of the reality of the pressing social need implied by the notion of 'necessity' in this context.

 **Decipher**

This paragraph, and those following, reveal the importance of the Convention concept of the "margin of appreciation".

Consequently, Article 10 (2) leaves to the Contracting States a margin of appreciation. This margin is given both to the domestic legislator ('prescribed by law') and to the bodies, judicial amongst others, that are called upon to interpret and apply the laws in force.

49. Nevertheless, Article 10 (2) does not give the Contracting States an unlimited power of appreciation. The Court, which, with the Commission, is responsible for ensuring the observance of those States' engagements, is empowered to give the final ruling on whether a 'restriction' or 'penalty' is reconcilable with freedom of expression as protected by Article 10. The domestic margin of appreciation thus goes hand in hand with a European supervision. Such supervision concerns both the aim of the measure challenged and its 'necessity'; it covers not only the basic legislation but also the decision applying it, even one given by an independent court. In this respect, the Court refers to Article 50 of the Convention ('decision or ... measure taken by a legal authority or any other authority') as well as to its own case-law.

The Court's supervisory functions oblige it to pay the utmost attention to the principles characterising a 'democratic society'. Freedom of expression constitutes one of the essential foundations of such a society, one of the basic conditions for its progress and

for the development of every man. Subject to Article 10 (2), it is applicable not only to 'information' or 'ideas' that are favourably received or regarded as inoffensive or as a matter of indifference, but also to those that offend, shock or disturb the State or any sector of the population. Such are the demands of that pluralism, tolerance and broadmindedness without which there is no 'democratic society'. This means, amongst other things, that every 'formality', 'condition', 'restriction' or 'penalty' imposed in this sphere must be proportionate to the legitimate aim pursued.

From another standpoint, whoever exercises his freedom of expression undertakes 'duties and responsibilities' the scope of which depends on his situation and the technical means he uses. The Court cannot overlook such a person's 'duties' and 'responsibilities' when it enquires, as in this case; whether 'restrictions' or 'penalties' were conducive to the 'protection of morals' which made them 'necessary' in a 'democratic society'.

50. It follows from this that it is in no way the Court's task to take the place of the competent national courts but rather to review under Article 10 the decisions they delivered in the exercise of their power of appreciation.

However, the Court's supervision would generally prove illusory if it did no more than examine these decision in isolation; it must view them in the light of the case as a whole, including the publication in question and the arguments and evidence adduced by the applicant in the domestic legal system and then at the international level. The Court must decide, on the different data available to it, whether the reasons given by the national authorities to justify the actual measures of 'interference' they take are relevant and sufficient under Article 10 (2).

51. Following the method set out above, the Court scrutinised under Article 10 (2) the individual decisions complained of, in particular, the judgment of the Inner London Quarter Sessions.

The said judgment is summarised above. The Court reviewed it in the light of the case as a whole; in addition to the pleadings before the Court and the Commission's report, the memorials and oral explanations presented to the Commission between June 1973 and August 1974 and the transcript of the proceedings before the quarter sessions were, inter alia, taken into consideration.

52. The Court attaches particular importance to a factor to which the judgment of 29 October 1971 did not fail to draw attention, that is, the intended readership of the Schoolbook. It was aimed above all at children and adolescents aged from 12 to 18. Being direct, factual and reduced to essentials in style, it was easily within the comprehension of even the youngest of such readers. The applicant had made it clear that he planned a wide-spread circulation. He had sent the book, with a press release, to numerous daily papers and periodicals for review or for advertising purposes. What is more, he had set a modest sale price (30 pence), arranged for a reprint of 50,000 copies shortly after the first impression of 20,000 and chosen a title suggesting that the work was some kind of handbook for use in schools.

Basically the book contained purely factual information that was generally correct and often useful, as the quarter sessions recognised. However, it also included, above all in the section on sex and in the passage headed 'Be yourself' in the chapter on pupils, sentences or paragraphs that young people at a critical stage of their development could have interpreted as an encouragement to indulge in precocious activities harmful for them or even to commit certain criminal offences. In these circumstances, despite the variety and the constant evolution in the United Kingdom of views on ethics and education, the competent English judges were entitled, in the exercise of their discretion, to think at the relevant time that the Schoolbook would have pernicious effects on the morals of many of the children and adolescents who would read it.

However, the applicant maintained, in substance, that the demands of the 'protection of morals' or, to use the wording of the 1959/1964 Acts, of the war against publications likely to 'deprave and corrupt', were but a pretext in his case. The truth of the matter, he alleged, was that an attempt had been made to muzzle a small-scale publisher whose political leanings met with the disapproval of a fragment of public opinion. Proceedings were set in motion, said he, in an atmosphere little short of 'hysteria', stirred up and kept alive by ultra-conservative elements. The accent in the judgment of 29 October 1971 on the anti-authoritarian aspects of the Schoolbook showed, according to the applicant, exactly what lay behind the case.

The information supplied by Mr. Handyside seems, in fact, to show that letters from members of the public, articles in the press and action by Members of Parliament were not without some influence in the decision to seize the Schoolbook and to take criminal proceedings against its publisher. However, the Government drew attention to the fact that such initiatives could well have been explained not by some dark plot but by the genuine emotion felt by citizens faithful to traditional moral values when, towards the end of March 1971, they read in certain newspapers extracts from the book which was due to appear on 1 April. The Government also emphasised that the proceedings ended several months after the 'campaign' denounced by the applicant and that he did not claim that it had continued in the intervening period. From this the Government concluded that the 'campaign' in no way impaired dispassionate deliberation at the quarter sessions.

For its part the Court finds that anti-authoritarian aspects of the Schoolbook as such were not held in the judgment of 29 October 1971 to fall foul of the 1959/1964 Acts. Those aspects were taken into account only in so far as the appeal court considered that, by undermining the moderating influence of parents, teachers, the Churches and youth organisations, they aggravated the tendency to 'deprave and corrupt' which in its opinion resulted from other parts of the work. It should be added that the revised edition was allowed to circulate freely by the British authorities despite the fact that the anti-authoritarian passages again appeared there in full and even, in some cases, in stronger terms. As the Government noted, this is hard to reconcile with the theory of a political intrigue.

The Court thus allows that the fundamental aim of the judgment of 29 October 1971, applying the 1959/1964 Acts, was the protection of the morals of the young, a legitimate purpose under Article 10 (2). Consequently the seizures effected on 31 March and 1 April 1971, pending the outcome of the proceedings that were about to open, also had this aim.

53. It remains to examine the 'necessity' of the measures in dispute, beginning with the said seizures.

If the applicant is right, their object should have been at the most one or a few copies of the book to be used as exhibits in the criminal proceedings. The Court does not share this view since the police had good reasons for trying to lay their hands on all the stock as a temporary means of protecting the young against a danger to morals on whose existence it was for the trial court to decide. The legislation of many Contracting States provides for a seizure analogous to that envisaged by section 3 of the English 1959/1964 Acts.

...

67. Having found no violation of ... the Convention, the Court concludes that the question of the application of Article 50 does not arise in this case.

This case is significant for the way in which the court sets out the idea that freedom of expression was wide and must include the ability to express ideas that may be offensive as well as those that reassure. This statement of high principle did not actually assist Handyside, however, because the court were prepared to give the UK state a very significant "margin of appreciation" in determining when it was necessary for policy reasons to interfere with Article 10 rights.

The following case also illustrates how, when it comes to issues of morality and religious sensibilities, the Strasbourg court has generally given a generous margin of appreciation to domestic states.

***Wingrove v United Kingdom* (1997) 24 EHRR 1**

Panel: The President, Judge Bernhardt; Judges Thór Vilhjálmsson, Pettiti, De Meyer, Morenilla, Freeland, Mifsud Bonnici, Gotchev and Lõhmus

Statute: European Convention on Human Rights Article 10

Facts: The applicant produced a video, Visions of Ecstasy, which was refused a classification certificate on the ground that it infringed the criminal law of blasphemy. It depicted a female character in a sexual act with the crucified Christ.

JUDGMENT

Alleged Violation of Article 10 of the Convention

35. The applicant alleged a violation of his right to freedom of expression, as guaranteed by Article 10 of the Convention...

36. The refusal by the British Board of Film Classification to grant a certificate for the applicant's video work Visions of Ecstasy, seen in conjunction with the statutory provisions making it a criminal offence to distribute a video work without this

certificate, amounted to an interference by a public authority with the applicant's right to impart ideas. This was common ground between the participants in the proceedings.

To determine whether such an interference entails a violation of the Convention, the Court must examine whether or not it was justified under Article 10(2) by reason of being a restriction "prescribed by law", which pursued an aim that was legitimate under that provision and was "necessary in a democratic society".

Whether the interference was "prescribed by law"

37. The applicant considered that the law of blasphemy was so uncertain that it was inordinately difficult to establish in advance whether in the eyes of a jury a particular publication would constitute an offence. Moreover, it was practically impossible to know what predictions an administrative body—the British Board of Film Classification—would make as to the outcome of a hypothetical prosecution. In these circumstances, the applicant could not reasonably be expected to foresee the result of the Board's speculations. The requirement of foreseeability which flows from the expression "prescribed by law" was therefore not fulfilled.

38. The Government contested this claim: it was a feature common to most laws and legal systems that tribunals may reach different conclusions even when applying the same law to the same facts. This did not necessarily make these laws inaccessible or unforeseeable. Given the infinite variety of ways of publishing "contemptuous, reviling, scurrilous, or ludicrous matter relating to God, Jesus Christ, or the Bible", it would not be appropriate for the law to seek to define in detail which images would or would not be potentially blasphemous.

39. The Commission, noting that considerable legal advice was available to the applicant, was of the view that he could reasonably have foreseen the restrictions to which his video work was liable.

40. The Court reiterates that, according to its case law, the relevant national "law", which includes both statute and common law, must be formulated with sufficient precision to enable those concerned—if need be, with appropriate legal advice—to foresee, to a degree that is reasonable in the circumstances, the consequences which a given action may entail. A law that confers a discretion is not in itself inconsistent with this requirement, provided that the scope of the discretion and the manner of its exercise are indicated with sufficient clarity, having regard to the legitimate aim in question, to give the individual adequate protection against arbitrary interference.

Decipher

This description of prescribed by law has its origin in The Sunday Times v United Kingdom (1979-80) 2 EHRR 245. The protection against arbitrary point was further developed in Gillan v United Kingdom (2010) 50 EHRR 45.

41. It is observed that, in refusing a certificate for distribution of the applicant's video on the basis that it infringed a provision of the criminal law of blasphemy, the British Board of Film Classification acted within its powers under section 4(1) of the 1984 Act.

42. The Court recognises that the offence of blasphemy cannot by its very nature lend itself to precise legal definition. National authorities must therefore be afforded a degree of flexibility in assessing whether the facts of a particular case fall within the accepted definition of the offence.

43. There appears to be no general uncertainty or disagreement between those appearing before the Court as to the definition in English law of the offence of blasphemy, as formulated by the House of Lords in the case of *Whitehouse v. Gay News Ltd and Lemon*. Having seen for itself the content of the video work, the Court is satisfied that the applicant could reasonably have foreseen with appropriate legal advice that the film, particularly those scenes involving the crucified figure of Christ, could fall within the scope of the offence of blasphemy.

The above conclusion is borne out by the applicant's decision not to initiate proceedings for judicial review on the basis of counsel's advice that the panel's formulation of the law of blasphemy represented an accurate statement of the law.

44. Against the foregoing background it cannot be said that the law in question did not afford the applicant adequate protection against arbitrary interference. The Court therefore concludes that the impugned restriction was "prescribed by law".

Whether the interference pursued a legitimate aim

45. The applicant contested the Government's assertion that his video work was refused a certificate for distribution in order to "protect the right of citizens not to be offended in their religious feelings". In his submission, the expression "rights of others" in the present context only refers to an actual, positive right not to be offended. It does not include a hypothetical right held by some Christians to avoid disturbance at the prospect of other people's viewing the video work without being shocked.

In any event—the applicant further submitted—the restriction on the film's distribution could not pursue a legitimate aim since it was based on a discriminatory law, limited to the protection of Christians, and specifically, those of the Anglican faith.

46. The Government referred to the case of *Otto-Preminger Institute v. Austria* where the Court had accepted that the respect for the religious feelings of believers can move a State legitimately to restrict the publication of provocative portrayals of objects of religious veneration.

47. The Commission considered that the English law of blasphemy is intended to suppress behaviour directed against objects of religious veneration that is likely to cause justified indignation amongst believing Christians. It follows that the application of this law in the present case was intended to protect the right of citizens not to be insulted in their religious feelings.

48. The Court notes at the outset that, as stated by the Board, the aim of the interference was to protect against the treatment of a religious subject in such a manner as to be calculated (that is, bound, not intended) to outrage those who have an understanding of, sympathy towards and support for the Christian story and ethic, because of the contemptuous, reviling, insulting, scurrilous or ludicrous tone, style and spirit in which the subject is presented.

This is an aim which undoubtedly corresponds to that of the protection of "the rights of others" within the meaning of paragraph 2 of Article 10. It is also fully consonant with the aim of the protections afforded by Article 9 to religious freedom.

49. Whether or not there was a real need for protection against exposure to the film in question is a matter which must be addressed below when assessing the "necessity" of the interference.

50. It is true that the English law of blasphemy only extends to the Christian faith. Indeed the anomaly of this state of affairs in a multidenominational society was recognised by the Divisional Court in *R. v. Chief Magistrate, Ex parte Choudhury*. However, it is not for the European Court to rule in abstracto as to the compatibility of domestic law with the Convention. The extent to which English law protects other beliefs is not in issue before the Court which must confine its attention to the case before it.

The uncontested fact that the law of blasphemy does not treat on an equal footing the different religions practised in the United Kingdom does not detract from the legitimacy of the aim pursued in the present context.

51. The refusal to grant a certificate for the distribution of Visions of Ecstasy consequently had a legitimate aim under Article 10(2).

Whether the interference was "necessary in a democratic society"

52. The Court recalls that freedom of expression constitutes one of the essential foundations of a democratic society. As paragraph 2 of Article 10 expressly recognises, however, the exercise of that freedom carries with it duties and responsibilities. Amongst them, in the context of religious beliefs, may legitimately be included a duty to avoid as far as possible an expression that is, in regard to objects of veneration, gratuitously offensive to others and profanatory.

53. No restriction on freedom of expression, whether in the context of religious beliefs or in any other, can be compatible with Article 10 unless it satisfies, inter alia, the test of necessity as required by the second paragraph of that Article. In examining whether restrictions to the rights and freedoms guaranteed by the Convention can be considered "necessary in a democratic society" the Court has, however, consistently held that the Contracting States enjoy a certain but not unlimited margin of appreciation. It is, in any event, for the European Court to give a final ruling on the restriction's compatibility with the Convention and it will do so by assessing in the circumstances of a particular case, inter alia, whether the interference corresponded to a "pressing social need" and whether it was "proportionate to the legitimate aim pursued".

Decipher

The language of pressing social need and proportionate to the legitimate aim pursued has its genesis in Smith and Grady v United Kingdom (2000) 29 EHRR 493.

54. According to the applicant, there was no "pressing social need" to ban a video work on the uncertain assumption that it would breach the law of blasphemy; indeed, the overriding social need was to allow it to be distributed. Furthermore, since adequate protection was already provided by a panoply of laws—concerning, inter alia, obscenity, public order and disturbances to places of religious worship—blasphemy laws, which are incompatible with the European idea of freedom of expression, were also superfluous in practice. In any event, the complete prohibition of a video work that contained no obscenity, no pornography and no element of vilification of Christ was disproportionate to the aim pursued.

55. For the Commission, the fact that Visions of Ecstasy was a short video work and not a feature film meant that its distribution would have been more limited and less likely to attract publicity. The Commission came to the same conclusion as the applicant.

56. The Government contended that the applicant's video work was clearly a provocative and indecent portrayal of an object of religious veneration, that its distribution would have been sufficiently public and widespread to cause offence and that it amounted to an attack on the religious beliefs of Christians which was insulting and offensive. In those circumstances, in refusing to grant a classification certificate for the applicant's video work, the national authorities only acted within their margin of appreciation.

57. The Court observes that the refusal to grant Visions of Ecstasy a distribution certificate was intended to protect "the rights of others", and more specifically to provide protection against seriously offensive attacks on matters regarded as sacred by Christians. The laws to which the applicant made reference and which pursue related but distinct aims are thus not relevant in this context.

As the observations filed by the intervenors show, blasphemy legislation is still in force in various European countries. It is true that the application of these laws has become increasingly rare and that several States have recently repealed them altogether. In the United Kingdom only two prosecutions concerning blasphemy have been brought in the last 70 years. Strong arguments have been advanced in favour of the abolition of blasphemy laws, for example, that such laws may discriminate against different faiths or denominations—as put forward by the applicant—or that legal mechanisms are inadequate to deal with matters of faith or individual belief—as recognised by the Minister of State for the Home Department in his letter of 4 July 1989. However, the fact remains that there is as yet not sufficient common ground in the legal and social orders of the Member States of the Council of Europe to conclude that a system whereby a State can impose restrictions on the propagation of material on the basis that it is blasphemous is, in itself, unnecessary in a democratic society and thus incompatible with the Convention.

58. Whereas there is little scope under Article 10(2) of the Convention for restrictions on political speech or on debate of questions of public interest, a wider margin of appreciation is generally available to the Contracting States when regulating freedom of expression in relation to matters liable to offend intimate personal convictions within the sphere of morals or, especially, religion. Moreover, as in the field of morals, and perhaps to an even greater degree, there is no uniform European conception of the requirements of "the protection of the rights of others" in relation to attacks on their religious convictions. What is likely to cause substantial offence to persons of a particular religious persuasion will vary significantly from time to time and from place to place, especially in an era characterised by an ever growing array of faiths and denominations. By reason of their direct and continuous contact with the vital forces of their countries, State authorities are in principle in a better position than the international judge to give an opinion on the exact content of these requirements with

regard to the rights of others as well as on the "necessity" of a "restriction" intended to protect from such material those whose deepest feelings and convictions would be seriously offended.

This does not of course exclude final European supervision. Such supervision is all the more necessary given the breadth and open-endedness of the notion of blasphemy and the risks of arbitrary or excessive interferences with freedom of expression under the guise of action taken against allegedly blasphemous material. In this regard the scope of the offence of blasphemy and the safeguards inherent in the legislation are especially important. Moreover the fact that the present case involves prior restraint calls for special scrutiny by the Court.

59. The Court's task in this case is to determine whether the reasons relied on by the national authorities to justify the measures interfering with the applicant's freedom of expression are relevant and sufficient for the purposes of Article 10(2) of the Convention.

60. As regards the content of the law itself, the Court observes that the English law of blasphemy does not prohibit the expression, in any form, of views hostile to the Christian religion. Nor can it be said that opinions which are offensive to Christians necessarily fall within its ambit. As the English courts have indicated, it is the manner in which views are advocated rather than the views themselves which the law seeks to control. The extent of insult to religious feelings must be significant, as is clear from the use by the courts of the adjectives "contemptuous", "reviling", "scurrilous", "ludicrous" to depict material of a sufficient degree of offensiveness.

The high degree of profanation that must be attained constitutes, in itself, a safeguard against arbitrariness. It is against this background that the asserted justification under Article 10(2) in the decisions of the national authorities must be considered.

61. Visions of Ecstasy portrays, inter alia, a female character astride the recumbent body of the crucified Christ engaged in an act of an overtly sexual nature, the national authorities, using powers that are not themselves incompatible with the Convention, considered that the manner in which such imagery was treated placed the focus of the work "less on the erotic feelings of the character than on those of the audience, which is the primary function of pornography". They further held that since no attempt was made in the film to explore the meaning of the imagery beyond engaging the viewer in a "voyeuristic erotic experience", the public distribution of such a video could outrage and insult the feelings of believing Christians and constitute the criminal offence of blasphemy. This view was reached by both the Board of Film Classification and the Video Appeals Committee following a careful consideration of the arguments in defence of his work presented by the applicant in the course of two sets of proceedings. Moreover, it was open to the applicant to challenge the decision of the Appeals Committee in proceedings for judicial review.

Bearing in mind the safeguard of the high threshold of profanation embodied in the definition of the offence of blasphemy under English law as well as the State's margin of appreciation in this area, the reasons given to justify the measures taken can be considered as both relevant and sufficient for the purposes of Article 10(2).

Furthermore, having viewed the film for itself, the Court is satisfied that the decisions by the national authorities cannot be said to be arbitrary or excessive.

Conclusion

65. Against the foregoing background the national authorities were entitled to consider that the impugned measure was justified as being necessary in a democratic society within the meaning of paragraph 2 of Article 10. There has therefore been no violation of Article 10 of the Convention.

This case takes a very similar line, in the UK context, to the leading Strasbourg case of *Otto-Preminger Institute v Austria* (1995) 19 EHRR 3. As with that case, the decision in *Wingrove* can arguably be criticised for over-extending the protection given to religious sensitivities, through very generous use of the margin of appreciation technique. The court in this case seemed to be saying that the English law on blasphemy did not stop free expression about Christianity and other religious themes, as long as they were polite ones, which appears to run counter to some of the basic principles laid down in *Handyside*.

The following two cases are far more concerned with the political sphere and indicate that in this context, the courts tend to take a more robust view in practice and not just in theory about free expression.

***Jersild v Denmark* (1995) 19 EHRR 1**

Panel: The President, Judge Ryssdal; Judges Bernhardt, Gölcüklü, Macdonald, Russo, Spielman, Valticos, Martens, Palm, Pekkanen, Loizou, Morenilla, Lopes Rocha, Wildhaber, Mifsud Bonnici, Makarczyk, Gotchev, Repik and Philip

Statute: European Convention on Human Rights Article 10

Facts: The applicant was a journalist working for Danish public broadcasting on the current affairs programme 'Sunday News Magazine'. The editors decided to produce a documentary on the Greenjackets, a right-wing group which openly described themselves as racists. Jersild contacted representatives of the group and invited three of them to take part in a television interview. During the interview the three Greenjackets made abusive and derogatory remarks about immigrants and ethnic groups in Denmark. Following the programme the interviewees were convicted of a violation of the Danish Penal Code. The applicant was also convicted of aiding and abetting them. Before the Danish courts Jersild argued that he could not in any way be compared to the other three defendants, whose views he completely rejected. He appealed through the domestic courts but the critical issue remained fixed: the Danish law, as drafted, seemed to impose something akin to strict liability on people in his type of situation.

JUDGMENT

Alleged violation of Article 10

...

27. It is common ground that the measures giving rise to the applicant's case constituted an interference with his right to freedom of expression.

It is moreover undisputed that this interference was "prescribed by law", the applicant's conviction being based on Articles 266(b) and 23(1) of the Penal Code. In this context, the Government pointed out that the former provision had been enacted in order to comply with the UN Convention. The Government's argument, as the Court understands it, is that, whilst Article 10 of the Convention is applicable, the Court, in applying paragraph 2, should consider that the relevant provisions of the Penal Code are to be interpreted and applied in an extensive manner, in accordance with the rationale of the UN Convention. In other words, Article 10 should not be interpreted in such a way as to limit, derogate from or destroy the right to protection against racial discrimination under the UN Convention.

Finally it is uncontested that the interference pursued a legitimate aim, namely the "protection of the reputation of rights of others". The only point in dispute is whether the measures were "necessary in a democratic society".

28. The applicant and the Commission were of the view that, notwithstanding Denmark's obligations as a Party to the UN Convention (see paragraph 21 above), a fair balance had to be struck between the "protection of the reputation or rights of others" and the applicant's right to impart information. According to the applicant, such a balance was envisaged in a clause contained in Article 4 of the UN Convention to the effect that "due regard" should be had to "the principles in the Universal Declaration of Human Rights and the rights ... in Article 5 of [the UN] Convention" . The clause had been introduced at the drafting stage because of concern among a number of States that the requirement in Article 4(a) that "States Parties ... shall declare an offence punishable by law all dissemination of ideas based on racial superiority or hatred" was too sweeping and could give rise to difficulties with regard to other human rights, in particular the right to freedom of opinion and expression. In the applicant's further submission, this explained why the Committee of Ministers of the Council of Europe, when urging Member States to ratify the UN Convention, had proposed that they add an interpretative statement to their instrument of ratification, which would, *inter alia*, stress that respect was also due for the rights laid down in the European Convention.

The applicant and the Commission emphasised that, taken in the context of the broadcast as a whole, the offending remarks had the effect of ridiculing their authors rather than promoting their racist views. The overall impression of the programme was that it sought to draw public attention to a matter of great public concern, namely racism and xenophobia. The applicant had deliberately included the offensive statements in the programme, not with the intention of disseminating racist opinions, but in order to counter them through exposure. The applicant pointed out that he tried to show, analyse and explain to his viewers a new phenomenon in Denmark at the time, that of violent racism practised by inarticulate and socially disadvantaged youths. Joined by the Commission, he considered that the broadcast could not have had any significant detrimental effects on the "reputation or rights of others". The interests in protecting the latter were therefore outweighed by those of protecting the applicant's freedom of expression.

In addition the applicant alleged that had the 1991 Media Liability Act been in force at the relevant time he would not have faced prosecution since under the Act it is in principle only the author of a punishable statement who may be liable. This undermined the Government's argument that his conviction was required by the UN Convention and "necessary" within the meaning of Article 10.

29. The Government contended that the applicant had edited the Greenjackets item in a sensationalist rather than informative manner and that its news or information value was minimal. Television was a powerful medium and a majority of Danes normally viewed the news programme in which the item was broadcasted. Yet the applicant, knowing that they would incur criminal liability, had encouraged the Greenjackets to make racist statements and had failed to counter these statements in the programme. It was too subtle to assume that viewers would not take the remarks at their face value. No weight could be attached to the fact that the programme had given rise to only a few complaints, since, due to lack of information and insufficient knowledge of the Danish language and even fear of reprisals by violent racists, victims of the insulting comments were likely to be dissuaded from complaining. The applicant had thus failed to fulfil the "duties and responsibilities" incumbent on him as a television journalist. The fine imposed upon him was at the lower end of the scale of sanctions applicable to Article 266(b) offences and was therefore not likely to deter any journalist from contributing to public discussion on racism and xenophobia; it only had the effect of a public reminder that racist expressions are to be taken seriously and cannot be tolerated.

The Government moreover disputed that the matter would have been dealt with differently had the 1991 Media Liability Act been in force at the material time. The rule that only the author of a punishable statement may incur liability was subject to exceptions; how the applicant's case would have been considered under the 1991 Act was purely a matter of speculation.

The Government stressed that at all three levels the Danish courts, which were in principle better placed than the European Court to evaluate the effects of the programme, had carried out a careful balancing exercise of all the interests involved. The review effected by those courts had been similar to that carried out under Article 10; their decisions fell within the margin of appreciation to be left to the national authorities and corresponded to a pressing social need.

...

31. A significant feature of the present case is that the applicant did not make the objectionable statements himself but assisted in their dissemination in his capacity of television journalist responsible for a news programme of Danmarks Radio. In assessing whether his conviction and sentence were "necessary", the Court will therefore have regard to the principles established in its case law relating to the role of the press.

The Court reiterates that freedom of expression constitutes one of the essential foundations of a democratic society and that the safeguards to be afforded to the press

are of particular importance. Whilst the press must not overstep the bounds set, inter alia, in the interest of "the protection of the reputation and right of others", it is nevertheless incumbent on it to impart information and ideas of public interest. Not only does the press have the task of imparting such information and ideas: the public also has a right to receive them. Were it otherwise, the press would be unable to play its vital role of "public watchdog". Although formulated primarily with regard to the print media, these principles doubtless apply also to the audio-visual media.

In considering the "duties and responsibilities" of a journalist, the potential impact of the medium concerned is an important factor and it is commonly acknowledged that the audio-visual media have often a much more immediate and powerful effect than the print media. The audio-visual media have means of conveying through images meanings which the print media are not able to impart.

At the same time, the methods of objective and balanced reporting may vary considerably, depending among other things on the media in question. It is not for this Court, nor for the national courts for that matter, to substitute their own views for those of the press as to what technique of reporting should be adopted by journalists. In this context the Court recalls that Article 10 protects not only the substance of the ideas and information expressed, but also the form in which they are conveyed.

The Court will look at the interference complained of in the light of the case as a whole and determine whether the reasons adduced by the national authorities to justify it are relevant and sufficient and whether the means employed were proportionate to the legitimate aim pursued. In doing so the Court has to satisfy itself that the national authorities did apply standards which were in conformity with the principles embodied in Article 10 and, moreover, that they based themselves on an acceptable assessment of the relevant facts.

The Court's assessment will have regard to the manner in which the Greenjackets feature was prepared, its contents, the context in which it was broadcast and the purpose of the programme. Bearing in mind the obligations on States under the UN Convention and other international instruments to take effective measures to eliminate all forms of racial discrimination and to prevent and combat racist doctrines and practices, an important factor in the Court's evaluation will be whether the item in question, when considered as a whole, appeared from an objective point of view to have had as its purpose the propagation of racist views and ideas.

32. The national courts laid considerable emphasis on the fact that the applicant had himself taken the initiative of preparing the Greenjackets feature and that he not only knew in advance that racist statements were likely to be made during the interview but also had encouraged such statements. He had edited the programme in such a way as to include the offensive assertions. Without his involvement, the remarks would not have been disseminated to a wide circle of people and would thus not have been punishable.

The Court is satisfied that these were relevant reasons for the purposes of paragraph 2 of Article 10.

33. On the other hand, as to the contents of the Greenjackets item, it should be noted that the TV presenter's introduction started by a reference to recent public discussion and press comments on racism in Denmark, thus inviting the viewer to see the programme in that context. He went on to announce that the object of the programme was to address aspects of the problem, by identifying certain racist individuals and by portraying their mentality and social background. There is no reason to doubt that the ensuing interviews fulfilled that aim. Taken as a whole, the feature could not objectively have appeared to have as its purpose the propagation of racist views and ideas. On the contrary, it clearly sought—by means of an interview—to expose, analyse and explain this particular group of youths, limited and frustrated by their social situation, with criminal records and violent attitudes, thus dealing with specific aspects of a matter that already then was of great public concern.

The Supreme Court held that the news or information value of the feature were not such as to justify the dissemination of the offensive remarks. However, in view of the principles stated in paragraph 31 above, the Court sees no cause to question the Sunday News Magazine staff members' own appreciation of the news or information value of the impugned item, which formed the basis for their decisions to produce and broadcast it.

34. Furthermore, it must be borne in mind that the item was broadcast as a part of a serious Danish news programmes and was intended for a well-informed audience.

The Court is not convinced by the argument, also stressed by the national courts, that the Greenjackets item was presented without any attempt to counterbalance the extremist views expressed. Both the TV presenter's introduction and the applicant's conduct during the interviews clearly dissociated him from the persons interviewed, for example by describing them as members of "a group of extremist youths" who supported the Klu Klux Klan and by referring to the criminal records of some of them. The applicant also rebutted some of the racist statements for instance by recalling that there were black people who had important jobs. It should finally not be forgotten that, taken as a whole, the filmed portrait surely conveyed the meaning that the racist statements were part of a generally anti-social attitude of the Greenjackets.

Admittedly the item did not explicitly recall the immorality, dangers and unlawfulness of the promotion of racial hatred and of ideas of superiority of one race. However, in view of the above-mentioned counter-balancing elements and the natural limitations on spelling out such elements in a short item within a longer programme as well as the journalist's discretion as to the form of expression used, the Court does not consider the absence of such precautionary reminders to be relevant.

35. News reporting based on interviews, whether edited or not, constitutes one of the most important means whereby the press is able to play its vital role of "public watchdog". The punishment of a journalist for assisting in the dissemination of statements made by another person in an interview would seriously hamper the contribution of the press to discussion of matters of public interest and should not be envisaged unless there are particularly strong reasons for doing so. In this regard the

Court does not accept the Government's argument that the limited nature of the fine is relevant; what matters is that the journalist was convicted.

There can be no doubt that the remarks in respect of which the Greenjackets were convicted were more than insulting to members of the targeted groups and did not enjoy the protection of Article 10. However, even having regard to the manner in which the applicant prepared the Greenjackets item, it has not been shown that, considered as a whole, the feature was such as to justify also his conviction of, and punishment for, a criminal offence under the Penal Code.

36. It is moreover undisputed that the purpose of the applicant in compiling the broadcast in question was not racist. Although he relied on this in the domestic proceedings, it does not appear from the reasoning in the relevant judgments that they took such a factor into account.

37. Having regard to the foregoing, the reasons adduced in support of the applicant's conviction and sentence were not sufficient to establish convincingly that the interference thereby occasioned with the enjoyment of his right to freedom of expression was "necessary in a democratic society"; in particular the means employed were disproportionate to the aim of protecting "the reputation or rights of others". Accordingly the measures gave rise to a breach of Article 10 of the Convention.

In some ways *Jersild* appears to represent a victory for freedom of expression and responsible journalism. Arguably, though, he won the case primarily because the Strasbourg court decided that the mistake of the Danish courts was simply to misunderstand what his intentions had been in making the programme. Indeed, the structure of the domestic law was effectively to deny such an inquiry at all.

The last case is a domestic UK case which contains some very important comments from the higher judiciary about the importance of freedom of expression as a means by which to safeguard and promote other rights, in this context the right to a fair legal process.

Regina v Secretary of State for the Home Department ex parte Simms and others [2000] 2 AC 115

Panel: Lord Browne-Wilkinson, Lord Steyn, Lord Hoffmann, Lord Hobhouse of Woodborough and Lord Millett

Statute: European Convention on Human Rights Article 10

Facts: The applicants were prisoners convicted of murder, who had made unsuccessful applications for leave to appeal against conviction. They were in contact with journalists who were interested in covering their stories relating to their claims of innocence. However, the Home Secretary adopted a policy excluding all 'professional' visits by journalists to prisoners in order to maintain proper control and discipline, unless a special undertaking was signed. The prisoners were granted permission to apply for judicial review of the Secretary of State's decision to deny access to the journalists, on the grounds that the prohibition appeared to represent an excessive interference with a prisoner's right to free speech.

LORD STEYN

1. The lawfulness of the Home Secretary's policy

Freedom of expression

The starting point is the right of freedom of expression. In a democracy it is the primary right: without it an effective rule of law is not possible. Nevertheless, freedom of expression is not an absolute right. Sometimes it must yield to other cogent social interests. Article 10 of the European Convention for the Protection of Human Rights and Fundamental Freedoms (1953) (Cmd. 8969) is in the following terms:

[Lord Steyn set out Article 10 and continued]

In *Attorney-General v. Guardian Newspapers Ltd. (No. 2)* [1990] 1 A.C. 109, 283-284, Lord Goff of Chieveley expressed the opinion that in the field of freedom of speech there was in principle no difference between English law on the subject and article 10 of the Convention. In *Derbyshire County Council v. Times Newspapers Ltd.* [1993] A.C. 534, 550-551 Lord Keith of Kinkel, speaking for a unanimous House, observed about article 10:

"As regards the words 'necessary in a democratic society' in connection with the restrictions on the right to freedom of expression which may properly be prescribed by law, the jurisprudence of the European Court of Human Rights has established that 'necessary' requires the existence of a pressing social need, and that the restrictions should be no more than is proportionate to the legitimate aim pursued."

In that context Lord Keith observed that he reached his conclusion on the issue before the House without any need to rely on the Convention. But he expressed agreement with the observation of Lord Goff of Chieveley in the *Guardian Newspapers* case and added "that I find it satisfactory to be able to conclude that the common law of England is consistent with the obligations assumed by the Crown under the Treaty in this particular field." I would respectfully follow the guidance of Lord Goff of Chieveley and Lord Keith of Kinkel.

Freedom of expression is, of course, intrinsically important: it is valued for its own sake. But it is well recognised that it is also instrumentally important. It serves a number of broad objectives. First, it promotes the self-fulfilment of individuals in society. Secondly, in the famous words of Holmes J. (echoing John Stuart Mill), "the best test of truth is the power of the thought to get itself accepted in the competition of the market:" *Abrams v. United States* (1919) 250 U.S. 616 , 630, *per* Holmes J. (dissenting). Thirdly, freedom of speech is the lifeblood of democracy. The free flow of information and ideas informs political debate. It is a safety valve: people are more ready to accept decisions that go against them if they can in principle seek to influence them. It acts as a brake on the abuse of power by public officials. It facilitates the exposure of errors in the governance and administration of justice of the country: see Stone, Seidman, Sunstein and Tushnet, Constitutional Law, 3rd ed. (1996), pp. 1078-1086. It is this last interest which is engaged in the present case. The applicants argue that in their cases the criminal justice system has failed, and that they have been wrongly convicted. They

Alert

seek with the assistance of journalists, who have the resources to do the necessary investigations, to make public the wrongs which they allegedly suffered.

The value of free speech in a particular case must be measured in specifics. Not all types of speech have an equal value. For example, no prisoner would ever be permitted to have interviews with a journalist to publish pornographic material or to give vent to so-called hate speech. Given the purpose of a sentence of imprisonment, a prisoner can also not claim to join in a debate on the economy or on political issues by way of interviews with journalists. In these respects the prisoner's right to free speech is outweighed by deprivation of liberty by the sentence of a court, and the need for discipline and control in prisons. But the free speech at stake in the present cases is qualitatively of a very different order. The prisoners are in prison because they are presumed to have been properly convicted. They wish to challenge the safety of their convictions. In principle it is not easy to conceive of a more important function which free speech might fulfil.

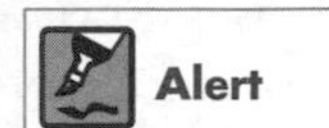

(b) Miscarriages of justice identified by investigative journalism

My Lords, the members of the Court of Appeal were under the impression, and acted on the basis, that it was not necessary for a prisoner to have an oral interview with a journalist since he can correspond with a journalist, and in that way advance his argument for the thorough investigation and possible eventual reopening of his case. As a result of the appeal to the House there is now available material which the Court of Appeal had no opportunity to consider. First, Mr. Woffinden, the journalist in the *Simms* case, has provided details of some 60 cases over the last 10 years where journalists played a substantial role in identifying miscarriages of justice which led to the quashing of the convictions. In the absence of contrary information I regard this document as relevant material tending to establish in a general way the value of investigative journalism in exposing miscarriages of justice. Secondly, and more importantly, an affidavit by Gareth Peirce, an experienced and distinguished practitioner, was placed before the House. Gareth Peirce has acted in more than 20 references to the Court of Appeal in which convictions were eventually quashed. She advised on the setting up of the Criminal Cases Review Commission and subsequently conducted training exercises for the new commissioners and caseworkers. She was asked to discuss the importance of the role of the press in undoing wrongful convictions and did so. Despite the length of the quotation it is necessary to set out in full the core passages in her affidavit. She listed following factors as "important and universal:"

"(a) There is no legal aid for investigations. (On the rare occasions that the green form scheme has allowed for extensions, these amount to little more than several hours' work by a solicitor.) (b) I am informed by the Criminal Cases Review Commission that more than 90 per cent. of applicants are not represented by solicitors. (c) The criteria for referring cases to the Court of Appeal are interpreted as requiring new evidence or new and important considerations of substance. (d) Any commitment to attempting to undo a wrongful conviction is a substantial one; as a solicitor, I am aware that each such commitment will involve me in enormous personal expenditure of time and money, as well as anxiety and responsibility above even the norm in defending cases. No one would contemplate such a commitment unless they had the clearest possible view at the outset of the appropriateness of their efforts. Such a view can only be properly arrived at by meeting the individuals concerned and discussing their predicament with them. (e) There is no difference in the approach of members of the press to that of solicitors; the commitment of an author to writing a book about a case, of a journalist to writing an insightful article, or a television company to the making of a programme involves a major deployment of resources, budgets and time. Each task demands that those making such a decision believe that their choice is an appropriate one. Such a decision is almost impossible if the individual cannot be seen; where it remains impossible, that the individual's case is the less likely to be taken up by that section of the press that might have become interested in the abstract. (f) Although the Criminal Cases Review Commission was expected to be able to conduct investigations into cases far more pro-actively than the Home Office had been able, it finds itself seriously under-resourced and underfunded. The report of its chairman this year to the House of Commons Home Affairs Committee spoke of incoming cases being required to wait at least two years before they can be assigned to a case worker. The cases with the best opportunity remain those which have arrived at the commission fully researched and investigated with new evidence compellingly presented. Resources available to the press, in particular (but not exclusively) the large budgets available to television programmes, are clearly the most significant chance of discovering new evidence, particularly where expensive expert research requires commissioning. As important, however, is the potential interest of smaller, local newspapers and journals, which can provoke interest in the relevant area and prompt fresh evidence."

Gareth Peirce then described in compelling detail how the above factors have been relevant in five particular cases "as well as in many others of which these are examples". Counsel for the Home Secretary was given leave to challenge this affidavit if it was thought proper to do so. There has been no challenge. I have no hesitation in accepting that the general picture sketched by Gareth Peirce, as well as her discussion of particular cases, is correct. On any view this is powerful evidence.

Two important inferences can and should be drawn. First, until the Home Secretary imposed a blanket ban on oral interviews between prisoners and journalists in or about 1995, such interviews had taken place from time to time and had served to identify and undo a substantial number of miscarriages of justice. There is no evidence that any of these interviews had resulted in any adverse impact on prison discipline. Secondly, the evidence establishes clearly that without oral interviews it is now virtually impossible under the Home Secretary's blanket ban for a journalist to take up the case of a prisoner who alleges a miscarriage of justice. In the process a means of correcting errors in the functioning of the criminal justice system has been lost.

(c) The counter-arguments on behalf of the Home Secretary

For my part I am reasonably confident that once it is accepted that oral interviews with prisoners serve a useful purpose in exposing potential miscarriages of justice the Home Secretary would not wish his present policy to be maintained. But, if I am mistaken in that supposition, my view is that investigative journalism, based on oral interviews with prisoners, fulfils an important corrective role, with wider implications than the undoing of particular miscarriages of justice. Nevertheless, I must directly address the counter arguments advance by the Home Secretary.

Latham J. was unimpressed with the reasons advanced in opposition to the applicants' limited claim in the first affidavit of Audrey Wickington. In my judgment the judge was right. The two new affidavits make a case that any oral interviews between prisoners and journalist will tend to disrupt discipline and order in prisons. In my view these affidavits do not take sufficient account of the limited nature of the applicants' claims, viz to have interviews for the purpose of obtaining a thorough investigation of their cases as a first step to possibly gaining access through the Criminal Cases Review Commission to the Court of Appeal (Criminal Division). The affidavits do not refute the case that until 1995 such interviews enabled a substantial number of miscarriages to be undone. Moreover, they do not establish that interviews confined to such limited purposes caused disruption to prison life. In any event, the affidavits do not establish a case of pressing need which might prevail over the prisoners, attempt to gain access to justice: see decision of the Court of Appeal in *Reg. v. Secretary of State for the Home Department, Ex parte Leech* [1994] Q.B. 198, the correctness of which was expressly accepted by counsel for the Home Secretary.

Counsel for the Home Secretary relied on the decision of the United States Supreme Court in *Pell v. Procunier* (1974) 417 U.S. 817. The case involved a ban by prison authorities of face to face interviews between journalists and inmates. The background was a relatively small number of inmates who as a result of press attention became virtual "public figures" within prison society and gained a disproportionate notoriety and influence among their fellow inmates. The evidence showed that the interviews caused severe disciplinary problems. By a majority of five to four the Supreme Court held the ban to be constitutional. The majority enunciated an approach of a "measure of judicial deference owed to corrections officials." This approach was followed in *Turner v. Safley* (1987) 482 U.S. 78 where the Supreme Court upheld restrictions on correspondence between inmates. In *Pell v. Procunier* the Supreme Court was faced with a very particular and intolerable situation in the Californian prison service where there had been virtually unlimited access by journalists to inmates. Nobody suggests anything of the kind in the present case. While the inmates in *Pell v. Procunier* no doubt wished to air their general grievances, there is nothing in the report to indicate that the prisoners wanted interviews with journalists for the specific purpose of obtaining access to an appeal process to challenge their convictions. And, in any event, the approach of judicial deference to the views of prison authorities enunciated in *Pell v. Procunier* does not accord with the approach under English law. It is at variance with the principle that only a pressing social need can defeat freedom of expression as explained in the *Derbyshire case* [1993] A.C. 534, 550h-551a, the *Leech case* [1994] Q.B. 198, 212e-f, and *Silver v. United Kingdom* (1980) 3 E.H.R.R. 475, 514-515, paras. 372-375 (the commission); (1983) 5 E.H.R.R. 347, 377, para. 99(e) (the court). It is also inconsistent with the principle that the more substantial the interference with fundamental rights the more the court will require by way of justification before it can be satisfied that the interference is reasonable in a public law sense: *Reg. v. Ministry of Defence, Ex parte Smith* [1996] Q.B. 517, 554e-f. In my view *Pell v. Procunier* does not assist.

(d) Conclusion

On the assumption that paragraphs 37 and 37A should be construed as the Home Secretary contends, I have no doubt that these provisions are exorbitant in width in so far as they would undermine the fundamental rights invoked by the applicants in the present proceedings and are therefore ultra vires.

2. The interpretation of paragraphs 37 and 37A

It is now necessary to examine the correctness of the interpretation of paragraphs 37 and 37A, involving a blanket ban on interviews, as advanced by the Home Secretary. Literally construed there is force in the extensive construction put forward. But one cannot lose sight that there is at stake a fundamental or basic right, namely the right of a prisoner to seek through oral interviews to persuade a journalist to investigate the safety of the prisoner's conviction and to publicise his findings in an effort to gain access to justice for the prisoner. In these circumstances even in the absence of an ambiguity there comes into play a presumption of general application operating as a constitutional principle as Sir Rupert Cross explained in successive editions of his classic work: Statutory Interpretation, 3rd ed. (1995), pp. 165-166. This is called "the principle of legality": Halsbury's Laws of England, 4th ed. reissue, vol. 8(2) (1996), pp. 13-14, para. 6. Ample illustrations of the application of this principle are given in the speech of Lord Browne-Wilkinson, and in my speech, in *Reg. v. Secretary of State for the Home Department, Ex parte Pierson* [1998] A.C. 539, 573g-575d, 587c-590a. Applying this principle I would hold that paragraphs 37 and 37A leave untouched the fundamental and basic rights asserted by the applicants in the present case.

The only relevant issue in the present proceedings is whether paragraphs 37 and 37A are ultra vires because they are in conflict with the fundamental and basic rights claimed by the applicants. The principle of legality justifies the conclusion that paragraphs 37 and 37A have not been demonstrated to be ultra vires in the cases under consideration.

3. The disposal of the appeal

My Lords, my judgment does not involve tearing up the rule book governing prisons. On the contrary I have taken full account of the essential public interest in maintaining order and discipline in prisons. But, I am satisfied that consistently with order and discipline in prisons it is administratively workable to allow prisoners to be interviewed for the narrow purposes here at stake notably if a proper foundation is laid in correspondence for the requested interview or interviews. One has to recognise that oral interviews with journalists are not in the same category as visits by relatives and friends and require more careful control and regulation. That is achievable. This view is supported by the favourable judgment of past experience. Moreover, in reality an oral interview is simply a necessary and practical extension of the right of a prisoner to correspond to journalists about his conviction: compare *Silver v. United Kingdom*, 3 E.H.R.R. 475 (the commission); 5 E.H.R.R. 347 (the court) and Livingstone & Owen, Prison Law, 2nd ed. (1999), pp. 228-230, paras. 7.30-7.33.

The criminal justice system has been shown to be fallible. Yet the effect of the judgment of the Court of Appeal is to outlaw the safety valve of effective investigative journalism. In my judgment the conclusions and reasoning of the Court of Appeal were wrong.

Declarations should be granted in both cases to the effect that the Home Secretary's current policy is unlawful, and that the governors' administrative decisions pursuant to that policy were also unlawful. I would allow both appeals.

Although this case was largely analysed and determined under a more orthodox, judicial review approach as the relevant events occurred before the coming into force of the Human Rights Act, it nevertheless contained some very important principles relating to freedom of expression. In particular it reinforces the impression, gained from other cases with more political content, such as *Jersild,* that the courts will tend to be readier to uphold this right when it fulfils a functional role, in this case by exposing possible miscarriages of justice.

Further Reading

Lewis, Tom and Cumper, Peter 'Balancing freedom of political expression against equality of political opportunity: the courts and the UK's broadcasting ban on political advertising', [2009] *PL* 89

Tierney, Stephen J.A. 'Press freedom and public interest: the developing jurisprudence of the European Court of Human Rights', [1998] 4 *EHRLR* 419

Jones, Timothy H. 'The devaluation of human rights under the European Convention, [1995]' *PL* 430

Part C

Administrative Law

13

Principles and Procedure of Judicial Review

Topic List

Alex Lawson and Christopher Costigan

Introduction

Judicial review has assumed huge constitutional importance in providing an external check on the power of the executive. In a highly centralised system, where the only meaningful separation of powers occurs between the judiciary and the other organs of state, judicial review has assumed the mantle of constitutional check and balance.

Three introductory observations about judicial review are worth making. First, judicial review only ever involves review of the executive's actions. The doctrine of parliamentary sovereignty means that the actions of the legislature are not reviewable. The second point is related. When the executive is subjected to judicial review, it is usually because it is acting in a way that infringes on the proper role of Parliament. Finally, there was little statutory basis for judicial review when is started to proliferate in the latter half of the twentieth century. It was essentially premised upon judges assuming that they enjoyed an innate power of review over executive action. However, it has been tolerated by the other branches of government and there has never been a serious legislative attempt to abolish judicial review, although strict application of the theory of parliamentary sovereignty would allow for this. In any event, when there have been specific legislative attempts to oust judicial review jurisdiction, the courts have demonstrated impressive willpower and ingenuity in circumventing them.

The cases below are split into two sections. The first deals with whether or not judicial review is available against a defendant, which must be a 'public body'. This is referred to as the issue of amenability to judicial review. The second section deals with the question of whether a claimant has standing to bring a claim.

1 Amenability to Judicial Review

R v Panel of Takeovers and Mergers ex p Datafin [1987] QB 815

Panel: Sir John Donaldson MR, Lloyd and Nicholls LJJ

Facts: The titular panel in this case was unusual in that it had not been created under statutory or common law powers. Rather, it had been created as a self-regulatory body, after various companies and financial institutions had set up an organisation to regulate members of its own industry. The question before the court was whether the proper test for amenability to judicial review was based on the source of the powers a body enjoyed or on the nature of that power. (The traditional view would have focused on the former which would have meant that the Panel's actions would have been unreviewable.)

LORD JUSTICE LLOYD

There have been a number of cases since the decision of the House of Lords in O'Reilly v. Mackman [1983] 2 A.C. 237 in which it has been necessary for the courts to consider the new-found distinction between public and private law. In most of them, objection has been taken by the defendant that the plaintiff has sought the wrong remedy. By seeking a remedy in private law, instead of public law, the plaintiff has, so it has been said, deprived the defendant of the special protection afforded by R.S.C., Ord. 53. The formalism thus introduced into our procedure has been the subject of strong criticism by Sir Patrick Neill in a Child & Co. Oxford Lecture given in 1985, and by other academic writers. The curiosity of the present case is that it is, so to speak, the other way round. The plaintiff is seeking a remedy in public law. It is the defendant who asserts that the plaintiff's remedy, if any (and Mr. Alexander for the panel concedes nothing), lies in private law. Mr. Alexander has cast away the protection afforded by R.S.C., Ord. 53 in the hope, perhaps, that the panel may in the words of Mr. Lever be subject to no law at all.

On this part of the case Mr. Alexander has advanced arguments on two levels. On the level of pure policy he submits that it is undesirable for decisions or rulings of the panel to be reviewable. The intervention of the court would at best impede, at worst frustrate, the purposes for which the panel exists. Secondly, on a more technical level, he submits that to hold that the panel is subject to the supervisory jurisdiction of the High Court would be to extend that jurisdiction further than it has ever been extended before.

On the policy level, I find myself unpersuaded. Mr. Alexander made much of the word "self-regulating." No doubt self-regulation has many advantages. But I was unable to see why the mere fact that a body is self-regulating makes it less appropriate for judicial review. Of course there will be many self-regulating bodies which are wholly inappropriate for judicial review. The committee of an ordinary club affords an obvious example. But the reason why a club is not subject to judicial review is not just because it is self-regulating. The panel wields enormous power. It has a giant's strength. The fact that it is self-regulating, which means, presumably, that it is not subject to regulation by others, and in particular the Department of Trade and Industry, makes it not less but more appropriate that it should be subject to judicial review by the courts.

It has been said that "it is excellent to have a giant's strength, but it is tyrannous to use it like a giant." Nobody suggests that there is any present danger of the panel abusing its power. But it is at least possible to imagine circumstances in which a ruling or decision of the panel might give rise to legitimate complaint. An obvious example would be if it reached a decision in flagrant breach of the rules of natural justice. It is no answer to say that there would be a right of appeal in such a case. For a complainant has no right to appeal where the decision is that there has been no breach of the code. Yet a complainant is just as much entitled to natural justice as the company against whom the complaint is made. Nor is it any answer that a company coming to the market must take it as it finds it. The City is not a club which one can join or not at will. In that sense, the word "self-regulation" may be misleading. The panel regulates not only itself, but all others who have no alternative but to come to the market in a case to which the code applies.

Mr. Alexander urged on us the importance of speed and finality in these matters. I accept that submission. I accept also the possibility that unmeritorious applications will be made from time to time as a harassing or delaying tactic. It would be up to the court to ensure that this does not happen. These considerations are all very relevant to the exercise of the court's discretion in particular cases. They mean that a successful application for judicial review is likely to be very rare. But they do not mean that we should decline jurisdiction altogether.

So long as there is a possibility, however remote, of the panel abusing its great powers, then it would be wrong for the courts to abdicate responsibility. The courts must remain ready, willing and able to hear a legitimate complaint in this as in any other field of our national life. I am not persuaded that this particular field is one in which the courts do not belong, or from which they should retire, on grounds of policy. And if the courts are to remain in the field, then it is clearly better, as a matter of policy, that legal proceedings should be in the realm of public law rather than private law, not only because they are quicker, but also because the requirement of leave under R.S.C., Ord. 53 will exclude claims which are clearly unmeritorious.

So I turn to Mr. Alexander's more technical argument. He starts with the speech of Lord Diplock in Council of Civil Service Unions v. Minister for the Civil Service [1985] A.C. 374, 409:

"For a decision to be susceptible to judicial review the decision-maker must be empowered by public law (and not merely, as in arbitration, by agreement between private parties) to make decisions that, if validly made, will lead to administrative action or abstention from action by an authority endowed by law with executive powers, which have one or other of the consequences mentioned in the preceding paragraph. The ultimate source of the decision-making power is nearly always nowadays a statute or subordinate legislation made under the statute; but in the absence of any statute regulating the subject matter of the decision the source of the decision-making power may still be the common law itself, i.e., that part of the common law that is given by lawyers the label of 'the prerogative.' Where this is the source of decision-making power, the power is confined to executive officers of central as distinct from local government and in constitutional practice is generally exercised by those holding ministerial rank."

On the basis of that speech, and other cases to which Mr. Alexander referred us, he argues (i) that the sole test whether the body of persons is subject to judicial review is the source of its power, and (ii) that there has been no case where that source has been other than legislation, including subordinate legislation, or the prerogative.

I do not agree that the source of the power is the sole test whether a body is subject to judicial review, nor do I so read Lord Diplock's speech. Of course the source of the power will often, perhaps usually, be decisive. If the source of power is a statute, or subordinate legislation under a statute, then clearly the body in question will be subject to judicial review. If, at the other end of the scale, the source of power is contractual, as in the case of private arbitration, then clearly the arbitrator is not subject to judicial review: see *Reg. v. National Joint Council for the Craft of Dental Technicians (Disputes Committee), Ex parte Neate*[1953] 1 Q.B. 704.

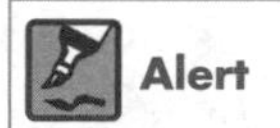
Alert

But in between these extremes there is an area in which it is helpful to look not just at the source of the power but at the nature of the power. If the body in question is exercising public law functions, or if the exercise of its functions have public law consequences, then that may, as Mr. Lever submitted, be sufficient to bring the body

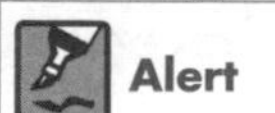
Alert

within the reach of judicial review. It may be said that to refer to "public law" in this context is to beg the question. But I do not think it does. The essential distinction, which runs through all the cases to which we referred, is between a domestic or private tribunal on the one hand and a body of persons who are under some public duty on the other. Thus in *Reg. v. Criminal Injuries Compensation Board, Ex parte Lain* [1967] 2 Q.B. 864 Lord Parker C.J., after tracing the development of certiorari from its earliest days, said, at p. 882:

"The only constant limits throughout were that [the tribunal] was performing a public duty. Private or domestic tribunals have always been outside the scope of certiorari since their authority is derived solely from contract, that is, from the agreement of the parties concerned."

To the same effect is a passage from a speech of Lord Parker C.J. in an earlier case, to which we were not, I think, referred, Reg. v. Industrial Court, Ex parte A.S.S.E.T.[1965] 1 Q.B. 377, 389:

"It has been urged on us that really this arbitral tribunal is not a private arbitral tribunal but that in effect it is undertaking a public duty or a quasi-public duty and as such is amenable to an order of mandamus. I am quite unable to come to that conclusion. It is abundantly clear that they had no duty to undertake the reference. If they refused to undertake the reference they could not be compelled to do so. I do not think that the position is in any way different once they have undertaken the reference. They are clearly doing something which they are not under any public duty to do and, in those circumstances, I see no jurisdiction in this court to issue an order of mandamus to the industrial court."

More recently, *in* Reg. v. British Broadcasting Corporation, Ex parte Labelle[1983] 1 W.L.R. 23, Woolf J. had to consider an application for judicial review where the relief sought was an injunction under R.S.C., Ord. 53, r. 1(2). The case was brought by an employee of the B.B.C. In refusing relief, Woolf J. said, at p. 31:

"Ord. 53, r. 1(2) does not strictly confine applications for judicial review to cases where an order for mandamus, prohibition or certiorari could be granted. It merely requires that the court should have regard to the nature of the matter in respect of which such relief may be granted. However, although applications for judicial review are not confined to those cases where relief could be granted by way of prerogative order, I regard the wording of Ord. 53, r. 1(2) and section 31(2) of the Act of 1981 as making it clear that the application for judicial review is confined to reviewing activities of a public nature as opposed to those of a purely private or domestic character. The disciplinary appeal procedure set up by the B.B.C. depends purely upon the contract of employment between the applicant and the B.B.C., and therefore it is a procedure of a purely private or domestic character."

So I would reject Mr. Alexander's argument that the sole test whether a body is subject to judicial review is the source of its power. So to hold would in my judgment impose an artificial limit on the developing law of judicial review. ...

I now turn to the second of Mr. Alexander's two arguments under this head. He submits that there has never been a case when the source of the power has been other than statutory or under the prerogative. There is a certain imprecision in the use of the term "prerogative" in this connection, as Professor Sir William Wade makes clear in another Child & Co. Oxford Lecture, "Procedure and Prerogative in Public Law" (1985) 101 L.Q.R. 180. Strictly the term "prerogative" should be confined to those powers which are unique to the Crown. As Professor Wade points out, there was nothing unique in the creation by the government, out of funds voted by Parliament, of a scheme for the compensation of victims of violent crime. Any foundation or trust, given sufficient money, could have done the same thing. Nor do I think that the distinction between the Criminal Injuries Compensation Board and a private foundation or trust for the same purposes lies in the source of the funds. The distinction must lie in the nature of the duty imposed, whether expressly or by implication. If the duty is a public duty, then the body in question is subject to public law.

So once again one comes back to what I regard as the true view, that it is not just the source of the power that matters, but also the nature of the duty. I can see nothing in *Reg. v. Criminal Injuries Compensation Board, Ex parte Lain* [1967] 2 Q.B. 864 which contradicts that view, or compels us to decide that, in non-statutory cases, judicial review is confined to bodies created under the prerogative, whether in the strict sense, or in the wider sense in which that word has now come to be used. Indeed, the passage from Diplock L.J.'s judgment, at p. 884, which Sir John Donaldson M.R. has already read, points in the opposite direction.

***R v Disciplinary Committee of the Jockey Club ex p Aga Khan* [1993] 1 WLR 909**

Panel: Sir Thomas Bingham MR, Farquharson and Hoffmann LJJ

Facts: The horse Aliysa won the Oaks at Epsom but, during a routine urine test, was found to have camphor in its system (a substance banned by the Jockey Club). As part of its role, the Jockey Club set up a disciplinary committee which found that the horse should be disqualified and the trainer fined £200. As an organisation the Jockey Club was 'officially responsible for the proper organisation, administration and control of all horse racing, race meetings and racehorse training in the United Kingdom', incorporated in 1970 under Royal Charter (although the Charter gave it no extra powers over those it already exercised). The Jockey Club's rules were brought to bear mainly through contracts with racecourse managers, owners, trainers and jockeys.

SIR THOMAS BINGHAM MR

Conclusions

I have little hesitation in accepting the applicant's contention that the Jockey Club effectively regulates a significant national activity, exercising powers which affect the public and are exercised in the interest of the public. I am willing to accept that if the Jockey Club did not regulate this activity the government would probably be driven to create a public body to do so.

But the Jockey Club is not in its origin, its history, its constitution or (least of all) its membership a public body. While the grant of a Royal Charter was no doubt a mark of official approval, this did not in any way alter its essential nature, functions or standing. Statute provides for its representation on the Horserace Betting Levy Board, no doubt as a body with an obvious interest in racing, but it has otherwise escaped mention in the statute book. It has not been woven into any system of governmental control of horseracing, perhaps because it has itself controlled horseracing so successfully that there has been no need for any such governmental system and such does not therefore exist. This has the result that while the Jockey Club's powers may be described as, in many ways, public they are in no sense governmental. The discretion Conferred by section 31(6) of the Supreme Court Act 1981 to refuse the grant of leave or relief where the applicant has been guilty of delay which would be prejudicial to good administration can scarcely have been envisaged as applicable in a case such as this.

I would accept that those who agree to be bound by the Rules of Racing have no effective alternative to doing so if they want to take part in racing in this country. It also seems likely to me that if, instead of Rules of Racing administered by the Jockey Club, there were a statutory code administered by a public body, the rights and obligations conferred and imposed by the code would probably approximate to those conferred and imposed by the Rules of Racing. But this does not, as it seems to me, alter the fact, however anomalous it may be, that the powers which the Jockey Club exercises over those who (like the applicant) agree to be bound by the Rules of Racing derive from the agreement of the parties and give rise to private rights on which effective action for a declaration, an injunction and damages can be based without resort to judicial review. It would in my opinion be contrary to sound and long-standing principle to extend the remedy of judicial review to such a case.

It is unnecessary for purposes of this appeal to decide whether decisions of the Jockey Club may ever in any circumstances be challenged by judicial review and I do not do so. Cases where the applicant or plaintiff has no contract on which to rely may raise different considerations and the existence or non-existence of alternative remedies may then be material. I think it better that this court should defer detailed consideration of such a case until it arises. I am, however, satisfied that on the facts of this case the appeal should be dismissed.

1.1 Standing in Judicial Review: Sufficient Interest

1.1.1 Sufficient Interest: The Requirements

IRC v National Federation of Self-Employed and Small Businesses [1982] AC 617

Panel: Lord Wilberforce, Lord Diplock, Lord Fraser of Tullybelton, Lord Scarman and Lord Roskill

Statute: Senior Courts Act 1981 s 31(3)

Facts: The case concerned the liability to tax of about 6,000 casual workers in the newspaper print industry on Fleet Street. They had falsified pay dockets so that the Inland Revenue could not trace them for tax purposes. The Inland Revenue discovered this practice and entered into an agreement with their trade unions. The agreement stipulated that, if the workers gave a proper account of the tax year 1977 – 1978, the Revenue would not enquire about previous years' tax returns. The National Federation of Self-Employed and Small Businesses Ltd applied to the court for a judicial review of this decision by the Revenue. In an *ex parte* hearing, they were granted leave, but at the *inter partes* hearing the Divisional Court found that the Federation did not have "sufficient interest" in accordance with s 31(3). The point was taken as a preliminary issue and an appeal to the Court of Appeal was allowed. The Inland Revenue further appealed.

LORD WILBERFORCE

There may be simple cases in which it can be seen at the earliest stage that the person applying for judicial review has no interest at all, or no sufficient interest to support the application: then it would be quite correct at the threshold to refuse him leave to apply. The right to do so is an important safeguard against the courts being flooded and public bodies harassed by irresponsible applications. But in other cases this will not be so. In these it will be necessary to consider the powers or the duties in law of those against whom the relief is asked, the position of the applicant in relation to those powers or duties, and to the breach of those said to have been committed. In other words, the question of sufficient interest can not, in such cases, be considered in the abstract, or as an isolated point: it must be taken together with the legal and factual context. The rule requires sufficient interest in the matter to which the application relates. This, in the present case, necessarily involves the whole question of the duties of the Inland Revenue and the breaches or failure of those duties of which the respondents complain.

LORD SCARMAN

The interest

The sufficiency of the interest is, as I understand all your Lordships agree, a mixed question of law and fact. The legal element in the mixture is less than the matters of fact

> and degree: but it is important, as setting the limits within which, and the principles by which, the discretion is to be exercised. ...
>
> My Lords, I will not weary the House with citation of many authorities. Suffice it to refer to the judgment of Lord Parker C.J. in *Reg. v. Thames Magistrates' Court, Ex parte Greenbaum*, 55 L.G.R. 129, a case of certiorari; and to words of Lord Wilberforce in *Gouriet v. Union of Post Office Workers* [1978] A.C. 435, 482, where he stated the modern position in relation to prerogative orders: "These are often applied for by individuals and the courts have allowed them liberal access under a generous conception of locus standi." The one legal principle, which is implicit in the case law and accurately reflected in the rule of court, is that in determining the sufficiency of an applicant's interest it is necessary to consider the matter to which the application relates. It is wrong in law, as I understand the cases, for the court to attempt an assessment of the sufficiency of an applicant's interest without regard to the matter of his complaint. If he fails to show, when he applies for leave, a prima facie case, or reasonable grounds for believing that there has been a failure of public duty, the court would be in error if it granted leave. The curb represented by the need for an applicant to show, when he seeks leave to apply, that he has such a case is an essential protection against abuse of legal process. It enables the court to prevent abuse by busybodies, cranks, and other mischief-makers. I do not see any further purpose served by the requirement for leave.

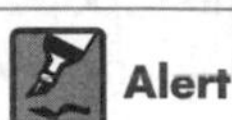

Their Lordships in this case, known colloquially as the *Fleet Street Casuals* case, made it clear that a broad view would be taken on standing and that, if a claim disclosed some potential basis, then leave should be granted. However, implicit in Lord Scarman's speech is a three questioned approach to standing: (1) because the applicant must have a sufficient interest *in the matter to which the application relates* (the exact wording of s 31(3)), there must be some logical connection between the claimant and the claim; (2) the merits of the case must be shown, *prima facie*; and (3) the court will exclude busybodies, cranks and mischief-makers.

The cases that follow deal with how a claimant can show such a logical connection.

1.1.2 Logical Connection: Individuals

The easiest way of showing a logical connection is to show that the claimant is directly affected by the decision. This can be seen in the case of *R v Secretary of State for Home Department ex p Venables* [1998] AC 407, where the killers of the toddler Jamie Bulger applied for judicial review of their tariff set by the Home Secretary. They were accepted as having standing as they were 'directly affected' by the imposition of the tariff period.

However, it should be noted that the rules on standing in judicial review are far wider than those for Human Rights Act cases. While showing that a claimant is directly affected is the easiest way to establish the logical connection, it is by no means the only one. For example in *R v Somerset CC ex p Dixon* [1998] Env LR 111, the applicant was granted leave in relation to an environmental matter where Sedley J said:

'Public law is not at base about rights... it is about wrongs – that is to say misuses of public power... If an arguable case of such misuse can be made out on an application for leave, the court's only concern is to ensure it is not being done for an ill motive'.

In *R v Felixstowe Justices ex p Leigh* [1987] QB 582 it was held that the public interest in open justice would entitle a journalist to bring an action against the Felixstowe magistrates for withholding the names of the bench in a trial for gross indecency. In *R v Secretary of State for Foreign and Commonwealth Affairs ex p Rees-Mogg* [1994] QB 552 Lord Rees-Mogg wished to challenge the ability of the government to ratify the Maastricht Treaty. In his judgment Lloyd LJ said:

'There is no dispute as to the applicant's locus standi... we accept without question that Lord Rees-Mogg brings the proceedings because of his sincere concern for constitutional issues'.

However, the rules on standing do still impose a limit beyond just rejecting cranks or those that cannot show a prima facie case. In particular, where policy reasons dictate, third parties may be excluded, as in the following case where Jamie Bulger's father also attempted, from a notably different perspective, to challenge the tariff imposed on Venables and Thompson.

***R (on the Application of Ralph Bulger) v The Secretary of State for the Home Department, The Lord Chief Justice of England and Wales* [2001] EWHC Admin 119, [2001] 3 All ER 449**

Panel: Rose LJ, Sullivan and Penry-Davey JJ

Statute: Senior Courts Act 1981 s 31(3)

Facts: Ralph Bulger was the father of Jamie Bulger, a toddler killed by two older children. After the killers' conviction and sentence, a tariff period was imposed, before which their release would not be considered. Ralph Bulger had been invited to make representations to be considered by the Home Secretary before setting the tariff. Ralph Bulger applied for judicial review on the basis that the period was too lenient. The key issue was whether he had a 'sufficient interest'.

LORD JUSTICE ROSE

18. The second question which, to my mind, arises is whether the claimant has standing to challenge the tariff which the Lord Chief Justice has fixed. This is not a point which initially any counsel (save Mr Fitzgerald QC to a limited extent) sought to take against the claimant. But it is a point which the court took because it appears to be of considerable potential importance. In his reasons, the Lord Chief Justice said that he had invited representations from the family as to the impact of the death on them but this "is not an invitation for the family to indicate their views as to what they would regard as an appropriate tariff".

19. This approach is entirely in accordance with the decisions of the Court of Appeal, Criminal Division in *R v Nunn* [1996] 2 Cr App R(S) 136, and *R v Perks* [2000] Crim

LR 606. The reasons were explained by Mr Justice Judge (as he then was) giving the court's judgment in *Nunn* at page 140:

"We mean no disrespect to the mother and sister of the deceased, but the opinions of the victim, or the surviving members of the family, about the appropriate level of sentence do not provide any sound basis for reassessing a sentence. If the victim feels utterly merciful towards the criminal, and some do, the crime has still been committed and must be punished as it deserves. If the victim is obsessed with vengeance, which can in reality only be assuaged by a very long sentence, as also happens, the punishment cannot be made longer by the court than would otherwise be appropriate. Otherwise cases with identical features would be dealt with in widely differing ways leading to improper and unfair disparity, and even in this particular case, as the short judgment has already indicated, the views of the members of the family of the deceased are not absolutely identical.

If carried to its logical conclusion the process would end up by imposing unfair pressures on the victims of crime or the survivors of a crime resulting in death, to play a part in the sentencing process which many of them would find painful and distasteful. This is very far removed from the court being kept properly informed of the anguish and suffering inflicted on the victims by the crime."

20. It is true, as Mr Newman submits, that the threshold for standing in judicial review has generally been set by the courts at a low level. This, as it seems to me, is because of the importance in public law that someone should be able to call decision makers to account, lest the rule of law break down and private rights be denied by public bodies: see, for example, the discussion in Wade and Forsyth Administrative Law (8th edition) at pages 667–688. But in the present matter the traditional and invariable parties to criminal proceedings, namely the Crown and the defendant, are both able to, and do, challenge those judicial decisions which are susceptible to judicial review as, for example, the many authorities on the meaning of the words "relating to trial on indictment" in section 29(3) of the Supreme Court Act 1981 amply illustrate.

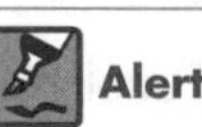

21. It follows that in criminal cases there is no need for a third party to seek to intervene to uphold the rule of law. Nor, in my judgment, would such intervention generally be desirable. If the family of a victim could challenge the sentencing process, why not the family of the defendant? Should the Official Solicitor be permitted to represent the interests of children adversely affected by the imprisonment of their mother? Should organisations representing victims or offenders be permitted to intervene? In my judgment, the answer in all these cases is that the Crown and the defendant are the only proper parties to criminal proceedings. A proper discharge of judicial functions in relation to sentencing requires that the judge take into account (as the Lord Chief Justice said he did in this case) the impact of the offence and the sentence on the public generally, and on individuals, including the victim and the victim's family and the defendant and the defendant's family. The nature of that impact is properly channelled through prosecution or defence.

1.1.3 Logical Connection: Representative Groups

***R v Liverpool Corporation ex p Liverpool Taxi Fleet Operators' Association* [1972] 2 QB 299**

Panel: Lord Denning MR, Roskill LJ and Sir Gordon Willmer

Facts: The issue in this case was the number of taxicabs on the streets of Liverpool. Since 1948 the Liverpool Corporation had limited the number of taxis to 300 and the taxi owners wanted it to remain at this figure. However, despite an assurance to the contrary, the Council decided to increase the number of licences. The Operator's Association, a representative group of taxi drivers, sought to review that decision. A key question for the court was whether the group, as opposed to the individual members of the group who were directly affected, had standing.

LORD DENNING MR

This case concerns the number of taxicabs on the streets of Liverpool. Since 1948 the Liverpool Corporation have limited the number of taxicabs to 300. The taxicab owners want it to remain at 300. They point out that in recent years a great number of private hire cars have come on to the streets. These private hire cars are not licensed.

There is no control over them. These vehicles do not have to come up to any required standard. The taxi drivers feel that they are taking custom which should belong to them. The mischief is such that the Liverpool Corporation are promoting a Bill before Parliament to bring these private hire cars under control.

In addition the Liverpool Corporation have passed a resolution to increase the number of taxicabs. The owners seek to prohibit them from doing so. They say the corporation passed the resolution without hearing their case properly and contrary to an undertaking.

...

In the middle of 1970, when the owners heard that the corporation proposed to increase the number of taxicabs, their association took up the matter. On July 24, 1970, the Town Clerk of Liverpool wrote to the solicitors for the taxicab owners' association, saying:

"No decision has been taken on the number of hackney carriage plates and, before any such decision was taken, you have my assurance that interested parties would be fully consulted."

That was reaffirmed on October 28, 1970, when the town clerk wrote:

"I have no doubt that your clients will be given an opportunity to make representations, at the appropriate time, should they wish to do so."

In July 1971 the matter was considered by a sub-committee of the corporation. The taxicab owners were represented by counsel. The subcommittee recommended an increase above 300, to the extent that there should be 50 more in the year beginning in January 1972 (making 350) and a further 100 in the year beginning January 1973 (making 450), and thereafter an unlimited number.

On August 4, 1971, that recommendation came up for consideration by the city council themselves. The minutes were approved subject to some matters being sent back. In addition the chairman of the committee, Alderman Craine, gave an undertaking (which was put into writing by the town clerk in a letter on August 11, 1971):

"The chairman of the committee gave an undertaking in council that no plates in addition to the existing 300 would be issued until proposed legislation had been enacted and had come into force."

After the meeting on August 4 the alderman came out to the representatives of the taxicab proprietors. The treasurer of the association asked: "Is it right, Alderman Craine, that no licences will be issued until legislation controlling private hire vehicles is in force?" The alderman replied: "I have just stated that publicly. I have just made an announcement to that effect."

So there was a clear undertaking, namely, no more than 300 licences until the legislation about private hire cabs was in force. It was expected that the bill would be introduced towards the end of 1971, passed in 1972, and in force early in 1973.

So things should have rested there till 1973. But not a bit of it. Behind the scenes the corporation seem to have been advised that that undertaking was not lawful and they ought not to hold themselves bound by it. So, without a word to the taxicab owners or their association, a sub-committee met on November 16, 1971. They rescinded the earlier resolution and put forward a new recommendation, namely, that from January 1, 1972, a further 50 licences would be issued bringing the total to 350: and that from July 1, 1972, a further 50, bringing the total to 400: and no limit from January 1, 1973.

The taxicab owners got indirectly to hear of that recommendation. (They were never told officially.) So their solicitors asked for a further hearing. They asked if there were any new facts and requested that their clients should be given an opportunity of making further representations. On December 7, 1971, the town clerk replied:

"There are no new important material facts. If there are any new material facts of which you have become aware, please let me have details of them by return."

The meeting was to be on the next day, December 8. So it was quite impossible for the owners to make any reply by return.

On December 8 the committee met. They confirmed the sub-committee. On December 22 the city council met. They confirmed the committee and adopted the recommendation. The result was that the corporation resolved to increase the number from 300 to 350 from January 1 to July 1972, and to 400 from July 1, 1972, to December 31, 1972, and thenceforth unlimited. That was quite contrary to the undertaking which had been most explicitly given in August.

On getting to know of this, the taxicab owners moved the Divisional Court ex parte for orders of prohibition and certiorari. The Divisional Court refused the application. We desired to hear the corporation. So notice was served on them. We have had the full argument before us today.

First I would say this: when the corporation consider applications for licences under the Town Police Clauses Act 1847, they are under a duty to act fairly. This means that they should be ready to hear not only the particular applicant but also any other persons or bodies whose interests are affected. In *Rex v. Brighton Corporation, ex parte Thomas Tilling Ltd.* (1916) 85 L.J.K.B. 1552, 1555 Sankey J. said:

"Persons who are called upon to exercise the functions of granting licences for carriages and omnibuses are, to a great extent, exercising judicial functions; and although they are not bound by the strict rules of evidence and procedure observed in a court of law, they are bound to act judicially. It is their duty to hear and determine according to law, and they must bring to that task a fair and unbiased mind."

It is perhaps putting it a little high to say they are exercising judicial functions. They may be said to be exercising an administrative function. But even so, in our modern approach, they must act fairly: and the court will see that they do so.

To apply that principle here: suppose the corporation proposed to reduce the number of taxicabs from 300 to 200, it would be their duty to hear the taxicab owners' association: because their members would be greatly affected. They would certainly be persons aggrieved. Likewise suppose the corporation propose to increase the number of taxicabs from 300 to 350 or 400 or more: it is the duty of the corporation to hear those affected before coming to a decision adverse to their interests. The Town Clerk of Liverpool was quite aware of this and acted accordingly. His letters of July 24, 1970, and October 28, 1970, were perfectly proper.

...

Alert

The writs of prohibition and certiorari lie on behalf of any person who is a "person aggrieved," and that includes any person whose interests may be prejudicially affected by what is taking place. It does not include a mere busybody who is interfering in things which do not concern him; but it includes any person who has a genuine grievance because something has been done or may be done which affects him... . The taxicab owners' association here have certainly a locus standi to apply for relief.

As a result of this case it can be taken that, where a group of individuals, all of whom are directly affected by the relevant decision, challenge the decision as a representative group, they will be able to establish a logical connection between themselves and the decision.

1.1.4 Logical Connection: Pressure Groups

While representative groups have been allowed standing, pressure groups have been treated differently as they are unlikely to be in a position where all of the membership is directly affected. The absence of anyone who could show they were directly affected by the relevant decision was a key reason for the refusal of standing in the next case, which can be seen as the low watermark in the otherwise liberal approach the judiciary has taken to standing.

R v Secretary of State for the Environment ex p Rose Theatre Trust Co Ltd [1990] 1 QB 504

Panel: Schiemann J

Statute: Senior Courts Act 1981 s 31(3)

Facts: During development of a site in Southwark, south London, some remains of the Rose Theatre, (where Marlowe's plays and some of Shakespeare's plays had been first performed), were uncovered. The Secretary of State refused to add the remains to the schedule of monuments of national importance, which would have required the landowner to preserve the remains. A group of interested persons established the Rose Theatre Trust to ensure the preservation of the remains and eventually applied for judicial review of the Secretary of State's refusal. The matter of the Trust's standing was raised.

MR JUSTICE SCHIEMANN

...I go on to consider what logically I ought perhaps to have considered first, namely, does the applicant have any standing to move for judicial review. I introduce this section of my judgment by pointing out something which may well surprise many laymen and some lawyers who do not practise in this branch of the law.

Inevitably, in the tide of human affairs decisions are from time to time reached which are unlawful, occasionally by someone who knows he is acting unlawfully but more usually by someone who does not know this. The law provides in general that even an unlawful decision is to be treated as lawful until such time as the court, at the suit of someone with a sufficient interest in the matter to which the application relates, allows an application to quash that decision. Often the law provides a time limit or other conditions which have to be complied with before the court is empowered to quash an admittedly unlawful decision. The reason for that, at first sight, surprising willingness of the law to treat the admittedly unlawful as lawful is that in many fields, if it were otherwise, uncertainty and, at times, complete chaos would result.

Suppose a decision to build a motorway turns out, once it has been built, to have been unlawful because the Secretary of State took into account something which he ought not to have done? If everyone could challenge an unlawfully granted planning permission for a house, what would be the position of the innocent first or subsequent purchaser? These are the types of problems with which the concept of standing is concerned.

...

There is no doubt that, in the early part of this decade, the High Court was fairly liberal in its interpretation of who had "a sufficient interest" to be able to apply for judicial review...

The leading case on this branch of the law is *Reg. v. Inland Revenue Commissioners, Ex parte National Federation of Self-Employed and Small Businesses Ltd.* [1982] A.C. 617. In that case, which concerned the right of the federation to apply for a declaration that the Inland Revenue had acted unlawfully in granting an amnesty to the Fleet Street casuals, five separate speeches were delivered by the five Law Lords who decided the case. I do not propose to lengthen this judgment by a close analysis of what each Law Lord said but I think the following propositions, to put it no higher, are not inconsistent with that case. 1. Once leave has been given to move for judicial review, the court which hears the application ought still to examine whether the applicant has a sufficient interest. 2. Whether an applicant has a sufficient interest is not purely a matter of discretion in the court. 3. Not every member of the public can complain of every breach of statutory duty by a person empowered to come to a decision by that statute. To rule otherwise would be to deprive the phrase "a sufficient interest" of all meaning. 4. However, a direct financial or legal interest is not required. 5. Where one is examining an alleged failure to perform a duty imposed by statute it is useful to look at the statute and see whether it gives an applicant a right enabling him to have that duty performed. 6. Merely to assert that one has an interest does not give one an interest. 7. The fact that some thousands of people join together and assert that they have an interest does not create an interest if the individuals did not have an interest. 8. The fact that those without an interest incorporate themselves and give the company in its memorandum power to pursue a particular object does not give the company an interest.

The applicant's argument on standing runs essentially like this. 1. When scheduled monument consent is sought anybody who wishes to make representations to the Secretary of State can do so and the Secretary of State must consider any such representations once made ... to the Act of 1979. 2. Therefore Parliament recognised that everyone has an interest in the preservation of monuments considered by the Secretary of State to be of national importance and everyone has a legitimate expectation to be consulted on such a matter. 3. The Secretary of State considers the Rose Theatre to be a monument of national importance. 4. At the stage when he is considering whether or not to schedule a monument considered by him to be of national importance, the area of discretion left to the Secretary of State is a very small one and therefore it would be artificial to make a distinction so far as standing is concerned between the position at the scheduling stage and the position at the scheduled monument consent stage. (I interpose to point out - and it will be evident - that earlier on in this judgment I rejected this particular submission.) 5. Therefore, the court should recognise that everyone has a sufficient interest to challenge, by way of judicial review, the lawfulness of the Secretary of State's decision in deciding not to schedule. 6. Although as a matter of form the applicant is a company, as a matter of substance the company is merely the corporate expression of the wills and desires of persons of undoubted expertise and distinction in the fields of archaeology, the theatre, literature and other fields and includes local residents, the local Member of Parliament and so on. These are not mere busybodies. 7. The very fact that the Secretary of State has answered with care the representations made by those whose will the applicant embodies gives them a sufficient interest for the purpose of this application. 8. There is no evidence of any rival organisation which claims to represent the public in relation to the Rose Theatre and thus if this application is struck down for lack of standing then the legality of the Secretary of State's decision is unlikely to be tested in the courts. It was implicitly but not expressly suggested that the Attorney-General is unlikely to act ex officio and unlikely to give his fiat for a relator action which, however, in the present case has not been sought.

The history of how persons gathered together to try to preserve the remains of the Rose Theatre and how the applicant company came to be formed is set out in Mr. Grayling's affidavit. Mr. Goldsmith submitted that the applicant company had even less of a claim to standing than those who agreed that a company should be used as a vehicle for the campaign. This raises points of some difficulty. It was, I think, accepted on behalf of the applicant that the company could have no greater claim to standing than the members of the campaign had before the company was made into the campaign's vehicle. In any event I so hold. It would be absurd if two people, neither of whom had standing could, by an appropriately worded memorandum, incorporate themselves into a company which thereby obtained standing.

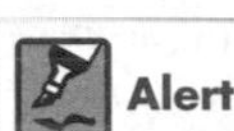

That being so, I propose first to examine the question of standing, leaving aside the fact of incorporation. I raised with Mr. Griffiths, who replied on behalf of the applicant (Mr. Sullivan being detained elsewhere), whether, if I found that no individual in the campaign has standing, he would submit that the agglomeration of individuals might have a standing which any one individual lacked. He replied that he did not so submit. I can therefore consider the question of standing by considering whether an individual of acknowledged distinction in the field of archaeology, of which the company has several amongst its members, has sufficient standing to move for judicial review of a decision not to schedule.

Applying the approach indicated in the propositions enumerated earlier on in this judgment it seems to me that the decision not to schedule is one of those governmental decisions in respect of which the ordinary citizen does not have a sufficient interest to entitle him to obtain leave to move for judicial review. Clearly a person cannot obtain a sufficient interest by writing a letter to the Secretary of State. I approach with reluctance the submission that because the Secretary of State sent a considered reply, that gives the recipient an interest which he would not have had if no reply had been sent beyond a formal acknowledgement. If the court were to sanction such an argument it might cause the decision makers to be less helpful to the general public. Further, what about the man who appears in the decision maker's office, the man who telephones the decision maker and so on?

None of these points are unanswerable but I hope my reluctance to go down this path is at least understandable. In any event, I do not consider that an interested member of the public who has written and received a reply in relation to a decision not to schedule a site as an ancient monument has sufficient interest in that decision to enable him to apply for judicial review.

Finally, I ought to say that I recognise the force of Mr. Sullivan's submission that since an unlawful decision in relation to scheduling either has been made (if the earlier part

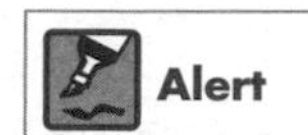

of my judgment be wrong) or may well be made in the future, my decision on standing may well leave an unlawful act by a minister unrebuked and indeed unrevealed since there will be those in the future who will not have the opportunity to ventilate - on this hypothesis - their well-founded complaints before the court.

This submission is clearly right. The answer to it is that the law does not see it as the function of the courts to be there for every individual who is interested in having the legality of an administrative action litigated. Parliament could have given such a wide right of access to the court but it has not done so. The challenger must show that he "has a sufficient interest in the matter to which the application relates." The court will look at the matter to which the application relates - in this case the non-scheduling of a monument of national importance - and the statute under which the decision was taken (in this case the Act of 1979) and decide whether that statute gives that individual expressly or impliedly a greater right or expectation than any other citizen of this country to have that decision taken lawfully. We all expect our decision makers to act lawfully. We are not all given by Parliament the right to apply for judicial review.

Since, in my judgment, no individual has the standing to move for judicial review it follows, from what I ruled earlier, that the company created by those individuals has no standing. In consequence I need not and I do not consider the effect of the interposition of the company in the present case.

I therefore reject this application on the dual grounds that the applicant has no standing to make it and that in any event it has no legal merits.

This case can also be seen to give rise to concerns about the rule of law, because the effect of it was that a minister could act unlawfully without the possibility of redress in the courts. However, as will be seen the next two cases, the courts have subsequently moved away from the restrictive approach of Schiemann J.

R v Inspectorate of Pollution ex p Greenpeace Ltd (No 2) [1994] 4 All ER 329

Panel: Otton J

Statute: Senior Courts Act 1981 s 31(3)

Facts: British Nuclear Fuels Limited held licences to dispose of nuclear waste at the Sellafield facility in Cumbria. BNFL obtained a variation of the licence and Greenpeace sought to challenge this decision through judicial review.

MR JUSTICE OTTON

Locus standi

Mr George Newman Q.C., leading counsel on behalf of BNFL, the party directly affected by the decision under review, submits that in principle and on authority Greenpeace have failed to establish a sufficient interest in the matter to which the application relates and that accordingly the grant of leave should be set aside and in the exercise of my discretion I should disallow the application on that ground, however I may have found on the merits of the case.

In advancing this argument Mr Newman was careful to preface his submissions by emphasising that this issue does not question the sincerity of Greenpeace and its supporters for the causes it supports. BNFL do not seek to question the legitimacy of Greenpeace's objectives and views. The question at issue is not the extent of its reputation and the extent to which it is known nationally and internationally or the integrity of its aims.

Leading counsel took me through an extensive and helpful review of the authorities on the point, which included:

...

In particular he relied upon the speeches in the House of Lords in *R. v. IRC ex parte Nfse*. This concerned a decision by the IRC in respect of the tax affairs of the "Fleet Street Casuals" not to investigate tax lost in earlier periods. The applicants were a Federation representing the self-employed and small businesses. It was held that the applicants did not have a sufficient interest in the matter to which the application related. The Federation was merely a body of tax payers which had shown no sufficient interest in that matter to justify their application for relief and the Federation had completely failed to show any conduct of the revenue which was ultra vires or unlawful. In particular he relied upon extracts from three of the speeches. Lord Wilberforce said:

It would be necessary to consider the powers or duties in law of those against whom the relief is asked, the position of the applicant in relation to those powers of duties, and the breach of those said to have been committed.

From Lord Diplock:

The questions (1) what was the public duty of the board of inland revenue of which it was alleged to be in breach, and (2) what was the nature of the breaches which were relied upon by the federation ... need to be answered in the instant case before it is possible to say whether the federation have "a sufficient interest in the matter to which the application relates ...

and *per* Lord Fraser:

the correct approach ... is ... to look at the statute under which the duty arises, and to see whether it gives any express or implied right to persons in the position of the applicant to complain of the alleged unlawful act or omission.

He also submitted that the analysis of Schiemann J. in *ex parte Rose Theatre Company* was a correct statement in principle...

Leading Counsel takes as his starting point the context of the 1960 [Radioactive Substances] Act. He submits that Parliament's purpose in passing the statute is to permit such activities subject to regulation by the designated statutory authorities, not to forbid them altogether.

There are built into the statutory framework, provisions for consultation in respect of new authorisations and even variations. Thus, there is no express or implied right to persons in the position of Greenpeace to complain of the alleged unlawful act or omission. He analysed the position of Greenpeace in relation to the statutory duties and powers. He emphasised that Greenpeace's primary object is:

In the United Kingdom and internationally to promote, encourage, further, establish, procure and achieve the protection of wildlife and the elimination of threats and damage to the environment or the global environment of the earth.

Thus Greenpeace asserts that it represents a wider public interest. This demonstrates that the complaint is in furtherance of Greenpeace's general campaign against the use of radioactive material and the disposal of radioactive waste. Greenpeace merely subscribes to a different view as to the risks associated with such activities from that formed by the authorities charged by statute to regulate and control these activities. Thus Greenpeace's complete opposition to authorising the disposal of radioactive waste is fundamentally incompatible with the statutory scheme adopted by Parliament in 1960 Act. The fact that an individual or a pressure group has commented on a proposed decision and those comments have been considered by the statutory authorities does not confer on the individual or pressure group a sufficient interest in the decision to challenge the decision by proceedings for judicial review. To hold otherwise, he submits, would be to discourage the statutory authorities from inviting or considering comments from the public beyond their statutory obligations to do so.

He further analyses the challenge to the lawfulness of the procedure and comments: "This is the classic case of the busybody. The nub of Greenpeace's complaint is that, although it has itself the opportunity to make comments the decision is flawed because some person or body should have been consulted. Allegations that procedural rights have not been respected are properly vindicated by those entitled to those rights and not by a pressure group which itself has no practical complaint."

In any event, he submits the case does not fall within the exceptional category envisaged by the House of Lords of "flagrant and serious breaches of the law" or "exceptionally grave or widespread illegality" or "a most extreme case" which would justify an exceptional approach to the question of "sufficient interest": See *R. v. IRC ex parte Nfse.*

Conclusions

The requirement of a sufficient interest emerges from section 31(3) Supreme Court 1981...

In reaching my conclusions I adopt the approach indicated by Lord Donaldson M.R. in R. v. Monopolies and Mergers Commission ex parte Argyle Group:

The first stage test which is applied on the application for leave, will lead to a refusal if the applicant has no interest whatsoever and is, in truth, no more than a meddlesome busybody. If, however, an application appears otherwise to be arguable and there is no other discretionary bar, such as dilatoriness on the part of the applicant, the applicant may expect to get leave to apply, leaving the test of interest or standing to be re-applied as a matter of discretion on the hearing of the substantive application. At this stage, the strength of the applicant's interest is one of the factors to be weighed in the balance ...

This approach was followed and developed by Purchas L.J. in *R. v. Department of Transport ex parte Presvac Engineering Ltd* when after considering the decision of the House of Lords in the "*Fleet Street Casuals*" case he said:

Personally I would prefer to restrict the use of the expression locus standi to the threshold exercise and to describe the decision at the ultimate stage as an exercise of discretion not to grant relief as the applicant has not established that he had been or would be sufficiently affected.

Thus I approach this matter primarily as one of discretion. I consider it appropriate to take into account the nature of the applicant and the extent of the applicant's interest in the issues raised, the remedy Greenpeace seeks to achieve and the nature of the relief sought.

In doing so I take into account the very nature of Greenpeace. Lord Melchett has affirmed thus:

Greenpeace International has nearly 5 million supporters worldwide; Greenpeace UK has over 400,000 supporters in the United Kingdom and about 2,500 of them are in the Cumbria region, where the BNFL plant is situated. Greenpeace is a campaigning organisation which has as its prime object the protection of the natural environment.

Greenpeace International has also been accredited with consultative status with the United Nations Economic and Social Council (including United Nations General Assembly). It has accreditation status with the UN Conference on Environment and Development. They have observer status or right to attend meetings of 17 named bodies including Parcom (Paris Convention for the Prevention of Marine Pollution from Land Based Sources).

BNFL rightly acknowledge the national and international standing of Greenpeace and its integrity. So must I. I have not the slightest reservation that Greenpeace is an entirely responsible and respected body with a genuine concern for the environment. That concern naturally leads to a bona fide interest in the activities carried on by BNFL at Sellafield and in particular the discharge and disposal of radioactive waste from their premises and to which the respondents' decision to vary relates. The fact that 400,000 supporters in the UK carries less weight than the fact that 2,500 of them come from the Cumbria region. I would be ignoring the blindingly obvious if I were to disregard the fact that those persons are inevitably concerned about (and have a genuine perception that there is) a danger to their health and safety from any additional discharge of radioactive waste even from testing. I have no doubt that the issues raised by this application are serious and worthy of determination by this court.

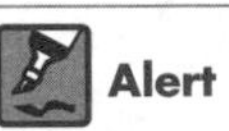

It seems to me that if I were to deny standing to Greenpeace those they represent might not have an effective way to bring the issues before the court. There would have to be an application either by an individual employee of BNFL or a near neighbour. In this case it is unlikely that either would be able to command the expertise which is at the disposal of Greenpeace. Consequently a less well-informed challenge might be mounted which would stretch unnecessarily the court's resources and which would not afford the court the assistance it requires in order to do justice between the parties. Further, if the unsuccessful applicant had the benefit of legal aid it might leave the respondents and BNFL without an effective remedy in costs. Alternatively, the individual (or Greenpeace) might seek to persuade H.M. Attorney General to commence a relator action which (as a matter of policy or practice) he may be reluctant to undertake against a government department (see the learned commentary by Schiemann J. on "locus standi". Neither of these courses of action would have the advantage of an application by Greenpeace, who, with its particular experience in environmental matters, its access to experts in the relevant realms of science and technology (not to mention the law) is able to mount a carefully selected, focused, relevant and well-argued challenge. It is not without significance that in this case the form 86 contains 6 grounds of challenge but by the time it came to the substantive hearing before me, the Greenpeace "team" (if I can call them that) had been able to evaluate the respondents' and BNFL's evidence and were able to jettison 4 grounds and concentrate on 2. This responsible approach undoubtedly had the advantage of sparing scarce court resources, ensuring an expedited substantive hearing and an early result (which it transpires is helpful to the respondents and to BNFL). ...

I also take into account the nature of the relief sought. In the *"Fleet Street Casuals"* case the House of Lords expressed the view that if mandamus were sought that would be a reason to decline jurisdiction. Here, the primary relief sought is certiorari (less stringent) and, if granted, the question of an injunction to stop the testing pending determination of the main applications would still be in the discretion of the court. I also take into account the fact that Greenpeace has been treated as one of the consultees during the consultation process and that they were invited (albeit with other non-consultees) to comment on the "minded to vary" letter.

It follows that I reject the argument that Greenpeace is a "mere" or "meddlesome busybody". I regard the applicants as eminently respectable and responsible and their genuine interest in the issues raised is sufficient for them to be granted locus standi.

I should add that Lord Roskill in *"Fleet Street Casuals"* approved the commentary to Order 53 of the Supreme Court Practice that the question of whether the applicant has a sufficient interest appear to be:

A mixed question of fact and law; a question of fact and degree and the relationship and the applicant and the matter to which the application relates, having regard to all the circumstances of the case. Thus it must not be assumed that Greenpeace (or any other interest group) will automatically be afforded standing in any subsequent application for judicial review in whatever field it (and its members) may have an interest. This will have to be a matter to be considered on a case by case basis at the leave stage and if the threshold is crossed again at the substantive hearing as a matter of discretion.

I also bear this consideration in mind when I respectfully decline to follow the decision of Schiemann J. in *Rose Theatre*. Suffice it to say that the circumstances were different, the interest group had been formed for the exclusive purpose of saving the Rose

Theatre site and no individual member could show any personal interest in the outcome. In any event his decision on the locus standi point (as indeed is mine) was not central to his decision.

In exercising my discretion I would grant Greenpeace standing in this case. ... In the event, having granted in my discretion Greenpeace leave to make this application on behalf of its members on these matters of considerable interest to the public, I cannot find for Greenpeace on the merits of the application. It must therefore be refused.

As can be seen, a more liberal approach to standing was taken in the *Greenpeace* case. Although one of the main reasons was that 2,500 regional members of Greenpeace were directly affected by the decision, three other important factors were also taken into account: (1) the size of Greenpeace's membership generally (around 400,000); (2) Greenpeace's national and international reputation; and (3) Greenpeace's undoubted expertise which was seen to have been of valuable assistance to the court.

R v Secretary of State for Foreign and Commonwealth Affairs ex p World

Development Movement Ltd [1995] 1 WLR 386

Panel: Rose LJ and Scott Baker J

Statute: Senior Courts Act 1981 s 31(3)

Facts: This action came about as a result of the Foreign Secretary's decision to grant aid for the building of the Pergau Dam in Malaysia, despite evidence that there would be much cheaper ways of producing electricity in that country. The World Development Movement Ltd, a group campaigning to increase the amount and quality of overseas aid generally, challenged the Foreign Secretary's decision. The Foreign Secretary questioned the applicant's standing. In this case the respondents submitted, and the applicant accepted, that neither the body itself nor any of its members were directly affected. However, if WDM did not have standing, it was unlikely that any other body would be able to challenge the decision.

LORD JUSTICE ROSE

The affidavit of Mr. Jackson, the applicants' campaign co-ordinator, describes the applicant company. It is a non-partisan pressure group, over 20 years old and limited by guarantee. It has an associated charity which receives financial support from all the main United Kingdom development charities, the churches, the European Community and a range of other trusts. About 60 per cent. of its total income comes from members and supporters. The council of the applicants has cross-political party membership, and, indeed, historically, a Member of Parliament from each of the three main political parties has sat on the council. There are 7,000 full voting members throughout the United Kingdom with a total supporter base of some 13,000. There are 200 local groups whose supporters actively campaign through letter writing, lobbying and other democratic means to improve the quantity and quality of British aid to other countries. It conducts research and analysis in relation to aid. It is a founder member of the Independent Group on British Aid, which brings academics and campaigners together. It has pressed the British Government, the European Union, the banks and other businesses for better trade access for developing countries. It is in regular contact with the O.D.A. and has regular meetings with the minister of that department, and it makes written and oral submissions to a range of select committees in both Houses of Parliament. It has run all-party campaigns against aid cuts in 1987 and 1992.

Internationally, it has official consultative status with U.N.E.S.C.O. and has promoted international conferences. It has brought together development groups with the O.E.C.D. It tends to attract citizens of the United Kingdom concerned about the role of the United Kingdom Government in relation to the development of countries abroad and the relief of poverty abroad.

Its supporters have a direct interest in ensuring that funds furnished by the United Kingdom are used for genuine purposes, and it seeks to ensure that disbursement of aid budgets is made where that aid is most needed. It seeks, by this application, to represent the interests of people in developing countries who might benefit from funds which otherwise might go elsewhere.

If the applicants have no standing, it is said that no person or body would ensure that powers under the Act of 1980 are exercised lawfully. For the applicants, Mr. Pleming submitted that the respondent himself, in a written statement of 2 March 1994, has expressly accepted that the matter is "clearly of public and parliamentary interest." It cannot be said that the applicants are "busybodies," "cranks" or "mischief-makers." They are a non-partisan pressure group concerned with the misuse of aid money. If there is a public law error, it is difficult to see how else it could be challenged and corrected except by such an applicant. He referred the court to a number of authorities: *Reg. v. Inland Revenue Commissioners, Ex parte National Federation of Self-Employed and Small Businesses Ltd.* [1982] A.C. 617, in particular the speech of Lord Wilberforce, at p. 630E, and the speech of Lord Diplock where there appears this passage, at p. 644:

"It would, in my view, be a grave lacuna in our system of public law if a pressure group, like the federation, or even a single public-spirited taxpayer, were prevented by outdated technical rules of locus standi from bringing the matter to the attention of the court to vindicate the rule of law and get the unlawful conduct stopped. The Attorney-General, although he occasionally applies for prerogative orders against public authorities that do not form part of central government, in practice never does so against government departments. It is not, in my view, a sufficient answer to say that judicial review of the actions of officers or departments of central government is unnecessary because they are accountable to Parliament for the way in which they carry out their functions. They are accountable to Parliament for what they do so far as regards efficiency and policy, and of that Parliament is the only judge; they are responsible to a court of justice for the lawfulness of what they do, and of that the court is the only judge."

Mr. Pleming also referred to *Reg. v. Monopolies and Mergers Commission, Ex parte Argyll Group Plc.* [1986] 1 W.L.R. 763. Sir John Donaldson M.R., when referring to the provision of Ord. 53, r. 3(7), said, at p. 773:

"The first stage test, which is applied upon the application for leave, will lead to a refusal if the applicant has no interest whatsoever and is, in truth, no more than a meddlesome busybody. If, however, the application appears to be otherwise arguable and there is no other discretionary bar, such as dilatoriness on the part of the applicant, the applicant may expect to get leave to apply, leaving the test of interest or standing to be re-applied as a matter of discretion on the hearing of the substantive application. At this second stage, the strength of the applicant's interest is one of the factors to be weighed in the balance."

There is a reference to Professor Wade's work on *Administrative Law*, 5th ed. (1982), pp. 587–591, to which I shall come later.

Mr. Pleming also referred to *Reg. v. Secretary of State for Social Services, Ex parte Child Poverty Action Group* [1990] 2 Q.B. 540, where that group were held to have a sufficient interest or standing. He referred also to *Reg. v. Inspectorate of Pollution, Ex parte Greenpeace Ltd. (No. 2)* [1994] 4 All E.R. 329, in particular to passages in the judgment of Otton J., at pp. 350 and 351, which it is unnecessary to read. Finally on this aspect, he invited the court's attention to *Reg. v. Secretary of State for Foreign and Commonwealth Affairs, Ex parte Rees-Mogg* [1994] Q.B. 552, 562A, where Lloyd L.J. delivering the judgment of the Divisional Court (comprised of himself, Mann L.J. and Auld J.), accepted that the applicant had standing "because of his sincere concern for constitutional issues." The question of lawfulness being for the court, Mr. Pleming submitted that the court in its discretion should accept the standing of the applicants. If they cannot seek relief, he said, who can? Neither a government nor citizen of a foreign country denied aid is, in practical terms, likely to be able to bring such a challenge.

For the respondent, there is no evidential challenge to the applicants' standing. Mr. Richards made submissions on sufficiency of interest, not with a view to preventing the court from considering the substantive issue as to the validity of the decision, but because sufficiency of interest goes to the court's jurisdiction: see *per* Woolf L.J. in *Reg. v. Secretary of State for Social Services, Ex parte Child Poverty Action Group* [1990] 2 Q.B. 540, 556E–F. The applicants, Mr. Richards submitted, are at the outer limits of standing. He submitted, and indeed Mr. Pleming accepted, that neither the applicants, nor any of its individual members, have any direct personal interest in funding under the Act of 1980, but they seek to act in the interest of potential recipients of aid overseas. Mr. Richards submitted that this is too remote an interest to be sufficient, and he contrasted Greenpeace members, some of whom, as Otton J. pointed out, were liable to be personally directly affected by radioactive discharge.

Mr. Richards accepted that the requirements of standing will vary from case to case and that the court may accord standing to someone who would not otherwise qualify, where exceptionally grave or widespread illegality is alleged. He referred in *Reg. v. Inland Revenue Commissioners, Ex parte National Federation of Self-Employed and*

Small Businesses Ltd. [1982] A.C. 617 to that part of Lord Diplock's speech at p. 637D, which shows that his comments, at p. 644E–G, which I have read are obiter. He referred to the speeches of both Lord Wilberforce, at p. 633B, and Lord Fraser of Tullybelton, at p. 646G, to the effect that a United Kingdom taxpayer's interest, which is no more than that of taxpayers in general, is insufficient to confer standing, save in an extreme case. If no United Kingdom taxpayer could raise the matter, this not being an exceptional case, the applicants, submitted Mr. Richards, cannot be in a better position.

It is to be observed, in passing, that there are dicta since Ex parte National Federation of Self-Employed and Small Businesses Ltd. which are in favour of according standing to a single taxpayer in an appropriate case: see Reg. v. Her Majesty's Treasury, Ex parte Smedley [1985] Q.B. 657, per Slade L.J., at 670B, and per John Donaldson M.R., at p. 667F. There is, submitted Mr. Richards, "a certain tension" between what Lloyd L.J. said in Reg. v. Secretary of State for Foreign and Commonwealth Affairs, Ex parte Rees-Mogg [1994] Q.B. 552, 562 and what Sir John Donaldson M.R. said in Reg. v. Monopolies and Mergers Commission, Ex parte Argyll Group Plc. [1986] 1 W.L.R. 763, 774A. The rules of standing should not, submitted Mr. Richards, be allowed to evolve further so as to embrace the applicants.

For my part, I accept that standing (albeit decided in the exercise of the court's discretion, as Sir John Donaldson M.R. said) goes to jurisdiction, as Woolf L.J. said. But I find nothing in *Reg. v. Inland Revenue Commissioners, Ex parte National Federation of Self-Employed and Small Businesses Ltd.* [1982] A.C. 617 to deny standing to these applicants. The authorities referred to seem to me to indicate an increasingly liberal approach to standing on the part of the courts during the last 12 years. It is also clear *from Ex parte National Federation of Self-Employed and Small Businesses Ltd.* that standing should not be treated as a preliminary issue, but must be taken in the legal and factual context of the whole case: see *per* Lord Wilberforce, at p. 630D, Lord Fraser, at p. 645D and Lord Scarman, at p. 653F.

Furthermore, the merits of the challenge are an important, if not dominant, factor when considering standing. In Professor Wade's words in Administrative Law, 7th ed. (1994), p. 712: "the real question is whether the applicant can show some substantial default or abuse, and not whether his personal rights or interests are involved."

Leaving merits aside for a moment, there seem to me to be a number of factors of significance in the present case: the importance of vindicating the rule of law, as Lord Diplock emphasised [1982] A.C. 617; the importance of the issue raised, as in Ex parte Child Poverty Action Group [1990] 2 Q.B. 540; the likely absence of any other responsible challenger, as in Ex parte Child Poverty Action Group and Ex parte Greenpeace Ltd. (No. 2) [1994] 4 All E.R. 329; the nature of the breach of duty against which relief is sought (see per Lord Wilberforce, at p. 630D, in Ex parte National Federation of Self-Employed and Small Businesses Ltd.); and the prominent role of these applicants in giving advice, guidance and assistance with regard to aid: see Ex parte Child Poverty Action Group [1990] 2 Q.B. 540, 546H. All, in my judgment, point, in the present case, to the conclusion that the applicants here do have

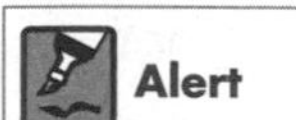
Alert

a sufficient interest in the matter to which the application relates within section 31(3) of the Supreme Court Act 1981 and Ord. 53, r. 3(7).

It seems pertinent to add this, that if the *Divisional Court in Ex parte Rees-Mogg* [1994] Q.B. 552, eight years after *Ex parte Argyll Group Plc.* [1986] 1 W.L.R. 763, was able to accept that the applicant in that case had standing in the light of his "sincere concerns for constitutional issues," a fortiori, it seems to me that the present applicants, with the national and international expertise and interest in promoting and protecting aid to underdeveloped nations, should have standing in the present application.

Despite there being no member of the WDM directly affected, the court was able to grant leave on the basis that (1) the rule of law would be in danger if there was no one capable of challenging the decision, and in this case there was no other responsible challenger (as there had been in the case of *Bulger*, a judgment also delivered by Rose LJ). This approach can be contrasted with Schiemann J's judgment in *Rose Theatre*. (2) The general importance of the issue raised. (3) The nature of the breach. (4) The prominent role of the applicant organisation in relation to the issue under examination, which echoes the point from *Greenpeace* that expertise, which can assist the court, may also be a factor in establishing a logical connection.

1.2 Conclusion

Therefore, in order to proceed to consider the substantive grounds on a claim for judicial review, there are four procedural hurdles that must be gone through:

- The defendant must be amenable to judicial review
- The claimant must have a sufficient interest in the matter
- The matter must be brought within the time limit
- There must be procedural exclusivity (the issue must be a matter of public law)

If there is an ouster clause on the facts then this should also be considered as a preliminary issue.

Further Reading

Cane, Peter *Administrative Law*, (4th Edition), Chapters 2, 3, 4 and 6

Cane, Peter 'Standing up for the public', [1995] *PL* 276

Lord Hope of Craighead, 'Mike Tyson comes to Glasgow – a question of standing', [2001] *PL* 294

14

Illegality

Topic List

1 Errors of Fact
2 Relevant Considerations
3 Delegation
4 Improper Purpose

Alex Lawson and Christopher Costigan

Introduction

The classic definition of illegality was given by Lord Diplock in *Council of Civil Service Unions v Minister for the Civil Service* [1985] AC 374 where he said

> 'By "illegality" as a ground for judicial review I mean that the decision-maker must understand correctly the law that regulates his decision-making power and must give effect to it.'

This concept, however, does not have just one element, but can be subdivided into six discrete ways in which a decision may be tainted by illegality:

1. True Ultra Vires;
2. Errors of Law and Errors of Fact;
3. Relevant/Irrelevant Considerations;
4. Improper Purpose;
5. Delegation of Discretion; and
6. Fettering of Discretion.

However, it is important to note that, as with all the grounds for judicial review, while they can be broken down into useful categories, they are not mutually exclusive; instead they work on a continuum. At the margins of each there is usually an overlap and so the same decision may be tainted by illegality in several different ways.

This chapter will focus on errors of fact, relevant considerations, delegation and improper purpose, but you should note that all the sub-heads of illegality are important and you must have a thorough understanding of them all.

1 Errors of fact

The courts' attitudes to errors of fact have evolved over time. They were initially reluctant to review errors of fact at all, on the basis that judicial review is not supposed to involve the substitution of the original decision maker's judgment with that of the judges. It was felt that the original decision maker was closer to the factual situation and that, if the courts tried to take over this position, they would not be as competent or as knowledgeable – and would then open themselves up to public criticism.

The problem with this laudable aim is that it enabled some flawed decisions to go unchallenged despite the factual errors at issue being glaringly obvious. Addressing this, the courts began to find circumstances where they could review errors of fact.

The first two types of reviewable factual errors are precedent (jurisdictional) facts, and facts with no supporting evidence (where one is entitled to conclude no evidence had been adduced, because none exists). The third type is the most interesting – mistake of facts. As we shall see in the next case, it now seems clear that this area of factual error is open for review.

E v Secretary of State for the Home Department [2004] QB 1044

Panel: Lord Phillips of Worth Matravers MR, Mantell and Carnwath LJJ

Facts: The case was brought by foreign nationals seeking asylum. Their claims were rejected and they appealed to the Immigration Appeal Tribunal on the basis of factual errors made by the decision maker. The Tribunal decided it could not hear their claims in relation to mistakes of fact. This was probably correct under the law governing the jurisdiction of the Tribunal, but the Court of Appeal was asked to consider whether or not the mistake of fact that the appellants wished to challenge could be raised as a free-standing claim, entirely separate from the statutory requirements which would preclude it. The Court of Appeal answered in the affirmative and indicated this would also apply to mainstream judicial review cases.

LORD JUSTICE CARNWATH

Introduction

This is the judgment of the court. These two appeals have been heard together because they raise a common issue as to the powers of the Immigration Appeal Tribunal ("IAT") and the Court of Appeal (a) to review the determination of the IAT, where it is shown that an important part of its reasoning was based on ignorance or mistake as to the facts; and (b) to admit new evidence to demonstrate the mistake.

...

Appeal on law, and judicial review

There was some discussion in the present case as to whether the grounds upon which the court may question a decision of the IAT differ materially, depending on whether the case comes before the court as an application for judicial review, or as an appeal on a point of law. It would certainly be surprising if the grounds for judicial review were more generous than those for an appeal. In practice, such cases only come by way of judicial review because the IAT has refused leave to appeal, and its refusal can only be challenged in that way. There is certainly no logical reason why the grounds of challenge should be wider in such cases.

More generally, the history of remedies in administrative law has seen the gradual assimilation of the various forms of review, common law and statutory. The history was discussed by the Law Commission in its Consultation Paper Administrative Law: Judicial Review and Statutory Appeals (1994) (No 126), Parts 17-18. The appeal "on a point of law" became a standard model (supplanting in many contexts the appeal by "case stated")... . In other statutory contexts (notably, planning, housing and the like), a typical model was the statutory application to quash on the grounds that the decision was "not within the powers of the Act": see e g *Ashbridge Investments Ltd v Minister of Housing and Local Government* [1965] 1 WLR 1320. Meanwhile the prerogative writ procedures were remodelled into the modern judicial review procedure. In *R v Hull University Visitor, ex p Page* [1993] AC 682, the House of Lords acknowledged the evolution of a common set of principles "to ensure that the powers of public decision-making bodies are exercised lawfully": p 701, per Lord Browne-Wilkinson.

Thus, in spite of the differences in history and wording, the various procedures have evolved to the point where it has become a generally safe working rule that the substantive grounds for intervention are identical. (The conceptual justifications are another matter; see, for example, the illuminating discussion in Craig, Administrative Law, 5th ed (2003), pp 476ff.) The main practical dividing line is between appeals (or review procedures) on both fact and law, and those confined to law. The latter are treated as encompassing the traditional judicial review grounds of excess of power, irrationality, and procedural irregularity. This position was confirmed in *R v Inland Revenue Comrs, Ex p Preston* [1985] AC 835, 862 (a tax case), where Lord Templeman said:

"Appeals from the general commissioners or the special commissioners lie, but only on questions of law, to the High Court by means of a case stated and the High Court can then correct all kinds of errors of law including errors which might otherwise be the subject of judicial review proceedings ..."

...

Incorrect basis of fact

Can a decision reached on an incorrect basis of fact be challenged on an appeal limited to points of law? This apparently paradoxical question has a long history in academic discussion, but has never received a decisive answer from the courts. The answer is not made easier by the notorious difficulty of drawing a clear distinction between issues of law and fact: see Craig, Administrative Law, 5th edition , p 488 and *Moyna v Secretary of State for Work and Pensions* [2003] 1 WLR 1929, 1935, para 22ff, per Lord Hoffmann.

The debate received new life following the affirmative answer given by Lord Slynn in *R v Criminal Injuries Compensation Board, Ex p A* [1999] 2 AC 330. In that case the claimant had claimed compensation on the basis that in the course of a burglary she had been the victim of rape and buggery. She was examined five days after the burglary by a police doctor who reported that her findings were consistent with the allegation of buggery. However, at the hearing of her claim that report was not included in the evidence, and the board was given the impression by the police witnesses that there was nothing in the medical evidence to support her case. The claimant did not ask for the report, but, in Lord Slynn's words, at p 343:

"having been told that she should not ask for police statements as they would be produced at the hearing, it would not be surprising that she assumed that if there was a report from the police doctor, it would be made available with the police report."

One of the issues discussed in detail in argument was whether the decision could be quashed on the basis of a mistake, in relation to material which was or ought to have been within the knowledge of the decision maker: see pp 333-336. Lord Slynn thought it could. He said, at pp 344-345:

"Your Lordships have been asked to say that there is jurisdiction to quash the board's decision because that decision was reached on a material error of fact. Reference has been made to Wade & Forsyth, Administrative Law, 7th ed (1994) , pp 316-318 in which it is said: 'Mere factual mistake has become a ground of judicial review, described as "misunderstanding or ignorance of an established and relevant fact", [*Secretary of State for Education and Science v Tameside Metropolitan Borough Council* [1977] AC 1014, 1030], or acting "upon an incorrect basis of fact" ... This ground of review has long been familiar in French law and it has been adopted by statute in Australia. It is no less needed in this country, since decisions based upon wrong facts are a cause of injustice which the courts should be able to remedy. If a "wrong factual basis" doctrine should become established, it would apparently be a new branch of the ultra vires doctrine, analogous to finding facts based upon no evidence or acting upon a misapprehension of law.' De Smith, Woolf & Jowell, Judicial Review of Administrative Action, 5th ed (1995) , p 288: 'The taking into account of a mistaken fact can just as easily be absorbed into a traditional legal ground of review by referring to the taking into account of an irrelevant consideration, or the failure to provide reasons that are adequate or intelligible, or the failure to base the decision on any evidence. In this limited context material error of fact has always been a recognised ground for judicial intervention.' For my part, I would accept that there is jurisdiction to quash on that ground in this case..."

Alert

However, Lord Slynn "preferred" to decide the instant case on the alternative basis that there had been a breach of the rules of natural justice amounting to "unfairness". ...

None the less, he considered that the police "do have a special position in these cases", and he noted the evidence that the board is "very dependent on the assistance of and the co-operation of the police who have investigated these alleged crimes of violence". He said, at p 346:

"In the present case, the police and the board knew that [A] had been taken by the police to see a police doctor. It was not sufficient for the police officer simply to give her oral statement without further inquiry when it was obvious that the doctor was likely to have made notes and probably a written report."

He concluded, at p 347:

"I consider therefore, on the special facts of this case and in the light of the importance of the role of the police in co-operating with the board in the obtaining of evidence, that there was unfairness in the failure to put the doctor's evidence before the board and if necessary to grant an adjournment for that purpose. I do not think it possible to say here that justice was done or seen to be done."

The other members of the House agreed with Lord Slynn's reasoning, thereby (as I read the speeches) endorsing his "preferred" basis of unfairness. Only Lord Hobhouse of Woodborough made any direct reference to the question of review for "error of fact", specifically reserving that issue for consideration in the future: p 348e.

The same statement on that question was repeated by Lord Slynn, in another context, in *R (Alconbury Developments Ltd) v Secretary of State for the Environment, Transport and the Regions* [2003] 2 AC 295, 321, para 53. He referred to the jurisdiction to quash for "misunderstanding or ignorance of an established and relevant fact", as part of his reasons for holding that the court's powers of review (under a statutory procedure to quash for excess of power) met the requirements of the European Convention for the Protection of Human Rights and Fundamental Freedoms. This part of his reasoning was not in terms adopted by the other members of the House of Lords. The point was mentioned by Lord Nolan and Lord Clyde. Lord Nolan put it in somewhat narrower terms; he said, at p 323, para 61:

"But a review of the merits of the *decision-making process* is fundamental to the courts' jurisdiction. The power of review may even extend to a decision on a question of fact. As long ago as 1955 your Lordships' House, in *Edwards v Bairstow* [1956] AC 14, a case in which an appeal (from general commissioners of income tax) could only be brought on a question of law, upheld the right and duty of the appellate court to reverse a finding of fact which had no justifiable basis."

He saw Edwards v Bairstow as an illustration of "the generosity" with which the courts have interpreted the power to review questions of law, corresponding to a "similarly broad and generous approach" in the development of judicial review [2003] 2 AC 295, 323, para 62. Lord Clyde referred to Lord Slynn's statement on this issue in the Criminal Injuries Compensation Board case [1999] 2 AC 330, commenting [2003] 2 AC 295, 355, para 169, that it was: "sufficient to note ... the extent to which the factual areas of a decision may be penetrated by a review of the account taken by a decision maker of facts which are irrelevant or even mistaken ..."

In the present case E and R rely on Lord Slynn's statement as representing the law. Mr Kovats, for the Secretary of State, contents himself with the observation that the *Criminal Injuries Compensation Board* case is "not in point" because it was a judicial review case, and Lord Slynn's statement was obiter. For the reasons already given, we do not think the fact that the *Criminal Injuries Compensation Board* case was a judicial review case is an adequate ground of distinction. Indeed, Lord Slynn himself (and Lord Clyde) treated it as no less relevant to a statutory review procedure in the *Alconbury case* [2003] 2 AC 295. The fact that the statement was obiter means of course that it is not binding on us, but does not detract from its persuasive force, bearing in mind also the authority of the textbooks cited by him.

Although none of the parties found it necessary to examine in any detail the authorities referred to in argument in the *Criminal Injuries Compensation Board case* [1999] 2 AC 330 or in the textbooks, it seems to us difficult to avoid such examination, if we are to address properly the issue in these appeals. Fortunately the ground is very well covered, not only in the textbooks, but also in two excellent articles: by Timothy H Jones, "Mistake of Fact in Administrative Law" [1990] PL 507; and by Michael Kent QC (no doubt stimulated by his unsuccessful advocacy in the *Criminal Injuries Compensation Board* case itself) "Widening the Scope of Review for Error of Fact" [1999] JR 239. The authorities are helpfully summarised in Michael Fordham's invaluable Judicial Review Handbook, 3rd ed (2001) , pp 730-732: see also Demetriou & Houseman "Review for Error of Fact—A Brief Guide" [1997] JR 27. Michael Kent includes a useful comparison with the concept of "manifest error" as applied by the Court of Justice of the European Communities. He concludes [1999] JR 239, 243:

"A cautious extension of the power of the court on judicial review to reopen the facts might now be appropriate. This would need to be limited to cases where the error is manifest (not requiring a prolonged or heavily contested inquiry), is decisive (on which the decision turned) and not susceptible of correction by alternative means ..."

That is not dissimilar to the formulation approved by Lord Slynn, although he required that the error should be "material", rather than "decisive". Before reaching a conclusion that mistake of fact is now a ground for judicial review in its own right, it is necessary to review briefly the authorities mentioned in those articles. Two main points emerge: first, that widely differing views have been expressed as to the existence or scope of this ground of review; but, secondly, that, in practice, this uncertainty has not deterred administrative court judges from setting aside decisions on the grounds of mistake of fact, when justice required it.

Differing views

First, there have been several judicial statements by eminent judges on both sides of the debate. The narrower view is exemplified by a recent statement of Buxton LJ, under the heading "Error of fact as a ground for judicial review?" in *Wandsworth London Borough Council v A* [2000] 1 WLR 1246, 1255-1256:

"The heading of this section of this judgment is, deliberately, the same as that of an important section in de Smith, Woolf & Jowell, Judicial Review of Administrative Action, 5th ed (1995), p 286, paras 5-091 and following. That section shows the difficult and elusive nature of this question, viewed as a general issue. However, if our present case is properly analysed the dilemma does not arise. While there may, possibly, be special considerations that apply in the more formalised area of planning inquiries, as suggested by de Smith, Woolf & Jowell, p 287, para 5-092, n75; and while the duty of 'anxious scrutiny' imposed in asylum cases by *R v Secretary of State for the Home Department, Ex p Bugdaycay* [1987] AC 514 renders those cases an uncertain guide for other areas of public law; none the less de Smith, Woolf & Jowell's analysis shows that there is still no general right to challenge the decision of a public body on an issue of fact alone. The law in this connection continues, in our respectful view, to be as stated for a unanimous House of Lords by Lord Brightman in *R v Hillingdon London Borough Council, Ex p Puhlhofer* [1986] AC 484, 518: 'it is the duty of the court to leave the decision [as to the existence of a fact] to the public body to whom Parliament has entrusted the decision-making power save in a case where it is obvious that the public body, consciously or unconsciously, are acting perversely'."

He adopted the observations of Watkins LJ (sitting with Mann LJ) in *R v London Residuary Body, Ex p Inner London Education Authority* The Times, 24 July 1987 , quoted in the Judicial Review Handbook , p 730:

"Of course, a mistake as to fact can vitiate a decision as where the fact is a condition precedent to an exercise of jurisdiction, or where the fact is the only evidential basis for a decision or where the fact was as to a matter which expressly or impliedly had to be taken into account. Outside those categories we do not accept that a decision can be flawed in this court, which is not an appellate tribunal, upon the ground of mistake of fact."

The clearest articulation of the alternative view (before the *Criminal Injuries Compensation Board case* [1999] 2 AC 330) was that of Scarman LJ in the Court of Appeal, in *Secretary of State for Education and Science v Tameside Metropolitan Borough Council* [1977] AC 1014, 1030. (This can be taken as having been implicitly endorsed by Lord Slynn, since it was cited by Wade & Forsyth, Administrative Law in the extract quoted by him: see above para 46.) The question in the *Tameside* case was whether the Secretary of State was entitled to hold that the council reacted "unreasonably" in reversing plans of the previous administration to make all the schools in their area "comprehensive". One issue was the practicability of carrying out the necessary selection process within the available time. On the material available to the Court of Appeal, it appeared that the Secretary of State had "either misunderstood or was not informed" as to the professional advice available to the authority on this issue; and that he had wrongly "jumped to the conclusion" that the proposals were unworkable: see pp 1031c, 1032h. Scarman LJ, at p 1030, did not accept that the scope of judicial review was as limited as suggested by counsel for the Secretary of State:

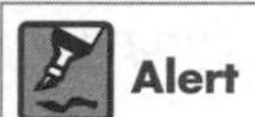

"I would add a further situation to those specified by him: misunderstanding or ignorance of an established and relevant fact. Let me give two examples. The fact may be either physical, something which existed or occurred or did not, or it may be mental, an opinion. Suppose that, contrary to the minister's belief, it was the fact that there was in the area of the local education authority adequate school accommodation for the pupils to be educated, and the minister acted under the section believing that there was not. If it were plainly established that the minister was mistaken, I do not think that he could substantiate the lawfulness of his direction under this section. Now, more closely to the facts of this case, take a matter of expert professional opinion. Suppose that, contrary to the understanding of the minister, there does in fact exist a respectable body of professional or expert opinion to the effect that the selection procedures for school entry proposed are adequate and acceptable. If that body of opinion be proved to exist, and if that body of opinion proves to be available both to the local education authority and to the minister, then again I would have thought it quite impossible for the minister to invoke his powers under section 68."

In the House of Lords, Lord Wilberforce [1977] AC 1014, 1047d-e referred to the need for "proper self-direction" as to the facts. But he made no direct reference to the observations of Scarman LJ, and it may be (as was the view of Buxton LJ: see the *Wandsworth case* [2000] 1 WLR 1246, 1256d) that he was thinking only of the limited forms of factual review later summarised by Watkins LJ in *R v London Residuary Body, Ex p Inner London Education Authority* The Times, 24 July 1987. The House of Lords held that the Secretary of State had acted unlawfully, principally on the ground that the Secretary of State had set the criterion of unreasonableness too low.

More recently, in *R v Independent Television Commission, Ex p Virgin Television Ltd* The Times, 17 February 1996 cited in Demetriou & Houseman, "Review for Error of Fact—A Brief Guide" [1997] JR 27, 31, para 28, Henry LJ distinguished between mistakes of fact "not grave enough to undermine the basis of a multi-faceted decision", and "misapprehension of the facts which form the foundation of the commission's decision"; only the latter would justify intervention by the court on judicial review.

Timothy H Jones in "Mistake of Fact in Administrative Law" [1990] PL 507 notes that another leading proponent of the wider approach, Sir Robin Cooke, in the New Zealand Court of Appeal, adopted Scarman LJ's formulation, saying: "To jeopardise validity on the ground of mistake of fact the fact must be an established one or an established and recognised opinion; and ... it cannot be said to be a mistake to adopt one of two differing points of view of the facts, each of which may be reasonably held." *(New Zealand Fishing Industry Association Inc v Minister of Agriculture and Fisheries* [1988] 1 NZLR 544 , 552.)

There was however no majority on this issue in the New Zealand Court of Appeal: see Jones [1990] PL 507, 514-515. ...

Underlying principle

As the passage cited by Lord Slynn shows, the editors of the current edition of de Smith, Woolf & Jowell, Judicial Review of Administrative Action (unlike Wade & Forsyth, Administrative Law) are somewhat tentative as to whether this is a separate ground of review, at para 5-094:

"The taking into account of a mistaken fact can just as easily be absorbed into a traditional legal ground of review by referring to the taking into account of an irrelevant consideration, or the failure to provide reasons that are adequate or intelligible, or the failure to base the decision upon any evidence."

We are doubtful, however, whether those traditional grounds provide an adequate explanation of the cases. We take them in turn. (i) Failure to take account of a material consideration is only a ground for setting aside a decision, if the statute expressly or impliedly requires it to be taken into account: *In re Findlay* [1985] AC 318, 333-334, per Lord Scarman That may be an accurate way of characterising some mistakes; for example, a mistake about the development plan allocation, where there is a specific statutory requirement to take the development plan into account (as in the *Hollis case* 47 P & CR 351. But it is difficult to give such status to other mistakes which cause unfairness; for example whether a building can be seen (*Jagendorf's case* [1987] JPL 771), or whether the authority has carried out a particular form of study (the *Simplex case* 57 P & CR 306). (ii) Reasons are no less "adequate and intelligible", because they reveal that the decision-maker fell into error; indeed that is one of the purposes of requiring reasons. (iii) Finally, it may be impossible, or at least artificial, to say that there was a failure to base the decision on "*any* evidence", or even that it had "no justifiable basis" (in the words of Lord Nolan: see above). In most of these cases there is *some* evidential basis for the decision, even if part of the reasoning is flawed by mistake or misunderstanding.

In our view, the *Criminal Injuries Compensation Board case* [1999] 2 AC 330 points the way to a separate ground of review, based on the principle of fairness. It is true that Lord Slynn distinguished between "ignorance of fact" and "unfairness" as grounds of review. However, we doubt if there is a real distinction. The decision turned, not on issues of fault or lack of fault on either side; it was sufficient that "objectively" there was unfairness. On analysis, the "unfairness" arose from the combination of five factors: (i) an erroneous impression created by a mistake as to, or ignorance of, a relevant fact (the availability of reliable evidence to support her case); (ii) the fact was "established", in the sense that, if attention had been drawn to the point, the correct position could have been shown by objective and uncontentious evidence; (iii) the claimant could not fairly be held responsible for the error; (iv) although there was no duty on the Board itself, or the police, to do the claimant's work of proving her case, all the participants had a shared interest in co-operating to achieve the correct result; (v) the mistaken impression played a material part in the reasoning.

...

In our view, the time has now come to accept that a mistake of fact giving rise to unfairness is a separate head of challenge in an appeal on a point of law, at least in those statutory contexts where the parties share an interest in co-operating to achieve the correct result. Asylum law is undoubtedly such an area. Without seeking to lay down a precise code, the ordinary requirements for a finding of unfairness are apparent from the above analysis of the Criminal Injuries Compensation Board case. First, there must have been a mistake as to an existing fact, including a mistake as to the availability of evidence on a particular matter. Secondly, the fact or evidence must have been "established", in the sense that it was uncontentious and objectively verifiable. Thirdly, the appellant (or his advisers) must not been have been responsible for the mistake. Fourthly, the mistake must have played a material (not necessarily decisive) part in the tribunal's reasoning.

2 Relevant Considerations

When trying to establish what are, and what are not relevant considerations for a decision maker to take into account, regard must first be had to any relevant statute itself. In *Hanks v Minister of Housing and Local Government* [1963] 1 QB 999 Megaw J said:

'...[I]f it be shown that an authority exercising a power has taken into account as a relevant factor something that which it should not properly have taken into account in deciding whether or not to exercise the power, then the exercise of the power, normally at least, is bad. Similarly, if the authority fails to take into account as a relevant factor something which is relevant, and which it ought to have taken into account, the exercise of the power is normally bad'.

However, while it is clear that a decision will be flawed where an irrelevant factor is taken into consideration, or a relevant factor is not taken into consideration, there is a third category where the decision-maker has a discretion. This category was described by Simon-Brown LJ, in *R v Somerset CC ex parte Fewings* [1995] 1 WLR 1037 as an area in which '...the decision-maker may have regard if in his judgment and discretion he thinks right to do so. There is, in short, a margin of appreciation in which the decision-maker may decide just what considerations should play a part in his reasoning process'.

R v Somerset County Council ex p Fewings [1995] 1 WLR 1037

Panel: Sir Thomas Bingham MR, Simon Brown and Swinton Thomas LJJ

Facts: Under the Local Government Act 1972 s 120(1)(b), local councils were tasked with managing their land for "the benefit, improvement or development of their area.". Somerset County Council bought a strip of land and banned stag hunting on it, which effectively prevented all hunts. It became apparent that their main reason for banning the hunts was ethical opposition to the practice. The question was whether or not this fell within the terms of their powers under the legislation, or whether morality was an irrelevant factor.

SIR THOMAS BINGHAM MR

The parties to this appeal are, on one side, the Somerset County Council and, on the other, representatives of the Quantock Staghounds ("the hunt"). The issue which divides them is whether the county council acted lawfully when it resolved, on 4 August 1993, that:

"This council, as landowners, with immediate effect, resolves to ban the hunting of deer with hounds on the county council owned land at Over Stowey Customs Common."

The hunt say that the resolution was unlawful, because based on considerations which members of the county council were not permitted to take into account. Laws J. agreed with them, and accordingly quashed the county council's decision. The county council say that the decision was lawful and that the judge erred in holding otherwise. That is the issue now before us.

...

In 1921 the county council acquired land known as the Quantock Lodge Estate. Most of this land was thereafter let by the county council on a long lease to the Forestry Commission. Under this lease the commission enjoyed the right to permit or prohibit the hunting of deer, and it has permitted this land to be used for that purpose. Some of the land was farmland, let to tenant farmers: sporting rights over this land were reserved to the county council, which has in practice left the decision whether to permit hunting on their land to the tenant farmers, who have chosen to do so. Part of the land acquired by the county council was Over Stowey Customs Common ("the common"), the land which is (alone) the subject of these proceedings. The common is a long, thin strip of land, about 148 acres in area, which almost bisects the territory over which red deer have for many years been hunted by staghounds. It forms a very small proportion of this territory, but the evidence suggests that the common is so placed as seriously to impede the conduct of the hunt if use of this land is forbidden. The common is part of a larger area designated by the Countryside Commission as an area of outstanding natural beauty under 4 section 87 of the National Parks and Access to the Countryside Act 1949.

...

On 2 April 1986 the planning and transportation committee considered whether deer hunting on the common should be banned. Papers before the committee rehearsed arguments for and against a ban. The committee resolved that it would not at that stage exercise its right to ban hunting on the common, but would await the outcome of a deer survey and agreement of a common land management plan. The management plan was prepared. In 1992 and 1993 a study and a working party report were commissioned by the National Trust, and these prompted a report to the Quantock Hills joint liaison group (a local body on which local authorities and the Countryside Commission were represented). This report was directed to the issue whether hunting should continue to be permitted on the common. The group concluded by a majority that it should. This report was also before the environment committee of the county council on 7 July 1993 when the committee resolved to recommend the county council to continue to permit hunting.

When the county council met on 4 August 1993 this recommendation was before it. But the leader of the council moved, as an amendment, the motion quoted at the outset of this judgment, which was carried by a majority of 26 to 22. This decision followed a debate lasting some 1 hours, said to have been of a very high quality. Although we have only an impressionistic note of the debate, the drift of the argument is clear. Some speakers urged, at times using strong and emotive language, that hunting deer with hounds involved an unacceptable degree of cruelty, which they and others found offensive and which they felt the county council should not permit on its land. Others argued that hunting was a more humane way of controlling the size of the herd than any other, and that it was only the existence of the hunt which preserved the deer from piecemeal and often cruel destruction by local farmers. Reference was made to alternative means of culling deer, and dispatching accidental casualties, if hunting were not permitted. It is common ground on this appeal (and the judge held) that the majority who supported the ban were moved to do so by their belief that hunting involved unacceptable and unnecessary cruelty to the red deer who were the victims of the chase. I shall hereafter refer to this, for convenience, as "the cruelty argument."

It appears from the note that in his opening remarks the leader of the county council referred to its clear right to control its own land. His motion made reference to the county council "as landowners." After the meeting of the county council, in answer to a complaint by the Quantock deer management and conservation group that it had not been consulted, the council replied:

"it is for every landholder to decide (within the general framework of the law) what activities he or she wishes to allow on his [or her] land. In this case the county council took the view that it did not wish to allow deer hunting on this piece of land."

The judge was at pains to emphasise [1995] 1 All E.R. 513, 515–516 what these proceedings are not about. This is so important that I must repeat it.

The point is often made that unelected unrepresentative judges have no business to be deciding questions of potentially far-reaching social concern which are more properly the preserve of elected representatives at national or local level. In some cases the making of such decisions may be inescapable, but in general the point is well made. In the present case it certainly is. The court has no role whatever as an arbiter between those who condemn hunting as barbaric and cruel and those who support it as a traditional country sport more humane in its treatment of deer or foxes (as the case may be) than other methods of destruction such as shooting, snaring, poisoning or trapping. This is of course a question on which most people hold views one way or the other. But our personal views are wholly irrelevant to the drier and more technical question which the court is obliged to answer. That is whether the county council acted lawfully in making the decision it did on the grounds it did. In other words, were members entitled in reaching their decision to give effect to their acceptance of the cruelty argument?

Alert

In seeking to answer that question it is, as the judge very clearly explained, at pp. 523–525, critical to distinguish between the legal position of the private landowner and that of a land-owning local authority. To the famous question asked by the owner of the vineyard ("Is it not lawful for me to do what I will with mine own?" St. Matthew, chapter 20, verse 15) the modern answer would be clear: "Yes, subject to such regulatory and other constraints as the law imposes." But if the same question were posed by a local authority the answer would be different. It would be: "No, it is not lawful for you to do anything save what the law expressly or impliedly authorises. You enjoy no unfettered discretions. There are legal limits to every power you have." As Laws J. put it, at p. 524, the rule for local authorities is that any action to be taken must be justified by positive law.

1043 The positive law in issue in this case is agreed by the parties to be section 120(1)(b) of the Local Government Act 1972. That provides:

"(1) For the purposes of ...

(b) the benefit, improvement or development of their area, a principal council may acquire by agreement any land, whether situated inside or outside their area."

At first sight this section has little to do with the present case, since we are not dealing with the acquisition of land but with the management or use of land which the county council acquired over 70 years ago. But the county council is a principal council within the statutory definition; we have been referred to no statutory provision or rule of law more closely in point; any other provision, unless more specific, would be bound to require powers to be exercised for the public good; and it seems perhaps reasonable to accept that the purposes for which land may be acquired are or may often be those to which the land should be applied after acquisition. I would therefore agree with Laws J. [1995] 1 All E.R. 513, 525, adapting his language a little, that the primary question in this case is whether the councillors' acceptance of the cruelty argument is capable of justifying the ban as a measure which conduces to "the benefit, improvement or development of their area" within section 120(1)(b) of the Act.

"Did they reach a decision on grounds which transgressed the fetter or limit which Parliament had imposed upon them, so that there was no positive legal justification for what they did?" See p. 525.

It is noteworthy that section 120(1) does not provide that principal councils may acquire land for the purposes of the benefit, improvement or development of that land. The reference is to the benefit, improvement or development of their area. That indicates that the draftsman was concerned not merely with improved husbandry of particular land but with wider questions of public benefit. The power to acquire land outside the council's area reflects the same intention. So a principal council would, it would seem, be authorised, in the absence of more specific provisions, to acquire land outside its area to be used as an adventure training or fieldcraft centre, or perhaps as a home for the elderly, if to do so would benefit its area.

...

Laws J. held the county council's resolution to be an unlawful exercise of power for reasons which he succinctly summarised [1995] 1 All E.R. 513, 529–530:

"What then is the true scope of the words in section 120(1)(b) 'the benefit, improvement or development of their area?' In my judgment, this language is not wide enough to permit the council to take a decision about activities carried out on its land which is based upon freestanding moral perceptions as opposed to an objective judgment about what will conduce to the better management of the estate. Section 120(1)(b) is not within the class of provisions which require the decision-maker to have regard to moral considerations as such. A prohibition on hunting, which manifestly interferes with the lawful freedom of those who take part in the sport, could only be justified under the subsection if the council reasonably concluded that the prohibition was objectively necessary as the best means of managing the deer herd, or was otherwise required, on objective grounds, for the preservation or enhancement of the amenity of their area. The view that hunting is morally repulsive, however pressing its merits, has nothing whatever to do with such questions. Section 120(1)(b) confers no entitlement on a local authority to impose its opinions about the morals of hunting on the neighbourhood. In the present state of the law those opinions, however sincerely felt, have their proper place only in the private conscience of those who entertain them. The council has been given no authority by Parliament to translate such views into public action; there is nothing in the section to indicate that it has."

...

Mr. Supperstone, for the county council, submitted that the judge had construed section 120(1)(b) too narrowly. It was, he reminded us, common ground that "the benefit ... of their area" included wildlife benefit: see [1995] 1 All E.R. 513, 523. Those who accepted the cruelty argument were, he said, entitled to give effect to their view that the use of the county council's land for hunting was not for the benefit of the area, and the judge was wrong to treat that expression as applying to the management of the herd alone. He argued that on an issue of this kind county councillors were bound, and if not bound entitled, to have regard to the ethical arguments for and against hunting and the judge had been wrong to treat such considerations as irrelevant. Where power had been entrusted to a popular assembly, the court should be slow to interfere with the exercise of that power.

For the hunt, Mr. Beloff supported the judge's reasoning. The issue was a short point of statutory construction and the judge had construed the section correctly. Acceptance of the cruelty argument had nothing to do with the benefit of the area. The resolution was an impermissible attempt by those who accepted the cruelty argument to outlaw an activity very recently regulated by Parliament in the Deer Act 1991. In resolving as it did the county council acted as if it enjoyed the free discretion of a private landowner and without regard to the constraints which bound a local authority.

I accept the county council's basic contention that the judge put too narrow a construction on the words "the benefit ... of their area." The draftsman would have been pressed to find broader or less specific language. I would not accept the judge's view that the cruelty argument, or the contrary argument that hunting is a less cruel means of controlling the herd than available alternatives (also, in the judge's terms, a moral argument), is necessarily irrelevant to consideration of what is for the benefit of the area. That is in my opinion to place an unwarranted restriction on the broad language the draftsman has used.

There is, however, as I think, a categorical difference between saying "I strongly disapprove of X" and saying "It is for the benefit of the area that X should be prohibited." The first is the expression of a purely personal opinion which may (but need not) take account of any wider, countervailing argument. There are, for example, those so deeply opposed to the capital penalty on moral grounds that no counter-argument (however cogent) could shake their conviction. The second statement is also the expression of a personal opinion, but involves a judgment on wider, community-based grounds of what is for the benefit of the area. Both statements may of course lead to the same conclusion, but they need not. There is nothing illogical in saying "I strongly disapprove of X, but I am not persuaded that it is for the benefit of the area that X should be prohibited." Thus a person might be deeply opposed to the capital penalty but conclude that it would not be for the benefit of the community to prohibit it so long as its availability appeared to deter the commission of murder.

The question therefore arises whether, in resolving as it did on 4 August 1993, the county council exercised its power to further the object prescribed by the statute, the benefit of the county council area. I conclude that it did not, for these reasons.

(1) At no point, before or during the debate, was the attention of the council drawn to what is now agreed to be the governing statutory provision. The minds of councillors were never drawn to the question they should have been addressing. As the judge observed [1995] 1 All E.R. 513, 523F: "It follows that if the ban was lawful, it was so more by good luck than judgment."

(2) A paper circulated to county councillors with the agenda concluded:

"In the final analysis people go hunting primarily because they find it a sport they enjoy. The county council must come to a decision, as the National Trust report said, 'largely on the grounds of ethics, animal welfare and social considerations ...' which are matters for members to decide."

I accept that animal welfare and social considerations were relevant matters to take into account, and I have accepted that ethical considerations could be. But this statement does not express or exhaust the statutory test, and could well be read as an invitation to councillors to give free rein to their personal views.

(3) The reference in the resolution to the county council "as landowners," and the statement in the letter (quoted ante, p. 1042C–D), written after the resolution, that it was for every landowner to decide what activities he wished to allow on his land, appear to equiparate the positions of private and local authority landowners. This in my view reflected a failure to appreciate the overriding statutory constraint.

(4) The lack of reference to the governing statutory test was not in my view a purely formal omission, for if councillors had been referred to it they would have had to attempt to define what benefit a ban would confer on the area and conversely what detriment the absence of a ban would cause. It may be that they could have done so, but as it was they did not need to try. The note certainly suggests that the debate ranged widely, and reference was made to "economic grounds" and "social damage" as well as to the cruelty argument and the contrary moral argument. But the note also suggests that expressions of purely personal opinion loomed large: "rituals unwholesome instincts," "systematically torture," "barbaric and amusement," "uniquely abhorrent," "pleasure torturing animals." In the absence of legal guidance, it was not, I think, appreciated that personal views, however strongly held, had to be related to the benefit of the area.

...

For the reason given, ...I would dismiss this appeal.

3 Delegation

It is a fundamental principle of administrative law that the person seized with discretion should be the person to exercise it. This was confirmed in the following case.

Lavender v Minister of Housing and Local Government [1970] 1 WLR 1231

Panel: Willis J

Facts: the Minister of Housing and Local Government refused Lavender's application for planning permission to develop land for use as a quarry, after hearing objections from the Minister of Agriculture. The decision was challenged on the grounds that the Minister of Housing and Local Government had effectively delegated the decision to the Minister of Agriculture.

MR JUSTICE WILLIS

...

The Minister gave his decision on April 14, 1969. The letter set out verbatim the inspector's conclusions and proceeded in paragraph 3 as follows:

"3. The Minister has considered his inspector's conclusions and appreciates his reason for not making a recommendation. He notes that the inspector would have recommended that the appeal should be allowed if the 'agricultural reservations' were not to be regarded as inviolable and he appreciates that the proposals for restoring the land after working have been very carefully thought out. Nevertheless, in weighing the need for sand and gravel against the preservation of high quality agricultural land he has had to take note of the fact that the appeal site lies within the 'agricultural reservations' which the Waters Committee recommended should be reserved indefinitely for agriculture.

"It is the Minister's present policy that land in the reservations should not be released for mineral working unless the Minister of Agriculture is not opposed to working. In the present case the agricultural objection has not been waived and the Minister has, therefore, decided not to grant planning permission for the working of the appeal site," and he dismissed the appeal. It is those last two sentences in the decision letter which lie at the heart of the matter in issue; and it is submitted, first of all, by Mr. Frank, for the applicants, that they show, in this case that the Minister had so fettered his own discretion to decide the appeal by the policy which he had adopted that the decisive matter was not the exercise of his own discretion upon a consideration of the report and other material considerations, but the sustained objection of the Minister of Agriculture. In effect he says that the decision was not that of the Minister of Housing and Local Government, the authority entrusted with the duty to decide, but of the Minister of Agriculture, who had no status save perhaps in a consultative capacity and certainly no status to make the effective decision.

...

In general support of his main submission, Mr. Frank has referred me to Professor de Smith's well known work *Judicial Review of Administrative Action,* 2nd ed. (1968), pp. 292–297, and to certain of the cases cited therein. He really puts his argument in two ways — (1) that the Minister has fettered his discretion by a self created rule of policy, and (2) that the Minister, who has a duty to exercise his own discretion in determining an appeal, has in this case delegated that duty to the Minister of Agriculture, who has no such duty and is, statutorily, a stranger to any decision.

...

The duties of the Minister and their extent in relation to a matter such as the appeal in the present case comprising in a hybrid form both administrative and quasi-judicial functions were enunciated by Lord Greene M.R. in a well known passage in *B. Johnson & Co. (Builders) v. Minister of Health* [1947] 2 All E.R. 395, 397:

"The duty placed on the Minister with regard to objections is to consider them before confirming the order. He is also to consider the report of the person who held the inquiry. Having done that, his functions are laid down by the last words of the paragraph, viz., 'and may then confirm the order either with or without modification.' Those words are important, because they make it clear that it is to the Minister that Parliament has committed the decision whether he will or will not confirm the order after he has done all that the statute requires him to do. There is nothing in that paragraph, or anywhere else in the Act, which imposes on the Minister any obligation with regard to the objections, save the obligation to consider them. He is not bound to base his decision on any conclusion that he comes to with regard to the objections, and that must be so when one gives a moment's thought to the situation. The decision whether to confirm or not must be made in relation to questions of policy, and the Minister, in deciding whether to confirm or not, will, like every Minister entrusted with administrative duties, weigh up the considerations which are to affect his mind, the preponderating factor in many, if not all, cases being that of public policy, having regard to all the facts of the case."

...

Can there, nevertheless, come a point ... when the court can interfere with a Ministerial decision which, ex facie, proceeds upon a consideration of the inspector's report and concludes by applying Ministerial policy?

Mr. Frank submits that such a point can be reached and has been reached in this case. It is reached, he says, adopting the words of Professor de Smith in his book, *Judicial Review of Administrative Action,* at p. 294, if a tribunal, entrusted with a discretion as the Minister was in the present case, disables itself from exercising that discretion in a particular case by the prior adoption of a general policy. In *Rex v. Port of London Authority, Ex parte Kynock Ltd.* [1919] 1 K.B. 176, Bankes L.J. said, at p. 184:

"In the present case there is another matter to be borne in mind. There are on the one hand cases where a tribunal in the honest exercise of its discretion has adopted a policy, and, without refusing to hear an applicant, intimates to him what its policy is, that, after hearing him, it will in accordance with its policy decide against him, unless there is something exceptional in his case ... On the other hand there are cases where a tribunal has passed a rule, or come to a determination not to hear an application of a particular character by whomsoever made."

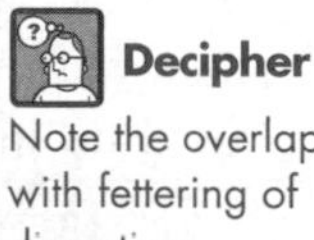

Decipher

Note the overlap with fettering of discretion.

In another licensing case, *Reg. v. Flintshire County Council Licensing (Stage Plays) Committee, Ex parte Barrett* [1957] 1 Q.B. 350, where the decision was given in the interests of consistency, Jenkins L.J. said, at pp. 367, 368:

"Then they went on ... to conclude ... that the Queen's Theatre licence must follow the fate of the Pavilion Theatre licence, because it was essential that the same rule should be applied in all cases or, in other words, that the committee should be consistent. I cannot think that that method fulfils the requirement that the matter should be heard and determined according to law ... It seems to me that it wrongly pursues consistency at the expense of the merit of individual cases."

I have referred to those two cases since they were relied on by Mr. Frank, but I am inclined to agree with Mr. Slynn that the considerations applicable to licensing cases are not of much assistance when considering the scope of a Minister's duties within a statutory framework.

The nearest case to the present which was referred to in argument on this aspect of the case is *Myton Ltd. v. Minister of Housing and Local Government* (1963) 61 L.G.R.

556. It concerned an application to develop land in an area of Leeds affected by what was known as a "sketch plan" for a green belt, in other words tentative proposals made ex parte without having reached the stage of being part of the development plan. The argument, which did not in the result succeed, was that there was a duty on the Minister to address his mind to the question whether the appeal site was required for the green belt and, if the circumstances justified it, to allow development, and that he had failed in this duty. Widgery J. said, at pp. 561, 562:

"I accept Mr. Bridge's contention that there is such a duty on the Minister. I think that it would be lamentable if in circumstances where a sketch plan has been prepared and where there is in effect a tentative proposal for a green belt, all applications for development within that green belt area should be automatically and peremptorily refused merely because provision of a green belt was in contemplation... The local planning authority's decision in this case is not for review before me, but I am bound to observe that the very speed with which they disposed of the application at least raises some suspicion that they dealt with the matter as being already prejudged by the fact that the land was within the sketch plan green belt."

It is, of course, clear that if the Minister has prejudged any genuine consideration of the matter before him, or has failed to give genuine consideration to, inter alia, the inspector's report, he has failed to carry out his statutory duties properly. *Franklin v. Minister of Town and Country Planning* [1948] A.C. 87.

In the present case, Mr. Frank does not shrink from submitting that the decision letter shows that no genuine consideration was given to the question whether planning permission could, in the circumstances, be granted. I have carefully considered the authorities cited by counsel, but I have not found any clear guide to what my decision should be in this case. I have said enough to make it clear that I recognise that in the field of policy, and in relation to ministerial decisions coloured or dictated by policy, the courts will interfere only within a strictly circumscribed field: see per Lord Greene M.R. in *Associated Provincial Picture Houses Ltd. v. Wednesbury Corporation* [1948] 1 K.B. 223, 228. It is also clear, and is conceded by Mr. Slynn, that where a Minister is entrusted by Parliament with the decision of any particular case he must keep that actual decision in the last resort in his own hands: see *Rex v. Minister of Transport, Ex parte Grey Coaches*, "The Times," March 19, 1933. I return, therefore, to the words used by the Minister. It seems to me that he has said in language which admits of no doubt that his decision to refuse permission was solely in pursuance of a policy not to permit minerals in the Waters agricultural reserve to be worked unless the Minister of Agriculture was not opposed to their working. Mr. Slynn submits that, read as a whole, the decision letter should be taken as implying some such words as:

"I have gone through the exercise of taking all material considerations into account, but you have not persuaded me that this is such an exceptional case as would justify me in relaxing my policy; therefore I stick to it and apply it."

If that were the right construction perhaps Mr. Slynn would be justified in saying that there was no error in law. But in my judgment the language used is not open to any such implication. There is no indication that this might be an exceptional case such as would or could induce the Minister to change his policy. It is common ground that the Minister must be open to persuasion that the land should not remain in the Waters reservation. How can his mind be open to persuasion, how can an applicant establish an "exceptional case" in the face of an inflexible attitude by the Minister of Agriculture? That attitude was well known before the inquiry, it was maintained during the inquiry, and presumably thereafter. The inquiry was no doubt, in a sense, into the Minister of Agriculture's objection, since, apart from that objection, it might well have been that no inquiry would have been necessary, but I do not think that the Minister after the inquiry can be said in any real sense to have given genuine consideration to whether on planning (including agricultural) grounds this land could be worked. It seems to me that by adopting and applying his stated policy he has in effect inhibited himself from exercising a proper discretion (which would of course be guided by policy considerations) in any case where the Minister of Agriculture has made and maintained an objection to mineral working in an agricultural reservation. Everything else might point to the desirability of granting permission, but by applying and acting on his stated policy I think the Minister has fettered himself in such a way that in this case it was not he who made the decision for which Parliament made him responsible. It was the decision of the Minister of Agriculture not to waive his objection which was decisive in this case, and while that might properly prove to be the decisive factor for the Minister when taking into account all material considerations, it seems to me quite wrong for a policy to be applied which in reality eliminates all the material considerations save only the consideration, when that is the case, that the Minister of Agriculture objects. That means, as I think, that the Minister has by his stated policy delegated to the Minister of Agriculture the effective decision on any appeal within the agricultural reservations where the latter objects to the working. I am quite unable to accept that in these circumstances, the public inquiry could be justified, as Mr. Slynn submits, as giving the Minister of Agriculture the opportunity to hear the case and, if he thought right, to waive his objection. Unless there was a real chance that he would do so — and it seems to me clear beyond question that there was not — the inquiry was quite futile in my view, certainly as a means of providing the Minister with the material on which he could have exercised, and should have exercised, a genuine, unfettered discretion.

...

On the main ground on which this case has been argued, ... I am satisfied that the applicants should succeed. I think the Minister failed to exercise a proper or indeed any discretion by reason of the fetter which he imposed upon its exercise in acting solely in accordance with his stated policy; and further, that upon the true construction of the Minister's letter the decision to dismiss the appeal, while purporting to be that of the Minister, was in fact, and improperly, that of the Minister of Agriculture, Fisheries and Food.

Alert

The ruling in *Lavender* prohibits delegation to another agency. However, executive decision makers often find that the number of decisions they have to make outstrips their capacity to make them: it would be physically impossible (and scarcely good use of their time) for the Home Secretary or one of her deputy ministers to read everyone's passport application.

For this reason an important exception to the "no delegation" rule can be found in the case of *Carltona Ltd v Commissioners of Works* [1943] 2 All ER 560.

***Carltona v Commissioners of Works* [1943] 2 All ER 560**

Panel: Lord Greene MR, Goddard and Du Parcq LJJ

Facts: Carltona Ltd had its factory premises requisitioned as part of the war effort. The company applied for a declaration, *inter alia*, that the Commissioners had never brought their minds to bear on the question of the requisition and therefore the order for requisition was flawed. The Divisional Court rejected its application and Carltona Ltd appealed.

LORD GREENE MR

...[T]he next point which was taken was that the requisition itself was bad quite apart from the notice because the persons constituting the requisitioning authority never brought their minds to bear on the question. That argument is based, as it seems to me—and I say this without the slightest disrespect to the argument—upon a complete misapprehension as to the facts. It appears to have been thought at the time of the trial that the proper persons to take into consideration the question of exercising the power under this regulation were the Commissioners of Works themselves, a body which, as I have said, never meets. If that idea ever was put forward, and I am not quite sure whether it was or not, a moment's consideration will show that the argument cannot be supported for the very simple reasons, first, that the person who has the statutory power to act for the Commissioners of Works is the First Commissioner, and, secondly, that the person acting for the First Commissioner in this matter was the assistant secretary. There is no point in the argument at all that the Commissioners of Works as such did not take the matter into consideration, nor is there, in my opinion, any substance in the argument that, at any rate, the First Commissioner did not personally direct his mind to the matter.

In the administration of government in this country the functions which are given to ministers (and constitutionally properly given to ministers because they are constitutionally responsible) are functions so multifarious that no minister could ever personally attend to them. To take the example of the present case no doubt there have been thousands of requisitions in this country by individual ministers. It cannot be supposed that this regulation meant that, in each case, the minister in person should direct his mind to the matter. The duties imposed upon ministers and the powers given to ministers are normally exercised under the authority of the ministers by responsible officials of the department. Public business could not be carried on if that were not the case. Constitutionally, the decision of such an official is, of course, the decision of the minister. The minister is responsible. It is he who must answer before Parliament for anything that his officials have done under his authority, and, if for an important matter he selected an official of such junior standing that he could not be expected competently to perform the work, the minister would have to answer for that in Parliament. The whole system of departmental organisation and administration is based on the view that ministers, being responsible to Parliament, will see that important duties are committed to experienced officials. If they do not do that, Parliament is the place where complaint must be made against them.

Carltona appears to establish that delegation within a department is acceptable (as compared to between departments as in *Lavender*). In the case of *R v Secretary of State for the Home Department ex parte Doody* [1993] AC 157, which dealt with whether the Secretary of State for the Home Department could delegate the function of setting a tariff period for life sentence prisoners, the Court of Appeal said: 'there is no express or implied requirement in the Criminal Justice Act 1967 that a decision fixing the tariff period, or for that matter a decision to release a prisoner on licence, must be taken by the Secretary of State personally' (per Staughton LJ). This seems to suggest that, unless delegation is excluded specifically or by necessary implication, no power is non-delegable within a department. This approach was adopted on appeal to the House of Lords ([1994] 1 AC 531) by Lord Griffiths (para 565, 566), with whom their other Lordships simply agreed. However, in this case the power was delegated to a junior minister, and it was pointed out that a junior minister is still a Minister of the Crown responsible to Parliament. Whether the power could have been exercised by an official at civil service level was not dealt with.

Such cases prompted Freedland to comment that 'it is preferable to see the [Parliamentary] draftsmen as employing a notation or code whereby the entrusting of a discretion to a government department is expressed by conferring that discretion upon the minister concerned' (see [1996] PL 19 at p 22). In this way, any power conferred on the minister would be at all times exercisable by his department, but would maintain the distinction between departments identified in *Lavender*.

4 Improper Purpose

The classic exposition of improper purpose was given in the case of *Padfield v Minister of Agriculture, Fisheries and Food* [1968] AC 997.

Padfield v Minister of Agriculture, Fisheries and Food [1968] AC 997

Panel: Lord Reid, Lord Morris of Borth-y-Gest, Lord Hodson, Lord Pearce and Lord Upjohn

Facts: The Minister was given discretion to set up a committee of investigation on a complaint regarding the milk marketing scheme. The scheme created nine regions and milk producers in those regions had to sell their milk to the Milk Marketing Board, which had fixed the price for milk several years before, by reference to transport costs. The south-eastern region wished to amend the scheme, but could not get a majority on the Board so made a complaint to the Minister. The Minister refused to refer the matter to a committee of investigation, and an application for mandamus (the old name for a mandatory order) was made to the court. The House of Lords concluded that the Minister had acted for an improper purpose.

LORD REID

The question at issue in this appeal is the nature and extent of the Minister's duty under section 19 (3) (b) of the Act of 1958 in deciding whether to refer to the committee of investigation a complaint as to the operation of any scheme made by persons adversely affected by the scheme. The respondent contends that his only duty is to consider a complaint fairly and that he is given an unfettered discretion with regard to every complaint either to refer it or not to refer it to the committee as he may think fit. The appellants contend that it is his duty to refer every genuine and substantial complaint, or alternatively that his discretion is not unfettered and that in this case he failed to exercise his discretion according to law because his refusal was caused or influenced by his having misdirected himself in law or by his having taken into account extraneous or irrelevant considerations.

In my view, the appellants' first contention goes too far. There are a number of reasons which would justify the Minister in refusing to refer a complaint. For example, he might consider it more suitable for arbitration, or he might consider that in an earlier case the committee of investigation had already rejected a substantially similar complaint, or he might think the complaint to be frivolous or vexatious. So he must have at least some measure of discretion. But is it unfettered?

It is implicit in the argument for the Minister that there are only two possible interpretations of this provision either he must refer every complaint or he has an unfettered discretion to refuse to refer in any case. I do not think that is right. Parliament must have conferred the discretion with the intention that it should be used to promote the policy and objects of the Act, the policy and objects of the Act must be determined by construing the Act as a whole and construction is always a matter of law for the court. In a matter of this kind it is not possible to draw a hard and fast line, but if the Minister, by reason of his having misconstrued the Act or for any other reason, so uses his discretion as to thwart or run counter to the policy and objects of the Act, then our law would be very defective if persons aggrieved were not entitled to the protection of the court. So it is necessary first to construe the Act.

Alert

When these provisions were first enacted in 1931 it was unusual for Parliament to compel people to sell their commodities in a way to which they objected and it was easily foreseeable that any such scheme would cause loss to some producers. Moreover, if the operation of the scheme was put in the hands of the majority of the producers, it was obvious that they might use their power to the detriment of consumers, distributors or a minority of the producers. So it is not surprising that Parliament enacted safeguards.

...

The effect of these sections is that if, but only if, the Minister and the committee of investigation concur in the view that something is being done contrary to the public interest the Minister can step in. ...

I must now examine the Minister's reasons for refusing to refer the appellants' complaint to the committee. ...

The first reason which the Minister gave in his letter of March 23, 1965, was that this complaint was unsuitable for investigation because it raised wide issues. Here it appears to me that the Minister has clearly misdirected himself. Section 19 (6) contemplates the raising of issues so wide that it may be necessary for the Minister to amend a scheme or even to revoke it. Narrower issues may be suitable for arbitration but section 19 affords the only method of investigating wide issues. In my view it is plainly the intention of the Act that even the widest issues should be investigated if the complaint is genuine and substantial, as this complaint certainly is.

Then it is said that this issue should be "resolved through the arrangements available to producers and the board within the framework of the scheme itself." This re-states in a condensed form the reasons given in paragraph 4 of the letter of May 1, 1964, where it is said "the Minister owes no duty to producers in any particular region," and reference is made to the "status of the Milk Marketing Scheme as an instrument for the self-government of the industry," and to the Minister "assuming an inappropriate degree of responsibility." But, as I have already pointed out, the Act imposes on the Minister a responsibility whenever there is a relevant and substantial complaint that the board are acting in a manner inconsistent with the public interest, and that has been relevantly alleged in this case. I can find nothing in the Act to limit this responsibility or to justify the statement that the Minister owes no duty to producers in a particular region. The Minister is, I think, correct in saying that the board is an instrument for the self-government of the industry. So long as it does not act contrary to the public interest the Minister cannot interfere. But if it does act contrary to what both the committee of investigation and the Minister hold to be the public interest the Minister has a duty to act. And if a complaint relevantly alleges that the board has so acted, as this complaint does, then it appears to me that the Act does impose a duty on the Minister to have it investigated. If he does not do that he is rendering nugatory a safeguard provided by the Act and depriving complainers of a remedy which I am satisfied that Parliament intended them to have.

...

I have found no authority to support the unreasonable proposition that it [the Minister's discretion] must be all or nothing - either no discretion at all or an unfettered discretion. Here the words "if the Minister in any case so directs" are sufficient to show that he has some discretion but they give no guide as to its nature or extent. That must be inferred from a construction of the Act read as a whole, and for the reasons I have given I would infer that the discretion is not unlimited, and that it has been used by the Minister in a manner which is not in accord with the intention of the statute which conferred it.

In this case the purpose of the Act was to enable the Minister to correct faults in the system. The Minister's reasons for rejection, namely that the complainer should use the democratic mechanism of the Board, was clearly erroneous as his power had been conferred to enable him to correct errors brought about by that process. The argument that a decision upholding the complaint would force him to act was clearly flawed (see Lord Reid). As a result of this case a committee was set up and upheld the complaint, but the Minister then disregarded its recommendations.

The view that the decision maker must follow the purpose of the Act can also be seen in *Fewings*. In that case Sir Thomas Bingham MR said that, while the moral considerations could be relevant to the council's analysis, there was 'a categorical difference between saying 'I strongly disapprove of X' and saying 'It is for the benefit of the area that X be prohibited'. Further support was given to the principle that the purpose of an Act must be followed was given in *Congreve v Home Office* [1976] QB 629 where Lord Denning MR said: 'the Minister relies on the intention of Parliament. But it was not the policy of Parliament that he was seeking to enforce. It was his own policy. And he did it in a way which was unfair and unjust.'

Further Reading

Freedland, "The rule against delegation and the *Carltona* doctrine in an agency context" [1996] *PL* 19

Jones, Timothy H "Mistake of Fact in Administrative Law" [1990] *PL* 507

Kent, Michael QC, "Widening the Scope of Review for Error of Fact" [1999] *JR* 239

15

Unreasonableness

Topic List

1 *Wednesbury* Unreasonableness
2 Reformulation: Irrationality
3 The Rise of Proportionality

Alex Lawson and Christopher Costigan

1 *Wednesbury* Unreasonableness

The seminal case on unreasonableness is *Associated Picture Houses Ltd v Wednesbury Corporation* [1948] 1 KB 223 and any discussion of the area should start there.

Associated Provincial Picture Houses Ltd v Wednesbury Corporation [1948] 1 KB 223

Panel: Lord Greene MR, Somervell LJ and Singleton J

Facts: Under the Sunday Entertainments Act 1932 s 1(1) local authorities were given power to grant licences for film performances under the Cinematograph Act 1909 and to allow a licensed place to be open and used on Sundays, "subject to such conditions as the authority think fit to impose." The Picture House was granted a licence to open on Sundays, but the local authority granted this subject to the condition that 'no children under the age of fifteen years shall be admitted to any entertainment whether accompanied by an adult or not'. The Picture House brought an action for judicial review on the basis that the decision of the local authority was unreasonable.

LORD GREENE MR

...[W]e have heard in this case a great deal about the meaning of the word "unreasonable."

It is true the discretion must be exercised reasonably. Now what does that mean? Lawyers familiar with the phraseology commonly used in relation to exercise of statutory discretions often use the word "unreasonable" in a rather comprehensive sense. It has frequently been used and is frequently used as a general description of the things that must not be done. For instance, a person entrusted with a discretion must, so to speak, direct himself properly in law. He must call his own attention to the matters which he is bound to consider. He must exclude from his consideration matters which are irrelevant to what he has to consider. If he does not obey those rules, he may truly be said, and often is said, to be acting "unreasonably." Similarly, there may be something so absurd that no sensible person could ever dream that it lay within the powers of the authority. Warrington L.J. in *Short v. Poole Corporation* gave the example of the red-haired teacher, dismissed because she had red hair. That is unreasonable in one sense. In another sense it is taking into consideration extraneous matters. It is so unreasonable that it might almost be described as being done in bad faith; and, in fact, all these things run into one another.

In the present case, it is said by Mr. Gallop that the authority acted unreasonably in imposing this condition. It appears to me quite clear that the matter dealt with by this condition was a matter which a reasonable authority would be justified in considering when they were making up their mind what condition should be attached to the grant of this licence. Nobody, at this time of day, could say that the well-being and the physical and moral health of children is not a matter which a local authority, in exercising their powers, can properly have in mind when those questions are germane to what they have to consider. Here Mr. Gallop did not, I think, suggest that the council

> were directing their mind to a purely extraneous and irrelevant matter, but he based his argument on the word "unreasonable," which he treated as an independent ground for attacking the decision of the authority; but once it is conceded, as it must be conceded in this case, that the particular subject-matter dealt with by this condition was one which it was competent for the authority to consider, there, in my opinion, is an end of the case. Once that is granted, Mr. Gallop is bound to say that the decision of the authority is wrong because it is unreasonable, and in saying that he is really saying that the ultimate arbiter of what is and is not reasonable is the court and not the local authority. It is just there, it seems to me, that the argument breaks down. It is clear that the local authority are entrusted by Parliament with the decision on a matter which the knowledge and experience of that authority can best be trusted to deal with. The subject-matter with which the condition deals is one relevant for its consideration. They have considered it and come to a decision upon it. It is true to say that, **if a decision on a competent matter is so unreasonable that no reasonable authority could ever have come to it, then the courts can interfere**. That, I think, is quite right; but to prove a case of that kind would require something overwhelming, and, in this case, the facts do not come anywhere near anything of that kind. I think Mr. Gallop in the end agreed that his proposition that the decision of the local authority can be upset if it is proved to be unreasonable, really meant that it must be proved to be unreasonable in the sense that the court considers it to be a decision that no reasonable body could have come to. It is not what the court considers unreasonable, a different thing altogether. If it is what the court considers unreasonable, the court may very well have different views to that of a local authority on matters of high public policy of this kind. Some courts might think that no children ought to be admitted on Sundays at all, some courts might think the reverse, and all over the country I have no doubt on a thing of that sort honest and sincere people hold different views. The effect of the legislation is not to set up the court as an arbiter of the correctness of one view over another. It is the local authority that are set in that position and, provided they act, as they have acted, within the four corners of their jurisdiction, this court, in my opinion, cannot interfere.

In giving the judgment of the court, Lord Greene MR, set out two propositions for the term 'unreasonable'. His first definition was that 'a person entrusted with a decision must, so to speak, direct himself properly in law. He must call his own attention to the matters which he is bound to consider. He must exclude from his consideration matters which are irrelevant to what he has to consider. If he does not obey these rules, he may truly be said, and often is said, to be acting 'unreasonably''. This first definition is very restricted, and not properly to be considered a separate head of challenge: Lord Greene MR is simply saying that, if the decision is tainted by illegality, it will be unreasonable.

However, Lord Greene MR's second definition can properly be said to be a separate head of challenge on an application for judicial review. Here, he said 'if a decision on a competent matter is so unreasonable that no reasonable authority could ever have come it, then the courts can interfere'. This formulation is what has properly become known as *Wednesbury* unreasonableness. For Lord Greene MR this represented a very high threshold for the challenging party to overcome, and he felt that for a decision maker to be acting unreasonably, this would require something 'overwhelming'.

2 Reformulation: Irrationality

However, while *Wednesbury* is the natural starting point, it is by no means the end. As with illegality, in the *GCHQ* case Lord Diplock also formulated his idea of the meaning of unreasonableness, rebranding it as 'irrationality'.

***Council of Civil Service Unions and Others v Minister for the Civil Service* [1985] AC 374**

Panel: Lord Fraser of Tullybelton, Lord Scarman, Lord Diplock, Lord Roskill and Lord Brightman

Facts: see Chapter X.

LORD DIPLOCK

By "irrationality" I mean what can by now be succinctly referred to as "*Wednesbury* unreasonableness" (*Associated Provincial Picture Houses Ltd. v. Wednesbury Corporation* [1948] 1 K.B. 223). It applies to a decision which is so outrageous in its defiance of logic or of accepted moral standards that no sensible person who had applied his mind to the question to be decided could have arrived at it. Whether a decision falls within this category is a question that judges by their training and experience should be well equipped to answer, or else there would be something badly wrong with our judicial system. To justify the court's exercise of this role, resort I think is today no longer needed to Viscount Radcliffe's ingenious explanation in *Edwards v. Bairstow* [1956] A.C. 14 of irrationality as a ground for a court's reversal of a decision by ascribing it to an inferred though unidentifiable mistake of law by the decision-maker. "Irrationality" by now can stand upon its own feet as an accepted ground on which a decision may be attacked by judicial review.

Whether there is any benefit in using the word 'irrational' is debatable. The eminent writers Wade and Forsyth certainly felt that unreasonableness was a better term, as they saw 'irrational' to mean devoid of reasons; whereas 'unreasonable' meant devoid of satisfactory reasons. And indeed in *R v Devonshire CC ex p G* [1989] AC 573, Lord Donaldson MR, said that he 'eschewe[d] the synonym of 'irrational', because, although it is attractive as being a shorter test than '*Wednesbury* unreasonable'... it is widely misunderstood by politicians, both local and national, and even more by their constituents, as casting doubt on the mental capacity of the decision-maker'. In fact, the term 'unreasonableness' has continued to be used by judges, and irrational can now be seen as just one way in which a decision may be deemed unreasonable in the *Wednesbury* sense.

3 The Rise of Proportionality

The concept of proportionality requires, in simple terms, that a sledgehammer is not used to crack a nut: that the measures adopted to achieve a goal do not go further than are necessary. The concept has long been used in continental Europe and, as a result of membership of the EEC (now EU) and the enactment of the Human Rights Act 1998, it is now used in domestic UK courts. A tension has developed between the English concept of *Wednesbury* unreasonableness and that of proportionality, and debate has arisen as to whether or not the latter doctrine (which is seen as being a stronger form of review) should now displace *Wednesbury*.

Regina (on the application of Daly) v Secretary of State for the Home Department [2001] UKHL 26, [2001] 2 AC 532

Panel: Lord Bingham of Cornhill, Lord Steyn, Lord Cooke of Thorndon, Lord Hutton and Lord Scott of Foscote

Facts: Daly was a prisoner. Prison policy dictated that his cell could be routinely searched without him being present. This was of particular concern for Daly as he had stored legal correspondence (between him and his lawyer) in his cell. Part of his claim clearly engaged Article 8 of the European Convention on Human Rights, but Daly also had a claim that the policy of blanket exclusion of prisoners during searches infringed more orthodox, common law principles.

LORD BINGHAM OF CORNHILL

1. My Lords, on 31 May 1995 the Home Secretary introduced a new policy ("the policy") governing the searching of cells occupied by convicted and remand prisoners in closed prisons in England and Wales. The policy was expressed in the Security Manual as an instruction to prison governors in these terms:

"17.69 Staff must accompany all searches of living accommodation in closed prisons with a strip search of the resident prisoner. 17.70 Staff must not allow any prisoner to be present during a search of living accommodation (although this does not apply to accommodation fabric checks). 17.71 Staff must inform the prisoner as soon as practicable whenever objects or containers are removed from living accommodation for searching, and will be missing from the accommodation on the prisoner's return. 17.72 Subject to paragraph 17.73, staff may normally read legal correspondence only if the Governor has reasonable cause to suspect that their contents endanger prison security, or the safety of others, or are otherwise of a criminal nature. In this case the prisoner involved shall be given the opportunity to be present and informed that their correspondence is to be read. 17.73 But during a cell search staff must examine legal correspondence thoroughly in the absence of the prisoner. Staff must examine the correspondence only so far as necessary to ensure that it is bona fide correspondence between the prisoner and a legal adviser and does not conceal anything else. 17.74 When entering cells at other times (eg when undertaking accommodation fabric checks) staff must take care not to read legal correspondence belonging to prisoners unless the Governor has decided that the reasonable cause test in 17.72 applies."

2. Mr Daly is a long-term prisoner. He challenges the lawfulness of the policy. He submits that section 47(1) of the Prison Act 1952, which empowers the Secretary of State to make rules for the regulation of prisons and for the discipline and control of prisoners, does not authorise the laying down and implementation of such a policy. But on this appeal to the House Mr Daly confines his challenge to a single aspect of the policy: the requirement that a prisoner may not be present when his legally privileged correspondence is examined by prison officers. He contends that a blanket policy of requiring the absence of prisoners when their legally privileged correspondence is examined infringes, to an unnecessary and impermissible extent, a basic right recognised both at common law and under the European Convention for the Protection of Human Rights and Fundamental Freedoms, and that the general terms of section 47 authorise no such infringement, either expressly or impliedly.

The origin of the policy

3. On 9 September 1994 six category A prisoners, classified as presenting an exceptional risk, escaped from the Special Security Unit at HMP Whitemoor. An inquiry led by Sir John Woodcock, formerly HM Chief Inspector of Constabulary, was at once set up. The report of the inquiry, presented to Parliament in December 1994 (Cm 2741), revealed extensive mismanagement and malpractice at Whitemoor. The escape had been possible only because prisoners had been able, undetected, to gather a mass of illicit property and equipment. This in turn had been possible because prisoners' cells and other areas had not been thoroughly searched at frequent but irregular intervals, partly because officers seeking to make such searches had been intimidated and obstructed by prisoners, partly because relations between officers and prisoners had in some instances become unacceptably familiar so that staff had been manipulated or "conditioned" into being less vigilant than they should have been in security matters.

4. In its report the inquiry team made a number of recommendations. One of these was that cells and property should be searched at frequent but irregular intervals. Following a strip search, each prisoner was to be excluded from his cell during the search, to avoid intimidation. The inquiry team gave no consideration at any stage to legal professional privilege or confidentiality. The policy was introduced to give effect to the inquiry team's recommendation on searching of cells.

The legal background

5. Any custodial order inevitably curtails the enjoyment, by the person confined, of rights enjoyed by other citizens. ...But the order does not wholly deprive the person confined of all rights enjoyed by other citizens. Some rights, perhaps in an attenuated or qualified form, survive... . And it may well be that the importance of such surviving rights is enhanced by the loss or partial loss of other rights. Among the rights which, in part at least, survive are three important rights, closely related but free standing, each of them calling for appropriate legal protection: the right of access to a court; the right of access to legal advice; and the right to communicate confidentially with a legal

adviser under the seal of legal professional privilege. Such rights may be curtailed only by clear and express words, and then only to the extent reasonably necessary to meet the ends which justify the curtailment.

...

The argument

13. The ambit of the present argument is very narrow. In the face of a compelling statement by Mr Narey, the Director General of HM Prison Service, Mr Daly accepts the need for random searches of prisoners' cells for the purpose of security, preventing crime and maintaining order and discipline. He accepts that such searches may properly be carried out in the absence of the resident prisoner. He accepts the need for prison officers to examine legal correspondence held by prisoners in their cells to make sure that it is bona fide legal correspondence and that such correspondence is not used as a convenient hiding place to secrete drugs or illicit materials of any kind, or to keep escape plans or any records of illegal activity. Thus he does not claim that privileged legal correspondence is immune from all examination. He contends only that such examination should ordinarily take place in the presence of the prisoner whose correspondence it is.

14. The Home Secretary for his part accepts that prison officers may not read a prisoner's privileged legal correspondence during a cell search carried out in the absence of the prisoner. But he relies on the statement of Mr Narey, who regards the right to examine such correspondence as necessary and regards the absence of the prisoner during the examination as a necessary feature of the policy. Mr Narey states:

"The aim of the search procedure is to prevent the concealment of material likely to endanger prison security, or the safety of others or which would contribute to criminal activity within the prison. These searches must be carried out in the absence of the prisoner in order to discourage prisoners from using intimidatory or conditioning tactics to prevent officers carrying out a full search of possessions. By 'conditioning tactics' I mean action by which prisoners seek to influence the future behaviour of prison officers. For example, a prisoner might create a scene whenever a particular item was searched, intending to cause prison officers not to search it in future on the ground that searching it was more trouble than it was worth. The policy also prevents prisoners from becoming familiar with searching techniques generally and those of individual officers."

Mr Narey goes on to state that alternative procedures have been considered within the prison service and rejected and states:

"The difficulty is that the prisoner's presence would compromise the policy's aims of preventing prisoners from intimidating or conditioning officers and from gaining familiarity with general and individual search techniques."

He goes on to say:

"The respondent [Secretary of State], the Prison Service and its staff, are mindful that the distinction between the examination of legal documents to confirm that they are bona fide and do not conceal anything illicit and the reading of legal documents (which current instructions expressly preclude other than by authority of a governor acting on received intelligence), is a fine one. However, anything of an illicit nature such as records of key codes or drug dealing can with ease be disguised as brief notations on what in every other respect is a legitimate legal document. It is the considered opinion of the respondent, of the Prison Service generally, and my own view, that the unreliability of current intelligence systems in prisons makes it unavoidable that we maintain the current position in an effort to deter concealments of this nature and the resultant threat to security and good order and discipline."

A record of illicit property found during cell searches year by year since 1993, appended to Mr Narey's statement, shows that the number of finds per year has very greatly increased since 1995, although the number of items which could be concealed in legal correspondence is relatively very small.

15. It is necessary, first, to ask whether the policy infringes in a significant way Mr Daly's common law right that the confidentiality of privileged legal correspondence be maintained. He submits that it does for two related reasons: first, because knowledge that such correspondence may be looked at by prison officers in the absence of the prisoner inhibits the prisoner's willingness to communicate with his legal adviser in terms of unreserved candour; and secondly, because there must be a risk, if the prisoner is not present, that the officers will stray beyond their limited role in examining legal correspondence, particularly if, for instance, they see some name or reference familiar to them, as would be the case if the prisoner were bringing or contemplating bringing proceedings against officers in the prison. For the Home Secretary it is argued that the policy involves no infringement of a prisoner's common law right since his privileged correspondence is not read in his absence but only examined.

16 I have no doubt that the policy infringes Mr Daly's common law right to legal professional privilege. This was the view of two very experienced judges in *R v Secretary of State for the Home Department, Ex p Simms* [1999] QB 349, against which decision the present appeal is effectively brought. At p 366, Kennedy LJ said:

"In my judgment legal professional privilege does attach to correspondence with legal advisers which is stored by a prisoner in his cell, and accordingly such correspondence is to be protected from any unnecessary interference by prison staff. Even if the correspondence is only inspected to see that it is what it purports to be that is likely to impair the free flow of communication between a convicted or remand prisoner on the one hand and his legal adviser on the other, and therefore it constitutes an impairment of the privilege."

Judge LJ was of the same opinion. At p 373, he said:

"Prisoners whose cells are searched in their absence will find it difficult to believe that their correspondence has been searched but not read. The governor's order will sometimes be disobeyed. Accordingly I am prepared to accept the potential 'chilling effect' of such searches."

In an imperfect world there will necessarily be occasions when prison officers will do more than merely examine prisoners' legal documents, and apprehension that they may do so is bound to inhibit a prisoner's willingness to communicate freely with his legal adviser.

17. The next question is whether there can be any ground for infringing in any way a prisoner's right to maintain the confidentiality of his privileged legal correspondence. Plainly there can. Some examination may well be necessary to establish that privileged legal correspondence is what it appears to be and is not a hiding place for illicit materials or information prejudicial to security or good order.

18. It is then necessary to ask whether, to the extent that it infringes a prisoner's common law right to privilege, the policy can be justified as a necessary and proper response to the acknowledged need to maintain security, order and discipline in prisons and to prevent crime. Mr Daly's challenge at this point is directed to the blanket nature of the policy, applicable as it is to all prisoners of whatever category in all closed prisons in England and Wales, irrespective of a prisoner's past or present conduct and of any operational emergency or urgent intelligence. The Home Secretary's justification rests firmly on the points already mentioned: the risk of intimidation, the risk that staff may be conditioned by prisoners to relax security and the danger of disclosing searching methods.

19. In considering these justifications, based as they are on the extensive experience of the prison service, it must be recognised that the prison population includes a core of dangerous, disruptive and manipulative prisoners, hostile to authority and ready to exploit for their own advantage any concession granted to them. Any search policy must accommodate this inescapable fact. I cannot however accept that the reasons put forward justify the policy in its present blanket form. Any prisoner who attempts to intimidate or disrupt a search of his cell, or whose past conduct shows that he is likely to do so, may properly be excluded even while his privileged correspondence is examined so as to ensure the efficacy of the search, but no justification is shown for routinely excluding all prisoners, whether intimidatory or disruptive or not, while that part of the search is conducted. Save in the extraordinary conditions prevailing at Whitemoor before September 1994, it is hard to regard the conditioning of staff as a problem which could not be met by employing dedicated search teams. It is not suggested that prison officers when examining legal correspondence employ any sophisticated technique which would be revealed to the prisoner if he were present, although he might no doubt be encouraged to secrete illicit materials among his legal papers if the examination were obviously very cursory. The policy cannot in my opinion be justified in its present blanket form. The infringement of prisoners' rights to maintain the confidentiality of their privileged legal correspondence is greater than is shown to be necessary to serve the legitimate public objectives already identified. I accept Mr Daly's submission on this point.

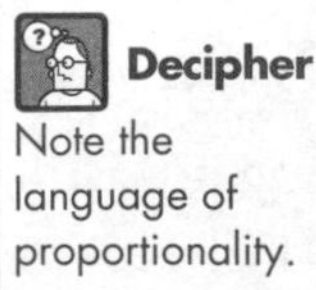

Note the language of proportionality.

20 I am fortified in reaching this view by four considerations, all of some importance in my opinion.

(1) Following a complaint to him about the policy by a prisoner other than Mr Daly in November 1995, the Prisons Ombudsman carried out a full inquiry and reported in November 1996. In his report the Ombudsman said:

"I entirely support the main thrust of Woodcock's recommendations regarding cell searching. It is apparent that prisoner intimidation was precluding the effective searching of prisoner accommodation in many establishments, and that this searching, which is essential for the safety and security of both staff and prisoners, is carried out far more effectively when the prisoner is absent. This procedure has also been assisted by the introduction of the volumetric control of prisoners' in-possession property. However, the legal privilege which must protect the confidentiality of correspondence between a solicitor and his client is too important to be sacrificed for the sake of expediency; whilst it would undoubtedly be easier for staff to search a prisoner's legal documents in his absence, this allows legal privilege to be compromised to an unacceptable degree. It is clear that, in complaining about the Prison Service's cell searching policy, [the prisoner] has raised a matter which has far-reaching consequences. I believe that his complaint is a valid one and that, in searching prisoners' legal papers in their absence, the Prison Service is compromising the legal privilege which ensures that correspondence between a solicitor and his client will remain confidential. I therefore uphold [the prisoner's] complaint. Security Group has previously drafted a revised version of section 68.3 of the Security Manual. This revised version allows the prisoner to remain in the cell while his legal documents are being searched, after which the documents are sealed in a box or bag, thus avoiding any possible compromise of legal privilege. I consider that the Security Manual should be amended to incorporate this revised method of cell searching."

(2) The Ombudsman's investigations revealed that, following a complaint by a prisoner confined in HMP Full Sutton, a procedure had been developed in that prison to meet the wishes of prisoners who objected to the searching of their legal documents in their absence. The procedure was that

"if the prisoner objects to his legal documents being searched in his absence DST [dedicated search team] staff place the documents in a bag, seal the bag using a numbered reception seal and give the prisoner a copy of the seal number. The bag is left in the prisoner's cell while the search is being carried out. When the prisoner returns, he checks the seal on the bag to ensure that it has not been tampered with and the documents are searched in his presence."

It does not appear that this procedure gave rise to difficulty in practice.

(3) The current standing order covering cell searches in Scotland provides that "When a cell is searched, this should be done by at least two officers, in the prisoner's presence." It is pointed out that the prison population in Scotland is small compared with that of England and Wales, there are very few high risk prisoners and escape is rare. No doubt the problem of control is less acute in Scotland than in England and Wales. But the Scottish experience does suggest that a policy which generally permits a prisoner to be present during the examination of his privileged legal correspondence,

unless there are, or are reasonably believed to be, good reasons for excluding him, is not unworkable in practice.

(4) While cell searches in recent years have led to the finding of very many more items of illicit property than in earlier years, only two such items have been identified as having been found among legal documents and the great majority of items found could not have been concealed in that way. It does not appear that legal files or bundles have been regarded by prisoners as a highly favoured hiding place for materials they are not permitted to hold.

21. In R v Secretary of State for the Home Department, Ex p Simms [1999] QB 349 and again in the present case, the Court of Appeal held that the policy represented the minimum intrusion into the rights of prisoners consistent with the need to maintain security, order and discipline in prisons. That is a conclusion which I respect but cannot share. In my opinion the policy provides for a degree of intrusion into the privileged legal correspondence of prisoners which is greater than is justified by the objectives the policy is intended to serve, and so violates the common law rights of prisoners. Section 47(1) of the 1952 Act does not authorise such excessive intrusion, and the Home Secretary accordingly had no power to lay down or implement the policy in its present form. I would accordingly declare paragraphs 17.69 to 17.74 of the Security Manual to be unlawful and void in so far as they provide that prisoners must always be absent when privileged legal correspondence held by them in their cells is examined by prison officers.

22. Although, in response to a request by the House during argument, counsel for Mr Daly proffered a draft rule which might be adopted to govern the searching of privileged legal correspondence, it would be inappropriate for the House to attempt to formulate or approve the terms of such a rule, which would call for careful consideration and consultation before it was finalised. It is enough to indicate that any rule should provide for a general right for prisoners to be present when privileged legal correspondence is examined, and in practice this will probably mean any legal documentation to avoid time-wasting debate about which documents are privileged and which are not. But the rule must provide for the exclusion of the prisoner while the examination takes place if there is or is reasonably believed to be good cause for excluding him to safeguard the efficacy of the search, and the rule must permit the prison authorities to respond to sudden operational emergencies or urgent intelligence.

23. I have reached the conclusions so far expressed on an orthodox application of common law principles derived from the authorities and an orthodox domestic approach to judicial review. But the same result is achieved by reliance on the European Convention. Article 8(1) gives Mr Daly a right to respect for his correspondence. While interference with that right by a public authority may be permitted if in accordance with the law and necessary in a democratic society in the interests of national security, public safety, the prevention of disorder or crime or for protection of the rights and freedoms of others, the policy interferes with Mr Daly's exercise of his right under article 8(1) to an extent much greater than necessity requires. In this instance, therefore, the common law and the Convention yield the same result. But this need not always be so. In *Smith and Grady v United Kingdom* (1999)

Decipher
Despite claiming this, you might query whether the earlier highlighted paragraph was based on English common law.

29 EHRR 493, the European Court held that the orthodox domestic approach of the English courts had not given the applicants an effective remedy for the breach of their rights under article 8 of the Convention because the threshold of review had been set too high. Now, following the incorporation of the Convention by the Human Rights Act 1998 and the bringing of that Act fully into force, domestic courts must themselves form a judgment whether a Convention right has been breached (conducting such inquiry as is necessary to form that judgment) and, so far as permissible under the Act, grant an effective remedy. On this aspect of the case, I agree with and adopt the observations of my noble and learned friends Lord Steyn and Lord Cooke of Thorndon which I have had the opportunity of reading in draft.

LORD STEYN

24. My Lords, I am in complete agreement with the reasons given by Lord Bingham of Cornhill in his speech. For the reasons he gives I would also allow the appeal. Except on one narrow but important point I have nothing to add.

25. There was written and oral argument on the question whether certain observations of Lord Phillips of Worth Matravers MR in *R (Mahmood) v Secretary of State for the Home Department* [2001] 1 WLR 840 were correct. The context was an immigration case involving a decision of the Secretary of State made before the Human Rights Act 1998 came into effect. The Master of the Rolls nevertheless approached the case as if the Act had been in force when the Secretary of State reached his decision. He explained the new approach to be adopted. The Master of the Rolls concluded, at p 857, para 40: "When anxiously scrutinising an executive decision that interferes with human rights, the court will ask the question, applying an objective test, whether the decision-maker could reasonably have concluded that the interference was necessary to achieve one or more of the legitimate aims recognised by the Convention. When considering the test of necessity in the relevant context, the court must take into account the European jurisprudence in accordance with section 2 of the 1998 Act."

These observations have been followed by the Court of Appeal in *R (Isiko) v Secretary of State for the Home Department* The Times, 20 February 2001 ; Court of Appeal (Civil Division) Transcript No 2272 of 2000 and by Thomas J in *R (Samaroo) v Secretary of State for the Home Department* (unreported) 20 December 2000.

26. The explanation of the Master of the Rolls in the first sentence of the cited passage requires clarification. It is couched in language reminiscent of the traditional *Wednesbury* ground of review (*Associated Provincial Picture Houses Ltd v Wednesbury Corpn* [1948] 1 KB 223), and in particular the adaptation of that test in terms of heightened scrutiny in cases involving fundamental rights as formulated in *R v Ministry of Defence, Ex p Smith* [1996] QB 517 , 554e-g per Sir Thomas Bingham MR. There is a material difference between the *Wednesbury* and *Smith* grounds of review and the approach of proportionality applicable in respect of review where Convention rights are at stake.

27. The contours of the principle of proportionality are familiar. In de Freitas v Permanent Secretary of Ministry of Agriculture, Fisheries, Lands and Housing [1999] 1

AC 69 the Privy Council adopted a three-stage test. Lord Clyde observed, at p 80, that in determining whether a limitation (by an act, rule or decision) is arbitrary or excessive the court should ask itself:

"whether: (i) the legislative objective is sufficiently important to justify limiting a fundamental right; (ii) the measures designed to meet the legislative objective are rationally connected to it; and (iii) the means used to impair the right or freedom are no more than is necessary to accomplish the objective."

Clearly, these criteria are more precise and more sophisticated than the traditional grounds of review. What is the difference for the disposal of concrete cases? Academic public lawyers have in remarkably similar terms elucidated the difference between the traditional grounds of review and the proportionality approach: see Professor Jeffrey Jowell QC, "Beyond the Rule of Law: Towards Constitutional Judicial Review" [2000] PL 671; Professor Paul Craig, *Administrative Law*, 4th ed (1999), pp 561-563; Professor David Feldman, "Proportionality and the Human Rights Act 1998", essay in *The Principle of Proportionality in the Laws of Europe* edited by Evelyn Ellis (1999), pp 117, 127 et seq. The starting point is that there is an overlap between the traditional grounds of review and the approach of proportionality. Most cases would be decided in the same way whichever approach is adopted. But the intensity of review is somewhat greater under the proportionality approach. Making due allowance for important structural differences between various convention rights, which I do not propose to discuss, a few generalisations are perhaps permissible. I would mention three concrete differences without suggesting that my statement is exhaustive. First, the doctrine of proportionality may require the reviewing court to assess the balance which the decision maker has struck, not merely whether it is within the range of rational or reasonable decisions. Secondly, the proportionality test may go further than the traditional grounds of review inasmuch as it may require attention to be directed to the relative weight accorded to interests and considerations. Thirdly, even the heightened scrutiny test developed in R v Ministry of Defence, Ex p Smith [1996] QB 517 , 554 is not necessarily appropriate to the protection of human rights. It will be recalled that in *Smith* the Court of Appeal reluctantly felt compelled to reject a limitation on homosexuals in the army. The challenge based on article 8 of the Convention for the Protection of Human Rights and Fundamental Freedoms (the right to respect for private and family life) foundered on the threshold required even by the anxious scrutiny test. The European Court of Human Rights came to the opposite conclusion: *Smith and Grady v United Kingdom* (1999) 29 EHRR 493. The court concluded, at p 543, para 138:

"the threshold at which the High Court and the Court of Appeal could find the Ministry of Defence policy irrational was placed so high that it effectively excluded any consideration by the domestic courts of the question of whether the interference with the applicants' rights answered a pressing social need or was proportionate to the national security and public order aims pursued, principles which lie at the heart of the court's analysis of complaints under article 8 of the Convention."

In other words, the intensity of the review, in similar cases, is guaranteed by the twin requirements that the limitation of the right was necessary in a democratic society, in the sense of meeting a pressing social need, and the question whether the interference was really proportionate to the legitimate aim being pursued.

28. The differences in approach between the traditional grounds of review and the proportionality approach may therefore sometimes yield different results. It is therefore important that cases involving Convention rights must be analysed in the correct way. This does not mean that there has been a shift to merits review. On the contrary, as Professor Jowell [2000] PL 671, 681 has pointed out the respective roles of judges and administrators are fundamentally distinct and will remain so. To this extent the general tenor of the observations in *Mahmood* [2001] 1 WLR 840 are correct. And Laws LJ rightly emphasised in *Mahmood* , at p 847, para 18, "that the intensity of review in a public law case will depend on the subject matter in hand". That is so even in cases involving Convention rights. In law context is everything.

LORD COOKE OF THORNDON

29. My Lords, having had the advantage of reading in draft the speeches of my noble and learned friends, Lord Bingham of Cornhill and Lord Steyn, I am in full agreement with them. I add some brief observations on two matters, less to supplement what they have said than to underline its importance.

30. First, while this case has arisen in a jurisdiction where the European Convention for the Protection of Human Rights and Fundamental Freedoms applies, and while the case is one in which the Convention and the common law produce the same result, it is of great importance, in my opinion, that the common law by itself is being recognised as a sufficient source of the fundamental right to confidential communication with a legal adviser for the purpose of obtaining legal advice. Thus the decision may prove to be in point in common law jurisdictions not affected by the Convention. Rights similar to those in the Convention are of course to be found in constitutional documents and other formal affirmations of rights elsewhere. The truth is, I think, that some rights are inherent and fundamental to democratic civilised society. Conventions, constitutions, bills of rights and the like respond by recognising rather than creating them.

31. To essay any list of these fundamental, perhaps ultimately universal, rights is far beyond anything required for the purpose of deciding the present case. It is enough to take the three identified by Lord Bingham: in his words, access to a court; access to legal advice; and the right to communicate confidentially with a legal adviser under the seal of legal professional privilege. As he says authoritatively from the woolsack, such rights may be curtailed only by clear and express words, and then only to the extent reasonably necessary to meet the ends which justify the curtailment. The point that I am emphasising is that the common law goes so deep.

32. The other matter concerns degrees of judicial review. Lord Steyn illuminates the distinctions between "traditional" (that is to say in terms of English case law, *Wednesbury*) standards of judicial review and higher standards under the European Convention or the common law of human rights. As he indicates, often the results are the same. But the view that the standards are substantially the same appears to have received its quietus in *Smith and Grady v United Kingdom* (1999) 29 EHRR 493 and

Lustig-Prean and Beckett v United Kingdom (1999) 29 EHRR 548. And I think that the day will come when it will be more widely recognised that Associated Provincial Picture Houses Ltd v Wednesbury Corpn [1948] 1 KB 223 was an unfortunately retrogressive decision in English administrative law, in so far as it suggested that there are degrees of unreasonableness and that only a very extreme degree can bring an administrative decision within the legitimate scope of judicial invalidation. The depth of judicial review and the deference due to administrative discretion vary with the subject matter. It may well be, however, that the law can never be satisfied in any administrative field merely by a finding that the decision under review is not capricious or absurd.

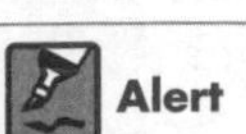
Alert

33. I, too, would therefore allow the present appeal.

While in *Daly* the relationship between unreasonableness and proportionality was discussed, the court was of the view that the claimant would have won his case using either approach. In other cases the tensions between the two approaches has been more evident and suggestions have been made that the time has come to dispense with unreasonablesness and to adopt proportionality as the single ground of review in all cases, whether they engage human rights or EU law or not. In particular, Lord Slynn in the case of *Regina (Alconbury Developments Ltd and Others) v Secretary of State for the Environment, Transport and the Regions* [2003] 2 AC 295 said:

'I consider that even without reference to the Human Rights Act 1998 the time has come to recognise that this principle [proportionality] is part of English administrative law not only when judges are dealing with Community acts but also when they are dealing with acts subject to domestic law. Trying to keep the *Wednesbury* principle and proportionality in separate compartments seems to me to be unnecessary and confusing'.

However, despite Lord Synn's comments and general sympathy for the contention, the Court of Appeal has confirmed that the *Wednesbury* concept does still apply and that, if proportionality is to supplant unreasonableness as a free standing ground of challenge in an action for judicial review, it is for the House of Lords to perform the 'burial rites' (see *R (on the application of Association of British Civilian Internees: Far East Region) v Secretary of State for Defence* [2003] QB 1397).

Academic commentary has focused on the relative merits of both principles.

Towards the nutcracker principle: reconsidering the objections to proportionality, Garreth Wong [2000] PL 92

In a much-quoted dictum, Lord Diplock picturesquely cautioned against using a "steam hammer to crack a nut, if a nutcracker would do". At that time, proportionality was not a general principle of judicial review, against which administrative conduct could be measured and disproportionate decisions could be struck down. It is unfortunate from the viewpoint of legal progress that official English legal doctrine today, 16 years after Lord Diplock uttered those words, remains blind to the concept of proportionality as a ground for judicial review. In stark contrast, the Court of Justice of the European

Community applies an explicit principle of proportionality, which has, "in varying degrees of intensity, affected virtually every area of administrative action governed by Community law and of Community legislation".

Many objections have been raised to an introduction of proportionality as an independent ground of judicial review in English administrative law. However, no critical overview exists of these criticisms. This article intends to remedy that defect by outlining the relevant arguments in this area, along with a consideration of their respective merits. The article also accommodates the recent and continuing discussion regarding the proper basis for judicial review and the proper place of the judiciary within the constitutional matrix. The latter debate has altered sufficiently the paradigm within which administrative law functions, so any consideration of the desirability of a judicial (and hence unilateral) incorporation of a principle of proportionality without the express permission of Parliament would need to take into account these recent developments.

In the following sections, I will contend that English administrative law has matured sufficiently to assimilate within the general system of judicial review a workable and independent control of proportionality, supplemental to the existing grounds of review.

The argument will be developed in three stages. First, a few words will be said concerning the current state of judicial review and the concept of proportionality. Secondly, the arguments in favour of the introduction of a control of proportionality will be outlined. Finally, the main objections against such introduction will be analysed, with attention paid to the recent constitutional debate and with reference to the legal system of the European Community.

The current situation

Judges in administrative law cases have always been careful of the distinction between review and appeal: courts will only pass judgment if the claim is one that goes essentially to the legality of the challenged administrative conduct and not to its merits, the latter being within the lawful discretion of the administration and hence the function of an administrative appeal. Of the different grounds on which judicial review of administrative action may be sought, a classic exposition can be found in Lord Diplock's speech in the *G.C.H.Q.* case, in which he distinguishes between procedural impropriety, illegality and irrationality. This last category is generally taken to be synonymous with the ground of review known as *Wednesbury* unreasonableness, helpfully defined as coming to "a conclusion so unreasonable that no reasonable authority could ever have come to it".

As a ground of review, proportionality would broadly involve the determination of the lawfulness of administrative conduct in the light of three criteria: (i) the administrative body must not have taken any action that went beyond what was necessary to achieve its aims, in the sense that it must have utilised the method least burdensome to affected persons (the necessity test), (ii) the means chosen must have been suitable for achieving those aims (the suitability test), and (iii) the body must have balanced proportionately the burdens thereby imposed on affected persons against the importance of the purposes it hoped to achieve (the balancing test). It should be noted that the role of the reviewing court is not to ensure that the right balance was struck between opposing interests, but rather to determine whether the decision thus made was in fact disproportionate. It is a form of negative control and therefore it would be more correct, strictly speaking, to talk of a test of *disproportionality,* rather than of proportionality.

The current authoritative determination of the status of proportionality in English law is *R. v. Secretary of State for the Home Department, ex p. Brind,* where a majority of the House of Lords denied that proportionality was at that time a separate ground of judicial review in general administrative law. Lord Ackner was concerned that such a test would mean that an "inquiry into and a decision upon the merits cannot be avoided", in the sense that the court would have to balance the pros and cons of the challenged decision. Lord Lowry felt that judges were not well equipped by training or experience to "decide the answer to an administrative problem where the scales are evenly balanced". However, Lords Roskill and Bridge left open the possibility that proportionality might at some point in the future be incorporated into English law, while Lord Templeman did not agree that proportionality was not part of English law. Nevertheless, explicit recognition of a general test of proportionality in judicial review has been slow.

Reasons for an incorporation of proportionality

(i) Dissatisfaction with Wednesbury

The first argument for the incorporation of proportionality as a ground of review lies in dissatisfaction with the *status quo,* a sentiment that has found recent expression in the House of Lords. Briefly, Jowell and Lester argue that *Wednesbury* unreasonableness as a ground of review is unsatisfactory for three reasons. First, invoking the mantra of *Wednesbury* unreasonableness does not in itself provide sufficient justification for judicial intervention in administrative decisions. Fairness and intellectual honesty demand an elaboration of *why* a decision was deemed unreasonable, not merely an assertion that the decision was irrational. Secondly, the test is unrealistic as courts in practice often set a variable standard of review, depending on the circumstances of the individual case, rather than a rigid one as the actual wording of the test suggests. Thirdly, the definition of *Wednesbury* unreasonableness is itself tautologous. To improve the state of substantive review, they suggest the articulation of independent principles, one of which is the principle of proportionality. "Justification by reference to principles is intellectually honest, avoiding as it must the obscurity of a vague test and openly revealing the true reasons for intervention". Moreover, the recognition of principles would also greatly strengthen the coherence and clarity of administrative law.

(ii) A legal patchwork

The second reason advanced for an incorporation of proportionality lies in the current landscape of English administrative law, which Lord Scarman once described as "an assortment of bits and pieces ... no more than an ad hoc bunch of restraints, controls, and procedures". At present, at least three distinct though overlapping groups of cases may be discerned within the rubric of general administrative law. The first includes those cases involving a European Community dimension. The second consists of those cases involving an alleged breach by an administrative body of rights protected under the Human Rights Act 1998. The third category is a residual one, consisting of those cases not falling under either of the previous two, where, as discussed above, proportionality is not recognised.

In contrast, the judiciary is obliged to apply a test of proportionality to all administrative decisions that fall under the rubric of Community law. The result is a legal patchwork lacking in principled distinctions, other than the fact that some areas are covered by the U.K.'s international obligations while others are not. The facts of the famous *German Beer* case will serve as an illustration. This concerned a German government blanket prohibition on all additives in beer sold domestically, including those approved by other Member States, ostensibly for the protection of public health. The Court of Justice declared the rule disproportionate. Though a selective ban on some additives might have been justified, a total ban was not, as international scientific research and data strongly suggested that the additives did not constitute a threat to public health, and in fact served a real need.

If the English government were to propagate such a nation-wide ban now, it is beyond doubt that national courts could use a control of proportionality to strike down such action. However, if the English government were to ban the use of additives in the *production* of domestic beer rather than its importation, courts would be unable to invoke proportionality, since this case would no longer fall under the umbrella of Community law. Prospective applicants would therefore be left without a remedy, unless they were able to bring such a case within the ambit of the other traditional grounds of judicial review. This would be in spite of the fact that in the first hypothetical example the affected interests are far more difficult to quantify, being in part the interests of foreign importers into England, whereas in the second, the interests involved encompass the immediate livelihood, economic loss and hardship of local producers.

The recent enactment of the Human Rights Act 1998 does not improve this legal collage. Though the Act itself does not explicitly enjoin the courts to apply a test of proportionality, it is arguable that it implicitly does so, and there are eminent voices, including the Lord Chancellor, who argue for judicial recognition and application of the test of proportionality, at least for cases that fall within the scope of the Act. This view seems to have found favour among the judiciary–in *R. v. Secretary of State for the Home Department, ex p. Simms and another,* Lord Hobhouse, agreeing with the conclusion of the majority, held unjustifiable an administrative policy in part because it was disproportionate. While Lord Steyn (with whom Lords Browne-Wilkinson and Hoffmann agreed) based his judgment more conservatively on *Wednesbury* grounds, it is significant to note that their Lordships, while overruling the earlier decision of the Court of Appeal, expressed no disapproval of the application by that court of an explicit test of proportionality.

Therefore, it seems that English courts are at present empowered to strike down disproportionate administrative decisions as long as the applicants can plead some relevant aspect of Community law, or point to some right protected under the Human Rights Act. However, administrative conduct falling outside these areas is arbitrarily immune from judicial inquiry on the grounds of proportionality. This lack of consistency smacks of artificially induced distinctions unfounded on any principled consideration. There is no justifiable difference between the two hypothetical examples outlined above the demands of justice remain the same in both cases regardless of the nationality of the producer. The extent of legal protection available to individuals should not vary depending on whether the particular facts of the instant case may be interpreted as involving some point of Community law, or whether a human right can be brought into play. If we agree with the fundamental axiom of justice that like should be treated alike, then as a matter of principle we must also concede that a control of proportionality should be available in English judicial review to all deserving cases.

Objections to an introduction of proportionality

Having outlined the reasons in favour of the introduction of a control of proportionality into English administrative law, we move on to a consideration of the main objections against such introduction. Three distinct but interrelated groups of arguments can be identified: first, that a control of proportionality is redundant and ultimately ineffective; secondly, that the introduction and use of proportionality as a head of review is inconsistent with the constitutional role of English courts; and finally, that the institutional framework of the judiciary renders the practical working of a test of proportionality difficult, if not nearly impossible.

(i) Wednesbury unreasonableness: redundancy and ineffectiveness

The first objection finds its expression in oft-repeated statements that English law already has a head of review broadly analogous to the test of proportionality: *Wednesbury* unreasonableness. There are two branches to this argument.

First, there are some who would question the use of proportionality as an independent head of review because they see it as a mere aspect or indication of irrationality. The judgment of Gibson L.J. in *R. v. General Medical Council, ex p. Colman*, for example, supports this view when the learned judge quoted approvingly the judgment of Lord Donaldson M.R. in *ex p. Brind* and concluded that proportionality was not an "an independent head of review" but "an aspect of the submission based on *Wednesbury* unreasonableness". Proponents of this view maintain that proportionality as a concept is ultimately redundant in a system with *Wednesbury* review.

The reasons against this position, namely the inadequacy, unreality and tautology of *Wednesbury* have already been considered above. However, more reasons can be adduced. By masking proportionality under a veneer of *Wednesbury* unreasonableness, one runs the risk of allowing judges to "obscure their social and economic preferences more easily" under the vagueness of the irrationality test than if their reasoning for intervention had to be "guided by established legal principle". A proper respect for the difference between review and appeal would argue in favour of introducing a more structured and transparent form of judicial control, rather than relying constantly on the "blunt tool" of *Wednesbury* unreasonableness. Encouraging transparent judgments, and hence confidence in an unelected judiciary possessing neither the purse nor the sword, are profound reasons in favour of incorporating a control of proportionality as an independent ground of review in its own right.

The second limb picks up where the first leaves off, and argues that although the *Wednesbury* test has some deficiencies, nevertheless a test of proportionality would be ineffective in solving those problems. Boyron asserts that the use of the term proportionality itself "does not provide an explanation, it needs to be reinforced with some other kind of justification" just like *Wednesbury,* and that a broad use of proportionality could prove to be another "ample cloak hiding prejudices or policy considerations".

Boyron's objection proves too much and too little at the same time. On the one hand, it proves too much in that the mere assertion of each and every ground of review, on its own, can be said to supply insufficient justification. For example, any judgment that annuls an administrative decision based on a bare repeated intonation of "irrelevant considerations" could justly be criticised for having no real explanatory force. There should be an attempt by the court to elucidate the purpose of the empowering legislation, to pinpoint the consideration the administrative body took into account in deciding but which the court considers to have been irrelevant, and to justify the irrelevancy by reference to the wording and purposes of the legislation. Mere incantation of any head of review is insufficient justification for judicial intervention.

On the other hand, the argument proves too little in that it fails to show that an introduction of proportionality would not be an improvement on general *Wednesbury* unreasonableness, in terms of enabling judges to give more reasoned, clear and principled decisions. Unreasonableness as a head of review has been said to include a cocktail of concepts, from proportionality to legal certainty, from proper respect for fundamental rights to the relevancy of considerations. Whether ultimately correct or not, the existence of such claims proves the malleability, vagueness and plasticity of the *Wednesbury* concept of unreasonableness. Proportionality by contrast is restricted to determining whether an appropriate balance was reached between means, goals, costs and benefits, and whether the method used was strictly necessary. Its incorporation as a relatively well-defined concept when compared to *Wednesbury* would undoubtedly aid in the rendering of clear, transparent and comprehensible judgments.

(ii) The constitutional conundrum

This next section goes on to consider the constitutional objections to a judicial introduction of proportionality. Two arguments are considered in this context. The first deals with the relationship between the judiciary and Parliament, and the second concerns itself primarily with the relationship between the judiciary and the executive.

(a) Parliamentary supremacy and the role of the judiciary.

In the context of objecting to an introduction of the French principle of proportionality into English administrative law, Boyron advances the reason that English courts hold an "inferior rank" to Parliament, which is supreme in that it can make and unmake any law. This position is made manifest in the constant reference during statutory interpretation to the intention of Parliament, which is an expression of the subordination of the judiciary to Parliament and the "desire of the judiciary to disavow a large creative role in the interpretation of statutes". Put in another way, the incorporation of a principle of proportionality, without express Parliamentary approval, would amount to judicial legislation by the back-door, and would therefore be contrary to the constitutional doctrine which gives Parliament a monopoly on legislative capacity.

Before engaging in the merits of this argument, it is worth noting that many current grounds of review are judicially developed notions, without Parliament's express seal of approval. "*Wednesbury* standards have not been voted in by Parliament", as Laws succinctly puts it. Both unreasonableness and the principles of natural justice, to give two instances, are grounds of review that are cornerstones of current judicial review. They were given life and nurtured by the courts, yet nowhere is it suggested that they are any less legitimate because of the lack of explicit legislative approval.

Boyron's argument is linked with a strict conception of the orthodox basis of judicial review. According to this view, judicial review of executive action is limited to policing the boundaries of the law granting the discretionary power, as divined from the wording of the legislation or presumed to be the intention of Parliament. Only these limits, and no other, may be enforced. Once outside these boundaries, administrative action is *ultra vires* and therefore unlawful. The relationship between these limits and Parliament's intent, as manifested in the wording of the empowering statute, is a direct one Parliament must have specifically intended every last aspect of the principles of good administration that the courts apply. Any unilateral judicial attempt to introduce a principle of proportionality would therefore amount to a usurpation of the legislative prerogative of Parliament.

This strict traditional rationale for judicial review has come under intense criticism in recent years. Besides the implausibility of the assumption that Parliament possesses a particular intent with regard to each and every principle of good administration the courts apply, the traditional theory cannot explain how extremely detailed judicial principles are seemingly derived from sometimes very generally worded legislation. Current supporters of the *ultra vires* basis of judicial review have instead embraced what has been dubbed the "modified theory of *ultra vires*", and propound an indirect relationship between judicial principles of good administration and Parliamentary intention. This argues that in the absence of contrary evidence, it is entirely sensible to assume that Parliament intends to legislate in conformity with the rule of law, one of the bed-rocks on which the British constitution rests, which presupposes that any exercise of governmental power be just and principled.

[Parliament] is therefore taken to withhold from decision-makers the power to act unfairly and unreasonably, while recognising that the detailed requirements of fairness and rationality can most appropriately be determined incrementally by the courts through the forensic process. Hence, Parliament grants to the judges a margin of freedom ... to set the precise limits of administrative power.

This view of the relationship between the judiciary and the supreme Parliament lends itself far more readily to a judicial incorporation of the principle of proportionality, without predictable accusations of judicial legislation. To the contrary, the introduction of a concept that requires the executive to wield its power in a fair, reasoned and balanced way with due regard to all interests affected would actually be a *fulfilment* of the duty delegated to the courts by Parliament to ensure proper respect for the law and the rule of law, by precisely delineating administrative discretion.

It should be borne in mind that this modified theory of *ultra vires* represents the most orthodox version of the *ultra vires* basis of judicial review still currently defensible. The other competing model is the common law theory of judicial review supported by Laws and Craig. Proponents of this theory argue that principles of judicial review are in reality the progeny of the common law and of judicial parenting Parliamentary intent had little or no role in their conception. Parliamentary supremacy is not, however, challenged on this view Parliament still retains the power to abolish these controls generally, or to make it unequivocal in legislation that some or all of these principles are not to apply in certain specific circumstances, and the courts will unhesitatingly obey such commands. However, in the absence of such explicit edicts, the courts will apply the common law principles of judicial review, developed on the grounds of justice and the rule of law. Therefore, there is even less difficulty reconciling unilateral judicial incorporation of proportionality with the constitutional role of judges if one subscribes to the common law theory of judicial review, since this admits of more room for judicial independence in shaping fundamental norms of administrative behaviour.

The debate over the proper basis for judicial review rages on, but what is common to both these camps is the recognition that the exact norms of proper administration are in reality developed by the judiciary, whether the justification for that lies in Parliament's implied delegation or in the innate vigour of the common law to fashion and apply new legal norms according to changing circumstances and the dictates of justice. Therefore, in the context of an introduction of proportionality into English administrative law, there can be no objection on the basis of Parliamentary supremacy and the proper role of the judiciary. Far from it, the proper role of judges would require that they be sensitive to the changing constitutional context in which they operate, and take note of developing principles of democratic government and administration, of which proportionality is one.

Therefore, it is time to shed the confines of the strict orthodox conception of *ultra vires,* and to recognise the court's constitutional role in shaping new principles of good administrative conduct. Unsupportable cries of judicial legislation and supremacism should not be a deterrent to an incorporation of a principle of proportionality.

(b) The separation of powers: blurring the appeal-review distinction.

As mentioned earlier, the judiciary's role is to review the *legality* of a contested administrative decision, and not to pass judgment on its *merits,* which is the domain of the executive. Courts may only police the legal boundaries of administrative decisions. The second argument contends that the use of proportionality by the courts would inevitably result in the judiciary usurping the role of the administration by making decisions for it, instead of merely ruling on the legality of contested decisions. A due respect for Parliamentary sovereignty would dictate that when Parliament bequeaths a power to an administrative body, it intends that body, and no other, to exercise that power. Moreover, public bodies are, by their function and position, more trained and knowledgeable in exercising their discretion in difficult administrative cases than are judges. Courts should respect the "division of function as between the administration and the judiciary" and therefore "it cannot be right for the judiciary to overturn such a decision merely because the court would have balanced the conflicting interests differently".

This argument, however convincing, rests on two assumptions. First, that the use of proportionality would involve review of administrative decisions on a threshold that is "considerably lower" than the current level of *Wednesbury* unreasonableness. Secondly, that this would result in courts trespassing on the allocated domain of the public body by inviting "review of the merits of public decisions" and involving the courts in "a process of policy evaluation". Both these assumptions are open to doubt.

With regard to the first assumption, two points can be made. First, eminent voices have proposed that English courts have always used a concept of proportionality in administrative law, albeit implicitly. For example, Lord Slynn's judgment in *ex p. ITF,* though on the face of it a straightforward application of the traditional *Wednesbury* test of unreasonableness, could be read instead as a covert application of the concept of proportionality. Besides adopting the variable "margin of appreciation" test, his Lordship, with whom Lords Nolan and Hope agreed, made liberal use of the concepts of balance and necessity, which as we have seen before, bear a marked resemblance to the concepts used in a test of proportionality. Therefore, in this view the introduction of proportionality would not involve a lowering of the threshold for judicial review beyond what is currently practiced covertly, and its recognition would promote the legitimacy and integrity of the judiciary by enabling judges to be explicit about their real reasons for their decisions.

Secondly, the terminology of proportionality has long been used explicitly in the area of excessive sanctions, in the sense that administrative conduct imposing excessive penalties in relation to the wrongdoing has been held to be amenable to judicial review on that basis.

With regard to the second assumption, even if one were to concede that a proportionality test would result in a lowering of the standard for judicial intervention in public decisions, it is by no means clear that this would necessarily result in the courts usurping the function of the administration by making decisions based on their merits. Three points can be made in response to this objection.

First, it is imperative to distinguish, on the one hand, judicial review which *considers* the merits of the decision to the extent to which their assessment is necessary to determine its legality, and on the other hand, judicial intervention which *makes* the decision for the public body by a substitution of judgment or assessment of facts to that put forward by the administration. The former is an entirely legitimate exercise of control and one that is already practiced to some extent in the *Wednesbury* unreasonableness ground of review it is impossible for a court to determine whether a decision was so unreasonable that no reasonable authority properly informed could have decided thus, unless the same court also gave some consideration to the substantive merits of the case. Similarity, a test of proportionality that considers the merits of a decision as a necessary prelude to a ruling on its legality is not trespassing on the domain of the administration; the actual decision still lies in the hands of the public body.

Secondly, it must be borne in mind that any tool of judicial review for checking government action may be applied with varying degrees of intensity. In the context of the *Wednesbury* doctrine, the courts have shown great care not to trespass on the administrative domain by applying different thresholds for judicial intervention depending on whether fundamental freedoms were challenged, in which case the court would exercise the most "anxious scrutiny", or whether the case involved high-level economic and social policy, in which case the court would be more reluctant to interfere. Just as "reasonableness means different things in different circumstances", so the courts should be able to apply a control of proportionality with varying degrees of intensity, depending on the subject-nature of the case. It is worth noting that the variable "margin of appreciation" test, formulated in *ex p. Smith,* has been recently confirmed and applied by the House of Lords in the cases of *ex p. Simms,* and *ex p. ITF.* There is no reason to presume that the courts will show any less finesse in using proportionality against the backdrop of their constitutional role than they currently do with *Wednesbury.*

In the context of Community law, a similar situation already exists. A survey of the relevant case law of the European Court of Justice reveals that the Court does not always apply the test of proportionality with the same degree of rigour in all cases. The Court takes a wide variety of factors into account when deciding the intensity with which it will consider the proportionality of a challenged measure, including not only the nature and importance of the interests of the applicant and the nature and importance of the administrative goal, but also the position and expertise of the court as against the decision-maker.

For example, the Court is usually content to grant Community institutions a wide margin of appreciation when reviewing cases involving complex economic situations, restricting itself to determining whether the decision "is manifestly inappropriate having regard to the objective which the competent institution is seeking to pursue", "contains a manifest error", or imposes burdens that were "*manifestly* out of proportion to the object in view". Equally, however, the Court has not been afraid to overturn Community measures, even in areas where the institutions have specifically been given a wide ambit of discretion with regard to complicated matters. Similarly, the Court is more critical when reviewing Member States' actions that seek to restrict the ambit of fundamental norms guaranteed by Community Treaties. Thus, a derogation from the free movement of workers, guaranteed by Article 39 (*ex* Article 48) of the E.C. Treaty, is only permissible if there exists a genuine and serious threat to public policy, and moreover only the least restrictive measure in the circumstances may be taken.

Thirdly, far from being a tool by which to encourage judicial meddling with the workings of the administration, a transparent and principled test of proportionality may actually have the reverse effect. Bearing in mind the current vague formulation of the *Wednesbury* ground of review, de Búrca suggests that "the more clearly the agreed standards or grounds of review can be articulated, the more clearly it can be seen whether a court is genuinely attempting to apply these in a structured way to the decision taken rather than substituting its overall judgment as to what would be a better or preferable decision". By requiring the courts to substantiate decisions to overturn administrative action in terms of suitability, necessity, balance or proportionality, one actually reduces the capacity of judges to deliver judgments on the merits of cases, a potential for abuse that is inherent in the amorphous formulation of the current *Wednesbury* ground of review.

In short, two points can be made. First, we would be doing a great disservice to the English judiciary not to attribute to them the same integrity and perceptiveness that their European Court counterparts demonstrate in applying a differential (and sometimes deferential) control of proportionality to difficult cases with variable subject-matters, especially since English courts already apply a variable standard of review in the context of *Wednesbury* unreasonableness. It is by no means an easy or uncontroversial task, but definitely a necessary one, and more importantly, one that the judiciary is equipped to deal with. Secondly, an incorporation of proportionality by no means constitutes judicial licence for wanton disregard for the prerogatives of the administration. This is summed up by Jowell and Lester, when they conclude that an incorporation of proportionality "by no means releases judges from their proper reserve in interfering with decisions on the ground of policy, or assessment of facts or merits ... Indeed, because proportionality advances a relatively specific legal principle ... it focuses more clearly than [the *Wednesbury* test] on the precise conduct it seeks to prevent ... By concentrating on the specific it is more effective in excluding general considerations based on policy rather than principle".

There is admittedly a danger that a judicial decision may restrict the range of reasonable (or proportionate) choices left to the administration to such an extent that it becomes a judicial decision in all but name. However, acknowledging the danger of judicial over-activism does not necessarily mean that recognition of proportionality is the last straw that would push substantive review over into the realms of appeal, nor does it mean that this danger does not already exist with the vagueness and elasticity of the *Wednesbury* doctrine. As Lord Cooke succinctly put it, "[j]udges are entirely accustomed to respecting the proper scope of administrative decisions. In my respectful opinion they do not need to be warned off the course by admonitory circumlocutions".

Institutional problems

The last group of objections to the incorporation of proportionality as a ground of review revolves around the difficulty the employment of the test will produce with regard to the surrounding institutional framework.

Adjudicative difficulties

First, there is the problem of adjudicative difficulties or competence. Due to the doctrine of the separation of powers, English judges are drawn from the ranks of distinguished court lawyers, not the civil service. The structural divorce of judges from the administration means judges often have very little expertise or practical knowledge of the wider problems of administration: "judges are not, generally speaking, equipped by training or experience, or furnished with the requisite knowledge and advice, to decide the answer to an administrative problem where the scales are evenly balanced". Therefore, this objection is not so much concerned with the appropriate constitutional role of the judiciary, as with the ability of judges to rule competently on matters that are not suited to the process of adversarial adjudication.

However, the severity of this problem can be exaggerated. First, if one were to consider the European Court of Justice, it immediately becomes obvious that over half of the past and present judges of the Court have been pure academicians or members of national judiciaries without any extensive political or administrative experience. Appointment to the Court is restricted to "persons ... who possess the qualifications required for appointment to the highest judicial offices in their respective countries or who are jurisconsults of recognised competence". Nowhere does it mention as a prerequisite extensive administrative experience. In fact, the majority of judges constituting the Court have always been former academics, and only relatively recently have ex-members of national judiciaries outnumbered them. Only a minority have held political or administrative posts prior to their appointment. Yet this did not stop the Court from developing a detailed doctrine of proportionality, nor does its composition deter it from applying such a control at present. Most significantly, much of the criticism directed towards the Court is aimed at its perceived political activism in the *way* it applies the test, and not towards its *competence* to apply the test in the first place. In actual fact, the Court tends to be "deferential in [its] review of cases which highlight ... the limited evidentiary and procedural processes of adjudication, and the difficulty of providing a defined individual remedy in contexts which involve complex political and economic policies".

Secondly, English judges are already very conscious of the limitations of the adversarial judicial process, and are generally wary of reviewing cases requiring detailed knowledge of and expertise in matters that the courts lack; "[i]t is not for the court to second-guess the judgment of a specialist tribunal".

Thirdly, what is perhaps the biggest flaw with the adjudicative-difficulties argument is that it applies equally well to domestic cases involving a Community dimension and those that fall under the Human Rights Act, and as we have seen, English courts are obliged to apply a control of proportionality to at least the first category of cases, if not also to the second. Admittedly, the application of a test of proportionality to such cases is not unproblematic. However, if one were to take the adjudicative-difficulties criticism seriously, then one should object to the courts applying proportionality in those cases as well. But nowhere is it suggested that the courts should decline to do so.

Most importantly, the mandate to apply proportionality in Community law cases, and perhaps cases under the Human Rights Act as well, originates from Parliament. It flows logically that, from a constitutional point of view, the supreme Parliament has considered the courts *capable* of exercising such control. Thus it is irrational to maintain that, on the one hand, the courts are sufficiently competent to apply a test of proportionality to some cases, while on the other hand, those same courts are inherently incompetent in respect of other cases. Either the courts are *capable* in terms of their abilities to apply such a test or they are not, regardless of whether Parliament has *instructed* them to. Therefore if we were really sincere about the adjudicative-difficulties objection, we should apply it across the board and maintain that courts should never apply a control of proportionality to Community law cases, contrary to Parliament's express instruction, because they are simply incompetent to do so. Of course, this position is indefensible, at least for those who still uphold the doctrine of Parliamentary supremacy while simultaneously recognising the legitimacy of decisions of domestic courts in such cases. Therefore there must be some concession that the judiciary is capable, or at least not totally incapable, of applying some sort of control of proportionality, even within the limited adjudicative framework.

Finally, the current mandatory application of a control of proportionality to Community law cases, and perhaps cases under the Human Rights Act as well, will in time attune and accustom English judges to the concept itself. This may make a practical reception of this principle into general administrative law easier and less fraught with difficulties. In any case, the concept of proportionality has been enshrined in the new Rules of Civil Procedure. Under the new Rules, all judges, from the county courts to the Court of Appeal, have to give effect to the overriding objective of enabling cases to be dealt with justly, of which proportionality is one consideration. Significantly, the Rules recognise that wider social and economic considerations have to be balanced against the single-minded pursuit of justice.

Therefore, at least for the sake of domestic adjudication of Community law and human rights issues as well as case-management under the new Rules, if not for the cause of extending proportionality into general administrative law, it is to be hoped that constant practice will iron out many of the operational problems currently attributed to its application.

In short, it is submitted that courts are already aware of the limitations of the adjudicative process, and the self-restraint present serves to prevent the judiciary overstepping its limits, in the event of an introduction of a control of proportionality. Moreover, the comparison with the European Court of Justice suggests that though a background in practical administration is an added bonus in members of the judiciary using a test of proportionality, it is by no means a necessary one. Finally, it is manifest that English courts are capable of utilising such a principle even within the acknowledged limitations of the adjudicative framework.

Scope of the review

The second problem is concerned with the question of where courts should draw the line in applying a test of proportionality: should they confine themselves to the particular administrative decision in question, or should they consider possible alternative measures, adopting the "necessity" test used by the Court of Justice? Both the latter, and to a lesser extent the former, will involve wider-ranging inquiries than are embarked on under the present grounds of review.

There are two aspects to this objection. First, "[a] good knowledge of the facts is essential in order for a principle of proportionality to work efficaciously", and though Order 53 provides for a court-ordered discovery of 108 documents, there are many judicial and extra-judicial statements to the effect that this provision should be used sparingly, because of the extra time and costs involved. The lack of information will therefore be an obstruction to a test of proportionality. Secondly, English courts "do not readily interfere in the weighing of factual evidence and are even less keen to dabble in the assessment of policy alternatives". Therefore in considering whether the appropriate balance was struck by an administrative decision, and when considering alternative strategies, the court will be impeded by the lack of information and a reluctance to enter into policy and factual inquiries in the first place.

However, the extent of this objection can be exaggerated. It is not a given that the traditional English judicial reluctance against ordering discovery of documents will extend uniformly to a new test of proportionality, where it is "necessary either for disposing fairly of the cause or matter or for saving costs". There are judicial indications that leave open the option for courts to order discovery "whenever, and to the extent that, the justice of the case requires". The 1988 Justice/All Souls Report actually encourages a more relaxed attitude to ordering discovery when necessary. Moreover, courts have been willing to allow cases to proceed outside the Order 53 procedure where it seems that a complex and detailed factual inquiry was necessary. Thus, it is possible to conduct factual inquiries essential for a proper consideration of the proportionality of an administrative decision, both within and without Order 53. The final point is that the scarcity of relevant information represents a practical obstacle to a working test of proportionality, one that is moreover capable of being overcome, and not a reason for dismissing outright the suggestion of incorporation of the concept.

Conclusion

The traditional objections to the incorporation of an independent concept of proportionality as a ground of review in general administrative law are no longer as cogent as they once were. Far from being redundant and ineffective, a structured concept of proportionality would in fact facilitate the delivery of clear and transparent judgments, especially when contrasted with the amorphous state of the existing *Wednesbury* ground of review. Moreover, within the constitutional framework as recently redefined in debate, the incorporation of proportionality would actually be a fulfilment of the role of the courts as guardians of the rule of law. It was argued above that a sensitive application of proportionality would not necessarily lead to the courts trespassing onto the merits of the decision, and in fact its use as a transparent and structured principle would encourage the reverse. Finally, it was canvassed that the courts are in fact capable of applying such a control in general administrative law, and that the judiciary is well aware of the limits of the institutional framework and the need for self-restraint in this regard. Furthermore, exposure to cases involving a Community element, an aspect of the Human Rights Act, and case-management under the new Civil Procedure Rules would inevitably acclimatise the judiciary to the application of proportionality.

In contrast, dissatisfaction with the existing grounds of review, particularly with the plastic *Wednesbury* principle, as well as the current arbitrary distinction between cases involving a Community aspect (and possibly those involving a right protected by the Human Rights Act), in which proportionality applies, and cases which do not, in which proportionality does not apply, argue persuasively for the extension of a principled and structured concept of proportionality into general administrative law.

It seems that judicial developments may have steamed on ahead of academic debate. The foregoing discussion may have been rendered otiose by the case of *ex p. ITF,* in which Lord Slynn, delivering the majority judgment, uses arguably the clearest expression of an implicit test of proportionality as a ground of review in general administrative law, while never explicitly labelling it as such. Nevertheless this article advocates an unambiguous and open judicial recognition of that principle, for all the reasons outlined above.

There will undoubtedly be problems and controversies in the application of a control of proportionality, just as with any other ground of review. It has never been contended that the principle is "some panacea which will serve to cure all ills". But is suggested that in the final analysis a control of proportionality will do more good than harm.

Proportionality has proven a useful judicial tool in many of the continental legal systems for keeping decision-makers within their designated bounds. It is to be hoped that some day before the passing of yet another 16 years, an English judge will be able to use the "nutcracker principle" for more than merely stopping over-enthusiastic public bodies from crushing nuts using steam hammers.

Given the combined effect of the decisions in *Brind* and *Daly*, which have confirmed the place of unreasonableness as the correct ground of review outside the ECHR or EU context, the position remains as outlined in Wong's article. However, the judiciary and academics are gradually moving to the idea that the two tests should become one.

Further Reading

Jowell, J ' Beyond the Rule of Law; towards constitutional Judicial review' [2000] *PL* 671

Elliott, M ' The Human Rights Act 1998 and the Standards of Substantive Review" [2001] *CLJ* 301

Hickman, T 'The substance and structure of proportionality' [2008] *PL* 694

16

Procedural Impropriety

Topic List

1 The Right to a Fair Hearing
2 The Duty to Give Reasons
3 The Rule Against Bias

Alex Lawson and Christopher Costigan

Introduction

In *GCHQ* Lord Diplock, having described illegality and unreasonableness, went on to say:

> 'I have described the third head as "procedural impropriety" rather than failure to observe basic rules of natural justice or failure to act with procedural fairness towards the person who will be affected by the decision. This is because susceptibility to judicial review under this head covers also failure by an administrative tribunal to observe procedural rules that are expressly laid down in the legislative instrument by which its jurisdiction is conferred, even where such failure does not involve any denial of natural justice.'

Lord Diplock is describing two different requirements under this head the duty to:

- Observe the common law rules of natural justice
- Comply with statutory procedural requirements

In relation to the second requirement, Lord Diplock is simply saying that a decision-maker must conform to the rules which Parliament lays down. If they fail to do so then the decision will be *ultra vires*. The relationship between this and illegality should be immediately obvious.

It is the first requirement which is of greater importance and which will be the focus of this chapter. The common law requirement of natural justice can be broadly split into two forms: the right to a fair hearing (*audi alterem partem*) and the rule against bias (*nemo judex in causa sua*). These concepts should be considered to be 'implied mandatory requirements, non-observance of which invalidates the exercise of power'.

1 The Right to a Fair Hearing

The right to a fair hearing is a broad category which (in addition to the right to a hearing in some form) actually encompasses five different rights: (1) to know the case against you; (2) to make representations; (3) to call witnesses; (4) to have legal representation; and (5) to be given reasons for a decision.

A key issue is when does the right to a fair hearing apply? It clearly applies to judicial decisions, but questions have been posed as to whether it applies also to decisions of an administrative nature. In *Cooper v The Board of Works for the Wandsworth District* 14 CB (NS) 180, Erle CJ found that a duty to hear the plaintiff was not restricted simply to those matters which were purely judicial in nature:

> 'I [do not] undertake the rest of my judgment solely upon the ground that the district board is exercising judicial discretion upon the point: but the law, I think, has been applied to many exercises of power which in common understanding would not be at all more a judicial proceeding than would be the act of the district board'.

Despite a clawing back on this position in the first half of the twentieth century the principle that a right to a fair hearing applies to all types of public law decisions was confirmed in *Ridge v Baldwin* [1964] AC 40.

In the aftermath of *Ridge*, though, a question arose as to whether the full gambit of rights relevant under this broad heading was available for all decisions or whether there was a sliding scale of fairness. In the Privy Council case of *Durayappah v Fernando* [1967] 2 AC 337, Lord Upjohn confirmed that the level of fairness owed in a case needed to take into account three factors. Depending where the claimant's case fell on a sliding scale of fairness, the appropriate content of fairness would vary accordingly. The more serious the issue, the more likely that the higher end rights – such as the right to call witnesses and be represented legally – would come into play.

The three factors to be taken into account and assessed were: firstly, what is the nature of the property, the office held, status enjoyed or services to be performed by the complainant of injustice (how important is the office, property etc.?). Secondly, in what circumstances or on what occasions is the person claiming to be entitled to exercise the measure or control entitled to intervene (how serious are the allegations?). Thirdly, when a right to intervene is proved, what sanctions in fact is the latter entitled to impose on the other (how severe is the sanction which could result?).

1.1 The Right to Know the Case Against You

'If the right to be heard is to be a real right which is worth anything, it must carry with it a right in the accused man to know the case which his made against him. He must know what evidence has been given and what statements have been made affecting him.'

These words, which exemplify the general principle, were spoken by Lord Denning in *Kanda v Government of Malaya* [1962] AC 322.

R v Governors of Dunraven School ex p B [2000] BLGR 494

Panel: Morritt, Brooke and Sedley LJJ

Facts: A schoolboy was permanently excluded following the theft of a teacher's handbag. B's expulsion was based on the witness statement of a pupil. B's parents were was not allowed to see the statement or to know who had made it. B brought a judicial review of the refusal to give him access to the statement.

LORD JUSTICE SEDLEY

...

Did the applicant have a fair hearing?

18. It is a proposition too obvious to require authority that what fairness demands in a particular situation will depend on the circumstances. In relation to permanent exclusion from a grant-maintained school Parliament has made it clear — as the common law would otherwise have done, given what is at stake in such cases — that the pupil,

through his or her parent, has a right to be heard. Such a right is worthless unless the parent knows in some adequate form what is being said against the child. Where what is being said has taken at least two different and arguably inconsistent forms, fairness will ordinarily require enough disclosure to reveal the inconsistency.

19. A second, related, principle is that it is unfair for the decision-maker to have access to damaging material to which the person at risk — here the pupil through his parent — has no access.

Alert

20. In my judgment both of these principles were breached in the course of the hearing before the governors. They were also breached in the hearing before the appeal committee... . Although this conclusion seems to me to follow from first principles — subject to one important matter, the protection of an informant, to which I shall come — it conforms to the view attributed to McCullough J in the report of *R v Governors of the London Oratory School, ex parte Regis* (1989) 19 Fam.L. 67:

"It was right that a boy facing possible expulsion should know the nature of the accusation against him; that he should have an opportunity to answer; and that he should appear before a tribunal that acted in good faith."

Collins J in *R v Governors of Bacon's College, ex parte W* [1998] ELR 488 applied these principles to facts not dissimilar to the present ones (adverse statements had not been seen by the pupil or his parents) and concluded:

"What is fair in any given case obviously depends upon the circumstances, but to rely on something by hearsay without seeing any of the material and without giving the parents the opportunity to see that material is unquestionably unfair."

The departmental guidelines adopt the same approach. They say:

"Written material must have been seen by all parties. If a new issue arises during the proceedings, parties should be given an opportunity to consider and comment on it."

21. But Mr Oldham has placed justifiable stress on one specific element of this case: the need to protect D from exposure as the informant and from consequent reprisal. Mr McManus submits that there was no such need: the school's own evidence suggests plainly that the Applicant and M already knew of D's role. But at the time of the head's decision and the governors' hearing this was very much a matter for the school's judgment, and it would be quite wrong for this court now to second-guess it.

22. Taking this, therefore, to have been a critical consideration, what was to be done? The problem is a recurrent one in criminal proceedings, where informers' identity is ordinarily protected on grounds of public policy but where the interests of justice occasionally require disclosure. Here the Crown has a painful but straightforward choice: to let the informer be named or (if without his evidence there is no triable case) to abandon the prosecution. The problem has also been usefully considered in the employment situation. In *Linfood Cash and Carry Ltd v Thomson* [1989] IRLR 235 the Employment Appeal Tribunal, under the presidency of Wood P, had to consider what a fair disciplinary procedure called for where employees were suspected of fraud on the

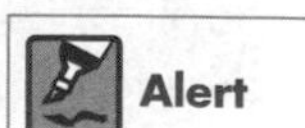
Alert

evidence of a fellow employee who, through fear, would not let his identity be known to the others. Wood P said:

"... a careful balance must be maintained between the desirability to protect informants who are genuinely in fear, and providing a fair hearing of issues for employees who are accused of misconduct. We are told that there is no clear guidance to be found from ACAS publications, and the lay members of this court have given me the benefit of their wide experience.

Every case must depend upon its own facts, and circumstances may vary widely — indeed with further experience other aspects may demonstrate themselves — but we hope that the following comments may prove to be of assistance:

1. The information given by the informant should be reduced into writing in one or more statements ...

In taking the statements the following seem important:

...

*(d) whether the informant has suffered at the hands of the accused or has any other reason to fabricate, whether from personal grudge or any other reason or principle.

...

5. If the informant is prepared to attend a disciplinary hearing, no problem will arise, but if, as in the present case, the employer is satisfied that the fear is genuine then a decision will need to be made whether or not to continue with the disciplinary process.

...

7. The written statement of the informant — if necessary with omissions to avoid identification — should be made available to the employee and his representatives.

8. If the employee or his representative raises any particular and relevant issue which should be put to the informant, then it may be desirable to adjourn for the chairman to make further inquiries of that informant."

23. It seems to me, with the caveats entered earlier, that this is helpful guidance as to what fairness may well demand in school exclusion cases. In the present case it supports my view that the governors needed to proceed in this way: first, if they wished to take D's account into consideration, which necessarily meant letting the pupil and his parent know what it was, they had to consider whether his identity could be concealed; if it could not, then they had to consider whether to go ahead without reliance on anything D had said (by, for example, simply considering the applicant's admission, albeit withdrawn by him, that he had been there) or to drop the case and reinstate the applicant. The one thing which in my judgment the governors could not fairly do was decide to take into account a written statement made by D which the applicant had not seen and D's oral testimony to them which the applicant had not heard. Nor would it have been fair to disclose these without also disclosing (to the governors as well as to the applicant) what D had originally said to the head teacher.

The case of *B* clearly demonstrates the broad principle applicable: that if the right to a fair hearing is to mean anything it must include the right to know the case against you. It would seem therefore, that knowing the case against you forms the minimum 'content' of fairness that should be available to those on the receiving end of a public law decision. However, this does not necessarily mean that an applicant is entitled to know all the precise details, as can be seen in the next case.

***R v Gaming Board for Great Britain, ex parte Benaim and Khaida* [1970] 2 QB 417**

Panel: Lord Denning MR, Lord Wilberforce and Phillimore LJ

Facts: Benaim and Khaida applied to the Gaming Board of Great Britain for a certificate of consent to apply for a licence for their premises, as required by the Gaming Act 1968. Their applications were rejected. The applicants made repeated requests to find out exactly why, all of which failed. They argued that they had a right to know, based on the procedural requirements of fairness; essentially the principle that everyone has the right know the case against them. The Board argued that they endeavoured to give applicants the best possible indication in this regard, but that requirements of confidentiality of sources and public interest meant that there was no such absolute right.

LORD DENNING MR

...[The Gaming Board] was set up by Parliament to cope with disreputable gaming clubs and to bring them under control. By bitter experience it was learned that these clubs had a close connection with organised crime, often violent crime, with protection rackets and with strong-arm methods. If the Gaming Board were bound to disclose their sources of information, no one would "tell" on those clubs, for fear of reprisals. Likewise with the details of the information. If the board were bound to disclose every detail, that might itself give the informer away and put him in peril. But, without disclosing every detail, I should have thought that the board ought in every case to be able to give to the applicant sufficient indication of the objections raised against him such as to enable him to answer them. That is only fair. And the board must at all costs be fair. If they are not, these courts will not hesitate to interfere.

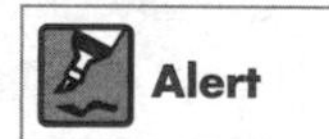

In this case, even though the allegations were perhaps as serious as in *B*, Lord Denning MR only effectively felt that the applicants were entitled to the 'gist' of the case against them. It will be noted however, that in this case the parties were 'mere applicants' for a licence; whereas in *B* something was being taken away, so the ramifications could be seen as more serious for the individual. When this is put into the *Durayappah* scale, the difference in treatment can be rationalised.

2 The Duty to Give Reasons

Continental jurisprudence has long asserted the requirement that sound decision making requires decision makers to give reasons. However, in English law the position has tended to rest firmly the other way: reasons are not generally required, unless there is some positive duty to do so. This was affirmed in the case of *R v Secretary of State for the Home Department ex p Doody* [1994] 1 AC 531.

R v Secretary of State for the Home Department ex p Doody [1994] 1 AC 531

Panel: Lord Keith of Kinkel, Lord Lane, Lord Templeman, Lord Browne-Wilkinson and Lord Mustill

Facts: The applicant had been convicted of murder and sentenced to a mandatory life sentence. The tariff period was set by the Home Secretary who refused to give reasons for how he had calculated the period of minimum detention. The applicant applied for judicial review.

LORD MUSTILL

Alert

...I accept without hesitation, and mention it only to avoid misunderstanding, that the law does not at present recognise a general duty to give reasons for an administrative decision. Nevertheless, it is equally beyond question that such a duty may in appropriate circumstances be implied, and I agree with the analyses by the Court of Appeal in *Reg. v. Civil Service Appeal Board, Ex parte Cunningham* [1991] 4 All E.R. 310 of the factors which will often be material to such an implication.

Alert

Turning to the present dispute I doubt the wisdom of discussing the problem in the contemporary vocabulary of "prisoner's rights," given that as a result of his own act the position of the prisoner is so forcibly distanced from that of the ordinary citizen, nor is it very helpful to say that the Home Secretary should out of simple humanity provide reasons for the prisoner, since any society which operates a penal system is bound to treat some of its citizens in a way which would, in the general, be thought inhumane. I prefer simply to assert that within the inevitable constraints imposed by the statutory framework, the general shape of the administrative regime which ministers have lawfully built around it, and the imperatives of the public interest, the Secretary of State ought to implement the scheme as fairly as he can. The giving of reasons may be inconvenient, but I can see no ground at all why it should be against the public interest: indeed, rather the reverse. This being so, I would ask simply: Is refusal to give reasons fair? I would answer without hesitation that it is not. As soon as the jury returns its verdict the offender knows that he will be locked up for a very long time. For just how long immediately becomes the most important thing in the prisoner's life. When looking at statistics it is easy to fall into the way of thinking that there is not really very much difference between one extremely long sentence and another: and there may not be, in percentage terms. But the percentage reflects a difference of a year or years: a long time for anybody, and longer still for a prisoner. Where a defendant is convicted of, say, several armed robberies he knows that he faces a stiff sentence: he can be advised by reference to a public tariff of the range of sentences he must expect; he hears counsel address the judge on the relationship between his offences and the tariff; he will often hear the judge give an indication during exchanges with counsel of how his mind is working; and when sentence is pronounced he will always be told the reasons for it. So also when a discretionary life sentence is imposed, coupled with an order under section 34. Contrast this with the position of the prisoner sentenced for murder. He never sees the Home Secretary; he has no dialogue with him: he cannot fathom how his mind is working. There is no true tariff, or at least no tariff exposed to public view which might give the prisoner an idea of what to expect. The announcement of his first review date arrives out of thin air, wholly without explanation. The distant oracle has spoken, and that is that.

My Lords, I am not aware that there still exists anywhere else in the penal system a procedure remotely resembling this. The beginnings of an explanation for its unique character might perhaps be found if the executive had still been putting into practice the theory that the tariff sentence for murder is confinement for life, subject only to a wholly discretionary release on licence: although even in such a case I doubt whether in the modern climate of administrative law such an entirely secret process could be justified. As I hope to have shown, however, this is no longer the practice, and can hardly be sustained any longer as the theory. I therefore simply ask, is it fair that the mandatory life prisoner should be wholly deprived of the information which all other prisoners receive as a matter of course. I am clearly of the opinion that it is not.

My Lords, I can moreover arrive at the same conclusion by a different and more familiar route, of which *Ex parte Cunningham* [1991] 4 All E.R. 310 provides a recent example. It is not, as I understand it, questioned that the decision of the Home Secretary on the penal element is susceptible to judicial review. To mount an effective attack on the decision, given no more material than the facts of the offence and the length of the penal element, the prisoner has virtually no means of ascertaining whether this is an instance where the decision-making process has gone astray. I think it important that there should be an effective means of detecting the kind of error which would entitle the court to intervene, and in practice I regard it as necessary for this purpose that the reasoning of the Home Secretary should be disclosed. If there is any difference between the penal element recommended by the judges and actually imposed by the Home Secretary, this reasoning is bound to include, either explicitly or implicitly, a reason why the Home Secretary has taken a different view. Accordingly, I consider that the respondents are entitled to an affirmative answer on the third issue.

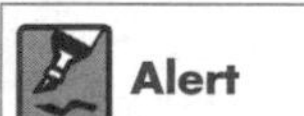
Alert

The case of *Doody* makes three important points. First, that there is no general duty in English law to give reasons. Second, however, that a duty will exist where there is to be a deprivation of liberty (as would normally apply to a trial judge from whom reasons are required). Finally, that where it might otherwise be impossible to mount a successful judicial review (because the grounds on which that review could take place would be unknown without them), the court may impose a duty. Within that argument certainly lays the seed of a general duty to give reasons.

Reg v Civil Service Appeal Board, Ex parte Cunningham [1991] 4 All ER 310

Panel: Lord Donaldson of Lymington MR, McCowan and Leggatt LJJ

Facts: The applicant was dismissed from his employment as a physical education officer after 23 years in the prison service. He applied to the Civil Service Appeal

Board who ruled that his dismissal was unfair and recommended reinstatement. The recommendation was rejected by the Home Secretary and so a monetary award was made by the board instead. The award was abnormally low and the Board refused to give reasons. Cunningham applied for judicial review.

LORD DONALDSON OF LYMINGTON MR

... I do not accept that, just because Parliament has ruled that some tribunals should be required to give reasons for their decisions, it follows that the common law is unable to impose a similar requirement upon other tribunals, if justice so requires. As Lord Bridge of Harwich put it in *Lloyd v. McMahon* [1987] A.C. 625, 702–703:

"My Lords, the so-called rules of natural justice are not engraved on tablets of stone. To use the phrase which better expresses the underlying concept, what the requirements of fairness demand when any body, domestic, administrative or judicial, has to make a decision which will affect the rights of individuals depends on the character of the decision-making body, the kind of decision it has to make and the statutory or other framework in which it operates. In particular, it is well-established that when a statute has conferred on any body the power to make decisions affecting individuals, the courts will not only require the procedure prescribed by the statute to be followed, but will readily imply so much and no more to be introduced by way of additional procedural safeguards as will ensure the attainment of fairness."

...

I then ask myself what additional procedural safeguards are required to ensure the attainment of fairness. The answer is, I believe, to be found in the judgment of Lord Lane C.J. in *Reg. v. Immigration Appeal Tribunal, Ex parte Khan (Mahmud)* [1983] Q.B. 790, 794–795 which I do not believe owed anything to the fact that immigration appeal tribunals are required by statute to give some reasons for their decisions:

"The important matter which must be borne in mind by tribunals in the present type of circumstances is that it must be apparent from what they state by way of reasons first of all that they have considered the point which is at issue between the parties, and they should indicate the evidence upon which they have come to their conclusions. Where one gets a decision of a tribunal which either fails to set out the issue which the tribunal is determining either directly or by inference, or fails either directly or by inference to set out the basis upon which they have reached their determination upon that issue, then that is a matter which will be very closely regarded by this court, and in normal circumstances will result in the decision of the tribunal being quashed. The reason is this. A party appearing before a tribunal is entitled to know, either expressly stated by the tribunal or inferentially stated, what it is to which the tribunal is addressing its mind. In some cases it may be perfectly obvious without any express reference to it by the tribunal; in other cases it may not. Secondly, the appellant is entitled to know the basis of fact upon which the conclusion has been reached. Once again in many cases it may be quite obvious without the necessity of expressly stating it, in other cases it may not."

Judged by that standard the board should have given outline reasons sufficient to show to what it was directing its mind and thereby indirectly showing not whether its decision was right or wrong, which is a matter solely for it, but whether its decision was lawful. Any other conclusion would reduce the board to the status of a free-wheeling palm tree.

The board's objection to giving reasons, which curiously is fully supported by both the official and the staff sides, is that this would tend to militate against informality and would lead to an undesirable reliance upon a body of precedent. I find this totally unconvincing. The evidence shows that those who advise applicants and departments do so frequently and must be well aware of the board's previous decisions and of the circumstances in which they were made. There must therefore already be a body of precedent. If the board has no regard to its previous decisions, it must be acting inconsistently and be failing to do justice as between applicants. This I am loath to believe. As to informality, no one has yet complained that the industrial tribunals lack informality, yet they give reasons for their decisions. A complaint of legalism is another matter, but there is no reason why the giving of brief reasons should lead to this most distressing of diseases.

LORD JUSTICE LEGGATT

...

I have not been much assisted by the articles relied on by Mr. Pannick, distinguished though their authors are, because they are recommending, advocating or protesting what the law ought to be: they are not intent on demonstrating what, in a context such as the present, the law is. But it seems obvious that for the same reason of fairness that an applicant is entitled to know the case he has to meet, so should he be entitled to know the reasons for an award of compensation, so that in the event of error he may be equipped to apply to the court for judicial review. For it is only by judicial review that the board's award can be challenged. The applicant has a right of appeal not by way of hearing de novo, as on appeal from a magistrates' court, but only if it can be shown that he has not been fairly treated by the board.

...

[T]he average compensation award by the board during 1988 was £2,201.56, while in the year ended 31 March 1988 the median award made by industrial tribunals in unfair dismissal cases was £1,865.

Apart from the fact that the periods are different, statistically it is unhelpful to compare an average with a median figure, and in any event it does nothing to dispel the belief that the compensation awarded to the applicant was, as his solicitors asserted, meagre. Applying "the rules and guidelines adopted by industrial tribunals," the applicant would have been entitled, as Lord Donaldson of Lymington M.R. has explained, to an award under sections 73(3) and 74(1) of the Employment Protection (Consolidation) Act 1978 of £12,108, without regard to any award of additional compensation under section 71(2)(b)(ii) of between £4,264 and £2,132.

Since the board recommended reinstatement it cannot be supposed that they arrived at their award of £6,500 by making a reduction as under sections 74(6) and 73(7B) on the ground that the dismissal was caused or contributed to by any action of the applicant.

> Mr. Laws argues that the applicant cannot succeed unless he can prove the existence of a statutory duty to give reasons or a legitimate expectation that he would be given them. I do not accept that the court's powers are so circumscribed. The fact that the board's principal function is to alleviate the rigour of summary dismissal does not mean that the person dismissed should not be accorded natural justice or that the board need not deal fairly with him. Without an obligation to give reasons the board's procedures cannot be checked, let alone challenged; and without reasons neither the person dismissed nor the court can tell whether to apply for or to grant judicial review.
>
> In relation to many, if not most, administrative decisions it may well be undesirable, for one reason or another, to give reasons. But there are not here, as in certain contexts there are, any valid grounds for adhering to the general rule that there is no duty to give reasons. On the contrary, there are here particular grounds for departing from the general rule. The applicant has a legitimate grievance, because it looks as though his compensation is less than it should be, and yet he has not been told the basis of the assessment.

Alert

> ...
>
> The cardinal principles of natural justice are that no one shall be judge in his own cause and that everyone is entitled to a hearing. But the subject-matter of the decision or the circumstances of the adjudication may necessitate more than that. An award of compensation by the board concerns the applicant's means of livelihood for the period to which the award relates. The board's determination binds the Home Office, and also the applicant subject to his right to challenge it by applying for judicial review. But that right is nugatory unless the award is so aberrant as to compel the inference that it must have been wrong, or unless the board explains how the figure was arrived at, so as to enable the applicant to tell whether the award can be successfully impugned.

Alert

> ...
>
> In my judgment the duty to act fairly in this case extends to an obligation to give reasons. Nothing more onerous is demanded of the board than a concise statement of the means by which they arrived at the figure awarded. Albeit for reasons which go wider than those relied on by the judge, I too agree that the appeal should be dismissed and cross-appeal allowed.

In *Cunningham* the latent argument suggesting a general duty to give reasons can also be seen. But additionally, as in *Doody*, it can be seen that the issues, when considered in relation to the *Durayappah* sliding scale approach, were at the higher level which increases the content of the right to a fair hearing and may justify the departure from the general rule that there is no duty to give reasons.

3 The Rule Against Bias

It is a fundamental tenet of administrative law that decisions should be made impartially and free from bias. Any decision maker is therefore to be disqualified from making a decision in which there is actual bias, and may be precluded if there is the appearance of bias. Bias can be split into two categories: personal interest, which will lead to the automatic disqualification of the decision maker; or other bias, which, depending on the circumstances, may lead to disqualification.

3.1 Automatic Disqualification: Personal Interest

The most obvious way in which a decision-maker may be shown to be automatically disqualified is if they have a pecuniary interest in the decision. The seminal case on pecuniary interest is that of *Dimes v Grand Junction Canal* (1852) 9 QB 469.

***Dimes v Grand Junction Canal* (1852) 10 ER 301**

Panel: Lord St Leonards LC, Parke B, Lord Brougham and Lord Campbell

Facts: Various orders were sought by the company Grand Junction Canal and granted by the Vice-Chancellor. The Lord Chancellor then affirmed the orders, but unbeknown to the applicant, the Lord Chancellor had a large financial interest in the company. Dimes appealed on the basis that the Lord Chancellor should be disqualified for bias and his affirmation of the orders set aside.

LORD CAMPBELL

I take exactly the same view of this case as do my noble and learned friends, and I have very little to add to their observations. With respect to the point upon which the learned Judges were consulted, I must say that I entirely concur in the advice which they have given to your Lordships. No one can suppose that Lord Cottenham could be, in the remotest degree, influenced by the interest that he had in this concern; but, my Lords, it is of the last importance that the maxim that no man is to be a judge in his own cause should be held sacred. And that is not to be confined to a cause in which he is a party, but applies to a cause in which he has an interest. Since I have had the honour to be Chief Justice of the Court of Queen's Bench, we have again and again set aside proceedings in inferior tribunals because an individual, who had an interest in a cause, took a part in the decision. And it will have a most salutary influence on these tribunals when it is known that this high Court of last resort, in a case in which the Lord Chancellor of England had an interest, considered that his decree was on that account a decree not according to law, and was set aside. This will be a lesson to all inferior tribunals to take care not only that in their decrees they are not influenced by their personal interest, but to avoid the appearance of labouring under such an influence. It is quite clear, likewise, I believe, that the orders of the Vice-Chancellor cannot be in the slightest degree affected by what the Lord Chancellor has done, nor can it be maintained that the Vice-Chancellor was acting merely as the Lord Chancellor's deputy when these orders and decrees were pronounced

An interesting case of automatic disqualification bias on a ground other than pecuniary interest can be seen in *R v Bow Street Metropolitan Stipendary Magistrate ex p Pinochet Ugarte (No 2)* [2000] 1 AC 119.

R v Bow Street Metropolitan Stipendary Magistrate ex p Pinochet Ugarte (No 2) [2000] 1 AC 119

Panel: Lord Browne-Wilkinson, Lord Goff of Chieveley, Lord Nolan, Lord Hope of Craighead and Lord Hutton

Facts: Senator Pinochet, the former dictator of Chile, was arrested after a Spanish judge issued a warrant for his extradition on charges of crimes against humanity. Senator Pinochet contended that he was immune from suit because of his role as a former head of state. The question for the UK court was the extent of that immunity. The case eventually came to the House of Lords. Before the case was heard, several human rights organisations, including Amnesty International, were allowed to intervene and were represented at the hearing. The House of Lords decided, by 3 – 2, that Senator Pinochet was not immune. Lord Hoffmann was the only judge not to give an opinion, but simply agreed with the majority. After the appeal had been completed, it was discovered that Lord Hoffmann was the director of a charitable subsidiary of Amnesty International, although he gained no pecuniary advantage from the post. Senator Pinochet then lodged a challenge that the decision of the House of Lords, or the opinion of Lord Hoffmann, should be set aside on the basis of bias; although he alleged no actual bias on the part of Lord Hoffmann.

LORD BROWNE-WILKINSON

The link between Lord Hoffmann and A.I.

It appears that neither Senator Pinochet nor (save to a very limited extent) his legal advisers were aware of any connection between Lord Hoffmann and A.I. until after the judgment was given on 25 November. Two members of the legal team recalled that they had heard rumours that Lord Hoffmann's wife was connected with A.I. in some way. During the Newsnight programme on television on 25 November, an allegation to that effect was made by a speaker in Chile. On that limited information the representations made on Senator Pinochet's behalf to the Home Secretary on 30 November drew attention to Lady Hoffmann's position and contained a detailed consideration of the relevant law of bias. It then read:

"It is submitted therefore that the Secretary of State should not have any regard to the decision of Lord Hoffmann. The authorities make it plain that this is the appropriate approach to a decision that is affected by bias. Since the bias was in the House of Lords, the Secretary of State represents the senator's only domestic protection. Absent domestic protection the senator will have to invoke the jurisdiction of the European Court of Human Rights."

After the representations had been made to the Home Office, Senator Pinochet's legal advisers received a letter dated 1 December 1998 from the solicitors acting for A.I. written in response to a request for information as to Lord Hoffmann's links. The letter of 1 December, so far as relevant, reads as follows:

"Further to our letter of 27 November, we are informed by our clients, Amnesty International, that Lady Hoffmann has been working at their international secretariat since 1977. She has always been employed in administrative positions, primarily in their department dealing with press and publications. She moved to her present position of programme assistant to the director of the media and audio visual programme when this position was established in 1994. Lady Hoffmann provides administrative support to the programme, including some receptionist duties. She has not been consulted or otherwise involved in any substantive discussions or decisions by Amnesty International, including in relation to the Pinochet case."

On 7 December a man anonymously telephoned Senator Pinochet's solicitors alleging that Lord Hoffmann was a director of the Amnesty International Charitable Trust. That allegation was repeated in a newspaper report on 8 December. Senator Pinochet's solicitors informed the Home Secretary of these allegations. On 8 December they received a letter from the solicitors acting for A.I. dated 7 December which reads, so far as relevant, as follows:

"On further consideration, our client, Amnesty International have instructed us that after contacting Lord Hoffmann over the weekend both he and they believe that the following information about his connection with Amnesty International's charitable work should be provided to you. Lord Hoffmann is a director and chairperson of Amnesty International Charity Ltd. ('A.I.C.L.'), a registered charity incorporated on 7 April 1986 to undertake those aspects of the work of Amnesty International Ltd. ('A.I.L.') which are charitable under U.K. law. A.I.C.L. files reports with Companies House and the Charity Commissioners as required by U.K. law. A.I.C.L. funds a proportion of the charitable activities undertaken independently by A.I.L. A.I.L.'s board is composed of Amnesty International's Secretary General and two Deputy Secretaries General. Since 1990 Lord Hoffmann and Peter Duffy Q.C. have been the two directors of A.I.C.L. They are neither employed nor remunerated by either A.I.C.L. or A.I.L. They have not been consulted and have not had any other role in Amnesty International's interventions in the case of Pinochet. Lord Hoffmann is not a member of Amnesty International. In addition, in 1997 Lord Hoffmann helped in the organisation of a fund raising appeal for a new building for Amnesty International U.K. He helped organise this appeal together with other senior legal figures, including the Lord Chief Justice, Lord Bingham. In February your firm contributed £1,000 to this appeal. You should also note that in 1982 Lord Hoffmann, when practising at the Bar, appeared in the Chancery Division for Amnesty International U.K."

Further information relating to A.I.C.L. and its relationship with Lord Hoffmann and A.I. is given below. Mr. Alun Jones for the C.P.S. does not contend that either Senator Pinochet or his legal advisers had any knowledge of Lord Hoffmann's position as a director of A.I.C.L. until receipt of that letter.

Senator Pinochet's solicitors informed the Home Secretary of the contents of the letter dated 7 December. The Home Secretary signed the authority to proceed on 9 December 1998. He also gave reasons for his decision, attaching no weight to the allegations of bias or apparent bias made by Senator Pinochet.

On 10 December 1998, Senator Pinochet lodged the present petition asking that the order of 25 November 1998 should either be set aside completely or the opinion of

Lord Hoffmann should be declared to be of no effect. The sole ground relied upon was that Lord Hoffmann's links with A.I. were such as to give the appearance of possible bias. It is important to stress that Senator Pinochet makes no allegation of *actual bias* against Lord Hoffmann; his claim is based on the requirement that justice should be seen to be done as well as actually being done. There is no allegation that any other member of the committee has fallen short in the performance of his judicial duties.

...

131 The parties' submissions

Miss Montgomery in her very persuasive submissions on behalf of Senator Pinochet contended (1) that, although there was no exact precedent, your Lordships' House must have jurisdiction to set aside its own orders where they have been improperly made, since there is no other court which could correct such impropriety; (2) that (applying the test in *Reg. v. Gough* [1993] A.C. 646) the links between Lord Hoffmann and A.I. were such that there was a real danger that Lord Hoffmann was biased in favour of A.I. or alternatively (applying the test in *Webb v. The Queen* (1994) 181 C.L.R. 41) that such links give rise to a reasonable apprehension or suspicion on the part of a fair minded and informed member of the public that Lord Hoffmann might have been so biased.

On the other side, Mr. Alun Jones accepted that your Lordships had power to revoke an earlier order of this House but contended that there was no case for such revocation here. The applicable test of bias, he submitted, was that recently laid down by your Lordships in *Reg. v. Gough* and it was impossible to say that there was a real danger that Lord Hoffmann had been biased against Senator Pinochet. He further submitted that, by relying on the allegations of bias in making submissions to the Home Secretary, Senator Pinochet had elected to adopt the Home Secretary as the correct tribunal to adjudicate on the issue of apparent bias. He had thereby waived his right to complain before your Lordships of such bias. Expressed in other words, he was submitting that the petition was an abuse of process by Senator Pinochet. Mr. Duffy for A.I. (but not for A.I.C.L.) supported the case put forward by Mr. Alun Jones.

Conclusions

...

2. Apparent bias

As I have said, Senator Pinochet does not allege that Lord Hoffmann was in fact biased. The contention is that there was a real danger or reasonable apprehension or suspicion that Lord Hoffmann might have been biased, that is to say, it is alleged that there is an appearance of bias not actual bias.

The fundamental principle is that a man may not be a judge in his own cause. This principle, as developed by the courts, has two very similar but not identical implications. First it may be applied literally: if a judge is in fact a party to the litigation or has a financial or proprietary interest in its outcome then he is indeed sitting as a judge in his own cause. In that case, the mere fact that he is a party to the action or has a financial or proprietary interest in its outcome is sufficient to cause his automatic disqualification. The second application of the principle is where a judge is not a party to the suit and does not have a financial interest in its outcome, but in some other way his conduct or behaviour may give rise to a suspicion that he is not impartial, for example because of his friendship with a party. This second type of case is not strictly speaking an application of the principle that a man must not be judge in his own cause, since the judge will not normally be himself benefiting, but providing a benefit for another by failing to be impartial.

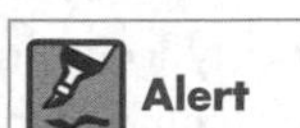

In my judgment, this case falls within the first category of case, viz. where the judge is disqualified because he is a judge in his own cause. In such a case, once it is shown that the judge is himself a party to the cause, or has a relevant interest in its subject matter, he is disqualified without any investigation into whether there was a likelihood or suspicion of bias. The mere fact of his interest is sufficient to disqualify him unless he has made sufficient disclosure: see *Shetreet, Judges on Trial* (1976), p. 303; De Smith, Woolf and Jowell, Judicial Review of Administrative Action, 5th ed. (1995), p. 525. I will call this "automatic disqualification".

In *Dimes v. Proprietors of Grand Junction Canal* (1852) 3 H.L.Cas. 759, the then Lord Chancellor, Lord Cottenham, owned a substantial shareholding in the defendant canal which was an incorporated body. In the action the Lord Chancellor sat on appeal from the Vice-Chancellor, whose judgment in favour of the company he affirmed. There was an appeal to your Lordships' House on the grounds that the Lord Chancellor was disqualified. Their Lordships consulted the judges who advised, at p. 786, that Lord Cottenham was disqualified from sitting as a judge in the cause because he had an interest in the suit. This advice was unanimously accepted by their Lordships. There was no inquiry by the court as to whether a reasonable man would consider Lord Cottenham to be biased and no inquiry as to the circumstances which led to Lord Cottenham sitting. Lord Campbell said, at p. 793:

"No one can suppose that Lord Cottenham could be, in the remotest degree, influenced by the interest he had in this concern; but, my Lords, it is of the last importance that the maxim that no man is to be a judge in his own cause should be held sacred. And that is not to be confined to a cause *in which he is a party* , but applies to a cause in which he has an interest." (Emphasis added.)

On occasion, this proposition is elided so as to omit all references to the disqualification of a judge who is a party to the suit: see, for example, *Reg. v. Rand* (1866) L.R. 1 Q.B. 230; *Reg. v. Gough* [1993] A.C. 646, 661. This does not mean that a judge who is a party to a suit is not disqualified just because the suit does not involve a financial interest. The authorities cited in the *Dimes* case show how the principle developed. The starting-point was the case in which a judge was indeed purporting to decide a case in which he was a party. This was held to be absolutely prohibited. That absolute prohibition was then extended to cases where, although not nominally a party, the judge had an interest in the outcome.

The importance of this point in the present case is this. Neither A.I., nor A.I.C.L., have any financial interest in the outcome of this litigation. We are here confronted, as was

Lord Hoffmann, with a novel situation where the outcome of the litigation did not lead to financial benefit to anyone. The interest of A.I. in the litigation was not financial; it was its interest in achieving the trial and possible conviction of Senator Pinochet for crimes against humanity.

By seeking to intervene in this appeal and being allowed so to intervene, in practice A.I. became a party to the appeal. Therefore if, in the circumstances, it is right to treat Lord Hoffmann as being the alter ego of A.I. and therefore a judge in his own cause, then he must have been automatically disqualified on the grounds that he was a party to the appeal. Alternatively, even if it be not right to say that Lord Hoffmann was a party to the appeal as such, the question then arises whether, in non-financial litigation, anything other than a financial or proprietary interest in the outcome is sufficient automatically to disqualify a man from sitting as judge in the cause.

Are the facts such as to require Lord Hoffmann to be treated as being himself a party to this appeal? The facts are striking and unusual. One of the parties to the appeal is an unincorporated association, A.I. One of the constituent parts of that unincorporated association is A.I.C.L. A.I.C.L. was established, for tax purposes, to carry out part of the functions of A.I. those parts which were charitable which had previously been carried on either by A.I. itself or by A.I.L. Lord Hoffmann is a director and chairman of A.I.C.L., which is wholly controlled by A.I., since its members (who ultimately control it) are all the members of the international executive committee of A.I. A large part of the work of A.I. is, as a matter of strict law, carried on by A.I.C.L. which instructs A.I.L. to do the work on its behalf. In reality, A.I., A.I.C.L. and A.I.L. are a close-knit group carrying on the work of A.I.

However, close as these links are, I do not think it would be right to identify Lord Hoffmann personally as being a party to the appeal. He is closely linked to A.I. but he is not in fact A.I. Although this is an area in which legal technicality is particularly to be avoided, it cannot be ignored that Lord Hoffmann took no part in running A.I. Lord Hoffmann, A.I.C.L. and the executive committee of A.I. are in law separate people.

Then is this a case in which it can be said that Lord Hoffmann had an "interest" which must lead to his automatic disqualification? Hitherto only pecuniary and proprietary interests have led to automatic disqualification. But, as I have indicated, this litigation is most unusual. It is not civil litigation but criminal litigation. Most unusually, by allowing A.I. to intervene, there is a party to a criminal cause or matter who is neither prosecutor nor accused. That party, A.I., shares with the government of Spain and the C.P.S., not a financial interest but an interest to establish that there is no immunity for ex-heads of state in relation to crimes against humanity. The interest of these parties is to procure Senator Pinochet's extradition and trial a non-pecuniary interest. So far as A.I.C.L. is concerned, clause 3(c) of its memorandum provides that one of its objects is "to procure the abolition of torture, extra-judicial execution and disappearance." A.I. has, amongst other objects, the same objects. Although A.I.C.L., as a charity, cannot campaign to change the law, it is concerned by other means to procure the abolition of these crimes against humanity. In my opinion, therefore, A.I.C.L. plainly had a non-pecuniary interest, to establish that Senator Pinochet was not immune.

That being the case, the question is whether in the very unusual circumstances of this case a non-pecuniary interest to achieve a particular result is sufficient to give rise to automatic disqualification and, if so, whether the fact that A.I.C.L. had such an interest necessarily leads to the conclusion that Lord Hoffmann, as a director of A.I.C.L., was automatically disqualified from sitting on the appeal? My Lords, in my judgment, although the cases have all dealt with automatic disqualification on the grounds of pecuniary interest, there is no good reason in principle for so limiting automatic disqualification. The rationale of the whole rule is that a man cannot be a judge in his own cause. In civil litigation the matters in issue will normally have an economic impact; therefore a judge is automatically disqualified if he stands to make a financial gain as a consequence of his own decision of the case. But if, as in the present case, the matter at issue does not relate to money or economic advantage but is concerned with the promotion of the cause, the rationale disqualifying a judge applies just as much if the judge's decision will lead to the promotion of a cause in which the judge is involved together with one of the parties. Thus in my opinion if Lord Hoffmann had been a member of A.I. he would have been automatically disqualified because of his non-pecuniary interest in establishing that Senator Pinochet was not entitled to immunity. Indeed, so much I understood to have been conceded by Mr. Duffy.

This case is very unusual on its facts and should be construed narrowly, a point with Lord Browne-Wilkinson was at pains to make in his speech. It has, however, established that personal interest bias is not necessarily limited to examples of pecuniary interest (although it will be very rare for the kind of interest in the *Pinochet* case actually to be found in a given situation). It is important to appreciate the context of the *Pinochet* case too; this was a symbolically very significant and politically contentious case and so the need for the highest possible degree of impartiality was vital. Even the remotest suggestion or appearance of bias could not be countenanced in that rare situation.

3.2 Non-automatic Disqualification Bias

Porter v Magill [2002] 2 AC 357

Panel: Lord Bingham of Cornhill, Lord Steyn, Lord Hope of Craighead, Lord Hobhouse of Woodborough and Lord Scott of Foscote

Facts: Shirley Porter, former leader of Westminster City Council, had been accused and found guilty of wilful misconduct in the exercise of public powers, leading to the imposition of a high personal, financial surcharge. The issue of bias arose against the District Auditor, Magill, who it was alleged had pre-judged the issue against her.

LORD HOPE OF CRAIGHEAD

Apparent bias

99. The test for apparent bias which the auditor sought to apply to himself, and was applied in its turn by the Divisional Court, was that which was described in *R v Gough* [1993] AC 646 by Lord Goff of Chieveley where he said, at p 670:

"I think it unnecessary, in formulating the appropriate test, to require that the court should look at the matter through the eyes of a reasonable man, because the court in cases such as these personifies the reasonable man; and in any event the court has first to ascertain the relevant circumstances from the available evidence, knowledge of which would not necessarily have been available to an observer in court at the relevant time. Finally, for the avoidance of doubt, I prefer to state the test in terms of real danger rather than real likelihood, to ensure that the court is thinking of possibility rather than probability of bias. Accordingly, having ascertained the relevant circumstances, the court should ask itself whether, having regard to those circumstances, there was a real danger of bias on the part of the relevant member of the tribunal in question, in the sense that he might unfairly regard (or have unfairly regarded) with favour, or disfavour, the case of a party to the issue under consideration by him ..."

100. The "reasonable likelihood" and "real danger" tests which Lord Goff described in *R v Gough* have been criticised by the High Court of Australia on the ground that they tend to emphasise the court's view of the facts and to place inadequate emphasis on the public perception of the irregular incident: *Webb v The Queen* (1994) 181 CLR 41, 50, per Mason CJ and McHugh J. There is an uneasy tension between these tests and that which was adopted in Scotland by the High Court of Justiciary in *Bradford v McLeod* 1986 SLT 244. Following Eve J's reference in *Law v Chartered Institute of Patent Agents* [1919] 2 Ch 276 (which was not referred to in *R v Gough*), the High Court of Justiciary adopted a test which looked at the question whether there was suspicion of bias through the eyes of the reasonable man who was aware of the circumstances: see also *Millar v Dickson* 2001 SLT 988, 1002-1003. This approach, which has been described as "the reasonable apprehension of bias" test, is in line with that adopted in most common law jurisdictions. It is also in line with that which the Strasbourg court has adopted, which looks at the question whether there was a risk of bias objectively in the light of the circumstances which the court has identified: *Piersack v Belgium* (1982) 5 EHRR 169, 179-180, paras 30-31; *De Cubber v Belgium* (1984) 7 EHRR 236, 246, para 30; *Pullar v United Kingdom* (1996) 22 EHRR 391, 402-403, para 30. In *Hauschildt v Denmark* (1989) 12 EHRR 266, 279, para 48 the court also observed that, in considering whether there was a legitimate reason to fear that a judge lacks impartiality, the standpoint of the accused is important but not decisive: "What is decisive is whether this fear can be held objectively justified."

101. The English courts have been reluctant, for obvious reasons, to depart from the test which Lord Goff of Chieveley so carefully formulated in *R v Gough*. In *R v Bow Street Metropolitan Stipendiary Magistrate, Ex p Pinochet Ugarte (No 2)* [2000] 1 AC 119, 136a-c Lord Browne-Wilkinson said that it was unnecessary in that case to determine whether it needed to be reviewed in the light of subsequent decisions in Canada, New Zealand and Australia. I said, at p 142f-g, that, although the tests in Scotland and England were described differently, their application was likely in practice to lead to results that were so similar as to be indistinguishable. The Court of Appeal, having examined the question whether the "real danger" test might lead to a different result from that which the informed observer would reach on the same facts, concluded in *Locabail (UK) Ltd v Bayfield Properties Ltd*[2000] QB 451, 477 that in the

overwhelming majority of cases the application of the two tests would lead to the same outcome.

102. In my opinion however it is now possible to set this debate to rest. The Court of Appeal took the opportunity in *In re Medicaments and Related Classes of Goods (No 2)*[2001] 1 WLR 700 to reconsider the whole question. Lord Phillips of Worth Matravers MR, giving the judgment of the court, observed, at p 711a-b, that the precise test to be applied when determining whether a decision should be set aside on account of bias had given rise to difficulty, reflected in judicial decisions that had appeared in conflict, and that the attempt to resolve that conflict in *R v Gough* had not commanded universal approval. At p 711b-c he said that, as the alternative test had been thought to be more closely in line with Strasbourg jurisprudence which since 2 October 2000 the English courts were required to take into account, the occasion should now be taken to review *R v Gough* to see whether the test it lays down is, indeed, in conflict with Strasbourg jurisprudence. Having conducted that review he summarised the court's conclusions, at pp 726-727:

"85. When the Strasbourg jurisprudence is taken into account, we believe that a modest adjustment of the test in *R v Gough* is called for, which makes it plain that it is, in effect, no different from the test applied in most of the Commonwealth and in Scotland. The court must first ascertain all the circumstances which have a bearing on the suggestion that the judge was biased. It must then ask whether those circumstances would lead a fair-minded and informed observer to conclude that there was a real possibility, or a real danger, the two being the same, that the tribunal was biased."

103. I respectfully suggest that your Lordships should now approve the modest adjustment of the test in *R v Gough* set out in that paragraph. It expresses in clear and simple language a test which is in harmony with the objective test which the Strasbourg court applies when it is considering whether the circumstances give rise to a reasonable apprehension of bias. It removes any possible conflict with the test which is now applied in most Commonwealth countries and in Scotland. I would however delete from it the reference to "a real danger". Those words no longer serve a useful purpose here, and they are not used in the jurisprudence of the Strasbourg court. The question is whether the fair-minded and informed observer, having considered the facts, would conclude that there was a real possibility that the tribunal was biased.

This last sentence is now the test applied when considering non-automatic disqualification bias.

Further Reading

Blom-Cooper, Louis 'Bias: malfunction in judicial decision-making', [2009] *PL* 199

Williams, David 'Bias; the judges and the separation of powers', [2000] *PL* 45

Campbell, N R 'The duty to give reasons in administrative law', [1994] *PL* 184

17

Legitimate Expectation

Topic List

Alex Lawson and Christopher Costigan

Introduction

Legitimate expectations arise out of a promise on the part of a public body that the claimant can expect to be fulfilled, or a practice on the part of a pubic body which the claimant can expect to continue. The term legitimate expectation has its origin in the case of *Schmidt and Another v Secretary of State for Home Affairs* [1969] 2 Ch 149.

***Schmidt and Another v Secretary of State for Home Affairs* [1969] 2 Ch 149**

Panel: Lord Denning MR, Russell and Widgery LJJ

Facts: The applicants were aliens who were in the UK to study at the Hubbard School of Scientology. Their visas had expired and they were seeking permission to remain to complete their studies. However, the Home Secretary had removed the School from the list of educational establishments for which visas could be granted and so the applications were refused. Schmidt, and another 50 students in a similar position, applied to the court on the basis that they had a legitimate expectation to be heard before their application was refused.

LORD DENNING MR

The speeches in *Ridge v. Baldwin* [1964] A.C. 40 show that an administrative body may, in a proper case, be bound to give a person who is affected by their decision an opportunity of making representations. It all depends on whether he has some right or interest, or, I would add, some legitimate expectation, of which it would not be fair to deprive him without hearing what he has to say.

While the applicants in *Schmidt* lost their case, it was established that an action could lie, not on the basis of an existing public law right, but on the basis of the public body's own actions giving rise to a legitimate expectation. That legitimate expectations exist independently of the traditional grounds of review was confirmed by Lord Fraser in *A-G of Hong Kong v Ng Yuen Shiu* [1983] 2 AC 629, where he said '"legitimate expectations" in this context are capable of including expectations which go beyond enforceable legal rights, provided they have some reasonable basis'.

1 Substantive Legitimate Expectation

In the genesis of legitimate expectation it seems clear that protection was anticipated to be through the imposition of a procedural requirement: normally a duty to be heard, which existing public law rights (ie those associated with the idea of procedural impropriety) would not otherwise provide. However, in subsequent case law it has become clear that in certain circumstances the substance of the expectation can also be protected by the courts.

Regina v North and East Devon Health Authority, ex parte Coughlan [2001] QB 213

Panel: Lord Woolf MR, Mummery and Sedley LJJ

Facts: Coughlan had been severely disabled in a road accident and had to live in a hospital. With her agreement, the health authority moved her to Mardon House, a residential care home for the long-term disabled, on the basis that it would be her 'home for life'. Later, the health authority sought to close Mardon House and Coughlan brought an action on the basis that she had been given a legitimate expectation that she could stay in Mardon House for life. Significantly here, however, she sought not just consultation before the decision was determined but also the right actually to stay in the home: in other words, the substance of the legitimate expectation itself.

LORD WOOLF MR handed down the following judgment of the court.

This is the judgment of the court to which all members of the court have contributed.

...

C. The promise of a home for life

50. The health authority appeals on the ground that the judge wrongly held that it had failed to establish that there was an overriding public interest which entitled it to break the "home for life" promise. In particular, the judge erred in concluding that the health authority had applied the wrong legal test in deciding whether the promise could or should be broken and that it had wrongly diluted the promise and treated it as merely a promise to provide care. It contends that it applied the correct legal test and that the promise had, in the decision-making process, been plainly and accurately expressed and given appropriate prominence.

51. It is also contended that the judge failed to address the overwhelming evidence on the urgent need to remedy the deficiencies of the reablement service and of the serious and acute risks to the reablement service if the status quo at Mardon House were maintained. If he had addressed that issue he would and should have concluded that the health authority was entitled to decide that such consideration pointed inexorably to the closure decision

52. It has been common ground throughout these proceedings that in public law the health authority could break its promise to Miss Coughlan that Mardon House would be her home for life if, and only if, an overriding public interest required it. Both Mr Goudie and Mr Gordon adopted the position that, while the initial judgment on this question has to be made by the health authority, it can be impugned if improperly reached. We consider that it is for the court to decide in an arguable case whether such a judgment, albeit properly arrived at, strikes a proper balance between the public and the private interest.

...

The judgment

54. It is also helpful to set out the views of the judge on this issue. The judge regarded as "the proper starting point" the question of what effect did the "promise for life" have in law. He held that it was a clear promise to Miss Coughlan and the other patients that Mardon House would be a permanent home for them; that a decision to break it, if unfair, would be equivalent to a breach of contract; that a public authority could reasonably resile from such a promise where the overriding public interest demanded it; and that the health authority had failed to discharge the burden of establishing that there were "compelling circumstances" amounting to an overreaching public interest. The health authority had concluded that, in its scale of priorities, reablement came higher than Miss Coughlan and her fellow patients. The "promise for life" was a relevant consideration. The judge concluded as follows:

"Consideration of the promise had to start with a proper understanding of the promise. It was a promise to provide care at Mardon House but the health authority wrongly treated it as merely a promise to provide care. That meant that the authority's attitude to the place where care was to be provided was flawed from the start."

Legitimate expectation—the court's role

55. In considering the correctness of this part of the judge's decision it is necessary to begin by examining the court's role where what is in issue is a promise as to how it would behave in the future made by a public body when exercising a statutory function. In the past it would have been argued that the promise was to be ignored since it could not have any effect on how the public body exercised its judgment in what it thought was the public interest. Today such an argument would have no prospect of success, as Mr Goudie and Mr Gordon accept.

56. What is still the subject of some controversy is the court's role when a member of the public, as a result of a promise or other conduct, has a legitimate expectation that he will be treated in one way and the public body wishes to treat him or her in a different way. Here the starting point has to be to ask what in the circumstances the member of the public could legitimately expect. In the words of Lord Scarman in *In re Findlay* [1985] AC 318, 338, "But what was their *legitimate* expectation?" Where there is a dispute as to this, the dispute has to be determined by the court, as happened in *In re Findlay*. This can involve a detailed examination of the precise terms of the promise or representation made, the circumstances in which the promise was made and the nature of the statutory or other discretion.

57. There are at least three possible outcomes. (a) The court may decide that the public authority is only required to bear in mind its previous policy or other representation, giving it the weight it thinks right, but no more, before deciding whether to change course. Here the court is confined to reviewing the decision on Wednesbury grounds (*Associated Provincial Picture Houses Ltd v Wednesbury Corpn* [1948] 1 KB 223). This has been held to be the effect of changes of policy in cases involving the early release of prisoners: see *In re Findlay* [1985] AC 318 ; *R v Secretary of State for the Home Department, Ex p Hargreaves* [1997] 1 WLR 906. (b) On the other hand the court may

decide that the promise or practice induces a legitimate expectation of, for example, being consulted before a particular decision is taken. Here it is uncontentious that the court itself will require *the opportunity for consultation* to be given unless there is an overriding reason to resile from it (see *Attorney General of Hong Kong v Ng Yuen Shiu* [1983] 2 AC 629) in which case the court will itself judge the adequacy of the reason advanced for the change of policy, taking into account what fairness requires. (c) Where the court considers that a lawful promise or practice has induced a legitimate expectation of a benefit which is substantive, not simply procedural, authority now establishes that here too the court will in a proper case decide whether to frustrate the expectation is so unfair that to take a new and different course will amount to an abuse of power. Here, once the legitimacy of the expectation is established, the court will have the task of weighing the requirements of fairness against any overriding interest relied upon for the change of policy.

58. The court having decided which of the categories is appropriate, the court's role in the case of the second and third categories is different from that in the first. In the case of the first, the court is restricted to reviewing the decision on conventional grounds. The test will be rationality and whether the public body has given proper weight to the implications of not fulfilling the promise. In the case of the second category the court's task is the conventional one of determining whether the decision was procedurally fair. In the case of the third, the court has when necessary to determine whether there is a sufficient overriding interest to justify a departure from what has been previously promised.

59. In many cases the difficult task will be to decide into which category the decision should be allotted. In what is still a developing field of law, attention will have to be given to what it is in the first category of case which limits the applicant's legitimate expectation (in Lord Scarman's words in *In re Findlay* [1985] AC 318) to an expectation that whatever policy is in force at the time will be applied to him. As to the second and third categories, the difficulty of segregating the procedural from the substantive is illustrated by the line of cases arising out of decisions of justices not to commit a defendant to the Crown Court for sentence, or assurances given to a defendant by the court: here to resile from such a decision or assurance may involve the breach of legitimate expectation: see *R v Grice* (1977) 66 Cr App R 167; cf *R v Reilly* [1982] QB 1208, *R v Dover Magistrates' Court, Ex p Pamment* (1994) 15 Cr App R(S) 778, 782. No attempt is made in those cases, rightly in our view, to draw the distinction. Nevertheless, most cases of an enforceable expectation of a substantive benefit (the third category) are likely in the nature of things to be cases where the expectation is confined to one person or a few people, giving the promise or representation the character of a contract. We recognise that the courts' role in relation to the third category is still controversial; but, as we hope to show, it is now clarified by authority.

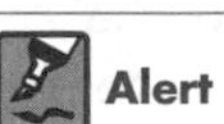

60. We consider that Mr Goudie and Mr Gordon are correct, as was the judge, in regarding the facts of this case as coming into the third category. (Even if this were not correct because of the nature of the promise, and even if the case fell within the second category, the health authority in exercising its discretion and in due course the court

would have to take into account that only an overriding public interest would justify resiling from the promise.) Our reasons are as follows. First, the importance of what was promised to Miss Coughlan (as we will explain later, this is a matter underlined by the Human Rights Act 1998); second, the fact that promise was limited to a few individuals, and the fact that the consequences to the health authority of requiring it to honour its promise are likely to be financial only.

The authorities

61. Whether to frustrate a legitimate expectation can amount to an abuse of power is the question which was posed by the House of Lords in *R v Inland Revenue Comrs, Ex p Preston* [1985] AC 835 and addressed more recently by this court in *R v Inland Revenue Comrs, Ex p Unilever plc* [1996] STC 681. In each case it was in relation to a decision by a public authority (the Crown) to resile from a representation about how it would treat a member of the public (the taxpayer). It cannot be suggested that special principles of public law apply to the Inland Revenue or to taxpayers. Yet this is an area of law which has been a site of recent controversy, because while *Ex p Preston* has been followed in tax cases, using the vocabulary of abuse of power, in other fields of public law analogous challenges, couched in the language of legitimate expectation, have not all been approached in the same way.

62. There has never been any question that the propriety of a breach by a public authority of a legitimate expectation of the second category, of a *procedural* benefit—typically a promise of being heard or consulted—is a matter for full review by the court. The court has, in other words, to examine the relevant circumstances and to decide for itself whether what happened was fair. This is of a piece with the historic jurisdiction of the courts over issues of procedural justice. But in relation to a legitimate expectation of a substantive benefit (such as a promise of a home for life) doubt has been cast upon whether the same standard of review applies. Instead it is suggested that the proper standard is the so-called *Wednesbury* standard which is applied to the generality of executive decisions. This touches the intrinsic quality of the decision, as opposed to the means by which it has been reached, only where the decision is irrational or (per Lord Diplock in *Council of Civil Service Unions v Minister for the Civil Service* [1985] AC 374, 410) immoral.

...

64. It is axiomatic that a public authority which derives its existence and its powers from statute cannot validly act outside those powers. This is the familiar ultra vires doctrine adopted by public law from company law (*Colman v Eastern Counties Railway Co* (1846) 10 Beav 1). Since such powers will ordinarily include anything fairly incidental to the express remit, a statutory body may lawfully adopt and follow policies (*British Oxygen Co Ltd v Board of Trade* [1971] AC 610) and enter into formal undertakings. But since it cannot abdicate its general remit, not only must it remain free to change policy; its undertakings are correspondingly open to modification or abandonment. The recurrent question is when and where and how the courts are to intervene to protect the public from unwarranted harm in this process. The problem can readily be seen to go wider than the exercise of statutory powers. It may equally arise

in relation to the exercise of the prerogative power, which at least since *R v Criminal Injuries Compensation Board, Ex p Lain* [1967] 2 QB 864, has been subject to judicial review, and in relation to private monopoly powers: *R v Panel on Take-overs and Mergers, Ex p Datafin plc* [1987] QB 815.

65. The court's task in all these cases is not to impede executive activity but to reconcile its continuing need to initiate or respond to change with the legitimate interests or expectations of citizens or strangers who have relied, and have been justified in relying, on a current policy or an extant promise. The critical question is by what standard the court is to resolve such conflicts. It is when one examines the implications for a case like the present of the proposition that, so long as the decision-making process has been lawful, the court's only ground of intervention is the intrinsic rationality of the decision, that the problem becomes apparent. Rationality, as it has developed in modern public law, has two faces: one is the barely known decision which simply defies comprehension; the other is a decision which can be seen to have proceeded by flawed logic (though this can often be equally well allocated to the intrusion of an irrelevant factor). The present decision may well pass a rationality test; the health authority knew of the promise and its seriousness; it was aware of its new policies and the reasons for them; it knew that one had to yield, and it made a choice which, whatever else can be said of it, may not easily be challenged as irrational. As Lord Diplock said in *Secretary of State for Education and Science v Tameside Metropolitan Borough Council* [1977] AC 1014, 1064:

"The very concept of administrative discretion involves a right to choose between more than one possible course of action upon which there is room for reasonable people to hold differing opinions as to which is to be preferred."

But to limit the court's power of supervision to this is to exclude from consideration another aspect of the decision which is equally the concern of the law.

66. In the ordinary case there is no space for intervention on grounds of abuse of power once a rational decision directed to a proper purpose has been reached by lawful process. The present class of case is visibly different. It involves not one but two lawful exercises of power (the promise and the policy change) by the same public authority, with consequences for individuals trapped between the two. The policy decision may well, and often does, make as many exceptions as are proper and feasible to protect individual expectations. The departmental decision in *Ex p Hamble (Offshore) Fisheries Ltd* [1995] 2 All ER 714 is a good example. If it does not, as in *Ex p Unilever plc* [1996] STC 681, the court is there to ensure that the power to make and alter policy has not been abused by unfairly frustrating legitimate individual expectations. In such a situation a bare rationality test would constitute the public authority judge in its own cause, for a decision to prioritise a policy change over legitimate expectations will almost always be rational from where the authority stands, even if objectively it is arbitrary or unfair. It is in response to this dilemma that two distinct but related approaches have developed in the modern cases.

67. One approach is to ask not whether the decision is ultra vires in the restricted *Wednesbury* sense but whether, for example through unfairness or arbitrariness, it

amounts to an abuse of power. The leading case on the existence of this principle is *Ex p Preston* [1985] AC 835. It concerned an allegation, not in the event made out, that the Inland Revenue Commissioners had gone back impermissibly on their promise not to reinvestigate certain aspects of an individual taxpayer's affairs. Lord Scarman, expressing his agreement with the single fully reasoned speech (that of Lord Templeman) advanced a number of important general propositions. First, he said, at p 851:

"... I must make clear my view that the principle of fairness has an important place in the law of judicial review: and that in an appropriate case it is a ground upon which the court can intervene to quash a decision made by a public officer or authority in purported exercise of a power conferred by law."

Second, Lord Scarman reiterated, citing the decision of the House of Lords in *R v Inland Revenue Comrs, Ex p National Federation of Self-Employed and Small Businesses Ltd* [1982] AC 617, that a claim for judicial review may arise where the Commissioners have failed to discharge their statutory duty to an individual or "have abused their powers or acted outside them". Third, that "unfairness in the purported exercise of a power can be such that it is an abuse or excess of power".

68. It is evident from these passages and from Lord Scarman's further explanation of them that, in his view at least, it is unimportant whether the unfairness is analytically within or beyond the power conferred by law: on either view public law today reaches it. The same approach was taken by Lord Templeman, at p 862:

"Judicial review is available where a decision-making authority exceeds its powers, commits an error of law, commits a breach of natural justice, reaches a decision which no reasonable tribunal could have reached, or abuses its powers."

69. Abuses of power may take many forms. One, not considered in the *Wednesbury case* [1948] 1 KB 223 (even though it was arguably what the case was about), was the use of a power for a collateral purpose. Another, as cases like *Ex p Preston* [1985] AC 835 now make clear, is reneging without adequate justification, by an otherwise lawful decision, on a lawful promise or practice adopted towards a limited number of individuals. There is no suggestion in *Ex p Preston* or elsewhere that the final arbiter of justification, rationality apart, is the decision-maker rather than the court. Lord Templeman, at pp 864-866, reviewed the law in extenso, including the classic decisions in *Laker Airways Ltd v Department of Trade* [1977] QB 643; *Padfield v Minister of Agriculture, Fisheries and Food* [1968] AC 997; *Congreve v Home Office* [1976] QB 629 and *HTV Ltd v Price Commission* [1976] ICR 170 ("It is a commonplace of modern law that such bodies must act fairly... and that the courts have power to redress unfairness": Scarman LJ at p 189.) He reached this conclusion, at pp 866-867:

"In principle I see no reason why the [taxpayer] should not be entitled to judicial review of a decision taken by the commissioners if that decision is unfair to the [taxpayer] because the conduct of the commissioners is equivalent to a breach of contract or a breach of representation. Such a decision falls within the ambit of an abuse of power for which in the present case judicial review is the sole remedy and an appropriate remedy. There may be cases in which conduct which savours of breach of [contract] or breach of representation does not constitute an abuse of power; there may be circumstances in which the court in its discretion might not grant relief by judicial review notwithstanding conduct which savours of breach of contract or breach of representation. In the present case, however, I consider that the [taxpayer] is entitled to relief by way of judicial review for 'unfairness' amounting to abuse of power if the commissioners have been guilty of conduct equivalent to a breach of contract or breach of representations on their part."

The entire passage, too long to set out here, merits close attention. It may be observed that Lord Templeman's final formulation, taken by itself, would allow no room for a test of overriding public interest. This, it is clear, is because of the facts then before the House. In a case such as the present the question posed in the *HTV case* [1976] ICR 170 remains live.

70. This approach, in our view, embraces all the principles of public law which we have been considering. It recognises the primacy of the public authority both in administration and in policy development but it insists, where these functions come into tension, upon the adjudicative role of the court to ensure fairness to the individual. It does not overlook the passage in the speech of Lord Browne-Wilkinson in *R v Hull University Visitor, Ex p Page* [1993] AC 682, 701, that the basis of the "fundamental principle ... that the courts will intervene to ensure that the powers of public decision-making bodies are exercised lawfully" is the *Wednesbury* limit on the exercise of powers; but it follows the authority not only of *Ex p Preston* [1985] AC 835 but of Lord Scarman's speech in *R v Secretary of State for the Environment, Ex p Nottinghamshire County Council* [1986] AC 240, 249, in treating a power which is abused as a power which has not been lawfully exercised.

71. Fairness in such a situation, if it is to mean anything, must for the reasons we have considered include fairness of outcome. This in turn is why the doctrine of legitimate expectation has emerged as a distinct application of the concept of abuse of power in relation to substantive as well as procedural benefits, representing a second approach to the same problem. If this is the position in the case of the third category, why is it not also the position in relation to the first category? May it be (though this was not considered in *In re Findlay* [1985] AC 318 or *Ex p Hargreaves* [1997] 1 WLR 906) that, when a promise is made to a category of individuals who have the same interest, it is more likely to be considered to have binding effect than a promise which is made generally or to a diverse class, when the interests of those to whom the promise is made may differ or, indeed, may be in conflict? Legitimate expectation may play different parts in different aspects of public law. The limits to its role have yet to be finally determined by the courts. Its application is still being developed on a case by case basis. Even where it reflects procedural expectations, for example concerning consultation, it may be affected by an overriding public interest. It may operate as an aspect of good administration, qualifying the intrinsic rationality of policy choices. And without injury to the *Wednesbury* doctrine it may furnish a proper basis for the application of the now established concept of abuse of power.

...

Fairness and the decision to close

83. How are fairness and the overriding public interest in this particular context to be judged? The question arises concretely in the present case. Mr Goudie argued, with detailed references, that all the indicators, apart from the promise itself, pointed to an overriding public interest, so that the court ought to endorse the health authority's decision. Mr Gordon contended, likewise with detailed references, that the data before the health authority were far from uniform. But this is not what matters. What matters is that, having taken it all into account, the health authority voted for closure in spite of the promise. The propriety of such an exercise of power should be tested by asking whether the need which the health authority judged to exist to move Miss Coughlan to a local authority facility was such as to outweigh its promise that Mardon House would be her home for life.

84. That a promise was made is confirmed by the evidence of the health authority that:

"the applicant and her fellow residents were justified in treating certain statements made by the health authority's predecessor, coupled with the way in which the authority's predecessor conducted itself at the time of the residents' move from Newcourt Hospital, as amounting to an assurance that, having moved to Mardon House, Mardon House would be a permanent home for them."

And the letter of 7 June 1994 sent to the residents by Mr Peter Jackson, the then general manager of the predecessor of the health authority, following the withdrawal of John Grooms stated:

"During the course of a meeting yesterday with Ross Bentley's father, it was suggested that each of the former Newcourt residents now living at Mardon House would appreciate a further letter of reassurance from me. I am writing to confirm therefore, that the health authority has made it clear to the community trust that it expects the trust to continue to provide good quality care for you at Mardon House for as long as you choose to live there. I hope that this will dispel any anxieties you may have arising from the forthcoming change in management arrangements, about which I wrote to you recently."

As has been pointed out by the health authority, the letter did not actually use the expression "home for life."

85. The health authority had, according to its evidence, formed the view that it should give considerable weight to the assurances given to Miss Coughlan; that those assurances had given rise to expectations which should not, in the ordinary course of things, be disappointed; but that it should not treat those assurances as giving rise to an absolute and unqualified entitlement on the part of the Miss Coughlan and her co-residents since that would be unreasonable and unrealistic; and that:

"if there were compelling reasons which indicated overwhelmingly that closure was the reasonable and—other things being equal—the right course to take, provided that steps could be taken to meet the applicant's (and her fellow residents') expectations to the greatest degree possible following closure, it was open to the authority, weighing up all these matters with care and sensitivity, to decide in favour of the option of closure."

Although the first consultation paper made no reference to the "home for life" promise, it was referred to in the second consultation paper as set out above.

86. It is denied in the health authority's evidence that there was any misrepresentation at the meeting of the board on 7 October 1998 of the terms of the "home for life" promise. It is asserted that the board had taken the promise into account; that members of the board had previously seen a copy of Mr Jackson's letter of 7 June 1994, which, they were reminded, had not used the word "home"; and that every board member was well aware that, in terms of its fresh decision-making, the starting point was that the Newcourt patients had moved to Mardon on the strength of an assurance that Mardon would be their home as long as they chose to live there. This was an express promise or representation made on a number of occasions in precise terms. It was made to a small group of severely disabled individuals who had been housed and cared for over a substantial period in the health authority's predecessor's premises at Newcourt. It specifically related to identified premises which it was represented would be their home for as long as they chose. It was in unqualified terms. It was repeated and confirmed to reassure the residents. It was made by the health authority's predecessor for its own purposes, namely to encourage Miss Coughlan and her fellow residents to move out of Newcourt and into Mardon House, a specially built substitute home in which they would continue to receive nursing care. The promise was relied on by Miss Coughlan. Strong reasons are required to justify resiling from a promise given in those circumstances. This is not a case where the health authority would, in keeping the promise, be acting inconsistently with its statutory or other pubic law duties. A decision not to honour it would be equivalent to a breach of contract in private law.

87. The health authority treated the promise as the "starting point" from which the consultation process and the deliberations proceeded. It was a factor which should be given "considerable weight", but it could be outweighed by "compelling reasons which indicated overwhelmingly that closure was the reasonable and the right course to take". The health authority, though "mindful of the history behind the residents' move to Mardon House and their understandable expectation that it would be their permanent home", formed the view that there were "overriding reasons" why closure should nonetheless proceed. The health authority wanted to improve the provision of reablement services and considered that the mix of a long stay residential service and a reablement service at Mardon House was inappropriate and detrimental to the interests of both users of the service. The acute reablement service could not be supported there without an uneconomic investment which would have produced a second class reablement service. It was argued that there was a compelling public interest which justified the health authority's prioritisation of the reablement service.

88. It is, however, clear from the health authority's evidence and submissions that it did not consider that it had a legal responsibility or commitment to provide a *home* , as distinct from care or funding of care, for the applicant and her fellow residents. It considered that, following the withdrawal of the John Grooms Association, the provision of care services to the current residents had become "excessively expensive,"

having regard to the needs of the majority of disabled people in the authority's area and the "insuperable problems" involved in the mix of long-term residential care and reablement services at Mardon House. Mardon House had, contrary to earlier expectations, become:

"a prohibitively expensive white elephant. The unit was not financially viable. Its continued operation was dependent upon the authority supporting it at an excessively high cost. This did not represent value for money and left fewer resources for other services."

The health authority's attitude was that:

"It was because of our appreciation of the residents' expectation that they would remain at Mardon House for the rest of their lives that the board agreed that the authority should accept a continuing commitment to finance the care of the residents of Mardon for whom it was responsible."

But the cheaper option favoured by the health authority misses the essential point of the promise which had been given. The fact is that the health authority has not offered to the applicant an equivalent facility to replace what was promised to her. The health authority's undertaking to fund her care for the remainder of her life is substantially different in nature and effect from the earlier promise that care for her would be provided *at Mardon House*. That place would be her home for as long as she chose to live there.

89. We have no hesitation in concluding that the decision to move Miss Coughlan against her will and in breach of the health authority's own promise was in the circumstances unfair. It was unfair because it frustrated her legitimate expectation of having a home for life in Mardon House. There was no overriding public interest which justified it. In drawing the balance of conflicting interests the court will not only accept the policy change without demur but will pay the closest attention to the assessment made by the public body itself. Here, however, as we have already indicated, the health authority failed to weigh the conflicting interests correctly. Furthermore, we do not know (for reasons we will explain later) the quality of the alternative accommodation and services which will be offered to Miss Coughlan. We cannot prejudge what would be the result if there was on offer accommodation which could be said to be reasonably equivalent to Mardon House and the health authority made a properly considered decision in favour of closure in the light of that offer. However, absent such an offer, here there was unfairness amounting to an abuse of power by the health authority.

The case of *Coughlan* established three different ways in which a legitimate expectation may be protected according to Lord Woolf MR in para 58 of his judgment, but it is not clear in exactly what circumstances an expectation would fall into each of the three categories. In the case of *R v Secretary of State for Education ex p Begbie* [2000] 1 WLR 1115, Laws LJ gave valuable guidance on this point.

Regina v Secretary of State for Education and Employment ex p Begbie [2000] 1 WLR 1115

Panel: Peter Gibson, Laws and Sedley LJJ

Facts: This case involved the assisted places scheme under which some students were supported financially by the state to allow them to attend private schools. When in opposition before 1997 the Labour Party had committed itself to disband the scheme but, both before and after the election, had indicated that no student who was currently in the scheme would be adversely affected until their placement ceased. Begbie's daughter was at an all-through school (a school which provided both primary and secondary education), and thought that she would be able to attend the school until 18. However, the new Labour Education Secretary, David Blunkett, determined that her education would only be funded until the end of primary school age. The applicant applied for judicial review on the basis of a legitimate expectation.

LORD JUSTICE LAWS

I agree that this appeal should be dismissed... . I would add a few words of my own upon the application of the legal principles relating to legitimate expectations... .

Abuse of power has become, or is fast becoming, the root concept which governs and conditions our general principles of public law. It may be said to be the rationale of the doctrines enshrined in *Associated Provincial Picture Houses Ltd. v. Wednesbury Corporation* [1948] 1 K.B. 223 and *Padfield v. Minister of Agriculture, Fisheries and Food* [1968] A.C. 997, of illegality as a ground of challenge, of the requirement of proportionality, and of the court's insistence on procedural fairness. It informs all three categories of legitimate expectation cases as they have been expounded by this court in *Reg. v. North and East Devon Health Authority, Ex parte Coughlan* [2000] 2 W.L.R. 622.

The difficulty, and at once therefore the challenge, in translating this root concept or first principle into hard clear law is to be found in this question, to which the court addressed itself in the *Coughlan* case: where a breach of a legitimate expectation is established, how may the breach be justified to this court? In the first of the three categories given in *Ex parte Coughlan*, the test is limited to the *Wednesbury* principle. But in the third (where there is a legitimate expectation of a substantive benefit) the court must decide "whether to frustrate the expectation is so unfair that to take a new and different course will amount to an abuse of power:" [2000] 2 W.L.R. 622, 645, para. 57. However the first category may also involve deprivation of a substantive benefit. What marks the true difference between the two? In the *Coughlan* case this court allotted the facts of the case before it to the third category, for these reasons, at p. 646, para. 60:

"First, the importance of what was promised to Miss Coughlan... second, the fact that promise was limited to a few individuals, and the fact that the consequences to the health authority of requiring it to honour its promise are likely to be financial only."

Fairness and reasonableness (and their contraries) are objective concepts; otherwise there would be no public law, or if there were it would be palm tree justice. But each is a spectrum, not a single point, and they shade into one another. It is now well established that the *Wednesbury* principle itself constitutes a sliding scale of review, more or less intrusive according to the nature and gravity of what is at stake: see for example, in the field of human rights, the observations of Sir Thomas Bingham M.R. in *Reg. v. Ministry of Defence, Ex parte Smith* [1996] Q.B. 517. The court's review of the authorities in the *Coughlan* case [2000] 2 W.L.R. 622 shows, as was said at p. 648, para. 69, that abuse of power may take many forms; and, at p. 651, para. 74: "Nowhere in this body of authority, nor in *Reg. v. Inland Revenue Commissioners, Ex parte Preston* [1985] A.C. 835, nor in *In re Findlay* [1985] A.C. 318, is there any suggestion that judicial review of a decision which frustrates a substantive legitimate expectation is confined to the rationality of the decision. But in *Reg. v. Secretary of State for the Home Department, Ex parte Hargreaves* [1997] 1 W.L.R. 906, 921, 925 Hirst L.J. (with whom Peter Gibson L.J. agreed) was persuaded to reject the notion of scrutiny for fairness as heretical, and Pill L.J. to reject it as wrong in "principle".

The court proceeded, at p. 652, para. 76 to distinguish *Reg. v. Secretary of State for the Home Department, Ex parte Hargreaves* [1997] 1 W.L.R. 906 on the basis that: "fairness in the statutory context required more of the decision-maker than in *Ex parte Hargreaves* where the sole legitimate expectation possessed by the prisoners had been met".

As it seems to me the first and third categories explained in the Coughlan case [2000] 2 W.L.R. 622 are not hermetically sealed. The facts of the case, viewed always in their statutory context, will steer the court to a more or less intrusive quality of review. In some cases a change of tack by a public authority, though unfair from the applicant's stance, may involve questions of general policy affecting the public at large or a significant section of it (including interests not represented before the court); here the judges may well be in no position to adjudicate save at most on a bare Wednesbury basis, without themselves donning the garb of policy-maker, which they cannot wear. The local government finance cases, such as *Reg. v. Secretary of State for the Environment, Ex parte Hammersmith and Fulham London Borough Council* [1991] 1 A.C. 521, exemplify this. As Wade and Forsyth observe (Administrative Law, 7th ed. (1994), p. 404):

"Minister's [sic] decisions on important matters of policy are not on that account sacrosanct against the unreasonableness doctrine, though the court must take special care, for constitutional reasons, not to pass judgment on action which is essentially political."

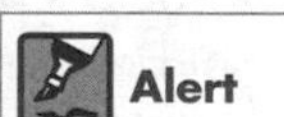

In other cases the act or omission complained of may take place on a much smaller stage, with far fewer players. Here, with respect, lies the importance of the fact in the Coughlan case [2000] 2 W.L.R. 622 that few individuals were affected by the promise in question. The case's facts may be discrete and limited, having no implications for an innominate class of persons. There may be no wide-ranging issues of general policy, or none with multi-layered effects, upon whose merits the court is asked to embark. The court may be able to envisage clearly and with sufficient certainty what the full consequences will be of any order it makes. In such a case the court's condemnation of what is done as an abuse of power, justifiable (or rather, falling to be relieved of its character as abusive) only if an overriding public interest is shown of which the court is the judge, offers no offence to the claims of democratic power.

There will of course be a multitude of cases falling within these extremes, or sharing the characteristics of one or other. The more the decision challenged lies in what may inelegantly be called the macro-political field, the less intrusive will be the court's supervision. More than this: in that field, true abuse of power is less likely to be found, since within it changes of policy, fuelled by broad conceptions of the public interest, may more readily be accepted as taking precedence over the interests of groups which enjoyed expectations generated by an earlier policy.

The present case does not lie in the macro-political field. It concerns a relatively small, certainly identifiable, number of persons. If there has been an abuse of power, I would grant appropriate relief unless an overriding public interest is shown, and none to my mind has been demonstrated. But the real question in the case is whether there has been an abuse of power at all. The government's policy was misrepresented through incompetence. It is not in truth a case of change of policy at all. Mrs. Begbie, who has conducted herself throughout with dignity, restraint, and a clarity of mind which contrasts with the letter to her from the Secretary of State of 11 March, did not alter her or her daughter's position in reliance on the misrepresentation. The mistake was corrected five weeks or so after the "Teed" letter. The issue is whether the correction amounted to an abuse of power; or whether the Secretary of State should be compelled to allocate public resources to the grant of assisted places inconsistently with his perfectly lawful policy.

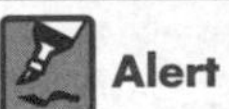

If there had been reliance and detriment in consequence, I would have been prepared to hold that it would be abusive for the Secretary of State not to make the earlier representations good. But there has not. Bitter disappointment, certainly; but I cannot see that this, though it excites one's strongest sympathy, is enough to elevate the Secretary of State's correction of his error into an abuse of power. We do not sit here to punish public authorities for incompetence, though incompetence may most certainly sometimes have effects in public law.

For my part I am driven, with great regret, to conclude, as I have said, that this appeal must be dismissed.

The implication of the above decision is of course, not that pre-election promises are worthless before the law. It is rather that pre-election promises made in opposition are worthless before the law. The sound technical reason for this is that such promises are not being made by a public authority. Therefore, they are not governed by the law on judicial review. This fits in neatly with the policy reason underlying this: it is unrealistic to hold opposition politicians to promises they made before they were in possession of all the information (which will only occur once they are in government).

***R (on the application of Bibi) v London Borough of Newham* [2001] EWCA Civ 607, [2001] 1 WLR 237**

Panel: Schiemann and Sedley LJJ and Blackburne J

Facts: The applicants were refugees who the local authority in Newham provided with temporary housing, after assessing them as being unintentionally homeless and in priority need. The local authority then promised them secure accommodation within 18 months in the belief that it was legally obliged to do so. It was subsequently found by the House of Lords that no such duty existed and so the council continued to provide them with temporary accommodation only. The applicants brought an action claiming that the council was obliged to follow through on its promise.

LORD JUSTICE SCHIEMANN delivering the judgment of the court

This is the judgment of the Court.

...

To what has the authority committed itself?

[46] We accept Mr Luba's submission that Newham's letter and subsequent conduct will have generated an expectation in each applicant, as in others in their situation, that Newham would be providing them with secure housing in the relatively near future. We agree too that such an expectation was legitimate, both in the sense that it was entirely reasonable for the applicants to entertain it and in the sense – which, as Mr Matthias submits, is equally fundamental to legitimacy – that it lay within the powers of the local authority both to make the representation and to fulfil it.

[47] The case has throughout been argued on the basis that the Authority acted lawfully in making the representations. No argument was advanced by Mr Matthias that the making of the representations was beyond the powers of the Authority, perhaps because it is always embarrassing for an authority to resist an application for judicial review by relying on its own illegalities. It would not be right for us to decide the case on the basis of such a possible argument and we do not do so.

[48] We proceed therefore on the basis that the Authority has lawfully committed itself to providing the applicants with suitable accommodation with secure tenure.

Has the authority acted unlawfully?

[49] Whereas in *Coughlan* [2000] 2 WLR 622 it was common ground that the authority had given consideration to the promises it had made, in the present cases that is not so. The Authority in its decision making process has simply not acknowledged that the promises were a relevant consideration in coming to a conclusion as to whether they should be honoured and if not what, if anything, should be done to assuage the disappointed expectations. In our judgment that is an error of law.

[50] The Authority should when considering the position of the applicants have borne in mind that a promise was made to each of them that they would be given secure tenancies and that these promises have to this day, many years after they were made, not been fulfilled. There is no indication that the Authority has ever come to a judgment as to what weight should be given to the fact that the promises were made. There is no reason why the applicants should be disadvantaged by the fact that the promises were made as a result of the Authority's misunderstanding of the law.

[51] The law requires that any legitimate expectation be properly taken into account in the decision making process. It has not been in the present case and therefore the Authority has acted unlawfully.

[52] It was submitted that neither applicant has changed his or her position on the strength of the expectation and therefore no weight ought to be given to the fact that the promises have not been fulfilled. We have already said that this factor does not rank as a legal inhibition on giving effect to the legitimate expectation. But what weight ought to be given to the lack of change of position?

[53] The fact that someone has not changed his position after a promise has been made to him does not mean that he has not relied on the promise. An actor in a play where another actor points a gun at him may refrain from changing his position just because he has been given a promise that the gun only contains blanks.

[54] A refugee such as Mr Al-Nashed might, had he been told the true situation, have gone to one of the bodies which assist refugees for advice as to where in England and Wales he might have better prospects; or have tried to find the deposit on an assured tenancy, with the possibility thereafter of housing benefit to help with the rent.

[55] The present case is one of reliance without concrete detriment. We use this phrase because there is moral detriment, which should not be dismissed lightly, in the prolonged disappointment which has ensued; and potential detriment in the deflection of the possibility, for a refugee family, of seeking at the start to settle somewhere in the United Kingdom where secure housing was less hard to come by. In our view these things matter in public law, even though they might not found an estoppel or actionable misrepresentation in private law, because they go to fairness and through fairness to possible abuse of power. To disregard the legitimate expectation because no concrete detriment can be shown would be to place the weakest in society at a particular disadvantage. It would mean that those who have a choice and the means to exercise it in reliance on some official practice or promise would gain a legal toehold inaccessible to those who, lacking any means of escape, are compelled simply to place their trust in what has been represented to them.

Lord Justice Schiemann's judgment confirmed the point which was hinted at by Lord Woolf MR in *Coughlan*: that detrimental reliance is not needed to found the expectation. But, as can also be seen from *Coughlan*, such reliance is likely to be seen as helpful to an applicant's case. This was given further force by Lord Hoffmann in *R (on the application of Bancoult) v Secretary of State for Foreign and Commonwealth Affairs* [2008] UKHL 61, [2009] 1 AC 453 where he said: 'It is not essential that the applicant should have relied upon the promise to his detriment, although this is a relevant consideration in deciding whether the adoption of a policy in conflict with the promise would be an abuse of power and such a change of policy may be justified in the public interest'.

2 Legitimate Expectation and Proportionality

As was seen when looking at the issue of unreasonableness, the concept of proportionality is starting to influence public law heavily and its relationship with traditional common law concepts is in a state of flux. The next case explores whether proportionality is the correct test to apply when considering whether a legitimate expectation should be frustrated.

***R (on the application of Nadarajah) v Secretary of State for the Home Department R (on the application of Abdi) v Secretary of State for the Home Department* [2005] EWCA Civ 1363, [2005] All ER (D) 283 (Nov)**

Panel: Laws and Thomas LJJ and Nelson J

Facts: Both applicants applied for asylum. They were found to have entered the UK from Germany and Italy respectively and the Home Secretary proposed to send them back to those countries to determine their applications. However, the Home Secretary had adopted a 'Family Links Policy' whereby, if an applicant's spouse was resident in the UK (as Nadarajah's was), or if an applicant was under the age of 18 and her parents were in the UK (as Abdi's were), their claims would be substantively determined in this country. The Home Secretary denied that the policy was relevant to either applicant for various reasons, and they claimed that this was a breach of their right to private and family life under article 8 of the European Convention and that they had a legitimate expectation that their claims would be substantively determined in the UK in line with the Family Links Policy.

LORD JUSTICE LAWS

...

67. In *Coughlan* (paragraph 71, cited above) Lord Woolf said of legitimate expectation, "[t]he limits to its role have yet to be finally determined by the courts. Its application is still being developed on a case by case basis." I do not begin to suggest that what follows fulfils the task. But although as I have said I would conclude the case in the Secretary of State's favour on the arguments as they stand, I would venture to offer some suggestions – no doubt obiter – to see if we may move the law's development a little further down the road, not least so as to perceive, if we can, how legitimate expectation fits with other areas of English public law.

68. The search for principle surely starts with the theme that is current through the legitimate expectation cases. It may be expressed thus. Where a public authority has issued a promise or adopted a practice which represents how it proposes to act in a given area, the law will require the promise or practice to be honoured unless there is good reason not to do so. What is the principle behind this proposition? It is not far to seek. It is said to be grounded in fairness, and no doubt in general terms that is so. I would prefer to express it rather more broadly as a requirement of good

administration, by which public bodies ought to deal straightforwardly and consistently with the public. In my judgment this is a legal standard which, although not found in terms in the European Convention on Human Rights, takes its place alongside such rights as fair trial, and no punishment without law. That being so there is every reason to articulate the limits of this requirement – to describe what may count as good reason to depart from it – as we have come to articulate the limits of other constitutional principles overtly found in the European Convention. Accordingly a public body's promise or practice as to future conduct may only be denied, and thus the standard I have expressed may only be departed from, in circumstances where to do so is the public body's legal duty, or is otherwise, to use a now familiar vocabulary, a proportionate response (of which the court is the judge, or the last judge) having regard to a legitimate aim pursued by the public body in the public interest. The principle that good administration requires public authorities to be held to their promises would be undermined if the law did not insist that any failure or refusal to comply is objectively justified as a proportionate measure in the circumstances.

69. This approach makes no distinction between procedural and substantive expectations. Nor should it. The dichotomy between procedure and substance has nothing to say about the reach of the duty of good administration. Of course there will be cases where the public body in question justifiably concludes that its statutory duty (it will be statutory in nearly every case) requires it to override an expectation of substantive benefit which it has itself generated. So also there will be cases where a procedural benefit may justifiably be overridden. The difference between the two is not a difference of principle. Statutory duty may perhaps more often dictate the frustration of a substantive expectation. Otherwise the question in either case will be whether denial of the expectation is in the circumstances proportionate to a legitimate aim pursued. Proportionality will be judged, as it is generally to be judged, by the respective force of the competing interests arising in the case. Thus where the representation relied on amounts to an unambiguous promise; where there is detrimental reliance; where the promise is made to an individual or specific group; these are instances where denial of the expectation is likely to be harder to justify as a proportionate measure. They are included in Mr Underwood's list of factors, all of which will be material, where they arise, to the assessment of proportionality. On the other hand where the government decision-maker is concerned to raise wide-ranging or "macro-political" issues of policy, the expectation's enforcement in the courts will encounter a steeper climb. All these considerations, whatever their direction, are pointers not rules. The balance between an individual's fair treatment in particular circumstances, and the vindication of other ends having a proper claim on the public interest (which is the essential dilemma posed by the law of legitimate expectation) is not precisely calculable, its measurement not exact. It is no surprise that, as I ventured to suggest in *Begbie*, "the first and third categories explained in the *Coughlan* case... are not hermetically sealed". These cases have to be judged in the round.

70. There is nothing original in my description of the operative principle as a requirement of good administration. The expression was used in this context at least as long ago as the *Ng Yuen Shiu* case, in which Lord Fraser of Tullybelton, delivering the judgment of the Privy Council, said this (638F):

> "It is in the interest of good administration that [a public authority] should act fairly and should implement its promise, so long as implementation does not interfere with its statutory duty."
>
> My aim in outlining this approach has been to see if we can conform the shape of the law of legitimate expectations with that of other constitutional principles; and also to go some small distance in providing a synthesis, or at least a backdrop, within or against which the authorities in this area may be related to each other. I would make these observations on the learning I have summarised earlier. First, there are some cases where, on a proper apprehension of the facts, there is in truth no promise for the future: *Ex p. Hargreaves;* see also *In re Findlay* [1985] AC 318. Then in *Ng Yuen Shiu* and *Ex p. Khan* the breach of legitimate expectations — of the standard of good administration — could not be justified as a proportionate response to any dictate of the public interest; indeed I think it may be said that there was no public interest to compete with the expectation. In *Coughlan* the promise's denial could not be justified as a proportionate measure. The three categories of case there described by Lord Woolf represent, I would respectfully suggest, varying scenarios in which the question whether denial of the expectation was proportionate to the public interest aim in view may call for different answers. In *Begbie*, the legitimate expectation was frustrated by the operation of statute. *Bibi* went off essentially on the basis that the authority had "simply not acknowledged that the promises were a relevant consideration in coming to a conclusion as to whether they should be honoured". Its primary importance arises from the court's comments on reliance, including its citation of Professor Craig. That there is no hard and fast rule about reliance to my mind illustrates the fact, which I have already sought to emphasise, that it is in principle no more than a factor to be considered in weighing the question whether denial of the expectation is justified — justified, as I would suggest, as a proportionate act or measure.
>
> 71. Applying this approach to the present case, I would arrive at the same result as I have reached on the arguments as they were presented. I am clear that the Secretary of State was entitled to decline to apply the original policy, construed as Stanley Burnton J construed it, in the appellant's case. I have already said that the Secretary of State acted consistently throughout. The appellant knew nothing of the Family Links Policy at the time of the February 2002 decision. He seeks the benefit, not of a government policy intended to apply to persons in his position but unfairly denied him, but the windfall of the Secretary of State's misinterpretation. There is nothing disproportionate, or unfair, in his being refused it. Nothing in Mr Husain's points seems to me to shift that position.

Although *Abdi* is a case with a human rights context, Laws LJ did not suggest that the proportionality approach is restricted to cases with a Convention element. This is a point raised, amongst others, in the next article.

Legitimate Expectations, ALBA Lecture (7 March 2006), Philip Sales

The Legal and Institutional Background

The doctrine of legitimate expectation operates as a control over the exercise of discretionary powers conferred upon a public authority. The typical reason why discretionary powers are conferred upon a public authority is to ensure that they are exercised having due regard to the particular circumstances of individual cases coming before the decision-maker – ie in circumstances where Parliament was not confident at the time of passing legislation in predicting all circumstances and how individual cases should be resolved. It is often difficult to tell in advance of concrete situations arising precisely how an authority should act; and that may be as true for the authority as for Parliament itself. This reasoning is inherent in the rule forbidding a public authority which has a discretion and adopts a policy as to its exercise from following that policy without having due regard to the specific facts of the particular case: *British Oxygen* [1971] AC 610.

The doctrine of legitimate expectation is the converse of this situation: it operates to say that, subject to certain conditions, a public authority which adopts a policy should be required to follow and apply that policy in cases subject to it, without being permitted to depart from it. It applies in cases where the decision-maker has committed itself in advance to a particular course of conduct in a particular class of case (defined in more or less general terms), without reference to the specific facts of individual cases. The key issue, therefore, in legal terms, is to explain by reference to normative considerations when and why (or why and, therefore, when) the policy maker will be required to follow its own pre-determination of the outcome of the case without being free just to change its mind when the specific facts of an individual case are before it.

In addressing that issue, it is important to understand that the problem which presents itself is one of public law, and that private law analogies are of limited assistance: see *R (Reprotech (Pebsham) Ltd v E Sussex CC* [2003] 1 WLR 348, HL, at [34] per Lord Hoffmann (indicating an important shift from the cases in the infancy of the development of the doctrine, where the private law analogy was used as the normative foundation for the doctrine: see esp. *Re Preston* [1985] AC 835, 865-7 per Lord Templeman). Viewed from the perspective of public law, the protection of legitimate expectations is both greater but also less than the protection of comparable interests under private law (particularly in contract or estoppel cases):

The protection is greater, in that in some cases no absolute promise or consideration or detrimental reliance may be required. It may be sufficient to say that the adoption of a policy by the decision-maker informs and strengthens the application of general requirements of lawful behaviour on the part of public authorities, including in particular (in the case of representations as to the procedure to be adopted) the requirement that a public decision-maker act fairly and (in the case of representations as to the substantive outcome in a class of case) the requirement that a public decision-maker act consistently and rationally (cf *Matadeen v Pointu* [1999] AC 98). In each sort of case, it seems that the specific adoption of a policy by the decision-maker will strengthen rights which the individual enjoys under general public law. But then, it is important to identify to what extent the adoption by the public authority of a policy in advance adds to the rights which the individual already enjoys under general public law.

The protection is less, in that the interest of the individual in having the policy or representation complied with in their case may be overridden by countervailing public interest considerations. Short of a binding private law contract or estoppel, the hands of the public authority are not absolutely bound by its advance declaration of how it will deal with particular cases. It can depart from its policy, if at the time of decision it considers that there is some overriding reason of the public interest which requires an approach different from that declared in general terms by it in advance. But then, it is important to identify to what extent it is open to the public authority which has made representations or adopted a policy in advance should have the freedom to depart from it.

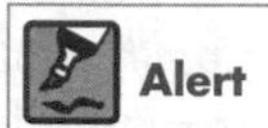

In institutional terms, where a public authority has conferred upon it a wide discretionary power covering a large number and variety of cases, it may be important for the public authority's own coherent and consistent approach to decision-making that it adopts a policy as to how it will act – at least in the usual run of cases. But, the greater the extent that the doctrine of legitimate expectations may result in the public authority's hands then being held by the courts to be tied in law, the greater the wariness authorities may have about adopting policies as to how they approach their decision-making in a particular area. Also, a public authority may, in practical terms, face the same sort of difficulty in predicting precisely in advance how its decision-making powers should be exercised in particular cases that Parliament faced when conferring discretionary powers upon it in the first instance: ie it cannot be known with certainty in advance how particular cases ought to be decided (which is at least part of the rationale for conferring a discretion in the first place, rather than Parliament itself prescribing in advance in legally binding legislation what the outcome should be in particular cases). Parliament having chosen to confer a discretion rather than creating a binding duty, it would be odd if the doctrine of legitimate expectations could operate so that the public authority itself, by adopting a policy, creates a binding duty for itself. Again, the more the doctrine operates to bind the hands of the public authority, the more it implicitly engages the courts and the decision-maker in creating something approaching the kind of binding duty which Parliament chose not to create.

Given these general points, one would expect the doctrine of legitimate expectations to develop by adaptation in the light of the weight of the conflicting public law reasons in favour of greater or less decision-making flexibility for public authorities at the point of actually deciding what to do in specific cases. In broad terms, it is submitted that this is what one finds in the case law.

A distinction between procedural and substantive legitimate expectations?

In general terms, it is desirable for public authorities to do what they have declared they will do. That assists citizens to plan their affairs and fosters trust and confidence in the administrative authorities. It can generally be said to be a feature of good administration that public bodies "deal straightforwardly and consistently with the public" (see *Abdi and Nadarajah v Secretary of State for the Home Department* [2005] EWCA Civ 1363, per Laws LJ at [68], where he describes it as a "requirement"). But these are factors which have to be balanced, at the level of legal principle, against competing factors, pointing in favour of the desirability of public authorities having flexibility to adapt to changing circumstances and changing assessments of the public interest – which is the main underlying reason they will have had a discretion conferred upon them. It can generally be said also to be a feature of good administration that public bodies accurately assess the overall public interest as to how their powers are exercised, in the light of all the relevant facts available to them at the time when they decide what to do. When taking account of this latter sort of consideration, I would suggest that it is very much stronger in the case of representations as to substantive outcomes rather than representations as to the decision-making procedure to be followed. That in turn suggests that it is important to maintain a distinction between procedural legitimate expectations and substantive legitimate expectations.

It is well known that the Court of Appeal in its seminal exposition in *R v N and E Devon Health Authority, ex p Coughlan* [2001] QB 213 emphasised the difference between procedural legitimate expectations (based on representations as to the procedure a public authority will follow before it takes a decision on the substantive merits of a particular case) and a narrower class of protected substantive legitimate expectations (based on representations as to the decision which a public authority will take on the substantive merits of a particular case). Where a public authority represents that a particular procedure will be followed before it decides what to do on the merits of an individual case, the intrusion on its decision-making discretion to decide what to do in that case having regard to the overall public interest is less where it is held to be bound by its representations than where it is held to be bound by its representations as to the substantive decision it will take. In the latter class of case (representations as to substantive outcome), the public authority is being held to its assessment of the overall public interest taken in advance (sometimes, a long time in advance) and in more or less general and abstract terms, and that advance and general assessment is found to trump the specific and precise assessment of the public interest which it makes when the particular facts of the individual case are directly before it – even though the public authority has not become functus officio simply by adoption of a policy.

Indeed, this difference between procedure and substantive outcome has for a long time lain at the heart of the development of public law more generally, and is reflected in the development by the courts of comparatively full and binding standards of fairness in the decision-making process (where the courts have taken themselves to be the primary decision-makers as to the content of those standards: see eg *R v Panel on Take-overs and Mergers, ex p. Guinness plc* [1990] 1 QB 146) as compared with relatively light standards of review as to the substantive merits as expressed, in particular, in the *Wednesbury* formula. The conflict of substantive legitimate expectations with the ability of a public authority to assess the balance of the public interest and how best to behave in the light of the actual circumstances of a particular case becomes particularly acute where the enforcement of the substantive legitimate expectation would involve the court in overriding the public authority's judgment how scarce resources should be utilised in the face of competing claims. That is a judgment which, on the face of it, Parliament has allocated to the public authority rather than the court, and where the public authority rather than the court is best placed to weigh all the competing considerations.

Given the nature of the analytical exercise when deciding whether and to what extent a public authority should be treated as bound by representations it has made in advance, and the balance which the doctrine of legitimate expectation has to strike in concrete terms between treating a public authority as bound by its earlier (rather than present) assessment of the overall public interest and allowing it freedom to decide how to behave in the light of its present assessment arrived at in light of the specific facts of particular cases, one would expect in principle to find a difference in approach as between procedural and substantive cases. The pressures for preserving freedom of choice for a public authority in the present are far less in the case procedural legitimate expectations than in the case of substantive legitimate expectations (directed to the outcome on the merits). The more a public authority is to be treated as bound by its advance decision as to the substantive merits, the more one would expect the conditions for that binding outcome to reflect the ability of the public authority to have accurately assessed in advance what the balance of the public interest should be and the clarity with which the public authority had in fact addressed that relevant question. That suggests that, where one is dealing with substantive legitimate expectations, the courts should focus very carefully on factors which affect the quality of the advance "decision" taken by the public authority, and the appropriateness of treating that advance "decision" as in some sense binding upon the public authority when taking an actual decision in a concrete case in the present. The more the public authority has, at the advance stage, had clearly in mind the particular ramifications of its representations or policy for the type of concrete decision which it eventually has to take and has deliberately chosen a particular outcome, the more readily one would regard it is as legitimate for the courts (having regard to other considerations, including the general desirability of public authorities abiding by pre-declared policies) to treat the public authority as in some sense bound by that advance "decision". Conversely, the further away one is from that situation, the stronger the argument for retention of freedom of action for the public authority in the light of full information about current circumstances.

This, I would suggest, is an important part of the analytical background to the stress in substantive legitimate expectation cases upon the quality of the information available to a public authority before it is treated as prima facie bound by advance representations it makes as to the substantive outcome in a case (see eg *R v IRC, ex p. MFK Underwriting Agencies Ltd* [1990] 1 WLR 1545), and upon the precision, clarity and limited focus of the representation relied upon (*MFK Underwriting*; *Coughlan* at [57]-[59]). Since the impact upon the general interest in an authority having freedom to determine and act upon the public interest as it determines it to be at the point of actual decision is much less where the authority's representation only goes to the procedure to be followed rather than the substantive outcome of any case, these strict requirements can be relaxed. It is more acceptable to require the authority to abide by its representations and policy when made in general terms and to the world at large.

Similarly, it is more acceptable for a legitimate expectation to be founded upon an established course of conduct in the past, rather than any specific promise as to conduct for the future: see eg *O'Reilly v Mackman* [1983] 2 AC 237, 275 (there is no authority which has found a substantive legitimate expectation to have emerged from past conduct: the closest example is *R v IRC, ex p Unilever plc* [1996] STC 681, which the Court treated not as a legitimate expectation case - even in the context of an extremely precise and focused course of conduct known by the IRC to have engendered very specific expectations on the part of the taxpayer claimant - but a case of conspicuous unfairness, tantamount to irrationality, in failing to follow the same established practice in relation to permitting tax rebate claims to be made in a particular way, so that the claims were defeated at huge cost to the taxpayer).

For reasons of both authority and principle, therefore, one might respectfully doubt whether an approach which seeks to assimilate the test for holding that a protected legitimate expectation has been created by representations by a public authority as to procedure ought to be adopted in relation to representations as to substantive merits: contrast *Abdi & Nadarajah v Secretary of State for the Home Department* [2005] EWCA Civ 1363 at [67]-[71] per Laws LJ, esp. at [69] ("The dichotomy between procedure and substance has nothing to say about the reach of the duty of good administration"). On the analysis presented above, the dichotomy between procedure and substance does have important things to say about the reach of the duty of good administration; and there is good reason why that dichotomy should inform the test for determining when a protected legitimate expectation will be held to have arisen.

How may a legitimate expectation be overridden?

In *Abdi and Nadarajah*, Laws LJ said at [68], "The principle that good administration requires public authorities to be held to their promises would be undermined if the law did not insist that any failure or refusal to comply is objectively justified as a proportionate measure in the circumstances." There are three problems with this part of the judgment which I would respectfully wish to focus on.

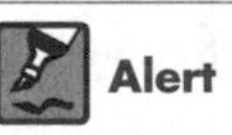
Alert

First, to the extent that (as Laws LJ does earlier in his judgment) one assimilates the test for a protected legitimate expectation to arise in a substantive expectation case with that for a procedural expectation, the adoption of a standard of proportionality represents a greater inroad by the courts into the practical decision-making powers of the public authority charged by Parliament with taking the decision in question. In relation to procedural expectations, the courts' authority to apply their own standards of fairness is well established (see *Guinness*, supra), and this represents a clearly acceptable practical compromise between fairness as a value of good administration and accurate substantive decision-making by the relevant public authority designated by Parliament as a competing value of good administration. It seems straightforward for the courts to extend that sort of approach to cover procedural legitimate expectations, and insist upon a high standard of justification (perhaps expressed in a proportionality rubric) before such legitimate expectations are overridden. To say that a departure from a substantive legitimate expectation can only be justified on a basis of proportionality, rather than by reference to an ordinary rationality standard, is much more questionable. To the extent that relatively restrictive criteria are applied before a substantive legitimate expectation is found to have arisen, such an intensive standard of review may be justified – and this was, in effect, the balance struck by the Court of Appeal in *Coughlan*. But if those restrictive criteria are to be relaxed (as Laws LJ suggests), it is not immediately obvious that the proportionality standard of review (if that is said to be different from ordinary rationality review) will be the appropriate one. At some point, argument about the relevant standard shades into the arguments about whether proportionality should be adopted as a general test of lawfulness under domestic administrative law.

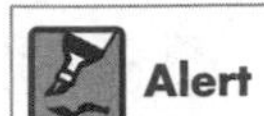

Second, one may doubt just how useful a test of proportionality will be in these cases. To say that the test is one of "proportionality" begs the question, proportionate to what? If it is said, "proportionate to a legitimate aim", one has to acknowledge that in some cases the legitimate aim will be extremely diffuse, to the point of not being a helpful analytical tool (eg a public authority, on consideration of the full facts, may simply decide it does not wish to expend limited public funds in a particular way; or there may be a change in the political complexion of a public authority, and it simply makes a different assessment of the public interest in a given case). Perhaps the test should be expressed more broadly, as one directed to severe and unjustifiable substantive unfairness which would be suffered by an individual if a public authority departs from its representation, with a focus then upon spelling out the factors (eg detrimental reliance, the nature of the public interest being pursued) relevant to such an assessment. Detrimental reliance was identified by Peter Gibson LJ as an important factor in substantive legitimate expectation claims in *R v Secretary of State for Education and Employment, ex p. Begbie* [2000] 1 WLR 1115, 1124.

A proportionality approach might be said to be rather narrowly expressed for other reasons as well. Sometimes, the reason that a legitimate expectation may be departed from is that the public authority behaves fairly in doing so, rather than because the departure is itself proportionate to some overriding public interest. It may be sufficient for a public authority to afford an individual to whom a representation has been made an indication that the public authority is minded not to adhere to its representation and an opportunity to make representations why the public authority should adhere to it. If the basis for a claim to a legitimate expectation is a representation by a public authority how it will act, there may well be situations in which it will be fair for the public authority to retreat from that position, provided that it affords the individual concerned an opportunity to make representations to persuade it otherwise. If there has been no detrimental reliance by the individual, and the public authority has acted fairly in this way, it is difficult to see why (in the ordinary case) it should be held bound by what it said some time ago. This point is underlined by the approach of the courts in relation to relief, particularly where a substantive legitimate expectation is concerned…

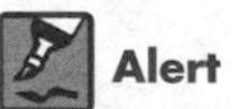

Third, a proportionality approach is difficult to reconcile with recent House of Lords authority. In *R (Mullen) v Secretary of State for the Home Department* [2005] 1 AC 1 the Secretary of State recognised that the claimant fell within the scope of his policy on payment of compensation to persons wrongfully convicted, but (since it was established that the claimant had in fact been involved in a terrorist related offence) did not wish to pay him compensation in respect of his wrongful conviction (ie wished to depart from his policy statement in light of the particular features of the claimant's case). The

Secretary of State gave the claimant an indication that he proposed to do that, invited representations on the point, and having considered the representations received decided that he would depart from his policy in that case. He did not withdraw or restate the general policy. The House of Lords held that the Secretary of State was entitled to decide not to apply his policy in the claimant's case, having afforded the claimant a fair opportunity to make representations on the point: on the substance of the decision, the House applied a rationality test (see esp. [58]-[62] per Lord Steyn).

The form of relief where there is a violation of a legitimate expectation

Ordinarily, in a procedural legitimate expectation case, the public authority will (absent some sufficiently compelling and overriding public interest) simply be required to comply with its representations (or established practice) as to the procedure it would follow. A failure to do so will be treated like a failure to comply with common law standards of fairness.

The position is more complicated in a substantive legitimate expectation case, where a representation as to the substantive outcome on the merits is concerned. It may be that the public authority will be held to be required actually to confer the substantive benefit as it has said it would. But that will bring the court into tension with other principles of public law, which require that the primary operative decision should be that of the public authority in the light of all the circumstances known at the time of the decision. Therefore, it is submitted that usually a particularly compelling interest of the individual will be required before the court may feel confident that it is appropriate to override the (current) decision of the local authority. The sort of interest which means that the fair balance to be struck between the interests of the individual (and general value in public authorities acting in accordance with their prior representations) and the public interest of flexibility of decision-making in the light of all the circumstances at the time of decision comes down in favour of compelling the public authority to act contrary to its present judgment and in line with its previously declared policy will usually be some form of detrimental reliance on the part of the individual. One may then become involved in a debate about the sort of detriment which ought to count for these purposes: compare *R (Bibi) v Newham LBC* [2002] 1 WLR 237 and *R (Rashid) v Secretary of State for the Home Department* [2005] EWCA Civ 744.

The tension referred to above becomes all the more acute when the enforcement of the substantive legitimate expectation according to its terms involves, in practice, the court allocating to the claimant some scarce resource, which will mean that other possibly deserving individuals will lose the opportunity to have that resource allocated to them. That was the position in *Bibi*, supra. The solution of the Court of Appeal was to meet that tension by declining to grant relief in substantive form by requiring the local authority to honour its promise, and instead granting relief in procedural form (obligation on local authority to reconsider claimant's case, with opportunity for representations, and a requirement to give reasons explaining any decision to depart from its promise). An important area for the future development of the law in relation to substantive legitimate expectations will be the articulation by the courts of the principles according to which the proper remedial reaction to a substantive legitimate expectation

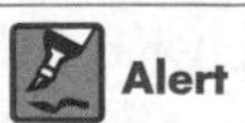

will be procedural in form, and those according to which the proper remedy will be direct enforcement of the public authority's promise or policy on the mandatory order of the court. Again, it is submitted that detrimental reliance is likely to be an important consideration in relation to this dividing line.

Further Reading

Sales, Philip and Steyn, Karen 'Legitimate expectations in English public law: an analysis', [2004] *PL* 564

Elliott, Mark 'Reflections on Abdi & Nadarajah: The Place of Abuse of Power and Proportionality', ALBA Lecture (7 March 2006),

Knight, C J S 'Expectations in transition: recent developments in legitimate expectations', [2009] *PL* 15